MERGERS AND ACQUISITIONS

LAW, THEORY, AND PRACTICE

■ ■ ■

Claire Hill

Professor and James L. Krusemark Chair in Law
University of Minnesota Law School

Brian JM Quinn

Associate Professor of Law
Boston College Law School

Steven Davidoff Solomon

Professor of Law
University of California, Berkeley School of Law

AMERICAN CASEBOOK SERIES®

WEST
ACADEMIC
PUBLISHING

American Casebook Series is a trademark registered in the U.S. Patent and Trademark Office.

© 2016 LEG, Inc. d/b/a West Academic
    444 Cedar Street, Suite 700
    St. Paul, MN 55101
    1-877-888-1330

West, West Academic Publishing, and West Academic are trademarks of West Publishing Corporation, used under license.

Printed in the United States of America

ISBN: 978-0-314-28906-3

ACKNOWLEDGMENTS

We are grateful for permission to use all or portions of the following:

Stephen M. Bainbridge, *The Geography of Revlon-Land,* 81 FORDHAM L. REV. 3277 (2013).

Stephen Bainbridge, *Did Facebook's Zuckerberg Just Have a Van Gorkom Moment?*, PROFESSORBAINBRIDGE.COM (April 18, 2012), http://www. professorbainbridge.com/professorbainbridgecom/2012/04/did-facebooks-zuckerburg-just-have-a-van-gorkom-moment.html.

Lucian A. Bebchuk, *Don't Make Poison Pills More Deadly*, N.Y. TIMES (February 7, 2013), http://dealbook.nytimes.com/2013/02/07/dont-make-poison-pills-more-deadly/?_r=0.

B. Jeffery Bell, *The Acquisition of Control of a United States Public Company*, MORRISON & FOERSTER (2015), http://media.mofo.com/files/ Uploads/Images/1302-The-Acquisition-of-Control-of-a-United-States-Public-Company.pdf.

Matthew D. Cain & Steven M. Davidoff (Solomon), *Form Over Substance? The Value of Corporate Process and Management Buy-outs*, 36 DEL. J. CORP. LAW 849 (2011).

Brett Carron & Steven M. Davidoff (Solomon), *Getting U.S. Security Holders to the Party: The SEC's Cross-Border Release Five Years On*, 12 U. PA J. INT'L ECON L. 455 (2005).

John C. Coffee, Jr. and Darius Palia, *The Impact of Hedge Fund Activism: Evidence and Implications.* (Sept. 14, 2014). European Corporate Governance Institute [ECGI]—Law Working Paper No. 266/2014; Columbia Law and Economics Working Paper No. 489.

Aswath Damodaran, *Facebook Buys Whatsapp for $19 billion: Value and Pricing Perspectives*, MUSINGS ON MARKETS (February 20, 2014), http://aswathdamodaran.blogspot.com/2014/02/facebook-buys-whatsapp-for-19-billion.html.

Steven M. Davidoff (Solomon), *Takeover Theory and the Law and Economics Movement*, in RESEARCH HANDBOOK ON THE ECONOMICS OF CORPORATION LAW (Edward Elgar Publishing; Claire Hill & Brett McDonnell eds., 2012).

Steven M. Davidoff (Solomon), Anil K. Makhija & Rajesh P. Narayanan, *Fairness Opinions in Mergers and Acquisitions*, in THE ART OF CAPITAL RESTRUCTURING: CREATING SHAREHOLDER VALUE THROUGH MERGERS AND ACQUISITIONS (H. Kent Baker, Halil Kiymaz, eds., 2011).

STEVEN M. DAVIDOFF (SOLOMON), GODS AT WAR: SHOTGUN TAKEOVERS, GOVERNMENT BY DEAL, AND THE PRIVATE EQUITY IMPLOSION (WILEY, 2009).

Steven M. Davidoff (Solomon), *Strine Strikes Again: Mercier, Et Al. v. Inter-Tel,* M&A LAW PROF. BLOG (August 21, 2007), http://lawprofessors. typepad.com/mergers/2007/08/strine-strikes-.html

Steven M. Davidoff (Solomon), *Better Know a Deal Structure,* M&A LAW PROF. BLOG, (October 22, 2007), http://lawprofessors.typepad.com/ mergers/2007/10/better-know-a–1.html.

Steven M. Davidoff (Solomon), *Nasdaq, Borse Dubai and Exon Florio,* M&A LAW PROF. BLOG (October 2, 2007) http://lawprofessors.typepad .com/mergers/2007/10/nasdaq-borse-du.html.

Steven M. Davidoff (Solomon), *Strine Strikes Again: Mercier, Et Al. v. Inter-Tel,* M&A LAW PROF. BLOG (August 21, 2007), http://lawprofessors. typepad.com/mergers/2007/08/strine-strikes-.html

Steven M. Davidoff (Solomon), *The SEC and the Failure of Federal Takeover Litigation,* 34 FLA. ST. U. LAW REV. 211 (2007).

Steven M. Davidoff (Solomon), *The Obsolescence of Rule 14e–5,* M&A LAW PROF. BLOG (July 1, 2007), http://lawprofessors.typepad.com/mergers /2007/07/the-obsolescenc.html.

Dissident Success Rate, Proxy Fights 2001–Present, FACTSET SHARKREPELLENT.NET.

Due Diligence Memo, PRACTICAL LAW, http://us.practicallaw.com/9-382-1874.

Daniel R. Fischel, *The Business Judgment Rule and the Trans Union Case,* 40 BUS. LAW. 1437 (1985).

Eduardo Gallardo and Joe Tillman, *No-Shops and Fiduciary Outs: A Survey of 2012 Public Merger Agreements,* GIBSON DUNN M&A REPORT (Winter 2013), http://www.gibsondunn.com/publications/Documents/MA Report-Winter2013.pdf.

Marilyn Geewax, *Can A Huge Hog Deal Pose A National Security Risk?,* NPR, May 13, 2013, http://www.npr.org/2013/05/31/187351539/can-a-huge-hog-deal-pose-a-national-security-risk.

Sal Guerrera, Lou R. Kling, Robert S. Saunders, Sarah M. Ward, Dohyun Kim, *Stapled Financing in the Aftermath of Delaware's Del Monte Decision,* SKADDEN, ARPS, MEAGHER, & FLOM LLP AND AFFILIATES (2012), http://www.skadden.com/newsletters/Skadden_2012_Insights_Capital_Markets.pdf.

David W. Healy, *Corporate and Securities Update: M&A Development—Deal Process and Protections,* FENWICK & WEST LLP

(2007), https://www.fenwick.com/FenwickDocuments/M-A_Developments _Deal_Process.pdf.

Claire Hill, *Bargaining in the Shadow of the Lawsuit: A Social Norms Theory of Incomplete Contracts*, 34 DEL. J. CORP. L. 191 (2009).

Claire Hill & Brett McDonnell, *Sanitizing Interested Transactions*, 36 DEL. J. CORP. L. 903 (2011).

Marshall Horowitz and Joshua Schneiderman, *Negotiating Investment Banking M&A Engagement Letters: Keeping the Investment Bank Incentivized While Protecting Your Interests*, SNELL & WILMER (Spring 2012), http://info.swlaw.com/reaction/2012/CorporateCommunicator_2012_ HTML/CC_Spring2012/CC_Spring2012_WEB.html.

Suneela Jain, Ethan Klingsberg & Neil Whoriskey, *Examining Data Points in Minority Buy-Outs: A Practitioners Report*, 36 DEL. J. CORP. LAW 939 (2011).

Charles Korsmo & Minor Myers, *Appraisal Arbitrage and the Future of Public Company M&A*, 92 WASH. U. L. REV. 1551 (2015).

L&W Capital Markets Group, *The Curious Case of How to Resell Securities Obtained in an M&A Transaction—Rules 144 and 145*, WORDS OF WISDOM—LATHAM & WATKINS LLP (August 11, 2010), http://www. wowlw.com/ma-issues/the-curious-case-of-how-to-resell-securities-obtained-in-an-ma-transaction-rules-144-and-145/.

Martin Lipton, *Bite the Apple; Poison the Apple; Paralyze the Company; Wreck the Economy*, HARVARD LAW SCHOOL FORUM ON CORPORATE GOVERNANCE AND FINANCIAL REGULATION (February 26, 2013), http://corpgov.law.harvard.edu/2013/02/26/bite-the-apple-poison-the-apple-paralyze-the-company-wreck-the-economy/.

Robert Little, *Private Placement of Publicly Traded Equity Securities as Consideration in an M&A Transaction after the JOBS Act*, THE SECURITIES REGULATION AND CORPORATE GOVERNANCE MONITOR— GIBSON DUNN (April 18, 2012), http://www.securitiesregulationmonitor. com/Lists/Posts/Post.aspx?ID=165.

Robert Little and James Moloney, *Private Placement of Publicly Traded Equity Securities as Consideration in an M&A Transaction after the JOBS Act*, THE SECURITIES REGULATION AND CORPORATE GOVERNANCE MONITOR—GIBSON DUNN (October 3, 2013), http://www.securities regulationmonitor.com/Lists/Posts/Post.aspx?List=f3551fe8-411e-4ea4-830c -d680a8c0da43&ID=216&Web=97364e78-c7b4-4464-a28c-fd4eea1956ac.

Jonathan Macey, *State Anti-Takeover Statutes: Good Politics, Bad Economics*, WISC. LAW REV. 467 (1988).

Model Stock Purchase Agreement, Second Edition: Letter of Intent, THE AMERICAN BAR ASSOCIATION, https://apps.americanbar.org/buslaw/blt/content/departments/2010/09/mspa-letter-of-intent.pdf.

Jonathan L.H. Nygren, *Addressing Financial Advisor Conflicts in the Wake of Del Monte and El Paso*, FAEGRE BAKER DANIELS (07/16/2012), http://www.faegrebd.com/18685.

PLC Standstill Agreement, PRACTICAL LAW, http://us.practicallaw.com/2-532-4753.

Proxy Fights, 2001–Present, FACTSET SHARKREPELLENT.NET.

Public Merger Timeline, PRACTICAL LAW, http://us.practicallaw.com/9-383-1095.

Brian JM Quinn, *MFW—Just Half a Loaf*, M&A LAW PROF. BLOG (March 18, 2014), http://lawprofessors.typepad.com/mergers/2014/03/mfw-just-half-a-loaf.html.

Brian JM Quinn, *Putting Your Money Where Your Mouth Is: The Performance of Earnouts in Corporate Acquisitions*, 81 U. CIN. L. REV. 127 (2013).

Brian JM Quinn, *Bulletproof: Mandatory Rules for Deal Protection*, 32 J. CORP. L. 865 (2007).

Michael K. Reilly, *The Post-Agreement Market Check Revisited*, POTTER ANDERSON & CORROON LLP (March 1, 2004), http://www.potteranderson.com/newsroom-publications-157.html.

Paul Rose, *On the Role and Regulation of Proxy Advisors*, 109 MICH. L. REV. FIRST IMPRESSIONS 62 (2011).

Christina M. Sautter, *Shopping During Extended Store Hours: From No Shops to Go-Shops—The Development, Effectiveness, and Implications of Go-Shop Provisions in Change of Control Transactions*, 73 BROOK. L. REV. 525 (2008).

SEC Amendments to Tender Offer "Best-Price" Rule Effective Today, GIBSON DUNN (Dec 8, 2006), http://www.gibsondunn.com/publications/pages/secamendmentstotenderofferbestpriceruleeffectivetoday.aspx.

Guhan Subramanian, Steven Herscovici, & Brian Barbetta, *Is Delaware's Antitakeover Statue Unconstitutional? Evidence from 1988–2008*, 65 BUS. LAW. 799 (2010).

Summary of SEC Regulation S, Dorsey and Whitney LLP (2005), http://www.dorsey.com/files/tbl_s21Publications%5CPDFUpload141%5C1052%5CSummary_of_SEC_Regulation_S.pdf.

Tender Offer Timeline with DGCL 251(h) Merger, PRACTICAL LAW, http://us.practicallaw.com/1-548-3827.

Robert H. Thompson & D. Gordon Smith, *Toward a New Theory of the Shareholder Role: "Sacred Space" in Corporate Takeovers*, 80 TEX. L. REV. 261 (2001).

U.S. Securities Laws Considerations and Options for Japanese Cash Tender Offers, Davis Polk & Wardwell LLP Client Memorandum (October 2009).

US M&A Revenue Ranking, Dealogic. 2014.

US M&A Volume Ranking—Announced Deals, Dealogic. 2014.

Eric H. Wang, *Mergers and Acquisitions Alert (US): Reviewing the M&A Nondisclosure Agreement*, DLA PIPER (August 8, 2012), https:// www.dlapiper.com/en/us/insights/publications/2012/08/reviewing-the-ma-nondisclosure-agreement/.

Marc Weingarten and Erin Magnor, *Second Generation Advance Notification Bylaws*, SCHULTE ROTH & ZABEL LLP (March 16, 2009), http://www.srz.com/Second-Generation-Advance-Notification-Bylaws-03-16-2009/.

Warren S. de Wied, *Proxy Contests*, PRACTICAL LAW (November 2010), http://us.practicallaw.com/6-503-6878.

Daniel E. Wolf, Joshua M. Zachariah, Jeffrey D. Symons, & David B. Feirstein, *Setting the Record (Date) Straight*, KIRKLAND & ELLIS LLP (April 17, 2013), http://www.kirkland.com/siteFiles/Publications/MAUpdate_041713.pdf.

SUMMARY OF CONTENTS

———

TABLE OF CONTENTS

PART II. ACCOUNTING AND VALUATION

PART III. DOING THE DEAL

TABLE OF CASES

The principal cases are in bold type.

MERGERS AND ACQUISITIONS
LAW, THEORY, AND PRACTICE

CHAPTER I

INTRODUCTION

■ ■ ■

A. HISTORY

Mergers and acquisitions (M&A) have a rich history in the American economy. Over the course of the past century and a half, merger activity has proceeded in waves, each wave inevitably followed by a regulatory response. Modern merger activity first emerged around the time of the Erie Wars of the late-nineteenth century. The succeeding trust era, characterized by monopolies and frenetic acquisition activity, resulted in new regulations in the 1890s and early nineteenth century. Merger activity created vast conglomerates during the 1960s. During the 1970s and 1980s, the leveraged buyout boom led to the development of modern M&A legal doctrine. The late 1980s and 1990s saw the embracing of new participants such as private equity firms. Today, the Internet Age and globalization have led to the current M&A market, characterized by transactions that are global, very large (multi-billion dollar), and sometimes both.[1]

1. THE BIRTH OF MODERN U.S. MERGER ACTIVITY: THE ERIE WAR

Following the Civil War and lasting through the Panic of 1873, the railroad industry underwent a period of explosive growth as federal money flowed into the South to rebuild railroad stock and West to open up the frontier. Estimates put the number of railroad companies at the time in the thousands. Simultaneously and in part to meet the needs of these new organizations, a national capital market, centered around the New York Stock Exchange, began to develop. It was at this point that the modern U.S. mergers and acquisitions market began. Yet, there was little law governing the field. The struggle for control of the Erie Railroad illustrates the unregulated nature of the takeover market during this period.

Commodore Cornelius Vanderbilt purchased control of the New York and Harlem Railroad and the New York and Hudson Railroad in 1862. His control became apparent in late 1867 when he was elected President

---

[1] *See generally* STEVEN M. DAVIDOFF (SOLOMON), GODS AT WAR: SHOTGUN TAKEOVERS, GOVERNMENT BY DEAL, AND THE PRIVATE EQUITY IMPLOSION (2009).

of New York Central Railroad and gained permission to consolidate his stakes into the New York Central and the Hudson River Railroad. By issuing "watered" stock, stock that is sold with a face value greater than its actual value, Vanderbilt was able to pay dividends to his shareholders even through the depression of the 1870s.

Meanwhile, the Erie Railroad, Vanderbilt's main competitor in the state, was controlled by Daniel Drew, a former cattle driver and notorious stock speculator who in earlier years had been Vanderbilt's rival in the steamboat industry. Drew was aided by two other well-known speculators, Jim Fisk and Jay Gould. The three became known as the "Erie Gang." Fisk was a stockbroker from Vermont who had a reputation for eccentricity. He was portrayed by Edward Arnold in the 1937 film, *The Toast of New York*. Gould was introverted and is often portrayed in contemporary media as a sinister, villainous genius. Prior to the struggle over control of the Erie Railroad, Fisk and Gould had already helped Drew sell Erie Railroad bonds for eight times their true value.

Vanderbilt was eager to expand and take control of the Erie Railroad. In 1868 he began purchasing as much of the Erie stock as he could get his hands on. Unfortunately, for the Commodore, the shares he was buying were 100,000 new shares converted by the Erie Gang from overvalued bonds. The Erie Gang simply responded to Vanderbilt's demand for Erie stock by printing more shares, a nearly endless supply. By issuing additional shares, the Erie Gang diluted Vanderbilt's position and thus prevented a takeover. The Erie Gang anticipated a maneuver that would become known in the modern era as a "poison pill" (see Chapter XV.D).

Upon discovering he had been cheated, Vanderbilt obtained a warrant to arrest Drew, Fisk, and Gould from his friend, Judge George Barnard. However, the trio escaped Manhattan by boat and took refuge in a hotel in Jersey City, New Jersey. The Erie Gang also took over $7 million of Erie Railroad's funds in addition to more unissued Erie Railroad stock. Vanderbilt was ready for battle, literally. The Commodore sent armed henchmen to attack the Erie Gang, but the gang fought back, even mounting cannons outside their refuge in New Jersey. The battle was ultimately won not with the sword, but with the pen and money: The Erie Gang, with the assistance of Senator William Tweed (aka "Boss Tweed") and a bribe of a half a million dollars, convinced the New York legislature to enact legislation validating their actions, leaving the Erie Gang in control.

Despite their legislative victory over Vanderbilt, the members of the Erie Gang saw only short-lived success:

> Drew, now replaced in top Erie leadership by Gould, turned to less successful exploits on Wall Street, where he was finally ruined in the Panic of 1873, left with little more than his Bibles,

hymnbooks, and sealskin coat. Fisk, the new vice-president, was known as "Prince of Erie" and had a marble and gilded office in Pike's Opera House, which he and Gould rented to Erie at the not too modest rate of $75,000 a month. He went on to be "Admiral" of his own steamship line and Colonel of the 9th Regiment, New York National Guard. But his flamboyant career was ended early in 1872, when he was shot by a rival for the affection of his favorite mistress, Josie Mansfield. The Erie Railroad lay in ruins, and Gould soon took his profits elsewhere.[2]

A New York Times article describes a famous Thomas Nash cartoon depicting the end of the Erie Gang's control:

> On March 11, 1872, the Erie Ring was broken and a new board of directors took over the Erie Railroad Company, with Gould formally resigning as president the next day. In the cartoon's background, the new board of directors takes the form of an incoming train whose path has been cleared by Justice at the switch. General John Dix (the engine) is the new president; S. L. M. Barlow (second car), the new counselor; William Watts Sherman (fifth car), the new treasurer; and O. H. P. Arches (sixth car), who spearheaded the takeover, was reelected vice-president. H. M. Otis was re-appointed secretary.

> Below Judge Barnard in the cartoon is David Dudley Field, chief counsel for both the Erie Ring and the Tweed Ring. . . . To the left of Field is his law partner, Thomas G. Shearman, whose upper body is obscured by the smoke and dust of the crash. In 1873, Shearman left Field to partner with John Sterling, and in 1875 counseled Gould on the financier's attempted takeover of the Union Pacific Railroad. Today, Shearman & Sterling is a prestigious, international law firm. . . . Plummeting upside down at the bottom of the picture is Jay Gould.[3]

---

[2]   JOHN F. STOVER, AMERICAN RAILROADS 105 (2d ed. 1997).

[3]   Robert C. Kennedy, *On This Day*, N.Y. TIMES, available at http://www.nytimes.com/learning/general/onthisday/harp/0330.html. The cartoon, reprinted from the article, is originally from Thomas Nast, *Justice on the Rail—Erie Railroad (Ring) Smash Up*, Harper's Weekly, Mar. 30, 1872.

2. FIRST AND SECOND WAVES OF U.S. MERGER ACTIVITY: THE RISE OF ANTITRUST REGULATION AND THE TRUSTBUSTERS

The first merger wave came in the late 1800s during the age of the corporate trusts. Large corporations combined to form trusts, merging diverse enterprises in order to control production and pricing. These combinations were in select industries such as oil, sugar, and steel, and were for the most part horizontal (that is, in the same industry), resulting in a highly concentrated industrial groups. John Moody calculated that during this first wave, roughly 5,300 industrial sites were consolidated into just 318 industrial trusts.[4] During this period, Standard Oil of New Jersey consolidated the oil industry and U.S. Steel, at the behest of J.P. Morgan, Sr., consolidated the steel industry; they each controlled over three quarters of their respective industries.

In response to this massive consolidation of industries into trusts and monopolies, Congress for the first time began to regulate takeovers from an antitrust perspective. Three key regulatory actions included the enactment of the Sherman Antitrust Act in 1905, the enactment of the Clayton Antitrust Act in 1914, and the creation of the Federal Trade Commission (FTC) in 1914.

a.   Sherman Antitrust Act

The Sherman Antitrust Act makes contracts, trusts, or conspiracies that unreasonably restrain competition and that affect interstate commerce illegal. The Act also makes it a felony to "monopolize, or attempt to monopolize, or combine or conspire with any other person or persons, to monopolize any part of the trade or commerce among the several States, or with foreign nations." (15 U.S.C. § 2).

Although the Sherman Act was enacted in 1890, the Department of Justice (DOJ) and the courts were reluctant to enforce it until Theodore Roosevelt became president.

> During the first decade of the Sherman Act's enforcement, the U.S. Supreme Court was indifferent to the creation and exercise of monopoly power. In cases such as United States v. E.C. Knight Co., the Court declined to prohibit consolidation of ninety-eight percent of the country's sugar refining capacity in the hands of the Sugar Trust. Almost another decade passed before the Court blocked a merger which would create a monopoly; in 1904, the Court ruled in favor of the DOJ in its Sherman Act challenge to the Great Northern and Northern Pacific railways combination. President Theodore Roosevelt, a man often depicted in political cartoons as the ultimate trustbuster, had urged the DOJ to sue the railways. In the 1904 election, Roosevelt described the Great Northern case as one of the "great achievements of [his] administration." Roosevelt's contemporaneous statements also recognized, however, that combinations could produce scale and scope efficiencies that benefited the consumer.[5]

---

[4]   *See* JOHN MOODY, THE TRUTH ABOUT THE TRUSTS: A DESCRIPTION AND ANALYSIS OF THE AMERICAN TRUST MOVEMENT 486 (1904).

[5]   Ilene Knable Gotts, et al., *Nature vs. Nurture and Reaching the Age of Reason: The U.S./E.U. Treatment of Transatlantic Mergers*, 61 N.Y.U. ANN. SURV. AM. L. 453, 456–57 (2005).

Although the effectiveness of President Roosevelt's actions to break up the trusts is debated, in the popular mind he is still viewed as the President who began and led the effort to do so.

Theodore Roosevelt[6]

Roosevelt aiming a cannon at the oil trust[7]

In 1911 perhaps the greatest victory of the trust busters occurred when the Supreme Court in *Standard Oil Co. of New Jersey v. United States,* 221 U.S. 1 (1911), ruled that the Standard Oil trust was illegal under the Sherman Antitrust Act. Standard Oil was subsequently split

---

6   T. Roosevelt Cartoon. *'Jiu-Jitsued': American cartoon,* c1906, available at http://fineart america.com/featured/1–t–roosevelt-cartoon-granger.html.

7   ST. LOUIS POST-DISPATCH, Nov. 1906.

up into thirty-four different companies. Nonetheless, trusts remained a significant public issue. In the 1912 Presidential campaign, Woodrow Wilson challenged Roosevelt's strategy regarding trusts.

> Like Roosevelt, Wilson viewed the growth of large corporations as an inevitable component of economic progress. And, like Roosevelt, he supported an active role for the government in overseeing the economic system. Unlike Roosevelt, however, Wilson shared Taft's view that the federal government should only police the activities of business, not direct the economy. Wilson believed that if the government could prevent the abuses of monopoly power, natural competition would prevail and make it unnecessary for the government to actively regulate the economy. Unlike Taft, however, Wilson did not wish to leave the policing to the judicial branch. He preferred instead the creation of administrative agencies with this oversight function. Wilson's philosophy, then, contained elements of both Lockean liberalism and republicanism. This combined philosophy relegated the government to playing a largely reactionary role—so long as business behaved properly, government would not interfere in its operations. The result was piecemeal regulation, rather than a central plan for coordinating the economy.[8]

A second wave of mergers began during Wilson's presidency, and continued until the Great Depression. During this period, heightened antitrust enforcement impeded horizontal mergers (mergers among competitors). Instead, during this wave the predominant transaction form was the vertical merger (mergers among companies in a supply chain), as oligopolies were formed. As noted, Wilson's presidency saw continued vigor in regulating and breaking up the trusts with the enactment of the Clayton Antitrust Act and the Federal Trade Commission Act.

b. Clayton Antitrust Act

The Clayton Antitrust Act, enacted in 1914, expanded on the Sherman Act. The Act made substantive additions related to four topics: price discrimination, exclusive dealings and tying, mergers and acquisitions, and corporate governance. However, despite its attempts to enhance the Sherman Act, the Clayton Antitrust Act came under fire for failing to do much of anything.[9]

---

[8] Deborah A. Ballam, *The Evolution of the Government-Business Relationship in the United States: Colonial Times to Present,* 31 AM. BUS. L. J. 553, 619–20 (1994).

[9] *See* Commentary, *Judicial Interpretation of § 7 of the Clayton Act,* 39 YALE L. J. 1042 (1930).

c.Federal Trade Commission

The FTC was created by the Federal Trade Commission Act; the Act was enacted in 1914, a month before the Clayton Act. The FTC is comprised of five commissioners, with no more than three commissioners from the same political party. Commissioners have staggered seven-year terms and are appointed by the President of the United States with consent by the Senate.[10] In addition to enforcing the Federal Trade Commission Act, the FTC was granted wide investigatory and supervisory powers relating to U.S. antitrust enforcement.

d.The Great Depression and Subsequent Reform

The stock market crash of 1929 brought on the Great Depression and exposed numerous fraudulent practices in the period leading up to the crash. For example, Goldman Sachs & Co. became embroiled in a scandal over the Goldman Sachs Trading Corp., an investment fund that collapsed in the Great Depression amid accusations of fraud and insider trading. These and other real and perceived abuses led Congress to pass the Securities Act of 1933 and Securities Exchange Act of 1934, among other laws. These two acts as amended over the years are now among the main federal laws regulating M&A activity.

3.THIRD WAVE OF U.S. MERGER ACTIVITY: THE CONGLOMERATES

By the early 1960s, large corporations were experiencing increased cash flows and skyrocketing stock prices. Rather than "waste" corporate cash by paying out dividends, management used excess funds to acquire other companies. However, the federal government began to vigorously enforce antitrust laws in the 1960s.[11] Government enforcement prevented mergers between companies in the same line of business. These events cued the conglomerate acquisition craze.

Conglomerate mergers involve two companies in unrelated businesses. A typical 1960s conglomerate merger involved a large corporation acquiring a smaller, poorly-managed corporation. The preeminent finance theorists of the time believed that conglomerates offered several benefits. First, a conglomerate would decrease its financial risk through diversification of businesses within a corporate umbrella. The conglomerate corporation would have many products across many markets, reducing the impact of a market downturn on corporate profits. Second, a corporation could expand its product lines and market share through a conglomerate merger. It was also theorized that economies of

---

[10]15 U.S.C. § 41 (2015).

[11]See Joseph C. Gallo, Kenneth Dau-Schmidt & Joseph L. Craycraft, *Department of Justice Antitrust Enforcement 1955–1997: An Empirical Study*, 17 REV. OF INDUS. ORG. 75 (2000).

scale would allow maximization of human capital and operational resources, allowing management knowledge and capital that could be shared across unrelated businesses.

At the height of the conglomerate craze, from 1967 to 1969, more than 10,000 companies were acquired; the total during the 1960s was approximately 25,000 acquisitions. These acquisitions gave rise to gigantic corporate conglomerates. Consider, for example, International Telephone and Telegraph Corporation, a manufacturer of telecommunications equipment and operating telephone systems:

> From 1960 to 1977, with Harold Geneen at the helm, ITT acquired more than 350 companies—at one time securing deals at the rate of one acquisition per week. The portfolio included well-known businesses such as Sheraton hotels, Avis Rent-a-Car, Hartford Insurance and Continental Baking, the maker of Wonder Bread. Under Geneen's management, ITT grew from a medium-sized business with $760 million in sales to a global corporation with $17 billion in sales.[12]

By the early 1970s, it was clear that the touted benefits of conglomerates were not being realized. Diversification of businesses within a corporate entity did not yield the expected profits. Conglomerates needed to "keep buying companies and writing up earnings. It was magic, until the pyramid became top-heavy and fell."[13] Companies' managements could not develop their vast empires and control the various enterprises within the empires. The conglomerate bubble burst. Corporations began exploring ways to divest business divisions and break conglomerates up into manageable segments. This gave rise to the fourth wave of takeover activity: "going-private" transactions.

4. FOURTH WAVE OF U.S. MERGER ACTIVITY: HOSTILE TAKEOVERS AND THE RISE OF PRIVATE EQUITY

In the 1970s and 1980s, takeover activity exploded into the popular consciousness. It was prominently featured not only in the media but also in Hollywood movies. Scholars, politicians, and market participants, also commented extensively on the subject. This period featured high-stakes hostile takeovers, defense mechanisms with evocative names such as the "poison pill," the dramatic rise of private equity, and innovative forms of financing, mainly the leveraged buy-out. The fourth wave of takeover

---

[12] *History of ITT*, International Telephone and Telegraph Corporation, available at http://www.itt.com/about/history/.

[13] JOHN BROOKS, THE GO-GO YEARS: THE DRAMA AND CRASHING FINALE OF WALL STREET'S BULLISH 60S 158 (1998).

activity focused on unwinding the 1960s corporate conglomerates. By 1977, fifty-three percent of all U.S. takeovers were the result of conglomerate divestitures—a sale of a company by a conglomerate. Conglomerate divestitures were given substantial impetus by the creation of the "junk bond" market by Drexel Burnham Lambert's Michael Milken and the ready financing junk bonds provided. Junk bonds are bonds rated below investment grade. Milken was able to attract sources of capital that had previously considered the junk bond market too risky. This new capital was available to fund merger and acquisition transactions, including some by acquirers that would otherwise have had difficulty obtaining capital from more traditional sources.

M&A activity was not limited to corporate divestitures. Conglomerate corporations came under siege during the early 1980s. Acquirers initiated unsolicited hostile acquisitions through cash tender offers financed by junk bonds with the aim of busting up under performing conglomerates. Contested tender offers increased from twelve in 1980 to forty-six in 1988.[14] No company was safe as acquirers aimed for bigger and bigger targets: of the Fortune 500 companies in 1980, at least twenty-eight percent were acquired by 1989.[15] Acquisition attempts were quick and public, often catching unsuspecting management off guard. T. Boone Pickens, Carl Icahn, Ronald Perelman, and other so-called "corporate raiders," developed innovative bidding tactics and takeover methods to enable them to expedite the acquisition process. In response, target boards implemented defensive measures, including poison pills, shark repellents, Pac-Man defenses, golden parachutes, and greenmail. These are discussed in Chapter XV.[16] The Delaware Court of Chancery approved the use of defensive mechanisms in hostile acquisitions, in particular poison pills, arming target boards with tools to fight raiders' bids. Indeed, M&A's core legal doctrines developed between the late 1970s and late 1980s as a result of the heightened number of takeovers and the creativity of bidders and targets. The fourth wave of takeover activity thus had a fundamental impact on modern M&A.

The 1980s also saw the rise of leveraged buyout firms, now known as private equity firms. Between 1985 and 1989, more than 1,625 private equity buy-outs or "going-private" transactions occurred. The 1980s private equity firms were "lean, decentralized organizations with

[14] MALCOLM SALTER & WOLF WINHOLD, MERGER TRENDS AND PROSPECTS OF THE 1980S 32 (1980).

[15] Andrei Shleifer & Robert W. Vishny, *Takeovers in the '60s and the '80s Evidence and Implications*, 12 STRATEGIC MGMT. J. 51, 53 (1991).

[16] M&A is—fortunately or unfortunately—jargon-filled. We generally define terms as we use them, but students may also want to refer to an online glossary such as Latham & Watkins' *Book of Jargon*, available at http://www.lw.com/bookofjargon-apps/BOJ–GlobalMandA for a particular definition.

relatively few investment professional and employees."[17] The first such firm was Kohlberg, Kravis, Roberts & Co. (KKR), formed in 1976. Private equity firms solicited investors, primarily pension funds, pooling their money to acquire underperforming companies. They charged annual management fees and acquisition fees as well as fees to monitor the companies they acquired. Private equity firms were thus intimately involved in the operations of these companies. Management accountability, operations outside of public markets, long-term financial goals, and leverage allowed private equity firms to realize high returns on their acquisitions.

KKR pioneered the private equity model using financing from pension funds and junk bonds. During the 1980s, KKR completed "nearly $60 billion in acquisitions, buying companies as diverse as Safeway Stores, Duracell, Motel 6, Stop & Shop, Avis, Tropicana, and Playtex."[18] In 1979, KKR completed its first major leveraged buy-out, of Houdaille Industries for $380 million. Fast forward ten years, KKR won a bidding war against a management buy-out group to purchase RJR/Nabisco in a then-record-setting $31.1 billion leveraged buyout. The RJR/Nabisco transaction was later memorialized in the book and movie, "Barbarians at the Gate." At the time, the leveraged buyout (LBO) was a new approach to financing acquisitions. In an LBO, private equity firms borrowed money against the target corporation's assets to finance the purchase of the target corporation. George Anders explained: "[a]s merchants of debt, the KKR men could control a giant company's stock and claim a fat share of eventual profits, at hardly any cost to themselves. All they needed was the audacity to propose and carry out these combinations of borrowed money and borrowed management."[19] Private equity firms obtained financing from large commercial banks, and from junk bonds, to make million- or billion-dollar hostile takeover offers. At one point Michael Milken and his Drexel associates underwrote $20 billion in junk bonds annually.[20]

KKR's takeover of RJR/Nabisco represented the last major leveraged-buyout transaction of the 1980s. In the late 1980s, the junk bond market crashed in part due to heavy saturation by the debt needed for the RJR/Nabisco deal. One news account described the junk bond market as

---

[17] Steven N. Kaplan & Per Stroemberg, *Leverage Buyouts and Private Equity*, 22 J. ECON. PERSP. 121, 123 (2009).

[18] GEORGE ANDERS, MERCHANTS OF DEBT: KKR AND THE MORTGAGING OF AMERICAN BUSINESS XV (1992).

[19] *Id.* at 21.

[20] *Id.* at 83. Michael Milken later pleaded guilty to six counts of securities law violations and was sentenced to ten years in prison, a sentence that was reduced to two years. He also paid $600 million in total fines and restitution.

"groaning under an avalanche of RJR Nabisco Inc. securities."[21] The private equity and leveraged buy-out acquisition wave was over, and takeover activity entered a quiet period.

5.   THE FIFTH WAVE OF U.S. MERGER ACTIVITY

The fifth wave of U.S. merger activity, ranging from approximately 1992 to 2001, has been described as the era of the "mega deal." During this period, companies of unprecedented global size and scale were created; the size and number of M&A deals was largely unprecedented as well.[22] Like the preceding waves, it was driven by the buoyancy of the stock market. This wave included the technology (or dot.com) bubble. It came to a halt due to the equity market collapse in 2000, when the bubble burst.

Throughout the fifth wave, there was a strong drive toward larger economies of scale. Several multinational conglomerates were created under the widely held belief that competitive advantage was best achieved through size. This belief motivated mergers between companies such as Chrysler and Daimler-Benz, Exxon and Mobil, Boeing and McDonnell Douglas, Morgan Stanley and Dean Witter, and AOL and Time Warner.[23] Large-scale transactions such as these required substantial financing. During this wave, debt became less common as a financing tool, and was replaced with equity.

The strategic transactions of the fifth wave were in part focused around inflated equity securities. During this wave, the stock market values of several large companies took off, and various market indices reached new highs. The technology or dot.com bubble, mentioned above, began in the late 1990s, popping in 2001.[24]

While each takeover wave may originate out of similar circumstances, the individual waves are typically characterized by different transaction types and industry concentrations. The fifth wave was no exception.

> Certain industries accounted for a disproportionate share of the total dollar volume of M&A in the United States during the fifth merger wave. In particular, banking and finance and

---

[21] *See* Robert Lenzer, *RJR Nabisco Issue May Bring Junk Bonds Into the Mainstream,* CHI. TRIB., Mar. 19, 1989, available at http://articles.chicagotribune.com/1989–03–19/business/89032 70950_1_ostrander-capital-rjr-nabisco-junk-bonds.

[22] *See* Marina Martynova & Luc Renneboog, *Takeover Waves: Triggers, Performance and Motives,* CentER Discussion Paper; Vol. 2005–107; TILEC Discussion Paper, Sept. 2005, available at https://pure.uvt.nl/portal/files/776337/107.pdf.

[23] *See* Martin Lipton, *The Davies Lecture at Osgoode Hall Law Sch., York Univ.: Merger Waves in the 19th, 20th and 21st Centuries,* CORNERSTONE BUS. SERVS. (Sept. 14, 2006), available at http://cornerstone-business.com/MergerWavesTorontoLipton.pdf.

[24] Mark L. Mitchell & J. Harold Mulherin, *The Impact of Industry Shocks on Takeover and Restructuring Activity,* 41 J. FIN. ECON. 193 (1996).

communications and broadcasting accounted for 26.5% of all U.S. deals over the period of 1993–2004. However, the percentage accounted for in these industries rose from a low of 7.5% in 1994 to a high of 41.9% of deals in 1999. This was caused by a combination of factors including the continued impact of deregulation and consolidation of the banking industry as well as the dramatic changes that were going on in telecom and Internet-related businesses. The fifth wave would have been different had it not been for the "inflating" yet short-lived impact of these sectors.[25]

Roll-ups and consolidations were also a significant feature of the fifth wave. These roll-ups involved the consolidation of fragmented industries through larger-scale acquisitions by companies called "consolidators." A group of investment banks began specializing in financing roll-ups and issuing stock in these newly consolidated companies. Roll-ups were intended to combine smaller companies into national-scale businesses so that these companies could market nationally rather than regionally. While these benefits existed in theory, the track record of many of these consolidation deals was poor.

During the fifth wave, M&A activity tended to occur between firms in related industries. We also saw the beginnings of international M&A, something that would come to define merger activity in the sixth wave. The onset of the new millennium, the bursting of the dot-com bubble, and the tightening of banking standards on issuing credit, all served to end the fifth wave of M&A.

6. THE SIXTH WAVE OF U.S. MERGER ACTIVITY: MODERN M&A ACTIVITY

The sixth wave of U.S. merger activity was an era of private equity and cross-border transactions that was relatively short, yet intense, ending abruptly with the financial crisis.

After the collapse of the technology bubble and subsequent global downturn, the U.S. entered a brief recession. The Federal Reserve System lowered its primary interest rate to combat the recession. As the economy recovered, merger activity began picking up. During 2004–2008, deal-making became a truly global business. The trade winds of globalization forced businesses to look beyond their national borders for a competitive advantage worldwide. This wave was boosted by the advent of global capital, increased hedge fund activity, an unprecedented wave of liquidity, and the availability of cheap credit due to low interest rates and

---

[25] PATRICK A. GAUGHAN, MERGERS, ACQUISITIONS, AND CORPORATE RESTRUCTURINGS 69 (5th ed. 2015).

global savings imbalances. Because of this liquidity and low interest rates, cash replaced stock as the primary acquisition currency.[26]

Private equity acquirers taking advantage of cheap credit drove the sixth wave. Private equity took off in this era, as shareholders looked to spread the ownership and day-to-day management of their companies between themselves and institutional investors.

> In the sixth wave private equity acquirers bought companies (or divisions of companies), waited for the rising market to push up the value of their acquisitions, and then spun them off. And although private equity companies were not new to the M&A market, private equity buyers became major players during this time due to the low cost of capital. Private equity investors backed more than half of the large transactions concluded in the period. These increasingly targeted technological firms—in deals like the $1.1 billion purchase of DoubleClick by Hellman & Friedman—or teamed up with fund mega-deals, such as the $10.4 billion acquisitions of SunGard Data Systems. And since the bulk of the financing that paid for these acquisitions was low-interest-rate debt, these firms were able to generate high returns for the equity holders upon disposal. Historically low interest rates therefore not only fueled the growth of the merger wave but also, for the first time, allowed private equity companies to play a significant role in the market.[27]

A substantial proportion of M&A activity in the sixth wave was cross-border transactions, reflecting the growing globalization of products, services, and capital markets. The sixth wave occurred in the context of deregulation in Asia, market integration in Europe, low interest rates, and a historically weak dollar.[28] The result was heightened cross-border investment. Developing nations' entry into the M&A market became increasingly important in modern M&A. During the sixth wave, China, India, and Brazil emerged as global players in trade and industry, making cross-cultural negotiation skills a central component of the cross-border M&A practice.

The sixth wave ended in 2008, as credit became more expensive, and more dramatically, as the financial crisis began. From 2008 to 2010, M&A activity sank to its lowest levels since 2004. As this book is being written in 2015, M&A activity is only now recovering to pre-financial crisis levels as companies remain hesitant to pursue risky M&A transactions and

---

[26] *See generally* George Alexandridis, et al., *How Have M&As Changed? Evidence from the Sixth Merger Wave,* 18 EUR. J. FIN. 663 (2012).

[27] KILLIAN J. MCCARTHY & WILFRED DOLFSMA, UNDERSTANDING MERGERS AND ACQUISITIONS IN THE 21ST CENTURY: A MULTIDISCIPLINARY APPROACH 26 (2013).

[28] DONALD DEPAMPHILIS, MERGERS, ACQUISITIONS, AND OTHER RESTRUCTURING ACTIVITIES (2d ed. 2008).

private equity's role remains diminished. Still, we are seeing some large scale M&A transactions occur as certain industries contract into a small number of key players, including the telecommunications and cable industries. Meanwhile, internet companies like Google and Facebook are reviving the conglomerate model through large-scale investment in a variety of different technologies.

B. DRIVERS OF MERGERS AND ACQUISITIONS

We have already seen that M&A activity often comes in waves. When stock markets are frothy and optimistic, M&A activity increases. Indeed, deal size and volume of activity is often taken as a rough proxy for health of financial markets and the economy in general. Large M&A transactions can certainly be headline getters, but does a multitude of large, high-profile transactions indicate that value is being created? The answer to this question depends in part on why parties decide to do deals.

1. THE ECONOMIC RATIONALES FOR MERGERS AND ACQUISITIONS

There are many reasons companies do a merger or undertake an acquisition. For example, as was the case in the first merger wave, industries may be prone to consolidation as industry players seek to use M&A as a way to gain scale or eliminate competition, either by acquiring competitors in horizontal mergers or by acquiring participants in the vertical supply chain. Alternatively, acquirers may be seeking to add complementary business units and seek "synergies" through the combination. There are other rationales as well. In the third merger wave, the age of the conglomerates, dealmakers pursued deliberate diversification strategies, and thus sought to combine seemingly unrelated operating units under the umbrella of a single holding company. In recent years, technology companies have pursued targets, often not for the technology the targets own or the products the targets make, but to get access to the target's human capital, through so called "acqui-hiring."

Some transactions may be best explained by reference to manager motivations. Managers may be motivated to merge or enter into acquisition transactions to build "empires" (the so-called "hubris hypothesis"). Such transactions may be less about efficiencies and more about managerial "agency costs" (that is, "costs" that reflect the ability of officers and directors to be advancing their own interests rather than those of the corporation and its shareholders). Agency costs can also lead to another important kind of transaction: the hostile takeover. Where incumbent managers underperform market expectations, shareholder activists or corporate raiders may have incentives to attempt to acquire the corporation over the objections of those managers. In the empire-building situations, the transaction is motivated by agency costs: the manager's empire is being created at his company's expense. In some hostile takeovers, agency costs play a different role: the transactions are intended to reduce or limit agency costs the acquirers believe are being imposed by incumbent management.

Depending on the motivation and the specific circumstances that drive the transaction in question, transactions may be more or less likely to be value creating. Deals are also subject to normal business and operational risk. Even a deal that was well-conceived and well-executed may be unsuccessful. When a buyer engages in an M&A transaction in order to move into a new or emerging business sector, the newly acquired technology or product may not be successful in the marketplace. Also, even if the target's product is the best one available, integration of merged entities can be a complicated process. Indeed, more than a few mergers have failed during the post-closing integration process. Besides operational challenges to integration, there may also be cultural challenges. These challenges may be hard to anticipate prior to a deal, but inability to address them after the deal closes may lead to deal failure. For instance, questions about pay levels and benefits packages for mid-level managers may not attract attention during the process of negotiating a transaction, but can cause significant discord after the closing.

Given the complexities involved, it is not surprising that economic studies of M&A do not provide a clear answer to the question "Does M&A create value?" M&A transactions almost always create "value" for the seller (target) insofar as the transactions are typically done at prices exceeding the target's pre-deal market price. (The excess over market price is known as a premium.) Studies of merger premia for targets find average premia in the range of thirty percent above pre-announcement trading prices. The more interesting question is whether targets are worth the premium paid for them. If acquirers (bidders) systematically overpay for targets, one might question whether more oversight by acquirer shareholders is appropriate. On the other hand, if sellers are systematically undercompensated for their stock in an M&A transaction, then one must question whether boards are living up to their obligations to seek the highest price reasonably available to shareholders.

An early review of studies of merger transactions observed:

> We have a conundrum. Ex ante, mergers appear to create value for bidder and target together that is substantial relative to the premerger worth of the target firm. That is, the financial markets appear to believe that bidders can wring a lot more value from the typical target's assets. Ex post, recent studies run

exactly in the opposite direction, indicating that mergers not merely fail to warrant acquisition premia but actually reduce the real profitability of acquired business units, increase the intra-industry dispersion of plants' productivity levels, and shrivel the acquiree's market share.[29]

Another review of fifty-four different economic studies assessing whether M&A transactions generated value for acquirers found that forty percent of the studies reported cumulative negative returns to acquirers from M&A activity.[30] In other words, acquirers on the whole paid too much for the companies they acquired. The balance of studies reviewed in this article reported zero or positive cumulative returns to acquirers. The mixed evidence with respect to the value of M&A for acquirers suggests that a measured view with respect to the value of doing deals may be appropriate, something that may be very easy to forget in the fast-moving, high-profile, and highly lucrative world of deal-making.

Why might acquirers pay too much? One hypothesis is that some CEOs are overconfident, and are particularly apt to pay too much when their companies have generated a great deal of cash flow.[31] But why would their shareholders allow this? If not infrequently, acquirers are paying too much, why are their shareholders not demanding acquisitions be curtailed? One article argues that acquirer shareholders expect their companies to overpay for something—if not an acquisition target, then something else—and that the acquirer's stock price takes that expectation into account.[32] Another explanation is that shareholders have too little say in these acquisitions, including too little power to stop them, a subject to which we will return in later Chapters.

2. WHEN M&A GOES WRONG: THE CASE OF AOL/TIME WARNER

AOL's acquisition of Time Warner in 2001, at the height of the dot com tech stock bubble, is perhaps the quintessential example of deal overreach and deal-making gone wrong. By the time the deal was unwound in 2013 with the spin-off of AOL from Time Warner, it was widely panned as one of the worst deals in history, resulting in the destruction of well over $100 billion in value. Before announcement of the transaction, Time Warner had been struggling for years to put together a strategy that would combine its content businesses with its cable

---

[29] Richard E. Caves, *Mergers, Takeovers, and Economic Efficiency*, 7 INT. J. IND. ORG. 151, 167 (1989).

[30] *See* Robert Bruner, *Where M&A Pays and Where It Strays: A Survey of the Research*, 16 J. APPLIED CORP. FIN. 63 (2004).

[31] *See* Ulrike Malmendier & Geoffrey Tate, *CEO Overconfidence and Corporate Investment*, 60 J. FIN. 2661(2005).

[32] Bernard Black, *Bidder Overpayment in Takeovers*, 41 STAN. L. REV. 597 (1989).

businesses. The vision motivating the deal, still radical at the time but almost obvious now, was that the future would see a rapid convergence around broadband content delivery via untraditional avenues like the nascent Internet. The 1989 merger between Time and Warner was motivated in part by this vision, as was Paramount's subsequent merger with Viacom.[33]

The AOL/Time Warner transaction involved two companies, one an upstart internet access provider and the other one of the oldest and most respected companies on the media landscape. At the time of the deal, AOL's market capitalization was more than double Time Warner's, but AOL had less than one-quarter the revenue of its new partner.[34] Although the deal was characterized as a "merger of equals" with the new board consisting of 16 members, half from the old boards of each of AOL and Time Warner, it was clearly perceived to be an acquisition of Time Warner by AOL using AOL's inflated stock as currency. When the deal was announced, Steve Case, co-founder of AOL proclaimed, "This is a historic moment in which new media has truly come of age."[35]

At the time, the deal was the largest deal ever—then valued at almost $350 billion. It was subject to criticism almost immediately.[36] Again, the deal could have been prescient: the future would be about broadband connections and content, and this transaction was seemed ideally situated to combine the two. Time Warner had a large base of cable subscribers who could be funneled into AOL's Internet network. Given AOL's email and instant messaging services (IM), customers might be locked in, thus generating real value for the merged company.

In reality, however, the government and the market were already moving to open up walled garden Internet services (i.e., internet services that kept customers effectively confined to their own internal websites). As a condition to approving the transaction, the FTC and the DOJ required that Time Warner open up its cable systems to competing Internet service providers. Combined with a market move away from ISP (Internet service provider) based email and messaging services towards portable, Internet-based services, much of the impetus for the transaction withered away.

---

[33] *See Paramount Communications, Inc. v. Time*, Inc., 571 A.2d 1140 (Del. 1989); *see also Paramount Communications v. QVC Network*, 637 A.2d 34 (Del. 1994), further discussed in Chapter XVIII.B.

[34] Richard Pérez-Peña, *Time Warner Board Backs AOL Spinoff*, N.Y. TIMES, May 28, 2009, available at http://www.nytimes.com/2009/05/29/business/media/29warner.html?_r=0.

[35] Tim Arango, *How the AOL-Time Warner Merger Went So Wrong*, N.Y. TIMES, January 10, 2010, available at http://www.nytimes.com/2010/01/11/business/media/11merger.html.

[36] At the time, reporter Kara Swisher derided the transaction, saying, "[a] company without assets is buying a company without a clue." KARA SWISHER & LISA DICKEY, THERE MUST BE A PONY IN HERE SOMEWHERE prologue (2003). Don Logan, head of Time Inc. responded thusly to news of the transaction: "Dumbest idea I had ever heard in my life." Arango, *supra* note 35.

Over the course of the next ten years, the combined AOL-Time Warner was unable to achieve anything near the promised benefits and its stock price reflected this failure to deliver.

Figure 1: Performance of Time Warner stock since 1993.

Zoom: 1d 5d 1m 3m 6m YTD 1y 5y 10y All
Jan 08, 1999 - Dec 12, 2014 -34.22 (-29.42%)

280
260
240
220
200
180
160
140
120
100
80
60
40

Merger   Spin Off

1999 2000 2001 2002 2003 2004 2005 2006 2007 2008 2009 2010 2011 2012 2013 2014

By 2009, AOL-Time Warner declared its intention to spin off AOL. As part of the spin off transaction, AOL-Time Warner changed its name back to Time Warner Inc., thus closing the book on AOL's acquisition of Time Warner and providing a final chapter for the story of the dot.com bubble.

3. THE REGULATORY DRIVERS OF M&A: THE CASE OF INVERSIONS

M&A can be motivated by factors generally considered positive ones for the overall economy, such as economies of scale or scope. But it can also be motivated by something which, from a societal perspective, may be a bit more complicated: "regulatory arbitrage," an attempt to reduce regulatory costs, including for this purpose taxes. The transaction at issue in *Smith v. Van Gorkom*, discussed in Chapter XVII.A, was in part driven by the target's desire to take advantage of investment tax credits that it could not fully utilize because it had insufficient taxable income, but that could be valuable to an acquirer.

During the writing of this textbook, one type of transaction in the news was the "inversion," in which a U.S. corporation acquires a foreign corporation and reincorporates in the foreign country, while maintaining its U.S. operations. The U.S. taxes a U.S. domiciled corporation's income wherever it is earned to the extent it is brought back to the U.S. Other countries do not have global tax systems, however. Consequently, following the inversion, the former-U.S. corporation no longer pays U.S. taxes on its global income, but only on its U.S. sourced income. Inversion transactions have been politically unpopular, with the U.S. corporations being accused of not "paying their fair share." How much of a difference the ability to reincorporate outside the U.S. makes for aggregate revenue collection by the U.S. Treasury is an interesting question—certainly, corporations have many ways to structure their operations in a manner that minimizes their operations and income in the US. After a flurry of inversion transactions in 2014, including AbbVie's announced $55 billion acquisition of Shire, the U.S. Treasury Department announced new regulations designed to halt these transactions. In the wake of these newly announced regulations, AbbVie terminated the acquisition. But at this writing, in November of 2015, inversions remain possible—and controversial. The pattern is familiar: a transaction that allows for tax savings is limited due to political pressure. Sometimes the limitation effectively ends the transactions, but sometimes not.

Many other transactions that are not done solely, or perhaps even principally, for tax reasons, nevertheless benefit enormously from tax effects. A notable example is a leveraged buyout (LBO). As we will see, in a LBO, a company is purchased from its shareholders, and much of the money paid to the shareholders is borrowed from a bank, to be repaid by the company. Generally, interest payments are deductible from a company's income, whereas dividends are not. All else equal, replacing dividend payments with interest payments will lower, often significantly, a company's tax burden, meaning that the amounts of foregone taxes are not available to meet the government's revenue needs.

C. A NOTE ON APPLICABLE LAW

What is the law of M&A? Many bodies of law are relevant. The most relevant, and the ones on which we will spend most of our time in this book, are state corporate law and federal securities law. Each state has its own corporate law. The state corporate law principally applies to corporations incorporated in that state, but has some provisions governing other corporations as well. (That internal affairs of corporations, including relationships among shareholders and the corporation, are principally governed by the law of the state of incorporation is called the "internal affairs doctrine.") Corporate law relevant to mergers and acquisitions includes the mechanics of how to merge, and when shareholders of a company that has merged can ask a court to appraise the value of their shares. It also includes law on governance matters such as elections, annual and special meetings, and access to corporate books and records; all of these can take on particular importance in the context of mergers and acquisitions.

State corporate law also has provisions relevant to corporate defenses against being taken over. Thirty nine states' corporate laws also include "anti-takeover" statutes, which apply to acquisitions of corporations that are either incorporated in the state or have some significant relationship to the state. We discuss these statutes further in Chapter XV.G. Corporate law, especially the corporate common law, establishes principles and provides examples for how corporate management must act when it wants to sell a corporation, when it wants to resist selling the corporation to anyone, or when it is choosing among potential buyers.

Our principal state law focus will be on the corporate law of Delaware, the Delaware General Corporation Law, Title 8 of the Delaware Code ("DGCL"). Why Delaware? A corporation is not required to incorporate in its principal place of business; indeed, a corporation need not have much of a relationship with the state in which it is incorporated except a "legal" one, maintaining a registered agent (who, among other things, can be served with process if the corporation is sued), filing documents, paying taxes, and, of course, complying with the provisions of the corporate law. In a state where the corporation does business but is not incorporated, it may, depending on state law and the scope of business, be required to register to do business as a foreign corporation in that state.

For a variety of historical reasons, today the majority of public companies incorporate in Delaware. According to the Delaware Secretary of State's website, "[t]oday, more than one million business entities have made Delaware their legal home . . . [M]ore than 60 percent of the Fortune 500 companies are incorporated in Delaware."[37] Delaware's advantages as a place of incorporation include the sophistication of its Court of Chancery and the predictability and, many would say, business-friendly nature, of its jurisprudence, and corporate lawyers' familiarity with the law, both the statute and the cases. Other states are also highly influenced by Delaware corporate law, with many non-Delaware court decisions making express reference to it.

The Delaware Chancery Court is the trial court below the Delaware Supreme Court. The Delaware Chancery Court consists of five members each appointed to twelve-year terms by the Delaware legislature. The Chancery Court is a court of equity specializing in corporate law disputes. This specialization gives the judges significant experience and knowledge in corporate matters. In addition, the five judges communicate extensively with the corporate bar, performing a similar function as a traditional regulator. This means that even though it is not the court of last resort in Delaware, the Chancery Court is extremely influential.

Delaware has a significant volume of M&A lawsuits, which has led its corporate law to be highly developed. Chapters XVI–XIX discuss many of the important cases. These cases are important not only in Delaware, but are also influential throughout the country. At present, litigation is almost inevitable for any transaction of an appreciable size: a recent

---

[37] From http://corplaw.delaware.gov/eng/why_delaware.shtml.

study found that in 2011, litigation occurred in ninety-two percent of transactions with a value greater than $100 million.[38]

Federal securities laws also play an important role in M&A regulation. These laws address:

- How a tender offer—which is, roughly speaking, a public purchase of a significant proportion of a public company's stock from its shareholders—must be conducted;

- The disclosures shareholders of public companies must receive in connection with votes on various matters relevant to mergers and acquisitions;

- Disclosures shareholders must get in connection with stock or debt issued in mergers and acquisition transactions; and

- The disclosures that must be made by those acquiring more than five percent of a public company; such acquisitions might presage an attempt to take over the company.

The federal securities laws are enforced by the Securities and Exchange Commission ("SEC"), which also has the power to promulgate rules and regulations under those laws. The SEC was established in 1934. Its mission is to "protect investors, maintain fair, orderly, and efficient markets, and facilitate capital formation."[39] You may be familiar with the SEC as the guardian of capital markets, prosecuting securities fraud. But the agency also regularly reviews disclosure by public issuers and is responsible for the general regulation of the stock markets. In M&A, the SEC has two primary roles: (1) to administer the proxy rules governing voting on mergers and acquisitions and (2) to administer the rules governing tender offers. For the most part, this involves reviewing disclosure filings by the parties. However, it can, although rarely does, involve an enforcement action for violating the substantive rules under the securities laws. The SEC also responds to letters sent by lawyers asking about the SEC's position on a particular matter. The lawyers request, and sometimes get, confirmation that if they proceed based on their interpretation of a rule, the SEC will "take no action." These letters are therefore called "no action letters."

The SEC also has a second, more prominent, enforcement role in M&A. Insider trading is common in companies involved or potentially involved in M&A. The SEC is concerned with the possibility of insider trading, and spends considerable resources investigating it. It may examine trading in the days and months prior to the announcement of an

---

[38] *See* Matthew D. Cain & Steven M. Davidoff Solomon, *A Great Game: The Dynamics of State Competition and Litigation*, 100 IOWA L. REV. 165 (2015).

[39] U.S. Sec. & Exch. Comm'n, *The Investor's Advocate: How the SEC Protects Investors, Maintains Market Integrity, and Facilitates Capital Formation*, available at http://www.sec.gov/about/whatwedo.shtml, (last visited Feb. 18, 2013).

acquisition. Often the SEC, together with the stock exchanges, will send requests to the parties to provide a list of people at the company and third-party advisors who worked on the transaction. The SEC uses this list as part of its investigation to spot unusual trading. Prosecutions for insider trading may be brought as a result.

In addition to Delaware and federal securities law, we will also touch on a few other bodies of law, particularly tax and antitrust law. M&A transactions always involve tax issues, and frequently involve antitrust issues: an M&A lawyer needs to be sensitive to these issues. We will also touch on some other laws which may be implicated in M&A transactions, especially laws requiring consents from various regulators.

Much of what M&A lawyers do is draft, negotiate and review contracts. Thus, contract law is relevant. That being said, we will touch very little on the specifics of contract law in this book, with one notable exception. M&A contracting is largely about parties' attempts to agree on and document the terms of their transaction. Contract law does not significantly constrain the contents of the agreement. But if the parties have a dispute, they may litigate. In resolving the litigation, the court will use traditional principles of contract interpretation. Our book contains cases and other material on possible (and sometimes conflicting) interpretations of contract language.

D. AN INTRODUCTORY NOTE ON VALUATION

Some students have never considered the value of investment assets. This note can safely be skipped by students familiar with the concept. We will cover valuation issues in depth in Chapter X.

In M&A, valuation is critically important. After all, no M&A transaction can be done unless the parties can agree on the value of the asset (business) to be sold or transferred. Yet, how much is something worth? Everyone has bought things. What they pay is, in a tautological sense, what the thing is worth to them. But how is that determined? A person might compute how much she can afford and how much "comparable" things cost (in her definition of comparable—how much more would one pay to see a performance live than watch a taped version?). But, for many things people buy, they don't consider how much someone else might pay them for the thing sometime in the future. They think about consumption, not investment. And for most things many people buy, the things are consumed and eventually wear out. The major exception is purchasing one's own home, which is partly consumption, partly investment; the house may very well come to be worth more as time goes on—the owner certainly hopes so—although it also costs money to maintain. When a person is deciding to buy a house, she may consider how much she would have had to pay in rent, how much she can afford, and generally, how much the house costs relative to other houses she has decided are desirable for various reasons particular to her situation. She may also consider what she knows of others' tastes—she may not want to buy a house that has some feature that she values but knows others value less, or not at all.

Especially when people are making major purchases, they may also take into account the circumstances of the seller. If the seller is "motivated"—a euphemism for eager or desperate to sell—the buyer will often expect to get a better deal. And of course the condition of what one is buying matters; obviously, all else equal, fixer-uppers cost less than houses in pristine condition.

Contrast the foregoing with a purchase of investment assets. While some such assets do double duty as consumption and investment assets (thoroughbred horses or "hobby" businesses such as winemaking; art collecting; and, occasionally, buying stock in some entity a person may have a particular attachment to, such as a sports team) many investment assets have no consumption value. What that means is that the asset is only worth the amount of money it will generate, either on an ongoing basis on by sale to someone else. How much will someone else pay? Again, that will be based on how much money the asset will generate on an ongoing basis or by sale to someone else. That value is "the present value of future cash flows"—the amount one would pay, today, in order to get the amounts of money in the future that the asset will generate. Of course, getting one hundred dollars in a year is worth less than getting one hundred dollars now. Getting one hundred dollars in two years is worth even less. Hence "present value." The "future cash flows" for a bond are straightforward—the bond will pay interest at a certain percent per year, for some number of years. There is some uncertainty as to what the "future cash flows" are for a stock, a subject to which we will return below. And "present value" also is scarcely a mechanically determinable amount: there is a discount for the future, but by how much? But conceptually, the valuation achieves the same outcome—the present value of the amount(s) to be generated in the future.

Where a seller is selling publicly traded stock on the stock market, she should be able to get the market price—the concept of a "motivated seller" as it is colloquially understood is not applicable. But where a seller has a larger chunk of stock to sell, or where a buyer seeks to acquire a larger chunk from one or more sellers, the price may differ from the market price. The buyer may, and typically will, place a higher value on a chunk of stock that enables him to get some influence over the company that he would over a much smaller amount. So, he might be willing to pay, for instance, an amount that far exceeds the market price, for each share of a larger bundle he can assemble. The excess amount is a "premium," discussed earlier in this Chapter and to be discussed extensively later in this book.

There might be other reasons, too, for valuations to vary based on the special circumstances of the buyer or seller. Perhaps some regulatory benefit, such as tax credits that cannot be utilized (such as those involved in the *Van Gorkom* case briefly discussed above and discussed extensively in Chapter XVII), is now available upon purchase of a company, but may soon become unavailable. Or perhaps the seller needs to divest itself of part of its business for antitrust reasons.

For public companies, which are subject to extensive public disclosure requirements, considerable information is readily available from which computations of value can be made. For private companies, the computation relies on information that may be far harder to get, and especially for smaller companies, that may be far less reliable. The private companies' accounting may be less sophisticated, and the "stick" represented by the penalties for violating the Federal securities laws' requirements that public disclosures be complete and accurate is not present.

A final point: the foregoing assumes that what is being bought and sold is the cash flows from some particular business that will be continued, albeit perhaps in somewhat of a different form. Companies may sell parts of a business, or equipment or other assets; in such cases, the valuation again gets at the present value of the future cash flows, but the computation may be quite different, insofar as the buyer may have very different plans for the business or assets than the seller did, such that the buyer's computation has much less of a relationship to the seller's computation than would be the case where the buyer is buying the whole business. Indeed, even the purchase of a whole business may be done by a buyer intending to very significantly alter how the business operates; in such cases, the cash flows achieved by the seller are not very relevant. This may, for instance, be the case with the acquisition of a small start-up company that is bought by a larger company that will significantly professionalize the business.

In this book we discuss some specifics of how valuation is done—by investment banks, courts, and parties buying and selling companies. Many different methods are used. These include comparing the business to other recently sold businesses determined in some manner to be comparable and determining the appropriate "industry multiple" by which to multiply this business's recent earnings. As we discuss in Chapter X, many courts have become increasingly sophisticated when called upon to assess valuation, making use of the leading expertise in finance.

E. THE DEALS IN THIS CASEBOOK

Throughout this book, we will use examples from recent deals. We have concentrated on a core group of M&A transactions. Each of the deals represents a different transactional situation that implicates its own legal and business questions and has different structuring and legal considerations. We include illustrative provisions from corporate documents, including deal documents, and communications with shareholders. Note that particularly in the case of deal documents, we sometimes simplify the provisions for ease of exposition.

The first type of transaction we focus on is a strategic acquisition, an acquisition by a company in a line of business that is related to or otherwise has synergies with the company it is acquiring (the target). Here we principally use Men's Wearhouse's June 18, 2014 acquisition of Jos. A. Bank. The Jos. A. Bank takeover battle involved, first, a "hostile" approach by Jos. A. Bank offering to acquire Men's Wearhouse. A hostile approach is typically one where the purported acquirer wishes to complete the transaction over the objections of the board of directors of the target. In the Jos. A. Bank transaction, after a lengthy series of back and forths, the parties agreed to a "friendly" transaction in which Men's Wearhouse would acquire Jos. A. Bank. The hunter became the hunted.

An offer we examine, made by a strategic buyer, is Valeant's hostile offer for the drug company Allergan. Valeant's offer did not succeed, and Allergan ended up selling itself to another drug company, Actavis, in a friendly transaction. We also look briefly at another Valeant deal, its acquisition of Salix, also a pharmaceutical company, as well as Facebook's acquisition of Instagram, also a strategic deal.

By contrast with strategic transactions, "financial" transactions are those in which the acquirer, typically a private equity fund, is in the business of buying and selling companies. Many of the deals discussed in this book, including the Dell transaction, discussed below, involved private equity buyers. We discuss the differences between strategic and financial transactions further in Chapter XI.B.3.

A third type of acquisition we examine involves companies that are being taken private by significant or controlling shareholders. A "going-private" or a "management buyout" transaction is a transaction in which a publicly traded corporation is acquired by a private buyer, often a controlling shareholder or a private equity firm with the participation of incumbent management. The surviving corporation is private. Because going-private transactions involve extinguishing the rights of public shareholders, they raise fiduciary duty issues vis-à-vis the shareholders who are being bought out. We discuss these types of transactions in

Chapter XIX.[40] For this type of transaction we also look at Dell's acquisition, by Silver Lake Partners, a private equity firm, and Michael Dell.

The Dell transaction, which closed on October 29, 2013, involved a major shareholder, Michael Dell, the company's founder, fourteen-percent shareholder and CEO, taking the company private together with Silver Lake. In the transaction, structured as a merger, shareholders other than Dell and Silver Lake got cash for their shares. The transaction was publicly opposed by Carl Icahn, a well-known shareholder activist, who has been in the business for more than 30 years. During the 1980s, activist investors like Mr. Icahn were known as "corporate raiders." Over the ensuing years, the role of activists like Mr. Icahn in promoting M&A activity and the market for corporate control, though still controversial, has become more accepted in the marketplace. We will discuss shareholder activism in Chapter XX.

In that Chapter, we will also examine shareholder activism aimed at influencing the governance of a target company. It implicates many of the same state and federal rules that govern M&A, and sometimes can involve a takeover transaction. In this regard we examine both the Dell transaction, in which Carl Icahn fought against the efforts of Michael Dell to take the company private, Valeant's hostile offer for Allergan, which was supported by the hedge fund Pershing Square, and the hedge fund Third Point's shareholder activism with respect to Sotheby's, the auction house.

QUESTIONS

1. Does the history of M&A suggest that it is too heavily regulated? Too lightly regulated?

2. Who are the intended beneficiaries of M&A regulation? Who should be the intended beneficiaries of M&A regulation?

3. What might make for a "good" M&A transaction?

4. How much do you think market forces reign in M&A transactions?

5. Some of the efficiencies achieved in M&A transactions might reflect lower costs because of a smaller workforce. Should law in any way attempt to discourage transactions that might increase unemployment?

6. To what extent should the law attempt to restrict transactions done wholly or partly for tax reasons?

---

[40] *See* U. S. Sec. & Exch.Comm'n, Going Private, http://www.sec.gov/answers/gopriv.htm for an explanation of going-private transactions.

PART I

DEAL STRUCTURES UNDER STATE AND FEDERAL LAW

■ ■ ■

CHAPTER II

DEAL STRUCTURES: INTRODUCTION TO MERGERS AND ASSET SALES

■ ■ ■

A. BUILDING YOUR DEAL VOCABULARY

This Part will discuss many different types of transactions. It will describe each type of transaction and set forth the applicable law. This Part will also discuss why parties might select one transaction form over another.

As you are reading this book, it is important to understand the vocabulary of deal lawyers and practitioners. For example, when deal lawyers say they are doing a "merger" they are actually referencing a particular type of transaction. Mergers can come in a variety of flavors, including reverse subsidiary mergers and forward subsidiary mergers, among others. Later in this Chapter you will be introduced in detail to the statutory basis for these merger transactions. Another common transaction is the "tender offer." A tender offer can come in two forms, an exchange offer or a cash tender offer. We will learn about the federal regulations governing these kinds of transactions later in this Part.

As you might expect, these terms have precise meanings. Indeed, M&A has an extensive vocabulary. When practitioners talk about deals, they are very careful to use the correct terms. This book will teach you about the law and practice of M&A; it will also teach you about the vocabulary of deal lawyers.

A variety of terms are used for the principal parties in mergers and acquisitions. A company making an acquisition can be called an acquirer, a purchaser, a buyer, or a bidder. As we will see, in a commonly used acquisition structure, a company forms a subsidiary, and the subsidiary is the actual acquirer. The company forming the subsidiary—the parent—will still for most purposes be called the acquirer (or buyer or purchaser or bidder). Another term, often used when a company is conducting its acquisition by means of a tender offer, is "offeror"—that term is sometimes used as a synonym for acquirer, purchaser, buyer or bidder. Yet another term used for some acquirers issuing securities as part of the transaction consideration is "issuers." One final point on acquirer terminology: the terms "bidder" and "offeror" (and of course bid and offer) are used in contexts where no deal is made—a company has, for instance, made a bid and been successfully rebuffed. Such a company is a "bidder" but not an "acquirer."

A company being acquired may be called a seller or a target. The paradigmatic use of "target" is when a company is pursued—targeted—for acquisition, especially if there are several interested acquirers. But the term can be used more broadly, as a synonym for "seller." That being said, note that, as with "bidder" and "offeror," a "target" is not always acquired—a target may successfully rebuff a hostile bid, and not become a seller.

The term "seller" may be, and commonly is, used for a company being acquired, even if the acquisition is being made via a transaction to which the company's owners—its shareholders—are not parties. (The transaction will typically have obtained shareholder approval, though.) In private company acquisitions, we distinguish between the company being sold (also often called the seller or target) and the selling shareholders; in such a transaction, the shareholders will be parties, and indeed, will typically play an important role in many aspects of the transaction.

B. STATUTORY MERGER

The statutory merger is the basic building block of most acquisition transactions.[1] The statutory merger derives its name from the fact that the procedure is explicitly authorized by the corporate statute. Under the broad umbrella of the statutory merger, there are a variety of different merger "flavors." There are "direct mergers," "triangular mergers," "reverse triangular mergers," "interspecies mergers," "mergers of equals," "short-form mergers," "squeeze-out mergers," etc. One should not let the overabundance of jargon in merger practice cause distress. All of the previously mentioned mergers are simply versions of the same transaction, the statutory merger.

1. DGCL SECTION 251

Every state corporate code, as well as the Model Business Corporation Act ("MBCA"), includes a merger provision which lays out in some detail the formalities of the merger process. For example, the DGCL provides for mergers of two domestic corporations under § 251. Section 251(a) provides:

---

[1] The statutory merger is also known by tax professionals as an "A" reorganization. To qualify as an A reorganization under the tax rules, a merger must constitute a statutory merger or consolidation. The determination as to whether an "A" reorganization under IRC § 368(a)(1)(A) is a taxable event to the shareholders of the seller depends on "continuity of interest" in the surviving corporation. In order for there to be continuity of interest, at least forty percent of the consideration received by the selling shareholders must be stock of the acquiring corporation. To the extent consideration received in such circumstances is stock of the acquirer, that portion is not taxable at the time of the transaction.

(a) Any 2 or more corporations existing under the laws of this State may merge into a single corporation, which may be any 1 of the constituent corporations or may consolidate into a new corporation formed by the consolidation, pursuant to an agreement of merger or consolidation, as the case may be, complying and approved in accordance with this section.

Section 251(a) includes some important jargon, which requires further definition. First, the "constituent corporations" are only those corporations directly involved in the transaction, not other affiliated corporate entities. Typically, in a direct merger, there are only two constituent corporations, usually the acquirer ("A") and the target ("T"), as diagrammed below:

Figure 1: Merger of T "with and into" A, with A and T as the constituent corporations. Following the transaction, A is the "surviving" corporation and T is the "disappearing" corporation.

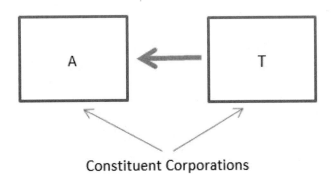

Constituent Corporations

In a direct merger, the target merges with and into the acquirer. The statute uses the language "merge into" to identify which corporation is the "surviving corporation" and which corporation is the "disappearing corporation," sometimes known as the "non-surviving corporation." In the typical direct merger, the acquirer will be the survivor and the target will be the disappearing corporation. We will learn more about the implications of a constituent corporation disappearing in a merger transaction later in this Chapter.

Almost all statutory transactions are done pursuant to a merger. However, the language of § 251(a) describes two distinct transactions. In addition to a merger, the statute also describes a "consolidation." In a consolidation, the constituent corporations combine to form a new, third entity, called the "resulting corporation."

Figure 2: Consolidation. In a consolidation, two constituent corporations (C and D) combine to form a new entity (E), the "resulting corporation."

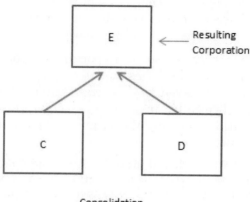

Consolidation

For either a merger or a consolidation, the merger provision lays out explicit procedures that must be accomplished before the transaction can be completed. First, the board of directors of each of the constituent corporations must adopt resolutions approving an agreement of merger or consolidation and declare the advisability of that agreement.[2] The agreement approved by the boards must include details about the transaction's terms, consideration, and the method of implementing the merger, including any conversion of stock of the constituent corporations. The statute is extremely liberal with respect to what constitutes adequate consideration for a merger. Almost anything can be used as consideration including cash, stock of the acquirer, stock of another corporation, assumption of indebtedness, etc. Because the merger transaction requires a vote of the shareholders, the statute permits amendments to the surviving corporation's certificate of incorporation in conjunction with the merger transaction. To the extent the transaction involves such amendments, those amendments must be spelled out in the merger agreement.

What sorts of amendments are typically made to certificates of incorporation in these contexts? In some instances, where a strategic acquirer is buying a private company, the private company's certificate of incorporation may be very long; in the transaction, a far shorter certificate is adopted. In other instances, parties aim to make other substantive changes to the certificate. Given that there is a vote on the merger in any event, the vote on the changes to the certificate is effectively "bundled" with the merger vote. In both instances, there may be provisions that are apt for the company pre-merger (or were apt at

---

²   Title 8 DGCL § 251(b).

some point in the past) that are no longer apt for the post-merged entity. For instance, some provisions that are appropriate for public companies, such as those relating to takeover defenses, are not needed for private companies. The merger may provide a good opportunity to bring provisions, such as indemnification provisions, up to the latest standards.

One example of a company making significant changes to its certificate of incorporation in a merger was Dell, when it went private in 2013. Prior to the merger, Dell's certificate of incorporation included provisions giving the board the right to issue series of preferred stock—these are not infrequently used as poison pills, discussed in Chapter XV.D. Once Dell became a private company, it had no further need for such provisions; consequently, the certificate of incorporation adopted in conjunction with the merger does not have them. But the new certificate has a provision giving shareholders the right to compete with the corporation under certain circumstances, something that may now be needed given that Dell is privately held following the transaction. The Online Appendix to this book contains Dell's certificate of incorporation in effect prior to the merger, and as of the effective time of the merger.

2. VOTING REQUIREMENTS

a. DGCL Voting Requirements

Section 251(c) requires that the merger agreement be submitted to the shareholders of each of the constituent corporations for approval at a shareholder meeting called for the purpose of approving the agreement. Approval of the agreement requires an affirmative vote of a majority of the outstanding shares of the corporation. Alternatively, the merger agreement may, if the constituent corporation's bylaws so allow, be approved by written consent pursuant to § 228.

Although the default rule under DGCL § 251(c) is that shareholders of each of the constituent corporations are required to vote to approve the merger, there are certain exceptions to this requirement. Under DGCL § 251(f), a vote of the shareholders of the surviving corporation is not required if in connection with the merger each of the following conditions is satisfied:[3]

---

[3] Title 8 DGCL § 251(f) states that "Notwithstanding the requirements of subsection (c) of this section, unless required by its certificate of incorporation, no vote of shareholders of a constituent corporation surviving a merger shall be necessary to authorize a merger if (1) the agreement of merger does not amend in any respect the certificate of incorporation of such constituent corporation, (2) each share of stock of such constituent corporation outstanding immediately prior to the effective date of the merger is to be an identical outstanding or treasury share of the surviving corporation after the effective date of the merger, and (3) either no shares of common stock of the surviving corporation and no shares, securities or obligations convertible into such stock are to be issued or delivered under the plan of merger, or the authorized unissued shares or the treasury shares of common stock of the surviving corporation to be issued or delivered under the plan of merger plus those initially issuable upon conversion of any other

- The company's certificate of incorporation is not amended;

- There is no change in the characteristics of the outstanding stock of the surviving corporation; and

- The surviving corporation does not issue more than twenty percent of its outstanding stock in connection with the transaction.

The last requirement, that the surviving company issue no more than twenty percent of its stock, is often what prevents § 251(f) from applying, such that a vote of the shareholders of the surviving corporation is required. For instance, if the surviving corporation had 100 shares of stock outstanding before the merger, § 251(f) would not be available if it issued twenty-one shares as consideration in the merger. Section 251(f) will also not apply where the surviving company amends its certificate of incorporation in connection with the merger.

If all three conditions of § 251(f) are met, then shareholders of the surviving corporation are not required to vote to approve the merger. This exemption from the voting requirement makes sense because a transaction in which all three conditions are met is likely not a transaction that will fundamentally alter the relationship of the survivor's shareholders to the corporation. An acquirer can thus "work around" the voting requirement by simply issuing less stock (or no stock) so long as the conditions are otherwise still met. Note, however, that the vote of shareholders of the disappearing corporation will always be required to approve the merger transaction.

After shareholder approval for the merger has been received, the merger transaction is not yet complete. The merger will only become effective upon the physical filing of a certificate of merger with the state pursuant to § 251(c). The certificate of merger contains very basic information about the transaction, including statements identifying the constituent corporations to the transaction as well as statements that the transaction has been approved by the shareholders of the constituent corporations and that copies of the merger agreement are available for inspection by former shareholders. The effect of the certificate of merger (a form of which is available in the Online Appendix to this book) is to put the state authorities on notice that two corporate entities have merged, and indicates to the state which of the two is the surviving corporation. Although filing the certificate is a ministerial act, it is an extremely important milestone in any merger transaction because none of the legal consequences of a statutory merger apply until after the filing is

shares, securities or obligations to be issued or delivered under such plan do not exceed 20% of the shares of common stock of such constituent corporation outstanding immediately prior to the effective date of the merger.

complete. As counsel to the acquirer, you will be required to file a certificate of merger with the state in order for the merger to be effective.

b. Stock Exchange Voting Requirements

Although a vote of the shareholders may not be required to approve a merger under state corporate law, the New York Stock Exchange (NYSE) or NASDAQ may still require one for companies whose stock is listed or quoted thereon. The vote requirement is most often triggered when an acquirer acquires a target for stock consideration in a reverse subsidiary merger (we will discuss the mechanics of reverse subsidiary mergers below). Under the NYSE and NASDAQ's listing rules, Rule 312 and Rule 4350(i) respectively, where greater than twenty percent of the outstanding shares are issued in connection with a merger transaction, the share issuance (but not the merger) will require a vote of a majority of shareholders voting at a meeting with a valid quorum.[4] Note that under state corporate law, no vote is required for issuance of authorized shares (that is, shares authorized in the certificate of incorporation). Such shares can normally be issued with a simple resolution of the board of directors. The exchange rules require a vote because the issuance of a large block of stock, although permissible under state law, is dilutive of incumbent shareholders. It is important to remember that this vote is a vote to approve only the issuance of stock in connection with a merger and not an approval of the merger transaction itself.

c. SEC Unbundling Requirements

In recent years, corporations have found it profitable to relocate their corporate headquarters overseas. By re-incorporating overseas, formerly U.S. corporations become subject to lower foreign corporate tax rates. The most common tactic in recent years to accomplish this tax saving move abroad is through a merger transaction called a "corporate inversion." In a simplified corporate inversion, the U.S. company acquires a foreign corporation, with the foreign corporation as the surviving corporation. Following the transaction, the surviving corporation undertakes a name change and takes on the name of the former U.S. corporation. Following the inversion, the U.S. corporation is now re-domiciled in a lower taxed foreign country.

This kind of transaction obviously raised political hackles. In response, the Obama Administration adopted a series of rules to make

---

[4] Previous iterations of this rule had required a majority of shareholders voting at a meeting where at least fifty percent of the shareholders were present. This could sometimes trip up parties with corporate bylaws with lower quorum requirements (e.g. thirty-three percent). For purposes of a valid vote under the exchange rules, these firms would have to comply with the requirements of the exchange rule rather than their own corporate bylaw. These rules have since been amended. The NYSE's new rule on this point, NYSE Rule 312.07, came into effect on July 11, 2013.

such transactions unpalatable. One such rule is a revision of the SEC's guidance on SEC Rule 14a–4(a)(3).[5] Rule 14a–4(a)(3) requires corporate issuers to "identify clearly and impartially each separate matter intended to be acted upon" on a proxy statement. The revision to this rule now requires:

> [I]f a material amendment to the acquiror's organizational documents would require the approval of its shareholders under state law, the rules of a national securities exchange, or its organizational documents if presented on a standalone basis, the acquiror's form of proxy must present any such amendment separately from any other material proposal, including, if applicable, approval of the issuance of securities in a triangular merger or approval of the transaction agreement in a direct merger.

Prior to revision of 14a–4(a)(3), the only one vote was required on in a typical merger was the shareholder vote required under state law. Under this new rule, intended to be a hurdle to slow down corporate inversions, managers would have to seek shareholder two votes in connection with an inversion. The first vote would be a shareholder vote under state law to approve the merger transaction. This first vote is all that would be required under state law to amend a certificate of incorporation in connection with the merger. The second vote would be required pursuant to the SEC's unbundling requirement to approve any material amendment to the certificate of incorporation in connection with a statutory merger.

3. LEGAL EFFECTS OF THE STATUTORY MERGER

There are a number of important legal consequences of a merger or a consolidation. The first and most important consequence of a merger is that upon the filing of the certificate of merger, the separate existence of all the constituent corporations shall cease and the constituent corporations shall be merged into one. Following the merger, by operation of law all the rights, privileges, powers, and assets of the disappearing corporation(s) shall be the rights, powers, and assets of the surviving corporation.[6] At the same time, the surviving corporation will be subject to all the restrictions, disabilities and duties of the disappearing

---

[5]   http://www.sec.gov/divisions/corpfin/guidance/exchange-act-rule-14a-4a3.htm.

[6]   In *Great Hill Equity Partners IV, LP v. SIG Growth Equity Fund I, LLLP,* 80 A. 3d 155 (Del. Ch. 2013), the question for the court was whether the attorney-client privilege of the seller passed to the buyer upon the closing. In *Great Hill*, the seller sought to prevent the buyer from getting post-closing access to privileged attorney-client communications of the seller. Attorneys for Great Hill asked the court to rule that when DCGL § 259 said all "privileges" it did not mean the seller's attorney-client privilege. That argument fell short. Then-Chancellor Strine noted that "[t]o indulge the Seller's argument would conflict with the only reasonable interpretation of the statute, which is that all means all as to the enumerated categories, and that this includes all privileges, including the attorney-client privilege."

corporation(s). All property, real, personal and mixed, and all debts due to any of the disappearing corporation(s) become by operation of law the property and debts of the surviving corporation. All rights of creditors on any property of the disappearing corporation(s) are preserved unimpaired, and all debts, liabilities and duties of the disappearing corporation(s) will be the debts, liabilities, and duties of the surviving corporation. These debts and obligations may be enforced against the surviving corporation to the same extent as if they had been originally contracted by the surviving corporation.

The general effect of these survival provisions is that parties cannot use the mechanics of a merger in order to avoid debts and creditors or contractual or other obligations. For example, in *Fitzsimmons v. Western Airlines*, 290 A.2d 682 (1972), Western Airlines merged with American Airlines, with American Airlines being the surviving corporation and Western Airlines being the disappearing corporation. Plaintiffs in the lawsuit were representatives of Western Airlines' mechanics union who sought a declaratory judgment from the court that their collective bargaining agreement with Western would survive the merger and that the agreement, including its arbitration provisions, would be binding on American Airlines. The Delaware Chancery Court in *Fitzsimmons* found:

> It is [. . .] a matter of statutory law that a Delaware corporation may not avoid its contractual obligations by merger; those duties "attach" to the surviving corporation and may be "enforced against it." In short, the survivor must assume the obligations of the constituent.

As a consequence, following the merger American Airlines was subject to the arbitration provisions of the collective bargaining agreement signed between Western Airlines and its labor unions. In the context of a more typical merger, § 259's survival provision means that where the target's contracts are silent with respect to the effects of a merger, the fact of the merger will result in the target's contracts becoming the contracts of the acquirer. Typical contracts that are passed to the acquirer in this manner will often include leases, licenses, vendor agreements, and employment agreements, among others.[7]

The same is true with respect to any civil, criminal, or administrative proceedings that the disappearing corporation is a party to prior to the merger. Where the disappearing corporation is a party to a civil, criminal

---

[7] Many commercial contracts include anti-assignment provisions that purport to restrict assignment of a contract in the event of a merger or a change of control. Absent such restrictions, the general rule under contract law is that contracts are assignable in a merger. However, this default rule with respect to the assignability of contracts is subject to an exception. Where the contract rights are "personal," for example rights related to intellectual property, courts have ruled that the default rule does not apply-that permission must be sought to assign such rights. *See PPG Industries v. Guardian Industries Corp.*, 597 F.2d 1090 (6th Cir. 1979); *see also SQL Solutions, Inc. v. Oracle Corp.*, 1991 WL 626458 (N.D. Cal. December 18, 1991).

or administrative matter, following the merger the surviving corporation is substituted for the disappearing corporation as if the merger had never taken place. An exception to this general rule is the derivative suit. In *Lewis v. Anderson*, 477 A.2d 1040 (Del. 1984), the Delaware Supreme Court ruled that following a merger, shareholder plaintiffs in the disappearing corporation lose standing under DGCL §§ 259, 261, and 327. This is so because plaintiffs in these cases are no longer shareholders of the corporation with the claim but rather, holders of rights to receive cash or stock of the surviving corporation. In any event, the loss of standing upon the effectiveness of the merger is one reason why merger litigation is often won and lost at the preliminary injunction stage.

4. OTHER TYPES OF STATUTORY MERGERS

a. Triangular Mergers

The statutory mergers described above are all "direct" mergers. They are known as direct mergers because the constituent corporations which are directly combining—that is, merging—in the transaction are operating companies. Direct mergers like the ones described above are not common. Rather, the "triangular" merger, sometimes referred to as a "subsidiary" merger, is the deal structure most commonly used. A triangular merger is one in which the acquirer incorporates a subsidiary that will act as one of the constituent corporations in the merger (the "merger subsidiary"). The sole purpose of this merger subsidiary is to act as a catalyst for the transaction. In a reverse subsidiary merger, the wholly-owned subsidiary then merges with and into a target entity. Following the merger transaction, the merger subsidiary disappears and the target survives as a wholly-owned subsidiary of the acquirer.

Figure 3: Reverse Triangular Merger. In the example below, the acquirer forms a wholly-owned subsidiary. This subsidiary and the target are the constituent corporations in a merger. The merger subsidiary merges with and into the target and then, as a result of the merger, the target is a wholly-owned subsidiary of the acquirer.

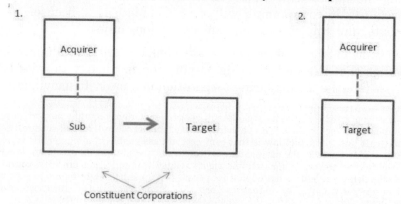

The merger between the target corporation and the wholly-owned subsidiary is itself a § 251 statutory merger. The transaction adopts the moniker of a triangular, or subsidiary, merger because the transaction involves a merger subsidiary wholly-owned by the ultimate acquirer and the structure of ownership results in the surviving corporation being held at arm's length by the acquirer. Triangular mergers where the target is the surviving corporation are known as reverse triangular mergers, or reverse subsidiary mergers (Figure 3). Triangular mergers where the merger subsidiary is the surviving corporation are known as forward triangular mergers, or forward subsidiary mergers (Figure 4).

Figure 4: Forward Triangular Merger. In the example below, the acquirer forms a wholly-owned subsidiary. This subsidiary and the target are the constituent corporations in a merger. The target merges with and into the merger subsidiary and then as a result of the merger, the merger subsidiary, a wholly-owned subsidiary of the acquirer, survives and the target has disappeared.

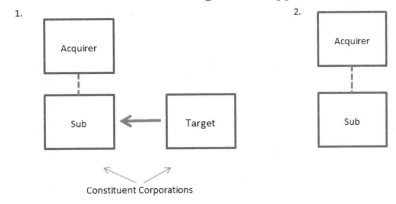

A triangular merger is generally preferred by dealmakers over a direct merger of the acquirer and target described in Figure 1. A triangular merger allows the acquirer to keep the assets and liabilities of the target at arm's length in a subsidiary corporation. . Between a reverse triangular merger and a forward triangular merger, the reverse triangular merger structure, a § 251 statutory merger between the target and a shell subsidiary of the acquirer where the target is the surviving corporation, is perhaps the most common structure used by dealmakers when engaging in merger transactions.

In addition to keeping the target's liabilities at a distance, there are a number of other reasons, both business and legal, why the reverse triangular merger structure is so often used. These include, but are not necessarily limited to, the following:

- Because § 251's voting and other requirements only apply to the constituent parties in a merger, the triangular structure dispenses with the need for a § 251 vote of the shareholders of the acquirer since it is not a constituent corporation in the merger transaction. As discussed above, other legal or stock exchange rules may still require that the acquirer have a shareholder vote, such as the NYSE and NASDAQ rules which require a shareholder vote if the acquirer issues greater than twenty percent of its outstanding stock or the requirement to have a vote to amend the parent's certificate of incorporation if it needs to authorize additional shares in connection with the transaction.

- Engaging in a merger at the subsidiary level requires little, if any, operational changes at the acquirer level. Consequently, it is administratively easier on the acquirer.

- There may be significant brand value in the target entity: a direct merger where the target entity disappears would destroy some of the value that the acquirer is seeking in the merger. By electing a structure that permits the target to survive, the acquirer is able to take advantage of that existing brand value.

- When the acquirer holds the target at arm's length as a subsidiary, the target can continue to operate independently of the acquirer, thus reducing the need to engage in integration of the entities' operations.

While the reverse triangular merger is the most common structure for the reasons listed above, there may be circumstances when dealmakers would prefer a forward triangular structure with the target corporation disappearing and the merger subsidiary surviving. The most common circumstance when this occurs is due to tax benefits, which are discussed briefly in Subsection E below. In addition, when the target has negative brand value, it may be in the best interests of the acquirer not to continue the brand of the target. For example, in 2001, Dynegy and Enron announced a transaction in which Enron was to be acquired by Dynegy in a forward triangular merger. The parties' intent was for Dynegy to acquire Enron while allowing the Enron brand to die. (The transaction never closed.)

b. Short Form Mergers

In § 253, the statute provides for a "short form merger." The short form merger provides a cost effective method of permitting firms with a controlling shareholder with at least ninety percent of the outstanding shares to eliminate or squeeze out the minority shareholders. A short form merger does not require a vote of the shareholders. In fact, such a vote, were it to occur, would have a pre-ordained result as at least ninety percent of the shares are owned by a controller. Rather, the § 253 short form merger is initiated by the parent corporation with the filing of a certificate of ownership and merger that sets forth the terms of a merger between the subsidiary and the parent or the subsidiary with any other controlled firm. The effect of the merger is to cash out the minority shareholders. Although such shareholders do not have the right to vote to approve the transaction as they would with any other statutory merger, they have the right to an appraisal if they believe the price to be paid to them in the merger was not fair value (see Chapter III on appraisal).

In 2013 the Delaware legislature adopted § 251(h), which provides for an alternative short form merger structure. Section 251(h) is used in combination with friendly tender offers, and permits a merger without a vote of the target shareholders if its conditions are satisfied. (The regulatory regime applicable to tender offers is discussed in Chapter V). In a tender offer, often less than 100 percent of the shares will be tendered. Squeezing out the remaining shareholders would require a shareholder vote unless the conditions for a § 253 short form merger are satisfied. Often not only would offerors not get 100 percent of the shares, they might not even meet the ninety percent threshold needed for a § 253 short form merger. To allow a merger without a shareholder vote under these circumstances, targets regularly granted "top-up options" to acquirers following completion of a friendly tender offer transactions. As the name suggests, top-up options are options for the amount of shares needed to "top up" the tender offeror's shareholdings to reach the ninety percent threshold. Having reached this level of ownership, the acquirer could then proceed with a § 253 short form merger.

Before the adoption of § 251(h), top-up options were commonly used. One article recounts the following history and statistics: "[s]urfacing in a handful of deals in 2000, it spread quickly. By 2004, one-third of tender offers included a top-up, according to MergerMetrics. By 2008, it was virtually 100 percent."[8]

One reason for the challenges against top-up options is the fact that in order to accomplish a top-up option and get an acquirer to at least 90%, it sometimes required the target to issue very large amounts of stock. These very large issuances caused potential issues with stock exchanges and caused concern that stockholders who do not tender might find themselves adversely affected in subsequent appraisal proceedings. Top-ups have been challenged in court. The validity of top-up options under certain conditions, including protection of non-tendering shareholders' rights in appraisal, has generally been upheld.[9]

---

[8]   Liz Hoffman, *Top-Up Option, We Hardly Knew Ye*, Law360, April 26, 2013, available at http://www.law360.com/articles/436259/top-up-option-we-hardly-knew-ye.

[9]   *Olson v. Ev3, Inc.*, 2011 WL 704409 (Del. Ch. 2011) (holding that a top-up option is lawful provided the option holder first possesses voting control and the value of the minority shares in appraisal are not adversely affected by the exercise of the option).

Adoption of § 251(h) by the Delaware legislature was intended to make the "top-up option" irrelevant. Under § 251(h), a vote is not required for a squeeze-out merger so long as the parties (the tender offeror and the target) first enter into a merger agreement in conjunction with the announcement of a tender offer. That merger agreement must specify that the transaction is governed by § 251(h), and that the acquirer will have voting control of the corporation following completion of the tender offer, and that the shares to be cancelled pursuant to § 251(h) will be converted into the right to receive the same consideration as shares tendered in the tender offer immediately prior to the § 251(h) short form merger. The tender offer itself must be for any and all of the target's shares.[10]

The § 251(h) structure is functionally equivalent to the top-up option but it sidesteps difficulties that made the top-up option unwieldy at times. To date, no state has adopted an equivalent to Delaware's § 251(h). In states which have not adopted the § 251(h) structure, top-up options are still viable methods for conducting a backend squeeze-out merger in which shareholder approval is not required following a friendly tender offer.

One of the first transactions to use DGCL § 251(h) was Paulson & Co.'s acquisition (through a wholly owned subsidiary) of Steinway Musical Instruments, Inc. by means of a friendly tender offer.

Given that § 251(h) had just recently been enacted, the merger agreement granted a top-up option, to be used if § 251(h) was not available. Here is relevant language from the offer to purchase sent by Paulson to Steinway shareholders:[11]

> If we acquire at least one Share more than 50% of the Shares on a fully-diluted basis in the Offer, in accordance with the terms of the Merger Agreement, we will complete the Merger without a vote of the stockholders of Steinway pursuant to Section 251(h) of the General Corporation Law of the State of Delaware (the "DGCL"). We do not foresee any reason that would prevent us from completing the Merger pursuant to Section 251(h) of the DGCL within one business day following the consummation of the Offer. However, in the event that we are unable for any reason to complete the Merger pursuant to Section 251(h) of the DGCL within one business day following the consummation of the Offer, and if we do not acquire at least one Share more than

---

[10] And the shares received in the tender offer must carry sufficient votes to approve the merger. In most cases, this simply means that a majority of shares must be tendered. But if a corporation's charter required a percentage greater than a majority to approve a merger, at least that percentage of shares would need to be tendered. DGCL § 251 (h)(3).

[11] The offer to purchase is available at http://www.sec.gov/Archives/edgar/data/911583/000119312513342308/d587541dex99a1a.htm.

90% of the Shares on a fully-diluted basis in the Offer, then the Purchaser will exercise the Top-Up Option (as described below), and thereafter effect the Merger pursuant to Section 253 of the DGCL without a vote of the stockholders of Steinway. Whether the Merger is effected pursuant to Section 251(h) or Section 253 of the DGCL, (i) stockholders of Steinway will be entitled to appraisal rights under Delaware law if they do not tender Shares in the Offer and (ii) stockholders of Steinway who do not validly exercise appraisal rights under Delaware law will receive the same cash consideration for their Shares as was payable in the Offer.

The offer to purchase summarizes the merger agreement and the tender offer, entered into at the time of the tender offer as required under § 251(h). Note, too, that as required by DGCL § 251(h), the merger is to be completed promptly after the tender offer is consummated, and that the non-tendering shareholders who do not exercise appraisal rights will receive the same consideration paid to shareholders who tendered in the offer.

c.   Interspecies Mergers

Until now, we have focused on the mechanics and the legal effects of statutory mergers where the constituent corporations are two Delaware corporations. However, mergers are not limited to transactions between domestic corporations. There are many "interspecies mergers" that involve mergers between corporations incorporated in different states, or mergers between different types of business organizations (e.g. an LLC merging with a corporation or a Delaware corporation merging with a California corporation). All of these types of mergers are permitted. However, they are covered under provisions of the code other than § 251. For example, § 252 covers mergers between Delaware corporations and "foreign" corporations.[12] The requirements to effectuate a merger under § 252 are substantially the same as for a merger under § 251. In addition to the requirements under the domestic law, the foreign corporation will also have to ensure that the merger complies with the interspecies merger provisions of its own jurisdiction.

C. MERGERS IN PRACTICE: THE DELL EXAMPLE

The following Section discusses the mechanics of a statutory merger using the example of Dell.

---

[12] "Domestic" corporations are incorporated in Delaware or the home jurisdiction. "Foreign" corporations are any corporations incorporated in a jurisdiction other than Delaware or the home jurisdiction. These include truly foreign corporations (e.g. incorporated in the U.K.) and corporations from other states (e.g. Nevada).

Typically, sections 1 and 2 of a merger agreement describe the merger transaction as well as the effect of the merger on the capital stock of the seller and whether and how the certificate of incorporation and the bylaws of surviving corporation will be affected by the merger transaction.

Below are excerpts of the Dell merger agreement. The merger is structured as a reverse subsidiary merger with the merger subsidiary disappearing and Dell continuing as the surviving corporation and wholly-owned subsidiary of the parent. The merger agreement lays out a number of the changes to be affected by the transaction. For example, the merger agreement describes amendments to the existing certificate of incorporation and bylaws, as well as designation of new directors for the surviving corporation. Upon the merger, the merger agreement provides that the directors of the merger subsidiary will become the directors of Dell and the previous directors of Dell will be out. Officers of Dell remain the same before and after the transaction.

There is a common misperception that in a merger transaction, the stock of the target corporation remains outstanding and that the merger involves an exchange of cash for the target's stock. What actually happens is a little more subtle than that. In a merger, the rights and status of stock of both the surviving and disappearing corporations are re-designated as specified in the merger agreement. In the Dell merger transaction, upon filing of the certificate of merger with the state, the publicly traded shares of Dell are cancelled and converted into the right to receive cash. Although the merger subsidiary disappears, its stock is converted into the entire stock of the surviving corporation. Following the transaction, former public shareholders of Dell are left holding rights to receive cash while the former shareholders of the merger subsidiary are left in control of Dell, the surviving corporation.

Below, you will find excerpts from the Dell merger agreement. Read the agreement to understand the mechanics of a merger transaction in practice:

DELL, INC. MERGER AGREEMENT

ARTICLE I

THE MERGER

Section 1.1 The Merger. On the terms and subject to the conditions set forth in this Agreement, and in accordance with the DGCL, at the Effective Time, <u>Merger Sub will merge with and into the Company [Dell], the separate corporate existence of Merger Sub will cease and the Company will continue its corporate existence</u> under Delaware law as the surviving corporation in the Merger (the "Surviving Corporation").

[This section describes the transaction that will occur. In this case, you can see that Section 1.1 describes a reverse triangular (subsidiary) merger in which a wholly-owned subsidiary of the acquirer is merged into the target, with the target surviving.]

Section 1.2 Closing. The closing of the Merger (the "Closing") shall take place at the offices of Debevoise & Plimpton LLP, 919 Third Avenue, New York, New York at 9:00 a.m. Eastern Time, on a date which shall be the second Business Day after the satisfaction or waiver (to the extent permitted by applicable Law) of the conditions set forth in Article VI (other than those conditions that by their nature are to be satisfied at the Closing, but subject to the satisfaction or waiver of such conditions) or at such other place, time and date as the Company and Parent may agree in writing; provided that without the prior written consent of Parent, the Closing shall not occur prior to the earlier of (x) a date during the Marketing Period specified by Parent on no fewer than two (2) Business Days' notice to the Company (it being understood that such date may be conditioned upon the simultaneous completion of the Parent Parties' financing of the transactions contemplated by this Agreement) and (y) the final day of the Marketing Period. *[Marketing Period is defined as the first twenty consecutive business days starting after the date of the agreement.]* The date on which the Closing actually occurs is referred to herein as the "Closing Date".

[This section describes the completion of the transaction, known as the Closing. The Closing can occur only after all the conditions precedent set forth in the merger agreement have been fulfilled or waived. Although the customary language of this provision describes an in-person closing in the offices of the acquirer's counsel, these days it is more likely that a transaction will close by e-mail without a ceremony.]

Section 1.3 Effective Time. Subject to the provisions of this Agreement, at the Closing, the Company shall cause a certificate of merger (the "Certificate of Merger") to be duly executed, acknowledged and filed with the Secretary of State of the State of Delaware in accordance with Section 251 of the DGCL. The Merger shall become effective at such time as the Certificate of Merger has been duly filed with the Secretary of State of the State of Delaware or at such later date or time as may be agreed by the Company and Parent in writing and specified in the Certificate of Merger in accordance with the DGCL (the effective time of the Merger being hereinafter referred to as the "Effective Time").

[After the closing has occurred, the acquirer will cause a Certificate of Merger to be filed with state authorities. Once this certificate has been accepted by the state, the merger is effective.]

Section 1.4 Effects of the Merger. The Merger shall have the effects set forth in this Agreement and the applicable provisions of the DGCL.

Section 1.5 Certificate of Incorporation and Bylaws of the Surviving Corporation. At the Effective Time, (a) the certificate of incorporation of the Surviving Corporation shall be amended and restated in its entirety to be in the form attached hereto as Exhibit A (the "Charter"), until thereafter amended, subject to Section 5.10, as provided therein or by applicable Law and (b) the by-laws of the Surviving Corporation shall be amended and restated, subject to Section 5.10, in their entirety to be in the form attached hereto as Exhibit B (the "Bylaws"), until thereafter amended as provided therein or by applicable Law.

[*In the course of a merger, the statute permits the surviving corporation to amend its certificate of incorporation as part of the transaction. Section 1.5 indicates that at the effective time of the merger, Dell will amend its certificate. The amended certificate is attached to the merger agreement as an exhibit.*]

Section 1.6 Directors. The directors of Merger Sub immediately prior to the Effective Time shall, from and after the Effective Time, be the directors of the Surviving Corporation and shall hold office until their respective successors are duly elected and qualified, or their earlier death, incapacitation, retirement, resignation or removal, in accordance with the Charter and Bylaws.

[*Section 1.6 specifies the identities of the board of directors of the surviving corporation. In this case, the directors of the target are replaced and the board of the merger sub becomes the board of the surviving corporation. In some cases, this provision is highly negotiated. More often in a reverse triangular merger, the board of the target is replaced by a board comprised entirely of employees of the acquirer.*]

Section 1.7 Officers. The officers of the Company immediately prior to the Effective Time shall, from and after the Effective Time, be the officers of the Surviving Corporation and shall hold office until their respective successors are duly elected or appointed and qualified, or their earlier death, incapacitation, retirement, resignation or removal, in accordance with the Charter and Bylaws.

[*Just as the directors can be replaced as part of the merger transaction, corporate officers can and often are replaced pursuant to this section of the merger agreement. In this case, the corporate officers of the target are not changed as part of the merger.*]

ARTICLE II

CONVERSION OF SHARES; EXCHANGE OF CERTIFICATES

Section 2.1 Effect on Capital Stock. At the Effective Time, by virtue of the Merger and without any action on the part of the Company or the Parent Parties or the holders of any securities of the Company or any other Person:

(a) Conversion of Common Stock. Each Share, other than Excluded Shares, Company Restricted Shares and Dissenting Shares, issued and outstanding immediately prior to the Effective Time shall be converted automatically into the right to receive $13.65 in cash [*Editor: the agreement was amended to raise the consideration to $13.75 per share, and a dividend of $.13 per share, for a total of $13.88 per share*], without interest (the "Merger Consideration"), whereupon all such Shares shall be automatically canceled upon the conversion thereof and shall cease to exist, and the holders of such Shares shall cease to have any rights with respect to such Shares other than the right to receive the Merger Consideration (less any applicable withholding Taxes), upon surrender of Certificates or Book-Entry Shares in accordance with Section 2.2.

. . . .

(c) Conversion of Merger Sub Common Stock. Each share of common stock, par value $0.01 per share, of Merger Sub issued and outstanding immediately prior to the Effective Time shall be converted into and become one validly issued, fully paid and nonassessable share of common stock, par value $0.01 per share, of the Surviving Corporation.

[*In a merger transaction, there is no actual purchase of the stock of the target corporation. Rather, coincident with the merger—and by operation of law—the rights of the stock of the constituent corporations are re-designated pursuant to the terms of this Section 2.1. The stock of the target outstanding immediately prior to the merger ceases to have any rights with respect to the surviving corporation and is converted into the right to receive the merger consideration. The stock of the disappearing merger subsidiary is re-designated as the stock of the surviving corporation. Following the transaction, shareholders of the target are holding stock representing a right to receive payment from the acquirer while the acquirer is holding the stock of the surviving corporation.*]

D. SALE OF ALL OR SUBSTANTIALLY ALL THE ASSETS

1. DGCL SECTIONS 271 & 275

Another common statutory transaction structure is the asset sale. Firms can sell assets at any time. In fact, sales of divisions or subsidiaries are not uncommon transactions. For the most part, sales of corporate assets are simply corporate actions taken in the ordinary course, and do not necessarily implicate the corporate law. Indeed, sale of a corporate asset differs little from the sale of any other property. It requires a title transfer and perhaps payment of sales tax. Statutory corporate law is implicated only when "all or substantially all the assets of the corporation" are being sold.[13] The underlying reason is that, like a merger, a sale of "all or substantially all the assets of the corporation" is a significant event in the lifecycle of the company, requiring shareholder approval.

A sale of all or substantially all the assets of a corporation is typically structured as two separate transactions undertaken very close in time. The first transaction is the actual sale of "all or substantially all the assets" of the corporation pursuant to § 271. This transaction is then immediately followed by a voluntary dissolution pursuant to § 275. Although the mechanics of this transaction are slightly more complicated, the result is functionally equivalent to a direct merger in that post-transaction, the seller no longer exists and the acquirer holds title to the seller's assets.

The asset sale, like the statutory merger, is a friendly transaction in that it may only be accomplished with the assent and cooperation of the seller's board of directors. The statute requires the target board recommend the transaction to its shareholders. In the typical asset sale, the buyer and the seller agree to an asset purchase agreement, which, like a merger agreement, outlines the terms and conditions of the sale. The agreement will usually describe with some level of specificity the assets to be sold to the buyer as well as the assets and liabilities to be left behind.

Unlike in a merger, where the assets of the seller become the assets of the buyer by operation of law upon consummation of the transaction, in the asset sale transaction, the title for each of the identified assets must be individually transferred to buyer. This makes the asset sale more cumbersome and slightly unwieldy. The asset sale also generates sales

---

[13] A sale of substantially all the assets of the corporation is known by tax professionals as a "C" reorganization. In order for an asset sale to be deemed a non-taxable event under IRC § 368(a)(1)(C), the acquiring corporation must acquire substantially all the assets of the seller in exchange solely for voting stock of the acquirer.

tax liabilities that are not present in a merger transaction. Notwithstanding these drawbacks, there are reasons why parties might opt to undertake a sale of substantially all the assets over a merger. First among these is the ability, subject to limitations discussed below, to leave certain liabilities behind.

The sale of all or substantially all the assets of a corporation is initiated by the board of directors of the selling corporation. The statute requires the board to adopt a resolution that "deems [the proposed asset sale] expedient and for the best interests of the corporation."[14] At the same board meeting, board members will typically adopt another resolution "deem[ing] it advisable in the judgment of the board" that the corporation be dissolved upon completion of the asset sale. The dual transactions are then sent to shareholders for votes. The affirmative vote of a majority of the outstanding stock of the corporation is required to adopt a resolution approving the sale of substantially all the assets of the corporation. Similarly, the affirmative vote of a majority of the outstanding stock of the corporation is required to adopt a resolution approving the voluntary dissolution of the corporation.

When the sale is effectuated, the designated assets of the seller are transferred to the buyer, and the seller receives the consideration. The consideration is used to pay off all the liabilities of the seller and then the balance is distributed to the seller's shareholders in the form of a special dividend. Immediately following the dividend payment, the seller files a certificate of dissolution with the state and its separate existence ends. The result of the transaction is that all or substantially all the assets of the seller are now in the hands of the buyer and the shareholders of the seller are holding consideration for their pro rata shares of the selling corporation. In effect, the result is the same as a direct merger. The transaction can be structured so that a subsidiary of the buyer is the actual acquirer; this yields the same result as a triangular merger.

---

[14] *See* Title 8 DGCL § 271(a).

Figure 5: Sale of All or Substantially All the Assets. This asset purchase is structured as a purchase through a wholly-owned acquisition subsidiary of the buyer. In exchange for cash consideration, all or substantially all the assets of the seller are transferred to the acquisition subsidiary of the buyer. Following the transaction, the former assets of the seller are held by the buyer's subsidiary. The seller holds cash and liabilities. The seller then pays off its creditors and distributes whatever cash is left to the shareholders in the form of a special dividend. Following this, the seller voluntarily dissolves.

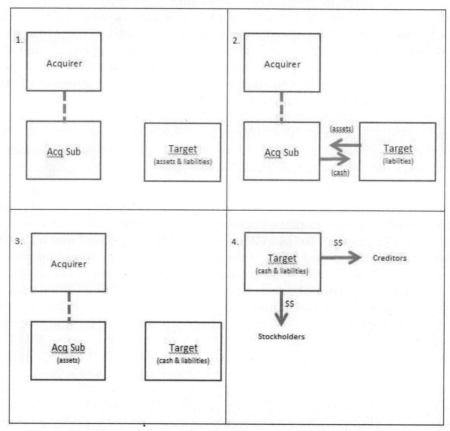

2. THE DEFINITION OF "ALL OR SUBSTANTIALLY ALL"

Sales of corporate assets are sometimes challenged by shareholders. The issues raised are often about whether the asset(s) sold by the corporation constituted "all or substantially all the assets" of the corporation. If they do, then shareholders have the right to vote to approve the transaction. If not, then boards are free to dispose of assets without the consent of shareholders. Consequently, what constitutes "all or substantially all the assets of the corporation" can be hotly contested. Take, for example, the case of *Hollinger v. Hollinger Int'l, Inc.*, 858 A.2d

342 (Del. 2004). In *Hollinger*, the board decided to sell certain assets of the corporation, including the high profile United Kingdom (U.K.) newspaper, The Telegraph (Hollinger also owned the Chicago Tribune and the Jerusalem Post). The controlling shareholder, who was temporarily unable to exert direct control over the corporation because of legal action against him at the time, sought to block the sale, claiming that Hollinger's Telegraph newspaper unit constituted "all or substantially all the assets" of the corporation, so a sale could not proceed without shareholder approval.

In deciding whether a vote of the shareholders was required, the Chancery Court relied on a test announced many years prior in *Gimbel v. Signal Companies, Inc.*, 316 A.2d 599 (Del. 1974). Section 271, the statute governing voting requirements for asset sales, does not require a vote when any major asset or trophy is sold; it requires a vote only when the assets to be sold, when considered quantitatively and qualitatively, amount to "all or substantially all" of the corporation's assets. In this case the Telegraph comprised fifty-six to fifty-seven percent of the assets of Hollinger Int'l as well as forty-nine percent of the earnings of the revenue.

The court in *Hollinger Int'l* stuck to the principle that if the sale is of assets quantitatively vital to the operation of the corporation and is out of the ordinary and substantially affects the existence and purpose of the corporation, then it is beyond the power of the board of directors. Assets are "quantitatively vital" to the corporation when they are necessary to the continuation of the corporation's life. Merely being an important or a large asset, or even more than fifty percent of net assets as was the case of the Telegraph, does not necessarily make the assets quantitatively vital. More is required. In addition, the transaction in question has to be out of the ordinary for the corporation. The modern corporate holding company structure, in which corporations move into and out of businesses through the purchase and sale of subsidiaries, makes it difficult these days to characterize the sale of any single subsidiary as "qualitatively vital" such that it affects the purpose and existence of the ongoing business enterprise.

When asked to decide whether a sale of Hollinger's Telegraph Group constituted a sale of substantially all the assets of Hollinger, which would have triggered the requirement for a shareholder vote, the court ruled that it did not. Certainly, the Telegraph was a high-profile asset that brought with it a high degree of social prestige in the U.K. for the controlling shareholder. However, social cachet and the ability to "have dinner with the Queen" is not the same as the asset being qualitatively vital to the corporation. Following the transaction, Hollinger remained an active participant in the publishing business, although now focused on different markets. The sale of the Telegraph division did not affect either the existence or the purpose of the corporation.

The court also ruled that the Telegraph Group was not quantitatively vital to the corporation as a whole. Although it did make up just over half of the corporation's assets at the time, the court noted that half is not "substantially all." Indeed, in selling the U.K. assets while holding onto U.S. based publishing assets, Hollinger retained the fastest growing assets in its portfolio. While certainly smaller post-transaction, with the growth prospects of the remaining assets there was no question that Hollinger would be in a position to continue profitably. Ultimately, the court concluded that the sale was not quantitatively vital under the *Gimbel* test; although the "Telegraph Group is somewhat more valuable than" the Chicago Tribune, it was not qualitatively vital since Hollinger Int'l could "continue as a profitable entity" after the Telegraph's sale.[15]

3. DE FACTO MERGER DOCTRINE

In some states, sales of all or substantially all the assets of a corporation not only require a shareholder vote but also give shareholders appraisal rights. But this is not true in all states. In those states, including Delaware, sales of all or substantially all assets do not give appraisal rights. Some shareholders in such states have nevertheless sought appraisal rights upon an asset sale, arguing that because the result is the same as a statutory merger, they should get the same such rights that they would get in a merger. Parties should not, according to the de facto merger doctrine, be able to avoid the protections afforded shareholders by reason of managers' decisions as to how to structure transactions. In a de facto merger, shareholders receive the same rights, including the right to an appraisal, that would otherwise be afforded them had the board of the seller elected to undertake the transaction as a merger and not an asset sale.

Some states have allowed shareholders to obtain appraisal rights under the de facto merger doctrine. But most states, including Delaware, do not.[16] Delaware follows the equal dignity doctrine. The equal dignity doctrine provides that each provision of the corporate statute has equal dignity before the law. Delaware courts will not penalize boards of directors who comply with one provision of the statute and not another,

---

[15] "Although both Groups are profitable, valuable economic assets and although the Telegraph Group is somewhat more valuable than the Chicago Group, International can continue as a profitable entity without either one of them."

[16] See *Hariton v. Arco Electronics, Inc.* 188 A.2d 123 (Del. 1963). The seminal case applying the de facto merger doctrine to allow shareholders to get appraisal rights in an asset sale is *Farris v. Glen Alden Corp.*, 143 A.2d 25 (Pa.1958), decided under Pennsylvania law. After that case, there have been various statutory amendments and cases which, together, make it seem as though the use of the de facto merger doctrine in Pennsylvania to obtain appraisal rights may be dead, or at least severely limited. See *Terry v. Penn Central Corp.*, 668 F. 2d 188 (3rd Cir. 1981).

and so will not apply the laws related to a merger to an asset sale (and vice versa). A leading case, *Hariton v. Arco Electronics, Inc.*, 188 A.2d 123, 125 (Del. 1963), quoted approvingly from an earlier case describing "the general theory" of Delaware corporate law, "that action taken pursuant to the authority of the various sections of that law constitute acts of independent legal significance and their validity is not dependent on other sections of the Act."

If a board decides not to structure its transaction as a statutory merger, but rather a sale of substantially all the assets of the corporation, and the corporation complies with the provisions of the statute with respect to that transaction, Delaware courts will not look through the transaction and provide shareholders with rights available only under another provision of the law. Rejection of the de facto merger doctrine and Delaware's embrace of the doctrine of equal dignity is extremely important for transaction planners. The doctrine of equal dignity provides transaction planners with sufficient certainty that should they desire to structure their transaction in a particular manner, courts will not disregard that considered choice.

The effect of the equal dignity doctrine is to give deal lawyers substantial latitude in how to structure transactions in order to avoid shareholder votes and appraisal rights. In the prior Sections, we have already seen that acquirers can avoid the need for a shareholder vote by structuring the transaction as a subsidiary merger. Lawyers can also choose between the merger structure and an asset sale to also avoid appraisal rights, and sometimes, a shareholder vote.

Most states, including Delaware, do allow creditors to use the de facto merger doctrine as a successor liability doctrine. Different states formulate the test differently, but all the tests seek to protect creditors from what might be considered an abuse, where the assets or operations that were their source of repayment have gone elsewhere and the liabilities have not been assumed. A related doctrine allows creditors to recover where the asset buyer is a "mere continuation" of the asset seller.[17] To the extent transaction planners opt for an asset sale structure solely to avoid the successor liability effects of § 259, then Delaware courts may look through the form of the transaction and assign liability to the successor entity.

---

[17] A seminal case on this matter is *Fehl v. SWC Corp.*, 433 F. Supp. 939 (D. Del. 1977). In *Fehl*, the court stated that "If the seller corporation is absorbed into the buyer, and if the seller's shareholders continue to have an ownership interest in the buyer, a merger may be found even though statutory requirements were not followed. Similarly, if a new corporation is formed to acquire the assets of an existing corporation, which then ceases to exist, the successor may be found to be a mere continuation of the predecessor." *See also Spring Real Estate LLC v. Echo/RT Holdings, LLC.*, CA No. 7994–VCN (Del. Ch. Dec. 31, 2013). *See generally* John Matheson, *Successor Liability*, 96 MINN. L. REV. 371 (2011).

4. FRAUDULENT CONVEYANCE

The most salient risk facing transaction planners when undertaking a sale of substantially all the assets of a company is the risk of fraudulent conveyance.[18] In part, that is because for many firms, tech firms in particular, a sale of substantially all the assets of the corporation is a viable alternative to bankruptcy proceedings. An asset sale may be considered fraudulent if at the time the transaction is undertaken, there was any actual intent to defraud creditors or if the consideration received for the assets was not of reasonably equivalent value. In order to sustain a fraudulent conveyance claim, the claimant must also show that after the sale the company was either insolvent (i.e., its liabilities exceeded its assets), or it was unable to continue to pay its debts in the ordinary course. In the event of a fraudulent conveyance, a creditor has the right to prevent transfers made with the intent defraud either present or future creditors. If the transaction has been consummated, then the action for fraudulent conveyance and consequent money damages is available against the board of the seller as well as the acquirer of the assets in question.

Fraudulent conveyance issues are common when there is an asset sale. A board will be concerned about future liability for selling an asset for inadequate value or otherwise assuring that the company is neither insolvent nor unable to pay its bills after the sale. To provide comfort on this issue, it is not uncommon for a board to request a "fraudulent conveyance" or "bulk sale" opinion from their lawyers in order to ensure that the board is sufficiently protected. The opinion will speak to the value of the asset being sold and consideration received in exchange, as well as the solvency and ability of the company to pay its bills after the transaction. In preparing this opinion the lawyers will rely on certificates as to the financial state of the company and value of the sold asset as provided by either corporate officers or external financial advisers. For a sample bulk sale opinion, see the Online Appendix.

E. TAX CONSIDERATIONS

Tax considerations often drive the structuring of transactions. For deal lawyers, perhaps one of the most significant tax points is the difference between the treatment of forward triangular mergers and reverse triangular mergers.

In a forward triangular merger, an acquirer can pay approximately fifty percent of the consideration in stock, and the stock component of the consideration will be considered a tax-free exchange. The effect of this is that the target's shareholders will not pay tax on the stock consideration

---

[18] Fraudulent conveyance is also a significant risk in the context of a LBO transaction.

they receive in the merger. The cash component, however, is always taxable. In a reverse triangular merger, an acquirer can only pay up to twenty percent of the consideration in ~~stock~~ for the stock component to be treated as non-taxable.

The net effect of this difference is that if the acquirer wants to pay more than twenty percent of the consideration in stock but still have a non-taxable stock component, the forward triangular merger is the only option.

Because of space limitations we do not include an extensive discussion of the tax treatment of M&A transactions in this casebook. However, we encourage you to take a corporate taxation class in order to familiarize yourself with these issues. The best transactional lawyers can work easily with both tax and corporate law principles in order to structure and complete transactions.

QUESTIONS

1.   What is the rationale for allowing mergers under some circumstances without a shareholder vote? Do you agree with the rationale? Do you think shareholders are adequately protected?

2.   Do you agree with Delaware's rejection of the de facto merger doctrine in the context of appraisal rights for asset sales? What are the benefits of allowing form to trump substance? The costs? What are the benefits of allowing equity to override statutes? The costs?

3.   Apex Tech and Beta Corp enter into a merger agreement. Pursuant to the agreement Apex will merge with and into Beta with Apex Tech as the disappearing corporation and Beta Corp as the surviving corporation. Shareholders of Apex Tech will receive cash as consideration for their stock. As part of the merger, the surviving corporation will formally amend its certificate of incorporation to change its name to ApexBeta Tech Corp. and increase the number of authorized shares. Do shareholders of Apex Tech have the right to vote on the transaction? Why or why not? Do shareholders of Beta Corp have the right to vote on the transaction? Why or why not?

4.   If in the question above the shareholders of Beta Corp are asked to vote on the transaction, what is the minimum number of votes in favor required at a duly called meeting of the shareholders for purposes of considering the merger agreement if you have the following information:

     a.   Number of Beta shares authorized: 10,000,000

     b.   Number of Beta shares outstanding: 8,000,000

     c.   Number of Beta shares present at meeting: 6,000,000

5.   Apex Tech and Beta Corp enter into a merger agreement. Pursuant to the agreement, Apex Acquisition Sub, a wholly owned subsidiary of Beta Corp, will merge with and into Apex Tech, with Apex Acquisition Sub as the

disappearing corporation and Apex Tech as the surviving corporation. Shareholders of Apex Tech will receive cash as consideration for their stock. Do shareholders of Apex Tech have the right to vote on the transaction? Why or why not? Do shareholders of Beta Corp have the right to vote on the transaction? Why or why not?

6.   Apex Tech and Beta Corp enter into a merger agreement. Pursuant to the agreement, Apex Acquisition Sub, a wholly owned subsidiary of Beta Corp, will merge with and into Apex Tech with Apex Acquisition Sub as the disappearing corporation and Apex Tech as the surviving corporation. Shareholders of Apex Tech will receive stock of Beta Corp as consideration for their stock. As a result of the transaction, former Apex Tech shareholders will hold 30% of the outstanding stock of Beta Corp. Do shareholders of Apex Tech have the right to vote on the transaction? Why or why not? Do shareholders of Beta Corp have the right to vote on the transaction? Why or why not?

7.   Apex Tech and Beta Corp enter into a merger agreement. Pursuant to the agreement Apex will merge with and into Beta with Apex Tech as the disappearing corporation and Beta Corp as the surviving corporation. Shareholders of Apex Tech will receive stock of Beta Corp as consideration for their stock. As a result of the transaction, former Apex Tech shareholders will hold 10% of the outstanding stock of Beta Corp. Do shareholders of Apex Tech have the right to vote on the transaction? Why or why not? Do shareholders of Beta Corp have the right to vote on the transaction? Why or why not?

8.   Delta LLC and Beta Corp enter into a merger agreement. Pursuant to the agreement Delta LLC will merge with and into Beta Corp with Delta LLC as the disappearing corporation and Beta Corp as the surviving corporation. Unitholders of Delta LLC will receive stock of Beta Corp as consideration for their units. As a result of the transaction, former Delta LLC unitholders will hold 10% of the outstanding stock of Beta Corp. Do unitholders of Delta LLC have the right to vote on the transaction? Why or why not? Do shareholders of Beta Corp have the right to vote on the transaction? Why or why not?

9.   Apex Tech and Beta Corp enter into an agreement pursuant to which Apex Tech agrees to sell substantially all of its assets to Beta Corp. Apex Tech will receive cash as consideration (which it may then distribute to its shareholders as a dividend). Do shareholders of Apex Tech have the right to vote on the transaction? Why or why not? Do shareholders of Beta Corp have the right to vote on the transaction? Why or why not?

10. Apex Tech and Beta Corp enter into an agreement pursuant to which Apex Tech agrees to sell substantially all of its assets to Beta Corp. Apex Tech will receive stock of Beta Corp as consideration, and Apex Tech will then dissolve. As a result of the transaction, former shareholders of Apex Tech will hold 25% of the stock of Beta Corp. Do shareholders of Apex Tech have the right to vote on the transaction? Why or why not? Do shareholders of Beta Corp have the right to vote on the transaction? Why or why not?

11. Apex Tech and Beta Corp enter into an agreement pursuant to which Apex Tech agrees to sell two of its four divisions to Beta Corp. The two divisions they are selling are the two original corporate divisions of Apex Tech from when Apex was a major force in the manufacture of electronic typewriters. Those divisions, which long made up the corporate identity, have hit on hard times recently. The two remaining divisions are almost equal in size to the original divisions but are in a totally different line of business. Apex Tech will receive cash as consideration. Do shareholders of Apex Tech have the right to vote on the transaction? Why or why not? Do shareholders of Beta Corp have the right to vote on the transaction? Why or why not?

12. Apex Tech agrees to sell substantially all its assets to Beta Corp. As part of the transaction, Beta Corp decides that there are a number of liabilities that it would like to leave behind. Is Beta Corp permitted to leave behind certain liabilities or is it required to take all of Apex's liabilities? If Beta is not required to accept all the Apex liabilities, what provisions must be made?

PROBLEMS

1. KKW, a private equity firm wishes to acquire the mining operations of Beta Corp., a publicly traded diversified conglomerate with mining operations (70% of revenues and profits) and a newspaper business (30% of revenues and profits). The mining operations of Beta Corp. have significant liabilities. KKW does not wish to assume these liabilities. The consideration is cash. Please recommend and diagram an acquisition structure for this deal. Please note which company's shareholders will be required to vote in the transaction.

2. Apex Tech, a publicly traded financial services company, wishes to acquire Beta Corp, a publicly traded diversified conglomerate. Apex Tech's general counsel comes to you and says that Apex Tech does not want to have its shareholders vote on the transaction. Please recommend and diagram an acquisition structure for this deal. Does it matter what type of consideration Apex Tech offers?

3. Kappa Corporation, a Delaware corporation, is publicly traded. It presently has 10 million shares outstanding; each share is traded on the NYSE, and the share price has been stable, at $100/share. Kappa has an additional 100,000 shares authorized. Kappa is interested in acquiring the Delta Corporation, and is considering how to structure the acquisition. Recently, Delta turned down a bid for $350,000,000 on grounds that it was too low, but stated that it was interested in being acquired for an appropriate price. On what matters might Kappa shareholders have a vote if Kappa uses its own stock in the transaction? Consider both a purchase of Delta's assets and a direct merger in which Kappa survives.

4. Using the information available in the Dole Merger Agreement in the Online Appendix (primarily Sections 1 and 2), draft a certificate of merger that complies with the requirements of DGCL § 251 as well as § 103.

5.   Using the information available in the Dole Merger Agreement in the Online Appendix, draft board resolutions for the board of the target firm that comply with the requirements of DGCL § 251.

CHAPTER III

APPRAISAL RIGHTS

■ ■ ■

Prior to the adoption of modern corporate law, fundamental corporate transactions such as mergers required unanimous consent of shareholders. Analytically, this made sense. A shareholder's relationship to the corporation was contractual in nature and a merger that forced an unwilling shareholder to accept consideration for her stock seemed counter to basic concepts of fair contractual relations. However, this unanimity requirement also gave hold-out shareholders, those unwilling to go along with a transaction, power to veto otherwise valuable transactions. Liberalized merger statutes reduced the vote required to approve merger transactions to a supermajority, and later, to a simple majority.[1]

While liberalization of merger approval requirements facilitated valuable transactions by eliminating the hold-out problem, it created a problem that unanimity rules were meant to prevent: how to deal with shareholders who oppose the merger because they do not believe the consideration offered represented fair value for their stock. The appraisal remedy was created to address this need. The appraisal remedy allows a shareholder who does not vote for the merger to "dissent." The dissenting shareholder can go to a court and demand that a fair price, which she believes is higher than the merger consideration, be paid for her shares.

The appraisal remedy's purpose is not to provide dissenting shareholders with an additional avenue to oppose a merger, but rather, to provide them with an orderly means of obtaining what a judge determines is fair value for their shares. Of course, a judge is rarely in a position to conduct such an appraisal on his or her own. Consequently, appraisal actions often become battles of valuation experts.

We will spend some time parsing the specifics of DGCL § 262, the Delaware law governing appraisal rights. This exercise is important because courts require scrupulous adherence to the statute's requirements in order to access the remedy. The Sections that follow lay out the appraisal process, the circumstances in which such rights are available, how shareholders can perfect their appraisal rights, and how courts determine fair value.

---

[1] *See* N.Y. BSC. LAW § 903; *see also* Title 8 DGCL § 251(c).

Appraisal rights for dissenting shareholders are not universally available in all transactions. Recall the discussion of asset sales in the previous Chapter: the Chapter noted that appraisal often is not available in a transaction structured as an asset sale. Indeed, not having appraisal rights may be a (if not *the*) principal reason for structuring a transaction in this manner. Tender offers—purchases directly from target shareholders, further discussed starting in Chapter V—also do not trigger appraisal rights, nor do certain mergers described below in which shareholders receive consideration for their shares in the form of stock rather than cash. Because the appraisal remedy is not universally available, it is important to have a firm understanding of when the statute makes the remedy available to dissenting shareholders.

A. PERFECTING APPRAISAL RIGHTS

Shareholders of a constituent corporation dissenting from a merger because they believe that the consideration offered in the merger is inadequate may be eligible to receive a judicial appraisal of their stock if they comply with the requirements of DGCL § 262.

1. WHO CAN EXERCISE APPRAISAL RIGHTS?

The right to receive an appraisal is a statutory right, like voting, conferred on record shareholders (those in whose name shares are held), rather than beneficial shareholders (those holding the ultimate economic interest). Most beneficial owners are not record owners; rather, their shares are held of record in "street name."[2] Historically, beneficial shareholders seeking an appraisal have had to do so with the consent and cooperation of the record holder. Because the record holder had to bring the action, the plaintiff in many appraisal cases was "Cede & Co.;" Cede, the nominee of Depository Trust Company (DTC), is by far the largest record shareholder on Wall Street.

Normally, record shareholders would agree to act as a nominal plaintiff in appraisal actions in order to provide beneficial shareholders with access to the proceeding and the remedy. But beneficial shareholders no longer need to proceed through their record owners. In 2007, after the *Transkaryotic* decision discussed later in this Chapter, Delaware amended § 262 to permit a person who is the beneficial owner of shares held either in a voting trust or by a nominee to file for an appraisal in her own name.

---

[2] "The street name registration system was created to facilitate securities trading, eliminate paperwork and preserve the confidentiality of beneficial owners' identities. DTC holds the shares on behalf of banks and brokers, which in turn hold on behalf of their clients (who are the underlying beneficial owners or other intermediaries)." John C. Wilcox, John J. Purcell III, & Hye-Won Choi, *"Street Name" Registration & The Proxy Solicitation Process* 12–3, available at http://www.sec.gov/comments/4–537/4537–25.pdf.

Appraisal rights are only available if shareholders are dissenting from a statutory merger accomplished pursuant to any of §§ 251–58, 263–64, or 267). This includes short form mergers: the § 253 short form merger and the § 251(h) short form merger. Appraisal rights are also available in statutory mergers between Delaware entities and non-Delaware entities, and between a corporation and an entity other than a corporation, such as a Limited Liability Company (LLC).

The Delaware statute does not provide appraisal rights for many other types of transactions, including a sale of all or substantially all the assets of the corporation pursuant to § 271 or a tender offer. Some other state statutes do provide appraisal rights for sales of assets. Moreover, as discussed in Chapter II, in some states, courts may apply the de facto merger doctrine to extend appraisal rights to transactions not structured as statutory mergers but having the same result. Because of its doctrine of independent legal significance, Delaware resists such extensions of statutory rights.

2.   DELL APPRAISAL RIGHTS

Below you will find the relevant language from the merger agreement for the 2013 Dell management buyout, in which Dell was "taken private." The excerpted provision describes the rights of shareholders to receive appraisal under the statute. In transactions where shareholders will have access to the statutory appraisal right, it is common to include a provision in the merger agreement describing the right. When you are reading this provision, note that it describes what is required under § 262. If Dell were incorporated in a state other than Delaware, this section would be drafted to reflect the requirements of that state's appraisal statute.

(d) Dissenters' Rights. Any provision of this Agreement to the contrary notwithstanding, Shares that are issued and outstanding immediately prior to the Effective Time and that are held by holders of such Shares who have (i) not voted in favor of the adoption of this Agreement or consented thereto in writing and (ii) properly exercised appraisal rights with respect thereto in accordance with, and otherwise complied with, Section 262 of the DGCL (the "Dissenting Shares") shall not be converted into the right to receive the Merger Consideration pursuant to Section 2.1(a). Holders of Dissenting Shares shall be entitled only to receive payment of the fair value of such Dissenting Shares in accordance with the provisions of such Section 262, unless and until any such holder fails to perfect or effectively withdraws or loses its rights to appraisal and payment under the DGCL. If, after the Effective Time, any such holder fails to perfect or effectively withdraws or loses such right, such

Dissenting Shares shall thereupon cease to be Dissenting Shares, including for purposes of Section 2.1(a), and shall be deemed to have been converted into, at the Effective Time, the right to receive the Merger Consideration as provided for in Section 2.1(a). At the Effective Time, the Dissenting Shares shall be automatically canceled and shall cease to exist and any holder of Dissenting Shares shall cease to have any rights with respect thereto, except the rights provided in Section 262 of the DGCL and as provided in the previous sentence.

3.   HOW DOES A SHAREHOLDER EXERCISE APPRAISAL RIGHTS?

Only shareholders who perfect their appraisal rights in accordance with the statute will have access to the appraisal remedy. The steps for perfecting appraisal rights are set forth below.

a.   The Obligation to Make a Written Demand for Appraisal

A shareholder of a constituent corporation engaged in a transaction for which appraisal rights are available who wishes to exercise those rights must make a written demand for an appraisal of his or her shares prior to the shareholder vote held on the transaction. The shareholder's written demand for an appraisal need not take any particular form, but it must be timely and "reasonably inform the corporation of the identity of the shareholder and that the shareholder intends thereby to demand [an] appraisal."

Consider, for example, the experience with appraisal proceedings in the Dell going-private transaction (from which the above language is taken). One Dell shareholder who had previously attempted to acquire Dell, Carl Icahn, opposed the transaction, asserting that the consideration being offered was inadequate. During the months preceding the shareholder vote to approve the going-private transaction, Mr. Icahn announced his intention to seek appraisal of his Dell shares, and urged other Dell shareholders to do the same. Below you will find the text of his letter to Dell shareholders, filed as part of his Schedule 13D on July 11, 2013. Notice how this letter instructs shareholders that they should make a written demand prior to the shareholder vote, and further instructs them as to how to make the demand, effectively telling them how to proceed so that they can comply with the requirements of DGCL § 262(d)(1).

FOR IMMEDITATE RELEASE

CARL C. ICAHN ISSUES OPEN LETTER TO STOCKHOLDERS OF DELL:

NO-BRAINER AT DELL

New York, New York—July 11, 2013—Carl C. Icahn and his affiliates today issued the following open letter to stockholders of Dell Inc.

Dear Fellow Dell Stockholders:

On rare occasions in investing, one comes across situations that are "no-brainers." In these situations the odds are greatly in your favor of making a profit while taking very little risk, and in some very rare situations, you can make a profit while taking no risk at all. Strangely, in my experience many investors miss the opportunity to take advantage of these situations.

When I first started Icahn & Co. in 1968 I discovered that you could purchase convertible bonds in companies and sell short the stock they converted into. If the market declined precipitously, the stocks you shorted would go down but the bonds would stop declining and trade as bonds. Few investors set up this riskless arbitrage because no one thought the market would go down enough to make a profit on the bonds. But the market crashed in 1969, and Icahn & Co. made 10 times its capital in its first year of existence.

Throughout my career I have constantly been on the lookout for situations where risk is very negligible compared to the reward. I believe that today a "no-brainer" exists at Dell. This is because if you own Dell and opt for appraisal rights, you have a rare opportunity to make a profit without taking risk. Under the law, if you are dissatisfied with the price that you are being forced to take in a "going-private" transaction that you did not vote for, you can go to court for an appraisal. The reason that doing this is a "no-brainer" is because the law allows you to change your mind up to 60 days after the transaction is consummated. All you have to do is notify Dell before the vote that approved the transaction.

In the case of Dell, even if the Michael Dell/Silver Lake offer of $13.65 is accepted by shareholders on July 18, Dell has indicated that the merger is expected to be consummated around October. If that is the case, and if you opt for appraisal, you will have until December to decide if you want the $13.65 or continue on with the appraisal process. You therefore have a free put under this example until December. You always have 60 days from the actual date that the merger is consummated to change your mind.

As in all "no-brainers," while there is no risk, it does not seem likely that you will make a profit either, so why bother— but appearances can be deceiving. On occasion these "no-brainers" make profits and sometimes huge ones. In the case of Dell, a great many things can occur between now and December to make this trade profitable. For one thing, Dell may want to settle with those seeking appraisal rights. Another possibility is that Dell paints a much rosier picture of the company's prospects when the approximately $16 billion loans that Michael Dell/Silver Lake need are being syndicated. We believe this will make it apparent that the company is worth far more than $13.65 and that can be taken advantage of to fight for a premium well over $13.65.

But remember, in order to take advantage of appraisal you must notify Dell of your intention to do so before the vote on the merger and you must not vote for the merger. If you don't do both of those things you cannot take advantage of the benefit of the "no-brainer" if that benefit becomes available.

In case you are interested, yesterday we opted for appraisal on the approximately 152 million shares that we own and we are in the process of delivering the applicable documents. You should be aware that you have only a few more days to exercise your appraisal rights.

THE PROCESS TO SEEK APPRAISAL RIGHTS TAKES TIME, SO ACT NOW IF YOU WISH TO PERFECT YOUR APPRAISAL RIGHTS AND IMMEDIATELY CONTACT YOUR BROKER AND OTHER ADVISORS. If you have any questions concerning appraisal rights or wish to seek help or information regarding appraisal rights, contact D.F. King & Co., Inc. at 1-800-347-4750 or dell@dfking.com. They will take your information and provide it to people at Icahn who will call you back.

For a detailed discussion of the process for perfecting and exercising appraisal rights, see page 180 of the Definitive Proxy Statement on Schedule 14A filed by Dell with the SEC on May 31, 2013.

We urge stockholders not to vote for the Michael Dell/Silver Lake transaction. And we urge those that are not voting for the transaction to take advantage of the "no-brainer." In our opinion this approach gives you two chances to win, THE FIRST CHANCE, and the one that we desire to have happen, is that the

Michael Dell/Silver Lake transaction is defeated, in which event we will move on to the annual meeting, giving shareholders the opportunity to elect our slate of directors and have the benefit of our previously described $14 Dell self-tender proposal. THE SECOND CHANCE comes if the Michael Dell/Silver Lake transaction is approved by the other stockholders and is consummated, in which event you will at least have a shot at the "no-brainer". Why miss that opportunity to have a second bite at the apple?

Sincerely Carl C. Icahn
Chairman
Icahn Enterprises, L.P.

Dell sent shareholders a response to Mr. Icahn's letter; the response is included in the Online Appendix. Dell's letter emphasized the risks and costs of pursuing appraisal, noting that if enough shareholders did not vote in favor of the merger, the merger would not occur, and appraisal rights would therefore not be available. The letter also discussed the length and expense of appraisal proceedings, and noted that the appraised value of Dell shares could be lower than the merger consideration.

b.   Must Remain a Shareholder

In addition to making a demand, in order for a shareholder to perfect her appraisal rights, the shareholder must also hold shares of stock on the date she makes a written demand for an appraisal, and continue to hold those shares through the effective date of the merger. Dissenting shareholders need not be shareholders on the date the merger agreement is announced, just on the date a written demand is made. The language of the statute permits beneficial holders to purchase shares of the target *after* announcement of the merger and then pursue an appraisal. This loophole in the statute has created an avenue for arbitrageurs to buy shares and then pursue appraisal actions when they believe the announced deal values justify the investment. This is called appraisal arbitrage (and is discussed in Section E below).

The dissenting shareholder is required to remain a shareholder through the pendency of the appraisal action. The shareholder may not pursue an appraisal action if she has sold her shares or accepted the merger consideration.[3]

----

[3]   Note that an amendment to Delaware law was proposed which would allow companies to pay a portion of the merger consideration—the portion which is "uncontested"—to shareholders pursuing appraisal. Shareholders "accepting" this consideration would not give up their rights to

c.   The Obligation Not to Vote Yes

A dissenting shareholder who wishes to preserve her appraisal rights must not vote in favor of the transaction. A dissenting shareholder need not vote "no." She may abstain (that is, her vote is "abstain" rather than "yes" or "no") or even not vote at all. But she cannot vote in favor of the transaction or provide her written consent. Notice that in Carl Icahn's letter to Dell shareholders, Mr. Icahn reminds shareholders:

> [I]n order to take advantage of appraisal you must notify Dell of your intention to do so before the vote on the merger and you must not vote for the merger. If you don't do both of those things you cannot take advantage of the benefit of the "no-brainer" if that benefit becomes available.

When a share is bought after the record date, and the buyer is seeking appraisal, must the buyer demonstrate that the shares the buyer bought were not voted for the merger? In other words, must the shares for which appraisal is sought be "traced" to such shares? The share was, after all, not voted by or at the direction of the buyer. The rise of appraisal arbitrage has brought this issue to the fore, as appraisal arbitrageurs buy shares, often after the record date, in order to bring appraisal actions.

The question has been answered in the negative. Recall that most shares are held of record by a nominee, often Cede & Co. Following an important decision by the Delaware Chancery Court, *In re: Appraisal of Transkaryotic Therapies, Inc.*, CA. 1554–CC., 2007 WL 1378345 (Del. Ch. May 2, 2007), for stock held in "fungible bulk," (that is, where beneficial shareholders have only book-entry positions representing their pro-rata portion of the record holder's aggregate holding in the security) the record holder must have refrained from voting the number of shares sufficient to cover the demand for appraisal. There are no stock tracing requirements. Provided a sufficient number of shares were either not voted or were voted no, a beneficial owner need not establish how particular shares for which it claims the right of appraisal were voted.

4.   THE STATUS OF SHAREHOLDERS EXERCISING APPRAISAL RIGHTS

Once a shareholder has perfected his appraisal rights in the manner described above, he is no longer a shareholder of the corporation. Rather, he has given up his right to hold stock, and has become an unsecured creditor of the corporation. Shareholders who seek an appraisal rather

---

pursue appraisal. The amendment was intended to limit the ultimate payout to shareholders pursuing appraisal, given that, as we will discuss in the text, the appraisal statute grants them interest in excess of five percent on the amounts of appraised value. Paying the uncontested portion immediately means the company will not have to pay interest on that portion, and thus reduces the amount the company might otherwise have to pay in any appraisal proceeding. As this textbook goes to press, the proposal is on hold.

than accept the merger consideration "lose the benefits of stock ownership: the right to vote stock and to receive dividends or other distribution[s]" from the corporation.[4] As unsecured creditors, dissenting shareholders must accept the credit risk that the corporation's fortunes will decline precipitously between the effective date and the date their shares are appraised by a court. Unlike other transaction-related litigation, appraisal litigation tends to have a longer time horizon, sometimes taking as much as two or three years to complete. For many shareholders otherwise eligible to pursue appraisal, the lengthy wait is too much of a risk to bear, and they may take the consideration should the transaction be consummated. Indeed, Carl Icahn, having made demand on Dell, voting no, and holding his stock through the effective date, decided against pursuing appraisal. The following tweet appeared on his twitter feed not long after the closing of the Dell transaction:

Carl Icahn   @Carl_C_Icahn I withdrew my demand for appraisal of my Dell shares. Based on our returns on capital, we believe we have better uses for $2 billion. 10:11 AM—4 Oct 2013

Mr. Icahn accepted his merger consideration and moved on. By the time he did so, and presumably in response to his criticisms of the deal mentioned above, and others' criticisms as well, the merger consideration had been increased, to a total of $13.88 per share.

5. PURSUING APPRAISAL RIGHTS

Shareholders who wish to proceed with an appraisal must, within 120 days of the effective date, commence the proceeding by filing a petition with the court. The statute permits the surviving corporation to file an appraisal petition with respect to shares held by shareholders who have complied with the requirements of § 262.

Within the first sixty days after filing their petition, dissenters may freely withdraw their petition and accept the merger consideration. After sixty days, dissenters may not withdraw without the approval of a judge; this requirement exists to guard against collusion between dissenters and the corporation in what essentially becomes class litigation.

6. DETERMINING FAIR VALUE

Once the formalities required under § 262 are accomplished, the court will conduct an appraisal proceeding and determine the "fair value"

---

[4]   *Alabama By-Products Corp. v. Cede & Co.*, 657 A.2d 254 (Del. 1995).

of the dissenters' stock at the time of the merger without giving effect to any value imputed by the announcement of the merger. As noted above, the proceeding often becomes an expensive battle of the experts, in which the arguments often resemble a seminar in corporate finance more than they do law. The court may determine that fair value is more or less than, or the same as, the consideration offered in the merger agreement.

A recent paper by Professors Charles Korsmo and Minor Myers[5] found that appraisal filings tend to target the deals that might be thought less likely to be offering fair value: they found that more appraisal filings were made in transactions involving lower premiums above pre-deal market value.

Figure 8
Transaction Premia Residuals for Transactions with Counseled Appraisal (gray), by four-week residual premia

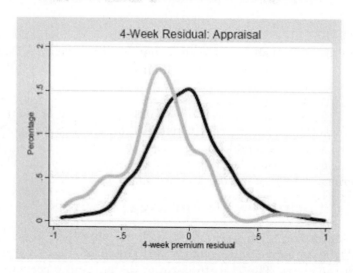

The gray line plots the residual premia for transactions that attracted a counseled appraisal petition, while the black line shows the same for transactions not attracting counseled petitions. (Counseled means that the shareholder is represented by a lawyer; "not counseled" means that the shareholder is acting pro se.) The consistent pattern in the data is that appraisal litigation involves transactions with strongly negative residual premia.

---

[5] Charles Korsmo & Minor Myers, *Appraisal Arbitrage and the Future of Public Company M&A*, 92 WASH. U. L. REV. 1551 (2015).

7. WHO EXERCISES APPRAISAL RIGHTS?

Exercising appraisal rights can be risky. In a shareholder class action for breach of fiduciary duty, the plaintiff's counsel usually is willing to work on a "contingency" basis, anticipating payment from the recovery or from the corporation. By contrast, in an appraisal action, the shareholder must initially pay her own legal expenses, and must hire and pay for experts to opine on valuation. The appraisal process can last for several years, and of course, the amount of any recovery is uncertain.

Indeed, when shareholders are considering whether to pursue an appraisal, the most important consideration is often cost. Appraisal proceedings are expensive. Because the issue before the court is the value of the stock, each side must hire and present expert witnesses. These experts offer opinions as to the fair value of the dissenter's holdings. Clearly, for shareholders with small amounts of stock who must bear the costs of pursuing the litigation, an appraisal proceeding rarely makes economic sense. However, dissenters may join together with other dissenters to form a class. By forming a single large block, smaller shareholders are able to share costs of litigation on a pro rata basis, thus reducing the economic disincentives of bringing such litigation. In addition, while each side in an appraisal typically bears its own costs, the court may, if it deems it equitable, assign the shareholders' costs to the corporation at the completion of litigation. Consequently, even small shareholders who believe the consideration offered in an appraisal is inadequate may have sufficient incentive to pursue statutory appraisal.

That being said, until recently, actions for appraisal had only been brought infrequently. Indeed, apart from Mr. Icahn's pursuit of appraisal rights for his Dell shares, such rights were pursued and perfected for only two percent of the Dell shares.

B. NOTICE REQUIREMENTS BY THE CORPORATION

Constituent corporations to a merger are required to provide notice to all record shareholders of their rights to dissent from the merger and receive an appraisal; the notice must be given at least twenty days prior to the meeting at which shareholders will vote on the merger (See the Dell shareholder notice above). Shareholders are thus on notice and can then take steps to perfect any appraisal rights they may have. The appraisal notice must include a copy of § 262 in its entirety. Failure to comply with the strict requirements can generate potentially significant liability for the surviving corporation, as *Berger v. PubCo.*, discussed in Section F. below, shows. The notice that Dell provided to its shareholders informing them of their appraisal rights in connection with its going-private transaction can be found in this textbook's Online Appendix.

C. IN WHAT TRANSACTIONS ARE APPRAISAL RIGHTS AVAILABLE?

The foregoing discussed for which what sorts of transactions appraisal rights are available and how such rights can be perfected. Whether appraisal rights are available is also affected by whether the stock a shareholder had in the entity being merged was public or private, and what sort of consideration the shareholder is to receive in the merger. As we shall see, there is far less concern that shareholders cannot receive fair value if they have, or are receiving, publicly traded stock. DGCL § 262(b) specifies mergers for which appraisal are available. To say that it is inartfully worded is a gross understatement, as you shall soon see.

§ 262.   Appraisal rights.

. . .

(b) Appraisal rights shall be available for the shares of any . . . stock of a constituent corporation in a merger . . . to be effected pursuant to § 251 [or other statutory merger]. . . .

(1) Provided, however, that . . . no appraisal rights under this section shall be available for . . . shares of [publicly traded] stock . . . ; and further provided that no appraisal rights shall be available for any shares of stock of the constituent corporation surviving a merger if the merger did not require for its approval the vote of the stockholders of the surviving corporation as provided in § 251(f) of this title.

(2) [However] . . . appraisal rights . . . shall be available for the shares . . . of a constituent corporation if the holders thereof are required . . . to accept for such stock anything except:

a.   Shares of stock of the corporation surviving or resulting from such merger. . . ;

b.   [Publicly traded] Shares of stock of any other corporation;

c.   Cash in lieu of fractional shares . . . ; or

d.   Any combination of the [above].

(3) [In a § 251(h), § 253 or other short-form merger], appraisal rights shall be available for [any] shares of a subsidiary [not owned by the parent immediately prior to the merger]

The structure of the statute is to first *grant* appraisal rights to statutory mergers, then to *limit* that grant, and then to restore rights, superseding the limit. Section 262(b) first grants the rights: appraisal rights are available to shareholders of constituent corporations in any statutory merger transaction. Section 262(b)(1) then limits the rights: no appraisal rights are available for any publicly-traded shares (recall that publicly traded for this purpose means (i) listed on a national securities exchange, or (ii) held of record by more than 2,000 holders) or shares of a surviving corporation where the shareholders were not required to vote.

Section 262(b)(2) then *restores* appraisal rights in some circumstances. Notwithstanding the restrictions in § 262(b)(1), appraisal rights are restored to shareholders of constituent corporations if they are required to accept as consideration in the merger anything other than stock of the surviving corporation (on grounds that the shareholder still has an interest in the company at issue) or publicly traded stock of another corporation. This latter provision is known as the "market out."

The rationale for this "market out" to the appraisal remedy is that shareholders do not need a court's protection if a public market exists into which they might sell their stock. The public market for the stock of the seller provides a valuation, which should be as good as, if not better than, a court's valuation. The appraisal remedy is better suited to situations where valuations may not be as reliable or as disinterested as market valuations, for example where the consideration being offered is the stock of a private company for which there is no readily accessible valuation. Some observers believe that this market out rationale is not satisfactory—that stock market prices are not reliable indicators of fair value. Indeed, when a Delaware court determines fair value, it specifically does not rely on stock market prices.

Notwithstanding the various exceptions to the appraisal rights provided for in § 262(b)(2), short form mergers pursuant to either §§ 253 and 251(h) are both eligible for appraisal rights. There is no market-out exception for these types of statutory mergers.[6]

The following summarizes the foregoing discussion of § 262(b), including the market out.

---

[6] A proposed amendment to Title 8 DGCL § 262 would require shares representing at least one percent of the outstanding stock or $1 million in merger consideration to perfect their appraisal rights in order for the appraisal remedy to be available to any shareholder. Under the proposal, shareholders seeking an appraisal in connection with short form mergers accomplished under §§ 253 or 267 would not be not subject to the minimum condition. Minimum conditions like this one are not uncommon in appraisal statutes. In general they are intended to improve efficiency of the process by ensuring that the remedy is available only when a significant number of shareholders believe the consideration offered in the transaction does not represent fair value for their shares. In this regard, the statutes deter nuisance suits. Critics argue that these statutes prevent shareholders from exercising legitimate claims for an arbitrary reason unrelated to the merits of an appraisal claim. As this textbook goes to press, the proposal is on hold.

Availability of appraisal rights:

1. Is the dissenting shareholder a shareholder of a constituent corporation in a statutory merger?

2. Did the dissenting shareholder have a vote in the merger?

If "no" to either of the above, then no appraisal rights are available. If "yes", then:

3. Does the dissenting shareholder hold stock of a publicly traded corporation?

   a. No. The shareholder has appraisal rights.

   b. Yes. Then the shareholder does not have appraisal rights, subject to the exception below.

4. Is the dissenting shareholder required to accept as consideration something other than stock of the surviving corporation or publicly-traded stock of a third corporation (e.g., cash or stock of a third company that is not publicly-traded)?

   a. Yes. The shareholder has appraisal rights.

   b. No. The shareholder does not have appraisal rights.

D. WHAT IS "FAIR VALUE"

Courts' views as to how to determine "fair value" in an appraisal have changed over time. In *Weinberger v. UOP, Inc.*, 457 A.2d 701 (Del. 1983), the Delaware Supreme Court rejected the use of the "Delaware block," or weighted average method, "wherein the elements of value, i.e., assets, market price, earnings, etc., were assigned a particular weight and the resulting amounts added to determine the value per share," in favor of methods that are more commonly used and accepted in the financial community. This more liberalized approach to valuation often includes, but is not limited to, the use of discounted cash flows as a methodology for appraising stock. We discuss these techniques further in Chapter X.

None of this is to say that the use of well-accepted valuation techniques brings certainty to the results of an appraisal proceeding, or indeed, to any sort of proceeding in which share value is relevant to the determination of damages. Even well-accepted valuation techniques offer a range of valuations, and sometimes quite a large range. Moreover, while appraisal rights should only entitle shareholders to the amount the company was worth pre-merger, such that shareholders do not share in post-merger gains, acquisitions are sometimes done in two stages: a tender offer in which the acquirer gains control, and second-step merger.

Once the acquirer has control it may be tempted to start implementing its proposed changes before it completes the second step merger. Certainly, it will be planning to do so. Implementing proposed changes to the corporation prior to completing the second step merger will give dissenting shareholders a right to claim part of the new value the acquirer's changes are expected to yield. There are cases suggesting that, if the plans are sufficiently developed, shareholders may also have a right to claim part of the new value generated by the acquirer's plans.[7]

While our detailed discussion of valuation is contained in Chapter X, a few other points should be made here. Appraisal decisions not infrequently discuss valuation methodology with great specificity. Courts are, after all, being called upon to make a decision after hearing from several well-credentialed experts with widely divergent views. Another important input the court will consider is the merger price itself. Insofar as it was arrived at through a vigorous and untainted process, it will be given "substantial evidentiary weight," although it will not be presumptively deferred to.

The following, from a 2013 case, *Huff Fund Investment Partnership v. CKx, Inc.*, CA No. 6844–VCG, 2013 WL 5878807 (Del. Ch. November 1, 2013), illustrates both of these propositions:

> The Petitioners are stockholders in a corporation, CKx, who have opted for appraisal rather than the cash-out price received in the sale of CKx to an acquirer. The sales process here has been challenged, reviewed and found free of fiduciary and process irregularities. The company was sold after a full market canvas and auction. Under our appraisal statute, I am to determine the fair value of the shares as a going concern. The parties have submitted expert valuations of the company, ranging from an amount below the sales price (submitted by the Respondents) to more than twice the sales price (submitted by the Petitioners). Our statute and the interpreting case law direct that I not rely presumptively on the price achieved by exposing the company to the market. I must evaluate "all relevant factors," and arrive at a going-concern value inclusive of any assets not properly accounted for in the sale, but exclusive of synergy value that may have been captured by the seller. In part, this directive represents the greater complexity in valuing, marketing and selling an ongoing corporate enterprise, in contrast to the simple sale of an asset, such as a parcel of real estate. Typically,

---

[7] The seminal case for the first proposition is *Cede & Co. v. Technicolor, Inc.*, 684 A.2d 289 (Del. 1996). A case holding that even unimplemented plans can be counted in company value is *Delaware Open MRI Radiology Associates, P.A. v. Kessler*, 898 A.2d 290 (Del. Ch. 2006).

therefore, this Court has relied on expert valuation, such as those employing discounted cash flow and comparable company analyses, [*both are discussed in Chapter X*] to determine statutory fair value. Even so, market value—where reliably derived—remains among the "relevant factors" for arriving at fair value. In this particular case, CKx presents significant and atypical valuation challenges . . . In particular, the unpredictable nature of the income stream from the company's primary asset renders the apparent precision of the expert witnesses' cash flow valuation illusory. Because neither party has presented a reasonable alternative valuation method, and because I find the sales price here a reliable indicator of value, I find that a use of the merger price to determine fair value is appropriate in this matter.

The *Huff Funds* court did, however, note that there was "limited evidence in the record concerning the existence and amount of synergies that Apollo [Apollo Global Management, a private equity fund] sought to realize in its acquisition of CKx." The court therefore allowed "the parties, if they so desire, the opportunity to provide additional evidence on this limited issue."

A 2015 case in which the court found that the merger price was the fair price was *In re Appraisal of Ancestry.com*, CA No. 8173–VCG (Del. Ch. January 30, 2015). In the *Ancestry* case, as in the *Huff Funds* case, the court had concerns with the expert valuations, and had praise for the process by which the merger process was reached. Vice Chancellor Glasscock noted that the process appeared to him "to represent an auction of the Company that is unlikely to have left significant stockholder value unaccounted for." He continued:

> I note that both [experts] are respected in their field, and well qualified to offer valuation opinions. [But] [n]either of [their] approaches gives great confidence in the DCF analysis of either expert, since both appear to be result-oriented riffs on the market price. Ultimately, I am faced with an appraisal action where an open auction process has set a market price, where both parties' experts agree that there are no comparable companies to use for purposes of valuation, and where management did not create projections in the normal course of business, thus giving reason to question management projections, which were done in light of the transaction and in the context of obtaining a fairness opinion. As [one of the experts] repeatedly testified, he saw it as his job to—torture the numbers until they confess[ed]. I note that (beyond any moral concerns) it is well-known that the problem with relying on torture is the possibility of *false* confession . . . Because the

inputs here . . . are problematic for the reasons addressed at length above, and because the sales process here was robust, I find fair value in these circumstances best represented by the market price.

In another appraisal case, *Golden Telecom, Inc. v. Global GT LP.*, 11 A.3d 214 (Del. 2010), the court found that the fair value of the shares ($125.49) was significantly in excess of the merger price ($105.00). The court discussed the appropriate deference to the merger price:

> Section 262(h) unambiguously calls upon the Court of Chancery to perform an independent evaluation of "fair value" at the time of a transaction. It vests the Chancellor and Vice Chancellors with significant discretion to consider "all relevant factors" and determine the going concern value of the underlying company. Requiring the Court of Chancery to defer—conclusively or presumptively—to the merger price, even in the face of a pristine, unchallenged transactional process, would contravene the unambiguous language of the statute and the reasoned holdings of our precedent. It would inappropriately shift the responsibility to determine "fair value" from the court to the private parties. Also, while it is difficult for the Chancellor and Vice Chancellors to assess wildly divergent expert opinions regarding value, inflexible rules governing appraisal provide little additional benefit in determining "fair value" because of the already high costs of appraisal actions. Appraisal is, by design, a flexible process. Therefore, we reject Golden's contention that the Vice Chancellor erred by insufficiently deferring to the merger price, and we reject its call to establish a rule requiring the Court of Chancery to defer to the merger price in any appraisal proceeding. . . . The Court of Chancery abuses its discretion only when either its factual findings do not have record support or its valuation is clearly wrong. This is a formidable standard and we accord Court of Chancery determinations of value a high level of deference on appeal. We defer because, over time, the Court of Chancery "has developed an expertise in cases of this type." In addition, while discharging its statutory mandate, it is entirely proper for the Court of Chancery to adopt one expert's model, methodology, and calculations if they are supported by credible evidence and the judge analyzes them critically on the record. As long as they are supported by the record, we will defer to the Court of Chancery's factual findings even if we might independently reach a different conclusion. Against this

background of deference, we find that the record supports the Vice Chancellor's findings of fact and valuation methods.[8]

The *Golden Telecom* case preceded *Huff Funds* and *Ancestry.com*. The latter two cases used the merger price as their touchstone for the appraisal award. This appears to represent the trend in Delaware, as the courts move away from awarding higher amounts in non-conflicted transactions where evidence suggests that the deal price was the product of a robust sales process. The reason for this Delaware turn is the rise of appraisal arbitrage, a strategy that has recently increased in popularity. Arbitrageurs buy shares of stocks in companies about to be merged in order to exercise appraisal rights (discussed further below). The recent moves by the Delaware courts can be seen as their attempt to make the appraisal arbitrage strategy less profitable.

E. APPRAISAL ARBITRAGEURS

For many years, appraisal was a lonely backwater for corporate work. The occasional disgruntled shareholder might file an appraisal petition, but in general, it was often easier for shareholders who had voted no on a transaction to simply take the merger consideration and move on to other investments. However, in recent years, there has been an upswing in interest in the appraisal remedy, led in part by growth of appraisal as an arbitrage opportunity.

Before *In re Transkaryotic Therapies*, in 2007, a shareholder's ability to use appraisal remedies was thought to require her to have been a shareholder before the record date for the meeting at which the merger was going to be voted upon, and to hold the stock through the effective date of the merger. However, *Transkaryotic* made it clear that the appraisal statute has no such requirement with respect to stock ownership prior to the record date. Rather, dissenters need only become shareholders before they make a written demand in advance of the shareholder meeting and then hold their stock through the effective date.

Transkaryotic announced a merger with Shire Pharmaceuticals in 2005. Ten days after the announcement of the record date for the merger, Transkaryotic announced "extraordinarily positive" results for its experimental drug. As a result, a merger priced at $37 no longer looked fair. Consequently, there was a significant arbitrage opportunity. The fair value of the stock immediately following announcement of the test results exceeded the consideration being offered in the merger. The increase in the value of Transkaryotic was in no way attributable to the merger. The unexpectedly positive results were the equivalent of finding gold. Predictably, investors, led by Carl Icahn, acquired Transkaryotic stock

---

[8]   *Golden Telecom, Inc. v. Global GT LP*, 11 A.3d 214, 219 (Del. 2010).

following the establishment of a record date and sought an appraisal for their newly acquired stock.

Transkaryotic argued that appraisal was not available—that the "arbitrageurs" had not complied with the requirements of DGCL § 262 because they were not shareholders as of the record date and they had not voted "no" in the shareholder vote. The court reminded the parties that voting "no" is not a requirement in the statute—that the statute simply requires a shareholder to (a) not vote in favor of the merger, to (b) make a written demand, and (c) to hold the stock through the effective date of the merger. The later-acquiring shareholders had complied with all these requirements. One more aspect of the case is of interest here. Recall that most shares are held of record by "Cede." Icahn and his fellow arbitrageurs could not prove that the particular shares beneficially owned by them were not voted yes. But the court held that " '[i]t is understood by now that an entity like Cede & Co. that is a record holder (but not beneficial holder) of a company's shares can vote certain of those shares against a merger, and others in favor, and seek appraisal as to the dissenting shares.' Thus, the fact that Cede voted shares in favor and against the merger does not preclude Cede from petitioning this Court for appraisal of those shares not voted in favor of the merger. It is uncontested that Cede voted 12,882,000 shares in favor of the merger and 16,838,074 against, abstained, or not voted in connection with the merger. It is further uncontested that Cede otherwise properly perfected appraisal rights as to all of the 10,972,650 shares that petitioners own and for which appraisal is now sought. . . . Cede may exercise appraisal rights for all 10,972,650 contested shares." The court held that provided the total number of shares seeking appraisal did not exceed the total number of "no" votes and abstentions, that the arbitrageurs would be permitted to pursue an appraisal remedy.

In a 2015 article, Professor Charles Korsmo and Minor Myers comment on the rise of appraisal arbitrage.

APPRAISAL ARBITRAGE AND THE FUTURE OF PUBLIC COMPANY M&A

Charles Korsmo and Minor Myers
92 WASH. U. L. REV. 1551 (2015)

[A]ppraisal activity involving public companies increased substantially starting in 2011, as measured both by the number of petitions filed and the value of the dissenting shares.

The most basic way to measure appraisal activity is by the raw counts of petitions filed. During our ten-year period of study, 129 appraisal petitions were filed in Delaware involving counseled petitioners. . . .

The recent change in appraisal activity becomes even more apparent when we compare appraisal claims to the number of appraisal-eligible mergers. From 2004 through 2010, the number of appraisal petitions moved roughly in tandem with the general level of merger activity, rising through 2007 and thereafter falling along with the number of mergers after the financial crisis. A more or less constant percentage of mergers attracted appraisal claims in this period. This pattern changed sharply, however, beginning in 2011. Despite a lower level of overall merger activity, the number of petitions filed in 2011 and 2012 matched the number filed at the peak of the pre-financial crisis merger wave, and the number of petitions in 2013 is larger still. . . .

Approximately 5% of appraisal-eligible transactions attracted at least one appraisal petition from 2004 through 2010. The appraisal rate more than doubled in 2011 and has continued to increase since then. By 2013, more than 15% of transactions attracted an appraisal petition. . . .

The values at stake in appraisal proceedings have also increased sharply in recent years. The 129 petitions we observed involved 106 separate transactions over our study period. The mean value of the foregone merger consideration in an appraisal dispute over the entire period was $30 million and does not appear to have followed any strong trend over time. When combined with the increase in the number of petitions over time, however, the total dollar amount at stake in appraisal proceedings in each year shows a large increase in recent years, particularly the most recent year. . . .

The amount of money involved in 2013 is nearly three times the amount involved in any prior year and ten times the 2004 amount. To some extent, this effect is driven by outliers. The largest appraisal case over our study period is Dell, a 2013 transaction where $654 million worth of shares dissented. The second largest is Transkaryotic Therapies, a 2005 transaction where $520 million worth of shares sought appraisal. But in some ways, excluding these two very large cases only makes the new trend clearer. Without Transkaryotic, the values at stake in appraisal never exceeded $300 million in any given year, while in 2013 the values at stake approach one billion dollars even excluding Dell. Most tellingly, over the ten year period, only eight appraisal cases have involved more than $100 million, and four of them were in 2013.

Perhaps the most remarkable thing about appraisal activity during the new 2011 to 2013 era is that, unlike 2007 and 2008, the increase in numbers and economic significance of appraisal does not coincide with an increase in merger activity. In other words, the rise in appraisal activity since 2011 appears to reflect a secular increase in interest in appraisal, rather than a mere cyclical phenomenon tied to the conditions of the merger market. For each year in our study period, we tallied the equity value of all appraisal-eligible transactions and then computed the percentage of value that sought appraisal. In 2013, 0.92% of the equity value dissented, more than three times higher than any prior year. Indeed, the percentage of dissenting equity value was never higher than 0.10% in any prior year except 2005, the year of Transkaryotic. . . .

In addition to the increasing volume of appraisal activity—measured both in number of petitions and the dollar values at stake—the profile of the public company appraisal petitioner has changed sharply in the recent period. In particular, petitioners have become increasingly specialized and sophisticated over our time period, with repeat petitioners increasingly dominating appraisal activity. Since 2011, more than 80% of appraisal proceedings have involved a repeat petitioner—that is, a petitioner who filed more than one appraisal petition across our study period. Three constellations of related funds appear more than ten times each. Perhaps the most striking result of our investigation is the increase in the economic significance of repeat players in appraisal.

The rise in repeat petitioner value beginning in 2010 is immediately apparent. Before 2010, appraisal appears to have been largely a one-off exercise for aggrieved stockholders. Repeat petitioners played a small role, and there is little evidence that funds were seeking appraisal as part of a considered investment strategy. Starting in 2010, however, and accelerating through 2013, the repeat petitioner dominates. Indeed, every appraisal case filed in 2013 involved at least one repeat petitioner.

By virtue of the unique standing requirements in appraisal, these specialized appraisal petitioners are typically able to invest in the target company after the announcement of the transaction they challenge. The decision to invest, then, is based on a calculation that the amount they will be able to recover in an appraisal proceeding in Delaware—via trial or settlement—will exceed the merger price by enough to offer an attractive return. This practice can be fairly characterized as appraisal arbitrage—by analogy to traditional merger arbitrage—and those who practice it may be termed appraisal arbitrageurs. . . .

Unlike in fiduciary litigation—where "professional plaintiffs" tend to be small shareholders with close ties to plaintiffs' firms—the repeat appraisal petitioners, especially at the top end of the field, appear to be sophisticated parties specializing in appraisal. For example, the largest repeat petitioner is Merion Capital, with over $700 million invested in appraisal claims. Merion has been involved in seven cases since 2010, with increasingly large amounts at stake. The fund is based in Pennsylvania and headed by Andrew Barroway, a successful plaintiffs' lawyer from Philadelphia. It made its first public appraisal investment in 2010, with $8.5 million at stake. After a number of appraisal petitions averaging around $50 million in value at stake during 2012 and 2013,

Merion reportedly raised a targeted amount of $1 billion for a dedicated appraisal fund in 2013. During 2013, it filed two appraisal petitions with an average value at stake of $177 million.

Another large and recent repeat petitioner is Verition Fund, a Greenwich-based fund that has been involved in four cases, all in 2013, with an average of $25 million at stake. Verition is managed by Nicholas Maounis, who formerly headed Greenwich-based Amaranth Advisors. Other recent entrants are Fortress Investment Group, a large publicly-traded hedge fund, and Hudson Bay Capital Management, both of whom filed large appraisal petitions in 2013.

Similarly, major mutual funds and insurance companies—two types of institutions that have entirely avoided standard stockholder litigation—have recently filed appraisal petitions. Much is often made of the involvement of institutional investors (or the lack thereof) in corporate governance. All too often in corporate litigation, the so-called "institutions" are akin to the Bailiffs' Retirement Fund of Chippewa Falls, while sophisticated financial players remain on the sidelines. The institutions that are beginning to specialize in appraisal, by contrast, are among the most sophisticated financial entities in the United States.

———————

The growth in appraisal arbitrage has been controversial, as acquirers view it as adding significant risk that they will have to pay a greater amount than anticipated. As discussed above, concerns over appraisal arbitrage may have led Delaware courts to give strong weight in appraisal actions to merger prices that are a result of a robust sales process. Concerns over appraisal arbitrage have also spurred proposals for reform of the appraisal rights statute.

F. QUASI-APPRAISAL PROCEEDINGS

As discussed above, "appraisal" is a specific statutory procedure under which certain shareholders can get courts to award them the "fair value" of their shares. There are other remedies that give shareholders similar rights in circumstances in which statutory appraisal would not be available.

In *Berger v. Pubco Corp.*, the court held that where shareholders were not provided full disclosure and hence had not been able to make a fully informed decision as to whether to seek appraisal, "quasi-appraisal" was an appropriate remedy. Strictly speaking, a quasi-appraisal is not an appraisal. It is open to the entire class of shareholders, not just those shareholders who did not vote in favor of the transaction. Quasi-appraisal is an equitable remedy that permits shareholders who might have otherwise sought appraisal the opportunity to receive an appraisal-like remedy notwithstanding the fact that they have not complied with the appraisal statute. In a quasi-appraisal action, shareholders are not required to opt in and do not have to escrow a portion of the merger proceeds in order to have their shares appraised.

BERGER V. PUBCO CORPORATION

Supreme Court of Delaware
976 A.2d 132 (2009)

JACOBS, JUSTICE.

FACTUAL AND PROCEDURAL BACKGROUND

Pubco Corporation ("Pubco" or "the company") is a Delaware corporation whose common shares were not publicly traded. Over 90 percent of Pubco's shares were owned by defendant Robert H. Kanner, who was Pubco's president and sole director. The plaintiff, Barbara Berger, was a Pubco minority shareholder.

Sometime before October 12, 2007, Kanner decided that Pubco should "go private." As the owner of over 90% of Pubco's outstanding shares, Kanner was legally entitled to effect a "short form" merger under 8 Del. C. § 253. Because that short form procedure is available only to corporate controlling shareholders, Kanner formed a wholly-owned shell subsidiary, Pubco Acquisition, Inc., and transferred his Pubco shares to that entity to effect the merger. In that merger, which took place on October 12, 2007, Pubco's minority shareholders received $20 cash per share.

Under the short form merger statute (8 Del. C. § 253), the only relevant corporate action required to effect a short term merger is for the board of directors of the parent corporation to adopt a resolution approving a certificate of merger, and to furnish the minority shareholders a notice advising that the merger has occurred and that they are entitled to seek an appraisal under 8 Del. C. § 262. Section 253 requires that the notice include a copy of the appraisal statute, and Delaware case law requires the parent company to disclose in the notice of merger all information material to shareholders deciding whether or not to seek appraisal.

In November 2007, the plaintiff received a written notice (the "Notice") from Pubco, advising that Pubco's controlling shareholder had effected a short form merger and that the plaintiff and the other minority stockholders were being cashed out for $20 per share. The Notice explained that shareholder approval was not required for the merger to become effective, and that the minority stockholders had the right to seek an appraisal. The Notice also disclosed some information about the nature of Pubco's business, the names of its officers and directors, the number of its shares and classes of stock, a description of related business transactions, and copies of Pubco's most recent interim and annual unaudited financial statements. The Notice also disclosed that Pubco's stock, although not publicly traded, was sporadically traded over-the-counter, and that in the twenty-two months preceding the merger there were thirty open market trades that ranged in price from $12.55 to $16.00 per share, at an average price of $13.32. Finally, the Notice provided telephone, fax and e-mail contact information where shareholders could request and obtain additional information.

In its summary judgment opinion, the Court of Chancery found that except for the financial statements, the disclosures in the Notice provided no significant detail. For example, the description of the Company comprised only five sentences, one of which vaguely stated that "[t]he Company owns other income producing assets." No disclosures relating to the company's plans or prospects were made, nor was there any meaningful discussion of Pubco's actual operations or disclosure of its finances by division or line of business. Rather, the unaudited financial statements lumped all of the company's operations together. The financial statements did indicate that Pubco held a sizeable amount of cash and securities, but did not explain how those assets were, or would be, utilized. Finally, the Notice contained no disclosure of how Kanner had determined the $20 per share merger price that he unilaterally had set.

As our law required, the company attached to the Notice a copy of the appraisal statute, but the copy attached was outdated and, therefore, incorrect. The appraisal statute had been updated by changes that became effective in August 2007—two months before the Notice was sent to shareholders—but the version attached to the Notice did not reflect those changes. Pubco never sent a corrected copy of the updated appraisal statute to its former minority stockholders.

On December 14, 2007, the plaintiff initiated this lawsuit as a class action on behalf of all Pubco minority stockholders, claiming that the class is entitled to receive the difference between the $20 per share paid to each class member and the fair value of his or her shares, irrespective of whether any class member demanded appraisal. . . .

ANALYSIS

[T]he issue presented here is: in a short form merger where the exclusive remedy is an appraisal, what is the consequence of the controlling stockholder's failure to disclose the facts material to an informed shareholder decision whether or not to elect that exclusive remedy? In the abstract, four possible alternatives present themselves . . .

[Two of the] alternatives advocated. . . are the two forms of "quasi-appraisal" remedy earlier described. The defendants argued, and the Court of Chancery agreed, that the appropriate remedy is the quasi-appraisal ordered in *Gilliland*. Under that remedial structure, fully informed minority shareholders who "opt in" and place into escrow a portion of the consideration they received may prosecute an action to recover the difference between adjudicated "fair value" and the merger consideration. The plaintiff advocated the second alternative form of "quasi-appraisal" remedy—a class action to recover the difference between "fair value" and the merger consideration, wherein the minority shareholders are automatically treated as members of the class with no obligation to opt in or to escrow any portion of the merger consideration. Under either structure, the only issue being litigated would be the appraised "fair value" of the corporation on the date of the merger, applying established corporate valuation principles. . . .

B. Discussion

. . .

(2) Selecting The Most Appropriate Alternative

. . . [We are required] to choose between the two dueling forms of quasi-appraisal advocated by the parties on this appeal. Both forms would entitle the minority stockholders to supplemental disclosure enabling them to make an informed decision whether to participate in the lawsuit or to retain the merger proceeds. Both forms would entitle those who elect to participate to seek a recovery of the difference between the fair value of their shares and the merger consideration they received, without having to establish the controlling shareholders' personal liability for breach of fiduciary duty. The difference between the two quasi-appraisal approaches is that under the defendants' approach (which the Court of Chancery approved), the minority shareholders who elect to participate would be required to "opt in" and to escrow a prescribed portion of the merger proceeds they received. Under the plaintiff's approach, all minority stockholders would automatically become members of the class without being required to "opt in" or to escrow any portion of the merger proceeds.

As thus narrowed, the final issue may be stated as follows: under the standard we have applied, which remedy is the more appropriate—the one that imposes the opt in and partial escrow requirements or the one that does not? Considerations of utility and fairness impel us to conclude that the latter is the more appropriate remedy for the disclosure violation that occurred here. Because neither the opt-in nor the escrow requirement is mandated as a matter of law and because those requirements involve different equities, we analyze each requirement separately.

We start with the "opt in" issue. The approach adopted by the Court of Chancery requires the minority shareholders to opt in to become members of the plaintiff class. The other choice would treat those shareholders automatically as members of the class—that is, as having already opted in. Those shareholders would continue as members of the class, unless and until individual members opt out after receiving the remedial supplemental disclosure and the Rule 23 notice of class action informing them of their opt out right. From the minority's standpoint, the first alternative is potentially more burdensome than the second, because shareholders that fail either to opt in or to opt in within a prescribed time, forfeit the opportunity to seek an appraisal recovery. On the other hand, structuring the remedy as an "opt out" class action avoids that risk of forfeiture, and thus benefits the minority shareholders. To the corporation, however, neither alternative is more burdensome than the other. Under either alternative the company will know at a relatively early stage which shareholders are (and are not) members of the class.

Given these choices, it is self evident which alternative is optimal. As between an opt in requirement that would potentially burden shareholders desiring to seek an appraisal recovery but would impose no burden on the corporation, and an opt out requirement that would impose a lesser burden on the shareholders but again no burden on the corporation, the latter alternative is superior and is the remedy that the trial court should have ordered.

That leaves the requirement that the minority shareholders electing to participate in the quasi-appraisal must escrow a portion of the merger proceeds that they received. The rationale for this requirement, as stated in *Gilliland*, is "to mimic, at least in small part, the risks of a statutory appraisal ... to promote well-reasoned judgments by potential class members and to avoid awarding a 'windfall' to those shareholders who made an informed decision [after receiving the original notice of merger] to take the cash rather than pursue their statutory appraisal remedy." [*Editor: Recall that in statutory appraisal proceedings, dissenting shareholders do not receive the merger consideration.*]

The defendants-appellees argue that it is fair and equitable to require the minority shareholders to escrow some portion of the merger proceeds. Otherwise (defendants say), the shareholders would have it both ways: they could retain the merger proceeds they received and at the same time litigate to recover a higher amount—a dual benefit they would not have in an actual appraisal. It is true that the minority shareholders would enjoy that "dual benefit." But, does that make it inequitable from the fiduciary's standpoint? We think not. No positive rule of law cited to us requires replicating the burdens imposed in an actual statutory appraisal. Indeed, our law allows the minority to enjoy that dual benefit in the related setting of a class action challenging a long form merger on fiduciary duty grounds. In that setting the shareholder class members may retain the merger proceeds and simultaneously pursue the class action remedy. The defendants cite no case authority, nor are we aware of any, holding that that in the long form merger context that benefit is inequitable to the majority shareholder accused of breaching its fiduciary duty.

Lastly, fairness requires that the corporation be held to the same strict standard of compliance with the appraisal statute as the minority shareholders. Our case law is replete with examples where dissenting minority shareholders that failed to comply strictly with certain technical requirements of the appraisal statute, were held to have lost their entitlement to an appraisal, and, consequently, lost the opportunity to recover the difference between the fair value of their shares and the merger price. These technical statutory violations were not curable, so that irrespective of the equities the unsuccessful appraisal claimant could not proceed anew. That result effectively allowed the corporation to retain the entire difference between fair value and the merger price attributable to the shares for which appraisal rights were lost. The appraisal statute should be construed even-handedly, not as a one-way street. Minority shareholders who fail to observe the appraisal statute's technical requirements risk forfeiting their statutory entitlement to recover the fair value of their shares. In fairness, majority stockholders that deprive their minority shareholders of material information should forfeit their statutory right to retain the merger proceeds payable to shareholders who, if fully informed, would have elected appraisal.

In cases where the corporation does not comply with the disclosure requirement mandated by *Glassman* [*Editor's note: as discussed below, Glassman held that so long as shareholders in a short form merger received "all the factual information material to [their] decision," their only remedy was appraisal. Glassman v. Unocal Exploration Corp.*, 777 A.2d 242, 248 (Del. 2001)], the quasi-appraisal remedy that operates in the fairest and most balanced way and that best effectuates the legislative intent underlying Section 253, is the one that does not require the minority shareholders seeking a recovery of fair value to escrow a portion of the merger proceeds they received. We hold, for these reasons, that the quasi-appraisal remedy ordered by the Court of Chancery was legally erroneous in the circumstances presented here.

To summarize: where there is a breach of the duty of disclosure in a short form merger . . .—the quasi-appraisal remedy for a violation of that fiduciary disclosure obligation—should not be restricted by opt in or escrow requirements.

G. APPRAISAL RIGHTS AND OTHER REMEDIES: WHEN ARE APPRAISAL RIGHTS EXCLUSIVE?

As discussed in Part IV of this book, a very important part of the law of mergers and acquisitions concerns the fiduciary duties of directors and officers. In general, where shareholders' only complaint is that the value offered them in a statutory merger was inadequate, then appraisal will be their exclusive remedy. However, shareholders in long-form statutory mergers who are otherwise entitled to appraisal are not foreclosed from pursuing the same sorts of remedies for harms attributed to violations of directors' fiduciary duties as shareholders who are not entitled to appraisal. These remedies are discussed further in Part IV of this book. As then-Vice Chancellor Strine noted in *Delaware Open MRI Radiology Associates, P.A. v. Kessler,* "[t]he resolution of this case is complicated by the presence of both an equitable entire fairness claim and a statutory appraisal claim. The key issues relevant to each type of claim are common, and the differing rubrics have relatively little influence on the bottom line outcome of the case, which turns on whether the merger was financially fair." That being said, as the Delaware Supreme Court stated in *Weinberger v. UOP, Inc.,* 457 A.2d 701 (Del. 1983):

> [w]hile a plaintiff's monetary remedy ordinarily should be confined to the more liberalized appraisal proceeding herein established, we do not intend any limitation on the historic powers of the Chancellor to grant such other relief as the facts of a particular case may dictate. The appraisal remedy we approve may not be adequate in certain cases, particularly where fraud, misrepresentation, self-dealing, deliberate waste of corporate assets, or gross and palpable overreaching are involved.

"Quasi-appraisal," as the determination of fair value in a proceeding that is not formally an appraisal proceeding is known, is still a likely remedy in these cases. But other types of remedies, such as recessionary damages, may be used instead. See *In re Orchard Enterprises, Inc. Stockholder Litigation,* 88 A.3d 1 (Del. Ch. 2014).

For short form mergers, appraisal is generally the exclusive remedy. Short form mergers, by their nature, reflect a certain amount of unfair dealing. Minority shareholders have no right to vote and are notified of the transaction only after it has occurred. Nevertheless, appraisal will generally be the exclusive remedy for minority shareholders cashed out in a short form merger. *Glassman v. Unocal Exploration Corp.,* 777 A.2d 242, 248 (Del. 2001), established the rule, and articulated when it did not apply: "[W]e hold that, absent fraud or illegality, appraisal is the exclusive remedy available to a minority stockholder who objects to a short-form merger." The exceptions, as discussed above, occur in situations where the corporation has not complied with its obligation under the statute and caselaw, including its obligation to timely give shareholders all material information to enable them to make a decision as to whether they want to seek appraisal. In *Pubco,* the exception yielded a quasi-appraisal.

H. DELAWARE AND THE MBCA COMPARED

This Chapter has principally discussed the Delaware appraisal statute and caselaw. Other states have regimes that differ from Delaware to varying degrees. Many are based on the Model Business Corporation Act (MBCA). The MBCA also provides appraisal rights for the shareholders of a company selling all or substantially all of its assets. Most states follow the MBCA in this respect.[9] The MBCA includes provisions not only for appraisal for asset sales, but also for certain share exchanges, certificate amendments, and some other events. See MBCA § 13.02. The MBCA also limits the market out exception. The market out exception does not apply for interested party transactions. See MBCA § 13.02(b)(4). There are differences between the MBCA and Delaware in other respects as well, including timing of payments and allocation of costs.[10]

Notwithstanding the differences, however, the rationale for providing an appraisal remedy is the same. Official Comment 1 to § 13.01 of the MBCA states that:

> Judicial appraisal should be provided by statute only when two conditions co-exist. First, the proposed corporate action as approved by the majority *[Editor: the MBCA does provide for appraisal in short-form mergers]* will result in a fundamental change in the shares to be affected by the action. Second, uncertainty concerning the fair value of the affected shares may cause reasonable persons to differ about the fairness of the terms of the corporate action. Uncertainty is greatly reduced, however, in the case of publicly traded shares. This explains both the market exception . . . and the limits provided to the exception.

QUESTIONS

Two companies, Alpha and Beta, both incorporated under Delaware law, wish to combine their operations. For each question, identify who has appraisal rights and why. In addition, please specify whether each company's shareholders have a vote or not.

1.   Beta will merge with and into Alpha under DGCL § 251. Both Alpha and Beta's shares are listed on the New York Stock Exchange. Neither company has more than 50 shareholders of record. In the merger, Beta's shares are cancelled and exchanged for cash paid by Alpha. Alpha's shares remain outstanding.

---

[9]   See MBCA § 13.02 Statutory Comparison, C.

[10]   *See generally* Mary Siegel, *An Appraisal Of The Model Business Corporation Act's Appraisal Rights Provisions*, 74 LAW & CONTEMP. PROBS. 231, 232–33 (2011).

2.   Beta will merge with and into Alpha under DGCL § 251. Alpha's shares are listed on the New York Stock Exchange. Beta's shares are not listed and Beta has a total of 50 shareholders. In the merger, Beta's shares are cancelled and exchanged for shares of Alpha. Alpha's shares remain outstanding. After the merger Beta's shareholders own 15% of Alpha.

3.   Beta will merge with and into Alpha under DGCL § 251. Neither Alpha's nor Beta's shares are listed; each has fewer than 50 shareholders. In the merger, Beta's shares are cancelled and exchanged for shares of Alpha. After the merger Beta's shareholders own 25% of Alpha. Alpha's shares remain outstanding.

4.   Beta will merge with and into a wholly-owned subsidiary of Alpha under DGCL § 251. Neither Alpha's nor Beta's shares are listed. Alpha has 50 shareholders of record while Beta has 3,000 shareholders of record. In the merger, Beta's shares are cancelled and exchanged for shares of Alpha. After the merger Beta's shareholders own 25% of Alpha.

5.   Beta will merge with and into Alpha under DGCL § 251. Alpha's shares are listed on the New York Stock Exchange. Beta's shares are not listed and Beta has a total of 50 shareholders. In the merger, Beta's shares are cancelled and exchanged for cash.

6.   Same facts as 5, but Beta's shares are listed on the New York Stock Exchange.

7.   Alpha will buy all of the assets and liabilities of Beta for cash. After the acquisition, Beta will dissolve and distribute all of the cash to its shareholders.

8.   Alpha owns 92% of Beta pre-merger. In the merger conducted under DGCL 253, all of the shares of Beta will be exchanged for shares of Alpha. Both Alpha and Beta are listed on the New York Stock Exchange.

9.   Same facts as 8, but Beta shareholders receive cash.

PROBLEM

The Gamma Corporation acquired 64% of the shares of the Beta Corporation, a publicly traded corporation, in a tender offer (to be discussed in Chapter V). The agreement did not provide for a top-up, nor did it provide for a merger without shareholder approval under DGCL § 251(h). A merger agreement is entered into under DGCL § 251, subject to shareholder approval, in which the remaining 36% of the Beta shareholders would receive shares of a private corporation previously wholly owned by Gamma, and Beta would be merged into Gamma. Before the tender offer, Gamma had prepared a plan that it expected to yield significant savings after a Gamma-Beta merger; it intended to put the plan into effect immediately upon consummation of the merger. Several months after the tender offer, the merger was approved by shareholders representing 98% of Beta's shares. After the merger, Gamma put its plan into place in the merged Gamma-Beta.

The plan proved extremely successful, and Gamma's shareholders benefitted enormously. Are appraisal rights available for this transaction? Assuming that the answer to this question is yes, as of what date will the appraised value of the Beta shares be computed?

Consider whether the following Beta shareholders are potentially able to get appraisal rights. Alice has held her Beta shares for several years. She abstained from voting on the merger. A week before the merger was consummated, she sold her shares to a colleague. Beth bought her shares after the notice to shareholders was sent. She initially sent in a proxy voting in favor of the merger, but revoked her proxy a week before the shareholders' meeting, and then voted against the merger. Is either of them potentially able to get appraisal rights?

CHAPTER IV

REGULATION OF MERGERS AND ACQUISITIONS UNDER FEDERAL LAW—SECTION 13(d)

■ ■ ■

A. WILLIAMS ACT HISTORY

In Chapter II, we introduced statutory mergers and asset sales. Those transaction forms are not the only ones available. Acquirers may also purchase the stock of the company they would like to acquire directly from its shareholders. In deals involving public companies, these purchases are typically accomplished using a "tender offer." A tender offer is an offer made directly to target shareholders to purchase their stock. By contrast with a statutory merger, in a tender offer there is no statutory role for the board of directors. Recall that in a merger pursuant to § 251, the board of the target, as a constituent party to the merger, must approve the merger and adopt a merger agreement; board approval is thus a prerequisite to a statutory merger. Because approval of the target's board is not required for a tender offer, tender offers are thus the preferred tool of hostile bidders, as discussed further in Chapter V.B. (All this being said, a friendly tender offer can be made in conjunction with entry by the offeror and target management into a merger agreement; these types of transactions are discussed in Chapter II.B.4.b, in the Section on two-step transactions; they will be discussed further in Chapter XIX.A)

Tender offers are regulated differently than statutory mergers. State laws play a smaller role while federal securities laws and regulations, notably the Williams Act of 1968, play a larger role. The Williams Act is part of the Securities Exchange Act of 1934 (the "'34 Act" or the "Exchange Act"), one of the two main federal securities law statutes. The other main federal securities law statute is the Securities Act of 1933 (the "'33 Act"). Both statutes, and the rules and regulations thereunder, include many provisions that deal with M&A. The '33 Act regulates the issuance of securities; thus, the '33 Act is relevant for M&A transactions when an acquirer is using stock to acquire another company. The '34 Act regulates transactions involving securities that have already been issued. Much of the federal securities law governing M&A transactions is found in the '34 Act and its rules and regulations. Our consideration of the

Williams Act is in this Chapter and the next Chapter. Our consideration of other relevant aspects of the federal securities laws is in Chapters VI and VII.

The Williams Act was enacted in response to an increased volume of hostile takeovers. In the 1960s, hostile acquirers not infrequently would "sweep" Wall Street, buying up shares quietly from a variety of sellers who did not know of the acquirer's plans or even its identity. Having acquired a "beachhead of ownership," an acquirer would make a cash tender offer that expired quickly, and was thus designed to pressure shareholders into tendering into the offer. These transactions were known as "Saturday Night Specials." The acquirer would announce a tender offer on a Friday for a limited number of shares, stating that the tender offer would close on the Monday. Shareholders would have to decide in a very short time whether they wanted to tender their shares and take the cash offered, or remain shareholders in an entity with an unidentified owner and an uncertain future. The Williams Act can be seen almost entirely as a response to this problem. The purpose of the Williams Act was to ensure "that public shareholders who are confronted by a cash tender offer for their stock will not be required to respond without adequate information."[1]

The Williams Act was not unopposed. Concerns were raised that regulating tender offers would inhibit such offers and entrench management. Indeed, the initial draft of the bill, proposed in 1965 by Senator Harrison A. Williams, Jr. (who was later convicted in the ABSCAM bribery scandal,[2] the subject of the 2013 film American Hustle), was expressly pro-management and anti-takeover. Describing the impetus for the bill, Sen. Williams decried "proud old companies reduced to corporate shells after white-collar pirates have seized control with funds from sources which are unknown in many cases, then sold or traded away the best assets, later to split up most of the loot among themselves."[3] The bill as originally proposed included a twenty day advance notice period before any person could acquire five percent ownership in a target whether by tender offer or in the open market. The SEC called the advance notice requirement "difficult," "burdensome," and "impossible," prompting Sen. Williams' original draft to be withdrawn. The Williams Act as revised and passed took, in Sen. Williams' words, "extreme care to avoid tipping the scales either in favor of management or

---

[1]   *Rondeau v. Mosinee Paper Co.*, 422 U.S. 49, 58 (1975), quoted in Andrew N. Vollmer & Paul R. Q. Wolfson, *The Williams Act: A Truly Modern Assessment*, http://corpgov.law. harvard.edu/2011/10/22/the-williams-act-a-truly-modern-assessment/.

[2]   He was convicted of bribery and conspiracy; he was to be expelled from the Senate, but resigned before this occurred. He was sentenced to three years' imprisonment and fined $50,000. *See* Douglas Martin, *Ex-Senator Harrison A. Williams Jr., 81, Dies; Went to Prison Over Abscam Scandal*, N.Y. TIMES, Nov. 20, 2001, available at http://www.nytimes.com/2001/11/20/nyregion/ ex-senator-harrison-a-williams-jr–81–dies-went-to-prison-over-abscam-scandal.html.

[3]   111 Cong. Rec. 28257 (1965). For more information see Vollmer & Wolfson, *supra* note 1.

in favor of the person making the takeover bids."[4] Whether the Williams Act in fact achieved this purpose is a matter of considerable debate, as research we will discuss below reveals.

The Williams Act has three types of provisions: disclosure requirements, substantive regulation of offers, and anti-fraud rules. Under Section 13(d), upon acquisition of more than five percent of a class of equity securities, the acquirer is required to making a filing on Schedule 13D disclosing specified information. Section 13(e) regulates issuer purchases of its own stock and going-private transactions (covered in Chapter XIX). Section 14(d) imposes both disclosure and substantive requirements on tender offers. Section 14(e) is an anti-fraud provision applicable to tender offers. We discuss Section 13(d) below; we discuss Section 14(d) and Section 14(e) in the next Chapter.

B. SECTION 13(d) REQUIREMENTS

Section 13(d) of the Williams Act is intended to be an early warning system. Recall that one of the problems with the Saturday Night Special was that bidders would surreptitiously and anonymously acquire stakes in companies and then surprise target boards and shareholders with a coercive offer with a very short fuse. The core of § 13(d) is thus a requirement that any person or group who acquires beneficial ownership of more than five percent of the equity securities of a publicly-traded company must file with the SEC a Schedule 13D disclosing its ownership, and providing certain other information thus providing target boards and shareholders with an early warning of potential acquirers on the horizon. The Schedule 13D must be filed ten days after any person acquires "directly or indirectly the beneficial ownership of any equity security" comprising more than five percent of that class of that equity security.

This seems like a fairly simple requirement, but its simplicity is deceptive. There are a host of complexities involved in important definitions such as the definitions of beneficial ownership and group for Schedule 13D filing purposes, as well as the specifics of what must be disclosed on the Schedule 13D. We will discuss each of these matters in this Section. For the full text of § 13(d) see the Online Appendix.

1. WHAT IS AN EQUITY SECURITY SUBJECT TO SECTION 13(d)?

The § 13(d) requirements apply to equity securities registered under § 12 of the Securities Exchange Act of 1934.[5] This includes securities of almost all publicly-traded companies listed on the NYSE or NASDAQ.

---

[4]   113 Cong. Rec. 24664 (1967).

[5]   They also apply to securities of certain insurance companies and closed-end investment companies. *See* § 13(d)(1)(a) of the Securities Exchange Act of 1934.

The definition of equity security includes common stock. It also includes securities convertible into equity securities, such as options, warrants, rights, and convertible debt instruments, but only if these come within Rule 13d–3. Rule 13d–3 states that a person only acquires beneficial ownership of securities convertible "within sixty days" into equity securities. This effectively means that many options and other convertible securities will not be counted for § 13 filing purposes since they are not exercisable or convertible within sixty days. Because of this definition, it is possible to enter into transactions involving securities convertible into an equity security or otherwise relating to that equity security which do not involve acquisition of the "equity security" and hence do not trigger a requirement to file a Schedule 13D. We discuss this issue below in the Subsection entitled Section 13(d) and Derivatives.

2. THE DEFINITION OF BENEFICIAL OWNER

To trigger § 13(d)'s filing requirement, a person must be the direct or indirect beneficial owner of the equity security at issue. Beneficial ownership is determined under Rule 13d–3 under the '34 Act, which provides that a beneficial owner is anyone who "directly or indirectly, through any contract, arrangement, understanding, relationship, or otherwise has or shares: (1) Voting power which includes the power to vote, or to direct the voting of, such security; and/or, (2) Investment power which includes the power to dispose, or to direct the disposition of, such security."

Note the use of "and/or": Either the power to vote (or influence the voting of) a security, or the power to sell or cause the sale of the security suffices. Note, too, the use of "shares"—sharing either or both of these powers suffices as well. Section 13(d) thus encompasses a person's ability not just to sell a security, but also to influence how the security is voted. As the District Court in *CSX Corp. v. Children's Investment Fund Management (UK), LLP, et al.* said:

> The SEC intended Rule 13d–3(a) to provide a "broad definition" of beneficial ownership so as to ensure disclosure "from all those persons who have the ability to change or influence control." This indeed is apparent from the very words of the Rule. By stating that a beneficial owner "includes" rather than "means" any person who comes within the criteria that follow, it made plain that the language that follows does not exhaust the circumstances in which one might come within the term. The phrases "directly or indirectly" and "any contract, arrangement, understanding, relationship, or otherwise" reinforce that point and demonstrate the focus on substance rather than on form or on the legally enforceable rights of the putative beneficial owner. It therefore is not surprising that the SEC, at the very adoption

of Rule 13d–3, stated that the determination of beneficial ownership under Rule 13d–3(a) requires:

> [a]n analysis of all relevant facts and circumstances in a particular situation . . . in order to identify each person possessing the requisite voting power or investment power. For example, for purposes of the rule, the mere possession of the legal right to vote securities under applicable state or other law . . . may not be determinative of who is a beneficial owner of such securities inasmuch as another person or persons may have the power whether legal, economic, or otherwise, to direct such voting.[6]

This is an extremely broad view of beneficial ownership, making for many potentially unclear cases. Record ownership, discussed in Chapter III, is straightforward—one is either a record owner, or one is not. But "indirect" ownership, or power via an "arrangement," "understanding," "relationship," or the more ephemeral, "influence," is not. A typical context in which the issue arises is when an acquirer obtains another shareholder's agreement to vote in favor of a transaction. The SEC has taken the position that the acquirer has "voting power" over the shares, and will require that a Schedule 13D be filed.

3. ACTING AS A GROUP

The broad construction of beneficial ownership is reflected in the Schedule 13D provisions which apply to "groups." In the most common situation, there is only one acquirer, who clearly has beneficial ownership. However, the § 13(d) rules were written to apply to parties who are acting as a group, so that their influence is known. The § 13(d) rules agglomerate the parties' holdings to determine whether the five percent threshold is met for purposes of the Schedule 13D filing requirements. Rule 13d–5 states that "[w]hen two or more persons agree to act together for the purpose of acquiring, holding, voting or disposing of equity securities of an issuer, the group formed thereby shall be deemed to have acquired beneficial ownership" of all of their equity securities. Besides its importance in the context of § 13(d) itself, the definition of a group under § 13(d) is also important because other transactions and corporate actions, including shareholder rights plans (also known as "poison pills"), often look to § 13(d) when defining or referring to groups for their own purposes.

If parties intend to act together, they will simply file their Schedule 13D as a group. But many parties do not want to be considered as a group

---

[6] *CSX Corp. v. Children's Investment Fund Management (UK), LLP*, et al., 562 F.Supp.2d 511, 540 (S.D.N.Y. 2008). The Second Circuit's opinion is at *CSX Corp. v. Children's Inv. Fund Management (UK), LLP,* 654 F.3d 276 (2d Cir. 2011).

for § 13(d) filing purposes yet still want to discuss or coordinate on issues concerning a target company ("the issuer"). This arises most prominently in shareholder activism situations, when multiple funds will buy stakes that individually would not meet the filing threshold but, in combination, do. They may want to interact with each other to coordinate their activities but at the same time avoid the § 13(d) group filing requirements. If there were no requirement to report group activities, activists and other potential acquirers might find it in their interests to assemble a large number of blocks, each less than five percent, and then coordinate their activities, all without alerting the board or the shareholders of the target.

In *CSX Corp. v. Children's Investment Fund Management (UK), LLP*, quoted above, CSX sued two shareholder activist hedge funds—The Children's Investment Fund (TCI) and 3G—who were seeking to remove and replace a number of CSX directors. The basis for CSX's suit was that the funds had violated § 13(d) by, among other reasons, failing to file a Schedule 13D after forming a group. The hedge funds denied they were a group at the time CSX claimed they were, saying that there were merely "relationships and communications among people and parallel investments in the same company." The hedge funds claimed that no specific arrangements had been made for the voting or sale of CSX shares under their control. The lower court in the Southern District of New York rejected this argument, stating:

> Section 13(d)(3) provides that "[w]hen two or more persons act as a partnership, limited partnership, syndicate, or other group for the purpose of acquiring, holding, or disposing of securities of an issuer, such syndicate or group shall be deemed a 'person' for the purposes of this subsection." The existence of a group turns on "whether there is sufficient direct or circumstantial evidence to support the inference of a formal or informal understanding between [members] for the purpose of acquiring, holding, or disposing of securities." Group members need not "be committed to acquisition, holding, or disposition on any specific set of terms. Instead, the touchstone of a group within the meaning of Section 13(d) is that the members combined in furtherance of a common objective." In this respect, an allegation that persons have formed a group "is analogous to a charge of conspiracy" in that "both assert that two or more persons reached an understanding, explicit or tacit, to act in concert to achieve a common goal." The requisite agreement "may be formal or informal, and need not be expressed in writing." The likelihood that any agreement in this case would be proved, if at all, only circumstantially is perhaps greater than usual because the parties went to considerable lengths to cover their tracks.

The Court already has made detailed findings concerning the defendants' activities and motives throughout the relevant period. The most salient points are summarized [below]:

- TCI and 3G have had a close relationship for years, in part because 3G's Synergy Fund is an investor in TCI.

- January 2007—Hohn and Behring discuss TCI's investment in CSX, including its approximate size.

- February 2007—3G begins buying CSX shortly after Behring's January conversation with Hohn.

- On or about February 13, 2007—Hohn speaks to his "friend Alex" Behring about CSX as a result of market excitement regarding CSX attributable in whole or part to 3G's heavy buying.

- At about the same time, Hohn begins tipping other funds to CSX, which continues for some time. This is an effort to steer CSX shares into the hands of like-minded associates.

- March 29, 2007—Amin and Behring meet.

- March 29, 2007—3G resumes CSX purchases after hiatus.

- March 29, 2007 through April 18, 2007—TCI increases its overall (shares plus swaps) position by 5.5 million shares, or 1.2 percent of CSX. 3G increases its position by 11.1 million shares, or 2.5 percent of CSX.

- August to September 2007—Hohn becomes concerned about possible reregulation. Both 3G and TCI reduce their CSX exposures, although 3G to a proportionately greater extent than TCI.

- Late September–October 2007—TCI tells D.F. King it probably will mount proxy contest. Hohn and Behring meet on September 26, 2007. Both TCI and 3G resume increasing their positions in the wake of the meeting. Both begin looking for director nominees.[7]

The lower court looked at the arrangements in the list above and inferred that the parties had an unstated "arrangement or understanding" with respect to CSX's shares, requiring a Schedule 13D to be filed. The filing was required even though there was no formal arrangement or understanding, and even though the parties, aware of the § 13(d) rules, had taken pains to avoid making any such arrangements.

---

[7] *CSX Corp. v. Children's Investment Fund Management (UK), LLP, et al.*, 562 F.Supp.2d 511, 552–53 (S.D.N.Y. 2008).

Nonetheless, the lower court felt that there were sufficient contacts to assume the existence of such an arrangement or understanding.

The Second Circuit rejected the lower court's conclusion that a group had been formed, stating that:

> [e]ndeavoring to meet the statutory standard, the District Court found that TCI and 3G formed a group, within the meaning of section 13(d)(3), "with respect to CSX securities," and that this group was formed no later than February 13, 2007. . . . Then, after identifying the Defendants' "activities and motives throughout the relevant period," . . . the Court stated, "These circumstances . . . all suggest that the parties' activities from at least as early as February 13, 2007, were products of concerted action. . . ."

> These findings are insufficient for proper appellate review. Although the District Court found the existence of a group "with respect to CSX securities," the Court did not explicitly find a group formed for the purpose of acquiring CSX securities. Even if many of the parties' "activities" were the result of group action, two or more entities do not become a group within the meaning of section 13(d)(3) unless they "act as a . . . group for the purpose of acquiring . . . securities of an issuer."[8]

The Second Circuit's decision endorses a narrower view of what constitutes a group for § 13(d) filing purposes, requiring that a documented arrangement or understanding be found. Nonetheless, despite the Second Circuit's decision, after the *CSX* case, shareholder activists have deliberately limited their contact with one another in order to avoid triggering the § 13(d) group requirements. Uncertainty exists because the SEC has failed to clarify this issue, and other courts may disagree with the Second Circuit, taking a view more akin to the lower court's expansive view in *CSX* of the circumstances under which a group will be deemed to have been formed.

4. WHEN MUST THE FILING BE MADE?

Section 13(d) and the rules and regulations thereunder provide that once the filing requirement is triggered, a filing must be made within ten calendar days. The filing is made to the SEC, to the issuer, and to each exchange on which the securities are traded. Between the moment the filing requirement is triggered and the moment the filing is required to be made, the acquirer is permitted to purchase additional securities.

---

[8] *CSX Corp. v. Children's Inv. Fund Management (UK) LLP,* 654 F.3d 276, 283–84 (2d Cir. 2011).

Both the ten day period and the ability of the acquirer to purchase additional shares during the interim period are the subject of vigorous debate. Companies have complained that shareholder activists and other acquirers can purchase shares surreptitiously during the interim period and frustrate the intent of § 13(d). An example illustrates the problem. In 2014, Pershing Square (a hedge fund) and Valeant (a pharmaceutical company) teamed up to purchase a stake in Allergan as a precursor to Valeant's unsolicited bid for Allergan. During the ten day time period between the day that Valeant and Pershing Square passed the five percent threshold and the day they were required to make Schedule 13D filings, the two parties were able to purchase an additional 4.7 percent of Allergan's stock, for a total stake of 9.7 percent. Allergan only learned of this stake after the ten day period elapsed and Pershing Square and Valeant filed their Schedule 13Ds, reporting the holding and indicating that the two were acting as a group for § 13(d) purposes.

In a petition to the SEC filed in 2011, several years before the Pershing Square and Valeant purchases, the law firm of Wachtell, Lipton Rosen & Katz requested that the SEC amend the § 13(d) rules to eliminate the ten day window and prevent further acquisitions until two business days after the filing of the Schedule 13D. The firm argued that full transparency for investors and companies required its proposed change, and that the "the ten-day reporting lag after the § 13(d) ownership reporting threshold is crossed facilitate[s] market manipulation and abusive tactics." The firm also stated that "[t]he pragmatic reasons which may have motivated the inclusion of a ten-day reporting lag in the Williams Act are simply obsolete. Changes in technology, acquisition mechanics and trading practices have given investors the ability to make these types of reports with very little advance preparation time."[9]

Shareholder activists and institutional investors have taken an opposing position, arguing that shortening the window would chill shareholder activism and hinder hostile bids. Shareholders would no longer be able to accumulate sufficiently large blocks to justify their activism. One opponent of the Wachtell Lipton proposal is Professor Lucian Bebchuk. In a newspaper column, he explained the reasons for his opposition:

> The SEC is planning to consider a rule-making petition, filed by a prominent corporate law firm, that proposes to reduce the 10-day period, as well as to count derivatives toward the 5 percent threshold. [*Editor: We will discuss the derivatives issue below.*] The push for tightening disclosure rules is at least partly driven

---

[9]   Wachtell, Lipton, Rosen & Katz, Petition for Rulemaking Under § 13 of the Securities Exchange Act of 1934, Mar. 7, 2011, available at https://www.sec.gov/rules/petitions/2011/petn4–624.pdf.

by the benefits that earlier disclosure would provide for corporate insiders. Supporters of the petition have made it clear that tightening disclosure requirements is intended to alert not only the market but also incumbent boards and executives in order to help them put defenses in place more quickly.

The drafters of the Williams Act envisioned a landscape that would allow outsiders who were not seeking to control a company to keep accumulating shares, provided that they made the required disclosures. But companies in the United States have been increasingly using poison pills . . . to limit the stakes of outside shareholders they disfavor.

Indeed, among the 637 companies with poison pills in the FactSet Systems database, 80 percent have plans with a threshold of 15 percent or less. No other developed economy grants corporate insiders the freedom to cap the ownership of blockholders they disfavor at such low levels.

The current ability of insiders to adopt . . . poison pills is a highly relevant factor for any assessment of the rules governing the relationship between incumbents and outside shareholders. In particular, the SEC should recognize that tightening disclosure requirements could impose costs on public investors and the economy by facilitating the use of such pills.

If the SEC does decide that tightening disclosure requirements is desirable, it should design the rules to avoid aiding the use of such poison pills. This could be done by limiting the application of tightened disclosure requirements to companies whose charters do not permit the use of . . . poison pills.

Proponents of the petition, which has thus far failed to attract any supportive comments from institutional investors, should endorse including such a limitation in any reform. Doing so is necessary to address concerns that tightened disclosure requirements might be aimed at protecting entrenched insiders rather than public investors.[10]

As this book goes to press, the SEC has not acted upon Wachtell Lipton's petition, and SEC officials have stated that the SEC has no current plans to act on this matter.

---

[10] Lucian A. Bebchuk, *Don't Make Poison Pills More Deadly*, N.Y. TIMES, Feb. 7, 2013, available at http://dealbook.nytimes.com/2013/02/07/dont-make-poison-pills-more-deadly/.

5. WHAT INFORMATION MUST THE FILING CONTAIN?

Section 13(d)(1) describes in general terms what sorts of information the required filing must contain. Schedule 13D sets forth the specific information to be included in the filing and a template for the Schedule. The Online Appendix includes the full form and instructions for Schedule 13D.

The main pieces of information required to be disclosed are:

a) The name, identity and background of the acquirer (Item 2)

b) The source of funds for the acquisition (Item 3)

c) The purpose of the acquisition (Item 4)

d) Any purchases or sales of securities in the last sixty days (Item 5)

(e) Any contracts of arrangements with respect to the securities of the issuer (Item 6)

By providing shareholders and the company with information about who has acquired their shares and what the acquirer's intent is, the Schedule 13D addresses the problem that motivated Section 13(d)'s adoption: the Saturday Night Special, in which an "unknown" acquirer with undisclosed intentions rapidly buys up shares of the target and then presents target shareholders with a coercive offer on a short fuse.

In drafting a Schedule 13D, the primary focus is the Item 4 disclosure concerning the purpose of the transaction. Item 4 requires the acquirer to describe any "plans or proposals" that may relate to different types of transactions described in the instructions to the schedule, including the acquisition of additional shares, or any merger, acquisition, or other extraordinary transaction.

A Schedule 13D filing must be amended if there is any material change in the information provided therein. Thus, if the filer's intent with respect to the issuer changes in any material respect, an amendment will be required. This is one reason why an acquirer may not want to pass the five percent threshold. Otherwise, its plans and proposals and negotiations with a target will have to be reflected "promptly" in updated Schedule 13D amendments. To minimize the need for subsequent amendments, acquirers filing their initial Schedule 13Ds will typically draft the Item 4 disclosure such that it provides maximum latitude for future actions without requiring an amendment.

The Item 4 disclosure from Valeant's Schedule 13D is set forth below (a full copy of the Schedule 13D is at the Online Appendix). This Schedule was filed on April 21, 2014, exactly ten days after Valeant acquired a greater than five percent interest in Allergan.

ITEM 4. Purpose of Transaction.

Valeant currently intends to propose a merger in which the Issuer's shareholders will receive a combination of cash and Valeant common shares. Valeant has not yet determined the amount of cash and number of Valeant common shares it will offer, but it currently expects the cash component will total around $15 billion. Barclays and Royal Bank of Canada have indicated they are prepared to deliver financing commitments covering the cash portion of the transaction at the time Valeant makes an offer.

Although Valeant currently expects to make an offer, it is under no obligation and provides no assurance it will do so. If Valeant fails to make an offer before May 2, 2014, Pershing Square will have the right to terminate the letter agreement described in Item 6 below and wind up PS Fund 1. [*Editor: PS Fund 1 LLC is an entity formed in connection with Pershing Square and Valeant's joint pursuit of a possible acquisition of Allergan. The letter agreement describes Valeant and Pershing Square's agreement as to various aspects of their arrangement with respect to Allergan.*]

In the course of pursuing a combination with the Issuer or otherwise, the Reporting Persons may consider, propose or take one or more of the actions described in subsections (a) through (j) of Item 4 of Schedule 13D. [*Editor: These items include acquisitions or dispositions of additional securities of the issuer, a merger of the issuer, a sale of a material amount of the assets of the issuer, a change in the issuer's board of directors, and a material change in the issuer's business.*]

Compare this to the Item 4 disclosure made by Pershing Square, Valeant's partner (a full copy of the full Schedule 13D is at the Online Appendix). The two were acting as a group for § 13(d) purposes but filed separate Schedule 13Ds:

ITEM 4. PURPOSE OF TRANSACTION

The Reporting Persons [Pershing Square, PS Management GP, LLC, and William Ackman, head of Pershing Square] believe that the Issuer's Common Stock is undervalued and is an attractive investment.

The Reporting Persons intend to engage in discussions with the Issuer and Issuer's management and board of directors, other stockholders of the Issuer and other persons that may relate to governance and board composition, management, operations, business, assets, capitalization, financial condition, strategic plans and the future of the Issuer. The Reporting Persons may also take one or more of the actions described in subsections (a) through (j) of Item 4 of Schedule 13D and may discuss such actions with the Issuer and Issuer's management and the board of directors, other stockholders of the Issuer and other persons.

The Reporting Persons intend to review their investments in the Issuer on a continuing basis. Depending on various factors and subject to the obligations described herein, including, without limitation, the Issuer's financial position and strategic direction, actions taken by the board, price levels of shares of Common Stock, other investment opportunities available to the Reporting Persons, concentration of positions in the portfolios managed by the Reporting Persons, market conditions and general economic and industry conditions, the Reporting Persons may take such actions with respect to their investments in the Issuer as they deem appropriate, including, without limitation, purchasing additional shares of Common Stock or other financial instruments related to the Issuer or selling some or all of their beneficial or economic holdings, engaging in hedging or similar transactions with respect to the securities relating to the Issuer and/or otherwise changing their intention with respect to any and all matters referred to in Item 4 of Schedule 13D.

Valeant currently intends to propose a merger in which the Issuer's shareholders will receive a combination of cash and Valeant common shares. Valeant has not yet determined the amount of cash and number of Valeant common shares it will offer, but it currently expects the cash component will total around $15 billion. Barclays and Royal Bank of Canada have indicated that they are prepared to deliver financing commitments covering the cash portion of the transaction at the time Valeant makes an offer.

Although Valeant currently expects to make an offer, it is under no obligation and provides no assurance it will do so.

———————————

The difference between the two Schedule 13Ds reflects the different goals of the two parties. Valeant is seeking to acquire Allergan while Pershing Square is an activist investor who may seek to make changes in Allergan and remain an investor even if Valeant's bid fails. Allergan therefore drafted its Schedule 13D disclosure much more broadly, to take all these possibilities into account.

6. WHEN MUST THE FILING BE UPDATED?

As discussed above, once the Schedule 13D filing is made, it must be amended "promptly" if there is any material change in the information contained therein. The previous Section discussed amendments to reflect a change in required disclosures under Item 4, the filer's plans and purposes with respect to the issuer. Amendments also must be filed to reflect material changes in ownership of the subject securities. Rule 13d–2 states that "an acquisition or disposition of beneficial ownership of securities in an amount equal to one percent or more of the class of securities shall be deemed 'material' for purposes of this Section; acquisitions or dispositions of less than those amounts may be material, depending upon the facts and circumstances." For example, a nine percent shareholder would need to amend her filing if she reduced her holdings to 7.9%, but if she reduced her holdings to 8.1%, she would only need to amend her filing if she concluded that not doing so would constitute a failure to state a material fact.

7. REMEDIES UNDER SECTION 13(d)

The SEC has clear enforcement rights under § 13(d), and can levy civil fines and obtain equitable relief for § 13(d) violations. Courts have also generally held that § 13(d) provides a private right of action. Issuers and security holders generally have been held to have such a right. Some courts have held that tender offerors also have a private right of action under § 13(d). The remedy most readily granted is corrective disclosure. But some courts have also allowed other injunctive relief such as "sterilization" of voting rights of shares. Some, although very few, courts have allowed a damages remedy. Most courts, however, have rejected claims for monetary damages in private suits under § 13(d).[11]

A case discussing private rights of action under § 13(d) is *In E.ON A.G. v. Acciona S.A.*[12] In that case, the court found that the right extended not only to issuers and shareholders, but also to tender offerors. The court discussed previous precedent holding that "the issuer 'can promptly and effectively police Schedule 13D filings.' " It noted that "[s]hareholders . . . rarely have the knowledge of the violation or the resources to engage in the complex and expensive litigation associated with enforcement of Williams Act disclosure," but that "a tender offeror has not only the resources, but also the self-interest which [the *GAF Co.* court [a Second Circuit decision, *GAF Corp. v. Milstein*, 453 F.2d 709 (2d Cir. 1971)] identified as 'vital to maintaining an injunctive action.' " The decision also discusses another Second Circuit decision, *Hallwood Realty*

---

[11] *See generally* American Law Reports, American Law Institute, *Availability of implied private action for violation of § 13 of Securities Exchange Act of 1934* (15 U.S.C.A. § 78m), 110 ALR Fed 758.

[12] *E.ON AG v. Acciona, S.A.*, 468 F. Supp. 2d 537 (S.D.N.Y. 2006).

Partners, L.P. v. Gotham Partners, L.P., 286 F.3d 613 (2d Cir. 2002), explaining why damages in a privately brought action under § 13(d) are generally not available:

> The aim of § 13(d) is to ensure that investors will be informed about purchases of large blocks of shares. In *GAF Corp.*, we found that this congressional purpose was furthered by providing issuers with the right to sue "to enforce [the] duties created by [the] statute," as the issuer "unquestionably is in the best position to enforce section § 13(d). The statute requires a copy of the statement to be sent by registered mail to the issuer ... and the issuer, in the course of constantly monitoring transactions in its stock, better than anyone else will know when there has been a failure to file." This court, however, expressly distinguished money damages from such injunctive relief, which furthers the object of § 13(d) by increasing honest disclosure for the benefit of investors without placing incumbent management in a stronger position than aspiring control groups. We noted that we were recognizing the rights of issuers "seeking equitable or prophylactic relief-not monetary damages-to take the necessary steps to effectuate the purposes of section 13(d)." In other words, in *GAF Corp.* we recognized that issuers have a private cause of action and standing to sue for injunctive relief because, inter alia, such relief increases the accurate information available to investors, while at the same time recognizing, in dicta, that monetary damages for issuers would not similarly benefit investors.

Recall that in the *CSX* case, discussed above, in addition to an injunction to correct the Schedule 13D, CSX attempted to obtain an injunction to sterilize (that is, prohibit the voting of) the shares of the hedge funds for purposes of an upcoming vote at CSX's annual meeting at which the two defendant hedge funds were trying to unseat a number of CSX directors. Despite finding a violation of § 13(d), the lower court did not grant the sterilization injunction since the corrective disclosure could be made in time for the shareholder meeting. Only if there was a threat of irreparable injury that an amendment could not correct would an injunction to sterilize the votes of shares be warranted. A goal of deterrence by providing a stronger penalty than merely corrective disclosure was not sufficient. The court stated, however, that if it were "free as a matter of law to grant such an injunction, whether on the basis that such relief is warranted to afford deterrence or on another basis, it would do so."[13]

---

[13] *CSX Corp. v. Children's Investment Fund Management (UK), LLP*, et al., 562 F.Supp.2d 511, 572 (S.D.N.Y. 2008).

8.   SECTION 13(d) AND DERIVATIVES

Section 13(d) only applies to equity securities. In today's capital markets it is possible to create a cash-settled derivative that mimics an equity security but does not actually qualify as an equity security for purposes of triggering the § 13(d) beneficial ownership requirement.

A cash settled derivative works as follows: An investor who wishes to invest in a particular company approaches an investment bank and arranges for a contract to be entered into between itself and the bank. The contract specifies the current trading price for the company's stock at the time the contract is entered into. The investment bank agrees to pay the investor the difference between that price and any increase at the termination date of the contract. The investment bank also agrees to pay the investor an amount equal to any dividend paid on the stock during the term of the contract. Conversely, the investor pays the investment bank the difference between the price specified in the contract and any decrease below that price. The investor also pays the bank interest on an amount equal to the price specified in the contract, as though it had bought the stock from the bank and borrowed money from the bank to do so. The net effect for the investor mimics ownership of the stock without actual ownership.

It is helpful to consider each component of the transaction separately. In accordance with standard usage, we will call the party who wishes to have the economic effect of owning the stock the "long" party, and the other party the "short" party (or counterparty). The following diagrams the cash flows going between the parties.

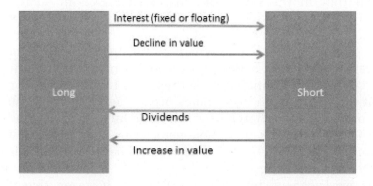

One effect of the cash-settled derivative is that it "locks up" a block of the company's stock equivalent to the ownership interest being replicated by the cash-settled derivative. An investment bank which is a party to a cash-settled derivative does not want to take the risk of an upturn in the company's stock. The bank therefore hedges its side of the transaction by purchasing an equivalent stake in the company's shares. The bank itself is exempt from the § 13(d) requirements because it is a financial institution engaged in a hedging operation. However, the bank can still vote these shares, and if the investor wants to unwind its cash-settled derivatives, the investor can quickly do so by purchasing the shares that the investment bank has on hand. This is well understood by both banks and sophisticated investors.

Because they technically seem to sidestep the § 13(d) rules, cash-settled derivatives have been used by activist hedge funds to accumulate stakes in companies without making Schedule 13D disclosure.

In *CSX,* discussed above, a court was called upon to weigh in on whether cash-settled derivatives qualified as "equity securities" under § 13(d). The lower court found that the funds' influence over the banks' (called the "short counterparties" in the opinion) securities made them beneficial owners of those securities. The lower court stated that:

> In the last analysis, there are substantial reasons for concluding that TCI is the beneficial owner of the CSX shares held as hedges by its short counterparties. The definition of "beneficial ownership" in Rule 13d–3(a) is very broad, as is appropriate to its object of ensuring disclosure "from all . . . persons who have the ability [even] to . . . influence control." It does not confine itself to "the mere possession of the legal right to vote [or direct the acquisition or disposition of] securities," but looks instead to all of the facts and circumstances to identify situations in which one has even the ability to influence voting, purchase, or sale decisions of its counterparties by "legal, economic, or other" means.
>
> On this record, TCI manifestly had the economic ability to cause its short counterparties to buy and sell the CSX shares. The very nature of the TRS transactions, as a practical matter, required the counterparties to hedge their short exposures. And while there theoretically are means of hedging that do not require the purchase of physical shares, in the situation before the Court it is perfectly clear that the purchase of physical shares was the only practical alternative. Indeed, TCI effectively has admitted as much. It did so by spreading its swap transactions among eight counterparties to avoid any one hitting the 5 percent disclosure threshold and thus triggering its own reporting obligation-a concern that was relevant only because TCI knew that the counterparties were hedging by buying shares. And it did so in closing argument, where its counsel said that the banks' purchases of CSX shares were "the natural consequence" of the swap transactions. Thus, TCI patently had the power to cause the counterparties to buy CSX. At the very least, it had the

power to influence them to do so. And once the counterparties bought the shares, TCI had the practical ability to cause them to sell simply by unwinding the swap transactions. Certainly the banks had no intention of allowing their swap desks to hold the unhedged long positions that would have resulted from the unwinding of the swaps.

The voting situation is a bit murkier, but there nevertheless is reason to believe that TCI was in a position to influence the counterparties, especially Deutsche Bank, with respect to the exercise of their voting rights.

TCI nevertheless argues strenuously against a finding that it has beneficial ownership of the shares, focusing heavily on the fact that it had no legal right to direct its short counterparties to buy or sell shares or to vote them in any particular way, indeed at all. Some amici, more cautiously, urge that any finding of beneficial ownership be rooted in unique facts of this case to avoid upsetting what they say is the settled expectation of the marketplace that equity swaps, in and of themselves, do not confer beneficial ownership of the referenced shares. They contend that a broader ruling could have extensive implications and that the subject therefore is dealt with more appropriately by administrative agency rule making than case-by-case adjudication. And the SEC Division of Corporation Finance argues-perhaps inconsistently with some of the Commission's past statements about the breadth of the definition of beneficial ownership-that there is no beneficial ownership where the short counterparties buy, sell, or vote their hedge shares as a result of their own economic incentives and not pursuant to legal obligations owed to their long counterparties, although it does not comment on the facts of this case. The Division, moreover, suggests that a contrary ruling would be novel and upset settled expectations of the market.

The focus on TCI's legal rights under its swap contracts, while those rights certainly are relevant, exalts form over substance. The securities markets operate in the real world, not in a law school contracts classroom. Any determination of beneficial ownership that failed to take account of the practical realities of that world would be open to the gravest abuse. Indeed, this Court is not alone in recognizing that abuses would be facilitated by a regime that did not require disclosure of the sort that would be required if "beneficial ownership" were construed as advocated by CSX.[14]

On appeal the Second Circuit stated that it was too divided to rule on the issue. However, Judge Ralph Winter issued a long concurrence in which he stated that the lower court decision was "flawed"—that "without an agreement between the long and short parties permitting the long party ultimately to acquire the hedge stock or to control the short party's voting of it, such swaps are not a means of indirectly facilitating a control transaction."[15]

The decision leaves the issue of cash-settled derivatives unsettled. A court in a particular case may follow Judge Winter's concurrence and hold that cash-settled derivatives do not trigger § 13(d) filing requirements absent a specific agreement to vote or sell the shares. Notably, the Dodd-Frank Act provided the SEC the ability to include these derivatives in § 13(d), implying that the power to do so did not exist before.[16] We believe that the issue will ultimately need to be resolved by the SEC, which as of this writing, has not acted.

C. SCHEDULE 13G

The § 13(d) rules allow certain securityholders to file a Schedule 13G instead of Schedule 13D if they intend to be passive investors. More specifically, Rule 13d–1 states that Schedule 13G is available for a person who "has acquired such securities [otherwise triggering the obligation to file a Schedule 13D] in the ordinary course of his business and not with the purpose nor with the effect of changing or influencing the control of the issuer, nor in connection with or as a participant in any transaction having such purpose or effect." Section 13G by its terms is generally limited to institutional investors, broker dealers, and banks.

Schedule 13G requires far less disclosure than does Schedule 13D. Unlike Schedule 13D, no Item 4 disclosure of purpose or intent is needed since the investor by definition has no such purpose or intent. Instead, the required disclosure is largely limited to the identity of the securityholder holding the issuer's shares and the amount of its holdings.

The requirements for filing Schedule 13G and amendments thereto are also far less exacting. Both the Schedule and amendments need only be filed within forty-five days after the end of the calendar year in which the need to file, or amend, arose. But if a Schedule 13G filer increases its

---

[14] *CSX Corp. v. Children's Investment Fund Management (UK), LLP*, et al., 562 F.Supp.2d 511, 545–47 (S.D.N.Y. 2008).

[15] *CSX Corp. v. Children's Inv. Fund Management (UK) LLP*, 654 F.3d 276, 288 (2d Cir. 2011).

[16] *See* Steven M. Davidoff, *Anticlimax in Long-Running CSX Railroad Court Case*, N.Y. TIMES, Jan. 17, 2014, available at http://dealbook.nytimes.com/2011/07/19/anticlimax-in-long-running-csx-court-case/.

ownership over ten percent, the Schedule 13G must be amended within ten calendar days after the month in which the change occurred. Moreover, if thereafter there are any increases or decreases of five percent or more in the filer's share ownership, an amendment must be filed within ten days after the end of the month in which the increase or decrease occurs. Finally, if the filer ceases to be a passive investor and comes to have a purpose or intent to change or influence control of the issuer, then it must convert to a Schedule 13D within ten business days.

The requirement of passivity and the concern that an attempt to influence, or even speak to, an issuer on governance or other matters may violate the Schedule 13G rules, leads most shareholder activist funds and even some institutional investors to file a Schedule 13D even when they might seem entitled to only file a Schedule 13G. The Gabelli Funds, for example, typically only file Schedule 13Ds to avoid signaling to issuers the investments in which they prefer to be more active, as well as to avoid the passivity requirement.

QUESTIONS

1.   If an employee has been awarded stock options equal to 15 percent of the outstanding shares of the company on a fully diluted basis, would that employee have to file a 13D? What issues would the employee have to consider in making a determination with respect to whether a filing is necessary? (To compute full dilution, you need to treat the number of shares for which the options could be exercised as being outstanding.)

2.   The 10 day filing window for Schedule 13D filings is controversial. Who would benefit and who would be harmed by such a move? Would reducing the window be consistent with the aims of the Williams Act? Do you think reducing the filing window is a good idea?

3.   What should the remedies be for a violation of § 13(d)? Should the remedies be different for private parties and for the SEC? Should money damages be available? If so, how would they be computed? How quick should judges be to sterilize voting rights? Should the remedy only be reserved for egregious cases?

4.   Consider the arrangement described in *CSX*. What are the best arguments that TCI has in fact formed a group with its counterparties? Would you favor a more or less expansive definition of the term "group" for purposes of § 13(d)? Why?

PROBLEMS

1.   You are the general counsel of Alpha hedge fund. Acme has acquired 3% of the outstanding common stock of Acme Corp. The head of Alpha approaches you and states that she wants to meet with Beta hedge fund to discuss potential changes to the management of Acme. Beta also

owns 3% of the outstanding common stock of Acme Corp. What advice would you give her about what can and cannot be discussed? Would you recommend that they meet?

2.   (Same facts as 1) After speaking with you, Beta and Alpha meet. At the meeting, representatives of Beta say to the head of Alpha that they want to work with Alpha to "shake up" the Acme Board. The head of Alpha says nothing, but nods her head in agreement. Are Alpha and Beta now required to file a Schedule 13D as a group? Why or why not?

3.   Instead of meeting with Beta, Alpha decides to pursue a stand-alone investment strategy. The head of Alpha comes to you and asks how Alpha can purchase another 10% of Acme without publicly disclosing this information? How would you recommend Alpha do this? What are the benefits and risks of this strategy?

4.   Your client is a hedge fund that has just purchased 7% of the outstanding shares of Acme Corp. Your client intends to continue to acquire shares of Acme on the open market. Your client has made it clear to you that it believes Acme is poorly managed and making strategic business decisions that have negatively impacted on its stock price. Your client believes that Acme and its shareholders would be better off if Acme were acquired by a strategic competitor. Draft an "Item 4" disclosure for your client's Schedule 13D.

CHAPTER V

REGULATION OF MERGERS AND ACQUISITIONS UNDER FEDERAL LAW— THE WILLIAMS ACT AND TENDER OFFERS

■ ■ ■

A. WHAT IS A TENDER OFFER?

The Williams Act imposes various requirements in connection with tender offers. But what is the definition of a "tender offer" for purposes of the Williams Act? An offer that an acquirer makes to all shareholders with a set time frame and at a fixed price for any and all shares of the target is almost certainly a tender offer both as understood by the capital markets and under the Williams Act. But what if an acquirer begins to buy up shares in a series of open market purchases without making a public announcement? What if those purchases are of shares held by private holders in privately negotiated transactions and not through an official exchange such as the NYSE at "take it or leave it" prices? Congress deliberately did not define what constituted a "tender offer." Instead, aware of "the almost infinite variety in the terms of most tender offers," it "left to the court and the SEC the flexibility to define the term."[1]

The leading case on the definition of tender offer under the Williams Act is *Wellman v. Dickinson*.[2] In *Wellman*, the court used an eight factor test to define a tender offer. These eight factors are whether the transaction: (1) involves an active and widespread solicitation of security holders; (2) involves a solicitation for a substantial percentage of the issuer's stock; (3) offers a premium over the market price; (4) contains terms that are fixed as opposed to flexible; (5) is conditioned upon the tender of a fixed number of securities; (6) is open for a limited period of time; (7) pressures security holders to respond; and (8) involves "public announcements of a purchasing program that precede or is coincident with a rapid accumulation of shares."

---

[1] *Full Disclosure of Corporate Equity Ownership in Corporate Takeover Bids*: Hearings on S. 510 Before the Subcommittee on Securities of the Senate Committee on Banking and Currency, 90th Cong., 1st Sess. 18 (1967) (statement of Manuel Cohen, Chairman, SEC), quoted in *Hanson Trust PLC v. SCM Corporation*, 774 F.2d 47, 56 (2d Cir. 1985).

[2] 475 F. Supp. 783 (S.D.N.Y. 1979), *aff'd* on other grounds, 682 F.2d 355 (2d Cir. 1982), *cert. denied,* 460 U.S. 1069 (1983).

In *Wellman*, a bidder, Sun Company, acquired a thirty-four percent stake in Becton, Dickinson & Company through private purchases. According to the court, the stake was acquired in part by having people telephone large shareholders of Becton, Dickinson:

> The callers followed the script. There were slight variations, but each solicitee was told that a non-disclosed purchaser, sometimes identified as in the top fifty of Fortune Magazine's 500, was looking for 20% of BD stock; that no transaction would be final unless 20% of the shares were acquired; that the $45 option was a top final price and the $40 option could be accepted with protection in the event shares were later bought at a higher figure; and that the desired 20% goal was within reach or that the order was filling up fast and a hurried response was essential. Each solicitee was asked to respond within one hour or less, although some were given until the next day. Sun was identified to a few institutions, but to most the purchaser's specific identity was not revealed.

The court held that Sun Company's purchases constituted a tender offer: "[I]t seems to me that the [eight factors] are the qualities that set a tender offer apart from open market purchases, privately negotiated transactions or other kinds of public solicitations. With the exception of publicity, all the characteristics of a tender offer, as that term is understood, are present in this transaction."[3]

Today, the issue of whether or not a bidder is making a tender offer under the Williams Act rarely arises. Bidders do not often take significant positions in a target prior to announcing their bid, and when they do, they mostly do so through open market purchases.[4] Nevertheless, understanding the *Wellman* factors is of key importance. Even though it may be clear that a tender offer is being made, the particular time when the offer is deemed to commence, and the extent to which the offeror's acquisitions of stock outside the tender offer (at, for instance, a previous or subsequent time) will nevertheless be deemed to be part of the tender offer, will be determined by the law defining tender offers.

B. WHEN IS A TENDER OFFER PREFERABLE TO A MERGER?

The typical acquisition structure is either a statutory merger described in Chapter II or a tender offer followed by a statutory merger, sometimes known as a "two-step" transaction. Various factors will

---

[3] *Id.* at 810; 824.

[4] Indeed, a Westlaw search conducted on January 17, 2015 shows that as of that date, *Wellman* had been cited by courts only 88 times, the last time in 2012.

determine which structure is more appropriate in a particular transaction.

A tender offer is a quicker mechanism to acquire control of a company than a merger requiring a shareholder vote. Rule 14e–1 requires a tender offer to be open a minimum of twenty business days from the date it is "first published or sent to security holders." This time period was specified to address the earlier concern with the Saturday Night Special that was the impetus of the Williams Act—shareholders coerced by short offering periods, typically over a weekend, to tender their shares without adequate time to consider the offer. By comparison, a merger typically takes two to three months to complete due to the mechanics of the shareholder vote process.

An important advantage of a merger is that it affects all the shares of a target, not just those of shareholders choosing to tender. While the tender offer provides a faster route to control, acquiring all of the shares in a tender offer for a public company is usually impossible. There will always be at least one non-tendering shareholder; more likely, there will be many more of them. Thus, one very common way to proceed in a friendly tender offer is a two-step process in which the acquirer achieves control in the first step through a tender offer, and then squeezes out the remaining shares "on the back end" in a short form merger. While, as we have learned in Chapter II, many mergers require approval of the target shareholders, short form mergers do not. There are two types of short form mergers potentially available to an acquirer in this context. If the acquirer acquires ninety percent or more of the target in the tender offer (or if the target has agreed to a "top up" to get the acquirer to the 90% threshold), then it can proceed with a § 253 short form merger. Alternatively, if the acquirer acquires more than fifty percent of the outstanding shares[5] and complies with the requirements of § 251(h), a short form merger under § 251(h) can be utilized to squeeze out the shareholders who did not tender into the offer. These short form mergers can be accomplished immediately after the tender offer closes; indeed, in the case of § 251(h), prompt consummation of the merger post tender offer is a requirement.

As we noted in Chapter II, at this writing other states do not have an analogue to § 251(h). If the target is not incorporated in Delaware and the acquirer has not received at least ninety percent of the stock in the offer (and does not have an agreement for a top-up), then a back-end merger will require a vote of the shareholders. A merger done in this way requires another one to two months, because of the time needed to file the necessary SEC documents and hold the vote. An acquirer may therefore prefer to structure a transaction as a merger if it does not expect to

---

[5] Or such greater percentage as may be required by the company's organizational documents.

acquire enough shares in the tender offer to exceed the short form squeeze-out threshold.

How does a top-up work? As discussed in Chapter II.B.4.b., in a friendly transaction, the target will often be willing to grant the tender offeror a "top-up" option by which the offeror can purchase from the target enough shares to bring its aggregate ownership up to at least ninety percent. In a recent case, *Olson v. EV3, Inc.*, 2011 WL 704409 (Del. Ch. Jan. 28, 2011), Vice Chancellor Laster described the role of the top-up option in a tender offer in the following way:

> The top-up option is a stock option designed to allow the holder to increase its stock ownership to at least 90 percent, the threshold needed to effect a short-form merger under Section 253 of the Delaware General Corporation Law (the "DGCL"), 8 Del. C. § 253. A top-up option typically is granted to the acquirer to facilitate a two-step acquisition in which the acquirer agrees first to commence a tender offer for at least a majority of the target corporation's common stock, then to consummate a back-end merger at the tender offer price if the tender is successful . . .

> The top-up option speeds deal closure if a majority of the target's stockholders have endorsed the acquisition by tendering their shares. Once the acquirer closes the first-step tender offer, it owns sufficient shares to approve a long-form merger pursuant to Section 251 of the DGCL, 8 Del. C. § 251. Under the merger agreement governing the two-step acquisition, the parties contractually commit to complete the second-step merger. A long-form merger, however, requires a board resolution and recommendation and a subsequent stockholder vote, among other steps. See *id.* § 251(b) & (c). When the deal involves a public company, holding the stockholder vote requires preparing a proxy or information statement in compliance with the federal securities law and clearing the Securities and Exchange Commission.

> The top-up option accelerates closing by facilitating a short-form merger. Pursuant to Section 253, a parent corporation owning at least 90% of the outstanding shares of each class of stock of the subsidiary entitled to vote may consummate a short form merger by a resolution of the parent board and subsequent filing of a certificate of ownership and merger with the Delaware Secretary of State. See 8 Del. C. § 253(a). This simplified process requires neither subsidiary board action nor a stockholder vote.

Vice Chancellor Laster wrote his opinion in *Olson* before § 251(h) was adopted. As discussed in Chapter II.B.4.b, § 251(h) eliminates the requirement for a shareholder vote in a back-end merger following a tender offer if the acquirer is able to obtain control through the tender offer. Consequently, while top-up options have disappeared in Delaware deals, they remain in deals for targets incorporated in states without a § 251(h) equivalent.

A merger may be a better choice than a tender offer if obtaining regulatory or other government clearances and consents will take a significant amount of time. A transaction cannot close without these consents. Until a tender offer closes, shareholders can withdraw their shares; shareholders thus can effectively veto the transaction throughout this time period. By contrast, in a merger, the necessary shareholder vote can occur while the regulatory and other clearances and consents are still pending; once the vote has occurred, even though the merger has not been consummated, shareholders cannot "withdraw" or otherwise rescind their votes. A merger may therefore be more desirable for a deal that is going to take a longer time to complete and is subject to some regulatory risk.

Other factors also influence the choice between a merger and a tender offer, including whether financing is being obtained to complete the offer or if the consideration is shares or cash. The need to obtain financing or to file and clear a registration statement with the SEC with respect to securities being offered in the deal may also delay the transaction and argue in favor of a merger.

Finally, as discussed earlier, in a tender offer, target board approval is not necessary. The offer is taken directly to shareholders. This means that for hostile bids, where the target's board is opposed to the transaction, the tender offer is the only structure available. We will discuss hostile tender offers further in Chapter XV. Another situation in which a tender offer is clearly preferable is where the deal is not hostile—and indeed, has been agreed upon—but the acquirer is concerned that a third party interloper may attempt to acquire the target. In both cases, a tender offer is preferable because it gives the acquirer control of the company on a faster timetable.

An example of the latter use of a tender offer is the private equity firm Apollo's Jan. 16, 2014, agreement to acquire Chuck E. Cheese. Apollo deliberately chose to complete the acquisition via a tender offer because of concerns about interlopers, starting its tender offer on Thursday, the day the deal was announced when the norm is for "the bidder [to] let a few days to a week elapse, as the lawyers rest up from the rush to get the deal signed and then turn to the tender offer papers." But, as the New York Times reported, in their rush, the lawyers were careless. "Chuck E. Cheese's parent is a Kansas corporation and Apollo is required under the tender offer documents to describe shareholders' appraisal rights. In the middle of describing Kansas appraisal rights in the tender offer to purchase, Apollo suddenly switche[d] to discussing the text of the

Delaware appraisal statutes and describe[d] the Kansas statute as the 'Delaware General Corporation Law.' "[6] The lawyers for Chuck E. Cheese quickly amended their tender offer documents to correct this mistake.

The haste may have worked. No subsequent bidder emerged for Chuck E. Cheese and it was acquired by Apollo.

C. SUBSTANTIVE RULES GOVERNING TENDER OFFERS

The Williams Act requires certain disclosures with respect to tender offers; it also imposes substantive requirements. The substantive requirements are set forth in § 14(d) and § 14(e) of the Securities Exchange Act of 1934 and the rules and regulations thereunder. The § 14(d) rules apply only to tender offers for more than five percent of a company's equity securities when that company's securities are registered with the SEC. However, the § 14(e) rules apply to all tender offers for any securities whether or not the issuer is public, as well as tender offers for less than five percent of an issuer's equity securities. As a practical matter, most tender offers are covered by both sets of rules. But transactions involving a private target or a tender offer for debt securities will only be subject to the § 14(e) rules.

1. COMMENCEMENT OF THE OFFER

A tender offer commences on the date that the bidder has first "published, sent or given the means to tender to security holders." (Rule 14d–2.) In practice, a buyer commences the tender offer by filing a Schedule TO with the SEC and publishing a summary advertisement in a national newspaper such as the New York Times or the Wall Street Journal. (Rule 14d–4.) Note that these rules have not been updated to reflect the impact of online publications; the publication of the offer must still be in a newspaper. The tender offer documents are mailed to security holders at the same time, or at a reasonable time thereafter.

Rule 14d–2, as initially promulgated in 1979, provided that upon announcing a tender offer, a bidder would have five business days to commence the offer or withdraw it. At the time, Rule 14d–2 stated that a tender offer announcement would be any statement which included: (1) the bidder's identity; (2) the identity of the target; (3) the amount and class of the securities sought; and (4) a price offered. This placed a significant burden on potential offerors, since they had to prepare and file all of the tender offer documents within five business days after any announcement. One effect of this rule was to push the practice of mergers

---

[6] Steven M. Davidoff, *Apollo Global Management is Sprinting to Acquire Chuck E. Cheese*, N.Y. TIMES, Jan. 17, 2014, available at http://dealbook.nytimes.com/2014/01/17/apollos-rush-to-get-the-chuck-e-cheese-deal-done/.

and acquisitions to larger law firms, which had the capacity to rapidly prepare and file the tender offer documents. Another was that it forced acquirers to be quite careful in phrasing their statements about any acquisition to avoid making an inadvertent public announcement of a tender offer, since making such an announcement would require them to very quickly file the necessary documents.

In 2000, the SEC amended Rule 14d–2 to eliminate the five business day rule. Instead, a public announcement is now defined as "any oral or written communication by the bidder, or any person authorized to act on the bidder's behalf, that is reasonably designed to, or has the effect of, informing the public or security holders in general about the tender offer." This definition of "public announcement" is quite broad, but with the five business day rule eliminated, the bidder is only required to commence the offer within a "reasonable amount of time."

In connection with the elimination of the five business day rule, the SEC also adopted Rule 14e–8. Rule 14e–8 makes it a fraudulent act for a person to announce a tender offer "without the intention to commence the offer within a reasonable time," with the intention of manipulating the offeror's or target's stock price, or without a reasonable belief that the offeror will have the means to complete the tender offer.

2. FILING REQUIREMENTS

The commencement of a tender offer triggers a requirement to file a Schedule TO with the SEC as soon as practicable on the date of commencement. (Rule 14d–3.) The bidder must also send a hard copy of the Schedule TO to the target at its principal executive office as well as the stock exchange where the target is listed and to any other bidder who has filed a Schedule TO for the target. Any amendment to the Schedule TO reporting any material changes in the information filed in the Schedule TO must promptly be filed with the SEC. Under Rule 14d–3, a final amendment reporting the results of the offer must also be filed with the SEC on Schedule TO.

3. DISSEMINATION

In practice, a buyer commences the tender offer by filing the Schedule TO with the SEC and publishing a summary advertisement in a national newspaper such as the New York Times or Wall Street Journal. Rule 14d–4. The tender offer documents are mailed at the same time or at a reasonable time thereafter to security holders. This is known as "short form" publication.

Following is the offer by Java Corp, a subsidiary of the Men's Wearhouse, to purchase all of the outstanding stock of Joseph A. Bank

Clothiers, as included in its public filings (and published in a major newspaper, the Wall Street Journal).

TENDER OFFER, JAVA CORP.
March 20, 2014

Second Amended and Restated Offer to Purchase for Cash
All Outstanding Shares of Common Stock
(Including the Associated Preferred Share Purchase Rights)
of
Jos. A. Bank Clothiers, Inc.
at
$65.00 Net Per Share
by
Java Corp.
A Wholly Owned Subsidiary of
The Men's Wearhouse, Inc.

**THE OFFER AND WITHDRAWAL RIGHTS EXPIRE AT
5:00 P.M., NEW YORK CITY TIME, ON APRIL 9, 2014,
UNLESS THE OFFER IS EXTENDED.**

Java Corp. (the "Purchaser"), a Delaware corporation and a wholly owned subsidiary of The Men's Wearhouse, Inc., a Texas corporation ("MW"), is offering to purchase all outstanding shares of common stock, par value $0.01 per share (together with the associated preferred share purchase rights, the "Shares"), of Jos. A. Bank Clothiers, Inc., a Delaware corporation ("JOSB"), at a price of $65.00 per share, net to the seller in cash, without interest and less any required withholding taxes (the "Offer Price"), upon the terms and subject to the conditions set forth in this Second Amended and Restated Offer to Purchase (as may be subsequently amended and supplemented from time to time, the "Offer to Purchase") and the related letter of transmittal that accompanies this Offer to Purchase (the "Letter of Transmittal") (which, together with any amendments or supplements thereto, collectively constitute the "Offer").

The Offer is being made pursuant to an Agreement and Plan of Merger (together with any amendments or supplements thereto, the "Merger Agreement"), dated as of March 11, 2014, by and among MW, JOSB and the Purchaser, pursuant to which, as soon as practicable after the completion of the Offer, subject to the satisfaction or waiver of certain conditions, the Purchaser will be merged with and into JOSB, with JOSB continuing as the surviving corporation and a wholly owned subsidiary of MW (the "Merger"). At the effective time of the Merger (the "Effective Time"), each Share issued and outstanding immediately prior to the Effective Time (other than (i) Shares held by JOSB or MW or any of their subsidiaries, all of which will be cancelled and will cease to exist, and (ii) Shares owned by holders who have properly exercised appraisal rights with respect thereto in accordance with Section 262 of the General Corporation Law of the State of Delaware (the "DGCL")) will be converted into the right to receive an amount in cash equal to the Offer Price.

THE BOARD OF DIRECTORS OF JOSB UNANIMOUSLY RECOMMENDS THAT YOU TENDER ALL OF YOUR SHARES INTO THE OFFER.

The board of directors of JOSB (the "JOSB Board") unanimously (i) determined that the Merger Agreement, the Offer, the Merger and the other transactions contemplated thereby, are advisable, fair to and in the best interests of JOSB and its stockholders, (ii) adopted and approved the Merger Agreement and the transactions contemplated thereby and (iii) resolved to recommend that the stockholders of JOSB accept the Offer and tender their Shares to the Purchaser pursuant to the Offer.

Consummation of the Offer is conditioned upon, among other things, (i) there being validly tendered and not validly withdrawn prior to the expiration of the Offer that number of Shares (excluding Shares tendered pursuant to guaranteed delivery procedures that have not yet been delivered in settlement or satisfaction of such guarantee) which, when added to the Shares already owned by MW and its subsidiaries (without duplication), represents at least a majority of the total number of outstanding Shares on a fully diluted basis, (ii) any waiting period (and any extension thereof) applicable to the consummation of the Offer under the Hart-Scott-Rodino Antitrust Improvements Act of 1976, as amended (the "HSR Act") having expired or been terminated, (iii) the absence of a Company Material Adverse Effect (as defined in the Merger Agreement) on JOSB, (iv) three business days having passed after completion of the Marketing Period (as defined in the Merger Agreement), (v) no applicable law, temporary restraining order, injunction or other judgment being and remaining in effect which has the effect of prohibiting or making illegal the consummation of the Offer, the Merger or the other transactions contemplated by the Merger Agreement and (vi) certain other customary conditions.

Consummation of the Offer is not subject to a financing condition.

This transaction has not been approved or disapproved by the Securities and Exchange Commission ("SEC") or any state securities commission, nor has the SEC or any state securities commission passed upon the fairness or merits of this transaction or upon the accuracy or adequacy of the information contained in this document. Any representation to the contrary is a criminal offense.

This Offer to Purchase and the related Letter of Transmittal contain important information, and you should carefully read both in their entirety before making a decision with respect to the Offer.

The Dealer Managers for the Offer are:

J.P. Morgan   BofA Merrill Lynch
March 20, 2014

IMPORTANT

Any stockholder of JOSB who desires to tender all or a portion of such stockholder's Shares in the Offer should either (i) complete and sign the accompanying Letter of Transmittal or a facsimile thereof in accordance with the instructions in the Letter of Transmittal, and mail or deliver the Letter of Transmittal together with the certificates representing tendered Shares and all other required documents to American Stock Transfer & Trust Company, LLC, the depositary for the Offer, or tender such Shares pursuant to the procedure for book-entry transfer set forth in "The Offer—Section 3—Procedure for Tendering Shares" or (ii) request that such stockholder's broker, dealer, commercial bank, trust company or other nominee effect the transaction for such stockholder. Stockholders whose Shares are registered in the name of a broker, dealer, commercial bank, trust company or other nominee must contact such person if they desire to tender their Shares. The associated preferred share purchase rights are currently evidenced by the certificates representing the Shares, and by tendering Shares, a stockholder will also tender the associated preferred share purchase rights. If a Distribution Date (as defined in "The Offer—Section 8—Certain Information Concerning JOSB—Preferred Share Purchase Rights") with respect to the Rights occurs, stockholders will be required to tender one associated preferred share purchase right for each Share tendered in order to effect a valid tender of such Share.

Any stockholder who desires to tender Shares and whose certificates representing such Shares are not immediately available, or who cannot comply with the procedures for book-entry transfer on a timely basis, may tender such Shares pursuant to the guaranteed delivery procedure set forth in "The Offer—Section 3—Procedure for Tendering Shares."

Any stockholder who has previously tendered Shares pursuant to the Offer and has not withdrawn such Shares need not take any further action in order to receive the offer price of $65.00 per Share, net to the seller in cash, without interest and less any required withholding taxes, if Shares are accepted for payment and paid for by the Purchaser pursuant to the Offer, except as may be required by the guaranteed delivery procedure, if such procedure was utilized.

Questions and requests for assistance may be directed to the Information Agent or to the Dealer Managers at their respective addresses and telephone numbers set forth on the back cover of this Offer to Purchase. Requests for copies of this Offer to Purchase, the related Letter of Transmittal, the Notice of Guaranteed Delivery and all other related materials may be directed to the Information Agent or brokers, dealers, commercial banks and trust companies, and copies will be furnished promptly at the Purchaser's expense. Additionally, this Offer to Purchase, the related Letter of Transmittal and other materials relating to the Offer may be found at http://www.sec.gov.

———————

A bidder can also commence a tender offer by printing the entire offer in a newspaper and filing a Schedule TO and foregoing mailing. This method was used in an earlier era, but is no longer used today.

The bidder's material must be sent to the target's shareholders. How does this happen? Upon the bidder's request, Rule 14d–5 requires the target either to mail the tender offer documents to the target's security holders or to provide the bidder with the names and addresses of such security holders. In practice, when getting a request from a hostile bidder, a target will almost always choose to mail the materials itself so as not to have to provide shareholder information to the bidder.

4. OFFER PERIOD

A tender offer must remain open for at least twenty business days from the date of commencement. (Rule 14e–1(a).) For purposes of this computation, the first day the tender offer is announced counts as a full day. (Rule 14d–2(a).)

5. SUBSEQUENT OFFERING PERIOD

In 2000 the SEC began allowing bidders to provide a subsequent offering period, lasting at least three business days, after the initial tender offer is completed. In order to be able to offer a subsequent offering period, (a) the initial offering period must have expired, (b) the offer must be for all the outstanding securities, (c) the bidder must immediately accept and promptly pay for the securities tendered during the initial offering period, (d) the bidder must immediately accept and promptly pay for all securities as they are tendered during the subsequent offering period, and (e) the bidder must offer the same amount and type of consideration in the initial and subsequent offering periods. (Rule 14d–11.) During the subsequent offering period no withdrawal rights are allowed; the period is primarily intended to allow remaining shareholders to tender so that the squeeze-out threshold can be achieved.

6. AMENDMENTS

If the bidder changes the consideration offered, the tender offer must remain open for an additional ten business days from the date the bidder first notifies shareholders of the change. (Rule 14e–1(b).) If there are any other material changes to the tender offer, the offer must be held open an additional five business days. (Rule 14d–4.)

Note that the additional time is not simply added onto the current offer period. So, for example, if a bidder launches a tender offer and after five business days increases the consideration offered, the ten business day period will not require an extension beyond the twenty business day period of the initial offering period. The bidder will therefore be able to complete its tender offer after twenty business days without delay.

7. ALL HOLDERS/BEST PRICE RULE

Rule 14d–10 sets forth the all-holders/best price rule. The all-holders part of the rule requires that the tender offer be open to all securityholders of the class of securities subject to the tender offer. The best price rule requires that the offeror pay to every securityholder tendering into the offer the highest price paid to any tendering securityholder. Some special issues concerning executive compensation and Rule 14d–10 are discussed below in All Holders/Best Price Rule: Special Issues.

8. WITHDRAWAL RIGHTS

A shareholder tendering her shares into a tender offer has the right to withdraw those shares at any time until the tender offer is completed. (Rule 14d–7.) This contrasts with the rules of many other countries, which do not permit the withdrawal of shares which have already been tendered. As a practical matter, however, the withdrawal rights rule does not come into play since institutional investors, who typically hold the bulk of shares in a public company, tend to wait until the last day of the offer to tender their shares. As noted above, withdrawal rights are not required during a subsequent offering period.

9. PRO RATION

A tender offer need not be for 100 percent of a company's shares; indeed, it can even be for a minority stake. But if a tender offer is not for all of a company's shares, Rule 14d–8 requires that the offeror acquire securities on a pro rata basis according to the number of shares tendered by each shareholder into the offer. How would this work in practice? See the following example:

A bidder makes a tender offer for twenty percent of the shares of target. Target has 100 shares outstanding; the bidder is seeking twenty shares. Thirty shares are tendered into the offer. To compute the percentage of shares purchased divide the number of shares sought by the number of shares tendered: 20/30 = .667, or 2/3rd. Accordingly, a shareholder who tenders three shares would have two purchased in the offer.

10. PURCHASES OUTSIDE THE OFFER

Rule 14e–5 prohibits the bidder from purchasing any securities outside the offer from the time a tender offer is announced until its completion. This rule is contrary to the rules in effect in most other countries, which allow these purchases. The practical effect of Rule 14e–5 is to prevent a tender offeror from acquiring shares outside of the offer.

The following post on the M&A Law Professor Blog illustrates some of these issues while providing further background on Rule 14e–5:

Rule 14e–5 was promulgated in 1969 as Rule 10b–13 to prohibit bidder purchases outside of a tender offer from the time of announcement until completion. The primary reason put forth by the SEC for barring these purchases in 1969 was that they "operate[ ] to the disadvantage of the security holders who have already deposited their securities and who are unable to withdraw them in order to obtain the advantage of possible resulting higher market prices." This is no longer correct; bidders are now obligated to offer unlimited withdrawal rights throughout the offer period. Moreover, Rule 10b–13 was issued at a time when targets had no ability to defend against these bidder purchases. They were yet another coercive and abusive tactic whereby the bidder could obtain control through purchases without the tender offer, thereby exerting pressure on stockholders to tender before the bidder terminated or completed its offer on the basis of these purchases. This is not feasible today. Poison pills and second and later generation state takeover statutes act to restrict these purchases to threshold non-controlling levels without target approval. In the wake of these developments, the original reasons underlying the promulgation of Rule 10b–13 no longer exist.

Moreover, Rule 14e–5, by its terms, acts to confine bidder purchases to periods prior to offer announcement. However, a bidder's capacity to make preannouncement acquisitions has been adversely effected by a number of subsequent changes in the takeover code, such as the Hart-Scott-Rodino waiting and review period requirements. These have combined to chill a bidder's ability to make preannouncement acquisitions or forthrightly precluded such purchases. Consequently, one study has recently reported that at least forty-seven percent of initial bidders have a zero equity position upon entrance into a contest for corporate control.

A bidder's preannouncement purchase of a stake in the target, known as a toehold, can be beneficial. The toehold purchase defrays bidder costs, incentivizes the bidder to complete the takeover, and reduces free-rider and information asymmetry problems. This can lead to higher and more frequent bids. Meanwhile, market purchases amidst a tender offer can provide similar benefits while providing market liquidity and confidence for arbitrageurs to fully act in the market.

Finally, Rule 14e–5 has never applied to bar purchases while a merger transaction is pending. Presumably, this path dependency was set in 1969 because a bidder in a merger situation requires acquiree agreement; the acquiree can therefore contractually respond to and regulate this conduct. But whatever the reason, today a bidder who runs a proxy contest without a tender offer is permitted post-announcement purchases during the contest. Unsolicited bidders will therefore initially characterize their offers as mergers in order to leave the option of such purchases. The result is preferential bias towards mergers over tender offers, discrimination which no longer seems sensical in a world where a takeover transaction will not succeed unless the original or replaced acquiree board agrees to it. Any prohibition on outside purchases should apply to both merger and tender offer structures or to neither.[7]

11. TARGET BOARD RESPONSE TO A TENDER OFFER

To ensure that securityholders have adequate information to decide whether or not to tender into the offer, the target is required under Rule 14e–2 to respond to the offer within ten days after the offer commences. Rule 14d–9 requires that the target respond by filing a Schedule 14D–9 with the SEC containing its recommendation as to whether shareholders should accept or reject the offer. The Schedule 14D–9 will also contain other information concerning the offer, including any compensation payable to the target's executives in connection with the offer. Rule 14d–9 also requires that the target file any communications concerning the tender offer with the SEC.

---

[7] Steven M. Davidoff, *The Obsolescence of Rule 14e–5*, M&A LAW PROF. BLOG, June 29, 2007, available at http://lawprofessors.typepad.com/mergers/2007/07/the-obsolescenc.html.

The typical initial response of a target when a tender offer is announced is to issue a "stop, look, and listen" communication. This is designed to inform the shareholders that they should wait until the company publishes its recommendation with respect to the offer and files a Schedule 14D–9. Rule 14d–9 specifically exempts such a statement from the communication filing requirements. Here is the stop, look, and listen communication from the Men's Wearhouse/Jos A. Bank hostile transaction:

Jos. A. Bank Urges Shareholders to Take No Action with Respect to Men's Wearhouse Tender Offer or Director Nominees

HAMPSTEAD, Md., Jan. 6, 2014 (GLOBE NEWSWIRE)—The Board of Directors of Jos. A. Bank Clothiers, Inc. (Nasdaq:JOSB) (the "Company") today confirmed that The Men's Wearhouse, Inc. (NYSE:MW) has commenced an unsolicited tender offer to acquire all outstanding common shares of the Company at a price of $57.50 per share.

The Board said that, consistent with its fiduciary duties, it will carefully review all aspects of the Men's Wearhouse offer in consultation with its financial and legal advisors and make a recommendation to shareholders, which will be outlined in a Statement on Schedule 14D–9 filed with the Securities and Exchange Commission on or before January 17, 2014.

The Company's stockholders are advised to take no action on the tender offer until the Company's Board of Directors has announced its recommendation to stockholders.

The date for the Company's 2014 annual meeting of shareholders has not yet been announced and shareholders are not required to take any action at this time with respect to the Men's Wearhouse nominees or otherwise. Additional information regarding the 2014 Annual Meeting will be provided at the appropriate time.

ADDITIONAL INFORMATION

This communication does not constitute an offer to buy or solicitation of an offer to sell any securities. The Company may file a solicitation/recommendation statement on Schedule 14D–9 with the U.S. Securities and Exchange Commission ("SEC"). Any solicitation/recommendation statement filed by the Company that is required to be mailed to stockholders will be mailed to stockholders of the Company. INVESTORS AND STOCKHOLDERS OF THE COMPANY ARE URGED TO READ THESE AND OTHER DOCUMENTS FILED WITH THE SEC CAREFULLY IN THEIR ENTIRETY WHEN THEY BECOME

AVAILABLE BECAUSE THEY WILL CONTAIN IMPORTANT INFORMATION. Investors and stockholders will be able to obtain free copies of these documents (when available) and other documents filed with the SEC by the Company through the web site maintained by the SEC at http://www.sec.gov. In addition, the Company may file a proxy statement with the SEC. Any definitive proxy statement will be mailed to stockholders of the Company together with a WHITE proxy card. INVESTORS AND SECURITY HOLDERS OF THE COMPANY ARE URGED TO READ THESE AND OTHER DOCUMENTS FILED WITH THE SEC CAREFULLY IN THEIR ENTIRETY IF AND WHEN THEY BECOME AVAILABLE BECAUSE THEY WILL CONTAIN IMPORTANT INFORMATION. Investors and security holders will be able to obtain free copies of these documents (if and when available) and other documents filed with the SEC by the Company through the web site maintained by the SEC at http://www.sec.gov. In addition, this document and other materials related to Men's Wearhouse's unsolicited proposal may be obtained from the Company free of charge by directing a request to the Company's Investor Relations Department, Jos. A. Bank Clothiers, Inc., 500 Hanover Pike, Hampstead MD 21074, 410.239.5715.

Note the legends in the "stop, look, and listen" communication above. These legends are required by the communication rules for tender offers and are discussed in Chapter VII.E.

12. ALL HOLDERS/BEST PRICE RULE: SPECIAL ISSUES

The SEC adopted the all-holders/best price rule in 1986 in response to the Delaware decision in *Unocal v. Mesa Petroleum* discussed in Chapter XVI. The rule made illegal a defensive tactic that the Delaware court had ruled was legal under the circumstances of the case: a target's right to exclude a hostile bidder from a tender offer made by the target for its own shares. From 1995 through 2002, a number of federal courts ruled that payments to executives in connection with an acquisition, such as golden parachute payments or change in control bonuses, might trigger the all-holders/best price rule. These courts held that if the compensation was an integral part of the tender offer, then it violated the rule that all tendering shareholders whose shares were accepted in the offer had to get the highest consideration paid to any shareholder in the offer. Other courts adopted a bright line test: so long as the compensation was not paid during the tender offer, there was no violation of the all-holders/best price rule.[8] This uncertainty led acquirers to spurn use of the tender offer structure for some time, to avoid the risk that an acquirer might have to pay the other security holders tendering in the offer the same price paid to the security holders getting a higher price—that is, the executives given golden parachutes or change in control bonuses. In 2006 the SEC adopted new rules to fix this problem. The new rules clarified that payments made as compensation were exempted from the best price rule. (See Rule 14d–10(d).) The SEC's reform changed practitioner views on when to use tender offers. According to FactSet MergerMetrics, in 2006 less than six percent of public acquisitions used a tender offer structure, a number that grew to sixteen percent in 2007 following adoption of the amendment to the best price rule.

D. TENDER OFFER TIMING

As noted above, a tender offer proceeds much more quickly than a merger that needs shareholder approval obtained via a proxy statement. Here is one possible timeline for a tender offer:

---

[8]   *See* the discussion in *Katt v. Titan Acquisitions Ltd.*, 244 F. Supp. 2d 841 (D. Tenn. 2003).

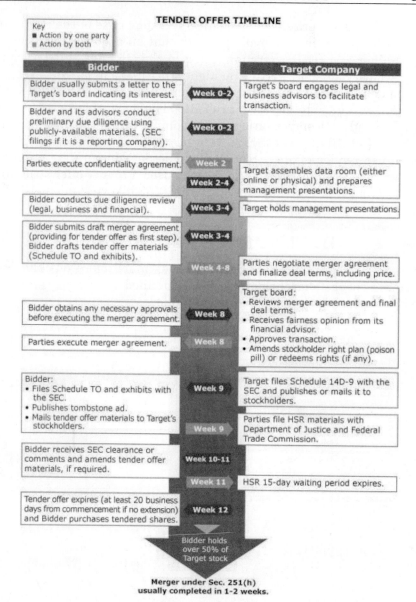

PLC, Tender Offer Timeline with DGCL 251(h) Merger

A tender offer moves more quickly because it need only be kept open for twenty business days. Antitrust clearance is not infrequently required for larger transactions, but it can often be obtained quickly. For cash tender offers, the waiting period is fifteen days, and it may be even shorter if a request for "early termination" is granted. We discuss the law at issue, the Hart-Scott-Rodino Antitrust Improvements Act of 1976, in Chapter VIII.A.

E. TENDER OFFER PRACTICALITIES

A tender offer involves many moving parts. In general, if the consideration consists solely of cash, the offer documents are relatively easy to prepare. They principally describe the offer itself, the mechanics of tendering, and the reasons to tender. If the consideration is securities, then the process can be much more arduous since it also involves the preparation, filing, and dissemination of a registration statement. (We discuss this process in Chapter VII.A). The following documents must be prepared in connection with the offer whether the consideration is cash or securities:

Schedule TO. This is the form required under Rule 14d–1 to be filed with the SEC on the date of commencement of the offer. This form sets forth the information required to be disclosed to shareholders in connection with the tender offer. As a practical matter, this information is usually incorporated "by reference" from the offer to purchase.

Offer to Purchase. The offer to purchase sets out the terms of the offer in a manner that conforms to the requirements of Schedule TO. The Offer to Purchase is filed as an exhibit to the Schedule TO and is incorporated by reference into the Schedule TO. It is the main document distributed to shareholders of the target company.

Broker-Dealer Letter. The investment banks representing the offeror in the tender offer are known as the dealer managers. The dealer managers will send this letter to broker-dealers and other organizations holding securities on behalf of shareholders. The letter instructs these entities to forward the tender offer material to their client shareholders. The tender offer materials to be forwarded include the offer to purchase and the following documents:

- *Letter of Transmittal.* For use by shareholders to instruct brokers and dealers to tender their shares.

- *Notice of Guaranteed Delivery.* To be used to accept an offer if share certificates and the other required tendering documents cannot be delivered to the depositary for the offer, or if the procedures for book-entry transfer cannot be completed, by the expiration of the tender offer.

- *To Our Clients Letter.* This is a form of letter which can be sent by the broker or dealer to the clients for whose accounts they hold shares registered in the broker-dealer's name or in the name of the nominee, in order to obtain instructions with respect to the offer.

Tombstone Ad. The tombstone is the advertisement published in the newspaper on the day the tender offer commences for purposes of Rule 14d–2.

Press Release. The offeror will issue a press release stating that the offer has commenced and directing security holders to the offering documents.

Schedule 14D–9. This is the target's response document; it must be filed by the target within ten days of the commencement of the offering. The Schedule 14D–9 contains the target board's recommendation to its shareholders with respect to the tender offer. In a friendly transaction, it is common for the Schedule 14D–9 to be filed and mailed to securityholders on the same day the tender offer commences.

Samples of all of these documents from Men's Warehouse's tender offer for Jos. A. Bank can be found in the Online Appendix.

F. EMPIRICAL EVIDENCE ON THE WILLIAMS ACT

The Williams Act should in theory have caused fewer tender offers to be made. Not only did it eliminate one easy avenue for such offers, the Saturday Night Special, it did so by imposing requirements that make transactions more costly and perhaps more uncertain. But, from the perspective of target shareholders, the offers that are made should be better ones, with higher premiums, since the shareholders' bargaining position should be better than it was when Saturday Night Specials were allowed.

Empirical studies and descriptive evidence support these theoretical predictions. In 1967, just before the 1968 enactment of the Williams Act, forty percent of takeovers were hostile, a number which quickly fell by 1969 to 8.3%. Professors Gregg Jarrell and Michael Bradley found that the average tender offer premium increased from thirty-two percent to almost fifty-three percent after the passage of the Williams Act.[9] Professor Robert Smiley also documented a significant deterrent effect on hostile bids from the Williams Act.[10] But Professors Kevin Nathan and Terrence O'Keefe found that premiums rose after the Williams Act for both mergers and tender offers and that the increase occurred after 1972,[11] something that B. Espen Eckbo calls "puzzling," saying that it may point to something else as the source of these findings.[12]

These findings cannot tell us how to appraise the aggregate effect of the Williams Act on tender offers. We cannot know whether the higher premiums compensate sufficiently for the lower number of offers; also,

---

[9] Gregg A. Jarrell & Michael Bradley, *The Economic Effects of Federal and State Regulations of Cash Tender Offers*, 23 J. LAW & ECON. 371 (1980).

[10] Robert Smiley, *The Effect of State Securities Statutes on Tender Offer Activity*, 19 ECON. INQUIRY 426 (1981).

[11] Kevin S. Nathan & Terrence B. O'Keefe, *The Rise in Takeover Premiums: An Exploratory Study*, 23 J. FIN. ECON. 101 (1989).

[12] B. Espen Eckbo, *Bidding Strategies and Takeover Premiums: A Review*, 15 J. CORP. FIN. 149 (2009).

beyond the immediate time frame after the adoption of the Williams Act, it is very difficult to know what would be happening with tender offers had the Williams Act not been adopted. Nonetheless, these findings do strongly suggest that parties' behavior as regards tender offers was substantially changed by the Williams Act.

QUESTIONS

1.   What are factors that favor using a merger structure? What are factors that favor using a tender offer?

2.   How do the "all-holders" and "best price" rules fit with the rationale of the Williams Act?

3.   Who is hurt if tender offers are made more expensive by the Williams Act? Who benefits?

PROBLEMS

Alpha, Inc. wishes to acquire Beta, Inc., a publicly traded firm incorporated in Delaware. The consideration is cash. There are no antitrust (competition) or other issues. The only possible delay in completion is expected to be for financing, which will take about one to two months to complete.

1.   Please advise your client whether a merger or tender offer structure should be used and explain why.

2.   How would your advice to your client change if you expected a lengthy antitrust review lasting for at least six months before a tender offer or merger could be completed?

3.   How would your advice to your client change if Beta was incorporated in a state other than Delaware and a shareholder owning 12% of Beta had publicly stated she was opposed to the acquisition? For these purposes assume there is no significant concern that another bidder might emerge.

4.   How would your answer to Problem 3 change if there were concerns about a hostile bidder?

5.   How would your answer to Problem 3 change if Beta were incorporated in Delaware?

CHAPTER VI

REGULATION OF MERGERS AND ACQUISITIONS UNDER FEDERAL LAW—PROXY RULES

■ ■ ■

A. OVERVIEW

In statutory mergers involving public companies, both federal securities laws and state corporate law play a role. Although federal securities laws do not govern the substantive features of the actual transaction, they do govern the process by which a board is permitted—or required—to communicate with its shareholders concerning a shareholder vote. The vote typically occurs because of state law requirements for a merger. Another reason for a vote includes a stock exchange requirement to approve the issuance of stock used as consideration in the merger. Alternatively, a company which is to issue stock to be used as consideration in a merger might need shareholder approval to amend its certificate of incorporation if it did not already have enough stock authorized. Note that in these latter two cases, the approval would be for the stock issuance or certificate amendment (or both), not the merger, unless the merger needed approval under state law.

By contrast, in a tender offer, there is no requirement for a shareholder vote. The shareholders are effectively "voting with their feet" by selling their shares. The proxy rules, which govern communications with shareholders in connection with a shareholder vote, therefore do not apply. While the tender offer itself does not require a shareholder vote, a subsequent back-end merger that is not a short form merger would require such a vote. If parties intended a two-step tender offer with a back-end long form merger, then federal proxy rules would apply to the vote on the back-end merger. The proxy rules are designed to ensure that when shareholders cast their vote either for or against a merger transaction, they are able to do so in a fully informed manner.

Almost all shareholder voting is done by proxy rather than in person; those with the right to vote give their "proxy" specifying how they would like their shares voted. For this reason, when votes are solicited, they are solicited via a "proxy statement." The federal securities laws governing the solicitation of shareholder votes are thus often collectively referred to as the proxy rules.

The following, written by a law firm practitioner, describes the key federal securities laws governing proxy solicitations.

PROXY CONTESTS

36–39
William S. de Wied, Wilson Sonsini Goodrich & Rosati P.C.
Practical Law Company (2010)

Key Legal Considerations

The solicitation of proxies is governed by Section 14 of the Securities Exchange Act of 1934, as amended (Exchange Act) and Regulation 14A under the Exchange Act. Key aspects of Regulation 14A include:

- The meaning of "solicitation."

- The ability to engage in solicitation before furnishing a proxy statement.

- Exemption of certain communications from the proxy rules.

- The content of the proxy statement and proxy card.

- Filing requirements for written soliciting materials.

- Disclosure and anti-fraud rules.

Solicitation Rules

The most important concept under the rules is the meaning of "solicitation." Pursuant to Rule 14a–1(l)(1), the terms "solicit" and "solicitation" include the following:

(i)   Any request for a proxy whether or not accompanied by or included in a form of proxy;

(ii) Any request to execute or not to execute, or to revoke, a proxy; or

(iii) The furnishing of a form of proxy or other communication to security holders under circumstances reasonably calculated to result in the procurement, withholding or revocation of a proxy.

The term "proxy" includes every proxy, consent or authorization (Rule 14a–1(f)). The SEC and the courts have broadly interpreted the term "reasonably calculated to result in the procurement, withholding or revocation of a proxy" to include communications prior to the commencement of a formal solicitation that appear to be designed to influence stockholders' voting decisions. Accordingly, communications that form part of a continuous plan that culminates in a formal solicitation and have the purpose or effect of influencing investors will be viewed as proxy solicitation.

However, the term "solicitation" does not include "[a] communication by a security holder who does not otherwise engage in a solicitation . . . stating how the security holder intends to vote and the reasons therefor" (Rule 14a–1(l)(iv)). Having influential investors publicly announce their voting intentions, as permitted by the rule, can be of significant value.

All written communications must be filed with the SEC on the date of first use, no later than 5:30 p.m. Eastern time. The term "written communication" is interpreted broadly to include all communications that are disseminated to the general public in any form other than orally and includes material such as press releases, slides, postcards, e-mails and internet postings. Scripts, prepared Q & A sheets or similar materials prepared for personal use generally do not need to be filed, unless they are given out to an audience or the press or otherwise distributed publicly. Similarly, if a document is widely distributed throughout the company, or provided to the IR department or other personnel for repeated use, it should be filed.

Once a solicitation begins, the company should assume that essentially all public or investor relations and employee communications could be viewed as solicitation activities and make the appropriate filings. Communications with customers and suppliers can also be viewed as solicitations depending on the circumstances. Therefore, the company should implement procedures to ensure appropriate vetting of communications with counsel to comply with the proxy rules.

Solicitation Prior to Furnishing the Proxy Statement

Rule 14a–12 permits parties to engage in solicitation activities before furnishing a proxy statement and without pre-clearance by the SEC, so long as each written communication includes:

(i) The identity of the participants in the solicitation and a description of their interests (by security holdings or otherwise) in the subject matter of the solicitation or a prominent legend indicating where security holders can find the information; and

(ii) A prominent legend advising security holders to read the proxy statement when it is available because it contains important information and explaining how investors can obtain the proxy statement and other relevant documents free of charge from the SEC's website or from the participant.

In addition, a definitive proxy statement must be sent or given to security holders before or at the same time forms of proxy are furnished to or requested from security holders.

Any soliciting material published, sent or given to security holders in accordance with Rule 14a–12(a) must be filed with the SEC on the date of first use under cover of Schedule 14A (Rule 14a–12(b)).

Important Exemptions

Rule 14a–2 sets out a number of exemptions from the proxy rules. Notably, Rule 14a–2(b) exempts from the proxy rules, other than the anti-fraud requirements of Rule 14a–9:

- Solicitations by certain persons not seeking proxy authority.
- Solicitations of ten or fewer stockholders (the "Rule of Ten").

Solicitations by Persons Not Seeking Proxy Authority

Any solicitation by or on behalf of a person who does not seek power to act as proxy and does not furnish or request a proxy is exempt from the proxy rules (Rule 14a–2(b)). Categories of persons who cannot rely on this exemption include:

- The issuer, its affiliates and their respective officers and directors.
- Any nominee for election.
- Any person being compensated by a person unable to rely on the exemption.
- Any Schedule 13D filer who has not disclaimed control intent.
- Any person with a substantial interest in the subject matter of the solicitation not shared pro rata with other holders.

Rule 14a–2(b) can be used by stockholders to encourage other holders to support one or other of the parties to the contest with minimal regulatory constraints. It can also be used in "withhold the vote" campaigns against the election of one or more directors or against a corporate transaction such as a merger.

Persons that rely on Rule 14a–2(b) and own shares (within the class being solicited) with a market value of more than $5 million must also file any written soliciting materials with the SEC within three days after the date of first use under cover of a Notice of Exempt Solicitation.

Rule of Ten

Any solicitation other than on behalf of the company where the total number of persons solicited is not more than ten is exempt from the proxy rules (other than the anti-fraud requirements). At companies with extremely concentrated share ownership, it may be possible to obtain the votes or consents needed to prevail in a contest without soliciting more than ten holders.

The Proxy Statement and Proxy Card

In a proxy contest, each side must file its proxy statement and form of proxy in preliminary form with the SEC at least ten calendar days before distributing a definitive proxy statement and form of proxy to investors (Rule 14a–6(a)). The SEC generally attempts to provide comments within the ten-calendar-day period.

The proxy statement must contain the information specified in Schedule 14A. For a proxy contest in connection with the annual meeting, the company's proxy statement will largely mirror the regular annual meeting proxy statement, other than any discussion of the election contest itself and any supporting information the company chooses to include in its proxy statement. Because the SEC does not require pre-clearance of soliciting materials other than the proxy statement and form of proxy, the parties generally include limited discussion of their respective campaign platforms in the proxy statement. Instead, the parties disseminate "fight letters" to investors which lay out, often with considerable dramatic flair, their core arguments (see Platform and Strategy). The first fight letter is generally disseminated on the day the definitive proxy statement is filed.

Rule 14a–4 specifies requirements for the form of proxy card. The proxy card must set forth each matter to be acted upon clearly and impartially, and provide a specifically designated blank space for dating the proxy card. The proxy card must provide a means for the person solicited to specify approval, disapproval or abstention as to each matter to be acted upon, except that in the case of election of directors the proxy card must provide a means to withhold authority from each individual nominee, and may provide a means to vote for the nominees as a group so long as it provides a similar means to withhold authority for the nominees as a group.

If a dissident is seeking fewer than all board seats (known as a short slate), it can round out its slate by including nominees named in the company's proxy statement in its proxy card (Rule 14a–4).

But the proxy card has important limitations. Generally, stockholders are faced with a mutually exclusive choice between executing the company's proxy card for some or all of its nominees or the dissident's proxy card for some or all of its nominees (plus the company's nominees used to round out the dissident's slate). Although the proxy card limits the choices available to stockholders as a matter of federal law, sophisticated institutions understand that, as a matter of state law, they can submit a ballot at the meeting selecting from both the company's and the dissident's nominees. However, this can be logistically challenging and is quite rare in practice.

In the course of a proxy contest, investors may receive multiple proxy cards from each side, and may, intentionally or inadvertently, submit more than one proxy card. The latest dated proxy card revokes any prior proxy. For more information on what information is required in an annual meeting proxy statement and proxy card, see Practice Notes, Proxy Statements.

Distribution of Proxy Materials; E-Proxy

Under Rule 14a–7, upon a written request by the dissident, the company is obligated to (at the company's option) either:

- Effect the mailing (or internet delivery) of the dissident's proxy materials.

- Provide to the dissident a list of record holders, non-objecting beneficial owners, and, if the company has elected to deliver proxy materials over the internet, the names of holders who have requested paper copies.

Because under state law (such as § 220 of the DGCL (8 Del. C. § 220)) the dissident generally has the ability to obtain a stockholder list for the purposes of soliciting proxies, the election under Rule 14a–7 is not particularly significant.

In 2007, the proxy rules were amended to provide for delivery of annual reports and proxy materials over the internet, thereby both streamlining the proxy process and reducing printing and mailing costs. To utilize e-proxy, the company must mail to security holders a notice of internet availability of proxy materials no later than 40 calendar days prior to the meeting date (Rule 14a–16(a)). If the company elects to use e-proxy, all of its proxy materials must be available on a website free of charge on or before the time the notice is sent, and all additional soliciting material must be available on the website on the day first sent to security holders or made public (Rule 14a–16(b)). The dissident has a choice to use e-proxy or paper delivery of materials and, if using e-proxy, must send its notice of internet availability of proxy materials by the later of 40 calendar days before the meeting or the date it files its definitive proxy statement as long as that filing occurs within days of the company's filing of its definitive proxy statement (Rule 14a–16(l)).

It is not necessarily to the company's advantage to use e-proxy in a proxy contest because it has been shown to lead to lower turnout of retail-held shares at shareholder meetings. In cases in which the company chooses to use e-proxy, a separate paper mailing to retail holders, or other additional solicitation efforts, may be important to maximize turnout by retail holders.

Disclosure and Anti-Fraud Rules

Rule 14a–9 prohibits making false and misleading statements of material fact in connection with any solicitation of proxies subject to Regulation 14A. The rule expressly states that the fact that proxy materials have been filed with or examined by the SEC does not constitute a finding that the materials are not false or misleading. The Supreme Court has held that a private right of action exists to remedy violations of Rule 14a–9 (see *J.I. Case v. Borak*, 377 U.S. 426 (1964)). The standard for materiality under Rule 14a–9 was clarified by the Supreme Court in *TSC Industries v. Northway*:

> An omitted fact is material if there is a substantial likelihood that a reasonable stockholder would have considered it important in deciding how to vote … [T]here must be a substantial likelihood that the disclosure of the omitted fact would have been viewed by the reasonable investor as having significantly altered the 'total mix' of information made available.

(See *TSC Industries v. Northway*, 426 U.S. 438 (1976).)

The SEC generally limits its role in proxy contests to:

- Reviewing materials for exaggerated or inflammatory statements.

- Requiring support for factual assertions and correction of statements expressed as fact which are matters of opinion rather than fact.

If a party believes the proxy materials of the other party violate Rule 14a–9, the SEC's general policy is to leave such matters to be addressed through litigation. A showing of scienter is not required in an action under Rule 14a–9. The range of potential remedies for violations of the Rule includes injunctive relief (which may include enjoining a party from soliciting proxies, enjoining the vote or requiring a new vote) and damages awards.

There is also an established body of case law in Delaware on the adequacy of disclosure in proxy statements, and the Delaware courts have shown themselves sensitive to the importance of full and fair disclosure in connection with elections of fiduciaries of the company. Whether considering litigation for federal or state law claims, however, in practice litigation is seldom a show stopper in a proxy contest. Except for the most egregious rule violations, the typical remedy is corrective disclosure. Since stockholders today are generally skeptical of the value of proxy litigation, a decision to litigate should be made only after a thorough analysis of the benefits and risks involved. The decision to litigate should be based on one principal criterion: whether it increases the chances for success in the proxy contest.

B. THE PROXY RULES IN PRACTICE

In a takeover of a public company involving a shareholder vote, there will always be a solicitation. The attorneys for the target and buyer therefore can simply prepare and file the proxy statement, and ensure that the necessary filings are made for any communications. The proxy rules are thus mainly a matter of timing and disclosure, provided there is no significant shareholder opposition. In short, the fact that there will be a solicitation requiring filings is a foregone conclusion.

The issues around solicitation and filings become more significant when a shareholder wishes to oppose the takeover, or when a shareholder activist is thinking about launching a campaign to nominate directors or attempting to proceed with a shareholder proposal. In such cases the "rule of ten" is particularly important. The "rule of ten" permits a shareholder to speak to up to ten other shareholders without triggering the filing and distribution requirements of the proxy rules. Similarly, a hostile bidder may take advantage of these rules to speak to shareholders before triggering the proxy requirements.

If a shareholder wishes to oppose a takeover by soliciting shareholders to vote "no," the federal proxy rules will apply. If the shareholder is going to solicit no votes, it will have to file and circulate a proxy statement. This is a significant cost and therefore a deterrent to such conduct.[1] These costs have arguably limited attempts to persuade shareholders to vote down takeovers: less than one percent of takeovers have been voted down by shareholders. Nonetheless, in recent years hedge funds which specialize in this conduct have become increasingly active. They will take positions in companies and agitate for a higher price or rejection of the transaction, and are willing to bear the expense. We further discuss this conduct in Chapter XX, on Shareholder Activism.

Often, a hostile tender offeror will run a proxy contest to replace the incumbent board, with the goal of placing new directors on the board who are more amenable to the hostile offeror's views. The tender offer/proxy contest combination is the preferred strategy for hostile acquirers who need to overcome takeover defenses, such as poison pills, in order for their offers to succeed. A proxy contest sponsored by a hostile offeror is subject to the proxy rules since it is a solicitation of shareholder votes.

---

[1] The shareholder bears the entire cost, but will only reap part of the benefit, since what he is attempting to do would affect the company as a whole and all of its shareholders.

C. THE MECHANICS OF THE SHAREHOLDER VOTE

There are many complex mechanics to be arranged in connection with the shareholder meeting to approve the transaction. These relate to, among other things, who votes, when the vote is held and when the necessary materials are required to be filed and distributed.

1. SETTING THE RECORD DATE

As the following memorandum notes, the process by which the record date is set is quite important because it determines which shareholders will vote at the meeting.

SETTING THE RECORD (DATE) STRAIGHT
Daniel E. Wolf, et al., Kirkland & Ellis LLP
May 6, 2013

A record date, often viewed in the merger context as a mere mechanic to be quickly checked off a "to do" list, creates a frozen list of stockholders as of a specified date who are entitled to receive notice of, and to vote at, a stockholders' meeting. A tactical approach to the timing of the record date can have strategic implications on the prospects for a deal's success, while the failure to comply with the rules relating to setting a record date could cause a significant delay in holding the vote, leaving the door open for a topping bidder or dissident stockholder to emerge or gather support. As a result, it is important that dealmakers understand the basic mechanics and rules of setting a record date and the tactical repercussions of the record date construct.

Starting first with the legal requirements, there are several key inputs that inform the mechanics of setting a record date, including laws of the company's state of incorporation, the company's organizational documents, federal securities laws, rules of the applicable securities exchange and the relevant merger agreement. Taken together, these requirements dictate the necessary procedural and governance steps for setting the record date and establish the minimum and maximum time periods between the record date and the meeting, as well as between the board action setting the record date and the record date itself.

The perils of failing to comply with formalistic legal requirements were highlighted in the *Staples* decision [*In re Staples, Inc. Shareholders Litigation*, 792 A.2d 934 (Del. Ch. 2001)] in 2001. Then-VC [Vice Chancellor] Strine, in a fact-intensive decision, enjoined the impending vote and required Staples to fix a new record date before proceeding with its meeting because he found that the power to set the record date had not been properly delegated by the board and contemporaneous documentation of the action setting the record date was absent. Similarly, failure to comply with technical SEC broker-search requirements in a timely manner for the requisite period ahead of the record date can have unforeseen consequences. In a number of cases, particularly where the deal is being contested, the SEC has commented on the failure to comply with these rules, resulting in a potential requirement to establish a new record date and postponement of the vote. . . .

Beyond the technical requirements, there are also strategically significant considerations in setting the record date because of its role in determining which stockholders are entitled to vote. On the most basic level, locking in the stockholder list provides the company and its advisers with a settled group of stockholders from whom they can solicit votes. More broadly, an early freezing of the voter base can impede dissident stockholders or competing bidders from buying in (or further buying in) after the record date and thereby seeking to influence the outcome of the vote because, as a general matter, the right to vote does not transfer with shares acquired after the record date. On the flip side, an early record date can exacerbate the risk of "empty voting" where stockholders who have sold their shares after the record date but before the meeting continue to have the right to vote for or against a deal despite lacking a corresponding economic interest in the company.

Motivated in part by a perceived need to address the potential mischief that can result from "empty voting," in 2009 Delaware adopted amendments to the DGCL allowing companies to bifurcate their record dates, setting one earlier record date for notice of the meeting and a later record date for the right to vote. While a later voting record date may alleviate the empty voting issue (or at least shorten the exposure period), the benefit might be outweighed by offsetting considerations. For example, the ability to solicit votes may be partially impaired because of the failure to get an early and fixed snapshot of the stockholder base and setting a bifurcated record date may (rightly or wrongly) signal to the market that the company is concerned about its ability to obtain the requisite vote.

The potential strategic implications of setting a record date become apparent when the record date has ramifications on the ability to delay a scheduled meeting date. The need or desire to delay a meeting can arise in a number of different circumstances—e.g., where a competing bid or other new information surfaces close to the scheduled meeting date or where the company has concerns about obtaining the required vote. As seen in the maneuvering over the delays in the stockholder votes at Dynegy and Cedar Fair in 2010, the ability of a company to delay the stockholder vote in the face of opposition to the proposed merger is significantly impacted by the effect of the delay on the existing record date as well as somewhat intricate legal distinctions under state law and the company's organizational documents. While producing the same outcome in terms of delaying the scheduled vote, the mechanic of delay— i.e., whether termed a postponement, adjournment or recess [*Editor: all of these are discussed in the next Subsection*]—may in fact determine whether the delay results in the need to set a new record date (and therefore a refreshed list of stockholders entitled to vote on the deal) and whether stockholder approval for the delay itself may be required. Parties should also be mindful that courts may critically review a decision to delay a meeting (and to preserve or, alternatively, update the record date) if the court determines that the intent of the delay and its impact on the record date, by postponement, adjournment or otherwise, was to frustrate the stockholder franchise or was an improper defensive tactic.

* * *

The inevitably unique facts of each deal will likely dictate the optimal record date for the stockholder meeting. Early attention to the record date question is advisable given the long lead-time under some of the procedural legal requirements mentioned above. Compliance with technical requirements and an awareness of strategic implications are necessary to ensure that parties don't fall prey to pitfalls inherent in treating setting the record date as a mere administrative task.

2. ADJUSTING THE RECORD AND MEETING DATES

In general, when a transaction the management favors is probably not going to be approved at the shareholder meeting, the company may seek to hold the meeting later than was originally scheduled. Adjournment is one way to achieve this. There are other ways as well: the meeting can be postponed, or there can be a recess. There are different legal rules and considerations applicable for each. A law firm memo provides additional detail:

> Public companies that are seeking stockholder approval of a contested business combination transaction have sometimes found it desirable to delay a previously scheduled meeting of stockholders. The company may wish to provide stockholders with additional time to consider new information (such as a new or revised acquisition proposal), may need additional time to solicit proxies, or may not have a quorum. Adjournment is the most traditional, and most accepted, method to delay a stockholder vote. In an adjournment, the meeting is convened without taking a stockholder vote, but then reconvened at a later time and date. However, a stockholder meeting also can be postponed or recessed. In a postponement, the previously

scheduled stockholder meeting is not convened, but is delayed to a subsequent time and date. In a recess, the stockholder meeting is convened, and then "recessed" without taking a stockholder vote and continued at a later time and date. The determination of whether a company can delay its previously scheduled stockholder vote, and the best method of doing so, requires a rigorous analysis of the company's charter and bylaws, applicable state or foreign law, the federal securities laws, and the agreements governing the transaction.[2]

The strategic implications of setting the record date and special meeting date to approve a transaction has led parties to agree that changes to these dates would be permitted in order to enhance the deals' prospects. Here is the provision from the merger agreement for the private equity firm Apollo Management's attempted (but ultimately unsuccessful) acquisition of Cedar Fair. Cedar Fair was a partnership and so the "shareholders" in this provision are unitholders.

> Section 5.04 <u>Unitholder Approval</u>. As promptly as practicable following the date of this Agreement and unless this Agreement has been validly terminated. . . . the Company shall call the Special Meeting to be held as soon as reasonably practicable after the date of this Agreement (and in any event within twenty (20) Business Days after the mailing of the Proxy Statement. . . . <u>provided</u>, <u>however</u>, that the Company may on one occasion postpone or adjourn the Special Meeting (i) to solicit additional proxies for the purpose of obtaining the Requisite Unitholder Vote, (ii) for the absence of a quorum, (iii) to allow reasonable additional time for the filing and mailing of any supplemental or amended disclosure which the Company has determined in good faith after consultation with outside legal counsel is necessary under applicable Law and for such supplemental or amended disclosure to be disseminated and reviewed by the Unitholders prior to the Special Meeting or (iv) if the Company has delivered the notice contemplated by <u>Section 5.02(e)</u> and the time periods contemplated by <u>Section 5.02(e)</u> have not expired; <u>provided</u>, <u>further</u>, that any such postponement or adjournment by the Company shall be for at least fifteen (15) Business Days. . . . unless otherwise agreed to in writing by Parent. Parent may request on one or, in the event of any of clauses (i)–(iii) above, more occasions that the Special Meeting be postponed or adjourned for up to fifteen (15) Business Days. . . . in which

---

[2]   Lois Herzeca and Eduardo Gallardo, *Delaying Judgment Day: How to Defer Stockholder Votes in Contested M & A Transactions*, 26 INSIGHTS: THE CORPORATE AND SECURITIES LAW ADVISOR, No. 3, 1, March 2012, available at http://www.gibsondunn.com/publications/Documents/HerzecaGallardo–DelayingJudgmentDay.pdf.

event the Company shall, in each case, cause the Special
Meeting to be postponed or adjourned in accordance with
Parent's request.

Cedar Fair Merger Agreement, dated Dec. 16, 2009.[3]

The provisions in the Cedar Fair deal became important when
shareholders objected to the price being offered by Apollo. The provisions
were invoked to adjourn the Cedar Fair meeting, but shareholders still
voted the transaction down.

Another transaction where these sorts of issues arose was The
Blackstone Group's purchase of Dynegy, a transaction which was opposed
by some Dynegy shareholders, including Carl Icahn. The night before the
meeting, Blackstone had increased its offer from $4.50 a share to $5 a
share; Dynegy wanted to give shareholders the opportunity to consider
the new offer. How should it proceed?

Dynegy needed to have the vote occur fairly soon, but not too soon.
Institutional investors generally vote by proxy, which are submitted well
before the meeting date. Institutional investors would need time to
reconsider their votes. Moreover, many institutional investors vote in
accordance with the recommendation of proxy advisory services such as
Institutional Shareholder Services ("ISS"). Those services, too, need time
to process any new information. Indeed, if the shareholder meeting is only
five days away or sooner, ISS will not change its recommendation. In the
case of Dynegy, ISS had already recommended the Blackstone deal, but
two other proxy advisory services, Glass Lewis and Proxy Governance,
had not.

In general, boards in such situations have a number of options to
avoid losing a shareholder vote. First, a board could convene and then
adjourn the shareholder meeting. Alternatively, a board could postpone
the meeting. Finally, a board could convene and then recess the meeting.

Dynegy could have adjourned the meeting, but decided against
proceeding in that manner. Its bylaws did "not provide clear authority for
adjournments . . . it was uncertain whether Dynegy could adjourn the
meeting without shareholder approval. But Dynegy did not want to hold
the vote because it likely would have lost."[4]

Another possibility was a postponement. Postponing a meeting is not
the same as an adjournment. Postponements are considered new
meetings, and require additional statutory notices sent "at least 20

---

[3] Available at http://www.sec.gov/Archives/edgar/data/811532/000090951809000914/
mm12–1709_8ke0201.htm.

[4] Steven M. Davidoff, *Dynegy's Unusual Approach to Delay a Vote,* N.Y. TIMES, Nov. 18,
2010.

calendar days prior to the date of the meeting." (DGCL § 251(c)). Thus, the vote would have been significantly delayed. Moreover, "Dynegy's proxy did not clearly spell out that the proxy stayed in effect for any postponement. A postponement would have also probably required Dynegy to refile its proxy and resolicit votes. This would push any meeting into [the next year] 2011." "Dynegy's lawyers . . . came up with a third option . . . The meeting was called to order but then a [recess] was called . . . until [7 days later] Nov. 23." DGCL § 231 (c) provides that the "date and time of the opening and the closing of the polls for each matter upon which the stockholders will vote at a meeting shall be announced at the meeting.

The meeting was "recessed," but when it resumed, it was still the same meeting, avoiding "the need for a vote on adjournment or postponement."[5]

The Dynegy shareholders still voted against the merger. Shortly thereafter Dynegy filed for bankruptcy.

3.   OTHER REQUIREMENTS

In addition to the record date, there are a number of other requirements relating to the shareholder meeting, including as to notice of the meeting, the record date, broker request forms, and proxy materials. Each of these requirements is addressed below.

Notice of Meeting. Under Delaware law, notice of the meeting must be no less than ten days and no more than sixty days from the actual meeting. (DGCL § 222(b)). Other states have similar requirements. The SEC requires that notice of the meeting be issued at least forty calendar days before the meeting date. (Rule 14a–16).

Record Date. The NYSE recommends that there be at least thirty days between the record date and the meeting date. NYSE Listed Manual Rule § 401.03. Delaware law also requires that the record date must be no less than ten days and no more than sixty days from the actual meeting. DGCL § 213. Under a recent rule change, a Delaware company can bifurcate its record date, setting a different, earlier date for notice of the meeting than the actual record date to determine who votes. Under the NYSE Rules, any change of record date requires ten days' notice. (NYSE Listed Company Manual Rule § 401.02.) The NYSE also requires that it be given notice ten days before the record date is set. There are no similar requirements under the NASDAQ rules, but in practice, companies listed on the NASDAQ will still follow the NYSE rules.

---

[5]   *Id.*

Broker Request Forms. These forms request the names and addresses of shareholders from brokers. They must be sent within twenty business days before the record date. (Rule 14a–13(a)(3).)

Proxy Materials. Proxy materials must be filed with the SEC in preliminary form ten days prior to the mailing of the definitive proxy. Rule 14a–6. The SEC does not specify how far in advance the proxy must be mailed, but if the e-proxy option is used- that is, the proxy materials are only available on the internet—shareholders must be given notice of the availability of the proxy statement at least forty calendar days before the meeting. In contrast to a tender offer, which requires the preparation of numerous documents, a proxy solicitation involves only the preparation of a proxy statement which is mailed to shareholders after review and clearance by the SEC.

A Sample Timeline for a special meeting to approve a merger which incorporates these rules could look like this:[6]

---

[6]   PLC Sample Proxy Timeline.

Public Merger Timeline

This timeline highlights the typical stages of a public merger. Like any acquisition, the timing varies from deal to deal and external factors can affect the timeline, such as regulatory approvals (for example, HSR, length of SEC review, buyer financing and third party consents). This timeline reflects two scenarios: one where the SEC reviews the proxy statement/prospectus (in blue); the other where the SEC clears the proxy statement/prospectus without a review (in green). This timeline assumes that the buyer does not require any financing and that the buyer's stockholders do not have to approve the merger. For an overview of public mergers, see Practice Note: Public Mergers: Overview.

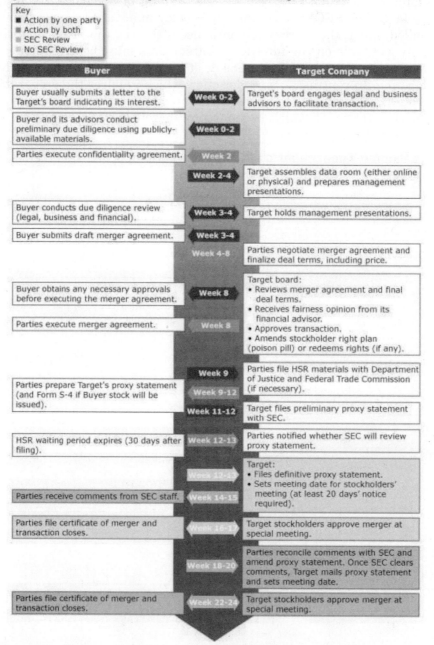

Key
- ■ Action by one party
- ■ Action by both
- ▦ SEC Review
- ▦ No SEC Review

Buyer		Target Company
Buyer usually submits a letter to the Target's board indicating its interest.	Week 0-2	Target's board engages legal and business advisors to facilitate transaction.
Buyer and its advisors conduct preliminary due diligence using publicly-available materials.	Week 0-2	
Parties execute confidentiality agreement.	Week 2	
	Week 2-4	Target assembles data room (either online or physical) and prepares management presentations.
Buyer conducts due diligence review (legal, business and financial).	Week 3-4	Target holds management presentations.
Buyer submits draft merger agreement.	Week 3-4	
	Week 4-8	Parties negotiate merger agreement and finalize deal terms, including price.
Buyer obtains any necessary approvals before executing the merger agreement.	Week 8	Target board: • Reviews merger agreement and final deal terms. • Receives fairness opinion from its financial advisor. • Approves transaction. • Amends stockholder right plan (poison pill) or redeems rights (if any).
Parties execute merger agreement.	Week 8	
	Week 9	Parties file HSR materials with Department of Justice and Federal Trade Commission (if necessary).
Parties prepare Target's proxy statement (and Form S-4 if Buyer stock will be issued).	Week 9-12	
	Week 11-12	Target files preliminary proxy statement with SEC.
HSR waiting period expires (30 days after filing).	Week 12-13	Parties notified whether SEC will review proxy statement.
	Week 12-13	Target: • Files definitive proxy statement. • Sets meeting date for stockholders' meeting (at least 20 days' notice required).
Parties receive comments from SEC staff.	Week 14-15	
Parties file certificate of merger and transaction closes.	Week 16-17	Target stockholders approve merger at special meeting.
	Week 18-20	Parties reconcile comments with SEC and amend proxy statement. Once SEC clears comments, Target mails proxy statement and sets meeting date.
Parties file certificate of merger and transaction closes.	Week 22-24	Target stockholders approve merger at special meeting.

QUESTIONS

1.   What is the timing difference between a proxy solicitation and a tender offer?

2.   James Whitehouse, an activist investor, recently appeared on television. During his appearance, Mr. Whitehouse encouraged all his fellow shareholders to vote against the incumbent board of Apex Tech at the upcoming shareholder meeting. Has Mr. Whitehouse engaged in a "solicitation"?

3.   What is the difference between a "postponement," an "adjournment," and a "recess"? How do those differences matter?

4.   What are the triggers for application of the proxy rules? How can someone avoid application of such rules and still speak to a select number of shareholders?

PROBLEMS

1.   Alpha hedge fund is planning to nominate three directors to the board of Beta Corp. Alpha wants to meet with shareholders of Beta to discuss this nomination and whether or not these shareholders will support Alpha. Would you recommend that Alpha proceed with these meetings? Are there any limitations you might suggest to avoid triggering the proxy rules?

2.   Alpha Corp. wants to acquire Beta Corp. In the merger, Alpha Corp. wants to pay the shareholders of Beta, except for Beta executives, $10 per share. The executives of Beta will receive stock in Alpha valued at $9.50 per share. Alpha is concerned that a competing bidder may emerge and wants to complete the acquisition as soon as possible. Would you recommend a tender offer or merger structure here? Give reasons for your answer.

CHAPTER VII

REGULATION OF MERGERS AND ACQUISITIONS UNDER FEDERAL LAW—REGISTERING STOCK

∎ ∎ ∎

A. SECTION 5 REGISTRATION

While some M&A transactions use cash as the acquisition consideration, other transactions use securities. Where securities are the transaction consideration, the transaction is subject to Section 5 of the Securities Act of 1933. Section 5 prohibits the offer or sale of a security unless the security is registered with the SEC, the transaction is exempt from registration, or the security being offered is exempt from registration. Prior to 1972, the SEC took the position that no "sale," occurred when securities were issued in connection with a merger or other business combination in which a shareholder vote was held. In 1972, the SEC adopted Rule 145 under the Securities Act, which rejected this position. Going forward, an issuer was required to register the securities issued in connection with a merger or business combination absent an applicable exemption.

Registration requires the preparation and filing with the SEC of a registration statement for the securities. The contents of the statement is specified by Form S–4, the form required for registering securities issued by a domestic issuer in connection with a merger, consolidation, or exchange offer. An exchange offer is a tender offer in which the consideration is stock, not cash. Shareholders receive one document—a proxy statement/prospectus—which includes the required disclosure for both the proxy solicitation and the securities issuance. The proxy statement/prospectus, filed under cover of Form S–4, includes a box to be checked to note that proxy disclosure is included.

Preparation of the registration statement can be time consuming. Moreover, the SEC is more likely to review and comment on registration statements than it is to review and comment on proxy statements. Transactions requiring a registration statement thus typically take a longer time to complete. Depending on the extent of SEC review, the time period may be one or two months. The Form S–4 must be filed with and declared effective by the SEC before it can be mailed to shareholders. All of this means that using stock as consideration in a merger transaction can be time consuming.

In 2000, in order to put exchange offers (where the securities for which the offer was being made were to be paid for with other securities) on a level footing with cash tender offers, the SEC adopted a rule providing that exchange offers can commence immediately upon filing the tender offer documentation. However, the transaction cannot close until the registration statement for the securities is declared effective.[1]

B. EXEMPT ISSUANCES

As noted above, the securities registration process in an acquisition requires that a Form S–4 be prepared and distributed to shareholders. Because doing so is a substantial undertaking, in an acquisition of a non-public company where securities consideration is being offered, M&A attorneys will typically attempt to find an exemption from registration. The following sections discuss the parameters of the most commonly applicable exemptions used in merger and acquisition transactions.

1. REGULATION D AND RULE 506

Regulation D and Rule 506 provide for an exemption under § 4(2) of the Securities Act for issuances not involving a public offering (e.g., where the offered securities are not publicly traded). Because Rule 506 is so flexible, it is used in almost all M&A transactions where an exemption for registration of securities to be issued in the transaction is sought. Rule 506 requires that sales of the securities only be made to "accredited investors," defined below, and no more than thirty-five "sophisticated" non-accredited investors, who the law deems to be capable of evaluating the merits of the securities. The rationale for this exemption is that the investors are deemed not to need the protections of registration because of their financial condition, investment sophistication, or both.

The following law firm memorandum sets forth the parameters of Regulation D and its role in an M&A transaction.

---

[1] *See generally* https://www.sec.gov/rules/final/33-7760.htm, describing the change and its rationale.

PRIVATE PLACEMENT OF PUBLICLY TRADED EQUITY SECURITIES AS CONSIDERATION IN AN M&A TRANSACTION AFTER THE JOBS ACT

Robert Little and James Moloney
GIBSON DUNN SECURITIES REGULATION AND
CORPORATE GOVERNANCE MONITOR
April 18, 2012

An issuer with equity securities that are publicly traded often seeks to use its equity securities as consideration in an acquisition of another business. If the target business is privately held, the acquirer may seek to privately place the equity securities with the owners of the target rather than registering the securities due to the lead-time required for the registration process or for other reasons. The following discussion addresses many of the securities law issues that public companies should consider when using privately placed equity as acquisition currency, including a discussion of upcoming changes in the private placement landscape precipitated by the Jumpstart Our Business Startups Act ("JOBS Act"), signed into law by President Obama on April 5, 2012.

Regulation D Compliance and "General Solicitation" Prohibition

Section 4(2) of the Securities Act of 1933 exempts "transactions by an issuer not involving any public offering" from the registration and prospectus delivery requirements of Section 5 of the Securities Act. Regulation D under the Securities Act (and particularly Rule 506 thereunder) provides a commonly relied upon safe harbor for private placement transactions, including for issuances of equity securities as consideration in business combinations. Rule 506 of Regulation D permits an issuer to sell an unlimited amount of its securities in a private placement to an unlimited number of "accredited investors" (as defined in Rule 501) and up to 35 non-accredited investors. Under Rule 506, each investor that is not an accredited investor, either alone or with his purchaser representative(s), must have such knowledge and experience in financial and business matters that he is capable of evaluating the merits and risks of the prospective investment. As a result, to confirm satisfaction of the investor suitability standards of Regulation D, the acquirer must determine whether the sellers are accredited investors or meet the financial and business sophistication requirements. The acquirer can make such determination by contacting each seller and requesting that each seller complete and return an investment questionnaire. If any seller is not an accredited investor, the acquirer can arrange for the appointment of a purchaser representative for such seller. If there are more than 35 non-accredited investors, or an unsophisticated non-accredited seller will not consent to the appointment of a purchaser representative, the acquirer must be prepared to pay the consideration to such seller(s) in cash or register the entire issuance of securities.

In its current form, Rule 506 also requires that offers and sales must satisfy all of the general terms and conditions of Rules 501 through 503 of Regulation D. Under Rule 502(c), one of the conditions to the availability of Regulation D is that the securities not be offered or sold by any form of "general solicitation." The SEC has stated that the determination of the presence or absence of a general solicitation is dependent on the facts and circumstances of each particular case. The SEC has taken positions in published materials that mailing written offers to acquire securities would not be deemed to constitute a general solicitation for purposes of Rule 502(c) if the issuer or its agent: (a) has a pre-existing relationship with the persons to whom the offer is directed of a nature that would enable the issuer to be aware of the financial circumstances or sophistication of such persons; and (b) believes that such persons have such knowledge and experience in financial and business matters that such persons are capable of evaluating the merits and risks of the proposed investment. In circumstances where the number of sellers is large and the acquirer has not been exposed to all of them during the negotiation process for the acquisition, the seller will not have a pre-existing relationship with each seller. Without this pre-existing relationship, acquirers historically have risked failing to comply with Rule 502(c)'s prohibition on general solicitation if the acquirer directly contacted each seller to determine such seller's investor suitability.

While this prohibition against general solicitation in Rule 502(c) historically has limited the ability of companies to issue privately placed equity securities to potential investors, including sellers in M&A transactions, forthcoming changes to Regulation D required by the JOBS Act will relax the restrictions on general solicitations in private placements under Rule 506. Specifically, Title II of the JOBS Act directs the SEC to revise Rule 506 to remove the prohibition against general solicitation or general advertising in offers and sales of securities made pursuant to Rule 506, provided that all purchasers of the securities are accredited investors. The JOBS Act also mandates that the SEC's rule revisions require issuers to take "reasonable steps" to verify that investors are accredited investors, using methods as determined by the SEC. The revisions to Regulation D required by the JOBS Act must be completed within 90 days following enactment of the JOBS Act, or July 4, 2012.

After the revisions to Regulation D are implemented and the general solicitation prohibition is eliminated for private placements conducted in reliance on Rule 506 in which all investors are accredited, issuers will be less restricted in the methods they may use in reaching out to potential investors, and concerns over whether a particular communication constitutes a "general solicitation" or that inadvertent general solicitation will make the Rule 506 safe harbor unavailable will be eliminated. In M&A transactions where the acquirer utilizes Rule 506, the acquirer will be free to contact directly all potential sellers in order to determine investor suitability, regardless of whether there is any pre-existing relationship. Importantly, however, even though Rule 506 provides that up to 35 non-accredited investors may invest if the non-accredited investors or their purchaser representative meet certain sophistication criteria, the JOBS Act's relief from the restrictions on general solicitation applies only if the purchasers of the securities are all accredited investors. Therefore, if the acquirer engages in a general solicitation of the potential sellers and finds that some of the equity owners of the target are not accredited investors, the acquirer will only be able to rely on the Rule 506 safe harbor if such owners do not receive equity consideration in the private placement (i.e., the acquirer must be prepared to pay the consideration in cash to sellers that are not accredited investors).

Other Regulation D Issues Applicable in M&A Transactions

The acquirer should ensure that the Regulation D offering of securities to the sellers is not integrated with any other securities offerings of the acquirer that would cause Regulation D not to be available for the private placement of securities to the sellers. In addition, the acquirer must file with the SEC a notice of sales on Form D no later than 15 calendar days after the first sale of the securities. Finally, the acquirer should be aware that its transfer agent will likely require an opinion of counsel with respect to the validity of the private placement as a condition to functioning as exchange agent or transfer agent with respect to the securities issued to the sellers.

Resales of Privately Placed Securities

Because the issuance of securities in the private placement is not registered under the Securities Act, such securities are "restricted securities" under Rule 144 of the Securities Act and are subject to holding period requirements and other resale restrictions. If the sellers demand liquidity in the securities prior to expiration of the applicable holding period, the acquirer can agree to file and cause to be declared effective within a certain time period a resale registration statement. The parties may negotiate penalty interest provisions that will apply if the acquirer does not meet filing and effectiveness deadlines for the resale registration statement.[2] [*Editor: See subsection C below for a discussion of Rule 144.*]

---

[2]   Available at http://www.securitiesregulationmonitor.com/Lists/Posts/Post.aspx?ID=165.

In a subsequent memorandum, the same authors further discuss Rule 506 after the adoption of the JOBS Act, and the implications for M&A transactions.

PRIVATE PLACEMENT OF PUBLICLY TRADED EQUITY SECURITIES AS CONSIDERATION IN AN M&A TRANSACTION AFTER THE JOBS ACT

Robert Little and James Moloney
GIBSON DUNN SECURITIES REGULATION AND
CORPORATE GOVERNANCE MONITOR
October 3, 2013

[I]n July 2013, the SEC adopted final rules (effective September 23, 2013) to eliminate the absolute prohibition against general solicitation in securities offerings conducted pursuant to Rule 506, as required by Section 201(a) of the JOBS Act. The following discussion updates our earlier post to address the legal and practical effects of these new rules for M&A transactions that include a private placement component. . . .

Importantly, the traditional Rule 506 safe harbor . . . [described in the memo quoted above] has been preserved intact as Rule 506(b), and issuers may continue to comply with its conditions, the most significant of which is the complete prohibition on the use of any form of general solicitation in the offering or sale of securities. As previously noted, when acquirers reach out to potential sellers to determine their sophistication they may risk violating the prohibition against general solicitation, unless the issuer or its agent has a pre-existing substantive relationship with the offerees.

The newly adopted rules create a new subsection (c) of Rule 506, which permits Rule 506 offerings that employ general solicitation methods if: (i) each purchaser in the offering is an accredited investor, or the issuer reasonably believes that each purchaser is an accredited investor at the time of the sale of the securities, and (ii) the issuer takes reasonable steps to verify that each purchaser is an accredited investor. This represents a seismic shift in the nature of allowable advertising and outreach in private offerings—including transactions in which unregistered equity securities may be offered as consideration in an acquisition, but the usefulness of the new Rule 506(c) will be constrained by the requirement that each offeree receiving unregistered equity securities must in fact be an accredited investor. Therefore, while an issuer-acquirer may now choose to engage freely in any "solicitation" or other efforts directed toward potential sellers to determine investor suitability, once the issuer has begun such a general solicitation, it may not then rely on Rule 506(c) to issue the equity securities to sellers that are not verified accredited investors. Furthermore, once a general solicitation has commenced, the issuer will no longer have the flexibility to go back and rely on Rule 506(b) or the traditional Securities Act Section 4(a)(2) private placement exemption as an alternative to the Regulation D safe harbor (given that the changes to Rule 506 specifically do not apply to Section 4(a)(2)). As a practical matter, if an acquirer chooses to engage in a general solicitation and cannot verify that each seller is accredited, then the acquirer should be prepared to pay cash consideration to any non-accredited investors. If so desired, the acquirer could also attempt to register the entire issuance of equity securities with the SEC, but of course the SEC may view the prior general solicitation as an "offer" in violation of the gun-jumping provisions of Section 5 of the Securities Act.

If the acquirer suspects that some of the sellers may not be accredited, but it still wants to use its privately-placed equity securities as acquisition currency, then it will need to follow the traditional model for engaging in such private placements—under Rule 506(b)—and avoid any type of general solicitation. This means that the issuer will need to have a pre-existing substantive relationship with each seller and the offering can include no more than 35 non-accredited investors. A purchaser representative may be used in order to establish the required pre-existing relationship or to validate the sophistication of any non-accredited sellers.[3]

The net effect of these rules is to give an issuer substantial leeway to issue securities to a small group of sellers in connection with an M&A transaction. Counsel should take care to limit the offering to accredited investors wherever possible in order to take advantage of the new general solicitation exemptions under the JOBS Act.

2. 3(a)(10) FAIRNESS HEARING PROCESS

One less common exemption sometimes used is the § 3(a)(10) fairness hearing. Section 3(a)(10) is a transaction exemption that allows securities to be issued exempt from the registration process if the issuance is approved by a court or an authorized governmental entity after a hearing. The following posting to the California Department of Corporations website describes the process in California.

California Corporations Code section 25142 allows companies interested in issuing securities in a merger or conducting an exchange of outstanding securities to seek a "fairness" hearing as part of its application for qualification of the offer and sale of securities. By this process, applicants may seek an exemption

---

[3] Available at http://www.securitiesregulationmonitor.com/Lists/Posts/Post.aspx?List=f35 51fe8–411e–4ea4–830c-d680a8c0da43&ID=216&Web=97364e78–c7b4–4464–a28c-fd4eea1956ac.

from federal registration as provided by Section 3(a)(10) of the Securities Act of 1933 through a state-law hearing on the fairness of the terms and conditions of the proposed issuance or exchange of securities.

California is one of only six states in the country that offer this kind of economical and equity-based review and approval process for the offer and sale of securities pursuant to a securities law. The fairness hearing process is used most often by companies for mergers and acquisition transactions. Fairness hearings provide a fast and cost-efficient alternative to federal registration, saving companies hundreds of thousands of dollars in federal registration costs. Many high-profile California companies have taken advantage of the fairness hearing process, and the Department of Business Oversight processes a significant volume of fairness hearings on an expedited basis.

Members of the private securities bar report that it can cost a substantial amount of money ($250,000 or more), as well as time (6 months or more), for a company to register a securities offering pursuant to federal securities laws. The fairness hearing process of the Department of Business Oversight allows a company to rely on an exemption from the federal registration requirements, thereby creating a significant savings in both cost and time for the business.[4]

As the California Secretary of State points out, the advantage of a fairness hearing is that the need to prepare and clear a registration statement for shareholders is obviated. Historically, an issuer would request a no-action letter from the SEC with respect to each § 3(a)(10) fairness hearing. The letter would seek the SEC's opinion on whether the fairness hearing would qualify for the exemption (this is the "no-action" in the no-action letter—that the SEC will not recommend enforcement action for failure to register the securities in reliance on the availability of the exemption).

The following is excerpted from a 1999 memo issued by the SEC discussing when the exemption is available. The memorandum noted that going forward, no-action guidance should be needed far less often since many sources of uncertainty had been eliminated.

Section 3(a)(10) of the Securities Act is an exemption from Securities Act registration for offers and sales of securities in specified exchange transactions. Before the issuer can rely on the exemption, the following conditions must be met.

---

[4]   CORPORATIONS FAIRNESS HEARINGS, CA. DEP'T BUS. OVERSIGHT, http://www.dbo.ca.gov/ ENF/FairnessHearings/ (last visited November 25, 2015).

- The securities must be issued in exchange for securities, claims, or property interests; they can not be offered for cash.

- A court or authorized governmental entity must approve the fairness of the terms and conditions of the exchange.

- The reviewing court or authorized governmental entity must:

  - find, before approving the transaction, that the terms and conditions of the exchange are fair to those to whom securities will be issued; and

  - be advised before the hearing that the issuer will rely on the Section 3(a)(10) exemption based on the court's or authorized governmental entity's approval of the transaction.

- The court or authorized governmental entity must hold a hearing before approving the fairness of the terms and conditions of the transaction.

- A governmental entity must be expressly authorized by law to hold the hearing, although it is not necessary that the law require the hearing.

- The fairness hearing must be open to everyone to whom securities would be issued in the proposed exchange.

- Adequate notice must be given to all those persons.

- There cannot be any improper impediments to the appearance by those persons at the hearing.

  The Section 3(a)(10) exemption is available without any action by the Division or the Commission. Issuers that are unsure of whether the exemption is available for a specific contemplated transaction may, however, seek the Division's views by requesting a "no-action" position from the Division.[5]

"Fairness" hearings raise interesting valuation issues relating to the substantive fairness of the transaction. By contrast, federal securities law does not make such "substantive" determinations of fairness and value.

---

[5]   SEC Division of Corporation Finance: *Revised Staff Legal Bulletin No. 3 (CF)*, (October 20, 1999), available at http://www.sec.gov/interps/legal/cfslb3r.htm. *See* SEC Division of Corporate Finance: No-Action, Interpretive & Exemptive Letters, http://www.sec.gov/divisions/corpfin/cf-noaction.shtml#3a10 for links to requests for no-action relief under 3(a)(10) that were granted.

The following describes the hearing on Facebook's $1 billion acquisition of Instagram using stock consideration issued pursuant to a fairness hearing before the California Department of Corporations:

> [W]e're sitting in what's called a Fairness Hearing. Trust me, it's very dry stuff . . . It's also something of a legal M&A fast track, a way of issuing Instagram its Facebook shares faster, while navigating around a lengthier, more expensive process that involves dealing with federal securities regulators. . . . [As expected,] the DoC [ruled] in favor of the deal, finding the acquisition "fair and equitable" for both parties. . . .

> More entertaining, however, is sitting back and watching the proceedings. A cadre of Facebook lawyers flank one side of the room, while Instagram's representative counsel sits on the other side of the table. . . . Instagram CEO Kevin Systrom sticks out above all, the lanky, 28-year-old soon-to-be multimillionaire standing tall above everyone else in the room by a good four inches.

> Virtually everyone, including Systrom, is wearing a tie, a stark contrast to the usual Silicon Valley setting, where hoodie- and T-shirt-clad engineers prevail over the Wall Street types in monkey suits.

> The two camps are here to discuss the nitty gritty details of the transaction. . . . DoC hearing officer Rafael Lirag asks Systrom how Instagram generates revenue: "That's a great question—as of right now we do not."

> Systrom [seems to be not fazed by the fact that Facebook's share price was then at 50% of its IPO price.]. . . . "I still believe firmly in the long-term value of Facebook."[6]

The Facebook/Instagram transaction attracted so much publicity that that the California regulator making the fairness determination issued a press release on the matter:

> (August 29, 2012)—The Department of Corporations determined Wednesday that the terms and conditions of Facebook Inc.'s acquisition of Instagram Inc. are fair to the Instagram shareholders and the Department will issue a permit that authorizes Facebook to issue stock for that acquisition. This determination constitutes the final regulatory approval required

---

[6] Mike Isaac, *As Face-tagram Deal Wraps Up, a Morning With Kevin Systrom and Facebook's Legal Team*, ALL THINGS DIGITAL, August 29, 2012, available at http://allthingsd.com/20120829/as-face-tagram-deal-wraps-up-a-morning-with-kevin-systrom-and-facebooks-legal-team/.

for the acquisition. Formal approval by Instagram's shareholders must still occur.

"Our role as the State's securities regulator is primarily to determine whether the transaction is fair to Instagram's 19 shareholders and the proposed exchange of securities meets that test," said Corporations Commissioner Jan Lynn Owen.

The finding came at the conclusion of a "Fairness Hearing" conducted under Section 25142 of the California Corporations Code.

The Fairness Hearing was conducted by a hearing officer and Department counsel as designated by Commissioner Owen. All 19 of Instagram shareholders were contacted and invited to participate in person or via telephone. Witnesses from both Facebook and Instagram presented testimony related to the fairness of the transaction.[7]

C. RESALES

One advantage of the § 3(a)(10) exemption is that it allows target shareholders to immediately resell the shares so long as they are not affiliates of any party to the transaction prior to the transaction, or the issuer after the transaction.[8]

By comparison, securities issued under Regulation D and the Rule 506 exemption are subject to resale restrictions as set forth in Rules 144 and 145. The ability to resell shares is of considerable value to target shareholders since it is the means by which they finally "cash out" and monetize their shares. In 2008, the rules were changed so that these securities would be more liquid and easier to resell.

The memorandum excerpted below discusses resale of securities issued in an M&A transaction and when a person can or cannot freely sell shares received in an M&A transaction.

THE CURIOUS CASE OF HOW TO RESELL SECURITIES OBTAINED IN AN M&A TRANSACTION— RULES 144 AND 145

Latham and Watkins Capital Markets Group
August 11, 2010

Can you freely resell stock acquired in a stock-for-stock merger? Here's how you go about sorting out the answer.

---

[7] California Department of Corporations Grants Permit to Facebook for Acquisition of Instagram, Aug. 29, 2012, available at http://www.dbo.ca.gov/Archives/Press/news/2012/Facebook_08–29–12.pdf.

[8] *See* Bulletin, *supra* note 5.

Do we need to worry whether the shareholder is an affiliate of the target? [*Editor: An affiliate for these purposes is a person in a relationship of control with the issuer; presumptively, executive officers, directors and 10% shareholders are affiliates.*]

Not any more, unless the transaction involves a "shell company" (other than a business combination related shell company), under the revisions to Rule 145 which took effect in February 2008. The only resale restrictions you need to worry about now are contained in Rule 144. For these purposes, it does not matter whether the transaction is registered (on Form S–4 or F–4) or unregistered (i.e., is a private exchange).

. . . But what about Rule 144?

To answer that question, you need to know whether the transaction is registered or unregistered, and in addition, whether the shareholder in question is or is not an affiliate of the issuer (i.e., an affiliate of the acquiring company). We will take each scenario in turn.

Scenario 1—*a Public Merger; Target Shareholder is Not an Affiliate*

This is the simplest scenario. The shareholder can freely resell his or her securities and Rule 144 does not apply because the securities were not issued in a private offering and therefore are not "restricted securities" within the meaning of Rule 144.

Scenario 2—*Private Merger; Target Shareholder is Not an Affiliate*

Rule 144 applies because the target shareholder takes restricted securities in the transaction. Under Rule 144, this means that the target shareholder will need to comply with the following holding period requirements:

- Six months if the issuer is an SEC reporting company and current in its filings; or

- One year if the issuer either is not an SEC reporting company or is not current in its SEC filings.

After one year, there are no restrictions on further resale.

Scenario 3—*Private Merger; Target Shareholder is an Affiliate*

Rule 144 applies again. This means that the target shareholder will need to comply with the following requirements:

- Holding period: The same provisions apply as outlined under Scenario 2 above.

- Volume limitations: In each three-month period, the total amount of securities of the class sold (restricted and unrestricted) cannot exceed the greater of (1) 1 percent of the total outstanding class of securities; or (2) the average

weekly trading volume on U.S. national securities exchanges
during the prior four weeks; or (3) if the securities sold are
debt securities, 10% of the principal amount of the tranche
attributable to the securities sold.

- Manner of sale: If the securities to be sold are equity
  securities, they must be resold in (1) unsolicited brokers'
  transactions; (2) transactions with a market maker; or
  (3) riskless principal transactions

- Notice of sale: If more than 5,000 shares or $50,000 worth of
  securities are resold in any three-month period, the seller
  must file a notice on Form 144 with the SEC.

Scenario 4—*Public Merger; Target Shareholder is an Affiliate*

This is apt to strike you as the most counterintuitive of the scenarios.
You would initially think that because the transaction is registered, the
affiliate should be freely able to resell the securities it acquires. You could
even continue to hold that view after looking at Rule 144, which does not
appear to address the question.

However, the right answer is that Rule 144 applies because securities
acquired by an affiliate in a registered transaction are considered control
securities subject to restrictions on resales even though they are not
restricted securities. Don't look for the definition of control securities in
Rule 144—it is not there.

In the case of control securities, there is no holding period.
Otherwise, all of the remaining requirements of Rule 144 apply as if the
affiliate were reselling restricted securities (volume limitations; manner
of sale requirements; notice of sale requirements).[9]

If the recipients of these securities cannot freely sell their shares
immediately after completion of the transaction, parties fairly often enter
into a "registration rights" agreement. This agreement will allow the
recipients of the securities to demand in certain circumstances that the
issuer register these securities. Often, if the issuer is a publicly traded
company which is eligible to file a short-form registration statement, then
the registration rights will be exercised immediately thereafter, again in
order to meet the needs of the sellers to have liquidity for their shares.

----

[9]   Available at http://www.wowlw.com/ma-issues/the-curious-case-of-how-to-resell-securities
-obtained-in-an-ma-transaction-rules-144-and-145/.

D.   THE CHOICE BETWEEN FORM S-4 AND FORM S-3

The requirements of registration and the resale restrictions have generally led practitioners to structure stock acquisitions in one of two ways:

First, in transactions where both the acquirer and the target are public, the acquirer will register its securities in connection with the completion of the transaction. To do this, the acquirer will typically file a Form S-4 and include the relevant information in the proxy statement/prospectus which is distributed to target shareholders. Because of the time delays inherent in issuing shares and SEC review of the registration statement, an acquisition of a public target with acquirer stock will almost always be structured as a merger rather than a tender offer. Only if the transaction is hostile will the tender offer structure will be used, in which case the information in the Form S-4 will be included in the offer to purchase/prospectus distributed to target shareholders.

Second, in transactions where the acquirer is public and the target is private, the acquirer will often seek to avoid having to file a Form S-4 and thereby delaying completion of the acquisition. The SEC has taken the position that Form S-4 is not suitable for private targets that, as is often the case, have a small number of shareholders, and that the target shareholders should be issued shares under Rule 506. The target shareholders will then own restricted stock which they cannot immediately sell. To solve this problem, the parties will negotiate a registration rights agreement which will require the acquirer to register the shares, typically immediately after completion of the transaction. In most cases, the acquirer will be able to register the shares using a relatively less cumbersome form, Form S-3. Alternatively, as discussed above, for California corporations, in lieu of using Rule 506, the acquirer can use the § 3(a)(10) fairness hearing procedure to obviate the need for registration.

In either of these cases, the acquirer is a publicly traded company. The situation is very different in the event the acquirer is a private company. Because a private company has yet to register its shares, the value of those shares remains uncertain, or at least does not have the benefit of a market price. In addition, where the acquirer is private, the acquirer has not yet had the opportunity to register any of its shares with the SEC. The registration process for an initial public offering of stock is much more onerous than registration of stock for a seasoned issuer. Consequently, private company acquirers very rarely use their own stock as consideration in an acquisition.

E. COMMUNICATION FILING REQUIREMENTS

Under the federal securities laws, communications made in connection with a business combination where either the target securities are registered under the Exchange Act or the acquirer is issuing securities are required to be filed with the SEC on or before the date of "first use." These rules also apply to any tender offer or proxy solicitation. The following SEC release describes these rules and the underlying rationale.

FINAL RULE: REGULATION OF TAKEOVERS AND SECURITY HOLDER COMMUNICATIONS

SEC Release No. 33–7760; 34–42055; IC–24107; File No. S7–28–98, RIN 3235–AG84
Effective January 24, 2000

1. Increased Communications Permitted Before Filing Disclosure Document

Today, merger and acquisition transactions are occurring at a faster pace, due in part to the rapid development of new technologies and advancements in communications. As a result of economic and regulatory pressures, many companies are releasing more information to the market before a registration, proxy or tender offer statement is filed publicly with us. In many cases, parties are releasing information on proposed transactions including pro forma financial information for the combined entity, estimated cost savings and synergies.... [P]arties to business combination transactions provide several reasons for the need to disclose information early, including the duty under Rule 10b–5 to disclose material information in a manner that is not misleading. We also recognize that parties may be subject to other regulatory requirements to disclose information to the markets early.

We are adopting, as proposed, non-exclusive exemptions under the Securities Act, proxy rules and tender offer rules that permit communications for an unrestricted length of time without a cooling-off period between the end of communications and filing. Written communications made in reliance on the exemptions must be filed.

One major benefit of permitting earlier communications is that more information will be available generally to all security holders, not simply to a limited audience of analysts and financially sophisticated market participants. Because the new rules do not require oral communications to be reduced to writing and filed, some selective disclosure may continue to occur. Nevertheless, the rules adopted today are designed to reduce selective disclosure by permitting widespread dissemination of information through a variety of media calculated to inform all security holders about the terms, benefits and risks of a planned extraordinary transaction. We believe that parties to business combination transactions generally wish to inform the marketplace at large about their deals, and will use the new rules to accomplish this end.

2. Eligibility

Our proposals did not make distinctions based on size and seasoned status. [*Editor: An issuer who meets certain minimum requirements as to its size and other matters—such issuers are allowed to file abbreviated disclosure documents in some contexts.*] Due to the extraordinary nature of business combination transactions, security holders and the markets need full and timely information regarding those transactions regardless of the size or seasoned status of the companies involved. We recognized the inherent difficulties in selecting the appropriate focus for purposes of applying an eligibility test (i.e., should you look at the status of the acquiror, the target or the combined entity?). All commenters who addressed the issue agreed with our view. Therefore, the exemptions are adopted as proposed, without any eligibility requirements.

3. Written Communications with Legend Filed on Date of First Use

We are adopting, as proposed, a condition to the communications exemptions that all written communications in connection with or relating to a business combination transaction be filed on or before the date of first use. In addition, all written communications must include a prominent legend advising investors to read the registration, proxy or tender offer statement, as applicable. We believe that a prompt filing requirement is necessary to protect security holders and assure that these communications are available to all investors on a timely basis. In most cases, this information will need to be filed electronically via the EDGAR System, and thus will be rapidly disseminated to the marketplace.

The filing requirement applies to written communications that are made public or are otherwise provided to persons that are not a party to the transaction. As a general matter, this would include, for example, scripts used by parties to the transaction to communicate information to the public and other written material (e.g., slides) relating to the transaction that is shown to investors. In contrast, internal written communications provided solely to parties to the transaction, legal counsel, financial advisors, and similar persons authorized to act on behalf of the parties to the transaction would not need to be filed. Also business information that is factual in nature and relates solely to ordinary business matters, and not the pending transaction, would not need to be filed. We expect that filing persons will apply traditional legal principles in determining whether a particular written communication is made in connection with or relates to a proposed business combination transaction.[10]

QUESTIONS

1.   What is the timing effect on an acquisition of including stock consideration (as opposed to paying all cash)? How does issuance of securities pursuant to the registration process (as opposed to the Rule 506 exemption) change this timing?

2.   When might the Rule 506 exemption be used?

3.   What is the effect of having unaccredited investors as part of the target's shareholders for purposes of the new solicitation rules?

4.   If you have received stock in a merger pursuant to a § 3(a)(10) fairness hearing exemption, can you sell it? Why or why not?

PROBLEMS

1.   Alpha, a publicly listed corporation incorporated in Delaware, wants to acquire Beta, a private corporation incorporated in California using a reverse subsidiary merger structure. Alpha wishes to pay stock consideration. Please advise Alpha on whether or not it should register the stock being issued and if not, what exemption it should rely upon. What are the pros and cons of each alternative?

2.   How does your answer to question 1 change if Beta is a Delaware corporation?

3.   How does your answer to question 1 change if Beta is a Delaware corporation and has 50 unaccredited shareholders?

4.   Alpha, a publicly listed corporation, acquires Beta, a private corporation pursuant to a reverse subsidiary merger. In the acquisition, Alpha issued stock consideration to Beta shareholders utilizing the Rule 506 exemption. After the merger there is one former Beta shareholder who now owns thirty percent of Alpha, Because of this ownership position the shareholder is considered to be an "affiliate" of Alpha under the federal securities laws. There are no other former Beta shareholders who are affiliates of Alpha. What are the post-merger restrictions, if any, on the Alpha shares now held by the former Beta shares?

---

[10]   Available at http://www.sec.gov/rules/final/33–7760.htm.

CHAPTER VIII

OTHER REGULATORY REQUIREMENTS

■ ■ ■

Most transactions involve a delay between signing or announcement of the transaction and the completion of the deal, also known as the closing. Especially for large deals, these delays can be lengthy. In part, the delays can be attributed to the mechanics of securing shareholder approval or SEC requirements to register stock to be used as consideration in the transaction. However, those requirements are not the only hurdles to getting a deal done. Several regulatory approvals are often required before a transaction is permitted to close. These approvals involve antitrust review and national security review, as well as sector-specific regulatory review. In addition to review by U.S. regulatory authorities, the globalized nature of modern commerce may also implicate international regulatory review even when the parties to the merger transaction are two U.S. corporations. Deal lawyers need to be aware of the various regulatory hurdles that specific transactions face and advise their clients accordingly.

What follows is an overview of the most common regulatory approvals needed in M&A transactions.

A. ANTITRUST CLEARANCE

Many sectors will have industry-specific regulators who must "clear" a transaction before a transaction is permitted to close. However, of all the various regulatory clearances required prior to closing, perhaps the most important is antitrust. Antitrust regulation crosses all industries and covers a broad spectrum of transaction types. Mergers, friendly tender offers, hostile tender offers, and equity investments, among others, are all potentially subject to antitrust review. Many horizontal deals between strategic competitors will have significant antitrust issues. Indeed, antitrust issues—and antitrust counsel—will often play an important role in the early stages of a transaction as both buyer and seller look towards post-signing regulatory issues. Many agreements will include antitrust closing conditions, reverse termination fees triggered upon failure to secure antitrust approval, and clauses that describe the efforts parties must make to deal with antitrust issues in the post-signing period. In Chapter XIV we discuss such clauses, including those requiring particular specified efforts, "best efforts" and even "hell-or-high-water" clauses requiring a party to do whatever the antitrust regulators require to close the transaction.

1. HART-SCOTT-RODINO PREMERGER NOTIFICATION

The most common regulatory review for an acquisition is pre-closing review required under the Hart-Scott-Rodino Antitrust Improvements Act of 1976 ("HSR"). Merger activity has always been a concern of U.S. antitrust laws. However, prior to the adoption of HSR, the only way for the government to enforce either the Sherman Act or the Clayton Act with respect to mergers was by filing a lawsuit after a transaction it considered to be anti-competitive had closed. Such lawsuits took years to prosecute, and during the ensuing time, the merged entities had time to establish themselves in the marketplace with customers, vendors, employees, etc. Even if the government were ultimately successful in its antitrust claims, the preferred remedy, a divestiture, was not easily accomplished.

The HSR Act established a premerger notification regime which requires that parties to mergers and acquisitions deals provide the FTC and the DOJ with certain information about the deals before they close. Such a transaction cannot close until the statutory waiting period of 30 days ends. Where there are no obvious antitrust issues implicated by the transaction, parties often request, and are granted, early termination of the waiting period.[1] In fiscal year 2013, 1,326 transactions were reported to the antitrust agencies. Of those, most requested early termination and most requests were granted (77% made requests, and 80.5% of the requests made were granted).[2] Of the 1,326 reportable transactions, 3.7% were subject to a "second request" for information and further investigation.

---

[1] *See generally* the FTC's webpage explaining the law and the process, at http://www.ftc. gov/tips-advice/competition-guidance/guide-antitrust-laws/mergers/premerger-notification-and-merger.

[2] FEDERAL TRADE COMMISSION, *Hart-Scott-Rodino Annual Report, Fiscal Year 2013*, 1, available at http://www.ftc.gov/system/files/documents/reports/federal-trade-commission-bureau-competition-department-justice-antitrust-division-hart-scott-rodino.s.c.18a-hart-scott-rodino-antitrust-improvements-act–1976/140521hsrreport.pdf.

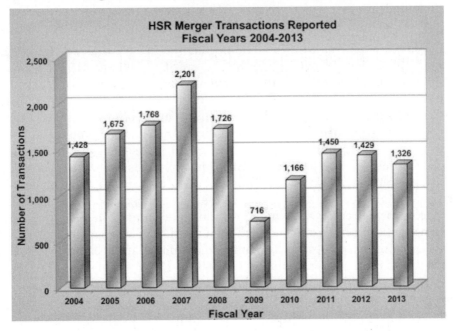

Figure 1: HSR Merger Transactions Reported.[3]

a.   Who Has to File?

The HSR Act requires a filing for any transaction (a "covered transaction") involving an acquisition of voting securities or assets, either directly or indirectly, that meets the test described in the next paragraph. The definition of covered transaction is intentionally broad. It includes mergers, tender offers, asset purchases, and other private acquisitions of stock.

Whether a covered transaction is required to make a premerger notification filing to the FTC and DOJ depends on a three-part test.[4] Part one relates to "commerce"—at least one of the parties to the transaction must be engaged in commerce or an activity affecting commerce. Part two relates to the size of the transaction. The size thresholds change annually. For 2014, the thresholds are as follows: If the transaction is valued at $75.9 million or less, then no filing is required. If the transaction is valued above $303.4 million then a filing with the FTC and DOJ is automatically triggered. If, however, the transaction is valued at more than $75.9 million and up to $303.4 million, then a filing is required only if the transaction meets the additional "size of person" test. The size of person test requires a filing if a transaction in this middle range

---

[3] *Id.* at 1.

[4] *See generally* FTC, Steps for Determining Whether an HSR Filing is Required, available at   http://www.ftc.gov/enforcement/premerger-notification-program/hsr-resources/steps-determining-whether-hsr-filing.

involves one party with annual net sales or assets of at least $151.7 million and another with at least $15.2 million in annual net sales or assets.[5]

Typically, parties to transactions that require a filing will make the filing immediately following announcement of the transaction. However, HSR does not require parties to wait until after a transaction is announced to make a filing. Parties may also make the necessary filings with the DOJ/FTC based on a letter of intent or an offer to acquire shares of the target. Because HSR requires filings from both the buyer and the target prior to closing a transaction, and because the definition of a covered transaction is so broad, HSR filings have also become a back door early warning system in the hostile deal context. A typical hostile acquirer might seek to keep its accumulation of target stock a secret until the acquirer is required to make a filing pursuant to a Schedule 13D. However, there are cases where the acquisition of voting securities by a hostile acquirer triggers the requirement to make an HSR filing *before* it triggers the requirement to make a Schedule 13D. In that case, the target gets early warning of the hostile acquirer's intentions as well as an opportunity to make its case to the DOJ/FTC as to why the hostile acquirer's proposed acquisition would be anti-competitive. The required HSR filing is one reason why hostile acquirers now rarely take "toeholds," or small entry-level ownership stakes, in potential targets.

Once a filing is made to the DOJ and the FTC, the parties making the filing are required to wait thirty days before the transaction can be closed. If the transaction is structured as a tender offer, then the statutory waiting period is only fifteen days. The waiting period is intended to provide the government with sufficient time to study the competitive effects of the transaction and the opportunity to intervene before the transaction has closed in the event the government determines the transaction may have anticompetitive effects. Once this waiting period has passed or the government has provided the parties with notice of an "early termination" of the waiting period if the parties so request (which, as noted above, most of them do), then the parties are free to close the transaction. If, during the course of the waiting period, the government believes the proposed transaction might violate the antitrust laws, the government can initiate a "second request" for information by issuing a subpoena.

After a second request has been made, parties are not permitted to close the transaction until they come into "substantial compliance" with

---

[5]   *See* FTC, *To File Or Not To File: When You Must File a PreMerger Notification Report Form* (2008), https://www.ftc.gov/sites/default/files/attachments/premerger-introductory-guides/guide2.pdf (on size of person test); see also Revised Jurisdictional Thresholds for Section 7A of the Clayton Act, 79 Fed. Reg. No. 15, http://www.ftc.gov/system/files/attachments/current-2014-thresholds/140123clayton7afrn.pdf (on 2014 filing thresholds).

the government's subpoena. The subpoena issued for a second request can require that the parties to an acquisition turn over substantial numbers of documents, requiring a team of lawyers to assemble a response and costing millions of dollars. Based on the lengthy investigative process of the second request, the government will decide whether it will initiate litigation to block the proposed transaction or will permit it to close without a challenge.

At this juncture, three points should be emphasized. First, transactions that require an HSR filing are not permitted to close until after the statutory waiting period ends. The waiting period can extend for months if a second request is made. Second, the HSR Act itself only allows the government to launch an investigation into the transaction. If the government wants to halt an acquisition, it will have to go to court and sue for an injunction or other remedy. Third, once the waiting period has elapsed, the parties may proceed to close the transaction. That the waiting period has elapsed does not necessarily mean that the transaction is in compliance with the antitrust laws. The government may initiate an investigation post-closing if it deems it necessary to do so.

b. "4(c)" Documents

As part of the initial filing with the DOJ/FTC, parties are required to submit copies of

> all studies, surveys, analyses and reports which were prepared by or for any officer(s) or director(s) (or, in the case of unincorporated entities, individuals exercising similar functions) for the purpose of evaluating or analyzing the acquisition with respect to market shares, competition, competitors, markets, potential for sales growth or expansion into product or geographic markets.[6]

These "4(c) documents", which include emails, PowerPoint presentations, and other types of reports, help the DOJ/FTC understand the competitive effects of the proposed transaction from the perspective of the parties doing the deal.

Getting an "inside" view on the competitive effects of a proposed transaction can be eye-opening. Take for example the case of Whole Foods' 2007 proposed acquisition of Wild Oats, a competitor. Prior to the transaction, Whole Foods' CEO e-mailed members of the board reasons for the proposed merger. They included some rather unwholesome views on the competitive nature of the proposed transaction:

---

[6]   FTC Item 4(c) Tip Sheet, available at https://www.ftc.gov/sites/default/files/attachments/hsr-resources/4ctipsheet.pdf.

After the merger, customers will have the choice, but of course the only choice is ours. We will obviously increase prices. . . .

This merger will give us leverage over customers, allowing us to raise our gross margins.

Elimination of an acquisition opportunity for a conventional supermarket—our targeted company is the only existing company that has the brand and number of stores to be a meaningful springboard for another player to get into this space. Eliminating them means eliminating this threat forever, or almost forever.

OATS remains a relevant competitor. By buying them we will greatly enhance our comps over the next few years and will avoid nasty price wars in Portland (both Oregon and Maine), Boulder, Nashville, and several other cities which will harm our gross margins and profitability. OATS may not be able to defeat us but they can still hurt us. Furthermore we eliminate forever the possibility of Kroger, SuperValu, or Safeway using their brand equity to launch a competing national natural/organic food chain to rival us.[7]

Clients, investment bankers, and deal counsel should be aware that their internal communications with respect to motivations to complete a particular transaction may be subject to review by the DOJ/FTC—and that language that might be wholly innocent and culturally acceptable in some places can look very different when viewed by antitrust counsel for the government. After three years of litigation, during which Whole Foods completed its acquisition of Wild Oats, Whole Foods and the DOJ agreed to a settlement. That settlement included the divestiture of thirty-two stores along with the Wild Oats brand.[8] Given the sensitive nature of internal communications and the likelihood that business people acting as internal advocates for any deal may be prone to careless rhetoric, having a frank, preventative, discussion with clients about 4(c) documents and the importance of HSR approvals in the deal process is critical.

c.   Transactions Not Subject to Filing Requirements

Because the net the DOJ/FTC casts is intended only to the capture the largest transactions or transactions involving the largest industry players, there are a significant number of potentially anticompetitive transactions for which no pre-closing filings will be required. The

---

[7]   FTC Complaint Against Whole Foods, available at http://www.ftc.gov/sites/default/files/documents/cases/2007/06/070605complaint.pdf.

[8]   FTC case summary available at http://www.ftc.gov/enforcement/cases-proceedings/0710114/whole-foods-market-inc-wild-oats-markets-inc.

exemption from submitting a premerger notification is not a more general exemption from the antitrust laws. Though a particular transaction may be too small to attract the attention of regulators prior to closing, if, post-closing, that transaction turns out to be anti-competitive, regulators may still enforce the antitrust laws against the parties. Consider two examples. The first is Election Systems & Software's acquisition (ES&S) of Premier Election Solutions from Diebold in 2009. At the time of the acquisition, Premier provided electronic voting machines to approximately twenty-three percent of the voting precincts in the United States. ES&S served forty-five percent of all the voting precincts in the United States. Because the size of the transaction fell below HSR's statutory trigger, the parties did not submit an HSR filing. However, in 2010, the DOJ examined the closed merger and determined that even though the parties had not violated any reporting requirements under HSR, the transaction nevertheless violated the antitrust laws. ES&S ultimately settled litigation with the government and divested itself of the acquired assets.[9]

In another transaction, BazaarVoice, a web-based customer review platform, purchased PowerReviews, a competitor. Again, the transaction was relatively small and fell below HSR's statutory triggers, so no filing was made prior to closing. Following closing of the transaction, the deal was investigated by the DOJ. The DOJ then sued BazaarVoice for violation of the antitrust laws in connection with the transaction. At trial, the DOJ submitted evidence of internal communications with respect to the PowerReview acquisition. These communications were damning to BazaarVoice's defense. Executives at BazaarVoice observed that acquisition of PowerReview would "[e]liminate [BazaarVoice's] primary competitor and provide relief from . . . price erosion."[10] BazaarVoice's CFO suggested that BazaarVoice could either compete against PowerReviews and "crush" them, or "dammit lets [sic] just buy them now." The result was that a court found BazaarVoice liable for violations of the antitrust laws and ordered divestiture of the PowerReviews assets.[11]

d. Gun Jumping

The HSR Act prohibits an acquirer from exercising "substantial operational control" over the target prior to expiration of the waiting period. "Gun jumping" is the term used by the DOJ/FTC to refer to a

---

[9]   DOJ Press Release announcing settlement: Press Release, Dep't of Justice, *Justice Department Requires Key Divestiture in Election Systems & Software/Premier Election Solutions Merger* (Mar. 8, 2010), available at http://www.justice.gov/opa/pr/justice-department-requires-key-divestiture-election-systems-softwarepremier-election.

[10]   Brian JM Quinn, *Courts Finds BazaarVoice violated Clayton Act, M&A Law Prof. Blog.* Jan. 13, 2014, http://lawprofessors.typepad.com/mergers/2014/01/bazaarvoice-violates-clayton.html.

[11]   *Id.* The judgment is available at http://www.justice.gov/atr/case-document/third-amended-final-judgment.

variety of actions that parties might enter into prior to closing to facilitate the merger and expedite the integration of the companies that could result in the acquirer having substantial operational control over the target. Examples of gun jumping include coordination between the acquirer and the target on prices or terms to be offered to customers for sales prior to closing the transaction. Coordinating negotiations with customers for sales to be made after the transaction closes may also be deemed to be gun jumping.

e. Penalties

Failure to comply with the requirements of the HSR Act can yield severe penalties. The maximum penalty for a failure to file is $16,000 per day until the violation is remedied. In recent years, several high profile defendants have found themselves inadvertently subject to sizable penalties for failure to file a legally mandated HSR notification. For example, Barry Diller, a well-known investor and member of the board of Coca-Cola, was fined $480,000 for failure to file when he acquired 725,000 shares of Coca-Cola over a two-year period. As a result of that acquisition, Mr. Diller held voting securities of more than $63.4 million, thus triggering the reporting requirements under HSR. Mr. Diller subsequently made a filing, but was still subject to sanction.[12] In another case, MacAndrews & Forbes acquired 800,000 shares of Scientific Games in early June of 2012. MacAndrews & Forbes failed to make a HSR filing until August 16, 2012. When it did, it was subject to a $720,000 fine.[13]

While the statutory penalties can be stiff, the FTC has discretion in how and when it seeks a sanction:

> In determining whether to seek civil penalties and at what level, the FTC considers several factors: did the parties fail to file as a result of understandable or simple negligence; did they promptly correct their mistake; have they gained any benefit (e.g., tax, contract or regulatory) by failing to file; and have they now implemented adequate safeguards to protect against future failures.[14]

---

[12] The FTC announcement, Fed. Trade Comm'n, *Barry Diller to Pay $480,000 to Settle FTC Allegations Related to Premerger Filing Requirements*, (July 2, 2013), is available at http://www.ftc.gov/news-events/press-releases/2013/07/barry-diller-pay–480000–settle-ftc-allegations-related-premerger.

[13] For the FTC press release, see Fed. Trade Comm'n, Investment Firm of MacAndrews & Forbes to Pay $720,000 Penalty to Resolve FTC Allegations Related to Premerger Filing Requirements (June 20, 2013), available at http://www.ftc.gov/news-events/press-releases/2013/06/investment-firm-macandrews-forbes-pay–720000–penalty-resolve-ftc.

[14] Cooley LLP, *Acquirers Beware: Inadvertent Failure to Submit HSR Filing Results in $720,000 Civil Penalty*, June 26, 2013, available at http://www.cooley.com/failure-to-submit-HSR-filing-results-in-penalty.

2. INTERNATIONAL ANTITRUST

Most countries have some version of antitrust, competition, or anti-monopoly law. While these laws obviously cover merger transactions involving two domestic parties in the relevant jurisdiction and also transactions where the target is located in the relevant jurisdiction and is being acquired by a foreign buyer, they may also reach out to cover transactions between two parties incorporated outside the relevant jurisdiction. The most significant non-U.S. antitrust reviews today are those by the European Union competition authority as well as those by Chinese anti-monopoly regulators. Other important jurisdictions for purposes of international antitrust often include Japan, Russia, and Brazil among others.

Historically, the European Union and United States antitrust authorities have coordinated their actions—but not always. The most notable disagreement was in 2001 when General Electric attempted to acquire Honeywell for $42 billion. The United States antitrust authorities cleared the transaction but it was subsequently blocked by the European Union. Since that time, however, the two have worked together with only rare disagreements. By contrast, the Chinese authorities are only beginning to assert their authority, with significant consequences for acquisitions. The following article discusses the role of the Ministry of Commerce (MOFCOM), a Chinese antitrust regulator, in Google's $12.5 billion acquisition of Motorola. Google had agreed to acquire Motorola, in significant part to acquire Motorola's many patents. Regulators from various countries had approved, as had shareholders.

> Google . . . waited . . . unable to close its acquisition until it obtains approval from Chinese regulatory authorities. . . .
>
> [MOFCOM] . . . has been increasingly aggressive in its enforcement actions since a Chinese antitrust law was enacted in 2008. The law requires that the ministry must approve any acquisition for antitrust purposes if the combined company would have about $63 million in Chinese sales and $1.5 billion in global sales. These are low thresholds that almost any large multinational acquisition meets these days.

China has not blocked many transactions, but it has blocked some, and has delayed others, in some cases requiring modifications before allowing a transaction to proceed. The article continues:

> Beijing is joining the club of influential regulators at a time when [U.S. and European] antitrust agencies are increasingly focusing on patent and patent rights.[15]

---

[15] On the manner in which "the Chinese antitrust regulators analyze intellectual property rights during its merger review," *see* Jing He, Su Sun, & Angela Zhang, *The Role of IPRs in*

. . . The question is whether the glacial pace of Chinese antitrust review is intentional or a simply a reflection of Beijing bureaucracy. Still, these are new laws, and the Ministry of Commerce appears to be gaining experience in how to act. And there are encouraging signs. China has signed a cooperation agreement with the European Union and the United States on antitrust matters.[16]

The Ministry of Foreign Trade and Economic Cooperation (MOFTEC), another of China's antitrust regulators, subsequently cleared Google's acquisition of Motorola with no conditions. Google has since sold Motorola's mobile business to Lenovo, keeping the patent portfolio.

A law firm memo notes that:

In 2014, MOFCOM took enforcement action to address competitive effects arising from five transactions, up from four such actions in 2013. MOFCOM permanently blocked one transaction—the P3 shipping joint venture—and imposed remedies upon four others . . . [T]hese decisions have deepened concerns that MOFCOM takes longer to review significant mergers than US and EU authorities and that the conclusions reached and remedies imposed often depart from other jurisdictions especially where Chinese competitors and national economic policy goals are significantly affected.

The memo also notes that "[i]n 2014, MOFCOM implemented final regulations designed to speed antitrust review for merger cases that raise no substantive antitrust issues" and some reviews have apparently gone more quickly than would previously have been the case. But it does sound a cautionary note: "Even though a transaction has been qualified as "simple," MOFCOM retains broad discretion to perform an in-depth merger review if it concludes that it is difficult to define the relevant market or where there are complaints of harm to consumers or Chinese "national economic development."[17]

China's Antitrust Merger Review, INTERNATIONAL COMMITTEE, ABA SECTION ON ANTITRUST LAW, March 2012, available at http://www.ei.com/downloadables/Su_Sun_Article.pdf.

[16] Steven M. Davidoff, *China Flexes Its Regulatory Muscle, Catching Google in Its Grip,* N.Y. TIMES, May 15, 2012, available at http://dealbook.nytimes.com/2012/05/15/china-flexes-its-regulatory-muscle-catching-google-in-its-grip/.

[17] *China Antitrust Review 2014,* Davis Polk & Wardwell, available at http://www.davispolk.com/sites/default/files/2015_01_27_China_Antitrust_Review_2014.pdf.

B. NATIONAL SECURITY REVIEW— EXON-FLORIO AMENDMENT

1. HISTORY

In the United States, the government is permitted to review—and reject—foreign acquisitions on national securities grounds. Almost all governments around the world reserve similar powers to themselves. A 1988 amendment to Section 721 of the Defense Production Act of 1950, known as the Exon-Florio Amendment (50 U.S.C. app. § 2170), governs the U.S's review. This law grants the President authority to block or suspend a merger, acquisition, or takeover by a foreign entity if there is "credible evidence" that a "foreign interest exercising control might take action that threatens to impair the national security" and existing provisions of law do not provide "adequate and appropriate authority for the President to protect the national security in the matter before the President."[18] The President has delegated this review process largely to an inter-governmental agency known as CFIUS. CFIUS stands for the Committee on Foreign Investment in the United States, an inter-agency committee chaired by the Secretary of Treasury. It is charged with administering the Exon-Florio Amendment.[19]

The current incarnation of the Exon Florio Amendment was enacted in 1988 in response to the 1987 attempt by Fujitsu, a Japanese electronics company, to acquire Fairchild Semiconductor Corporation. Congress responded by passing the Exon-Florio Amendment. Exon Florio was again amended in 2007 in The National Security Foreign Investment Reform and Strengthened Transparency Act. The bill further enhanced the CFIUS review process, and adds critical infrastructure, critical technologies, and foreign government-controlled transactions to the factors for review.[20] In any case, CFIUS can initiate a mandatory review of a transaction. Like the 1988 bill, the 2007 amendment was a response to perceived foreign investment "threats." This time it was the acquisition of Peninsular & Oriental Steam by Dubai Ports and the ensuing political brawl and heavy congressional protest which led to Dubai Ports terminating the U.S. component of its acquisition.

When representing a foreign acquirer, whether or not to make a voluntary filing with CFIUS is almost always a consideration, no matter what the industry. As you read through these materials, think about the extent to which when undertaking national security review of proposed

---

[18] 50 U.S.C. app. § 2170(d)(4).

[19] Portions of this Section are adapted from Steven M. Davidoff, *Nasdaq, Borse Dubai and Exon Florio*, M&A LAW PROFESSOR BLOG, October 2, 2007, available at http://lawprofessors. typepad.com/mergers/2007/10/nasdaq-borse-du.html.

[20] P.L. 110–49 (2007), amending 50 U.S.C. app. § 2170.

transactions the government is responding to true national security threats rather than responding to domestic political imperatives.

2.   EXTENT OF COVERAGE

Under the 2007 Amendment, a filing with CFIUS is voluntary and not obligatory. Why would a foreign acquirer make a voluntary filing that might cause the government to closely examine its proposed transaction? The benefit of making a voluntary CFIUS filing is that if the transaction is cleared, the government is forever foreclosed from unwinding it on national security grounds. A foreign acquirer will therefore typically prefer to make such a filing in order to clear the deck and avoid subsequent, unexpected review after the completion of the acquisition.

If a voluntary filing is made, the transaction is subject to an initial review period of thirty days, followed by a possible extended investigation period of no more than forty-five additional days. If, during the review period, the committee determines that the covered transaction does not represent a threat to any U.S. national security interests, the review is terminated and parties are informed in writing of the termination. If the committee determines that the covered transaction may in fact represent a threat to national security interests, the committee will refer the transaction to the President of the United States for a decision with respect to whether and how to permit the transaction to go forward.

3.   CFIUS IN PRACTICE

Referral to the President sounds rather extreme, and in fact, it very rarely happens. For example, in 2011 there were 114 CFIUS filings. Of those, forty-five were subject to a second review period. While four transactions were voluntarily withdrawn, no transactions were referred to the President.[21]

Depending on the domestic political situation and the parties involved, the review process can be politically charged. Moreover, many CFIUS filings are simply withdrawn prior to Presidential referral since acquirers do not want a public record that their acquisition has been rejected. In 2012, twenty-two CFIUS notices were voluntarily withdrawn while the President blocked only one transaction. That transaction was an order prohibiting the Chinese company Ralls Corporation from acquiring four wind farm companies located within the vicinity of

---

[21] *CFIUS Annual Report to Congress* (2011) available at http://www.treasury.gov/resource-center/international/foreign-investment/Documents/2012%20CFIUS%20Annual%20Report%20PUBLIC.pdf.

restricted air space at the Naval Weapons Systems Training Facility Boardman in Oregon.[22]

The government can at times take a broad—and arguably politically tinged—view of national security. Take, for example, the acquisition of Smithfield Foods by Shuanghui, a Hong Kong food producer. Although such a transaction does not immediately call to mind national security concerns, the prospect of a foreign buyer taking control of one the United States' largest food producer generated a good deal of political heat as the following news article explains:

> Americans do love their bacon, but is that romance a national security issue?
>
> Maybe.
>
> This week, China's biggest pork producer announced plans to buy Virginia-based Smithfield Foods Inc. Republican Sen. Charles Grassley of Iowa wants a national security review by an interagency panel known as the Committee on Foreign Investment in the U.S., or CFIUS.
>
> "To have a Chinese food company controlling a major U.S. meat supplier, without shareholder accountability, is a bit concerning," said Grassley, whose home state is a top pork producer.
>
> Hong Kong-based Shuanghui International Holdings doesn't object to Grassley's demand. In fact, the company is seeking a review of its planned acquisition of Smithfield, the biggest hog and pork producer in the world.
>
> By asking upfront for a CFIUS examination, Shuanghui may be able to build trust with U.S. officials and avoid angering Congress or the White House, said Timothy Keeler, a lawyer in Washington, D.C., who specializes in CFIUS filings.
>
> "Technically, the review is always a voluntary process," Keeler said. But companies that try to dodge it may risk drawing even tougher congressional scrutiny, which could discourage investors and scuttle a deal. "For any significant deal, it's prudent to go forward with a CFIUS review," he said.
>
> So what is CFIUS, and why does it have a say in the $4.72 billion cash deal that would mark the biggest-ever Chinese takeover of a U.S. company?

---

[22] Rachelle Younglai, *Obama Blocks Chinese Wind Farms in Oregon Over Security*, REUTERS, Sept. 28, 2012, available at http://www.reuters.com/article/2012/09/28/us-usa-china-turbines-idUSBRE88R19220120928.

CFIUS may not be a household name, but it has played a significant role in shaping foreign investments in this country for nearly four decades.

CFIUS has no enforcement power itself, but its website[23] says that if the committee uncovers a national security risk, it "may refer the case to the President for action." The White House then could issue an executive order to disrupt all or a portion of the deal. Overall, CFIUS's goal is to allow global trade and foreign investment to flourish, but only after taking into account loosely defined national security needs, such as maintaining production capacity for weapons, keeping sensitive information away from terrorists and protecting U.S. superiority in technologies that affect defense.

So what does any of that have to do with buying a pig in a poke?

The Shuanghui-Smithfield deal is of interest because it involves one of two key economic sectors that stir keen interest among lawmakers: energy and food.

In recent years, the spotlight often has focused on energy deals. For example, a few years ago when CNOOC Ltd., a Chinese-owned energy company, tried to buy California-based Unocal, Congress objected so strenuously that CNOOC withdrew its bid even before CFIUS could reach a conclusion.

Now the Shuanghui bid is stirring up concerns about food. Mountains of Smithfield hams end up on American dinner plates, and its bacon tops off millions of burgers each year. If that meat were diverted to China, would it drive up food prices for U.S. consumers?

Questions also are being raised about food purity. Shuanghui got caught up in the 2011 scandal that involved feeding dangerous additives to pigs set for slaughter.

"I have deep doubts about whether this merger best serves American consumers," U.S. Rep. Rosa DeLauro, a Connecticut Democrat, said in a statement.

And there is another worry: Some Smithfield Foods facilities are located near military bases, raising questions about spying. Similar concerns have tripped up previous transactions. . . .

Still, assuming no other bidders step forward with a better offer for Smithfield, Shuanghui is likely to win out, experts say.

---

[23] The website is at http://www.treasury.gov/resource-center/international/Pages/Committee-on-Foreign-Investment-in-US.aspx.

"It's a safe bet," said Mark Plotkin, co-chair of Covington & Burling's national security practice. The transaction may need some tweaks, such as selling off any hog farms located too near military facilities, but overall, "I don't see any obvious obstacles" that could kill the transaction, he said.

To reassure U.S. officials, Shuanghui says it will keep Smithfield at arm's length and has promised not to replace U.S. senior management.

No matter how the Smithfield review turns out, CFIUS itself is likely to continue receiving a lot of criticism for being too secretive. The committee, which sends classified reports to Congress, keeps its deliberations confidential. The veil is designed to protect military and proprietary information.

That lack of transparency only stokes the anger of CFIUS's critics. For example, the conservative editorial board of *The Wall Street Journal*—writing about the Smithfield deal—said "Washington protectionists and rural sentimentalists will certainly try" to use CFIUS's opaque process to derail the transaction.

But Plotkin says the panel has no choice but to do its work outside the spotlight. "The process *is* opaque," he said. "But it's hard to think of a national security review process anywhere in the world that is done in the sunlight."[24]

Ultimately, the Smithfield transaction was cleared. However, complaints remain that the CFIUS process is opaque and subject to political interference. In the case involving the President's blocking of the wind farm acquisition discussed above, the D. C. Circuit ultimately held that "the Presidential Order deprived Ralls of its constitutionally protected property interests without due process of law. . . . [D]ue process requires, at the least, that an affected party be informed of the official action, be given access to the unclassified evidence on which the official actor relied and be afforded an opportunity to rebut that evidence."[25] It remanded the matter "to the district court with instructions that Ralls be provided the requisite process set forth herein, which should include access to the unclassified evidence on which the President relied and an opportunity to respond thereto."

---

[24] Marilyn Geewax, *Can A Huge Hog Deal Pose A National Security Risk?*, NPR, May 13, 2013, available at http://www.npr.org/2013/05/31/187351539/can-a-huge-hog-deal-pose-a-national-security-risk.

[25] *Ralls Corp v. Committee on Foreign Investment in the United States*, No. 13–5315 at 36 (D.C. Cir. July 15, 2014). Ralls is an American corporation, incorporated in Delaware, owned by two foreign nationals.

C. OTHER U.S. REGULATORY REVIEWS

In addition to antitrust and national security review, there are a large number of industry specific regulatory approvals that may be required before a merger transaction is permitted to close. For example, transactions involving ownership of the broadcast spectrum will be subject to review by the Federal Communications Commission (FCC) prior to closing. The FCC is required under the law to find that the transaction is in "the best interests" of consumers. This can be a demanding standard, and the possibility, if not probability, that it would not be satisfied was a significant factor in Comcast abandoning its attempts to acquire Time Warner.

Transactions involving banks or other financial institutions will require approval by the Federal Reserve, Office of the Comptroller of the Currency, or the Federal Deposit Insurance Corporation, depending upon who is the institution's primary regulator. Transactions involving insurance companies may be subject to review and approval by state insurance regulators. Energy mergers may require the approval of the Federal Energy Regulatory Commission as well as state level energy regulators.

Some acquisitions, for example in the health sector, involve not-for-profit corporations. Acquisitions of not-for-profit corporations involve additional approvals by the state authorities that oversee the operation of the not-for-profit sector. With respect to hospital acquisitions, in particular, the role of religious organizations in the merger approval process cannot be overlooked. For example, Catholic-run hospitals, which comprise a large percentage of the hospital sector in the United States, cannot complete a merger with a secular hospital without the approval of the Vatican.

QUESTIONS

1. What are the criteria that would currently trigger the requirement to make a filing under the HSR Act? (You may have to look this up on the FTC website.)

2. Under what circumstances might you be able to structure a merger transaction that signs and closes on the same day?

3. Describe the various pre-merger approval regimes that might be applicable in the event Apex Energy, a foreign energy company, decides to acquire the Beta Corp, an electrical utility serving a major U.S. city.

4. Under what circumstances might the following transaction be subject to CFIUS review: acquisition of Delta, Inc., a popular social media app by a European buyer?

5.   Review the FCC's determination with respect to Comcast's proposed acquisition of Time Warner Cable (available on the FCC's website, Docket No. MB 14–57). Did the FCC determine that this transaction was in the "best interests" of the consumer?

PROBLEM

Heller, a citizen of Germany, acquired Epsilon Co. voting securities in a private placement transaction, and as a result of that transaction, held Epsilon Co. shares valued in excess of the $500 million. Heller has made it clear that he intends to gain a board seat and participate in the formulation, determination, or direction of the basic business decisions of Epsilon Co. as an Epsilon Co. board member. Heller has approached you as his counsel. Did the private placement transaction raise any concerns with respect to the various pre-merger notification regimes in the U.S.?

PART II

ACCOUNTING AND VALUATION

■ ■ ■

CHAPTER IX

ACCOUNTING

■ ■ ■

A. INTRODUCTION

An M&A transaction cannot occur without an agreement between the buyer and the seller over value. How is the assessment of a company's value made? A starting point is the company's financial statements: its balance sheet, income statement, and statement of cash flows.

The balance sheet is traditionally referred to as a "snapshot" of the company's condition at a particular point in time, recording the value of the company's assets and liabilities. The income statement tracks what has happened to a company over some period of time, usually a year. The statement of cash flows tracks the company's use of cash over time. It is needed because a balance sheet or income statement may not reflect the actual cash the company spends.

We will focus principally on the balance sheet and the income statement since these are of primary relevance in an M&A transaction. A simple balance sheet and income statement are set forth and discussed below. Our coverage below is introductory.[1] Still, business lawyers are increasingly expected to have basic accounting knowledge. We highly recommend that you take a class in accounting for lawyers.

B. THE BALANCE SHEET

A balance sheet reflects a company's assets and liabilities as of a certain date. More specifically, it is a view of the company's net worth computed using accounting rules. As we will discuss, accounting rules sometimes dictate that a company's assets be carried on its books at a value that differs from "fair market value." In particular, if an asset the company owns (for example, a building) or creates internally (for example some intellectual property company employees develop) appreciates in value, its accounting value may be less than its fair market value. Constructing the balance sheet is a mechanical exercise. Assets are recorded on the left hand side of the balance sheet. On the right side of the balance sheet, the company's liabilities and equity are recorded. The balance sheet identity: **assets = liabilities *plus* equity** captures the

---

[1]   A short and accessible discussion of financial statements and some related matters can be found on the SEC's website, at http://www.sec.gov/investor/pubs/begfinstmtguide.htm.

relationship between these three components. The three components are described in more detail below:

Assets. Assets are property, receivables and other items which can be converted into assets. Assets can be divided into current assets (assets which are cash or are expected to be converted into cash within a year), and fixed assets (assets that are "long term" such as intangibles and property).

Liabilities. Liabilities are obligations that a company is required to pay, such as debt, accounts payable and wages. Like assets, liabilities are divided into current liabilities (liabilities which are due within a year), and fixed liabilities (liabilities which are due in more than a year).

Shareholders' Equity. Equity is calculated according to our equation: **assets − liabilities = equity**. Equity is the capital of the corporation, and includes the corporation's earnings and the initial contribution of equity from the creation of the firm as well as any equity added in subsequent securities sales.

Below is a simple balance sheet as of the time the company has raised its initial funding, but before it commences operations, a time we call "year zero." The company has $1,000 in cash and no liabilities. $1,000 was raised by selling 100 shares at $10 apiece. The company's equity is therefore $1,000.

Year 0 Balance Sheet			
Assets	$1,000	Liabilities	$0
		Equity	$1,000
			$1,000

One year later, on the last day of year 1, the company buys a computer for $200, and a piece of real property for $250. The real property is bought using a loan due in five years with a 5% interest rate per annum. The company also earns $1,000. A balance sheet for year one of the company, dated as of the last date of its fiscal year, will look like this:

Year 1 Balance Sheet			
Assets		Liabilities	
Cash	$1,800	Current Liabilities	$0
Fixed Assets	$450	Long Term Liabilities	$250
		Equity	$2,000
			$2,250

Remember the balance sheet identity: **assets = liabilities plus equity**. In this case, the company has $2,250 worth of assets. This number equals the company's liabilities ($250) plus the company's equity ($2,000). The bank debt is classified as a long term liability since it is due more than a year in the future. (Recall that debt due in less than a year is classified as a current liability- this company has no such debt). Similarly, the computer and property are classified as fixed assets, since they are not readily convertible into cash. The business has an equity value of $2,000, but an enterprise value of $2,250. Enterprise value is the total value of the company—debt and equity—and is a metric used in M&A transactions to measure the total value of an acquisition. When a company is publicly traded, its enterprise value is typically calculated as the value of the traded equity plus the company's outstanding debt and any preferred stock.

In the next Subsection we look at the same business, but from the income side.

C. THE INCOME STATEMENT

The income statement is also known as the profit and loss statement, and is our primary tool for determining the success of the company. The income statement reflects the profit or loss of a business for a period of time, typically a fiscal year.

Below is an income statement for the business in Year 1.

Year 1 Income Statement	
Revenue	$6,300
Expenses	$5,000
Taxes	$300
Profit (Loss)	$1,000

The business had $6,300 of revenues, and $5,000 in expenses; it also paid $300 in taxes, earning a $1,000 profit.

In the year two income statement, the revenue is $9,000 but the profit is $1,338.

Year 2 Income Statement	
Revenue	$9,000
Expenses	$7,000
Interest	$13
Taxes	$600
Depreciation	$50
Profit (Loss)	$1,338

Why? The business has $7,000 in expenses, "depreciation" (explained below) of $50 for the computer, $12.50 in payments on interest for debt (rounded up to $13) and taxes of $600.

What is depreciation? A colloquial synonym is "wear and tear."[2] Many of a company's assets will be used over a period of time in the company's business. Rather than deducting the full cost of the asset when it is first acquired, the period of time the asset is expected to be used, otherwise known as its "useful life," is computed, based on accounting and tax rules, and the asset is "depreciated" over that time. For example, the computer our business bought will be depreciated over four years, $50 per year. Other depreciable assets are buildings, machinery, vehicles, furniture, and equipment as well as patents, copyrights, and computer software. Real property (i.e., land) is not a depreciable asset because in theory it lasts forever, rather than wearing out and needing to be replaced. Therefore, there is no line-item for depreciation of the land the company owns; rather, it is held as an asset on the balance sheet, at its purchase price, as part of the company's "fixed assets."

Note that the computer, too, will be included in the fixed assets, but not at its purchase price. Rather, it will be included at its purchase price less the amount by which it has been depreciated. This may or may not reflect the computer's actual value. There is no mechanism for adjusting the price for any increase in the computer's value. But if the company learns that the computer is worth less than the value at which the company has recorded it on its books—that its value is "impaired"—the

---

[2] The term is meant to capture that a company's assets wear out over time and will (at least in theory) become worthless. When the company first buys the asset, the asset is presumably worth what the company paid, but its value declines over time. Depreciation reflects that diminution of value when it is occurring, or at least approximately so, and that amount is the cost to be charged against the company's revenues at the correlative time. Consider a company that buys a machine for 50 that will last five years; assume the company has no other expenses and has revenue of 100 in each year. It is more accurate to describe the company as having made 90 in each of the five years than to describe it as having made 50 the first year and 100 in each of the succeeding 4 years: the machine was a cost of its making its revenues.

company may have to lower the asset's value on its books to reflect the impairment and record an expense for the amount of the impairment. (Impairment is discussed below.) Again, the converse is not true. Many assets are valued at "book," not at "market," and the fact that an asset may be worth more than its book value will in general not yield a revaluation upwards until the company sells the asset. At that point, the proceeds of the sale will be recorded as a gain to the extent that the sale price exceeded the value at which the company then carried the asset on its books. The term "book value" is sometimes used in cases and other relevant materials; it is helpful to have a sense of what it means and how it is different from market value.

When investors are valuing a company, they may look at the company's income statement and add back in certain items. The items most commonly added back are taxes, as well as interest on debt, depreciation and amortization. The abbreviation EBITDA is shorthand for this metric, and stands for earnings before (that is, adding back) interest, taxes, depreciation and amortization. EBITDA is a common multiple used to price businesses and in valuation, something we will examine in the next Subsection. What is the rationale for adding back these items? This company paid the taxes it paid, but there might be ways for the company to pay some other, perhaps smaller, amount of taxes. The same is true as to interest payments, discussed below—the company might be financed differently, with different interest payments, as well as depreciation and amortization. EBITDA is thus a useful metric for determining the core value of a business. Because these items are variable, EBIDTA, which subtracts them out, is often considered to be the true measure of the company's cash flows.

In the example above, the company's earnings are $1,338, with a firm EBITDA significantly higher at $2,000. The company has 100 shares outstanding, so the firm's earnings are $1.34 per share ($1,338 /100 shares) with an EBITDA per share of $200 ($2,000/100 shares).

Dealmakers sometimes refer to a transaction as either "accretive" or "dilutive." These terms refer to the effect of the transaction on the firm's earnings (EBITDA) per share. When a transaction is accretive, it means that the acquisition has the effect of increasing the combined (that is, post-merger) firm's EBITDA per share. When a transaction is dilutive, it means that the acquisition has the effect of decreasing the combined firm's EBITDA per share.

These are simple income statements and balance sheets, but they illustrate the basic principles behind accounting. For a real life example of a balance sheet and income statement please see the Online Appendix, which contains the financial statements for Dell in the year it was purchased.

D. A NOTE ON GOODWILL

The above discussion did not cover perhaps the most common intangible asset on a company's balance sheet—goodwill. One definition of goodwill is the intangible asset which is created when an acquirer acquires a target. The excess of the fair market value of the company over the fair market value of its total tangible assets less its total liabilities is goodwill. If a company has tangible assets with a fair market value of 150 and liabilities of 50, and a buyer pays 200, the buyer has paid 100 for the goodwill, and will record the 100 as an asset on its balance sheet.

For example, think about McDonald's Corporation. An enormous amount of McDonald's' value is in its expectation of future business—that it is very well known, and that many people eat there often. If you were to imagine trying to sell the assets of McDonald's piecemeal—the kitchens, furniture, and other hard assets—or even together but without the name, the price would be much lower than the price for the company "McDonald's" as a continuing business. To (over)simplify a bit, the difference is "goodwill." But McDonald's, having developed its own goodwill, cannot have goodwill on its financial statements, for reasons to be explained below. By contrast, a company that bought McDonald's would "allocate" on its balance sheet values for McDonald's tangible assets, and include another very large intangible asset, goodwill, representing the difference between the price it paid and the value it assigned to the tangible assets. If some very bad news came out about McDonald's that seemed as though it might adversely affect sales in the moderate term, the buyer of McDonald's might be forced to write down a portion of the goodwill as "impaired," a term explained further below when we discuss how acquirers account for purchases.

E. A NOTE ON CONTINGENCIES AND RESERVES

The assets we mentioned in subsections C and D above could be valued by, in the case of the computer, the purchase price, and in the case of goodwill, the excess of what a company paid to acquire another company over the value of the acquired company's hard assets less its liabilities. The specific numbers might be contested—maybe the company significantly overpaid for the computer, for instance, but the principle by which the valuation is made is straightforward. The liabilities we mentioned were amounts owing to a lender, and tax payments. The relevant amounts were all specified in the example: the amount of the loan, the interest rate, and the amount of the tax payment.

Contrast these sorts of items with another sort of item: the amounts a company might have to pay if it were sued. How would the amount be estimated? The company would have to estimate how likely the lawsuit was to be brought, how much legal fees might be, how likely it was to lose the suit, and how much a judgment might be. Clearly, the amount of possible future liabilities for lawsuits is highly relevant to a company's financial condition, but estimating the amount with any precision is impossible. There can be both reasonable disagreements and disagreements which are less reasonable, where a company would like to minimize the amount it records as a future liability even though it may think the amount should more accurately be higher.

Contingent liabilities present obvious valuation difficulties but even supposedly simpler accounting items, such as hard assets and tax liabilities, may be complicated to value. Further exploration of these issues is beyond the scope of this textbook, but it is important for you to be aware not only of the basics of accounting, but also the extent to which accounting is a matter of judgment. When dealmakers are considering whether to enter into a transaction and on what terms, they will use the valuation techniques discussed in Chapter X. But, even before making the kinds of computations involved, they will want to conduct due diligence on the financial statements, not only in order to understand the financial condition of the company, but also to understand the assumptions and judgments underlying the company's financial statements. The task is considerably assisted by requirements in the accounting rules that explanatory footnotes be included with the financial statements; you can see examples of these footnotes in the Dell financial statements included as part of the Online Appendix.

F. HOW IS ACCOUNTING USED IN M&A?

In M&A, accounting is used in multiple ways. First the financial statements are the primary way investors know about the financial condition and prospects of the company. The buyer and its advisors will work from the financial statements to understand the business of the company. Due diligence will be performed by the buyer and its accounting firm on the target to confirm the accuracy of the target's financial statements. If the target is a public company, this is an easier matter, as the company is already reporting its financial results to the SEC and undergoing regular audits. If the target is a private company, though, the financial statements may need significantly more due diligence to confirm their accuracy.

The lawyers will also negotiate representations and warranties in the merger agreement to confirm the accuracy of the financial statements. The target will typically represent in the merger agreement that all of its financial statements are true and correct in all material respects; there will also be a representation and warranty about the financial statements' compliance with generally accepted accounting principles, known as "GAAP." The target will typically represent that it has no material liabilities except as reflected on the financial statements. In these two representations, the target gives assurances to the buyer that the target's business reflects what the buyer perceives it to be based on the target's financial statements. In addition to specific representations and warranties concerning the financial statements, there are representations and warranties as to specific line-items such as inventory, debt, taxes, and other items. These types of representations and warranties are explored further in Chapter XIV, where we discuss the terms of merger agreements.

Lawyers also have to deal with accounting if the buyer is purchasing a company and issuing securities, something discussed in Chapter VII. A registration statement must be prepared for the buyer's securities; the statement will include audited financial statements. Additionally, pro forma financial statements reflecting the combined companies may be included in the registration statement. Pro forma financial statements are statements which include combined information as to the two businesses for prior years as well as future periods, and are designed to give shareholders a view of how the combined business operates. These financial statements will be prepared by the accounting firm, but the lawyers will work with the accountants on the accounting and SEC requirements for their preparation. Finally, if the transaction is defined as significant (measured by size) under SEC regulations, then the buyer will have to file pro forma financial statements for the business after the completion of the acquisition.

G. PURCHASE ACCOUNTING

Another significant issue in accounting and M&A is how a purchaser accounts for the purchase on its financial statements, including the treatment of goodwill. The following article provides historical context for this topic:

POOLING OR PURCHASE? A MERGER MYSTERY
John R. Walter
85 Fed. Reserve Bank of Richmond Economic Quarterly 27, 27–33 (1999)

On September 14, 1998, WorldCom merged with MCI to form MCI WorldCom, a global telecommunications giant.

On September 30, NationsBank of Charlotte, North Carolina, and BankAmerica of San Francisco merged to form BankAmerica, one of the largest banks in the United States. While each case involved the combination of two firms, each used a different accounting method. MCI WorldCom's merger announcement noted that the combination would be accounted for as a "purchase;" on the other hand, BankAmerica's merger used a method called "pooling of interests" accounting.

In May 1991, American Telephone and Telegraph (AT&T) acquired computer manufacturer NCR Corporation (formerly National Cash Register) for $110 per share, in what was to that date the largest-ever computer industry merger. Press reports indicated that during negotiations AT&T upped its offer by $5 per share, an increase of about $325 million, to secure NCR's cooperation in accounting for the acquisition as a pooling of interests.

Here is the mystery. AT&T paid the additional $325 million to use pooling accounting rather than the alternative—purchase accounting—a choice that affected accounting numbers but neither added assets, reduced liabilities, nor changed tax treatment. Why then was AT&T willing to expend an additional $325 million? Both anecdotal and empirical evidence indicate that AT&T's preference for pooling is not unusual. Corporate managers frequently go to some expense to employ pooling, though there are no obvious benefits.

These cases raise questions for those not acquainted with the features of merger and acquisition procedure. What are the differences between purchase and pooling of interests accounting? Should the choice of accounting method be of concern to analysts, investors, or others interested in business activity? Why are two different forms of accounting—purchase and pooling—used for otherwise similar acquisitions? This article addresses these questions.

1.   POOLING AND PURCHASE: THE NUTS AND BOLTS

Accountants attempt to report in balance sheets an accurate valuation of a firm's assets, liabilities, and equity. But how should accountants value a firm arising from the combination of two separate businesses? One approach is to simply sum the dollar amounts of assets, liabilities, and equity of the two firms as they stood before the combination. This is pooling of interests accounting. Or, since business combinations are typically one firm's purchase of another firm, another valid method would value the purchased firm at its purchase price, and add the purchase price to the assets of the acquiring firm, as one would if the acquisition were of a piece of equipment. In broad terms, the latter approach is purchase accounting. The financial statements of a combined firm will vary with the choice between pooling or purchase accounting. While accounting methods for business combinations have changed over time, under today's accounting rules both pooling and purchase are acceptable means of valuing combinations in the United States.

Pooling of Interests Accounting

As already implied, pooling of interests accounting is conceptually quite simple. When a business combination is completed, the balance sheet of the combined firm reflects assets, liabilities, and owners' equity at the sum of these accounts as recorded by the separate companies immediately before the combination was completed. Income statements will show income and expenses for the statement period in which the combination occurs as if the companies had been combined from the beginning of the period.

Purchase Accounting

Purchase accounting is somewhat more complicated. Under purchase accounting the acquiring and acquired firms are treated differently, so the first step is to identify which is which. FASB holds that in a typical combination the acquiring company pays out cash or other assets or issues the stock used in the acquisition and is the larger of the firms. Once acquirer and acquired are identified, accounting for the acquisition can proceed. The acquirer is to record on its books the acquisition at the price paid to the acquired firm's owners, using a two-step process. First, assets and liabilities from the acquired firm (target) are recorded on the acquirer's books at individual market values. Second, any positive difference between acquisition price and market value of net assets (assets minus liabilities) is recorded as an asset called goodwill. Once recorded, goodwill is depreciated by equal annual charges against the combined firm's earnings for a period of years over which, in the accountant's estimate, the combined firm benefits from the goodwill built by the acquired firm. The amortization period is limited to at most 40 years. If the market values of the acquired assets and liabilities are accurately measured, goodwill is the value of the acquired firm as a going concern. Alternatively, goodwill can represent promising products developed by the target, or the price the acquirer is willing to pay for economic gains, such as economies of scale, expected from the merger.

The following example may help illustrate purchase accounting. Assume Honest Auto Maintenance, Inc. (HAM), an auto repair shop management company, agrees to pay $100 million cash to acquire Wally's Import Repair, a regional chain. Following the acquisition, the assets and liabilities purchased in the acquisition are recorded on HAM's books at their current market values as determined by appraisers hired by HAM. The appraisers value the assets at $160 million and the liabilities at $90 million. So HAM has purchased net assets with a market value of $70 million ($160M–$90M). To record the difference between the market value of the net assets and the $100 million purchase price, $30 million of goodwill is recorded on HAM's balance sheet. For the next 40 years (the estimated life of the goodwill according to HAM's accountants) HAM will record on its income statement an after-tax expense of $750,000 ($30M/40 years), decreasing its reported net income each year by this amount.

2. THE MYSTERY: WHY DO ACQUIRERS PREFER POOLING?

The financial press and specialists in mergers and acquisitions maintain that acquirers prefer pooling to purchase accounting. Empirical analysis supports this view as well. It provides evidence that acquirers are willing to pay higher bid prices in acquisitions that are pooled than in those that use purchase accounting. Likewise, even though there can be additional costs of qualifying for pooling, discussed below, the current significant use of pooling argues for the presence of a fairly strong preference. So what benefit underlies this strong preference?

. . .

By All Logic, Acquirers Should Not Prefer Pooling to Purchase

The choice between pooling and purchase has no apparent economic consequences. Goodwill amortization charges are not cash flows and only serve to lower reported earnings. These charges have no effect on the current or future income produced by the activities of the firm. As a result, one would expect investors to ignore such changes to reported income and instead focus on changes in financial reports that signal changes in future income or in the health of the firm. While there appears to be abundant evidence of managers' preference for pooling, as previous sections have described, acquisitive managers should be indifferent between pooling and purchase if investors look beyond reported earnings.

Nevertheless, the question arises: Do investors have sufficient information with which to remove the distortion produced by the pooling-purchase choice? The answer is yes. Such information is typically available in proxy statements associated with an acquisition so that interested investors should be able to remove the effects of goodwill on future earnings.

. . .

In the post-World War II period, business combinations have received one of two accounting treatments, pooling of interests or purchase accounting. From the start, businesses preferred pooling and are apparently willing to pay for it, by most accounts because it allows them to report higher earnings. Yet that accounting choice neither increases assets, reduces liabilities, nor modifies tax treatment, so in theory it ought to be ignored by investors. The preference for pooling is especially puzzling since empirical research implies that investors are not swayed by whether merged firms employ pooling or purchase accounting. While the puzzle has yet to be solved analytically, there is a good chance that it will diminish in importance for business decisions. The Financial Accounting Standards Board has indicated that it may well eliminate pooling, bringing U.S. business combination accounting standards in line with those in other industrialized nations. This article suggests that while the elimination of pooling in favor of purchase accounting could produce benefits by requiring more complete disclosures in financial statements, it also might eliminate arrangements that owners and managers find to be cost-saving. Evidence that acquirers are willing to bear additional costs to pool, combined with the lack of a stock price penalty for poolers, at least hints at the presence of some as-yet-undetermined cost savings.[3]

The above article highlights a seeming mystery in M&A, the historical preference of acquirers for pooling accounting over purchase accounting. As the author discusses, the stated rationale made no sense, as the choice of accounting merely dictated the way goodwill was amortized—that is, spread over a period of time—on the income statement. Purchase accounting resulted in amortization which reduced income while pooling accounting did not. Yet, any sophisticated investor could calculate the difference. Still, acquirers were willing to pay for this simple numerical difference. To emphasize: the difference in "income" was an accounting difference, not a difference in the company's financial results. Purchase and pooling accounting could yield two different income figures for otherwise identical companies. But sophisticated investors would know the difference and simply adjust these numbers for purposes of their investment. Nonetheless, the need to present a higher number to the market seems to have been paramount.[4]

For this reason, among others, the Financial Accounting Standards Board (FASB) eliminated pooling accounting in June 2001. In connection with the elimination of pooling accounting, the FASB adopted a new standard for accounting for acquisitions in Statement of Financial Accounting Standards (SFAS) No. 141 "Business Combinations" and SFAS 142 "Goodwill and Other Intangible Assets." In general, the new standards require that an acquirer allocate the total purchase price to the acquired assets and liabilities of the target. The acquirer hires an appraisal or accounting firm to undertake this task. The purchase price will then be allocated by the firm and recorded on the balance sheet: to the tangible assets at their appraised value, with the remainder allocated to goodwill, an intangible asset. However, unlike the old purchase accounting, goodwill arising from an acquisition is no longer required to be amortized. Thus, the elimination of pooling accounting would not "reduce" earnings as much as it might initially have seemed. Instead of amortizing goodwill, each year the company must assess the value of the goodwill with its accountants and determine if its value is impaired.

---

[3] Available at https://www.richmondfed.org/publications/research/economic_quarterly/1999/winter/pdf/walter.pdf, some internal references omitted.

[4] For an explanation of pooling and other accounting techniques that "beautify" financial statements, see Claire A. Hill, *Why Financial Appearances Might Matter: An Explanation for 'Dirty Pooling' and Other Financial Cosmetics*, 22 DEL. J. CORP. L. 141 (1997). The explanation turns on an elaborate signaling game among market participants.

Goodwill is impaired if the fair market value of the acquired company, measured as of year-end, is below the acquisition cost. In such a case, goodwill will be impaired and reduced to the fair market value at the time is. Notably, adjustments to goodwill are only downward, not upward—if the value of the acquired company increases, goodwill is not similarly increased.

As the following article illustrates, companies may be loath to write down the value of goodwill, as doing so highlights a flawed acquisition:

> AOL Time Warner Inc. reported a 2002 net loss of $98.7 billion . . . The write-down [mostly of the value of AOL], creating the biggest annual corporate loss in history, was more than twice what Wall Street had anticipated.
>
> The huge loss underscores how much value has evaporated from what was once the largest, and most-heralded, merger in U.S. history. The merger . . . unraveled amid intense corporate infighting and a sharp slump in America Online's business a few months after the deal closed. AOL's stock price dropped sharply during the past 18 months, wiping out more than $100 billion in market value. . . .
>
> AOL has now written off most of the [AOL] goodwill. . . . [I]ts U.S. and world-wide subscriber numbers fell for the first time. . . . The charge also included a write-down in the value of the cable-TV unit and the music division.
>
> The charge also reveals how quickly the value of AOL's assets have plummeted. In August, Mr. Pace had said "it's . . . premature and inappropriate to take an impairment charge at this time." Some accounting specialists had predicted last year that the company would have to write down its intangible assets further by tens of billions of dollars . . . [T]he company's net worth . . . was [then] listed at $97.7 billion. . . . [and is now] down to $52.82 billion.[5]

QUESTIONS

1.   What is the balance sheet identity?

2.   If Alpha Corporation has assets worth $1 million and liabilities of $700,000, how much equity does Alpha Corporation have?

3.   If founders of Beta Co. contributed $50,000 in cash to the business and took on $250,000 in debt, what are the assets of Beta Co.?

---

[5]   Martin Peers & Julia Angwin, *AOL Posts a $98.7 Billion Loss On New Goodwill Write-Down*, WALL ST. J., Jan. 30, 2003, available at http://www.wsj.com/articles/SB1043702683178461304.

4. Why are accounting representations in merger agreements important? What role do you think the representation regarding the seller's accounting statements play in an M&A transaction?

5. Describe the concept of goodwill. What role does it play in mergers and acquisitions?

6. What is the difference between pooling and purchase accounting? Why might an acquirer wish to use pooling accounting?

7. If markets were efficient, how should they react to an acquirer's choice to pay more to acquire a company if it could get pooling treatment? Does the discussion in this chapter on pooling suggest that markets are efficient?

8. What is the impact of the decision to eliminate pooling accounting on the accounting for goodwill in an M&A transaction?

9. Delta Corp. announced its decision to enter into a merger agreement with Kappa Co. According to the Delta Co. press release, the transaction will be "accretive". What does that mean?

PROBLEMS

1. Below, please find a series of entries from Epsilon, Inc's books. Build a balance sheet using these entries:

   a. Mortgage loan to credit union: $250,000

   b. Paid in capital: $300,000

   c. Short term line of credit with commercial bank: $75,000

   d. Accounts receivable: $250,000

   e. Accounts payable: $80,000

   f. Cash account at bank: $235,000

   g. Retained earnings: $112,500

   h. Inventory: $340,000

2. Widget Co. is founded with a capital contribution of $50,000. In Year 1 it purchases a piece of property for $20,000 and 3 computers for $5,000. Widget Co. borrows $10,000 to purchase the property and loses $5,000 for the year. In year 2, Widget Co. sells the property for $25,000 and pays off the loan. Widget Co. earns $15,000 in Year 2 (including the gains from the property). Please prepare a balance sheet and income statement for Widget Co. for years 1 and 2.

CHAPTER X

VALUATION

■ ■ ■

A. INTRODUCTION

Accounting provides many of the inputs used in valuation. But valuation is how an acquirer determines how much it is willing to pay for a target—and how a target determines a price at which it can be acquired. Valuation has other uses with which lawyers should be familiar. As discussed in Chapter III, a determination of "fair value" in an appraisal proceeding entails valuation. Investment banks use valuation to deliver a fairness opinion to a board of directors (discussed further below).

There are many ways to value a company. One is to simply look at the price at which the company's shares trade on the stock market. But that price is for individual shares, the stock market price does not reflect the value of controlling the company. The price also does not reflect what somebody other than the present management might be able to do with the company. Indeed, virtually all acquisitions of public companies are done at prices higher than the share price. Moreover, what if the company is not publicly traded?

An analogy can be made to the purchase of a house. By some process-typically, a seller setting an asking price, a buyer offering a lower price, and the two parties bargaining, a price will be agreed upon. But is this agreed-upon price the value of the house? It is certainly one valuation. But a bank issuing a mortgage to the buyer will ask for an appraisal. An appraiser will appraise the value of the house by looking at comparable sales. This is another valuation method which may—or may not—arrive at the same price as the buyer and seller agreed to.

Valuation is not a science—rather, it is often called an "art." Valuations can change depending upon the valuation techniques, inputs and other choices the valuation expert (typically in an M&A transaction, the investment bank) makes. Ultimately, too, valuation cannot dictate the price a willing buyer and seller might agree upon. As you read through the next Section on different valuation techniques, think about the extent to which the techniques rely on assumptions that necessarily reflect judgment calls, including as to what will happen in the future.

B. VALUATION TECHNIQUES

How is valuation done? In the M&A context, there are a number of techniques, including discounted cash flow analysis, comparable company analysis, and premiums analysis. In these Sections we discuss each of these techniques, as well as others commonly used in M&A valuation. Our goal is not to teach you how to perform these valuations. That is the work of a corporate finance class. It is, rather, to familiarize you with these techniques and the role M&A lawyers play in valuation in various contexts, both before the deal and afterwards in appraisal and damages proceedings.

1. DISCOUNTED CASH FLOW ANALYSIS

The principal valuation technique in M&A is the discounted cash flow analysis. A discounted cash flow analysis calculates the present value of the future free cash flows of a company by discounting its cash flows at a particular discount rate. A discounted cash flow analysis is conducted by first estimating a company's future cash flows—the cash flows the company can be expected to produce in the future. Because a dollar today is worth more than a dollar tomorrow due to inflation and the opportunity cost of investing that dollar elsewhere, the stream of cash flows associated with the company is discounted to find its present value. For example, if you deposited $1,000 in a bank, it might earn 5% annual interest, or $50 in a year. Your $1,000 today would become $1,050 by next year. So, $1,050 next year has a present value of $1,000 now.

How is the discount rate determined? Typically, when valuing a company, the company's weighted average cost of capital, known as the "WACC," will be computed. A company's WACC is equal to the company's cost of capital for each of its various financing components—debt, equity or preferred securities—weighted by the proportion of each the company has assumed. Debt costs are relatively easy to compute. The computation uses the interest rate the company is currently paying or would be projected to pay in the market. But there is no easy way to compute the company's cost of equity, the return the company theoretically pays to its equity investors. Typically, the company's cost of equity is computed using the capital asset pricing model, a calculation of the company's cost of equity capital based on the company's return in relation to the stock market, a relationship generally known as beta.[1]

---

[1] The accepted industry method for computation of a discount rate is to compute the corporation's weighted average cost of capital ("WACC"), otherwise known as the corporation's opportunity cost of capital for its assets. WACC is typically computed in accordance with the following formula: Rdebt (1 − Tc) (D/V) + Requity (E/V) where Rdebt = rate of return on the corporation's debt; Requity = rate of return on the corporation's equity; D = value of the corporation's debt; E = value of the corporation's equity; V = D + E; and Tc = the corporation's marginal tax rate. The computation of WACC requires ascertainment of the rate of return on the corporation's equity. A corporation's return on equity can also be phrased as the risk premium of

To create a simple DCF model, the following steps are taken:

1. Estimate Future Cash Flows: The future cash flows of the company will be estimated, typically for a three or five year period.

2. Compute the Discount Rate: This is the WACC for the company.

3. Discount Future Cash Flows: The estimated cash flows of the company are discounted at the WACC to obtain the present value of these cash flows.

4. Estimate Terminal Value: The value of the cash flows beyond the estimated projections must be estimated. To do this, a terminal value of the company is estimated. This can be done using an exit multiple (such as a multiple of EBITDA) or another valuation technique.

5. Discount Terminal Value: The terminal value is then discounted to present value using the WACC.

6. Calculate the DCF value: The DCF value is computed by adding together the present value of the future cash flows and the terminal value.

We can calculate a very simple discounted cash flow for a taxi business that is operated by means of a phone app. Let us assume that the only asset of this business is the cab, that the owner can purchase the cab for $20,000 without any financing, and that no other capital is required to run this business. At the end of three years, the business will have a terminal value of $10,000. After investigating the taxi business under current conditions, we estimate that the business will generate the following net revenues in years 1, 2 and 3, respectively: $10,000, $12,000, and $15,000. The weighted average cost of capital, or the discount rate, is assumed to be 5%. Given those assumptions, the question for our business is whether the venture makes sense—or what is the net present value of the proposed business venture? The investment will make sense if the discounted cash flow of the business venture is greater than zero—that is, if the venture generates more surplus over time given its cost of capital. Given the estimated cash flows, the discounted cash flow value of our taxi business is $22,004. The venture is consequently an attractive investment.

---

the corporation's stock over and above the market risk premium which itself is the general return of the market over and above the risk free rate. There is debate and disagreement over the appropriate methodology to estimate a corporation's requity; however, industry practice is to use the capital asset pricing model ("CAPM"). The CAPM is calculated in accordance with the following formula: Requity = Rfree + Beta (Rmarket – Rfree) where Rfree = risk free rate (e.g., rate on governmental bonds); (Beta) = covariance between the market's return and the individual corporation's stock return; and Rmarket = return on the market. The foregoing is based on Steven M. Davidoff, *Fairness Opinions*, 55 AM. U.L.REV. 1557 (2006).

Discount Rate	5%			
Discounted Cash Flow				
Year	**0**	**1**	**2**	**3**
Earnings				
Revenue from Business		15,000	17,000	17,000
Terminal value				10,000
Expenses				
Vehicle Cost	20,000			
Operating Costs		5,000	5,000	2,000
Net Cash Flows	−20,000	10,000	12,000	25,000
Net Present Value	**$22,004**			

This was a simple DCF analysis. An example from the "real world" is the DCF analysis set forth below, prepared by J.P. Morgan in connection with its fairness opinion to the board of directors of Dell in connection with Dell's acquisition by Michael Dell and Silver Lake.

DELL DEFINITIVE PROXY STATEMENT[2]
67–68
May 31, 2013

Discounted Cash Flow Analysis

J.P. Morgan conducted a discounted cash flow analysis for the purpose of determining the fully diluted equity value per share for the Common Stock. A discounted cash flow analysis is a method of evaluating an asset using estimates of the future unlevered free cash flows generated by the asset and taking into consideration the time value of money with respect to those future cash flows by calculating their "present value." "Present value" refers to the current value of one or more future cash payments from the asset, which is referred to as that asset's cash flows, and is obtained by discounting those cash flows back to the present using a discount rate that takes into account macroeconomic assumptions and estimates of risk, the opportunity cost of capital, capitalized returns and other appropriate factors. "Terminal value" refers to the capitalized value of all cash flows from an asset for periods beyond the final forecast period.

---

[2]   Available at http://www.sec.gov/Archives/edgar/data/826083/000119312513242115/d505470 ddefm14a.htm.

J.P. Morgan calculated the unlevered free cash flows that the Company is expected to generate (i) during the time period from November 2012 through January 2016 on the basis of the BCG Base Case, the BCG 25% Case and the BCG 75% Case, and (ii) during the time period from November 2012 through January 2017 on the basis of the September 21 Case prepared by the management of the Company. J.P. Morgan calculated the unlevered free cash flows based upon the BCG 75% Case and the September 21 Case for informational purposes only. [*Editor: The BCG Case, BCG 25% Case, the BCG 75% Case and the September 21 Case are various estimates of the company's future performance. BCG is Boston Consulting Group, a management consulting firm hired in this deal by Dell.*]

J.P. Morgan also calculated a range of terminal asset values of the Company by applying an EV/EBITDA multiple ranging from 3.5x to 5.5x of the EBITDA of the Company as estimated for the terminal period. The unlevered free cash flows and the range of terminal asset values were then discounted to present values using a range of discount rates from 9.5% to 13.5%. The discount rates used by J.P. Morgan were informed based on the Capital Asset Pricing Model ("CAPM") methodology. CAPM methodology assumes the weighted average cost of debt and equity, according to the debt to equity ratio based on an assumed capital structure. Accordingly, J.P. Morgan reviewed the capital structure of the Company and of each of the selected companies identified above in "— Public Trading Multiples." To calculate a cost of equity, CAPM methodology requires adding (i) a risk-free rate to (ii) the product of an assumed beta range multiplied by an equity risk premium. In arriving at its selected beta range, J.P. Morgan reviewed the historical and Barra predicted betas for all of the selected companies identified above. However, because no selected company is exactly the same as the Company, J.P. Morgan believed that it was inappropriate to, and therefore did not, rely solely on the given historical and Barra predicted betas of the selected companies. Accordingly, J.P. Morgan also made qualitative judgments concerning differences between the business, financial and operating characteristics and prospects of the Company and the selected companies that could affect the betas of each in order to provide a context in which to consider the results of the quantitative analysis.

The present value of the unlevered free cash flows and the range of terminal asset values were then adjusted for the Company's estimated debt, cash and cash equivalents as of November 2, 2012 (as provided by the Company's management).

Case	Implied Valuation Range
BCG Base Case	$ 10.50 to $14.25
BCG 25% Case	$ 12.00 to $16.50
BCG 75% Case(1)	$ 15.00 to $21.25
September 21 Case(1)	$ 15.50 to $21.75

(1) Calculated for informational purposes only.

Reading through J.P. Morgan's calculations, you will note that instead of a specific price, the investment bank arrives at a range of valuations for Dell. This is because a discounted cash flow analysis is made using numbers that cannot be determined with certainty. Rather, the numbers used in the valuation model are estimated. In performing the analysis, three central choices are made, each of which can significantly affect the final valuation. These are the correct forecasted free cash flows to utilize, the appropriate discount rate, and the terminal value of the asset. Each of these choices requires an estimate made by the person performing the valuation. The forecasted free cash flows and the terminal value involve predictions as to the future performance of the company. These can vary widely, as the J.P. Morgan excerpt shows. The bank used four separate scenarios for Dell's future cash flows. In addition, depending upon the discount rate, the value will fluctuate tremendously. As the J.P. Morgan excerpt shows, the beta of the company must be calculated (beta is the covariance between the market's return and the individual corporation's stock return—for example, a stock with a beta of 1 can be expected to move with the market, whereas a stock with a beta of 2 will move twice as much as the market, and a stock with a beta of .5 will move half as much as the market). This involved the bank's own judgments as to the appropriate comparable companies. A different set of comparable companies would yield a different result. In the Dell valuation, J.P. Morgan ultimately used several different discount rates between 9.5% and 13.5%. The range of discount rates reflects J.P. Morgan's acknowledgment of uncertainty.

Thus, a discounted cash flow analysis yields a valuation that is at best a range of possible values. J.P. Morgan's DCF valuations of Dell fluctuated from $10.50 to $14.25 per share to $15.50 to $21.75 per share depending upon the assumptions that J. P. Morgan made. Note that at the time this analysis was done, Michael Dell and Silver Lake had agreed to pay $13.65 per share, on the low side of this range, which is perhaps one reason for the vehement shareholder opposition to this price (it was later renegotiated to $13.88 per share in the face of this opposition).

2. COMPARABLE COMPANY ANALYSIS

A comparable company analysis is another tool often used in M&A valuation involving public companies. A comparable company analysis compares the company being valued with selected similarly situated publicly traded companies. These companies are compared using price multiples of each company's stock against selected accounting ratios, such as price to future earnings, price to forecasted sales, or price to book value (explained in the last Chapter).[3] A comparable company analysis will often adjust the capital structure of each company in order to more accurately compare it with the company being valued.

The following is the comparable company analysis performed by J.P. Morgan for the board of directors of Dell in connection with Dell's acquisition by Michael Dell and Silver Lake. This analysis was included in the Dell Proxy Statement.

DELL DEFINITIVE PROXY STATEMENT
59–61
May 31, 2013

Public Trading Multiples

Using publicly available information, J.P. Morgan compared selected financial data of the Company with similar data for selected publicly traded companies engaged in businesses which J.P. Morgan judged to be comparable to the Company's businesses or aspects thereof. The companies selected by J.P. Morgan were:

	• Hewlett-Packard Company ("HP")
End-User Computing ("EUC")	• ASUSTEK Computer Inc.
	• Lenovo Group
	• Acer Incorporated
Software & Peripherals ("S&P")	• Insight Enterprises, Inc.
	• Avnet, Inc.
	• TechData Corp
	• Ingram Micro Inc.

---

[3] Certain ratios are considered particularly important in valuing companies; comparisons can easily be made among companies against which the company is being compared. Different ratios give information about different attributes of the company, such as its profitability or its debt levels. Students wanting to read more about ratios are directed to http://www.sec.gov/invest or/pubs/begfinstmtguide.htm, which provides some basic information. Another interesting link is at http://pages.stern.nyu.edu/~adamodar/New_Home_Page/AccPrimer/accstate.htm.

Enterprise
- Microsoft Corporation
- EMC Corporation
- NetApp Inc.
- Oracle Corporation
- Cisco Systems, Inc.
- International Business Machines Corp.

Services
- Wipro Limited
- Xerox Corporation
- Computer Sciences Corporation

Software
- BMC Software, Inc.
- Symantec Corporation
- CA, Inc.

These companies were selected by J.P. Morgan, based on its experience and familiarity with the Company's industry, because of similarities to the Company in one or more of their business, regional or end-market characteristics and, in certain cases, similarities to the Company based on operational characteristics and financial metrics.

For each selected company and the Company, J.P. Morgan calculated such company's expected earnings before interest, taxes, depreciation and amortization ("EBITDA") for the 2013 calendar year ("CY13E") (provided that, for the Company, expected EBITDA for its fiscal year ending January 31, 2014 was used as an approximation for calendar year). J.P. Morgan then divided each such company's Enterprise Value (as defined below) by its expected EBITDA for CY13E ("CY13E EV/EBITDA") and divided each such company's Cash Adjusted Enterprise Value (as defined below) by its expected EBITDA for CY13E ("CY13E Cash Adjusted EV/EBITDA"). For the Company, HP, the EUC companies and the Enterprise companies, J.P. Morgan also calculated on a rolling basis beginning in February 2010 each such company's Enterprise Value divided by expected EBITDA for the next twelve months ("NTM EV/EBITDA"). For purposes of this analysis, a company's "Enterprise Value" was calculated as the fully diluted common equity value of such company plus the value of such company's indebtedness and minority interests and preferred stock, minus such company's cash, cash equivalents and short-term and long-term liquid investments and its "Cash Adjusted Enterprise Value" was calculated as its Enterprise Value as adjusted for estimated costs associated with the repatriation of foreign cash, assuming a friction cost of 35%.

J.P. Morgan also calculated, for each selected company and the Company, the ratio of the closing price of such company's common stock to expected earnings per share for CY13E ("CY13E P/E"). J.P. Morgan also calculated, for the Company, HP, the EUC companies and the Enterprise companies on a rolling basis beginning in February 2010, the ratio of the closing price of such company's common stock to its expected earnings for the next twelve months per share ("NTM P/E"). For the S&P 500 J.P. Morgan used data from FactSet.

	Company	HP	EUC		S&P(1)		Enterprise		Services		Software	
			Range	Median	Range	Median	Range	Median	Range	Median	Range	Median
CY13E EV/ EBITDA	3.3x	3.7x	6.0x–7.8x	6.9x	4.2x–6.5x	4.8x	5.4x–9.0x	8.4x	4.1x–10.1x	5.5x	5.4x–7.6x	6.5x
CY13E Cash Adjusted EV/ EBITDA	4.3x	4.0x	6.0x–7.8x	6.9x	4.4x–6.5x	5.0x	5.6x–9.6x	8.9x	4.3x–10.1x	5.5x	5.6x–7.8x	6.9x
CY13E P/E	6.6x	4.9x	11.0x–25.0x	15.5x	7.7x–9.5x	9.0x	9.3x–20.5x	12.5x	7.2x–15.9x	14.3x	10.9x–13.7x	13.3x

The following table represents the results of J.P. Morgan's analysis of the NTM EV/EBITDA and NTM P/E multiples of comparable publicly traded companies and, with respect to NTM/PE only, for the S&P 500 as of February 1, 2013, November 30, 2012 and their one-, two- and three-year averages, compared to the Company's trading multiples as of January 11, 2013, the last trading day before media reports of a possible going-private transaction involving the Company were first published, and as of November 30, 2012, the last trading day before an analyst report was issued by Goldman Sachs suggesting that the Company might be a target for a leveraged buyout transaction and its one-, two-, and three-year averages (except with respect to the foregoing for the S&P 500, which is according to FactSet):

	Company		HP		EUC		Enterprise		S&P 500
	NTM EV/EBITDA	NTM P/E	NTM EV/EBITDA	NTM P/E	NTM EV/EBITDA	NTM P/E	NTM EV/EBITDA	NTM P/E	NTM P/E(1)
Current (2)	3.3x	6.6x	3.7x	4.9x	7.4x	12.2x	6.7x	12.0x	13.0x
Pre-GS Report	2.7x	5.8x	3.2x	3.8x	6.6x	11.7x	6.3x	11.3x	12.1x
1-year average	3.4x	6.6x	3.9x	4.9x	6.0x	11.4x	6.7x	11.9x	12.6x
2-year average	3.6x	7.4x	4.1x	5.8x	6.3x	11.1x	7.1x	12.5x	12.3x
3-year average	3.9x	8.4x	4.7x	7.0x	6.5x	11.2x	7.6x	13.2x	12.6x

For purposes of its analysis of each of the Company and the selected companies in the tables above, J.P. Morgan used estimates for EBITDA and earnings per share based on consensus analyst research estimates, and based on publicly available financial data, including Wall Street research estimates and FactSet, and, as appropriate, further adjusted to include stock-based compensation expense but exclude non-recurring items. (Non-recurring items are, as the name suggests, items that are not expected to recur. Examples might include losses from a natural disaster, or gains from the sale of the corporate headquarters; another name for these items is "extraordinary" items.)

J.P. Morgan selected certain reference ranges of multiples based on the multiples calculated for selected companies, and applied such ranges to various projections of EBITDA and earnings per share for the Company for the Company's fiscal year 2014 to calculate the Company's equity value per share. In calculating the implied equity value per share for the Company, J.P. Morgan reviewed five different cases, two of which, the Preliminary FY14 Internal Plan and the Preliminary FY14 Board Case (each as defined below), were prepared by the Company's management and three of which, the BCG Base Case, the BCG 25% Case and the BCG 75% Case (each as defined below), were prepared by BCG.

A summary of the implied valuation ranges of the Common Stock that J.P. Morgan derived based on the ratio of Enterprise Value to estimated EBITDA under each of the five cases, using a reference range of 3.5x to 5.5x, is set forth below:

Case	Implied Valuation Range
Preliminary FY14 Internal Plan	$ 12.00 to $17.25
Preliminary FY14 Board Case	$ 11.25 to $16.00
BCG Base Case	$ 10.50 to $15.00
BCG 25% Case	$ 12.00 to $17.25
BCG 75% Case(1)	$ 15.25 to $22.50

(1) Calculated for informational purposes only.

A summary of the implied valuation ranges of the Common Stock that J.P. Morgan derived based on the ratio of price per share to expected earnings per share under each of the five cases, using a reference range of 5.0x to 10.0x, is set forth below:

Case	Implied Valuation Range
Preliminary FY14 Internal Plan	$ 8.75 to $17.50
Preliminary FY14 Board Case	$ 8.00 to $16.00
BCG Base Case	$ 7.25 to $14.50
BCG 25% Case	$ 9.00 to $18.00
BCG 75% Case(1)	$ 13.00 to $26.00

(1) Calculated for informational purposes only.

The biggest decision to be made by a person performing a comparable company analysis is picking the appropriate comparable companies. Depending upon the selection, the valuation can change significantly. In addition, because not all companies have the same capital structure, in order to make proper comparisons between them, adjustments must be made so that each has a similar debt and equity profile. The adjustments to capital structure also can result in substantial variations in valuation, as illustrated in the above excerpt.

J.P. Morgan first compared Dell's stock price to the stock price of a number of companies in a variety of industries: End-User Computing, Software & Peripherals, and Enterprise Services Software as well as Hewlett-Packard on a stand-alone basis. J.P. Morgan then computed various multiples and compared them to the Dell multiple, the selected metric multiplied by the price being paid for Dell shares. J.P. Morgan found that the multiples in the other industries appeared to be higher than the Dell multiple.

J.P. Morgan next prepared an implied valuation range based on multiples of Enterprise Value to estimated EBITDA and estimated earnings per share. The companies used are not specified, but J.P. Morgan arrives at multiples of 3.5x to 5.5x for Enterprise Value to EBITDA and 5.0x to 10x for estimated earnings per share. J.P. Morgan then multiplied these numbers by the forecasted multiples to ultimately find a range of valuations from $8.75 to $17.50 to $13.00 to $26.00, a very wide range indeed. Again, compare this valuation range with the price at the time this analysis was performed ($13.65 per share) and the final renegotiated price at which the deal was done ($13.88 per share).

a. Premium Analysis

A premium analysis (sometimes called a "premiums analysis" or "premium paid analysis") compares the premium being paid in a transaction with historical premiums paid for selected, similarly-situated companies. The "premiums" are the amounts above market price; acquirers are getting control in these transactions, so the term "control premium" is sometimes used. Typically, a premium analysis is conducted side-by-side with a comparable company analysis, often utilizing the same corporate entities.

J.P. Morgan did not conduct a premium analysis for the Dell Board. However, the Dell board retained another investment bank, Evercore, to also provide a fairness opinion. The following is the premium analysis from the Dell transaction prepared by Evercore, taken from Dell's Proxy Statement.

DELL DEFINITIVE PROXY STATEMENT
71–72
May 31, 2013

Premiums Paid Analysis

Evercore reviewed the premiums paid for (i) all closed global transactions from January 1, 2002 through January 5, 2013 with enterprise values greater than $10.0 billion ("global transactions"), of which there were 126, (ii) global transactions with cash consideration only ("cash transactions") from January 1, 2002 through January 5, 2013, of which there were 50, (iii) global transactions involving strategic buyers ("strategic transactions"), from January 1, 2002 through January 5, 2013, of which there were 103, and (iv) global transactions involving financial sponsor buyers ("sponsor transactions") from January 1, 2002 through January 5, 2013, of which there were 23.

Using information from Securities Data Corp. and FactSet Research Systems, Inc., premiums paid were calculated as the percentage by which the per share consideration paid in each such transaction exceeded the closing price per share of the target companies one day, one week and four weeks prior to transaction announcements. The results of this analysis are provided in the table below:

	1 Day Prior	1 Week Prior	4 Weeks Prior
Global Transactions			
High	116.4%	123.6%	118.7%
75th Percentile	37.1%	39.9%	40.6%
25th Percentile	13.0%	15.7%	18.4%
Low	0.1%	1.0%	1.9%
Mean	27.7%	30.3%	32.2%
Median	24.5%	27.2%	28.0%

Cash Transactions

High	116.4%	123.6%	118.7%
75th Percentile	43.3%	51.1%	51.8%
25th Percentile	18.9%	18.9%	21.9%
Low	0.4%	1.0%	5.7%
Mean	33.8%	36.3%	38.8%
Median	28.0%	30.0%	32.8%

Strategic Transactions

High	116.4%	123.6%	118.7%
75th Percentile	38.0%	41.5%	43.0%
25th Percentile	14.1%	16.5%	17.9%
Low	0.1%	1.0%	3.3%
Mean	28.9%	31.7%	33.7%
Median	27.9%	28.4%	30.8%

Sponsor Transactions

High	45.1%	50.8%	47.2%
75th Percentile	31.2%	31.8%	33.1%
25th Percentile	10.5%	14.3%	19.6%
Low	4.4%	2.8%	1.9%
Mean	22.1%	24.3%	25.6%
Median	20.1%	22.8%	26.0%

Based on the above analysis and Evercore's professional judgment and experience, Evercore then applied a range of premiums derived from the selected transactions of: (1) 22.5% to 27.5% to the $10.97 closing price per share of the Company and the $7.63 enterprise value per share of the Common Stock (taking into account estimated net cash of the Company as of January 31, 2013 as provided by Company management), in each case, on January 4, 2013 (the date one week prior to the last trading day before media reports of a possible going-private transaction involving the Company were first published) and (2) 25.0% to 30.0% to the $10.67 closing price per share and the $7.33 enterprise value per share of the Common Stock (taking into account estimated net cash of the Company as of January 31, 2013 as provided by Company management), in each case, on December 11, 2012 (the date four weeks prior to the last trading day before media reports of a possible going-private transaction involving the Company were first published). Based on this analysis, Evercore derived the following range of implied equity values per share for the Company:

	Implied Equity Value Range Per Share
1 Week Prior to January 11, 2013	
Closing Price ($10.97)	$ 13.44–$13.99
Enterprise Value ($7.63)	$ 12.69–$13.07
4 Weeks Prior to January 11, 2013	
Closing Price ($10.67)	$ 13.34–$13.87
Enterprise Value ($7.33)	$ 12.50–$12.87

Evercore compared the results of this analysis to the $13.65 per share merger consideration to be received by the holders of Company common stock entitled to receive such consideration pursuant to the merger agreement, noting that the merger consideration is above the two implied valuation ranges that were derived from the enterprise value per share of the Common Stock and within the two other implied valuation ranges that were derived from the closing price per share of the Common Stock.

In its premiums analysis, Evercore ultimately chose to measure the comparable premiums as of one week and four weeks before the date of the first media reports that Dell might be acquired. J.P. Morgan picked a date before these reports emerged in order to examine Dell's stock price without the effect of rumors of an acquisition—such rumors would tend to push the price up. Evercore selected over 300 transactions which it deemed comparable and calculated the premiums paid for each, showing the mean, median, 75th and 25th percentile as well as the high and low premiums, in order to compare those premiums with the premium in the Dell transaction.

Evercore ultimately compared the Dell premium to a range of premiums, from 22.5% to 27.5% and 25.0% to 30.0%. Evercore did not explain how these numbers related to the ranges found in the premiums analysis. The ranges selected by Evercore appear to be on the low side of that range, which perhaps helps explain why the initial price for Dell elicited significant shareholder opposition.

b. Other Valuation Analyses

While DCF analysis, comparable company analysis and premiums paid analysis are the most commonly utilized valuation techniques in M&A, other analyses are sometimes employed. These include:

Break-up Analysis. A break-up analysis, sometimes called a sum-of-parts analysis, assumes that the different businesses of the corporation will be parceled out separately and sold as going concerns. It then values each of these businesses on a stand-alone basis to derive a value for the entire corporate entity.

Liquidation Analysis. A liquidation analysis assumes that the assets of the corporation will be sold separately in an orderly liquidation of the firm. It then values the assets of the corporation on this basis. It is different from a break-up analysis in that it assumes that each business entity will be liquidated rather than being sold as a going concern.

Leveraged Buy-Out Analysis. A leveraged buy-out analysis is utilized to determine the maximum price a financial sponsor such as a private equity firm can pay. The analysis will calculate the future financial cash flows of the company and the maximum debt feasible in order to service the debt and realize the private equity firm's minimum return.

Each of these techniques is utilized in a particular situation. For example, a break-up analysis will be utilized when the company is in several different businesses and a sale of each business may yield a higher price than the whole. Similarly, a liquidation analysis will be done when the company may not continue as a going concern. Finally, a leveraged buy-out analysis will be done when there is a private equity buyer, in order to determine the maximum amount the buyer can borrow to finance the purchase—an amount which determines the maximum amount the private equity firm can pay.

c.   A Note on Technology Valuations

The traditional tools of valuation cannot be used when dealing with high-growth internet and other technology and start-up companies. These companies often lack revenue (let alone profits) to do a discounted cash flow analysis. Facebook, for example, acquired Instagram for $1 billion despite the fact that Instagram had zero revenue. Comparable company analysis is also difficult as these companies are in new industries, without real peers. Because traditional valuation techniques are inappropriate, other valuation metrics are used. One technique is market share—how much of a market can a company capture? Uber was recently valued at $41 billion despite having no profits and little revenue. The basis for this valuation was investors' expectations that Uber would capture not just a large portion of the market for taxi services, but would also in effect create (and, presumably, capture a significant portion of) a new market. Another metric is "eyeball counts," measuring the number of users of an internet site or app. In an eyeball count valuation, the investor is paying for viewers, hoping that their views can be monetized at some later date. An eyeball count is one way noted valuation expert Aswath Damodoran justified the valuation underlying Facebook's acquisition of WhatsApp for over $20 billion despite WhatsApp's lack of revenue:

FACEBOOK BUYS WHATSAPP FOR $19 BILLION: VALUE AND PRICING PERSPECTIVES

Aswath Damodaran
MUSINGS ON MARKETS
Feb. 20, 2014

[T]here are two different processes at work in markets. There is the pricing process, where the price of an asset (stock, bond or real estate) is set by demand and supply, with all the factors (rational, irrational or just behavioral) that go with this process. The other is the value process where we attempt to attach a value to an asset based upon its fundamentals: cash flows, growth and risk. For shorthand, I will call those who play the pricing game "traders" and those who play the value game "investors", with no moral judgments attached to either. So, at the risk of ending up with a split personality, let me try looking at Facebook's acquisition of Whatsapp for $19 billion, with $15 billion coming from Facebook stock and $4 billion from cash, using both perspectives.

The Investor/Value View

I will start wearing my value cap. To justify a $19 billion value for a company in equity markets today, you would need that company to generate about $1.5 billion in after-tax income in steady state.

Value of equity = $19 billion

Implied required return on equity, given how stocks were priced on 1/1/14 = 8.00% (a 5% equity risk premium on top of a 3% risk free rate)

Steady state earnings necessary to justify value = $19 billion *.08 = $1.52 billion

Steady state pre-tax earnings needed to justify value, using an effective tax rate of 30%= $1.52 billion/(1 − .30) = $2.17 billion

That would translate into pre-tax income of about $2.2 billion and it is a lowball estimate of break even earnings, since the break even number will increase, the longer you have to wait for steady state and the more risk there is in the business model. Using a 10% required return (reflecting the higher risk) and building in a waiting period of 5 years before the income gets delivered increases the break-even income to $4.371 billion. You can try the spreadsheet with your inputs, if you so desire, to see what your break-even earnings estimate will be.

. . .

At this stage, if you are an investor, you have two choices. The first and less damaging one is to accept that social media investing is not your game and move on to other parts of the market, where you can find investments that you can justify with fundamentals. The second is to go from frustration (at being unable to explain the price) to righteous anger or indignation about bubbles, irrationality and short term traders to trading on that anger (selling short). I would strongly recommend that you not go down this path, since it will not only be damaging to your physical health (it is a sure fire way to ulcers and heart attacks) but it may be even more so for your financial health. While you may be right about the value in the long term, the pricing process rules in the near term.

The Trader (Pricing) View

Wearing my trading hat, though, the Facebook acquisition for Whatsapp may not only make complete sense, but it may actually be viewed as a positive. To understand why, I had to change my mindset from thinking about fundamentals (earnings/cashflows, growth and risk) to focusing on what the market is basing its price on. To find that "pricing" variable, I looked at the market prices of social media company, multiple measures of their success/activity and tried to back out the drivers of both price differences and price movements.

Making money is a secondary concern (at least for the moment): Markets (and investors) are not completely off kilter. There is a correlation between how much a company generates in revenues and its value, and even one between how much money it makes (EBITDA, net income) and value. However, they are less related to value than the number of users.

Returning to the Facebook/Whatsapp deal, it seems to me that Facebook is playing the pricing game, and that recognizing that this is a market that rewards you for having a greater number of more involved users, they have gone after a company (Whatsapp) that delivers on both dimensions. Here is a very simplistic way to see how the deal can play out. Facebook is currently being valued at $170 billion, at about $130/user, given their existing user base of 1.25 billion. If the Whatsapp acquisition increases that user base by 160 million (I know that Whatsapp has 450 million users, but since its revenue options are limited as a standalone app, the value proposition here is in incremental Facebook users), and the market continues to price each user at $130, you will generate an increase in market value of $20.8 billion, higher than the price paid. Are there lots of "ifs" in this deal? Sure, but it does simplify the explanation.[4]

Professor Damodaran raises a fundamental issue: what justifies acquisition prices a great deal higher than could be supported by traditional valuation techniques? In retrospect, some of these prices have

---

[4] http://aswathdamodaran.blogspot.com/2014/02/facebook-buys-whatsapp-for-19-billion.html.

been revealed to have been much too high: consider the AOL Time Warner deal we discussed, and, more broadly, the dot.com bubble, which burst in the early 2000s. Perhaps these deals are more amenable to traditional valuation techniques than optimists want to believe.

C. VALUATION IN PRACTICE

1. NEGOTIATING PRICE

In practice, how is valuation used to negotiate price? Investment bankers or company employees will prepare valuations. The negotiation team designated by the boards of the buyer and target will negotiate price based on these valuations. The final price is driven by negotiating dynamics.

In a "hot" auction with multiple bidders, the actual price paid may rise well above the investment bankers' valuation. For example, Hewlett Packard acquired 3Par, a cloud computing company for $32 per share. HP reached that price after a vigorous bidding contest with Dell. Dell had previously agreed to acquire 3Par in a friendly merger for $18 per share. 3Par sought and received valuation advice from Qatalyst, an investment bank. On its face, the $18 price represented a significant premium over the $9.65 per share closing price prior to the announcement of Dell's offer. In support of that transaction, Qatalyst conducted a discounted cash flow analysis of 3Par and estimated a range of values from $10.69 to $21.02. Qatalyst also did a comparable company analysis for 3Par and estimated a range of values from $6.85 to $12.72. Compared with these estimates, the $18 per share price negotiated with Dell seemed generous. One week after announcements of the Dell/3Par transaction, HP made a $24 per share offer for 3Par. Dell countered with $24.30. HP countered with $27, and Dell matched that bid. HP bumped its offer to $30 and then $32. The final price for 3Par was well in excess of even the most optimistic initial valuation estimates of 3Par's investment bankers. HP was willing to pay far above the "valuation" price because 3Par was a cloud computing company; cloud computing is a hot business area, and there were few companies available to be purchased.

Alternatively, with fewer bidders or a less scarce asset and the absence of an active bidding market, the parties may adhere more closely to their prepared valuations. Valuation thus becomes particularly important in acquisitions where there may be only one possible or likely buyer, such as freeze-outs or management buy-outs. In those cases, parties will heavily rely on their prepared valuations since the price negotiation is not apt to yield a different price.

A company may be willing to pay a particularly high price in order to keep another company out of the hands of a competitor. For example,

Google reportedly paid $966 million to acquire Waze, the crowd-mapping service with only 100 employees and revenue below $70 million per year. Google did so once Facebook and Apple, competitors of Google, also expressed interest in acquiring Waze. The experience of Waze and 3Par demonstrate that the final price paid depends on the method of sale, the number of potential bidders, and ultimately the price that a willing buyer will pay. These decisions are informed, but not dictated, by traditional valuation techniques. There may be an additional financial benefit available that the traditional techniques do not readily take into account and in particular, one that may be differentially available to particular buyers.

2. APPRAISAL RIGHTS

Recall from Chapter III that in a statutory appraisal action under § 262, the Delaware Chancery Court will determine the "fair value" of a dissenting shareholder's shares. As the following case excerpt shows, the determination of fair value in the context of an appraisal is an exercise in valuation. Note the extent to which the court discusses, in some cases quite critically, the specifics of the expert valuation opinions:

DOFT & CO. V. TRAVELOCITY.COM INC.

Delaware Court of Chancery
Civ.A. 19734 (2004)

LAMB, VICE CHANCELLOR.

I.

This is an appraisal action, pursuant to 8 Del. C. § 262, filed as a result of a merger that cashed-out the petitioners' shares at a price of $28 per share. Both parties presented expert testimony to determine the fair value of the shares as of the merger date. For the reasons herein, the court concludes that the fair value of the shares as of the merger date is $32.76.

II.

A. *Background*

1. *The Parties*

Travelocity.com Inc. ("Travelocity"), a Delaware corporation, is the surviving entity of a merger between it and Travelocity Holdings Sub Inc. ("Holdings"), a wholly owned subsidiary of Sabre Holdings Corporation ("Sabre"). Because Sabre, through Holdings, owned more than 90% of the outstanding shares of common stock of Travelocity, the merger was authorized by Sabre's board of directors pursuant to 8 Del. C. § 253 and became effective on April 11, 2002 (the "Merger Date"). As a result of the merger, Travelocity is (again) a wholly owned subsidiary of Sabre.

The petitioners owned 265,540 shares of Travelocity before the merger and were entitled to demand an appraisal of those shares pursuant to Section 253(d) of the DGCL. In accordance with 8 Del. C. § 262, the petitioners now seek a determination of, and payment for, the fair value of the Travelocity shares they held on the Merger Date.

. . .

The events of September 11, 2001. . . . created great uncertainty in the online travel business. Even though the industry slowed in the period after September 11, analysts predicted that the negative effect would be temporary. Travelocity, however, also faced strong competition in the market at this time. Expedia, Travelocity's main competitor, surpassed Travelocity as the industry leader in early 2002 and Orbitz, a then brand new travel services provider, had become the third largest online travel agent in less than a year. Expedia quickly became more successful than Travelocity because of its early implementation of the "merchant model." The merchant model is a business plan in which travel agencies purchase the airline tickets, hotel rooms or car rentals at a negotiated rate from the suppliers and then resell them directly to consumers at a higher price. In the traditional agency model then used by Travelocity, the travel agent merely serves as a liaison between the supplier and the customer and receives a commission for the sale. The merchant model generates higher profit margins and much higher cash flows than the traditional agency model because the travel agent controls the price and works directly with both the supplier and the consumer. [*Editor: The omitted text contains a discussion of more details as to challenges Travelocity faced, but also some reasons for optimism about Travelocity's prospects.*]

. . .

B.   *The Experts*

The petitioners' trial expert was William H. Purcell. Purcell has a B.A. in Economics from Princeton University and an M.B.A. from New York University. He has been an investment banker for more than 35 years. . . .

Purcell testified that the going concern value of Travelocity was at least $35 per share as of March 16, 2002. Purcell testified that he relied primarily on the most recent set of management projections in his valuation analysis. Purcell also looked to analyses performed by third parties to test the validity of his conclusions.

Travelocity's trial expert was Professor Paul A. Gompers of the Harvard Business School. Gompers has an A.B. in Biology from Harvard College, a M.Sc. in Economics from Oxford, and a Ph.D. in Business Economics from Harvard University. . . .

Gompers reviewed various documents and materials on the online travel industry in general, as well as internal documents of Sabre and Travelocity. He also conducted interviews with some Sabre and Travelocity personnel. Gompers reached the conclusion that the going concern value of Travelocity as of the Merger Date was $20 per share.

C. *The Valuation Methods Used*

Both experts used essentially the same methods to value Travelocity's stock; i.e. a discounted cash flow analysis ("DCF") and a comparable company analysis. In performing their comparable company analyses, both Purcell and Gompers used Expedia as the single comparable company. Despite the similar approaches taken, the results arrived at by Gompers and Purcell vary widely. Gompers opines that, on a DCF basis, Travelocity common stock was worth between $11.38 and $21.29 per share. Using the same methodology, but using different inputs, Purcell opines that a share of Travelocity common stock was worth between $33.70 and $59.95 as of the Merger Date. The two experts' comparable company analyses also yield significantly divergent results because they disagree about the appropriate discount to apply to reflect Travelocity's competitive disadvantages.

. . .

"In a statutory appraisal proceeding, both sides have the burden of proving their respective valuation positions by a preponderance of the evidence." The court may exercise independent judgment to assess the fair value of the shares if neither party meets its burden.

IV.

In determining the fair value of Travelocity's shares, the court may consider "proof of value by any techniques or methods which are generally considered acceptable in the financial community and otherwise admissible in court." Both parties used a DCF approach and a comparable company approach to value the shares. DCF involves projecting operating cash flows for a determined period, setting a terminal value at the end of the projected period, and then discounting those values at a set rate to determine the net present value of a company's shares. It is an exercise in appraising the present value at a set date of the expected future cash flows earned by the company. A DCF analysis is a useful tool for valuing shares and is frequently relied on by this court in appraisal actions.

The utility of a DCF analysis, however, depends on the validity and reasonableness of the data relied upon. As this court has recognized, "methods of valuation, including a discounted cash flow analysis, are only as good as the inputs to the model." The problem in this case is that the most fundamental input used by the experts—the projections of future revenues, expenses and cash flows—were not shown to be reasonably reliable.

Delaware law clearly prefers valuations based on contemporaneously prepared management projections because management ordinarily has the best first-hand knowledge of a company's operations. Here, management prepared the 5-year projections for the period 2002–2005 and gave them to Sabre for use in its routine planning processes. Often, projections of this sort are shown to be reasonably reliable and are useful in later performing a DCF analysis. In this case, however, the court is persuaded from a review of all the evidence that the Travelocity 5-year plan does not provide a reliable basis for forecasting future cash flows.

To begin with, Travelocity's management held the strong view that these projections should not be relied upon because the industry was so new and volatile that reliable projections were impossible. At trial, Punwani, Travelocity's CFO, characterized the 5-year projections as "simulations" and "thought studies" and said that they were never reviewed by any of the operating departments at Travelocity. Punwani further testified that because of the limited financial history of Travelocity, together with a rapidly evolving marketplace, it was difficult "to forecast the next quarter, let alone five years out." He also confirmed that the events of September 11 led to more doubt about the future of the industry and Travelocity's positioning in the market. . . .

Purcell's DCF relies more or less uncritically on the Travelocity 5-year plan. Purcell justifies his reliance on these projections because they were provided to Sabre for its 5-year planning and later used by Goldman Sachs in its presentations to Sabre. Punwani, however, explained at trial that these numbers were given to Sabre as a routine requirement for Sabre's internal planning process and with express caveats as to their reliability, and that he personally told both Sabre's CFO and controller that the numbers were only simulations. Moreover, Punwani was presented on cross-examination with several Sabre documents showing projections for Travelocity, and testified credibly that he had never seen the documents before nor was he familiar with how Sabre used Travelocity's projections in its business planning. Despite the normal preference for management projections, the court concludes that the petitioners failed to prove that Purcell's reliance on these projections was justified. Thus, the court must disregard Purcell's DCF analysis.

Gompers takes a different approach, after concluding that the 5-year projections were "merely meant as a rough plan and were considered to be optimistic targets" and not a reliable basis for a DCF analysis. Instead of eschewing a DCF analysis, however, Gompers sets about to create a new set of projections, covering periods of 10 and 15 years into the future, based on his expert analysis of Travelocity and post-merger discussions with certain members of its management. As a preliminary matter, this court is inherently suspicious of post-merger, litigation-driven forecasts because "[t]he possibility of hindsight bias and other cognitive distortions seems untenably high." As important, in this case, Gompers's exercise is strikingly at odds with the views of Travelocity management and Salomon that no one could reliably predict Travelocity's future cash flows.

The reliability of Gompers's projections is further undermined by the fact that he selectively picks and chooses variables from management's 5-year forecast that conveniently fit into his exercise in creating less "optimistic" projections. Although Gompers's valuation is facially more credible than Purcell's, in that he provides both the numerical calculations and the academic theories for his assumptions, his selective reliance on aspects of management's projections is suspect. Gompers starts reasonably by using Travelocity's 2002 revenue projection, adjusted for Travelocity's actual performance in the first three months of 2002. He then generates 10-year and 15-year revenue projections by assuming that the revenue growth rate will (i) decrease in a linear fashion to 17.2%, the 2005 revenue growth rate found in the 5-year forecast, and then (ii) will continue to slow in a linear fashion until it reaches the "steady state of growth" in 2011 or 2016. Gompers does not explain why only the 2005 growth rate from the Travelocity 5-year plan is reliable and ignores that the Travelocity 5-year plan predicted much higher intervening growth rates. Gompers then uses the operating margins found in the Travelocity 5-year plan through 2005 and uses the 2005 operating margin in perpetuity to derive his projections for operating income.

The respondents argue that this selective use of management projections is acceptable because "they are reasonable or somewhat optimistic" and that since the petitioner's valuation wholly relies on the Travelocity 5-year plan that it is somehow estopped from arguing that Gompers selective use is unacceptable. Neither of these arguments is persuasive. The only reasonable conclusion the court can draw from the record evidence is that no one, including Professor Gompers, is able to produce a reliable set of long-range projections for Travelocity, as of the Merger Date.

For these reasons, the court reluctantly concludes that it cannot properly rely on either party's DCF valuation.

The goal of the DCF method of valuation is to value future cash flows. Here, the record clearly shows that, in the absence of reasonably reliable contemporaneous projections, the degree of speculation and uncertainty characterizing the future prospects of Travelocity and the industry in which it operates make a DCF analysis of marginal utility as a valuation technique in this case. If no other method of analysis were available, the court would, reluctantly, undertake a DCF analysis and subject the outcome to an appropriately high level of skepticism. The court, however, now turns to the other method of valuation offered by the parties.

D.   *The Comparable Company Approach*

The comparable company approach entails the review of publicly traded competitors in the same industry, then the generation of relevant multiples from public pricing data of the comparable companies and finally the application of those multiples to the subject company to arrive at a value. The true utility of a comparable company approach is dependent on "the similarity between the company the court is valuing and the companies used for comparison." Both experts and Salomon use Expedia as the single comparable company in their analyses, but disagree on the appropriate discount to be applied to the multiples derived from their analyses of Expedia. The court agrees that Expedia is clearly comparable to Travelocity.

Gompers does not challenge Salomon's valuation, but he dismisses Purcell's valuation because "it is applied in an ad hoc manner with little understanding of the proper measure of comparison and the factors that affect comparable multiples." Gompers states that the discount to Expedia should be at least 40% and concludes that Travelocity's valuation as of the merger date is $22.08.

Purcell critiques Gompers's valuation in that it is significantly lower than any valuation done of Travelocity and, more importantly, inexplicably less than the $28 paid by Sabre in the merger. Purcell also criticizes Gompers's comparable company analysis in that it is "wildly divergent" from his DCF calculation when Gompers states that his comparable company valuation serves as a check on his DCF. Purcell states that a 10% discount to Expedia is appropriate and concludes that the value should be no less than $35 a share.

Salomon applies a 20%–30% discount range to Expedia and concludes that the appropriate value is between $24 and $32 a share. The independent valuation performed by Salomon provides the court with a neutral framework from which to analyze Purcell and Gompers's divergent values.

1.   *The Appropriate Discount*

The experts disagree on the appropriate discount that should be applied to Expedia as a comparable company. Purcell adopts Salomon's initial discount to Expedia of 10% and Gompers uses a minimum 40% discount. Salomon derives its discount range of 20% to 30% comparing the historical discounts of Travelocity's multiples of firm value to EBITDA and share price to estimated 2002 earnings per share relative to corresponding multiples for Expedia. The court finds Gompers's detailed analysis of Travelocity's risk and expected future growth rates reasonable. Furthermore, when asked why Salomon adjusted its initial discount rate, Zakkour testified at length about discussions with Travelocity's management as to the difficulties it faced in catching up to Expedia and successfully implementing a merchant model business. Gompers, like Zakkour, discusses the difference in the business models of the companies and the significance of this difference in the comparable company valuation.

Purcell relies on the early 2002 positive analyst research reports as proof that Travelocity should only be at a "moderate," if any, discount to Expedia. Purcell gives great weight to James Hornthal's testimony about Travelocity and its potential. Hornthal characterized the Expedia-Travelocity competition as a "cat-and-mouse game" where the two companies were "jockeying back and forth" in the market. Hornthal relies on the Site59 acquisition as a beacon of light for Travelocity in its ability to catch up to Expedia after Expedia had pulled ahead in the fourth quarter of 2001. Peluso's testimony on Site59's ability to "transform" Travelocity's business model is persuasive: the acquisition of Site59 while being a step in the right direction did not equal a fully operational merchant model business. Hornthal's optimistic view of Travelocity's ease in catching up to Expedia, on which Purcell relies, is too speculative when compared to the clear evidence in the record that Travelocity still faced significant challenges in the development of its merchant model business. Purcell also places great importance on the fact that Travelocity was going to meet or exceed its 2002 expectations, but Punwani testified that it was only going to meet its projections through strategic cost-cutting that could not be sustained long-term. Moreover, Salomon adjusted its initial 10% discount (on which Purcell relies) to a 20% to 30% range after discussing Travelocity's strengths and weaknesses with management. Therefore, the record shows that Purcell's assumptions vis-à-vis the appropriate discount to be applied in comparing the companies are unduly optimistic.

Gompers concludes that the discount to Expedia should be at least 40% because Travelocity had a higher cost of capital, a lower growth rate, and a lesser ability to generate cash. He states that at the time of the merger, "Travelocity had lost momentum and was facing new competition that made its prospects potentially tenuous." The record is clear that even though Travelocity was actively working to remedy its outdated model, it still faced significant challenges at the time of the merger. The court notes that there was no evidence presented at trial or in the record to quantify the actual cost of building a merchant model or any necessary technological upgrades. With all of these factors in mind, the court concludes that it should apply a 35% discount to the valuation multiples derived from the analysis of Expedia, to reflect that competitive obstacles

Travelocity confronted as of the Merger Date. This decision reflects the court's view that Gompers is substantially correct, albeit unduly pessimistic, in his critical comparison of Travelocity to Expedia. Instead of relying on Gompers's assessment that a discount of at least 40% is warranted, the court adopts, instead, the mid-point of Gompers's 40% and the high end of Salomon's 20%–30% range.

2. *Valuation Multiples*

Gompers and Purcell agree that firm value to EBITDA is the most important valuation metric. Purcell isolates firm value/ EBITDA as *"by far* the most relevant and important statistic for comparison purposes." Purcell argues that this is the most important statistic because Travelocity has a great deal of noncash expenses, including depreciation, amortization, and the amortization of intangibles such as goodwill. Gompers agrees with Purcell that the EBITDA multiples are the "preferred multiple to examine" because they "are closest to cash flow and are a better proxy for the firm's on-going concern value."

Zakkour testified in his deposition that even though a range of valuation metrics were used in Salomon's report, the most important valuation metric for comparing the companies was the price to earnings multiple because Travelocity was less profitable than Expedia. Zakkour further testified that Travelocity had a lot of work to do to catch up to Expedia, not only because Expedia was growing faster than Travelocity, but also because Travelocity had to basically transform its business model to remain competitive.

Based on the expert reports and Zakkour's testimony, the court isolates the 2002 EBITDA multiple and the price-to-earnings multiple as the most important multiples in calculating Travelocity's firm value. Since Purcell does not present any calculations to back up his comparable company valuation, the court looks to Gompers's analysis in deriving the correct multiples. Gompers provides detailed and reasonable calculations for both Travelocity and Expedia's financial multiples, and the court agrees that these multiples are appropriate in comparing the companies.

Discounting Expedia's EBITDA multiple (34.8x) by 35% produces an EBITDA multiple of 22.62x. Applying this multiple to Travelocity's expected 2002 EBITDA of $47.80 million yields a value of $1,081,236,000. Discounting Expedia's EPS multiple (50.77x) by 35% produces an EPS multiple of 33.00x. Applying this multiple to Travelocity's expected 2002 net earnings of $39.45 million yields a value of $1,301,850,000. The court gives 2/3 weight to the EBITDA calculation and 1/3 weight to the PE calculation, yielding an enterprise value of $1,154,774,000. To determine the equity value, Gompers adds back the cash of $114 million and subtracts out the debt of $4.03 million. This leads to an equity valuation of $1,264,744,000, or $25.20 per share.

E. *Application Of A Control Premium*

Delaware law recognizes that there is an inherent minority trading discount in a comparable company analysis because "the [valuation] method depends on comparisons to market multiples derived from trading information for minority blocks of the comparable companies." The equity valuation produced in a comparable company analysis does not accurately reflect the intrinsic worth of a corporation on a going concern basis. Therefore, the court, in appraising the fair value of the equity, "must correct this minority trading discount by adding back a premium designed to correct it."

The parties are silent on the proper application of a control premium. Purcell states summarily that if the court is to accept the theory that "some minority discount from going concern value" is appropriate in a comparable company analysis, then the correct valuation would be above his stated value. Salomon conducted a review of precedent minority squeeze-out transactions and found that the average premium paid for a control block when compared to the stock price was approximately 50%. Travelocity, however, is not directly comparable to the companies in Salomon's data survey. In fact, the online travel industry, as already discussed in great detail, is unique when compared generally to publicly traded companies. Moreover, the recent appraisal cases that correct the valuation for a minority discount by adding back a premium "that spreads the value of control over all shares equally" consistently use a 30% adjustment.

Relying on recent precedents, the court will adjust the $25.20 per share value by adding a 30% control premium. This results in a per share value of $32.76.

———————

The *Doft* case highlights a number of issues in valuation and appraisal actions. The first is the problem of valuing technology start-ups where traditional techniques like discounted cash flow analysis may be inapposite. The second is that given the large number of choices in valuation, appraisal actions are often reduced to a "battle of the experts," as dueling and markedly different valuations are put forth by each side. Sometimes, neither expert "wins" the battle: in some recent appraisal cases, *Huff Fund Investment Partnership v. CKx, Inc.* and *In Re Appraisal of Ancestry.Com., Inc.*, discussed in Chapter III, the court rejected the experts' valuations and used the merger price. Following is a criticism of the experts' methodology from the *CKx* opinion:

> First, I will not rely on either of Reilly's "guidelines" analyses: the guideline publicly traded company ("GPTC") analysis, or the guideline merged and acquired company ("GMAC") analysis.

"The true utility of a comparable company approach is dependent on the similarity between the company the court is valuing and the companies used for comparison." Here, the evidence is abundantly clear that the "guideline" companies used by Reilly are not truly comparable to CKx.

Second, the deficiencies of both DCF analyses lead me to conclude that they are unreliable measures of CKx's value. DCF, in theory, is not a difficult calculation to make—five-year cash flow projections combined with a terminal value are discounted to their present value to produce an overall enterprise value. However, without reliable five-year projections, any values generated by a DCF analysis are meaningless. The reliability of a DCF analysis therefore depends, critically, "on the reliability of the inputs to the model." Under Delaware appraisal law, "[w]hen management projections are made in the ordinary course of business, they are generally deemed reliable." But this Court has disregarded management projections where the company's use of such projections was unprecedented, where the projections were created in anticipation of litigation, or where the projections were created for the purpose of obtaining benefits outside the company's ordinary course of business.

In sum, judges, who are not experts or trained in valuation, are attempting to use highly technical and sometimes conflicting valuation techniques and expert valuations to determine one "fair" price for the target company's shares. Despite these issues, there has been no movement to reform how appraisal actions are conducted. Nonetheless, it appears that CKx and Ancestry.com do mark some degree of judicial reform. Going forward, absent a conflict or other issue with the transaction, Delaware judges appear ready to accept the merger price as the correct price in an appraisal action.

3. FAIRNESS OPINIONS

a. What Is a Fairness Opinion?

Another context in which valuation issues arise in M&A is fairness opinions. The following excerpt describes fairness opinions and their role in M&A transactions:

FAIRNESS OPINIONS IN MERGERS AND ACQUISITIONS

Steven M. Davidoff, et al.
in THE ART OF CAPITAL RESTRUCTURING: CREATING SHAREHOLDER VALUE THROUGH
MERGERS AND ACQUISITIONS (H. Kent Baker & Halil Kiymaz eds. 2011)

In a corporate control transaction, a fairness opinion is typically provided to a board, or a committee thereof, at the time of its consideration of the relevant transaction. The fairness opinion is usually delivered orally at this meeting by the investment bankers in attendance and confirmed in a subsequent, written letter addressed to the board from the investment bank. This two- or three-page letter sets forth the transaction terms, as well as the qualifications and assumptions underlying the investment bank's fairness determination. In fact, this is the letter's primary purpose—to manage and restrict the investment bank's liability for rendering the opinion. The laundry list of qualifications and assumptions is the bulk of the text. At the letter's end is one sentence wherein the fairness of the transaction at hand is opined. In a corporate control transaction, this is a statement that the consideration paid or received in the transaction is "fair from a financial point of view" to a specified party. The party is dependent upon the form and posture of the transaction, but the opinion is typically directed to the party receiving or paying the transaction consideration. For example, in an opinion delivered to a target board considering the transfer of corporate control through a corporate sale, the opinion would be directed toward the corporation's selling stockholders.

A fairness opinion is not an appraisal. It does not specify a set value or presume to be a determination of price. Instead, a fairness opinion is the opinion of a financial or other advisor that a specified transaction is within a range of values encompassing financial "fairness." A more specific definition of fairness in these circumstances is almost never proposed or spelled out. The definition of fairness varies in context and, in each instance, is subject to debate among practitioners and academics. In a corporate control transaction, one definition of fairness from a target's perspective is a minimum range of values that the corporation's unaffiliated stockholders could otherwise receive in a board-run auction process conducted in a fair, open, and equivalent manner. However, the definition of fairness depends upon the recipient as well as the transaction and its unique characteristics. To date, there is no agreed-upon standard definition among academics, practitioners, or standard-setters of what fairness is in any circumstance.

Liability concerns have driven the fairness opinion structure and form. Investment banks have eschewed definitional fairness since elaboration provides further facts and conclusions upon which to challenge the opinion's validity or preparation or to otherwise assert under the federal securities (and other disclosure-based laws) that it is a statement of fact rather than opinion. The qualification and assumptions are crafted responses designed in part to restrict or obviate past court attempts to broaden the courts' ability to review a fairness opinion analysis, as well as the scope of an investment bank's duty to the relevant corporation's stockholders.

Even the addressee—the board—is a source of liability concern. The board, rather than stockholders, is the addressee in order to provide a legal argument that stockholders cannot rely upon the opinion. Ultimately, while a full review of the fairness opinion form is beyond the scope of this chapter, some claim that these caveats and omissions eat up much of the worth of any fairness opinion. Recent evidence of this came from the Lazard fairness opinion to Bear Stearns shareholders with respect to the fairness of the consideration initially offered by J.P. Morgan. In that opinion, Lazard was able to conclude that J.P. Morgan's $2 a share price was fair, since Lazard assumed that the only alternative transaction was a bankruptcy where the equity holders received nothing (see Bear Stearns Companies Inc. Definitive Proxy Statement, 2008).

A fairness opinion delivered orally or in writing by the preparer at a board meeting is almost always, at least in a corporate control transaction, accompanied by a "board book." The board book details the underlying analyses conducted by the opiner used to arrive at and conclude financial fairness. The "meat" of the investment banker's work lies here. A well-advised board will review this book in connection with their receipt of a fairness opinion and question the bankers as to their derivation of fairness. The fairness opinion's meaning and worth, if any, lies in these actual analyses.

There are a number of different underlying valuation analyses upon which a fairness opinion can rest and which are set forth in this "board book." The most common and accepted techniques are discounted cash flow, comparable companies, premium, break-up, and liquidation analysis. The preparer of a fairness opinion will typically utilize a weighted combination of these to arrive at a fairness conclusion. However, in the investment banking community, no uniform, specific, and objective guidelines exist explaining the exact mix and weight to assign to each of these methods to arrive at fairness.

Each of the techniques is also prone to subjectivity. There is, however, no standard-setting or other body guiding these or other preparation decisions. This lends itself to valuation approach differences in each application and among institutions as each of them develops its own individual approach. For instance, Shaked and Kempainen's (2009) analysis of fairness opinions and the related proxy statement's description of the underlying analyses illustrate the considerable variation in the valuation techniques used and the assumptions underlying each valuation approach. They point out that the inadequate information available to shareholders regarding the inputs and valuation approaches used increases the difficulty for shareholders to determine if the board actually made the right decision.

The Online Appendix includes the fairness opinions given by J.P. Morgan and Evercore to the Dell board of directors. Also included in the Appendix are the presentations prepared by each firm for the board (the "board books") in connection with the fairness opinion, explaining the basis for the opinion. Note how short the fairness opinions are. Note, too, that they do not reference the board books.

b. Criticism of Fairness Opinions

Fairness opinions have been heavily criticized, mainly on grounds that the opinions purport to be far better grounded in objective metrics than they really are. For instance, Professors Bebchuk and Kahan criticize fairness opinion practice, noting the discretion inherent in the preparation of these opinions. In a law review article, they state:

> Because of this discretion, investment banks can arrive at widely differing estimates of 'fair price,' all of which would be reasonable and none of which could be shown to be 'wrong' (or unfair) under objective criteria. That financial analysts can regard widely differing figures as 'fair' is problematic for two reasons. First, the subjective nature of fairness opinions reduces their value. Even if an investment bank rendered an opinion based on its genuine beliefs about fair price, that would be just one bank's opinion. Since other analysts could (legitimately) arrive at very different opinions, no single opinion should receive excessive weight. Second, and more importantly, this discretion enables investment banks to act opportunistically. Investment bankers can formulate fairness opinions serving their and the managers' interests, rather than ones reflecting their best judgments of fair price. . . . [I]nvestment banks have strong incentives to write opinions that satisfy the managers who hire them and negotiate their fees[5]

Professors Carney and Elson also criticize fairness opinions, arguing that value is ultimately determined by the market. Elson argues that:

> [o]pinions on value are just that—opinions. Value is simply what one individual is willing to pay for a particular asset at a given point in time. . . . [Investors] make their own judgments on value

---

[5] Lucian A. Bebchuk & Marcel Kahan, *Fairness Opinions: How Fair Are They and What Can Be Done About It?*, 1989 DUKE L. J. 29–30 (1989).

when they decide to buy or sell based on their own conclusions on the financial information presented to them. It really matters little whether the opinion calls a price adequate or not. . . . [A suspect fairness opinion] is as necessary to valuation analysis as is the appendix to the human digestive system. Other than producing profits for the investment banking industry, it produces no benefit for the shareholders.[6]

Carney argues that "[a] good is only worth what a willing buyer will pay for it—no more, no less" and that fairness opinions are a "costly tax that legal rules impose on business transactions."[7] Why does Carney think fairness opinions exist? Not for the benefit of shareholders. Rather, they "exist for two reasons: a judicial belief in the determinacy of value, and legal rules that shelter the business judgment of a board when based on reliance on the opinions of experts."[8] He further suggests that the real function of fairness opinions is to encourage directors to take reasonable risks.

One of the co-authors of this book views fairness opinions more favorably. Professor Solomon highlights the subjectivity inherent in fairness opinions and the lack of set valuation standards but documents that these faults are commonly known in the marketplace. Solomon asserts that fairness opinions may be valued for other purposes. A fairness opinion's value may be in the underlying analysis and the tool it provides investment bankers to bargain over transaction price. Solomon agrees with the opinions' critics that fairness opinions themselves are a poor substitute for well-functioning market mechanisms, such as auctions and competitive bidding situations. But there are transactional contexts in which such mechanisms do not function well, if at all, such as freeze-out acquisitions by controlling shareholders. In such cases, fairness opinions are a needed substitute.

Despite being heavily criticized in the legal literature, fairness opinions are ubiquitous in public transactions. Professors Cain and Denis analyze a sample of 582 negotiated public transactions during the period from 1998 to 2005. They find that targets disclosed using a fairness opinion in ninety-six percent of transactions and acquirers in twenty-eight percent of transactions.[9]

---

[6] Charles M. Elson, *Fairness Opinions: Are They Fair or Should We Care?*, 53 OHIO ST. L.J. 951, 1002 (1992).

[7] William J. Carney, *Fairness Opinions: How Fair Are They and Why We Should Do Nothing About It*, 70 WASH. U. L. Q. 523, 527–28 (1992).

[8] *Id.* at 525.

[9] Matthew Cain & David J. Denis, *Information Production by Investment Banks: Evidence From Fairness Opinions*, 56 J. L. & ECON. 245 (2013).

c.　The Legal Reasons for Fairness Opinions

Legal reasons probably explain why fairness opinions are so commonly used despite the many critiques of such opinions. In *Smith v. Van Gorkom*, discussed in Chapter XVII, the Delaware Supreme Court found that the board of the Trans Union Corporation had breached its duty of care by approving the acquisition of a corporation (in a cash-out merger) in a manner that was not the product of an informed business judgment. The court held that the board's failure to obtain anything more than a "rough" and unquestioned estimate of possible value from the corporation's chief financial officer did not satisfy this duty. More was required. A target board, as part of its duty of care in a corporate change of control transaction, was obligated to duly inform itself of the corporation's sale value through a well-prepared financial analysis. While the court expressly said that a fairness opinion was not required as a matter of law, such opinions are now almost invariably obtained—and the reason given is the *Van Gorkom* opinion.

Why should *Van Gorkom* motivate a seller to get a fairness opinion? A key part of the decision relates to DGCL § 141(e), which provides that directors are:

> fully protected in relying in good faith ... upon such information, opinions, reports or statements presented to the corporation by any of the corporation's officers or employees or by any other person as to matters the member reasonably believes are within such other person's professional or expert competence.

The directors in *Van Gorkom* had claimed reliance on this statute based upon the advice of the corporation's chief executive and chief financial officers. While holding that the directors could not avail themselves of this protection in the case, the court did strongly imply that obtaining a thorough valuation study or a fairness opinion not only would satisfy the board's duty of care and duty to be duly informed as to corporate value but also would establish a sufficient basis to rely on § 141(e). Later Delaware court opinions would provide further support for this inference, particularly with respect to fairness opinions. The *Van Gorkom* case and DGCL § 141(e) are further discussed in Chapter XVII.

d.　The Role of Lawyers in Fairness Opinions

In recent years, fairness opinions have become more regulated due to a series of cases in the Delaware Chancery Court discussed in Chapter XII. In addition, the Financial Industry Regulatory Authority (the self-regulatory organization for the brokerage industry and stock exchanges) has adopted regulations requiring disclosure of conflicts of interest and investment bank compensation relating to fairness opinions.[10]

When lawyers represent investment banks giving fairness opinions, they serve as the investment banks' protective shield. Because transaction related litigation is a common prospect, investment banks hire their own legal advisors to advise them on their fairness opinion when the company to be acquired is public. The lawyer advises the investment bank on the structural issues of giving the fairness opinion, trying to ensure that all potential conflicts are vetted and disclosed. The lawyer also assists the investment bank in preparing the text of the fairness opinion and underlying board books. The lawyer reviews and may help draft the fairness opinion. Finally, the lawyer reviews, if not prepares, the disclosure of the fairness opinion and its underlying analysis in either the proxy or tender offer statement. The disclosure about the Dell valuations quoted above was prepared by J.P. Morgan and Evercore as part of their fairness opinions. The disclosure was included in Dell's proxy statement for its acquisition.

QUESTIONS

1. For what purposes are valuations used?

2. When might a transaction be done at a price that differs from a company's "valuation"?

3. What matters in valuation are most "subjective"? What matters are least subjective?

4. Reread the excerpts from the Dell valuation. Do you think the price negotiated initially for Dell ($13.25 per share) was appropriate? Do you think the banks thought that it was? Why do you think J.P. Morgan did not do a premiums analysis, but Evercore did?

5. How certain are you that the price arrived at by Vice Chancellor Lamb in the *Doft* case is correct? How certain do you think Vice Chancellor Lamb is?

6. What explains the wide gap in valuation between the two experts in *Travelocity.com*?

7. Do you agree that the "merger price" is the appropriate standard for "fair value" in most appraisal proceedings? Does this make an appraisal proceeding meaningless in most circumstances?

8. Do you think getting a fairness opinion adds any value for a company (as opposed to its directors)? If so, how?

9. What do you think would happen if there were no Delaware law on fairness opinions?

---

[10] FINRA Manual: 5150. Fairness Opinions, available at http://finra.complinet.com/en/ display/display_main.html?rbid=2403&element_id=6832.

PART III

DOING THE DEAL

■ ■ ■

CHAPTER XI

DECIDING TO DO A DEAL

■ ■ ■

A. MAKE OR BUY DECISIONS

For strategic acquirers, whether to engage in a merger transaction is a classic "make-or-buy" decision. When it is cost-effective to do so, firms will opt to grow organically, developing internal capacities and technologies to meet market challenges. However, at times, there may be necessary or desired capacities and technologies that exist external to the firm. Acquiring them through a merger may be more cost-effective than trying to develop them.[1] Firms face these make-or-buy decisions regularly as they expand vertically and horizontally, seeking economies of both scale and scope.

Cable television companies are good examples of companies pursuing expansion through horizontal mergers. When cable companies consider how to expand their reach, they typically have two choices. First, they might negotiate with individual municipalities in their targeted expansion areas and build new networks parallel to the existing networks. Alternatively, a cable company seeking to expand might acquire an existing company already operating in the location in which it wishes to expand. There are advantages and disadvantages to both strategies. In the end, when making their decision, company boards typically decide to acquire when the costs of acquiring are lower than the costs of investing the resources to move into the target business or market without an acquisition. As an industry, the cable industry has generally opted for acquisition as the more efficient answer to the make or buy question.

Companies sometimes seek to expand by acquiring smaller companies in their business segment, thereby reducing horizontal competition. These transactions are known as "roll-ups." For the past two decades, cable television companies have been aggressively acquiring smaller competitors and consolidating their coverage areas in roll-up transactions. While two decades ago, the cable television market was populated by hundreds of smaller providers and a dozen or so larger providers, by 2014 Comcast, Cox, Cablevision, and Time Warner Cable were the only significant players in the marketplace. Through a series of

---

[1]   *See* Ronald H. Coase, *The Nature of the Firm*, ECONOMICA (1938).

roll-up transactions, most of the smaller cable providers have been absorbed. Consider Comcast's attempt to acquire Time Warner Cable in 2014 for $45.2 billion. That attempt failed; at this writing, in late 2015, Charter Communications is now pursuing a merger with Time Warner Cable.

The pharmaceutical industry is another example of an industry in which a merger strategy has played an important role in answering the make-or-buy question. Over the past two decades, the industry has been steadily consolidating, with mergers among the largest fully-integrated pharmaceutical corporations. These transactions have been large by almost any measure. For example, in 2009 Pfizer acquired Wyeth Pharmaceuticals for $68 billion and Merck acquired Schering-Plough for $41 billion. In 2011 Sanofi acquired Genzyme for $20 billion. These transactions were motivated by a search for new products and a desire to generate additional economies of scale and scope. Not all pharmaceutical acquisitions are such large transactions, however. Developing new drugs is extremely expensive. Many research efforts fail to generate useful drug candidates. Big pharma will sometimes use acquisition strategies as a way of outsourcing research and development activities to start-up life sciences firms. By acquiring (or entering into long term licensing agreements with) successful start-up life science firms, both sides are able to benefit from decisions to buy new capabilities and technologies.

To merge or sell itself is typically one of the most important decisions in a company's life. These transactions are motivated by a variety of commercial and strategic considerations. Because of the significance of the merger or sale transaction, whether or not to engage in a merger or sale is highly scrutinized and regulated. That being said, regulators have, perhaps surprisingly, generally eschewed dictating to boards how they go about the process of buying or selling businesses. And as we will see, in making decisions with respect to corporate strategy, especially with respect to mergers and acquisitions, the board of directors plays a central role.

B. HOW TO SELL A COMPANY

1. GUIDING SALE PRINCIPLES

"We're not done!", Goldstone insisted. "Peter, we're willing to bid more. We'll bid more! What is this nonsense about starting an auction and shutting it down an hour later? There are no rules governing these procedures. We put in a bid saying we'll bid more, and we will. How can you do this? It's not fair!"

Atkins tried to calm the feverish lawyer but got nowhere.

"Peter you've got to keep the bidding open. You've got to keep the bidding open as long as people are willing to bid."[2]

Thus ended the bidding in 1988 for RJR Nabisco, as dramatized in the book and film *Barbarians at the Gate*. RJR Nabisco went private, in what was then the largest leveraged buyout deal, valued at over $25 billion. Two bidders, a management backed group and a private equity buyer, bid against each other in a managed bidding process. The board of RJR Nabisco ultimately decided to sell the company to the private equity buyer for $109/share, choosing that offer over the higher $112/share management offer.

As previously discussed, a company may decide to pursue expansion in its business area through an acquisition. Or it may simply see a good opportunity in making an acquisition, as is the case with private equity firms, which are in the business of seeking acquisition opportunities no matter the area. Below we focus on the seller's perspective, since sellers tend to have much more control over structuring the process than buyers do. Consider how one might sell an asset like a house. The asset might be advertised to various different types of potential buyers—for instance, those who might want to live in the house, those who might want to rent it out, and those who might want to tear it down and build something new on the land. All material information about the condition and history of the house is disclosed to any interested potential buyer. Multiple potential buyers place bids on the house, and the seller accepts the best offer. In the context of a sale of real estate, the open auction with multiple bidders may well be the best way to proceed. But there is no reason to suppose that this is true for the sale of a company. Deal lawyers say that there is "no single blueprint" a board must follow in selling a company.[3] While the "no single blueprint" mantra is meant to remind boards that they have a great deal of discretion in meeting their obligations under the *Revlon* standard, to be discussed in Chapter XVIII, it also suggests an obvious truth. There is no single best way to sell a company. What might work in one circumstance might not work in another. (By way of preview, when *Revlon* duties are triggered, a board must try to get the best price available for the shareholders. We will discuss when the duties are triggered in our coverage of *Revlon*, but for present purposes, the most common triggers are when a company initiates an active bidding process for itself, or there is to be a change in control or break-up.)

For example, in technology companies, the most valuable assets a firm has are not made of bricks and mortar; rather, they are the gray matter in the heads of the employees. The knowledge that the firm is for sale, and the employment uncertainty that often surrounds sales, could

---

[2]   BRYAN BURROUGH & JOHN HELYAR, BARBARIANS AT THE GATE 462 (1989).

[3]   *Barkan v. Amsted Indus., Inc.*, 567 A.2d 1279, 1286 (Del. 1989).

be enough to cause many of the most valuable employees of the firm to seek other, more secure, opportunities. Even if the most valuable talent stays, other important back-office functions, like human resources and finance, can be damaged by news of a potential sale of the company. In many sales, personnel in the back offices are the first people fired. Consequently, when news of a potential sale spreads, such personnel are often the first to leave for other opportunities. Departures of key personnel prior to a sale can negatively impact the value of the firm as a target. In the event a rumored sale does not occur, the departures of key personnel can be debilitating for the ongoing operation of the business.

The same calculus holds with respect to customers and vendors. Customers may be considering making significant long-term investments in products and technology sold by the target firm. If decision makers at the customer believe that the firm may be acquired and that the acquisition may result in significant changes, customers may not be willing to commit to purchases until this uncertainty is cleared up. The same is true for vendors and other partners who might be considering making significant investments related to the relationship with the target firm. They, too, might hold off on such investments until the future is clearer. Thus, issues surrounding customer and vendor retention may influence the decision of how to structure the sale process.

In theory, conducting a drawn-out public sale in these circumstances might lead to the highest price for the corporation. However, in practice, it could make achieving a decent sales price impossible. As the foregoing suggests, in many deals, particularly those involving technology companies, both speed and confidentiality in negotiating a transaction are important. The result not infrequently is a preference for single-bidder negotiations.

2. AUCTIONS VERSUS NEGOTIATIONS

As we have discussed, there are many ways to sell a company. One possibility is an auction process, like the one used by Sotheby's auction house to auction art, with many bidders making bids for the company and the winner being the highest bidder. Another possibility is to engage in negotiations with a single bidder, in the same way one typically sells a car. Both processes have their advantages and disadvantages. When deciding how to sell a company, boards need to choose among the many different possibilities a process that will get the best price for the company. In their paper, *How Firms Are Sold*, Professors Boone and Mulherin provide evidence that there is considerable variety in how companies are sold. Following is their description of their results from their sample of 400 firms:[4]

> The average selling firm . . . contacts nine potential bidders [,with] [r]oughly four . . . sign[ing] confidentiality agreements. On an average, 1.29 firms make a formal written private offer for the selling firm. For the large majority of firms . . . only [one] . . . bidder makes a public offer for the selling firm . . . only 51 of the 400 . . . takeovers had more than one public bidder.

> For the 202 takeovers classified as auctions, an average of 21 potential buyers are contacted and, on . . . average, roughly seven potential buyers sign confidentiality/standstill agreements. [*Editor: A standstill agreement is an agreement in which a buyer agrees not to make additional purchases of the selling firm's stock or take certain other actions furthering a potential acquisition of the selling firm.*] On . . . average, 1.57 bidders make private written offers and 1.24 bidders make public bids.

> For the 198 takeovers classified as a negotiation, the selling firm [usually] deals with only a single bidder. The average number contacted is slightly greater than 1; . . . [in] some cases . . . preliminary discussions with a second firm do not materialize or. . . an unsolicited offer was not considered by the selling firm. For all deals classified as negotiations, the selling firm signs a confidentiality agreement with . . . [one] bidder and receives only . . . [one] private written bid. The average number of public bidders for the negotiations is slightly above 1;[in] some cases . . . a public, unsolicited offer is rebuffed by the selling firm.

> [The sample includes transactions from 1989,] "the year with the fewest transactions," to 1997, "the year with the most transactions."] [T]wo-thirds of the transactions[were] announced [between] 1995 to 1999.

Professors Boone and Mulherin note that the choice of an auction structure or a negotiation in any particular sales transaction is related to characteristics such as the size and industry of the seller as well as the seller's previous relationship with the bidding firm.

In order to structure a value-maximizing auction, it is critical that the seller credibly commit to rules for the sales process.[5] If the seller is

---

[4]   Audra L. Boone & J. Harold Mulherin, *How Are Firms Sold?*, 62 J. FIN. 847, 851–52 (2007).

[5]   "If a buyer can accept an irrevocable commitment, in a way that is unambiguously visible to the seller, he can squeeze the range of indeterminacy down to the point most favorable to him." THOMAS C. SCHELLING, THE STRATEGY OF CONFLICT 24 (1960). *See also* Paul Milgrom, *Auctions and Bidding: A Primer*, 3 J. ECON. PERSP. 3 (1989).

unable to credibly commit to a sales process or auction rules, there are few incentives for buyers to submit their best bids when called upon. For example, if a seller asks for "best and final offers" from bidders, but bidders suspect that the seller will be open to entertaining later offers, because the seller's fiduciary duties require the seller's board to consider later offers, then there is little or no incentive for a bidder to make its "best and final offer" immediately. Rather, each bidder has an incentive to make a low bid and see if other, higher bids emerge before deciding whether to increase its bid. But, if the seller can credibly commit to auction rules that effectively close the bidding process, then its statements that buyers must make their best and final offers by a date certain can extract the best price possible from bidders, who know that later bids will not be entertained.

When a corporation is sold in bankruptcy, the court monitors the sales process. The processes adopted by bankruptcy courts are typically structured as public auctions, in which the buyer is determined through a sealed-bid auction. Because the court controls the sales process, it can credibly commit the seller to abide by specified rules for the auction process. Consequently, in bankruptcy an auction will be an optimal strategy for generating value. In a bankruptcy sale, the court will often seek out a "stalking horse" bidder, a bidder whose bid is intended to attract additional bidding. The stalking horse bidder is compensated by way of a modest termination fee that is payable to the stalking horse in the event the stalking horse's bid does not eventually win the auction. Unlike other circumstances where part of the rationale for using termination fees is to deter subsequent bidders, which we discuss in Chapter XVI.G.3, the termination fee in this circumstance exists solely to encourage the initial bidder to put together a bid that might stimulate an active auction process and to compensate the initial bidder in the event a subsequent bidder is successful.

Outside the bankruptcy context, the challenge for a seller's board is finding a way to credibly commit to rules for the sales process. The objective is to achieve the highest price for the seller's shareholders; it is critical, too, to avoid the downsides of premature public disclosure of a possible deal. Thus, one possibility is a controlled auction process. Investment bankers often play an important role in such a process. They approach potential acquirers. A subset of potential acquirers who are approached sign non-disclosure and standstill agreements with the seller, following which they are permitted to do due diligence, getting access to non-public information about the seller. The non-disclosure and standstill agreements permit the seller's board to exert some degree of control over the auction process by credibly committing bidders to particular sales strategies.[6] The standstill commits bidders to refrain from engaging in a hostile acquisition. If a bidder wants to acquire the seller, it is forced to do so through the sales process. In the controlled auction, as bidders receive more information about the seller, they are permitted to update their bids. As bids are updated, successive bidders are eliminated until ultimately, there are only a small number of bidders left. At that point, bidders are asked for their best and final offers and the sale is concluded. Unless the transaction is hostile, it will conclude with a definitive agreement. The definitive merger agreement is a highly negotiated document. The lawyers take the lead in negotiating the terms of the definitive merger agreement. Although the bidders at the table are constrained by the standstill agreements already in place, the winning bid is often granted certain deal protections in the definitive agreement to protect the bidder from last minute bids from parties not engaged in the sales process.[7]

Less formal than a controlled auction is the negotiated sales process. In negotiated sales, by contrast with an open auction with multiple bidders, the process typically involves only a single bidder. That there is only one bidder makes committing to rules for the sale difficult. Consequently, the negotiation is merely a back and forth. Negotiated sales will often start in the same manner as a controlled auction. First, an investment bank canvasses the market in search of potential bidders. Potential bidders interested in engaging in a negotiation then sign nondisclosure agreements that include standstills with the seller. Typically, a seller will not engage with more than two possible buyers at any given time. More often, sellers will engage in negotiations with a single buyer at this point. Where a seller negotiates with only a single buyer, sellers may attempt to create a false sense of competition by simultaneously pursuing an initial public offering (IPO) of the company while negotiating the sale. The incentive created by the IPO process is that the single buyer will have to offer a price high enough to dissuade the seller from taking the company public. At the conclusion of the negotiation, in the merger agreement, a seller will often give deal protections to the buyer. The process of canvassing the market before the onset of negotiations, as well as potentially parallel negotiations, assist the board in developing information about the value of the seller. Because of the extensive search and negotiation efforts sellers have made in this

---

[6]   For more on the use of standstill agreements, and the "don't-ask-don't-waive" structure in particular, see Chapter XIII.C.

[7]   The experience of BioClinica in its auction process is not uncommon. "Excel [BioClinica's investment bank] reached out to twenty-one separate entities during the auction process, several of whom signed NDAs with BioClinica. The auction was run by a committee of independent directors and supported by a fairness opinion from Excel. The directors were regularly apprised of their fiduciary duties. The auction resulted in a price of $7.25, which includes a premium of approximately twenty-five percent over the stock price." *In re BioClinica Shareholder Litigation*, Inc., No. CV 8272–VCG, 2013 WL 5631233 (Del. Ch. October 16, 2013), *7.

type of sales process, sellers' boards and courts can be reasonably assured that the sales are being done with adequate information about the value of the seller.

3. STRATEGIC VERSUS FINANCIAL BUYERS

Who are the potential buyers making acquisitions or entering into mergers? Some buyers are known as "strategic buyers." They are typically operating companies who may be interested in expanding "vertically"—up the chain, to suppliers, or down the chain, to customers, or "horizontally," into new regions or (related) fields. They may also be interested in complementing their own business by obtaining some capacity they do not presently have or excel in, or in eliminating competition. Some other potential buyers may include financial buyers, like private equity firms, for whom acquisition of the seller does not meet any strategic need, but rather, is a valuable financial investment in its own right because the financial buyer can use the cash flows from the seller to make a large return on a leveraged investment. Each of these types of buyers, strategic and financial, has its own characteristics that can affect the manner in which it enters the acquisition market.

For example, many transactions involving private equity buyers take the form of single bidder negotiated transactions without the benefit of a "pre-signing market check," an investigation of the market before the transaction is entered into, something we discuss further in Chapter XVIII. Private equity bidders are notorious for being unwilling to participate as bidders in auctions for target firms.[8] The reason for this unwillingness is that such bidders, like other financial buyers, are "common value" buyers rather than "private value" buyers. Financial buyers view target firms as little more than a stream of fungible cash flows. The value of any individual target is a function of the firm's cash flow, as it is or as could be improved by the sort of techniques financial buyers use. As a result, any target in the eyes of a financial buyer has a single, true objective value, but that value is unknown to bidders. Bidders can only make estimates of that value. Consequently, in a competitive auction, the winner of the auction is the bidder who may overestimate that objective value. This is the source of the "winner's curse."[9]

---

[8]   The late Teddy Forstmann, CEO of Forstmann Little & Co., once described his aversion to auctions by saying "I don't do auctions. I would sooner take my pants off in public." Dyan Machan, *A Hero Among Barbarians*, FORBES, Jul. 6, 1998, 134, http://www.forbes.com/forbes/1998/0706/6201132a.html.

[9]   Might there be another reason why private equity buyers might not be willing to participate in auctions? Interestingly, in 2014, some private equity firms, including Bain Capital, Silver Lake, and KKR, and Goldman, which did these sorts of deals through its buyout arm, settled, without admitting or denying, allegations that they had colluded with one another to keep prices of targets low, in some cases submitting joint bids, and in other cases, agreeing that in particular transactions, some of them would refrain from making bids so that one of the 'club' would not face competition from the others. *See* William Alden, *K.K.R., Blackstone and TPG*

Strategic buyers value targets differently than financial buyers. Strategic buyers are more likely to be "private value" bidders. In a private value transaction, the target has a value that is unique to each bidder. The source of the target's private value is often "synergies" and "cost savings" that can be attributed to combining the assets of the target with the buyer. Where bidders exhibit characteristics of private value bidders, such bidders are not averse to an active auction contest. In an open auction, the optimal bidding strategy is to pay no more than the bidder's private valuation for the target. In an auction, the winning bidder will pay one dollar more than the private value of the second highest bidder. Because each bidder's valuation is independent of any other bidder's valuation, private value auctions are less susceptible to the winner's curse than are common value auctions.

Because financial bidders face negative incentives to participate in auctions, they more often rely on bilateral negotiations when engaging in acquisitions. One significant problem from the seller's perspective is the lack of a mechanism within the sales process that would cause the buyer to reveal its private information about its valuation of the seller. Thus, when engaged in confidential single bidder negotiations, the seller's board may not be confident that it has negotiated the highest price available. However, in those cases, sellers might be able to rely on a "post-signing market check" to confirm the price negotiated by the seller's board. (The provisions at issue, "go-shop" provisions, are discussed in Chapter XVIII). Knowing that the contract price will be tested through an active shopping process following signing, buyers may have an incentive to put their best price forward during the bilateral negotiation so as to deter a subsequent active bidding contest for the seller.

4. NEGOTIAUCTIONS

Targets often use both auction and negotiation strategies to sell their companies, combining elements of the two to develop the best sale strategy. Professor Guhan Subramanian describes this sale process as a "negotiauction."[10] Professor Subramanian observes that many high-stakes negotiations, like merger negotiations, have significant auction elements to them, and many high-stakes auctions have important negotiation elements. In a typical auction setting, the rules of the sales process are set out ahead of time and are meticulously adhered to. Because the auction rules are credible, bidders have incentives to bid closer to their private valuations. On the other hand, negotiations are often conducted with few, if any, rules. In a negotiation, each party offers

Private Equity Firms Agree to Settle Lawsuit on Collusion, N.Y. TIMES, Aug. 7, 2014, available at http://dealbook.nytimes.com/2014/08/07/k-k-r-agrees-to-settle-lawsuit-on-private-equity-collusion/.

[10] GUHAN SUBRAMANIAN, NEGOTIAUCTIONS: NEW DEALMAKING STRATEGIES FOR A COMPETITIVE MARKETPLACE (2010).

something of value to the other party in exchange for something it values, but, as discussed above, it is harder for the seller to elicit bids closer to the bidder's private valuation.

Because the lines between the structures of the transactions are so blurred, Professor Subramanian's negotiauction term is quite apt when describing the transaction structure of a typical corporate merger. A negotiauction is a deal-making situation in which competitive pressure is coming both from interactions between the buyer and the seller and from interactions among bidders. A sale of corporate control often includes auction-like environments where multiple bidders submit bids in the absence of much information about competitors. It also includes a series of parallel bilateral negotiations where sellers attempt to use the competitive pressure of multiple bidders to extract additional value from the winning bidder in exchange for shutting down the sales process.

Consider the path taken by the board of Dollar Thrifty, the car rental company, in its acquisition by Hertz. The sale of Dollar Thrifty looks very much like a negotiauction. The board of Dollar Thrifty simultaneously used competitive pressures from bilateral negotiations as well as the competitive pressures between Hertz and Avis to extract value for its shareholders in a sale of control. The following description of Dollar Thrifty's sales process is taken from a Chancery Court opinion, *In re Dollar Thrifty Shareholder Litigation*. The Dollar Thrifty process is not only a good example of a negotiauction; it is also a good example of how a sales process with multiple bidders plays out in real life:[11]

> The 2007 acquisition of Vanguard Car Rental by Enterprise ignited discussions between the other major players in the industry about strategic combinations. In April 2007, Dollar Thrifty and Hertz began talks regarding a potential business combination. The two companies entered into a confidentiality agreement and conducted initial due diligence. Members of the two companies' senior management met to consider a possible transaction but shortly after the meeting the companies terminated their discussions.
>
> In October 2007, Dollar Thrifty received a non-binding indication of interest from Avis about a possible combination at a price of $44 per share with a 58% cash, 42% stock consideration mix. In December 2007, Avis lowered its offer to $35.50 at a time when Dollar Thrifty's stock was trading at $24.12 per share. In what would become a common refrain, Dollar Thrifty expressed a willingness to consider the offer but warned Avis that deal certainty was of "paramount importance." Avis would not agree to Dollar Thrifty's demands for a reverse termination fee payable

---

[11] *In re Dollar Thrifty Shareholder Litigation*, 14 A.3d 573 (Del. Ch. 2010).

in the event that antitrust approval was not received and in January 2008, the two companies mutually agreed to terminate discussions.

Three months later, in March 2008, Gary Paxton, the then President and CEO of Dollar Thrifty, contacted Mark Frissora, the CEO of Hertz, and Ronald Nelson, the CEO of Avis, to see if either would be interested in re-engaging in discussions about a merger. As a result of this overture, both Hertz and Avis indicated that they would be interested in such a transaction.

In April and May 2008, Dollar Thrifty again signed confidentiality agreements and began conducting due diligence with both Avis and Hertz. As a result, Dollar Thrifty received non-binding indications of interest from both companies in late May. Dollar Thrifty continued negotiations with both Avis and Hertz and in early June went so far as to provide both companies with a draft Agreement and Plan of Merger prepared by its outside counsel, Cleary Gottlieb Steen & Hamilton, LLP. Shortly thereafter, however, Avis advised Dollar Thrifty that it was no longer interested in pursuing a merger. When Avis walked away, Dollar Thrifty's shares were trading in the range of $10–15. In August 2008, Hertz also informed Dollar Thrifty that it was not interested in pursuing a transaction at that time. . . .

Shortly after [Scott] Thompson became CEO in October 2008, Frissora contacted him to discuss the possibility of reviving talks between Hertz and Dollar Thrifty.

On December 4, 2009, Frissora again reached out to Thompson about a possible merger between Dollar Thrifty and Hertz. The Board was apprehensive about reopening negotiations with Hertz in light of the failed talks in the past, but on December 7, Thompson communicated to Frissora that the Board was open to new merger talks, and on December 10, 2009, the two companies entered into a new confidentiality agreement. . . .

On December 22, 2009, Hertz made a formal expression of interest to acquire Dollar Thrifty at a price of $30 per share at a mix of 50% cash and 50% stock. Eight days later, on December 30, 2009, the Board met to consider Hertz's offer. At this meeting, Thompson advised the Board that one of the main concerns with a transaction with Hertz was "certainty of closing due to many factors, including regulatory review." Antitrust counsel from Cleary Gottlieb advised the Board on the regulatory issues and the Board asked questions of the lawyer. The Board was then advised by a different Cleary Gottlieb lawyer about its fiduciary obligations in connection with the offer, including in particular its *Revlon* duties.

The next day, Dollar Thrifty responded to Hertz, rejecting its offer but leaving open the possibility for further negotiations. Dollar Thrifty expressed a desire for a price "at least in the mid-thirties," expressed its preference for an all-cash offer, and conveyed that deal certainty was an important issue to the Board. In fact, in his December 31 letter to Frissora, Thompson stated that Dollar Thrifty "will require as a condition to proceeding with further discussions, confirmation that Hertz will bear the burden of any and all conditions imposed by any regulatory agency. . . ."

On January 7, 2010 Dollar Thrifty's and Hertz's financial advisors met to discuss the financial aspects of a possible deal. On January 18, senior management from the two companies met, and on January 25, Hertz submitted a revised offer to Dollar Thrifty.

The January 25 offer increased the price to $35 a share and changed the consideration mix to 60% cash and 40% stock. Hertz responded to Dollar Thrifty's antitrust concerns by offering that it was "prepared to use [its] reasonable best efforts to obtain regulatory clearance . . . including, if necessary, divesting assets. . . ."

On January 27, the Dollar Thrifty Board met to consider Hertz's latest offer. The bankers again presented materials relating to the economics of the transaction. The $35 price represented a premium of 44.5% to the January 25 stock price of $24.22, a 30.6% premium to the 30-day VWAP and a 62.3% premium to the 90-day VWAP.

After these deliberations, the Board chose not to accept Hertz's offer but authorized Thompson to execute a 45-day exclusivity agreement with Hertz and requested that management update the Board at least every two weeks on the progress of talks. On February 3, Dollar Thrifty and Hertz entered into an exclusivity agreement that expired at the end of March 17, 2010. On February 10 and 11, the senior management of Dollar Thrifty and Hertz met in person in Chicago to hash out a deal. On February 12, Thompson updated the Board via email that Hertz appeared serious about getting a deal done but that there was "no news on the anti trust [sic] front."

. . .

With the Hertz exclusivity agreement expired, and a viable offer to consider, the Dollar Thrifty Board met on March 24 and 25 in Dallas, Texas to discuss how best to move forward. [. . .]

The Board also again considered the possibility of making an overture to Avis now that Dollar Thrifty was no longer constrained by the exclusivity agreement. Thompson was concerned that trying to create an auction instead of dealing with Hertz alone posed real risks that no deal would get done with either potential buyer. JP Morgan and Goldman Sachs both expressed serious doubt that Avis could secure the necessary financing for a cash bid given the state of the credit markets and Avis's current leverage profile, and Cleary Gottlieb chimed in to discuss the need for Avis to obtain a shareholder vote if it was to use more equity-based consideration. This sparked a conversation about what sort of deal protections Dollar Thrifty would need to work into any deal with Avis to guard against the uncertainty created by these shortcomings.

The Board, however, was worried that a merger agreement with Hertz could chill a topping bid from Avis. . . .

Ultimately, the Board decided that negotiations with Hertz should continue, that no outreach to Avis should be made, and authorized Thompson to reopen the data room and to contact Hertz so that the companies could continue due diligence and resume negotiations.

On April 8, 2010, Dollar Thrifty proposed that Hertz pay a price of $44.96 per share with 50% cash, 50% stock consideration mix. The price represented a 25% premium to Dollar Thrifty's closing price on that day of $35.97. Hertz replied to the offer by shutting down its data room the next day and stopping due diligence. At the same time, Frissora attempted to set up a phone call with Thompson, but Thompson explained via email that "regrettably" his calendar would not allow him to talk until the week of April 26. Frissora responded that the $45 proposal was so far off the mark that Hertz was shutting down the process until Frissora and Thompson could come up with "some sort of a gap closure plan to see if this transaction still has legs."

On April 12, Frissora sent Thompson a letter communicating the results of a Hertz board meeting held that morning. Frissora stated that Hertz was still interested in acquiring Dollar Thrifty, but given what Hertz perceived as the material difference in valuation expectations between the two companies, that the Hertz board had decided to "step back from the transaction."

A Dollar Thrifty board meeting was scheduled for April 16. That Board meeting, however, never happened. Instead, Thompson and Frissora met on April 16 at the suggestion of JP Morgan to see if something could be worked out. At the April 16 meeting, Dollar Thrifty expressed willingness to do a deal with a price above $40 per share. Hertz countered with an offer of $38 per share, and the negotiations again broke down.

Very late in the negotiations with Hertz, Avis came back on the scene. It did so in a very oblique, awkward, and unclear manner. . . . [O]n April 12, Avis's CEO Nelson contacted Rob Sivitilli, an investment banker at JP Morgan, who was not working on the Dollar Thrifty deal to ask if Thompson would speak with Nelson. . . .

Meanwhile, on April 21, 2010 Frissora called Thompson to relay a new offer from Hertz. The terms of that offer were as follows: a price of $40 per share, with an 80% cash, 20% stock consideration mix; termination and reverse termination fees of 3.5% each; and an antitrust divestiture threshold set at the Advantage brand and/or other assets generating $100 million in revenue. Frissora conditioned his new offer on execution of a definitive merger agreement before Hertz announced its quarterly results on Monday, April 26. Frissora was eager to get the deal signed so that Hertz could announce the agreement along with its earnings. . . .

The Board was also advised by its financial advisors that Hertz was unlikely to go higher than its $40 offer. The financial advisors estimated that there was a better than 50/50 chance that Hertz would walk away at a price of $42, and that if the deal didn't close in this period Hertz would "probably go[ ] away for an 'extended period.'" Similarly, the advisors suggested that if Dollar Thrifty went for an extra dollar it would be difficult to get Hertz to agree to other contract provisions, which, as previously discussed, were important to Dollar Thrifty.

The Board decided that the time was right to sell and directed its legal advisors to finalize a merger agreement by April 25.

On April 25, the Board met to consider the final agreement. The Board again received guidance as to its fiduciary duties from Cleary Gottlieb. It again received presentations from its financial advisors in which JP Morgan and Goldman Sachs both separately advised the Board that the transaction price was fair to shareholders. Similarly, Cleary Gottlieb again spoke with the Board about antitrust risk and Hertz's related commitments in the Merger Agreement. Finally, the Board again focused on making sure that Avis would not be precluded from making an offer because of the agreement with Hertz.

On April 25, Hertz and Dollar Thrifty executed the Merger Agreement.

As you can see from the experience of Dollar Thrifty, the sales process is highly dynamic. Boards must be flexible and must respond to information as they receive it. In order to be successful in the sale process, it is critical that boards are able to rely on a strong team of advisers to counsel and guide them. In the next Section, we will introduce you to many of the most important players in the process.

QUESTIONS

1. What is the difference between a private value auction and a common value auction? How does it inform a target board's decision as to how to sell itself?

2. When should a target sell itself pursuant to an auction? When should it use a single-bidder negotiation?

3. How does a negotiauction differ from both a negotiation and an auction? Why might it be preferable to either a negotiation or an auction as a sales process?

4. Why did the Dollar Thrifty board decide not to reach out to Avis? Do you agree with the board's rationale?

5. What was the effect of the exclusivity agreement signed by Dollar Thrifty and Hertz?

CHAPTER XII

IMPORTANT ACTORS AND THEIR ROLES

■ ■ ■

A. ATTORNEYS

What do transactional lawyers do? Transactional lawyers advise on law. They must have a thorough knowledge of the relevant federal and state laws and rules. But they do much more. Transactional attorneys are also:

- *Issue Spotters.* Transactional attorneys must have the foresight and knowledge to spot significant issues in the transaction so that structuring and other legal decisions can be made.

- *Transaction Structurers.* Transactional attorneys structure the transaction, taking into account tax, accounting and other business factors.

- *Document Drafters.* Transactional attorneys draft the agreements related to the transaction as well as any public filings. Deals often require many long and complicated agreements, including acquisition agreements, voting agreements, employment agreements, and other agreements.

- *Party Planners.* A significant job of the transactional attorney in an acquisition is what is called "party planning" or "quarterbacking." Transactional attorneys coordinate the many attorneys working in specialized areas—tax, compensation and benefits, antitrust, environmental, and intellectual property—involved in the transaction. In addition, the transactional attorney coordinates with in-house counsel and the advisers, particularly the investment bank, working on the transaction.

- *Negotiators.* A good transactional attorney is also a good negotiator. In the transaction, much of the work of negotiating the merger agreement and ancillary documents is left to the transactional attorney, who must be good at her job to ensure an optimal outcome for her clients.

A successful transactional attorney is known for her problem solving skills and good judgment. The process need not be adversarial. Unlike in litigation, in transactional lawyering both sides can win by striking a deal for their respective clients which maximizes the value to each party. A large part of the negotiation process is bargaining. Each law firm has one or more "form" agreements that some of the firm's lawyers are familiar with from prior transactions. A lawyer starts with a form agreement that has provisions favorable to her side, and marks up the document to reflect the specifics of the transaction she is working on.[1] The final agreement will reflect the compromises and accommodations the parties reach— probably a considerable distance from where each party started out. In Anatomy of a Merger, the author, a very experienced corporate lawyer, describes the trajectory, pointing out to a junior lawyer his mistake in doing a first draft based on a contract that had actually been the culmination of negotiations:

> Now look fella, you'll just have to forgive my candor but time's short and this draft of the Proliferating-Suggestive agreement is an *inferior* job. . . . You [used] the final contract [for the Screwloose deal and] marked it up for purposes of this draft. Don't you realize that the final Screwloose agreement represented the culmination of three weeks of intensive negotiation on the part of a party smart seller's attorney? You've got to start with the first draft of the Screwloose contract![2]

The range of possibilities—and indeed, just how favorable to the drafting party's client the first draft will be—will be significantly informed by the client's needs, the specific nature of the transaction in question as well as the then-prevailing norms of the transacting community. Consequently, transactional lawyers must know the answer to the question "what is market"—what are the transaction terms accepted by and common in the market?

B. INVESTMENT BANKERS AND DEAL-MAKING

1. THE ROLE OF INVESTMENT BANKERS IN M&A

Investment banks and investment bankers play a key role in the mergers and acquisitions process, representing both buyers and sellers. What does this representation involve?

---

[1] For more on how documents for a particular transaction are generated from "forms," see Claire A. Hill, *Why Contracts are Written in Legalese*, 77 CHI. KENT. L. REV. 59 (2002); *see also* Claire A. Hill, *Bargaining in the Shadow of the Lawsuit: A Social Norms Theory of Incomplete Contracts*, 34 DEL. J. CORP. L. 191 (2009).

[2] JAMES C. FREUND, ANATOMY OF A MERGER: STRATEGIES AND TECHNIQUES FOR NEGOTIATION CORPORATE ACQUISITIONS 500 (1975)

a. Sell-Side Representation

An investment bank representing the target— taking what is known as a sell-side M&A advisory role—is in some respects like a real estate agent representing the seller of a home. Much like a real estate agent, the sell-side investment banker specializes in understanding the market, including potential buyers, prices, as well as sales processes. A sale process can be "targeted" to a known buyer or small number of potential buyers already identified. If the company has not already initiated contact with a buyer, the investment bank will use its knowledge of the industry and the universe of potential buyers, including the potential buyers' characteristics and willingness to bid for the target, to initiate contact with a small number of buyers, or even one potential buyer. Even if the company has initiated some contacts or negotiations with buyers, the bank may suggest and initiate more contacts and negotiations. The bank will advise the target in negotiating the target's sale using the bank's specialized knowledge and experience to get the best deal for the target. The investment banker's knowledge and informational advantages should allow a target to capture more gains.

A target can also sell itself in a "broad" process, where the universe of known buyers is requested to bid, typically through an auction. In this case, the investment bank will assist the target in identifying potential buyers and make efforts to have many of them participate in the sale process. In an auction process, the investment banker will prepare an offering letter, and conduct several rounds of bidding to help the target board identify a final bidder. As in a more targeted sale, the investment banker will assist the bidder in negotiating the final sale price using its specialized knowledge and experience.

No matter what sale process is utilized, a sell-side investment bank is guided by the fiduciary duties of the seller's board of directors in the context of a sale. Investment banks historically have assisted boards in meeting their fiduciary obligations by preparing a valuation of the target. The valuation is helpful both in the board's decision to sell the target, and in the negotiations on the terms of the sale itself. The case of *Smith v. Van Gorkom*, discussed in Chapter XVII, emphasized the importance of the bankers' role in assisting boards of directors to comply with their fiduciary obligations. The *Van Gorkom* court held that for a board to satisfy its duty of care, the board was required to inform itself with respect to the value of the company. One way of meeting the requirement to inform itself is for the board to obtain financial advice from an investment bank about the company's value. Such advice will typically involve the target's board of directors hiring an investment bank to provide a financial valuation and opinion. For that reason, the *Van Gorkom* case has sometimes been referred to by practitioners as the "Investment Bankers' Full Employment Act." Indeed, a study by

Professors Cain and Denis found that from 1998 to 2005, at least 96.4% of public targets were represented by an investment banker.[3]

Post-*Van Gorkom*, sell-side investment banks have had three distinct roles. First, investment banks have served their traditional role as informational intermediaries, using their contacts and knowledge to connect bidders and targets. Second, investment banks develop financial valuation and analysis to present to the target board for purposes of considering the value of the company and for negotiation of a sale price. Third, investment banks provide a fairness opinion to the target's board stating that the ultimate sale price being paid to the target's shareholders is "fair from a financial point of view." The value of these fairness opinions and the financial valuation that an investment bank provides to a company was discussed in Chapter X.C, which addressed fairness opinion and valuation practice more specifically.

b. Buy-Side Representation

If the investment bank is representing the buyer or a potential bidder, it will typically have two roles. First, the investment bank will assist in the buyer's assessment of valuation of the target. The investment bank will use its knowledge of the market and its experience to attempt to negotiate the lowest price possible that the buyer could pay. In practice, the buyer's and seller's investment banks typically negotiate a price acceptable to both companies. The process often entails a battle of valuation presentations, as the buyer's and the seller's banks present their dueling valuations to justify their requested prices. Unlike on the sell side, the law does not specifically require buyers to use investment banks in a buy-side role, and in fact, the use of banks on the buy side is not common. According to Professors Cain and Denis, 71.5% of buyers did not use investment banks for a fairness opinion in a purchase. Warren Buffett, the CEO of Berkshire Hathaway, has said that he will not use investment banks on the buy side because he does not see them adding significantly more value than his own staff can provide.[4] More generally, large corporations that have their own business development personnel in-house who can provide valuation analyses and knowledge of the industry often have little need of buy-side advice from an investment bank.

The second role of a buy-side investment banks is to provide financing for the purchase. This is often the primary reason a buyer will engage an investment bank. The buy-side investment bank will arrange for, or provide, the millions or even billions in financing necessary to

---

[3]   *See* Matthew D. Cain & David J. Denis, *Information Production by Investment Banks: Evidence from Fairness Opinions,* 56 J. L. & ECON. 245 (2013), at tbl 2.

[4]   *See* Andrew Ross Sorkin, *Buffet Casts a Wary Eye on Bankers*, N.Y. TIMES, Mar. 2, 2010, http://dealbook.nytimes.com/2010/03/02/buffett-casts-a-wary-eye-on-bankers/.

make the transaction occur. The transaction financing involved typically takes the form of loans or underwriting of a debt offering or a combination of the two. The ability to provide financing to buyers is an important business line for an investment bank, particularly since the fees for providing financing tend to be more lucrative than the fees for M&A advisory work.

2. THE CONCENTRATED NATURE OF M&A INVESTMENT BANKING

As the following table, setting forth M&A volume rankings for 2014, illustrates, the investment banking business is extremely concentrated:

	US M&A Volume Ranking – Announced Deals				
Rank	Advisor	Value $bn	Deals	% Share	Full Year 2013 Rank
1	Goldman Sachs	711.2	247	37.6	1
2	JPMorgan	526.5	174	27.8	2
3	Bank of America Merrill Lynch	491.1	157	25.9	4
4	Citi	442.9	157	23.4	7
5	Morgan Stanley	441.2	171	23.3	3
6	Barclays	412.9	157	21.8	5
7	Lazard	299.0	118	15.8	12
8	Deutsche Bank	240.8	122	12.7	9
9	Credit Suisse	232.5	129	12.3	10
10	Centerview Partners	230.9	36	12.2	13
11	UBS	120.8	69	6.4	6
12	Jefferies	113.5	108	6.0	18
13	Allen & Co	90.9	7	4.8	38
14	RBC Capital Markets	85.2	94	4.5	17
15	Wells Fargo Securities	83.1	71	4.4	16
16	PJT Capital	80.1	4	4.2	11
17	Perella Weinberg Partners	79.6	24	4.2	29
18	Evercore Partners	78.8	104	4.2	14
19	Greenhill & Co	52.5	35	2.8	20
20	Rothschild	40.0	44	2.1	21

Source: Dealogic

The investment banking business is dependent on the information and reputational networks these banks provide. That it is a concentrated business is thus not surprising. Note how high the aggregate market share is of the top five (and top ten) investment banks.

The Mergers and Acquisitions advisory business (discussed above) is also lucrative (even if not as lucrative as the financing business) as the following table, which sets forth revenue for the top investment banks from U.S. M&A, illustrates:

US M&A Revenue Ranking			
Rank	Bank	Revenue $m	% Share
1	Goldman Sachs	1,267	11.6
2	JPMorgan	1,095	10.0
3	Morgan Stanley	812	7.4
4	Bank of America Merrill Lynch	727	6.6
5	Barclays	716	6.5
6	Citi	540	4.9
7	Credit Suisse	500	4.6
8	Deutsche Bank	412	3.8
9	Lazard	387	3.5
10	Jefferies	373	3.4
11	Evercore Partners	342	3.1
12	Centerview Partners	297	2.7
13	Houlihan Lokey	243	2.2
14	UBS	234	2.1
15	Wells Fargo Securities	205	1.9
16	Moelis & Co	202	1.8
17	RBC Capital Markets	201	1.8
18	Qatalyst Partners	178	1.6
19	Stifel	139	1.3
20	Sandler O'Neill & Partners	107	1.0

Source: Dealogic

According to FactSet MergerMetrics, the median fees for investment banking services for a sell-side engagement in 2015 (through November 22, 2015) for a transaction valued over $100 million was $12 million. These fees are typically set as a percentage of the sale price, so the larger the transaction, the higher the fee. The fees are often contingent, only paid if a sale occurs.

3. INVESTMENT BANKS' ADDED VALUE

The foregoing discussion suggests that investment banks are hired in significant part for their reputation and information networks, both of which are sources of real added value. In the following excerpt, Professors Bill Wilhelm and Alan Morrison describe and explain how banks acquire and make use of these sources of value:

[T]he investment bank creates an environment within which mutual trust underpins agreements to find, and to pay for, price-relevant information. . . . Moreover, investment banks have traditionally relied upon tacit human skills that are hard-to-acquire and hard-to-prove or to disprove. The bank's ability to sell these skills again rests upon its reputation.

[Because] reputations are hard-to-acquire (and easy-to-lose) . . . new investment banks, which have no reputation, face a substantial barrier to entry. [This explains the high concentration within the industry]

The M&A advisory business relies upon human skill and judgment, and hence is at least as reputationally intensive [and highly concentrated] as the new issues business. . . . Many, though not all, of the top underwriters levered their reputational capital into a strong position in M&A advisory work. Moreover, some firms have largely specialized in M&A advisory services . . . Investment banks . . . have been joined in recent years by a new group of specialized 'boutique' banks that focus on M&A and corporate restructuring . . . founded by prominent bankers who have left bulge-bracket firms to start their own businesses. We argue that they chose to do so because it was very hard to combine their own, highly human-capital-based and reputationally intensive, specialisms with the emphasis upon scale and financial capital of the modern bulge-bracket firm.[5]

4.   A "REAL WORLD" VIEW OF INVESTMENT BANKS?

While Professors Morrison and Wilhelm depict investment bankers as adding value due to their reputational capital and expertise, some other commentators have more critical views. Indeed, there is a whole genre of books casting investment banks in a less-than wholly favorable, and sometimes quite unfavorable, light. Many of the books are written by bankers themselves. *Liar's Poker*, by Michael Lewis, is one of these books. Another is *The Accidental Investment Banker*, by Jonathan Knee. The critiques of these authors include arguments that bankers sometimes take advantage of their clients and otherwise engage in sharp dealing, that the atmosphere is banks is "less than professional," and that bankers' egos, especially the egos of more senior bankers, can sometimes cause difficulties.

An illustration of the latter is in this excerpt from *Barbarians at the Gate*, the story of the $25 billion takeover of RJR Nabisco. The excerpt details how a potential compromise between the two bidding parties to jointly buy RJR/Nabisco broke down in part because the investment banks financing the transaction could not agree on where each of their names would be placed on the ad (known as the "tombstone") announcing that they had financed the transaction.

The lead bank is so noted by placing its name first-on the left side-of the . . . tombstone advertisements that pack the Wall Street Journal and other financial publications. Being "on the left" of the tombstone thus has powerful symbolic significance in

---

[5]   ALAN D. MORRISON & WILLIAM J. WILHELM, JR., INVESTMENT BANKING: INSTITUTIONS, POLITICS, AND LAW 15–19 (Oxford 2007).

the bond world. . . . [It had been] agreed that Salomon and Shearson would co-run the books. Shearson would be on the left, Salomon on the right. That arrangement didn't bother Salomon . . . because Salomon's power in the bond world so overshadowed Shearson's that everyone would know who had really run the deal. . . . [But "w]ith Drexel on the left," Strauss [President of Salomon] said . . . *"we would have been perceived as an afterthought."* . . . [Salomon] was willing to sacrifice Johnson's [the CEO of RJR Nabisco] interests—indeed, the entire deal—to avoid the perception that it was taking a backseat to its hated rival, Drexel. . . . Gutfreund [Chairman of Salomon] and Strauss were prepared to scarp the largest takeover of all time because their firm's name would go on the right side, not the left side of a tombstone advertisement buried among the stock tables at the back of the Wall Street Journal and the New York Times.[6]

This interchange derailed a compromise that seemed imminent. Salomon ended up losing the deal for itself and for its client.

The Interaction of Lawyers and Investment Bankers

Lawyers work closely with investment bankers in the sale process in order to prevent real-world problems from creating legal difficulties. That mergers and acquisitions are highly regulated also assures that lawyers and bankers will interact regularly during the deal-making process. Lawyers' roles, and their interaction with investment bankers in the sale process, differ depending on whether their representation is sell-side or buy-side.

On the sell side, the sale process is typically run by the attorneys. They organize the process and coordinate the role of the investment bank. (By contrast, in Europe, the investment banks take primary responsibility for coordinating the sale process.) The interaction between the attorneys and bankers is more intense in a broad sale process than a narrow one, particularly if the sale is conducted using an auction. In a broad sale process, the attorneys will mark up and circulate a memorandum (the "bid procedures memorandum") which sets forth how potential bidders can submit a bid, and work with the investment bank to coordinate the bidding process. Regardless of the form of the process, the attorneys will work with the investment banks to negotiate confidentiality agreements with potential bidders. The attorneys will also review all of the "board books," the materials prepared by the bankers for presentation to the board, to make sure that these books accurately describe the proposed transaction and that the tone and language of the board books do not run afoul of antitrust laws in the event the board books must be turned over to relevant antitrust authorities.

---

[6] BRYAN BURROUGH & JOHN HELYAR, BARBARIANS AT THE GATE 325–26 (1990).

On the buy side, attorney involvement with investment bankers is more limited because the banks themselves have a smaller role. Still, in this context as well, attorneys will review the investment bank's presentations to the board of directors and be involved with and review the confidentiality agreements. Often, this work is done by in-house counsel with the advice of the outside attorneys. If the buyer is obtaining financing for the transaction, the interaction of attorneys and the investment bank on the buy side is more significant. The attorneys will work with the investment bank to negotiate the terms of the financing and prepare any necessary related documents, including loan documents, offering memorandum, and securities filings. The investment bank will also serve as the dealer-manager for any securities offering. This is a historical role that has no purpose now, but in prior years involved coordinating the offering for the buyer of their securities.

5. INVESTMENT BANKER CONFLICTS

Investment banks often have conflicts of interest. One reason for this is the highly concentrated nature of the investment banking industry. Indeed, the paradigmatic conflict is that the bank is representing both the target and the buyer in related or unrelated matters. But other conflicts are inherent in investment banker representation. For example, investment banks are typically only paid if a transaction closes. This creates an incentive for a banker to recommend a transaction that may not be optimal for the banker's client. Also, sell-side clients are typically one-off clients. A client who sells a firm, will not usually be in the market for additional sell-side services later. On the other hand, buyers are often serial participants in the market. Given this structure, a banker working on the sell side may negotiate less vigorously against a private equity firm or other repeat buyer because the private equity firm or other repeat buyer might be less likely to use the banker's services in the future if the repeat buyer views the banker as too aggressive. These conflicts are well known, and often acknowledged specifically by investment banks in their engagement letters or in the text of the fairness opinion.

Bankers attempt to manage these conflicts through disclosure to their clients and through a degree of self-regulation. While conflicted behavior may yield some short-term gain to the banker and perhaps the bank, it has been thought that the negative reputational consequences should restrain banks' opportunistic behavior, and should motivate investment banks to monitor their bankers. But some cases, discussed below, suggest that these theoretical constraints are not always as strong as they should be.

If a conflict of interest exists, rather than disqualifying the investment bank, the client may hire a second investment bank to validate the advice of the first bank and give a conflict-free fairness opinion. This practice has come under fire by some in the industry and among academics. The criticism is that the second bank will almost certainly come to the same "fairness" conclusion as the first bank given the latitude that the bank has in valuing the target for purposes of the fairness opinion. The target will thus expend a substantial additional amount of money paid to the second bank for a second opinion which accomplishes little.

a. The Move Toward Heightened Review of Advisor Conflicts

In recent years, the Delaware courts have been more carefully scrutinizing transactions for investment banker conflicts. Two recent cases highlight the problems of investment banker conflicts and Delaware's approach to resolving these problems.

In re Del Monte Foods Co. Shareholders Litigation, No. Civ. A. 6027–VCL, 2011 WL 2535256 (Del. Ch. June 27, 2011), arose from the $4 billion sale of Del Monte Foods Co. to a consortium of private equity firms led by Kohlberg Kravis Roberts & Co. (K.K.R.) In *Del Monte*, Vice Chancellor J. Travis Laster found on a preliminary record that the investment bank Barclays, with K.K.R.'s assistance, had rigged the Del Monte sale process to secure for itself a plum banking role and up to $24 million in extra fees. As the Vice Chancellor recounted the background of the case, in January 2010, Barclays, without Del Monte's knowledge, began to peddle a potential Del Monte buyout deal to a number of private equity firms, including K.K.R., a longtime Barclays client. Barclays was focused on providing the financing for the buyout, whoever the buyer was. After making its pitches, Barclays used its relationship with Del Monte to secure representation of the company in exploring its strategic alternatives, including a possible sale. Barclays then recommended that Del Monte limit its sale process to a small group of private equity firms that included the ones to which the bank had made its pitches. This first process was terminated by the Del Monte board after the board decided against a sale. Nevertheless, Barclays kept trying to arrange a Del Monte sale.

Vestar (another private equity firm) and K.K.R. had signed confidentiality agreements with Barclays that precluded them from teaming up to bid without Del Monte's approval. Nevertheless, Barclays arranged for Vestar and K.K.R. to make a joint bid. But Barclays did not disclose to Del Monte that it knew that Vestar and K.K.R. were working together in violation of the private equity firms' agreements with Del Monte. While the price was being negotiated, Barclays, with Del Monte's permission, switched sides and also advised K.K.R. and the buyout group (which now included Vestar) on financing. Barclays made $23.5 million for advising Del Monte on the sale. In addition, by providing financing to K.K.R. and its partners, Barclays received another fee in the range of $21 million to $24 million. Because Barclay's dual representation constituted a conflict, Del Monte hired a boutique investment bank, Perella Weinberg, to provide a second independent fairness opinion, for another $3 million. Vice Chancellor Laster concluded that "although Barclays' activities and nondisclosures in early 2010 are troubling, what indisputably crossed the line was the surreptitious and unauthorized pairing of Vestar with K.K.R. In doing so, Barclays materially reduced the prospect of price competition for Del Monte."[7] The case, brought by Del Monte's shareholders, was subsequently settled for $89.4 million, with Barclays Capital paying $23.7 million and Del Monte paying the remainder. Del Monte also refused to pay Barclay's fee of $21.5 million.

A year later, in 2012, Goldman Sachs & Co. was in the spotlight over Kinder Morgan's $21.1 billion acquisition of El Paso. Shareholders of El Paso sued to halt the merger, claiming misconduct by El Paso's board as well as El Paso's CEO Douglas Foshee, and Goldman Sachs, which was representing El Paso. In *In re El Paso Corp. Shareholder Litigation*, 41 A.3d 432 (Del. Ch. 2012), then-Chancellor Leo E. Strine, Jr. of the Delaware Court of Chancery took Goldman Sachs to task, largely agreeing with the plaintiffs' claims. El Paso failed to "cabin" Goldman Sachs's role despite the investment bank's clear conflict. Goldman was inherently conflicted because it represented El Paso for part of the time in the sale negotiations with Kinder Morgan and advised El Paso on a possible spinoff of its pipeline business. But Goldman's private equity arm also owned 19.1 percent of Kinder Morgan and had two appointees on Kinder Morgan's board. Although El Paso and Goldman took steps to manage this conflict, Chancellor Strine found that their efforts were ultimately not sufficient.

While the investment bank Morgan Stanley was hired as a second adviser to El Paso because of this conflict, Chancellor Strine concluded that Goldman still inappropriately continued to advise El Paso. Goldman also arranged the "remarkable feat" of limiting the scope of Morgan Stanley's engagement so that it got paid only if El Paso was sold but not if El Paso decided to engage in an alternative transaction, a spinoff of the pipeline business. This alternative transaction remained the exclusive domain of Goldman Sachs. Chancellor Strine described this arrangement as having the effect of giving Morgan Stanley an incentive to focus solely on a sale of El Paso to the detriment of what might be a bigger creator of shareholder value, a possible spinoff of the pipeline business.

Having concluded that both Goldman Sachs and El Paso's CEOs were inappropriately conflicted, Chancellor Strine then found "debatable negotiating and tactical choices" by El Paso, namely that the company failed to strongly challenge Kinder Morgan when it threatened to go

---

[7]   Steven M. Davidoff, *Del Monte Ruling Challenges Cozy Bids*, N.Y. TIMES, Feb. 15, 2011, available at http://dealbook.nytimes.com/2011/02/15/del-monte-ruling-challenges-cozy-buyout-bids/.

public with a hostile offer. Chancellor Strine did not enjoin the sale, but allowed the claims against El Paso, its officers and directors, and Goldman Sachs to proceed. The case was subsequently settled for $110 million.[8]

These two cases also highlight a new, potentially troublesome issue for investment banks: liability for aiding and abetting breaches of fiduciary duties by the board of directors. In prior years, banks had relied upon disclosures in their engagement letters to prevent them from being sued by shareholders of the companies that hired them. But their ability to prevent aiding and abetting suits is apparently diminishing. Consider in this regard the recent case involving Royal Bank of Canada's representation of Rural Metro. Vice Chancellor Laster of the Delaware Chancery Court found RBC liable for aiding and abetting the Rural Metro board's breaches of fiduciary duty in connection with the sale of Rural Metro at an inadequate price.[9] An article discussing the case asked:[10]

> [B]ecause of laws that make it virtually impossible to hold directors personally liable, Rural/Metro's board was able to settle a shareholders' lawsuit over the sale for just $6.6 million, most of which was paid by insurance, according to a source with knowledge of the lawsuit. The case shows just how greedy investment bankers can be, but is it right for the bank to be paying so much money and not the directors, particularly when it is the directors' misconduct that the bank's liability is based on?

The court's opinion recounts the history:

> The Board first formed the Special Committee in August 2010. Some weeks earlier, RBC had pitched Shackelton and DiMino [board members; DiMino was also the President and CEO of Rural Metro] on the possibility of Rural acquiring American Medical Response (AMR), Rural's lone national competitor in the ambulance business. AMR was a subsidiary of Emergency Medical Services Corporation (EMS), a publicly traded entity that seemed more interested in its higher margin medical services subsidiary. The Board created the Special Committee to oversee an approach to AMR.

The Special Committee consisted of Shackelton, DeMino and another board member, Davis.

---

[8]   *See generally* William W. Bratton & Michael L. Wachter, *Bankers and Chancellors*, 93 TEX L. REV. 1 (2014).

[9]   *In re Rural Metro Corporation Stockholders Litigation*, 88 A.3d 54 (Del. Ch. 2014).

[10]   Steven M. Davidoff, *Ruling Highlights Unequal Treatment in Penalizing Corporate Wrongdoers*, N.Y. TIMES, March 18, 2014, available at http://dealbook.nytimes.com/2014/03/18/ruling-highlights-unequal-treatment-in-penalizing-corporate-wrongdoers/.

Returning to the opinion:

> Shackelton, Davis, and DiMino each had personal circumstances that inclined them towards a near-term sale. Shackelton was a managing director of Coliseum Capital Partners, L.P. (Coliseum), a hedge fund he co-founded in 2006. . . . By 2010, Rural had grown to 22% of Coliseum's portfolio—twice the target size for a core position . . . Shackelton saw an M&A event as the next logical step for Coliseum's involvement with Rural.
>
> Davis had different reasons for favoring a sale. In fall 2010, Davis served on a dozen public company boards, which brought him into conflict with an ISS policy against "over-boarded" directors. . . . A sale of Rural would reduce his number of board seats, while letting him exit on a professional high note. It also would let Davis keep over $200,000 of Rural equity that would vest on a change of control, but which he would lose if he resigned voluntarily. Davis set a personal deadline of April 1 for Rural to announce a sale; otherwise, he would resign from the Board.
>
> DiMino was a late convert to the idea of a sale. During most of 2010, he favored keeping Rural independent. In September 2010, while Shackelton talked up the Company with private equity firms, DiMino politely resisted, arguing that the company was on a clear growth plan to increase revenue and EBITDA. . . . DiMino contrasted his assessment with what Shackelton and RBC thought, namely that now is the time to sell. DiMino changed his mind after his ["scathing"] six month performance review [which criticized his conduct in meeting with a prospective buyer of the Company]. . . . From that point on, DiMino supported a sale and deferred to Shackelton. According to Davis, self-interest also drove DiMino's change of heart: . . . I think at some point, he came to the conclusion he would be better off with a different Board, and a new owner would bring a different Board, on top of which he was going to prematurely cash out on the equity that he had received less than a year earlier. And probably if he was given the job back, would get more equity. It was a very good deal for him. . . .
>
> The Board [had] charged the Committee with retaining advisors and generating a recommendation on the best course of action. It did not authorize the Special Committee to pursue a sale. . . .

The Special Committee hired RBC as its advisor; RBC characterized its engagement as "sell side," advising on the sale of Rural Metro. RBC's aim, though, was not solely to sell Rural Metro. It had several other objectives, including some relating to EMS, which was putting itself up for sale at the same time.

> Internally, Munoz and his RBC colleagues realized that a private equity firm that acquired EMS might decide to buy Rural rather than sell AMR. Munoz and his colleagues recognized that if Rural engaged in a sale process led by RBC, then RBC could use its position as sell-side advisor to secure buy-side roles with the private equity firms bidding for EMS. RBC correctly perceived that the firms would think they would have the inside track on Rural if they included RBC among the banks financing their bids for EMS ... If RBC had not run the Rural process in parallel with the EMS process, other private equity players with equally large funds could have participated, forcing up the price. The timing of the Rural process also meant that Warburg [the private equity bidder who ultimately bought Rural] did not have to worry about strategic bidders [because of other developments involving those bidders].

Moreover, running the process in this way also limited the universe of buyers for Rural.

> It should have been clear from the outset, particularly to sophisticated market participants like Shackelton and RBC, that financial sponsors who participated in the EMS process would be limited in their ability to consider Rural simultaneously because they would be constrained by confidentiality agreements they signed as part of the EMS process and because EMS would fear that any participants in both processes would share EMS's confidential information with its closest competitor.

RBC led the last phase of the negotiations. RBC had significantly conflicting incentives: it only got paid if a deal got done, giving it an incentive to push for any deal rather than no deal, even a deal at a lower price than might be appropriate. In this case, RBC also wanted to get the financing business from Warburg. "Rather than pushing for the best deal possible for Rural, RBC did everything it could to get a deal, secure its advisory fee, and further its chances for additional compensation from Warburg."

> At the same time that RBC's leveraged finance bankers were engaging in last-minute lobbying with Warburg [to get its financing business], the RBC M & A team was working to lower the analyses in its fairness presentation to make Warburg's bid of $17.25 look more attractive.... [The court characterizes the information-provision by RBC to the board as seriously defective: no or not enough information, and also, some false information.] ... During the final negotiations over price, RBC took advantage

of the informational vacuum it created to prime the directors to support a deal at $17.25. . . .

RBC *created* the unreasonable process and informational gaps that led to the Board's breach of duty. At the outset, RBC knew that it was not disclosing its interest in obtaining a role financing the acquisition of EMS or how it intended to use the Rural process to capture the EMS financing business. RBC similarly knew that the Board and the Special Committee were uninformed about Rural's value when making critical decisions. RBC had not provided any preliminary valuation analysis since December 23, 2010, and had only provided its December 23 book to the Special Committee. Most egregiously, RBC never disclosed to the Board its continued interest in buy side financing and plans to engage in last minute lobbying of Warburg . . . As a result, it was natural for the Board to assume that Warburg's fully financed bid left RBC out of the picture and to send RBC to negotiate with Warburg. RBC knew and failed to disclose to the Board that on Saturday, March 26, 2011, senior bankers at RBC were engaged in a full-court press to convince Warburg to use RBC's staple financing or include RBC in the financing package. While those fevered efforts were underway, RBC was simultaneously revising its valuation of Rural downward. Munoz coordinated between the two groups but did not disclose RBC's activities to the Board.

. . .

RBC's actions led to (i) an ill-timed sale of Rural that did not capture value attributable to its acquisition strategy; (ii) a mismanaged sale process that generated only one final bid by a bidder that knew it had the upper hand in bidding and price negotiations; and (iii) uninformed board approval based on manipulated valuation analyses . . . [B]ut for RBC's actions, a fully-informed Board would have had numerous opportunities to achieve a superior result.[11]

The article quoted above that discusses the case concludes:

Given these facts, it was no surprise that Vice Chancellor Laster found RBC liable.

To find the investment bank liable, however, the judge also had to find misdeeds committed by the Rural/Metro board. Vice Chancellor Laster held that the Rural/Metro Board had breached its fiduciary duties because Mr. Shackelton and RBC effectively put the company up for sale without full board authorization and

---

[11] *In Re Rural Metro, supra* note 9.

that the board had failed to properly supervise RBC. He also concluded that the Rural Metro board did not have an "adequate understanding of the alternatives available to Rural" and that its decision to accept the Warburg offer was not reasonable because of a lack of sufficient information.[12]

Royal Bank of Canada was held liable for damages of $75.8 million. On appeal to the Delaware Supreme Court, the Chancery Court decision to impose damages on Royal Bank of Canada was upheld.[13]

In the wake of these opinions, investment banking conflicts are under harsh scrutiny, not only by courts but also by clients. The following article discusses the issue and best practices for boards in these situations:

ADDRESSING FINANCIAL ADVISOR CONFLICTS IN THE WAKE OF *DEL MONTE* AND *EL PASO*

Matthew Kuhn & Jonathan L. H. Nygren
Faegre Baker Daniels
July 19, 2012

Transactions involving financial advisor conflicts of interest and the role of boards of directors in policing these conflicts have occupied much of the news from the Delaware Court of Chancery during the last 18 months. The *Del Monte* opinion in particular makes clear that, despite the existence of conflicts of interest and efforts to conceal those conflicts, ultimately "the buck stops with the Board" when it comes to managing a financial advisor's conflicts of interest.

Boards Need to Understand and Assess the Incentives and Conflicts of Their Advisors

Engaging a financial advisor involves understanding the variety of activities and relationships of the advisor that can lead to actual or apparent conflicts of interest. There is no requirement that a company's financial advisor be free of conflicts, and boards of directors should keep in mind that not all conflicts, including equity interests in or loans to bidders, are of a sufficient size and nature to prevent the advisor from effectively representing the company.

In the wake of *Del Monte*, there was some speculation that, to ferret out conflicts of interest, companies might seek representations in engagement letters with investment banks regarding banks' prior activities with potential buyers. That approach has not become customary and is not necessary, but active questioning by boards of investment bankers regarding their relationship and activities with potential buyers

---

[12] Davidoff, *supra* note 10.

[13] *RBC Capital Markets, LLC v. Jervis*, No. 140, 2015, 2015 WL 7721882 (Del. Nov. 30, 2015).

should be part of evaluating any investment bank at the engagement stage in today's environment.

Incentives Created by Financial Arrangements Should Be Considered

Boards should be cognizant of, and give careful consideration to, the incentives created by the financial advisor's fee arrangements. In *El Paso*, although the court took issue with the company's engagement of Goldman Sachs given Goldman's unusually significant conflicts (noting that the company had prior relationships with several similarly qualified but substantially less conflicted investment banks), the court also criticized the board's failure to negotiate arrangements that would allow the company and its second financial advisor to explore, and be compensated for, an alternative transaction—the sale of its [pipeline] business—which might have maximized El Paso's value for its shareholders. The Chancery Court has repeatedly recognized that structuring financial advisor engagements with a significant success-based fee is acceptable, but boards should be aware of the impact of those fees on the advice the board may receive, especially if a second advisor is engaged.

Boards Should Address Advisor Conflicts as They Arise

In addition to simply identifying conflicts, *Del Monte* and *El Paso* emphasize the need for boards to understand and address those conflicts. In *Del Monte*, the court did not rule that the conflict created by Barclays "staple financing" for the company's buyer was impermissible per se; rather, the court faulted the board for allowing the conflict to arise when the company obtained nothing in return and because the conflict was not necessary to consummate the transaction.

In light of Goldman Sachs' conflicts in the El Paso transaction, El Paso's board took the appropriate step of engaging a second financial advisor in connection with the Kinder Morgan transaction. However, simply bringing a second advisor into a conflict situation does not adequately address the conflict if the second bank is not given sufficient authority to take actions that address the conflict that led to their engagement in the first place.

Conclusion

Financial advisor conflicts of interest are not new, but the degree of scrutiny they are receiving is increasing. Boards of directors and their advisors need to understand and address any conflicts of interest, manage their financial advisors and make sure any material conflicts are fully disclosed to shareholders.[14]

---

[14] Available at http://www.faegrebd.com/18685.

b.   The Issue of Sell-Side Financing

The *Del Monte and Rural Metro* cases illustrate the challenges associated with sell-side financing, sometimes called "stapled" financing, presents particular problems. Banks provide stapled financing when the target sells itself in a broad sales process, typically an auction. Banks offer such financing for two reasons. First, it allows for a quicker process, as each buyer does not need to line up its own financing, but can instead rely on the financing provided by the seller's investment bank. Second, it allows for uniform pricing by buyers since they are all using the same financing package. Many buyers, especially private equity firms, will need financing. As discussed in the preceding Chapter, each private equity buyer should have roughly the same value, a "common value," since there are no synergies or cost-savings that might make one such buyer have a higher valuation than another. Having one financing package should allow the target to analyze each bid and the financing risk on the same terms. But there are costs as well as benefits. With sell-side financing, the target's investment bank is inherently conflicted since it will switch sides once a deal is reached, representing the buyer in providing financing. Since the target's investment bank is providing the financing, it benefits if the deal is done at the lowest price possible, since this increases the chance that it will be repaid. But for the conflict, the target's bank would want the highest price possible for the target. The conflict is often dealt with by disclosure and the hiring of a second bank to provide a fairness opinion. But as the *Del Monte* and *Rural Metro* opinions show, this does not always eliminate the difficulties caused by the conflict. In the wake of these opinions, in which the Delaware courts closely scrutinized investment bank conflicts, boards are increasingly wary of sell-side financing. The following law firm memo sets forth the firm's view as to how boards should approach the possibility of sell-side financing by a target's bank:

> [B]oards of public targets should play an "active and direct role in the sale process." Specifically, in the stapled financing context, the board must decide, as a threshold matter, whether the benefits of the staple would outweigh the potential risks of conflicts. To make such a determination, the board typically will evaluate any prior or existing relationships that the financial advisor has with actual or potential bidders and determine whether any potential conflicts of interest are likely to develop, in each case carefully reflecting such consideration in its board minutes. In addition, the board must clearly demonstrate the benefits that would result from the staple, which may include (i) confidentiality (by reducing the need for the bidder to contact outside financing sources, the risk of leaks is reduced), (ii) speed (with financing in place, the bidder need not obtain its own

financing) and (iii) deal certainty (by having made committed debt financing available to qualified potential bidders on specified terms, the seller increases the likelihood that the transaction can be financed at an acceptable sale price). Another relevant consideration is the general availability in the market of financing to bidders.

Common Practices of Targets

After careful deliberation, if the board determines that the benefits justify the potential risks, it should actively pursue measures that minimize the possibility of such risks. Examples of ways a board can do this include:

- Clearly articulating to the financial advisor from the outset that the board will have the right to tell the advisor whether, and when, the advisor will be able to offer financing in the transaction;

- Obtaining representations from the financial advisor in an engagement letter or otherwise that the advisor has (i) disclosed to the target all communications that it has had with prospective buyers concerning the target prior to the date of the engagement letter and (ii) described any known conflicts;

- Considering hiring a second financial advisor to be involved in the sale process, including running any "go-shop" process and providing a second fairness opinion; and

- Considering a reduction in the fees payable to the investment bank providing buy-side financing to offset fees of the second financial advisor that may be required as a result of a conflict.[15]

c.   The Rise of Boutique Investment Banks

The prevalence of investment bank conflicts has spurred the rise of boutique investment banks. These smaller entities, which include Greenhill, Evercore, Moelis, Perella Weinberg, and Centerview, aim to solve the conflict problem by offering only advice and not providing financing. The following excerpt describes one such bank, Centerview Partners:

> As big investment banks wrestle with tarnished reputations and accusations of conflicts of interest, the allure of Wall Street boutiques only grows. They offer advice—nothing else—and have

---

[15] Skadden Arps Meager Slate & Flom, LLP, *Stapled Financing in the Aftermath of Delaware's Del Monte Decision Capital Market Insights* (2012), available at http://www.skadden.com/newsletters/Skadden_2012_Insights_Capital_Markets.pdf.

none of the other operations, such as trading, that breed conflicts. One firm little known outside of financial circles, Centerview Partners, has become a key player. Its bankers aren't just dealmakers; they're counselors to giant companies. And they're leading changes in corporate strategy as they establish new ways of handling nettlesome activist investors and create a fresh model for how companies and Wall Street interact.

Launched in 2006, Centerview is led by a roster of Wall Street veterans who left managerial roles at top banks. Centerview's partners are a seasoned group, mostly between the ages of 45 and 55, and their experience is proving a major advantage. For a small firm—its 22 senior bankers wouldn't even fill a department at Goldman Sachs—Centerview has worked on a remarkable number of trophy deals. It . . . has helped shepherd more than 30 transactions with a total value of more than $60 billion over the past 18 months.[16]

While boutique investment banks have carved out a niche, they have not significantly diminished the concentration in the industry, as the league tables in Subsection B.2 above show. Instead, they are often hired as a second bank to alleviate a conflict existing with the main investment bank advising a target or buyer. Market observers attribute the fact that the boutique banks have not gotten more of the larger investment banks' business to a number of factors, including the latter's greater informational networks and resources. The large investment banks are now almost all part of massive enterprises, bank holding companies, and can provide their own financing. Targets and buyers will often hire investment banks for financing purposes; they hire the banks for associated business as well, such as help with the sale, but they do so principally to cement the relationship and provide the banks with more business. For banks, this type of banking is called balance sheet banking because the bank is using its financing to insert itself into the transaction and get the associated non-financing business. By contrast, if a client retains a boutique bank like Centerview, it cannot use it for financing. (Indeed, in the mid-2015 deal between Heinz and Kraft, there were no big banks involved—only Centerview and Lazard—but this was a deal in which no financing was needed). Consider the Centerview banker's comments above about financing in this light.

---

[16] Shawn Tully, *Centerview Partners: Small Bank, Big Influence*, FORTUNE, Aug. 27, 2012, available at http://fortune.com/2012/08/27/centerview-partners-small-bank-big-influence/.

C. OTHER PROFESSIONALS

Attorneys and investment bankers are typically the two most important advisers in the merger and acquisitions process, but there are several other important actors.

1. ACCOUNTANTS

Accountants assist targets and buyers in the decision to enter into an M&A transaction and in completing any necessary filings with the SEC. In the assessment and due diligence phase, accountants for the buyer will evaluate the target's financial statements for their accuracy and validity. This is likely to be a more searching review for a private company than for a public company; a public company already regularly files reports with the SEC which include audited financial information. The reports are periodically reviewed by the SEC, and they are subject to the antifraud provisions of the federal securities laws. In addition, most public companies are audited by one of the "Big Four" accounting firms, Pricewaterhouse Coopers, Ernst & Young, Deloitte, and KPMG, who have significant reputational stake in ensuring they accurately report financial results for their clients. A buyer will thus often rely on the gatekeeping role of the target's accounting firm and the SEC, as well as the antifraud provisions. The buyer's accountants will thus only do limited due diligence, either before or after announcement of the transaction.

In contrast, if the target is private, it may be subject to only limited regulatory scrutiny. Moreover, it may have its accounting done by a smaller accounting firm without nearly as much reputational capital as one of the Big Four. Some targets may not even have audited financial statements. The buyer's accountants will therefore play a more significant role in private company acquisitions, doing far more extensive due diligence.

In cases where the buyer is acquiring the target in exchange for securities of the buyer, the target's accountants will need to do due diligence on the buyer, since the acquisition is now also an acquisition of an interest in the buyer by the target's shareholders. By contrast, if the buyer is only paying cash, the target has far less interest in the buyer, being more concerned that the buyer has the cash to close the transaction, and that there are no other reasons to suppose the transaction would not close.

Accountants prepare the necessary financial information for inclusion in the public filings for the acquisition. If the buyer is acquiring a public company by issuing securities, it will need to prepare a registration statement for the securities; the statement will include its audited financial statements. These financial statements will need to be reviewed and updated as necessary by the buyer's accountants. If the acquisition is large and significant enough, the registration statement will also need to include pro forma financial information reflecting the target and the buyer's businesses as combined, which will be prepared by the buyer's and target's accountants.[17] The buyer's accountants may also provide a "comfort letter" in connection with the registration statement. The comfort letter certifies that the financial information included in the registration statement is accurate. This is done in order to provide a "due diligence" defense to the directors of the company in connection with the inclusion of the financial statements in the registration statement, and the liability exposure that such inclusion creates under the securities laws.

2. PUBLIC RELATIONS

Public relations is an increasingly important component of the mergers and acquisitions process. While some companies prefer to do public relations through their own spokespeople, it is increasingly common for companies to hire a public relations adviser. The circle of public relations advisors in the mergers and acquisitions world is concentrated; the top firms include Brunswick Group, Sard Verbinnen & Co., and Joele Frank Wilkinson Bremmer Katcher. What accounts for the rise in public relations? Telling a coherent and positive story to the public and shareholders in contexts such as transactions with a significant regulatory component, hostile bids, and situations involving shareholder activists has become increasingly important.

In all of these contexts, the bulk of which involve public companies, the public relations firm will coordinate publicity with the media but also with shareholders. The public relations team will take an active role in "selling" the transaction to shareholders and regulators. In the case of a target fighting off a hostile bid or a shareholder activist, the public relations firm will assist the target in the public component of its defense. Attorneys often work with their client's media personnel behind the scenes, often speaking to media and shareholders to explain transaction points. In addition, in significant public transactions, the public relations team will work with the advisors prior to the announcement of the transaction in order to plan post-announcement publicity and media.

3. PROXY SOLICITORS AND INFORMATION AGENTS

Proxy solicitors assist a company in soliciting shareholders to vote on a merger transaction. As is typical in mergers and acquisitions, the business is concentrated, with the top three proxy solicitors being DF King & Co., Inc., Innisfree M&A, and MacKenzie Partners Inc.

---

[17] For more on "significance" for this purpose, see SEC Regulation S–X Rule 3–05 (17 C.F R. Part 210).

A proxy solicitor's job typically has three components. First, the proxy solicitor will assist the company in determining which shareholders are eligible to vote. This is more difficult than you might think. Most shareholders of record of the company are brokerage firms. The actual (or beneficial) shareholders hold their shares in the name of such brokerages (even the brokerage firms often hold shares in the name of a central nominee known as Cede & Co.). While the identity of a company's record shareholders is fairly stable over time, because of the high volume of trading, the identities of a company's beneficial shareholders is more difficult to ascertain. The proxy solicitor helps the company determine who beneficially owns record holders' shares and thus has the right to vote on the proposed merger. The proxy solicitor's second role is to count votes—to assist the company in determining how the shareholder vote is progressing, and whether the management's proposed merger is winning or losing. Because management controls the corporate election process, the board is aware of the results. The voting process can involve a decision to delay, which may be in the form of a postponement, adjournment, or recess of the shareholder meeting. If there is to be a delay, the relationship between the proxy solicitors and the board becomes extremely important. The solicitor's third role is to advise the company as to tactics and strategies to win shareholder votes.

If an acquisition is consummated via a tender offer, the proxy solicitor will serve as the information agent. The information agent serves roughly the same role as a proxy solicitor in a merger; they assist shareholders in tendering into the offer (rather than, as in the case of a merger, in voting), and assist the company in locating shareholders to be solicited to tender into the offer. The proxy solicitor or information agent serves as a public face of the transaction and can assist shareholders, answering their questions about the transaction or helping them respectively, vote or tender their shares.

4. PROXY ADVISORY FIRMS

Proxy advisory firms are perhaps the most controversial non-party participants in the M&A process. For a fee, proxy advisory firms advise institutional shareholders on how to vote their shares, not only in such "ordinary" matters as the election of directors, but also on mergers and acquisitions. In recent years, proxy advisory firms have also made recommendations as to whether shareholders should tender their shares in a tender offer.

The largest proxy advisory firm is Institutional Shareholder Services (ISS); the second largest is Glass Lewis. These proxy advisory firms are quite influential. One study has found that on average they sway six to ten percent of the vote in director elections.[18] Another study has found that they can sway anywhere from twelve to twenty-three percent of the vote on a merger.[19] Their important role, and the fact that they are for-profit businesses, has led many commentators to argue that proxy advisory services are not sufficiently regulated. The following excerpt discusses the issues raised by the role, use, and influence of proxy advisory firms:

> Commentators have identified a number of concerns with proxy advisors and the corporate governance industry in which they operate. One is the inherent conflict of interest in the business model of many of these firms—providing governance advice to corporate clients while also providing voting advice to investor clients—which gives reason to doubt the accuracy of their ratings and advice.

> The corporate governance ratings industry itself is a market response: firms effectively resolve the collective action problem faced by institutional investors who have a fiduciary duty to vote proxies in the best interests of their beneficiaries. But the market for governance ratings is not working as it should: ratings firms produce poor-quality ratings whose validity cannot be tested because the underlying metrics are proprietary and are not disclosed. Even if they were disclosed, it is likely that we would end up merely assuring ourselves that none of them are very useful.

> Another pressure point is the institutional investor client of corporate governance ratings firms. If these investors do indeed have a fiduciary duty to their beneficiaries, that duty should not be assumed to have been met by a casual acceptance of a proxy recommendation without some assurance that the mechanisms that produced the recommendation are both reliable and free of conflict. The SEC has spoken to the conflicts issue in a pair of letters to ISS and Egan-Jones. The ISS letter states:

> Consistent with its fiduciary duty, an investment adviser should take reasonable steps to ensure that, among other things, the [proxy advisory firm] can make recommendations for voting proxies in an impartial manner and in the best interests of the adviser's clients. The investment adviser should also assess whether the proxy voting firm has fully implemented the conflict procedures.

---

[18] *See* Stephen Choi, Marcel Kahan & Jill Fisch, *The Power of Proxy Advisors: Myth or Reality?*, 59 EMORY L.J. 869, 906 (2010).

[19] See Jill E. Fisch, Sean J. Griffith & Steven Davidoff Solomon, *Confronting the Peppercorn Settlement in Merger Litigation: An Empirical Analysis and a Proposal for Reform*, 93 TEX. L. REV. 557 (2015).

In the end, despite guidance such as the ISS letter, I think the SEC has not adequately encouraged investors to scrutinize not just potential conflicts of interest, but also the content of the advice they receive from corporate governance raters and proxy advisors. Unless the SEC provides better guidance on what such scrutiny should entail and undertakes a sustained enforcement program to detect and discipline fiduciaries who fail to meet their duties, the beneficiaries of the funds these institutional investors manage will suffer.[20]

The collective action problem that Professor Rose identifies is that institutional investors like Fidelity Investments can hold thousands of shares throughout its hundreds of mutual funds, but it will not be worthwhile for Fidelity to expend the resources to analyze each matter on which they have a shareholder vote. Their stake in each company is small relative to their overall size and to the size of the companies; certainly, they could not significantly affect the outcome of the vote. But by using a proxy advisory firm, Fidelity will expect that other institutional investors are voting similarly. Fidelity will also avoid expending resources to analyze each matter on which there is a vote. Fidelity and other such investors can thus be seen as outsourcing their fiduciary duties to appropriately supervise their investments.

Professor Rose criticizes the proxy advisory industry, and by implication institutional investors, for relying upon general corporate governance ratings, which empirical studies have been found to be flawed. The same criticisms have been leveled at the proxy advisory firms' recommendations on M&A transactions. The SEC is expected to address calls to further regulate the proxy advisory business in the coming years. Regulation might, for instance require institutional investors to offer better justifications for following the recommendations made by proxy advisory firms. Such a requirement would significantly curtail such firms' influence.

QUESTIONS

1.   After reading the memorandum discussing the avoidance of conflicts in providing sell-side financing, and the precautions recommended, do you think the Delaware approach to conflicts and investment banks is too strict or otherwise unnecessary? What is the goal of Delaware's approach?

2.   What other advantages do you see to hiring of a traditional investment bank over a boutique bank?

---

[20] Paul Rose, *On the Role and Regulation of Proxy Advisors*, MICH. L. REV. FIRST IMPRESSIONS 62 (2014), available at http://repository.law.umich.edu/cgi/viewcontent.cgi?article=1026&context=mlr_fi.

PROBLEM

You are representing a target in a sale process via an auction. The general counsel comes to you and says that the investment bank representing the company wants to provide stapled financing. The general counsel wants to know the issues with doing this and whether it is something they should do "legally." He tells you that management appears particularly keen on doing this since it will allow them to better assess the bids. When you remark that there have been some problems with this in the past, the general counsel remarks: "Well, my executives really want to do this so find a way. In particular, I don't see why this is different than any other conflict where we can simply acknowledge it. After all, we pay a success fee to investment banks all the time . . . isn't that a conflict? Can't we just retain a second bank for the fairness opinion?" Please write a short memo to your client discussing whether stapled financing is different and recommending a way that he can use this device. Conclude the memo with your advice to the partner as to whether your firm should recommend against using stapled financing.

CHAPTER XIII

PRELIMINARY NEGOTIATIONS

■ ■ ■

In a friendly transaction, the process to sell or buy a company may begin with casual interactions which lead to the signing of formal transaction documentation.[1] A target or buyer will hire an investment bank and other advisors such as attorneys and accountants. The target and potential buyer(s) will negotiate and execute a confidentiality agreement to allow for the orderly exchange of information. Due diligence, the buyer's investigation of the target, will occur next. Additionally, a letter of intent may be entered into to guide the parties in their negotiation of a definitive transaction. All of this may occur very quickly. Some tasks may be done in-house and others may be outsourced to outside counsel or other deal advisers. What follows describes this process, including the more significant issues—and pitfalls—that may arise.

A. INVESTMENT BANKER ENGAGEMENT LETTER

No lengthy highly-negotiated letter precedes the engagement of transactional lawyers. However, companies will negotiate engagement letters with investment banks. Sometimes these letters are negotiated in-house before the lawyers get involved, but other times, the company will use its outside M&A counsel. The investment banker's in-house counsel will typically present its standard form of engagement letter for clients to sign, often resisting any change to the letter, particularly the indemnification provisions, on grounds that the letter's provisions are "standard." The following excerpt discusses some of the most common issues that arise in negotiating an engagement letter. The Online Appendix includes an annotated form of an investment bank engagement letter which you may want to read in conjunction with this excerpt.

---

[1] Some of these interactions also occur in other types of M&A transactions such as those that start hostile but turn friendly. In this Chapter we will focus on "friendly" transactions and turn to other types of transactions in later Chapters. This Chapter's focus is principally on larger, public transactions. In a smaller private deal, there will often be fewer types of deal advisors. Moreover, where shares are not publicly traded, there is no need for a standstill.

NEGOTIATING INVESTMENT BANKING M&A ENGAGEMENT LETTERS: KEEPING THE INVESTMENT BANK INCENTIVIZED WHILE PROTECTING YOUR INTERESTS

Marshall Horowitz & Joshua Schneiderman
Snell & Wilmer Corporate Communicator
Spring 2012

The investment banker has approached your company, laid out a compelling case for why a sale at this time might make sense for your company, and has convinced you to plant a "for sale" sign in your corporate offices and test the market. The investment banker has served up his firm's "standard engagement letter," and asked that you sign it so you can partner up and kick off the process.

At this point you are conflicted—you know this investment banker is supposed to be "on your side" and "working for you" and you certainly do not want to start the relationship on the wrong foot. At the same time, there are a number of provisions in the engagement letter that make you uneasy, and you wonder whether they are customary or if there is room for negotiation ... [W]e highlight below several aspects of the engagement letter that should be evaluated with care and that have room for negotiation.

Fees

... The fee payable to the investment banker in an engagement letter is most likely calculated as a percentage of the price for which the company is sold. While an investment banker should always be working to get the company the greatest value in the sale, it is not uncommon to tweak the fee structure to give the bank some extra encouragement. One way to accomplish this is through a progressive fee schedule (sometimes referred to as a "Reverse Lehman" formula), where the success fee percentage increases as the sale price crosses certain thresholds. Under certain circumstances, minimum and/or maximum fees might be appropriate. . . .

In addition, while it is common for an investment banker to receive an upfront retainer and a success fee upon consummation of a transaction, occasionally an engagement letter will call for milestone payments at other points in time. If the banker has proposed a structure that incorporates milestone payments, and that is something a company is willing to consider, it is best to ensure that the milestone payments are only earned upon the achievement of legally meaningful and objective events. For instance, if the banker has asked for a milestone payment upon the signing of a letter of intent or term sheet, a company will likely want to resist this point, as letters of intent and term sheets are often nonbinding. While a letter of intent may be meaningful from a moral perspective, it typically only requires the parties to continue to negotiate in good faith, which would leave the company paying an investment banker fee with no assurance that it actually has a binding transaction. . . .

Carveouts from the Definition of "Transactions"

The engagement letter will typically provide that the investment banker will be entitled to its fee upon consummation of a "transaction." In a sale context, the term "transaction" will usually be defined to cover the sale of all or part of the capital stock of a company, the merger of a company with an acquirer, or a purchaser's acquisition of all or substantially all of a company's assets. Depending on a company's circumstances, however, there may be a number of transactions that it will want carved out from the definition of "transactions."

. . . [For instance, i]t is not uncommon to list on a schedule to the engagement letter a number of parties with whom the company has already had discussions about a sale transaction and to specify that a sale to, or combination with, any of those listed entities will not be considered a "transaction" for which the investment banker will be entitled to a fee . . .

Services

One important component in an engagement letter is a description of the services that the investment banker will provide in connection with the engagement. This list of services may include reviewing a company's financials and comparing them to industry data, identifying and approaching potential purchasers, coordinating potential buyers' due diligence efforts and assisting in negotiations . . .

Term, Termination and Tail

Most investment banks structure the term of the engagement in such a way that it will perpetually renew absent some affirmative action by the company to terminate the engagement. For instance, the engagement letter might provide that the engagement lasts for six months, but that it automatically renews for additional successive one-month periods if neither party provides written notice of its intent to terminate the engagement. Provisions such as this are notorious for catching up with unwitting companies who forget to notify their investment banker of their intent to terminate the engagement . . . In addition, and almost without fail, an investment banker will insist that the engagement letter include a "tail period." The tail period is a period of time after the termination of the engagement during which, upon the completion of a transaction, the investment banker would still be entitled to its fee.

Indemnification

. . . In general, there is relatively little room for negotiation of the indemnification provision. The investment banker will generally insist on being indemnified for any liability it incurs in connection with or as a result of the engagement other than any liability resulting from its own willful misconduct or gross negligence. This standard is common across banks, and it would be highly unusual for a bank to agree to accept liability for any conduct on its part that does not rise to this level. While a company may have some success tinkering with the terms of the indemnification provision on the margins, banks are typically very reluctant to deviate from their standard language.[2]

B. NON-DISCLOSURE AND CONFIDENTIALITY AGREEMENTS

Parties—both targets and potential buyers—are typically concerned about confidentiality. A target may not want those working for, or dealing with, it to know that it may be for sale; even if that fact is known, a target does not want the information it is providing to potential buyers to become more generally known. Potential buyers may not want their interest in acquiring the target to be public. This is so for many reasons, including that a potential buyer presumably does not want to signal to other bidders that the target is for sale. A confidentiality agreement, also known as a non-disclosure agreement ("NDA"), functions to ensure that any exchange of information between the target and the potential buyer is kept confidential.

A form of confidentiality agreement is included in the Online Appendix. You may wish to review it in conjunction with the memo below, which covers key points of negotiation between a target and possible bidder.

REVIEWING THE M&A NONDISCLOSURE AGREEMENT
Eric H. Wang
Mergers and Acquisitions Alert (US)
August 8, 2012

A nondisclosure agreement, often referred to as an NDA or a confidentiality agreement, is typically the first agreement to be entered into in a mergers and acquisitions transaction. The agreement is designed to protect the confidentiality of information exchanged in connection with the consideration and negotiation of the transaction and information

---

[2]   Available at http://info.swlaw.com/reaction/2012/CorporateCommunicator_2012_HTML/CC_Spring2012/CC_Spring2012_WEB.html.

exchanged in the course of a party's due diligence review of the other. In a situation where a party is presented with the other side's form NDA, a careful review is warranted.

Set forth below is a summary checklist and commentary concerning some of the more important items to consider when reviewing an NDA. The checklist and commentary refer to "Providers" and "Recipients," regardless of which part is the buyer or seller. That is because while the selling party generally is the "Provider," in some situations, such as where the buying party is issuing its equity as part of the transaction consideration, the buyer may also providing substantial amounts of confidential information to the seller for the seller's due diligence on the buyer. Where the italicized prefaces "Providers should" or "Recipients should" advocate actions to take in your review, keep in mind that business reasons may dictate the importance of certain provisions and the lesser relevance of others. The checklist does not contain every matter you may desire to negotiate and is not a substitute for review by sophisticated M&A counsel—it is merely intended to address some of the more common issues you should be aware of in reviewing an NDA.

General

Providers and Recipients should

Confirm that the form of NDA used is a proper one, as often parties mistakenly start with an NDA that is designed for providing information to vendors or with another short-form NDA that is not tailored for an M&A transaction.

Definition of confidential information

Providers should

Confirm that the definition of "confidential information" sufficiently covers the information and materials to be provided (and, to the extent applicable, confidential information that may have been previously provided).

Consider removing legending requirements (that any written materials be marked "confidential" or that oral statements be reduced to writing and so marked to be considered confidential) to avoid accidental failures to legend leading to unprotected confidential information.

Consider having any subset of extremely confidential information being supplied (such as pricing information, patent information, or source code) carved out and addressed separately under a special NDA implementing careful controls and procedures to limit the distribution and access of the information to those advisors or agreed upon personnel of the Recipient whom the Provider believes cannot exploit the information commercially, especially where the Recipient is a close competitor.

Remove any "residual" clause which allows the Recipient to use, in future products or services, all information retained in the memory of the Recipient's employees which was obtained from reviewing the confidential information.

Recipients should

Confirm that the exclusions from what is considered confidential information properly reflect the principle that information should not be protected if it was created or discovered by the Recipient prior to, or independent of, any involvement with the disclosing party.

Use of confidential information

Providers should

Confirm that there exists language limiting the use of the confidential information to that contemplated (evaluation of the specific transaction) and not for any other purpose.

Confirm that there exists language clarifying that no license is being granted to the Recipient or its representatives to use the confidential information except for the specific purpose of evaluating the transaction, and that no license is being granted to any of the Provider's intellectual property.

Confirm that the Recipient is responsible/liable for its representatives' proper use of the confidential information to the extent that the Provider does not request such representatives to be parties to the NDA.

If the Provider is a publicly traded company, confirm that the Recipient will not use confidential information in violation of applicable securities laws.

Consider implementing controls and procedures to limit the distribution and access of the information if there is extremely confidential information being supplied or if the Recipient is a close competitor, but where these factors do not arise to the level of affording treatment of the more sensitive portion under a special NDA.

Confirm there exists language clarifying that information provided does not constitute any representation or warranty of the Provider but that such representations and warranties are limited to what is provided for in the definitive agreement.

Non-disclosure of discussions

Providers should

Confirm that the NDA contains language clarifying that the fact of discussions between the parties regarding the transaction is confidential, especially if the Provider is a publicly traded company.

If the Provider is the selling company in an auction context, attempt to retain some limited ability to disclose the fact that the Recipient is bidding or, to the extent possible, to disclose the terms of any bid made by Recipient.

Recipients should

Confirm that the NDA contains language clarifying that the discussions between the parties regarding the transaction are confidential, including the identity of the parties and the terms of any bid if the Recipient is the acquiring company.

If the Recipient is the acquiring company and needs financing for the transaction, obtain a carve out allowing information to be disclosed to financiers.

Legally required disclosures

Providers should

Consider requiring the Recipient to fully cooperate with the Provider in obtaining any applicable protective order if requested.

Recipients should

Confirm there exists an exception to the NDA allowing the Recipient to disclose information which is legally required to be disclosed.

Return or destruction of materials

Providers should

Confirm there exists language providing for the return or destruction of any written confidential information provided.

If a copy is to be retained for archival/evidentiary purposes, confirm that this is kept by outside counsel.

Recipients should

Consider ensuring outside counsel the right to retain one copy for archival/evidentiary purposes.

Confirm that the Recipient is permitted to destroy or certify destruction of information to satisfy obligation.

Non-solicitation/employment

Providers should

Confirm that the NDA contains language providing for protection against the Recipient's solicitation of the Provider's employees for some amount of time (the typical range is six months to two years; one year is common) as well as against solicitation of former employees recently departed (six months is common).

The Recipient may argue strongly against this because it is a large entity that will have difficulty keeping track of solicitation and hiring activities. If this occurs, consider these alternatives: limiting scope of non-solicit to "key" employees or those Recipient had contact with or were identified during the diligence process, or limiting the interaction between both parties' employees by restricting which Provider employees the Recipient will be allowed to contact.

Recipients should

Consider a limiting provision that would apply only to "key" employees or employees of the Provider who Recipient had contact with or were identified to the Recipient during the diligence process.

Confirm that there exists a carve out for general solicitation not directed at Provider employees.

Consider removing this provision altogether if it concerns a large entity that would have difficulty keeping track of solicitation and hiring activities.

Term

Providers should

Consider language providing that the NDA does not expire, as what is confidential now may need to remain just as confidential many years from now.

Consider setting an unlimited term for trade secrets.

Recipients should

Consider limiting the NDA to a specific time period (range is generally one to five years).

Remedies

Providers should

Confirm there exists language having the Recipient acknowledge and agree that monetary damages are insufficient to remedy breach of the NDA, and that the Provider is entitled to equitable relief in addition to any other remedies.

Miscellaneous provisions applicable to providers and recipients

Privileged information. Consider language stating that disclosure is not deemed to have waived or diminished attorney-client privilege, attorney work-product protection, or any other privilege or protection applicable to the confidential information, which relies upon a form of the joint defense doctrine. Note that effectiveness of this provision is not certain.

Other

Binding agreement. Confirm that language exists clarifying that the NDA does not constitute an agreement to enter into or even negotiate a transaction, as sometimes courts have found an agreement to negotiate absent such language.

Standstill provisions. These provisions are only applicable where the target company is publicly traded or likely to be public soon, and, due to their complexity, these provisions should be carefully addressed and reviewed by sophisticated M&A counsel.

No-shop. The seller should delete provisions restricting it from shopping as these are not typically agreed to until at least a term sheet or basic transaction terms are agreed upon.[3]

A key consideration in the negotiation of a confidentiality agreement is the definition of the "Transaction" that the agreement covers. A confidentiality agreement in an M&A transaction will typically contain a provision requiring the possible bidder to only use the information obtained from the target, known as "Evaluation Materials," to evaluate a possible "Transaction," as defined in the agreement. If a target limits the use of the information to a "negotiated transaction" the agreement may subsequently prevent the bidder from launching a hostile or unsolicited takeover if negotiations break down. The bidder is now in possession of information about the target and can be accused of "using" that information for other than a permitted purpose, namely an unsolicited or hostile, as opposed to a friendly and negotiated, takeover.

A second possible issue for a potential buyer relates to the actual confidentiality requirements. A bidder may come into possession of material non-public information of the target after executing a confidentiality agreement. If talks break down and the bidder subsequently makes a hostile bid, again the bidder may not use the target's information for the hostile bid. Even if the bidder could make a

---

[3]   Available at http://www.dlapiper.com/en/us/insights/publications/2012/08/reviewing-the-ma-nondisclosure-agreement/.

hostile bid, under the securities laws, it may be required to disclose in its filings related to the hostile bid all material, non-public information concerning the target in its possession. Such disclosure, however, is prevented by the confidentiality agreement. The bidder may thus be unable to make the necessary filings to commence the hostile bid.

The following case touches on these issues, and shows how a target can use provisions in a confidentiality agreement as a shield, stopping a hostile or unsolicited bid. The confidentiality agreements at issue can be found in the Online Appendix. As you read the case, also note the close textual analysis engaged in by the court, and consider what that analysis suggests for your task as the lawyer charged with negotiating the contract language at issue.

MARTIN MARIETTA MATERIALS, INC. v. VULCAN MATERIALS COMPANY

Supreme Court of Delaware
68 A.3d 1208 (2012)

JACOBS, JUSTICE:

[T]he Court of Chancery enjoined Martin, for a four month period, from continuing to prosecute its pending Exchange Offer and Proxy Contest to acquire control of Vulcan. That injunctive relief was granted to remedy Martin's adjudicated violations of two contracts between Martin and Vulcan: a Non-Disclosure Letter Agreement (the "NDA") and a Common Interest, Joint Defense and Confidentiality Agreement (the "JDA"). Martin appealed to this Court from that judgment. . . . [The judgment is affirmed]

THE FACTS

A. *Background Leading to the Confidentiality Agreements*

Vulcan and Martin are the two largest participants in the United States construction aggregates industry. That industry engages in mining certain commodities and processing them into materials used to build and repair roads, buildings and other infrastructure. Vulcan, a New Jersey corporation headquartered in Birmingham, Alabama, is the country's largest aggregates business; and Martin, a North Carolina corporation headquartered in Raleigh, North Carolina, is the country's second-largest.

Since the early 2000s, Vulcan and Martin episodically discussed the possibility of a business combination, but the discussions were unproductive and no significant progress was made. In 2010, Ward Nye, who had served as Martin's Chief Operating Officer since 2006, was appointed Martin's Chief Executive Officer ("CEO"). After that, Nye and Vulcan's CEO, Don James, restarted merger talks. In early April 2010, Vulcan's investment banker at Goldman Sachs first "test[ed] out" the new

Martin CEO's interest. Nye's positive response prompted a meeting with James later that month, which led to more formal discussions.

At the outset Nye was receptive to a combination with Vulcan, in part because he believed the timing was to Martin's advantage. Vulcan's relative strength in markets that had been hard hit by the financial crisis, such as Florida and California, had now become a short-term weakness. As a result, Vulcan's financial and stock price performance were unfavorable compared to Martin's, whose business was less concentrated in those beleaguered geographic regions. To Nye, therefore, a timely merger—before a full economic recovery and before Vulcan's financial results and stock price improved—was in Martin's interest. Moreover, Nye had only recently been installed as Martin's CEO, whereas James, Vulcan's CEO, was nearing retirement age with no clear successor. To Nye, that suggested that a timely merger would also create an opportunity for him to end up as CEO of the combined companies.

Relatedly, although Nye was willing to discuss a possible merger with his Vulcan counterpart, he was not willing to risk being supplanted as CEO. The risk of Nye being displaced would arise if Martin were put "in play" by a leak of its confidential discussions with Vulcan, followed by a hostile takeover bid by Vulcan or a third party. . . .

Understandably, therefore, when Nye first spoke to Vulcan's banker, Goldman Sachs, in April 2010, he stressed that Martin was not for sale, and that Martin was interested in discussing the prospect of a friendly merger, but not a hostile acquisition of Martin by Vulcan. As the Chancellor found, Nye's notes prepared for a conversion with Vulcan's banker made it clear that "(i) Martin . . . would talk and share information about a *consensual* deal only, and not for purposes of facilitating an *unwanted* acquisition of Martin . . . by Vulcan; and even then only if (ii) absolute confidentiality, even as to the fact of their discussions, was maintained." When James and Nye first met in April 2010, they agreed that their talks must remain completely confidential, and they operated from the "shared premise" that any information exchanged by the companies would be used only to facilitate a friendly deal.

To secure their understanding, Nye and James agreed that their respective companies would enter into confidentiality agreements. That led to the drafting and execution of the two Confidentiality Agreements at issue in this case: the NDA and the JDA.

B. *The NDA*

[T]he NDA prohibited both the "use" and the "disclosure" of "Evaluation Material," except where expressly allowed. Paragraph 2 permitted either party to *use* the other party's Evaluation Material, but "*solely for the purpose of evaluating a Transaction*." Paragraph 2 also categorically prohibited either party from *disclosing* Evaluation Material to anyone except the receiving party's representatives. The NDA defined "Evaluation Material" as "any nonpublic information furnished or communicated by the disclosing party" as well as "all analyses, compilations, forecasts, studies, reports, interpretations, financial statements, summaries, notes, data, records or other documents and materials prepared by the receiving party . . . that contain, reflect, are based upon or are generated from any such nonpublic information. . . ." The NDA defined "Transaction" as "a possible business combination transaction . . . between [Martin] and [Vulcan] or one of their respective subsidiaries."

Paragraph 3 of the NDA also prohibited the disclosure of the merger negotiations between Martin and Vulcan, and certain other related information, except for disclosures that were "legally required." Paragraph 3 relevantly provided that:

Subject to paragraph (4), each party agrees that, without the prior written consent of the other party, it . . . will not disclose to any other person, *other than as legally required,* the fact that any Evaluation Material has been made available hereunder, that discussions or negotiations have or are taking place concerning a Transaction or any of the terms, conditions or other facts with respect thereto (including the status thereof or that this letter agreement exists).

Paragraph 4 defined specific conditions under which "legally required" disclosure of Evaluation Material (and certain other information covered by Paragraph 3) would be permitted:

In the event that a party . . . [is] requested or required (by oral questions, interrogatories, requests for information or documents in legal proceedings, subpoena, civil investigative demand or other similar process) to disclose any of the other party's Evaluation Material or any of the facts, the disclosure of which is prohibited under paragraph (3) of this letter agreement, the party requested or required to make the disclosure shall provide the other party with prompt notice of any such request or requirement so that the other party may seek a protective order or other appropriate remedy and/or waive compliance with the provisions of this letter agreement. If, in the absence of . . . the receipt of a waiver by such other party, the party requested or required to make the disclosure . . . should nonetheless, in the opinion of such party's . . . counsel be legally required to make the disclosure, such party . . . may, without liability hereunder, disclose only that portion of the other party's Evaluation Material which such counsel advises is legally required to be disclosed. . . .

As the Chancellor found, "Paragraph (4) establishes the Notice and Vetting Process for disclosing Evaluation Material and Transaction

Information that would otherwise be confidential under the NDA in circumstances [where] a party is 'required' to do so in the sense that the party had received an External Demand." The Chancellor further concluded that Ms. Bar's addition of the words "Subject to paragraph (4)" at the beginning of NDA paragraph (3), is "most obviously read as being designed to prevent any reading of ¶ 3 that would permit escape from ¶ 4's narrow definition of legally required and ¶ 4's rigorous Notice and Vetting Process."

C. *The JDA*

Because the parties were exploring a combination of the two largest companies in their industry, antitrust scrutiny appeared unavoidable. After the NDA was signed, the two companies' inside and outside counsel met to discuss that issue. The discussions implicated nonpublic, privileged information and attorney work-product, leading Martin and Vulcan also to execute the JDA (which was drafted by outside counsel) to govern those exchanges.

The JDA, like the NDA, prohibits and limits the use and the disclosure of information that the JDA describes as "Confidential Materials." The critical prohibitions and limitations are found in JDA Paragraphs 2 and 4. Paragraph 2 prohibits the disclosure of Confidential Materials without "the consent of all Parties who may be entitled to claim any privilege or confidential status with respect to such materials. . . ." JDA Paragraph 4 relevantly provides that "Confidential Materials will be used, consistent with the maintenance of the privileged and confidential status of those materials, solely for purposes of pursuing and completing *the Transaction.*" The JDA defines "Transaction" as "a *potential transaction being discussed* by Vulcan and Martin[ ] . . . involving the combination or acquisition of all or certain of their assets or stock. . . ."

D. *Martin's Use and Disclosure of Vulcan's Information Covered by the NDA and JDA*

After the JDA and the NDA were executed, Vulcan provided to Martin nonpublic information that gave Martin a window into Vulcan's organization, including detailed confidential information about Vulcan's business, revenues, and personnel. . . .

The Court of Chancery found, and Martin does not dispute, that Martin used and disclosed Vulcan's nonpublic information in preparing its Exchange Offer and its Proxy Contest to oust some of Vulcan's board members (collectively, the "hostile takeover bid"). . . . [At a certain point in March 2011, the talks were floundering but Martin wanted to do a deal.] Martin and its bankers began using Vulcan's confidential, nonpublic information to consider alternatives to a friendly deal. . . . Four months later, Martin launched its unsolicited Exchange Offer.

As a regulatory matter, an exchange offer carries a line-item requirement under federal securities law to disclose past negotiations. Martin announced its Exchange Offer on December 12, 2011, by sending Vulcan a public "bear hug" letter and filing a Form S–4 with the [SEC]. ["Martin's Form S–4 disclosed not only the history of the negotiations, but also other detailed information that constituted "Evaluation Material" and "Confidential Materials" under the respective Confidentiality Agreements."] On January 24, 2012, Martin announced its Proxy Contest and filed a proxy statement in connection therewith.

Both before and after Martin commenced its hostile takeover bid, Martin disclosed Vulcan's nonpublic information, first to third party advisors (investment bankers, lawyers and public relations advisors), and later publicly. Martin did that without Vulcan's prior consent and without adhering to the Notice and Vetting Process mandated by the NDA. . . . [N]o effort was made to shield these advisors from receiving Evaluation Material or information relating to James' and Nye's negotiations.

The disclosures by Martin to the SEC, the Chancellor found, "were . . . a tactical decision influenced by [Martin's] flacks," . . . "exceeded the scope of what was legally required," and involved "selectively using that [Evaluation] Material and portraying it in a way designed to cast Vulcan's management and board in a bad light, to make Martin['s] own offer look attractive, and to put pressure on Vulcan's board to accept a deal on Martin['s] terms."

Lastly, the Chancellor found that after it launched its hostile takeover bid, Martin disclosed Evaluation Material and other confidential information "in push pieces to investors, off the record and on the record communications to the media, and investor conference calls."

We conclude . . . that the Chancellor . . . correctly concluded (*inter alia*) that: (i) the JDA prohibited Martin from using and disclosing Vulcan Confidential Materials to conduct its hostile bid; (ii) the NDA prohibited Martin from disclosing Vulcan Evaluation Material without affording Vulcan pre-disclosure notice and without engaging in a vetting process; (iii) Martin breached the use and disclosure restrictions of the JDA and the disclosure restrictions of the NDA; and (iv) injunctive relief in the form granted was the appropriate remedy for those adjudicated contractual violations.

ANALYSIS

B. *Martin's Violations of the JDA*

The Chancellor determined that Martin, in making its hostile bid, both "used" and "disclosed" Vulcan Confidential Materials in violation of the JDA. That agreement (the trial court found) unambiguously prohibits the use of "Confidential Materials" without Vulcan's consent, except "for purposes of pursuing and completing the Transaction," which the JDA defines as "a potential transaction being discussed by Vulcan and Martin. . . ." The Court of Chancery found as fact that "the only transaction that was 'being discussed' at the time the parties entered into the JDA was a negotiated merger," and that "neither [the] Exchange Offer nor [the] Proxy Contest . . . was 'the' transaction that was 'being discussed' at the time that the JDA was negotiated."

Martin asserts that those determinations are reversibly erroneous . . . First, Martin claims, the court erred in concluding that the only transaction "being discussed" when the parties entered into the JDA was a negotiated merger. Second, Martin advances the related claim that, even if "Transaction" meant a negotiated transaction, Martin committed no contractual breach, because "the JDA expressly allows the use of [protected] information 'for purposes of *pursuing and completing* the Transaction,'" and Martin's hostile bid "ultimately will facilitate . . . a negotiated transaction." . . . [T]hese claims lack merit.

The trial court properly found that the relevant operative language of the JDA—"a potential transaction being discussed"—is unambiguous, and Martin does not seriously contend otherwise. The only remaining dispute, accordingly, is factual: what transaction was "being discussed?" The *only* transaction being discussed, the trial court found, was a negotiated merger. To say that that finding is not "clearly wrong" would be an understatement: the finding is amply supported by the evidence. Nye told Vulcan that Martin was not for sale. Nye told Vulcan that Martin was interested in discussing the prospect of a merger, *not* an acquisition, whether by Vulcan or otherwise. And, Nye described the transaction under discussion as a "modified merger of equals."

Equally unpersuasive is Martin's alternative contention that even if "Transaction" means a negotiated merger, Martin did not violate the JDA's use restriction, because the JDA expressly allowed Martin to use Confidential Materials "for purposes of pursuing and completing the Transaction," and Martin's hostile bid "ultimately will facilitate . . . a negotiated transaction." That claim fails because the Chancellor found as fact that the only transaction being discussed would be "friendly" or "negotiated." That finding expressly and categorically excluded Martin's "hostile bid or a business combination . . . effected by a pressure strategy." We uphold the Chancellor's factual finding that the transaction "being discussed" for purposes of the JDA's "use" restriction did not encompass a merger accomplished by means of hostile tactics. Martin's second claim of error, therefore, fails for the same reason as its first. . . . [*Editor: Discussion of a third reason omitted.*] For these reasons, we uphold the Chancellor's conclusion that Martin used and disclosed Vulcan Confidential Materials in violation of the JDA.

C. *Martin's Violations of the NDA*

. . . The Chancellor found as fact that Martin disclosed Vulcan confidential information, including Evaluation Material, in the course of pursuing its hostile bid, and Martin does not contest that finding. Rather, Martin's claim before us is that its disclosure of Vulcan confidential information was permitted by Paragraph 3 of the NDA. . . .

[W]e conclude, as a matter of law based upon the NDA's unambiguous terms, that: (i) Paragraph 3, of itself, does not authorize the disclosure of "Evaluation Material," even if such disclosure is otherwise "legally required;" (ii) Paragraph 4 is the only NDA provision that authorizes the disclosure of Evaluation Material; (iii) any disclosure under Paragraph 4 is permitted only in response to an External Demand and after complying with the pre-disclosure Notice and Vetting Process mandated by that paragraph; and (iv) because no External Demand was made and Martin never engaged in the Notice and Vetting Process, its disclosure of Vulcan's Evaluation Material violated the disclosure restrictions of the NDA.

. . . The Court of Chancery found as fact that Martin disclosed Evaluation Material in the course of conducting its hostile bid, without having received an External Demand and without having engaged in the Notice and Vetting Process. Martin has not challenged that finding. We therefore uphold the Court of Chancery's determination that Martin breached the NDA's disclosure restrictions.

C. STANDSTILLS

A potential bidder for a public company may, or may not, be willing to agree to include a standstill provision in its confidentiality agreement with the target. As mentioned earlier, a standstill provision generally provides that a potential bidder will not attempt to acquire the target without the target's prior approval for a specified period of time. A standstill may also contain a "don't ask/don't waive" provision which prohibits the potential bidder from requesting that the target board waive the standstill. The latter provision avoids forcing the board to consider a proposal from the potential bidder, even one that the board's fiduciary duties might have forced it to accept; we discuss board fiduciary duties further in Part IV. As discussed further below, the rationale for "don't ask/don't waive" provisions is that they motivate bidders to make their best offers in the sales process itself rather than waiting until the process is completed and simply topping the then-highest bid. The following is a common form of standstill agreement in an NDA:

9. Unless approved in advance in writing by the board of directors of the Company, the Recipient agrees that neither it nor any of its Representatives acting on behalf of or in concert with the Recipient (or any of its Representatives) will, for a period of [ ] year[s] after the date of this Agreement, directly or indirectly:

(a) make any statement or proposal to the board of directors of any of the Company, any of the Company's Representatives or any of the Company's stockholders regarding, or make any public announcement, proposal or offer (including any "solicitation" of "proxies" as such terms are defined or used in Regulation 14A of the Securities Exchange Act of 1934, as amended) with respect to, or otherwise solicit, seek or offer to effect (including, for the avoidance of doubt, indirectly by means of communication with the press or media) (i) any business combination, merger, tender offer, exchange offer or similar transaction involving the Company or any of its subsidiaries, (ii) any restructuring, recapitalization, liquidation or similar transaction involving the Company or any of its subsidiaries, (iii) any acquisition of any of the Company's loans, debt securities, equity securities or assets, or rights or options to acquire interests in any of the Company's loans, debt securities, equity securities or assets, (iv) any proposal to seek representation on the board of directors of the Company or otherwise seek to control or influence the management, board of directors or policies of any of the Company, (v) any request or proposal to waive, terminate or amend the provisions of this Agreement or (vi) any proposal, arrangement or other statement that is inconsistent with the terms of this Agreement, including this Section 9(a);

(b) instigate, encourage or assist any third party (including forming a "group" with any such third party) to do, or enter into any discussions or agreements with any third party with respect to, any of the actions set forth in clause (a) above;

(c) take any action which would reasonably be expected to require the Company or any of its affiliates to make a public announcement regarding any of the actions set forth in clause (a) above; or

(d) acquire (or propose or agree to acquire), of record or beneficially, by purchase or otherwise, any loans, debt securities, equity securities or assets of the Company or any of its subsidiaries, or rights or options to acquire interests in any of the Company's loans, debt securities, equity securities or assets

[, except that Recipient may beneficially own up to ___% of each class of the Company's outstanding loans, debt securities and equity securities and may own an amount in excess of such percentage solely to the extent resulting exclusively from actions taken by the Company].

[The foregoing restrictions shall not apply to any of the Recipient's Representatives effecting or recommending transactions in securities (A) in the ordinary course of its business as an investment advisor, broker, dealer in securities, market maker, specialist or block positioner and (B) not at the direction or request of the Recipient or any of its affiliates.]

(e) Notwithstanding the foregoing provisions of this Section 9, the restrictions set forth in this Section 9 shall terminate and be of no further force and effect if the Company enters into a definitive agreement with respect to, or publicly announces that it plans to enter into, a transaction involving all or a controlling portion of the Company's equity securities or all or substantially all of the Company's assets (whether by merger, consolidation, business combination, tender or exchange offer, recapitalization, restructuring, sale, equity issuance or otherwise).][4]

This provision effectively forces all the bidding parties who have signed agreements containing this provision to make their best bid because they know that they will not get another opportunity to bid once the formal process ends. Of course, this provision cannot preclude another bidder, one who has not signed an NDA, from making a higher bid after a winner emerges from the auction process. A buyer will often resist entering into a standstill because it thereby becomes foreclosed from initiating an unsolicited or hostile bid if negotiations break down. Conversely, a target will often insist on a standstill as the price of conducting negotiations and providing confidential information.

Delaware courts have struggled with enforcement of standstills given that they can prevent a bidder from making a higher bid. This is especially true in the context of a sale of control, when boards may be under fiduciary obligations, discussed in Chapter XVIII, to seek out the highest price reasonably available for shareholders.[5]

The first case to address this issue was not in Delaware. Rather, it involved two Canadian companies. Sunrise Senior Living Real Estate Investment Trust (Sunrise), a Toronto Stock Exchange listed company,

---

[4]   PLC Standstill Agreement.

[5]   The material in this subsection is adapted from material prepared by Professor Sean Griffith. *See also* Graham P.C. Gow, Brian C. Graves & R. Paul Streep, *Standstill Agreements in Auctions—Lessons from the Sunrise/Ventas Decision*, McCarty Tétrault LLP, May 31, 2007, available at http://www.mccarthy.ca/article_detail.aspx?id=3580.

put itself up for auction in November 2006.[6] Seven parties, including Ventas Inc. and Health Care Property Investors Inc. (HCP), signed confidentiality agreements. The confidentiality agreements signed by Ventas and HCP contained standstill provisions prohibiting them from making a proposal to acquire securities or assets of Sunrise for 18 months without Sunrise's prior written consent.[7]

Ultimately, the interested parties were winnowed down to Ventas and HCP, and Ventas made a proposal to acquire Sunrise's assets for $15 per unit. HCP did not submit a final bid. As a result, Ventas and Sunrise entered into a purchase agreement in January 2007 containing a no-shop provision (providing that Sunrise would limit its dealings with other potential acquirers. We discuss no-shop provisions in Chapter XVIII.B) with a customary fiduciary out (also discussed in Chapter XVIII.B, a provision allowing directors to proceed with another transaction if so required by their fiduciary duties). Ventas was given matching rights should a superior proposal arise—that is, rights to match any competing bid; if Ventas did not match the bid, Sunrise could terminate the purchase agreement upon paying a termination fee equal to 3.5% of the transaction value, and enter into an agreement with the new bidder. The purchase agreement also contained a provision, not expressly subject to the fiduciary out, that required Sunrise to not waive or fail to enforce the standstill provisions in any confidentiality agreements signed with third parties. The relevant provisions are excerpted below:

> 4.4 (1) Following the date hereof, Sunrise REIT shall not, directly or indirectly, through any trustee, officer, director, agent or Representative of Sunrise REIT or any of its Subsidiaries, and shall not permit any such Person to,
>
>> (i) solicit, initiate, encourage or otherwise facilitate (including by way of furnishing information or entering into any form of agreement, arrangement or understanding or providing any other form of assistance) the initiation of any inquiries or proposals regarding, or other action that constitutes, or may reasonably be expected to lead to, an actual or potential Acquisition Proposal,
>>
>> (ii) <u>participate in any discussions or negotiations in furtherance of such inquiries or proposals or regarding an actual or potential Acquisition Proposal or release any</u>

---

[6]   *See* Ventas, Inc. v. Sunrise Senior Living Real Estate Investment Trust, 2007 ONCA 205 DATE: 20070323 DOCKET: C46790 & C46791 (affirming the lower court's decision to enforce the standstill).

[7]   Significantly, however, the standstill provision in the Ventas confidentiality agreement differed from the HCP confidentiality agreement in that Ventas' standstill provision terminated if a third party made a bid for Sunrise or if Sunrise entered into a purchase agreement with a third party. The HCP standstill contained no such limitation.

Person from, or fail to enforce, any confidentiality or standstill agreement or similar obligations to Sunrise REIT or any of its Subsidiaries,

(iii) approve, recommend or remain neutral with respect to, or propose publicly to approve, recommend or remain neutral with respect to, any Acquisition Proposal,

. . . or

(v) withdraw, modify or qualify, or publicly propose to withdraw, modify or qualify, in any manner adverse to the Purchasers, the approval or recommendation of the Board (including any committee thereof) of this Agreement or the transactions contemplated hereby.

(2) Notwithstanding anything contained in Section 4.4(1), until the Unitholder Approval, nothing shall prevent the Board from complying with Sunrise REIT's disclosure obligations under applicable Laws with regard to a bona fide written, unsolicited Acquisition Proposal or, following the receipt of any such Acquisition Proposal from a third party (that did not result from a breach of this Section 4.4), from furnishing or disclosing non-public information to such Person if and only to the extent that:

(i) the Board believes in good faith (after consultation with its financial advisor and legal counsel) that such Acquisition Proposal is consummated could reasonably be expected to result in a Superior Proposal. . .

(3) Notwithstanding anything contained in Section 4.4(1), until the Unitholder Approval, nothing shall prevent the Board from withdrawing or modifying, or proposing publicly to withdraw or modify its approval and recommendation of the transactions contemplated by this Agreement, or accepting, approving or recommending or entering into any agreement, understanding or arrangement providing for a bona fide written, unsolicited Acquisition Proposal (that did not result from a breach of this Section 4.4) ("Proposed Agreement") if and only to the extent that:

. . .

(ii) the Board, believes in good faith (after consultation with its financial advisor and legal counsel) that such Acquisition Proposal constitutes a Superior Proposal and has promptly notified the Purchasers of such determination,

. . .

(7) Sunrise REIT shall, as promptly as practicable, notify the Purchasers of any relevant details relating to any Acquisition Proposal. . . .

(8) Sunrise REIT shall

. . .(v) <u>not amend, modify, waive or fail to enforce any of the standstill terms or other conditions included in any of the confidentiality agreements between Sunrise REIT and any third parties</u>.

Subsequently, HCP offered to acquire Sunrise for $18 per unit on terms identical to the Ventas/Sunrise transaction, subject to its concluding an agreement with the management company of Sunrise's properties. Sunrise did not immediately treat this proposal as a superior proposal because of the uncertainty created by this condition. The parties then made various applications to court, essentially to determine whether Sunrise could entertain the HCP offer. The *Ventas* court held that the standstill was enforceable as a simple agreement among the parties. The fact that Sunrise shareholders would lose out on a higher bid did not warrant nullifying this agreement. In the wake of this decision, Sunrise was obligated to enforce the standstill with HCP, despite the apparent superiority of the HCP proposal. Ultimately, however, Ventas increased its offer to $16.50 per unit, the Sunrise unitholders approved the transaction, and the sale was completed in April 2007.

In 2012, the Delaware Chancery Court considered a related issue. In March 2011, Quest Diagnostics Inc., a Delaware corporation, and Celera Corp., a Delaware corporation, entered into a merger agreement providing for the acquisition of Celera by a subsidiary of Quest for approximately $680 million. The acquisition agreement resulted from a bidding process in which Celera's financial advisors had contacted nine potential bidders, five of which (Illumina, Inverness, Lab Corp., Qiagen, and Quest) performed at least some measure of due diligence. In exchange for access to diligence information, all five of these companies entered into confidentiality agreements. The confidentiality agreements contained standstill provisions which expressly prohibited them from making offers for Celera shares without an express invitation from the Board, a restriction known as a "don't ask/don't waive" provision.[8]

When Quest emerged from this process as the winning bidder, the resulting acquisition was structured as a front-end tender offer, followed by a second-step squeeze-out merger. The merger agreement contained several deal-protection measures, including a termination fee of $23.45 million or about 3.5% of the total transaction value and a no-shop

---

[8] A target board has fiduciary duties to consider any offer to acquire the company. The "don't ask" part of the standstill is designed to prevent this duty from ever being triggered unless the target board specifically requests such an offer.

provision requiring Celera to terminate any existing discussions with, and not to solicit competing offers from, potential bidders other than Quest.

When the merger was challenged in shareholder litigation, plaintiffs argued that the combination of the no-shop provision with the "don't ask/don't waive" provision was particularly onerous because it prevented Celera's board from entering into discussions with the most likely competing bidders. The litigation was ultimately settled for non-monetary consideration including: (1) reduction of the termination fee (from $23.45 million to $15.6 million); (2) modification of the no-solicitation provision to invite competing offers from the potential bidders subject to the "don't ask/don't waive" provisions; (3) a seven day extension of the tender offer; and (4) additional disclosures about the transaction process and financial analysis.

In approving the settlement (and plaintiffs' attorneys' fees of $1.3 million), the court noted that:

> The Settlement Agreement provides Celera stockholders with two categories of benefits, the first of which is therapeutic changes to the terms of the Merger. Specifically, Defendants agreed to waive the Don't-Ask-Don't-Waive Standstills, to reduce the Termination Fee from $23.45 million to $15.6 million, and to extend the closing of the tender offer by one week.

> In waiving the Don't-Ask-Don't-Waive Standstills, ... Defendants invited back to the bargaining table the four bidders arguably most likely to make a superior offer (because they already had performed some due diligence and perhaps could evaluate more quickly whether to make a competitive offer). . . Similarly, . . .[l]owering a termination fee reduces the barrier to making a superior offer in the first place and increases the amount of the superior offer's consideration that would go directly to shareholders. Lastly, extending the closing date of the tender offer afforded potential bidders more time to conduct due diligence and consider whether to make a competing bid.

> . . . I also note that, as to a handful of the Plaintiffs' claims, the therapeutic deal changes may represent the maximum relief that Plaintiffs could have obtained. For example, Plaintiffs may have been able to show that the combined potency of the Don't-Ask-Don't-Waive Standstills and the No Solicitation Provision was problematic. The terms of the Don't-Ask-Don't-Waive Standstills restricted the potential bidder from, among other things, acquiring, offering to acquire, or soliciting proxies of Celera securities in any manner (including by assisting others to do any of the same) without the Company's express written invitation.

Furthermore, the affected bidders had agreed "not to request the Company (or its directors, officers, employees or agents), directly or indirectly, to amend or waive any provision of [the relevant standstill terms] (including this sentence)." Viewed in isolation, these Don't-Ask-Don't-Waive Standstills arguably foster legitimate objectives, "ensuring that confidential information is not misused, establishing rules of the game that promote an orderly auction, and giving the corporation leverage to extract concessions from the parties who seek to make a bid." Similarly, the No Solicitation Provision, viewed in isolation, appears legitimate; although it prevented the Company from contacting potentially interested parties, including the previously identified parties, it also contained a "fiduciary out" permitting the Board to waive the Don't-Ask-Don't-Waive Standstills if strict compliance with the Merger Agreement would violate the Board's fiduciary duty to maximize shareholder value.

Taken together, however, the Don't-Ask-Don't-Waive Standstills and No Solicitation Provision are more problematic. "[The Delaware Supreme] Court has stressed the importance of the board being adequately informed in negotiating a sale of control: 'The need for adequate information is central to the enlightened evaluation of a transaction that a board must make.'" Here, the Don't-Ask-Don't-Waive Standstills block at least a handful of once-interested parties from informing the Board of their willingness to bid (including indirectly by asking a third party, such as an investment bank, to do so on their behalf), and the No Solicitation Provision blocks the Board from inquiring further into those parties' interest. Thus, Plaintiffs have at least a colorable argument that these constraints collectively operate to ensure an informational vacuum. Moreover, the increased risk that the Board would outright lack adequate information arguably emasculates whatever protections the No Solicitation Provision's fiduciary out otherwise could have provided. Once resigned to a measure of willful blindness, the Board would lack the information to determine whether continued compliance with the Merger Agreement would violate its fiduciary duty to consider superior offers. Contracting into such a state conceivably could constitute a breach of fiduciary duty.

To be clear, I do not find, either in the circumstances of this case or generally, that provisions expressly barring a restricted party from seeking a waiver of a standstill necessarily are unenforceable. Such a ruling should be made, if ever, only on the merits of an appropriately developed record, especially because those provisions may be relatively common. Rather, based on the issues it redresses, I find this aspect of the settlement consideration to be valuable. Had Plaintiffs succeeded on this claim, the likely remedy would have been an injunction against enforcing the Standstill agreements. Therefore, Defendants' agreement to waive voluntarily those problematic contractual provisions mooted Plaintiffs' claims in this regard.

Similarly, to the extent that Plaintiffs complained of a deficient or disloyal market check, the likely remedy would have been limited injunctive relief, long enough to recreate an active market check but "without blocking the deal and sending the parties back to the drawing board." Where a company has been exposed to the market and potential transactions shopped for some time, even an egregious case of process defects probably would have led to an injunction of only twenty days or so. Furthermore, where no rival bidder has made its presence known, preliminary injunctive relief may be completely illusory.[9]

The *In re Celera* case was followed by a set of bench rulings issued in November 2012, in which the Delaware Court of Chancery temporarily enjoined a merger between Complete Genomics, Inc. and BGI-Shenzhen pending corrective disclosure regarding, among other things, BGI's willingness to employ Genomics' current CEO and let him operate Genomics as an independent entity under BGI ownership. As further discussed below, the court further enjoined Genomics from enforcing a confidentiality agreement with a third-party bidder that contained a "don't ask/don't waive" provision. The court also sharply criticized a provision restricting the Genomics' board's ability to change its recommendation.

Genomics was a Delaware corporation headquartered in California that had developed a unique DNA sequencing technology. Its products generated significant revenues, but the company faced severe financial distress. As a result, in June 2012, Genomics publicly announced that it was pursuing strategic alternatives and contacted 42 parties that might be interested in an equity investment, a strategic partnership, or an acquisition. Of these 42 parties, nine parties signed confidentiality agreements; four of the confidentiality agreements contained standstill agreements that prohibited the potential bidder from making any *public* request to be released from the standstill agreement. The number of parties interested in bidding, however, dwindled to eight by the time the Genomics board asked for nonbinding proposals, with six parties proposing equity investments and two proposing transactions. Genomics

---

[9] *In re Celera Corporation Shareholder Litigation*, Civ. No. 6304–VCP, at 51–55 (Del. Ch. March 23, 2012). In a later decision, the Delaware Supreme Court, en banc, affirmed in part and reversed in part. The reversal was to allow one party to opt out of the settlement. *In re Celera Corporation Shareholder Litigation*, 59 A. 3d 418 (Del. 2012).

pursued discussions with all parties, but focused on the two parties proposing transactions. Upon the withdrawal of one of those parties after being refused exclusivity by the Genomics board, BGI emerged as the sole remaining bidder.

In September 2012, the Genomics board approved a merger agreement where Genomics would be acquired by BGI in a two-step transaction. In the first step, an acquisition subsidiary of BGI would launch a tender offer for Genomics shares at $3.15 per share in cash and, if a majority of the shares were tendered, the parties would effect a second-step merger for the same consideration. The $3.15 share price reflected a 54% per share premium over the stock price on the day before the public announcement that Genomics was exploring strategic alternatives. Moreover, BGI further agreed to provide $30 million in bridge financing until closing of the merger. The merger agreement contained a variety of deal protections, including a 4.8% break-up fee (and if a topping bidder emerged, BGI could convert the bridge loan into shares of Genomics and also participate in the higher topping price), a prohibition on terminating the merger agreement to accept a superior proposal and restrictions on the Genomics board's ability to change its recommendation of the merger agreement or waiving any standstill agreements. Hence, short of a breach by BGI or an injunction order by a court, the only way Genomics could get out of the merger agreement was if the offer was not completed by the "outside date."

In its ruling, the court declined to enjoin the deal protection provisions, although it did call into question the ability of the board to restrict its ability to change its recommendation. However, when the court subsequently discovered that at least one potential bidder had entered into a "don't ask/don't waive" standstill, the court enjoined Genomics from enforcing the standstill agreement. In its November 27 ruling, the court held:

> In my view, a Don't-Ask-Don't-Waive Standstill resembles a bidder-specific no-talk clause. In *Phelps Dodge Corporation v. Cyprus Amax*, Chancellor Chandler considered whether a target board had breached its fiduciary duties by entering into a merger agreement containing a no-talk provision. Unlike a traditional no-shop clause, which permits a target board to communicate with acquirers under limited circumstances, a no-talk clause— and here I'm quoting from the Chancellor—"not only prevents a party from soliciting superior offers or providing information to third parties, but also from talking to or holding discussions with third parties." . . .

> The Chancellor concluded that there was a reasonable probability that for the target board to have agreed to such a

provision violated its ongoing—and again, I'm quoting—"duty to take care to be informed of all material information reasonably available." This was because the target board's agreement to disable itself from engaging in a dialogue with potential acquirer under any circumstances whatsoever was the legal equivalent of willful blindness.

Subsequent Delaware decisions have endorsed the *Phelps Dodge* analysis. . . .

In holding that the no-talk provision compromised the target board's ongoing obligation to remain informed, Chancellor Chandler in *Phelps Dodge* focused on the target's ability to decide whether to negotiate with third parties and whether the provision impermissibly prevented the board "from meeting its duty to make an informed judgment with respect to even considering whether to negotiate with a third party." . . . As Chancellor Chandler noted, a board doesn't necessarily have an obligation to negotiate. . . .

Regardless, a board does have an ongoing statutory and fiduciary obligation to provide a current, candid and accurate merger recommendation. A board has an ongoing fiduciary obligation to review and update its recommendation. . . .

Maintaining a current and candid merger recommendation is part of the director's duty of disclosure. . . . Put simply, Delaware law requires that a board of directors give a meaningful, current recommendation to stockholders regarding the advisability of a merger including, if necessary, recommending against the merger as a result of subsequent events. . . .

Chancellor Allen made the same comment in his 2000 Business Lawyer article where he pointed out, "A board may not suggest or imply that it is recommending the merger to the shareholders if in fact its members have concluded privately that the deal is not now in the best interest of the shareholders."

What these decisions and these authorities show is that the board has an ongoing statutory and fiduciary obligation with respect to the merger recommendation. So regardless of whether a no-talk provision, as in *Phelps Dodge*, or a Don't Ask, Don't Waive provision here, would create problems for the decision to negotiate, and certainly *Phelps Dodge* holds that it would, those provisions interfere with the target ability to determine whether to change its merger recommendation because they absolutely preclude the flow of incoming information to the board.

So in my view, by analogy to *Phelps Dodge*, a Don't Ask, Don't Waive Standstill is impermissible because it has the same disabling effect as the no-talk clause, although on a bidder-specific basis. By agreeing to this provision, the Genomics board impermissibly limited its ongoing statutory and fiduciary obligations to properly evaluate a competing offer, disclose material information, and make a meaningful merger recommendation to its stockholders. With respect to the Don't Ask, Don't Waive Standstill provision, therefore, the plaintiffs have established a reasonable probability of success on the merits that that provision represents a promise by a fiduciary to violate its fiduciary duty, or represents a promise that tends to induce such a violation. That's from Section 193 of the Restatement of Contracts.

. . .

In terms of the issue of irreparable harm, I think for purposes of the Don't Ask, Don't Waive Standstill, it's met. We just don't know and we would never be able to know unless Party J decides to cavalierly breach its own promise whether Party J would ever want to make some type of bid or other acquisition proposal. Yes, it would be nice to say confidently, as Mr. Aronstam [the lawyer for Complete Genomics] does, that this is a low likelihood event. Unfortunately, time-bound mortals aren't able to see the future. . . . This is a provision that flat-out prohibits, analogously to a bidder-specific no-talk clause, incoming information from that bidder under any circumstances. So just as that type of provision would create a situation that can't be remedied, likewise, here, I think that type of situation creates a situation that can't be remedied.[10]

As this book goes to press, the most recent case on this issue is *In re Ancestry.com Consolidated Shareholders' Litigation.*[11] In October 2012, Permira, a private-equity firm, agreed to pay $32 per share to acquire Ancestry.com, a 41% premium over the company's pre-sale closing price. Permira outbid TPG Capital and Providence Equity Partners in the sale process. Investors, however, challenged the transaction, arguing that Permira's bid had been improperly favored. There had been a "don't ask/don't waive" provision in the standstill, and there was vigorous debate as to how much the board had understood about the provision, how the provision had affected the sales process, and what concerning these (and other) matters had been disclosed to shareholders.

---

[10] *In re Complete Genomics, Inc. Shareholder Litigation*, C.A. No. 7888–VCL, AT 14–20 (Transcript, Nov. 27, 2012).

[11] CA. No. 7988–CS, 2012 WL 6971058 (Del. Ch., December 17, 2012). Chapter III discusses the appraisal action brought in connection with the transaction that was consummated.

With regard to the "don't ask/don't waive" provision, Chancellor Strine reasoned as follows:

. . . I know of no statute, I know of nothing, that says that these provisions are per se invalid. And I don't think there has been a prior ruling of the Court to that effect. . . .

And the *Celera* case expressly went out of its way to say it's not making a per se rule. I think what *Genomics* and *Celera* both say, though, is Woah, this is a pretty potent provision. And precisely because of this *Schnell* overlay, the equitable overlay of the law, directors need to use these things consistently with their fiduciary duties, and they better be darn careful about them. Because they're often used in cases like this which are governed by *Revlon* and the board's obligation to try to get the highest value.

And that obligation comes from the obvious reality that the board is saying to the shareholders, You should give up your continuing investment in the company right now for a sum certain. Which means that the directors are supposed to make sure that they've done everything reasonable to make sure that that price is as high as possible, that they give the shareholders full information about it, and when the shareholders vote, they know the risks.

So here we get a provision, and I'm not prepared to rule out that they can't be used for value-maximizing purposes. But the value-maximizing purpose has to be to allow the seller as a well-motivated seller to use it as a gavel, to impress upon the people that it has brought into the process the fact that the process is meaningful; that if you're creating an auction, there is really an end to the auction for those who participate. And therefore, you should bid your fullest because if you win, you have the confidence of knowing you actually won that auction at least against the other people in the process.

That's what I understand the additional part of this no-ask part of the waiver provision is. Not talking about the standstill itself, which gives the board the ability to control what happens with an offer. We're talking about the ability for someone to even ask for a waiver. And it's on this idea of we've identified the most likely potential bidders. In advance of any deal protections inhibiting them from making a bid, we're bringing them in. We think they're the most likely. We recognize that other people may come forward, and they'll be subject to different rules. But how do we, in a public company context, get these most likely bidders to actually put their full bid on the table rather than hold something in reserve? We can use this tool to gain credibility so that those final-round bidders know the winner is the winner, at least as to them.

That's what I understand the argument is around these things, in that you're running an auction. I'm not prepared to rule that out. I don't think the judges of this Court should be ruling that out. That sounds like if you want to say per se invalidity, that sounds like something for the Legislature to decide. But we do have an inescapable obligation to do what is the core job of this Court, which is to do that equitable overlay. Which is if you're going to use a powerful tool like that, are you using it consistently with your fiduciary duties, not just of loyalty, but of care?

And I think the plaintiffs here . . . have pretty obviously shown that this board was not informed about the potency of this clause. The CEO was not aware of it. It's not even clear the banker was aware of it. . . .

None of the board seems to be aware of this. The only way it has value as an auction gavel is if it has the meaning I've just described. It was not used as an auction gavel. And when Permira was signed up, Permira did not demand an assignment of it. And the board and its advisors did not waive it in order to facilitate those bidders which had signed up the standstills being able to make a superior proposal.

I think that probabilistically is a violation of the duty of care. I think what's more important is that I'm not prepared to allow this [the transaction] to go to a vote without the shareholders being told about that. I think . . . they should know about this.

[A]t least when the electorate votes—if these things are going to be used, and they're used for a gavel, then the electorate should know that with respect to the comfort they should take in the ability to make a superior proposal, they should understand that there is a segment of the market where that segment cannot take advantage of that; that the board made the cost/benefit trade-off that the best way to get the value was to draw the highest bid out from those people while they were in the process; that in order to do that, it had to incur the cost of giving to the winner the right to enforce it. But what you as a shareholder know is, We invited these people in on the front end. That's how we tried to maximize value. You still have the ability of somebody we didn't test the market with coming in, but you shouldn't assume that these other people can come in. That's if it's actually been assigned.

What's harder to explain is if the winning bidder didn't ask for the assignment, how it is that the seller—I admit I wouldn't do it until I signed the definitive acquisition agreement with Permira. I don't want to tip Permira, but I would have had you guys sign first. And then the nanosecond after you didn't sign, I would have sent a letter to all those people and said, We're waiving the sentence in your standstill that says, Blank has hereby waived. The remainder remains in force and effect. Which then makes clear to all of them that if they wish to ask for a waiver in order to make a superior proposal, that they are legally allowed to do that. That makes sense. That took this litigation for that to occur.

And so I think the plaintiffs have a point that there was—frankly, this was not used in a probabilistic way, in my view, in keeping with the duty of care that's required of directors during a *Revlon* process. . . .

I think that this was a process that had a lot of vibrancy and integrity to it, probabilistically. I think they tried to kick the tires. I think that . . . they were trying to get these buyers to pay as full a price as possible. They were trying to create a competitive dynamic.

Given that and given the ability of shareholders to vote for themselves, I'm disinclined to take it out of their hands. And I think that is what separates out the absence of having a bidder on the table. That's a very powerful dynamic, and it's one that this Court has to consider for the best interests of shareholders. That said, the shareholders should vote knowing the material facts. And I've identified two . . . flaws. And I believe that my balance of the harms calculus only works if the electorate in fact has that full information.

And so . . . I'm going to enjoin the deal subject to those disclosures [and some other disclosures not discussed here] being promptly made.

Courts are still struggling with the issue of "don't ask/don't waive" provisions in standstill agreements. Accordingly, well-advised boards of will be cautious in relying on such provisions, since enforcement is not assured. Transactional lawyers need, too, to be mindful to advise their clients that this area presents significant perils.

D. LETTERS OF INTENT/MOU

The following excerpt describes a letter of intent and many of the key issues arising from its negotiation.

PRELIMINARY NOTE, LETTER OF INTENT
ABA Model Stock Purchase Agreement, Second Edition

A letter of intent is often entered into between a buyer and a seller following the successful completion of the first phase of negotiations of an acquisition transaction. The letter generally, but not always, describes the purchase price (or a formula for determining the purchase price) and certain other key economic and procedural terms that form the basis for further negotiations. In most cases, the buyer and the seller do not yet intend to be legally bound to consummate the transaction and expect that the letter of intent will be superseded by a definitive written acquisition agreement. Alternatively, buyers and sellers may prefer a memorandum of understanding or a term sheet to reflect deal terms.

Although the seller and the buyer will generally desire the substantive deal terms outlined in a letter of intent to be nonbinding expressions of their then current understanding of the shape of the prospective transaction, letters of intent frequently contain some provisions that the parties intend to be binding. As discussed more fully below, the binding provisions of a letter of intent generally relate to the process of conducting the negotiations and proceeding towards a definitive agreement. What portions of the letter of intent should be binding or nonbinding and the risks of entering into a letter of intent at all are important issues with a heavy legal overlay. The level of detail in the letter of intent and which issues should be addressed or deferred are key strategic questions that should be discussed with the client, and their likely impact on the negotiation of the acquisition should be fully explored.

There are several reasons why letters of intent are used. A buyer and a seller frequently prefer a letter of intent to test the waters before incurring the costs of negotiating a definitive agreement and performing due diligence. The parties may also feel morally, if not legally, obligated to key terms once they are set down in writing. Sometimes the deal terms are sufficiently complicated that it is helpful to put them down in writing to ensure that the buyer and seller have consistent expectations. Signing a letter of intent at an earlier stage of the acquisition process, rather than waiting for the definitive agreement, can facilitate compliance with regulatory requirements. For example, a premerger notification form can be filed under the HSR Act upon entering into a letter of intent, thereby starting the clock on the applicable waiting period.

A signed letter of intent may also assist the buyer in convincing prospective lenders or investors to evaluate the transaction for the purpose of providing financing. The letter of intent often provides an outline for the transaction that can be used as the basis for drafting the definitive agreement. Letters of intent are also used to define the rights and obligations of the parties while a definitive agreement is being negotiated. For example, an exclusivity provision is often included, which prohibits the seller from negotiating with another party while negotiations with the buyer are ongoing. A letter of intent, either alone or in conjunction with a separate confidentiality agreement, will usually permit the buyer to inspect the target's properties and to review its operations and books and records while simultaneously restricting the buyer's ability to disclose and use the target's trade secrets and other proprietary information received during the negotiations. A letter of intent often covers how expenses of the acquisition and negotiations, such as fees and expenses of brokers, attorneys, and other advisors, will be paid and limits the rights of each party to publicize the acquisition or negotiations without the consent of the other party. A letter of intent may establish the time frame for conducting due diligence and closing the acquisition and certain other milestones and pre-conditions prior to the execution of a definitive agreement or the closing of the transaction.

Many commentators and business lawyers believe that the effect of a letter of intent is generally more favorable to the buyer than to the seller. An exclusivity provision in the letter of intent may prevent the seller from introducing other interested parties to the acquisition to enhance its negotiating position with the buyer. In those cases where a letter of intent is not used, the buyer might consider entering into a separate exclusivity agreement with the seller. If actual or suspected problems are uncovered during due diligence, the buyer may try to use that information to negotiate a lower purchase price or more favorable terms. A signed letter of intent, even if not binding, together with the buyer's inspection of the target's properties and review of its operations and books and records, often will create an expectation on the part of the target's employees, vendors, customers, lenders, or investors that a sale to the buyer will occur. Buyer's investigation of the target may also uncover information that can be used by the buyer to compete with the target if the sale is not consummated, even if the target receives protection against the disclosure or use by the buyer of the target's trade secrets and other proprietary information.

Although letters of intent are common, no consensus exists among business lawyers regarding their desirability. Many lawyers advise their clients that the great disadvantage of a letter of intent is that provisions intended by the parties to be nonbinding may be later found by a court to be binding. There is often an inherent conflict between the goals of the parties in negotiating a letter of intent. The buyer generally is most interested in securing exclusivity or other standstill types of provisions from the seller while seeking to maintain great flexibility regarding the purchase price and other key provisions that may be impacted by the results of the buyer's acquisition review of the target. The seller, on the other hand, generally will attempt to define more clearly the purchase price, limitations on its exposure with respect to the representations that will be part of the definitive agreement, and key terms of employment agreements, non-compete covenants, and other ancillary arrangements. If possible, the seller will prefer to avoid altogether, or to limit the scope of, any exclusivity commitment. The negotiation of a letter of intent can sometimes become bogged down in detailed discussions that are generally reserved to the negotiation of the definitive agreement. Because of these twin concerns of the possible, but unintended, binding nature of the letter of intent and the risk that the negotiation of the letter of intent will become mired in endless detail, lawyers often advise their clients to forgo a letter of intent and commence negotiation of a definitive agreement.

It is helpful at the outset to determine the client's desires as to whether a letter of intent is binding. For example, the acquisition may be so economically or strategically attractive that the client is willing, as a business decision, to risk being bound at this initial stage. The parties might also intend to be bound if the acquisition review has been completed and all economic issues have been settled. However, a fully binding letter of intent can lead to problems and unexpected results if the parties later are unable to agree to the terms of a definitive agreement. In that event, a court may impose upon the parties its interpretation of commercially reasonable terms for any unresolved issues. At the stage in the transaction when the letter of intent is signed, the transaction itself usually is still conditional in nature. Most often, many terms have not even been considered, much less discussed or settled. Moreover, due diligence is rarely completed at this stage and quite often not even commenced, and both parties may be oblivious to many potential pitfalls. Accordingly, the buyer may want to avoid specifics on many business deal points. This strategy may enhance the buyer's negotiating position by deferring discussions on these key issues until after the buyer has completed its due diligence and the seller's negotiating position has been compromised by executing a letter of intent. The seller, on the other hand, will want in most cases to resolve all important issues at the letter of intent stage when the seller may have its greatest negotiating leverage. For example, the seller may want to negotiate limitations with respect to its indemnification obligations in the letter of intent by providing for a cap, a basket, an expiration of the indemnification obligations, reliance on the indemnity provisions as the buyer's exclusive remedy, or some combination of these concepts. The seller may also seek to avoid guaranties and draconian escrows at the outset by facing these issues at the letter of intent stage.[12]

---

[12] Available at https://apps.americanbar.org/buslaw/blt/content/departments/2010/09/mspa-letter-of-intent.pdf.

A sample letter of intent is included in the Online Appendix. As the excerpt below notes, one of the key issues in such letters is the extent to which they bind either or both parties, either to the terms therein or even to a transaction. To limit the binding nature of a letter of intent, lawyers will sometimes negotiate a provision which states that the letter will not "give rise to any legally binding or enforceable obligation on any Party." However, even if a letter contains such a provision, an obligation to negotiate in good faith might nevertheless be found to exist. Such an obligation may arise by reason of the covenant of good faith and fair dealing, which is read into all agreements and cannot be waived.

In *Global Asset Capital, LLC v. Rubicon US REIT, Inc.*, No. 5071–VCL (Del Ch., Nov. 16, 2009), Vice Chancellor Laster considered the rights conferred by a letter of intent. Rubicon had faced a serious liquidity crisis, having insufficient cash to meet its current needs. It entered into a letter of intent with Global Asset Capital stipulating that Global Asset Capital would be a "stalking horse" if Rubicon filed for bankruptcy and subsequently auctioned itself off for sale. In the letter of intent, Rubicon agreed to a "no-shop," that Rubicon would not solicit competing bidders, and confidentiality provisions as well as the payment of a termination fee to Global Asset Capital if Rubicon later agreed to accept a competing bid. The letter provided that Rubicon and Global Asset Capital would negotiate the terms for Global Asset Capital's "stalking horse bid." When Rubicon secured financing, it ceased negotiating with Global Asset Capital. Global Asset Capital sued seeking a temporary restraining order (TRO) forcing Rubicon to negotiate with Global Asset Capital. In a bench decision, Vice Chancellor Laster granted the TRO, stating:

> . . . I believe at this stage of the case that it is a letter of intent that is sufficiently definite to give rise to rights on the part of the plaintiff. I am influenced in that regard not only by . . . cases . . . which I think set forth more fully how this Court regards both letters of intent as well as the duty to negotiate in good faith, which. . . is one that this Court recognizes, is one that is of commercial importance, and is one that this Court will protect.

> . . . . [I]n terms of the provisions of the agreement that are I think definite and certainly specific are the no-shop clause and the confidentiality provisions. There is obviously a hotly contested dispute of fact here as to whether those provisions were in fact breached. . . ., and also that the defendant did not negotiate in good faith, as required by the letter of intent. This brings me to the aspect of irreparable harm which is the far more critical one for this temporary restraining order. . . . Letters of intent mean something not only for the bankruptcy context, but for the M&A context and for our capital markets in general.

. . . [P]arties enter into letters of intent . . . because they create rights. Now, if parties want to enter into nonbinding letters of intent, that's fine. They can readily do that by expressly saying that the letter of intent is nonbinding, that by providing that, it will be subject in all respects to future documentation . . . I think this letter of intent is binding, although I will withhold a final decision on that. All I'm holding today is it's sufficiently binding to give rise to a colorable claim. But certainly, a no-shop provision, exclusivity provision, in a letter of intent is something that is important.[13]

Letters of intent are common in the deal-making world, particularly in the acquisitions of private companies, but they are fraught with risks. Clients may wish to document something short of a final agreement. Having done so, it is not clear to what extent their counterparties or the courts will consider them bound, or, for that matter, to what extent they will consider themselves bound—and to what terms.

E. DUE DILIGENCE

Once the confidentiality agreement and other preliminary arrangements are finalized, the next step is typically due diligence. In some ways, due diligence is the most important part of the M&A process. It is the process by which the potential bidder confirms (and to some extent obtains) its understanding of the business of the target, and the lawyers explore potential issues that may affect the transaction and the terms of the definitive acquisition agreement. The memorandum excerpted below outlines the due diligence process and what is expected in a public company deal:

DUE DILIGENCE FOR PUBLIC MERGERS AND ACQUISITIONS
PLC Practice Note

Due diligence is the investigation of a person or business. In the context of mergers and acquisitions, the parties use the due diligence process to gather information about each other and about the business being acquired. In a merger of equals or in instances where the buyer issues its securities as some or all of the merger consideration, the target company usually conducts due diligence on the buyer. However, the due diligence process is usually more significant for the buyer.

Reasons for Due Diligence

In any significant merger or acquisition, the buyer gathers information about what it is buying before making a commitment. The

---

[13] *Global Asset Capital, LLC v. Rubicon US Reit, Inc.,* CA No. 5071–VCL at 4–6 (Del. Ch. Nov. 16, 2009).

buyer uses this information to decide whether the proposed acquisition would make a sound commercial investment and to determine the issues relevant to the merger. In an extreme case, a buyer can decide to abandon the transaction after performing due diligence, but more commonly (in a negotiated deal) a buyer uses the information to negotiate certain contractual provisions (such as conditions to closing) or to adjust the merger consideration. Generally, the representations and warranties do not survive the closing in public mergers and a buyer is not protected against losses through indemnification provisions. As a result, completing a thorough due diligence investigation is of critical importance since the buyer cannot recover losses after closing. Because of the SEC's requirements, a significant amount of information about potential target companies is freely available to the public through the SEC's Electronic Data Gathering Analysis and Retrieval system, known as EDGAR).

Consequently, public company due diligence reviews usually proceed at a much quicker pace than that of a private company. In addition, a buyer considering a hostile takeover can conduct a due diligence review entirely from public sources and proceed without the cooperation of the target company's board of directors and management. A due diligence inquiry should determine the following key information about the target company:

- Confirm the assets and liabilities of the target company.

- Investigate any potential liabilities or risks.

- Confirm the value of the target company.

- Learn more about the operations of the target company.

- Identify any impediments to the transaction, such as third party consents or anti-takeover devices (such as a poison pill).

- Confirm information provided by the target company in its disclosure schedules.

- Identify steps necessary to integrate the target company.

Target Company Due Diligence

If the buyer intends to issue stock to the target company's shareholders as consideration or if the transaction involves a merger of equals, the target company needs to conduct a due diligence investigation. This is sometimes referred to as reverse due diligence. If the buyer intends to issue stock, the target company should:

- Confirm the value of the buyer' stock.

- Assess the economic risks of receiving the buyer's stock.

- Identify any impediments to the issuance.

- Identify any impediments to closing.

Scope of Due Diligence

Many factors determine the scope of a due diligence investigation. It is important to determine the scope at the outset because it influences the number of people needed, time requirements, need for outside experts and depth of review. Common factors that determine the scope of a due diligence review include:

- **Deal structure.** For example, in a reverse triangular merger, anti-assignment clauses pose no concern for the buyer (although change of control clauses are a concern).

- **Industry.** The industry of the target company can influence what areas of due diligence you concentrate on. For example, acquisition of a pharmaceutical company requires extensive intellectual property due diligence by the buyer.

- **Global presence.** If the target business has global operations, it is important to assess its compliance with the requirements of the Foreign Corrupt Practices Act of 1977

- **Competition.** If the buyer and target company compete with each other, they may want to (or be required by antitrust laws) keep certain information confidential (such as, pricing) until after the transaction is consummated (see Box, Competitively Sensitive Information).

- **Access to target company.** The target company often restricts access to the management of the business to only those necessary to facilitate the due diligence review to limit interference and preserve the confidentiality of the merger discussions.

- **Cost.** The buyer can limit the scope of the due diligence investigation to reduce its expenses. Sometimes, a buyer conducts its investigation in stages and only increases spending when the likelihood of consummation increases.

- **Time constraints.** The parties may wish to complete the transaction by a certain date (such as fiscal year end) or the target company may have enough bargaining power to limit the time allowed for due diligence (for example, in an auction). Also, because of the possibility of information leaks and the desire to maintain secrecy regarding the merger negotiations, timing becomes an important factor and it is usually in both parties' interest to quickly conclude the review and execute the definitive merger agreement.

Organizing the Due Diligence Process

Usually the corporate legal team (most often a junior corporate lawyer) acts as the "control center" for the buyer's due diligence process. This entails defining the due diligence task, requesting materials, distributing materials and ensuring communication among the due diligence team.

The Due Diligence Team

The make-up of the due diligence team depends on the specifics of the transaction, but usually includes legal, business, accounting and tax specialists. Generally, the legal team consists of corporate attorneys and other specialists (such as environmental, employee benefits, real estate, litigation and intellectual property attorneys). The buyer can conduct its own business due diligence or hire investment bankers or other consultants to review information. The buyer will usually also engage accountants and tax specialists to assist with the financial review of the target company. In some cases it may also be necessary to retain outside consultants in other areas such as regulatory compliance, environmental or insurance/risk management. If the target company conducts any operations outside of the US, the buyer may need to engage foreign or local counsel for diligence matters relating to those operations and confirm that no impediments to the transactions exist under applicable foreign laws (such as government or regulatory approvals).

Due Diligence Request

Although a large number of target company materials are available publicly, there is usually a significant amount of information that remains confidential or inaccessible. A buyer often submits a due diligence request for this confidential and inaccessible information. The due diligence request consists of a list of questions and requests for documents organized by topic. Examine the target company's public filings and agreements available on EDGAR (search the EDGAR Database) before making any due diligence requests. The initial due diligence request is usually supplemented by further requests as the negotiations proceed and the buyer learns more about the target company.

The size of a due diligence request depends on the scope of the due diligence review. The due diligence request list is typically shorter for public deals than private deals because counsel has already reviewed much of the material information by the time the request is submitted.

Sources of Information

Publicly Available Information

The bulk of due diligence review involves reading documents of the target company (for example, contracts, financial reports and corporate records). You can easily access much of this information by retrieving the target company's public SEC filings on EDGAR.

Documents

The target company (and its counsel) assemble due diligence documents and often store them on an online data site (also known as an electronic data room). Sometimes, particularly in smaller transactions, the target company can either send the buyer electronic or hard copies of documents. If the target company wants to limit dissemination of materials and control the review process, it can create a physical data room at its offices or the office of its attorney or investment banker.

When the materials are stored on an online data site, the target company determines and grants password protected access. You should determine which due diligence team members need access to the data site and then submit a comprehensive request for access to the target company.

Access to Management

Some information is difficult to learn from just reading documents. The buyer often asks to visit the target company site and talk with members of management. It can be helpful for some members of the legal team to participate in these meetings with management (sometimes called management presentations) to understand the operations of the business. For more insight into the target's legal framework and existing issues, buyer's counsel should meet, or hold a teleconference, with the target company's general counsel or other in-house legal staff at the outset of the due diligence review. The teleconference allows you to ask follow-up questions concerning due diligence materials and to receive complete answers based on your questions.

Distribution and Organization of Materials

If the due diligence materials are available electronically or sent in hard-copy form, they need to be distributed to the due diligence team. Usually a junior corporate attorney is responsible for distribution and organization of the materials.

Reviewing Materials: What to Look For

Categories of Materials and Common Issues

A corporate attorney encounters many different types of documents in a comprehensive due diligence review and should watch for many different kinds of issues, which are determined by the specifics of the transaction and target company. Some of the common categories of documents and common issues encountered in a due diligence review are listed below. This list does not include specialist areas such as, tax or employee benefits materials and is not intended to be exhaustive (see Specialist Review):

- **Organizational documents.** (For example, certificate of incorporation, bylaws, certificate of designation.) Common issues to consider include:

  - **Capitalization and equity ownership.** Is there a stockholder or group of stockholders that has control of, or a significant stake in, the target company? Are there any subsidiaries? What equity is outstanding? How much equity is authorized? Is there room for further issuances?

  - **Consent issues.** Are any votes or consents required in connection with the transaction? What actions require consent of stockholders or the board of directors?

  - **Special rights of stockholders.** Is there a poison pill? What are the triggering events? What is required to amend the plan or redeem the rights?

  - **Dividends.** What is the dividend policy? Can the board of directors change this policy without a vote?

  - **Unusual provisions.** Look for any provisions that could impact the transaction or future operation of the target company. For example, you should note if a stockholder is guaranteed representation on the board of directors.

- **Minutes of meetings of board of directors and committees of the board.** Common issues to consider include:

  - **Contingent liabilities.** Look for any discussions regarding claims against the target company or its management, defaults under agreements, threatened litigation, labor or employment concerns, and investigations involving the target company or its employees.

- **Contracts (for example, customer and supply contracts, operating contracts and licenses).** Common issues to consider include:

  - **Parties.** Who are the parties to the contract?

- **Change of control.** Is there a change of control provision? Does this transaction constitute a change of control?

- **Assignment.** Is the contract assignable? Is consent required? How is an assignment defined? Does the transaction structure require an assignment? Does a change of control constitute an assignment? See Box, Assignment and Change of Control.

- **Termination.** When does the contract terminate? Is there an automatic renewal provision? Can either party terminate without consent? Does a change of control give either party a right to terminate the contract?

- **Economics.** What are the basic economics of the contract? Are the economics of the contract fixed or do they fluctuate? How is the pricing determined?

- **Unusual provisions.** Look for any provisions that could impact the transaction or future operation of the target company. Are there any provisions restricting the target company or provide benefits to the other party? For example, you should note a most favored nation provision, non-compete provision or exclusivity provision.

Assignment and Change of Control

If a merger is structured as a forward merger or a forward triangular merger, third party consents are required for those target company contracts which contain anti-assignment clauses. Typically anti-assignment clauses are not triggered in reverse triangular mergers unless the contracts contain change of control clauses. In 2013, the Delaware Court of Chancery confirmed that reverse triangular mergers would not constitute an assignment by operation of law.

A change of control provision in an agreement gives the other party certain rights (such as consent, payment or termination) in connection with an acquisition transaction. Not all change of control provisions are triggered by the same action. A change of ownership, merger, sale of assets or change in board members can trigger a change of control. A change of control provision may not always be clearly labeled. It may actually be named as a change of control provision or it can be embedded in an assignment or termination section.

Specialist Review

Legal specialists (such as real estate, employment, intellectual property and environmental attorneys) and outside consultants (such as accountants and insurance specialists) conduct a portion of the due diligence review.

Impact on the Transaction

Due diligence is a necessary part of any significant acquisition. Your findings can impact the transaction in the following ways:

- **Merger Consideration.** If a due diligence finding affects the valuation of the target company, the buyer can adjust the merger consideration. For example, if you discover a previously unknown $10 million liability, the buyer can reduce its offer by that amount.

- **Representations and warranties.** A buyer often uses the representations and warranties as protection against unknown liabilities. Since the representation and warranties in public deals generally do not survive the closing, this protection only becomes relevant to "bring down" the representations and warranties from the period of signing through the closing. For example, if you discover during due diligence that certain permits are important to the operation of the business, the buyer would likely insist on a full representation and warranty that the target company is in compliance with all permits.

- **Disclosure schedules.** The buyer uses its due diligence review to verify the disclosure schedules. Ideally the buyer should have an opportunity to investigate anything the target company lists on the disclosure schedules. If the disclosure schedules do not agree with the buyer's due diligence findings, the buyer can negotiate to add or remove certain disclosures.

- **Deal termination.** In extreme situations, due diligence findings can cause a party to terminate the transaction (known as deal breakers).

- **Pre-closing covenants.** The due diligence findings can raise issues that the buyer wants the target company to correct before the closing.

Due Diligence Report

The ultimate product of a due diligence review is the due diligence report (also known as a due diligence memorandum). Due diligence reports range from an oral presentation to a lengthy document with detailed findings. You should ask your client what type of report they prefer at the start of the due diligence process.

Generally, the length and level of detail in the report corresponds with the scope of the due diligence review. As with the due diligence review, a junior corporate attorney usually coordinates the preparation of the report. Although each specialist usually writes up their own findings, you need to fit all of the pieces together into a coherent product. If the report is lengthy, it is helpful to provide an executive summary highlighting the significant findings and issues. The due diligence report should be clear and concise so that your client can assess any issues quickly. Drafting the due diligence report can become a time-consuming process as it involves drafting the corporate sections and refining and reformatting the specialist portions.[14]

In practice, the due diligence exercise focuses on two areas. The first is obtaining information concerning the company, including concerning its capital structure, material contracts and outstanding debt. The second is examining agreements for anti-assignment and change of control provisions which can be triggered if the transaction occurs. There are contexts in which this is particularly important. For instance, many pharmaceutical companies have intellectual property licenses which by their terms cannot be assigned or otherwise transferred in a change of control transaction. The existence of such provisions can prevent a transaction from occurring or significantly reduce the value of the acquired company. Due diligence, while time consuming and sometimes excruciatingly detail-intensive, translates into direct value for the client, and mistakes in the process can be quite costly.

QUESTIONS

1.   Why do you think that the lawyers for the investment banks resist any changes to the indemnification provisions in their engagement letters?

2.   Why is there is a negotiated engagement letter for the investment bank in an M&A transaction, but not the attorneys?

3.   What was the "error" of the lawyers for Martin Marietta and Vulcan? In other words, how did their negotiation of the two confidentiality agreements set the stage for the dispute which followed?

4.   How would you advise a buyer about how the definition of a "Transaction" should be worded in a confidentiality agreement post-*Vulcan v. Martin Marietta*? What would your advice be to a seller?

5.   What should you advise your client as to the consequences of entering into a confidentiality agreement and receiving material information if your client wants to preserve the option of undertaking an unsolicited or hostile bid?

---

14   Available at http://us.practicallaw.com/9-382-1874#a189987.

6. When is a don't ask/don't waive standstill illegal under Delaware law? What is the theoretical justification for a court to reject such a standstill?

7. When might a don't ask/don't waive standstill be justified? What is the theoretical justification for a court to accept such a standstill?

8. Do different Delaware Chancery Court judges approach the issues involved in standstills differently? If so, in what respects?

9. What would you advise a client about the validity of these measures after *In re Ancestry.com*?

10. What obligations does a letter of intent impose on the parties? How can transactional lawyers shift those obligations, if at all?

11. In *Rubicon,* why does Vice Chancellor Laster concern himself with whether provisions of the agreement are (sufficiently) definite or not?

12. As a transactional lawyer, how would you advise a client as to whether to enter into a letter of intent? Would it matter if your client were the prospective buyer or seller?

13. Examine the change of control provisions in the three contracts in the Diligence Section of the Online Appendix. What is the effect of each of these provisions, and how might they affect the structuring of a transaction?

PROBLEMS

1. Kappa Corp. has been approached by a private equity firm to acquire the company. Kappa's general counsel contacts you and informs you that management wants to hire an investment bank to represent it but only to sell the company in the next six months and not to explore a sale of the company's big software division. Kappa is eager to begin negotiations and Kappa's general counsel tells you not to spend too much time on this because they have a long-term relationship with the investment bank. You know this investment bank from prior transactions and expect to work with them again on many future transactions. The Online Appendix includes an annotated form of an investment bank engagement letter. Please mark it up to reflect the terms you would recommend that your client include in the letter. Be prepared to defend your choices and explain whether you think that negotiating this letter will be difficult and time-consuming. The client wants it signed tomorrow. (Annotated letter: http://www.kelrun.com/files/2013/05/Pear_AnnInvesLtr.pdf.)

For further guidance on these issues you may wish to read: Glenn D. West, Aaron J. Rigby and Emmanuel U. Obi, *Negotiating Investment Banking Engagement Letters: Avoiding Certain Traps for the Unwary Banker and Its Client,* available at http://www.weil.com/files/Publication/fada5a46–3e93–4e83–b6c8–52246c0ecffc/Presentation/PublicationAttachment/9e253cbf–8010–4d78–8dc2–7c44362c59b6/Engagement_Letters.pdf.

2.   You are an associate at a law firm retained by Alpha Co., a public company listed on the New York Stock Exchange. Alpha Co.'s board decided two weeks ago to explore a sale of the company. Alpha Co. then retained an investment bank which recommended that the company sell itself pursuant to an auction process.

Subsequently, the C.E.O. of Beta, Inc. contacted the C.E.O. of Alpha Co. and suggested that Beta, Inc. acquire Alpha Co. The Alpha Co. board has now decided to enter into negotiations with Beta, Inc. for an acquisition and suspend the auction process.

The general counsel of Alpha Co. calls you and states that she sent over a form of Confidentiality Agreement to the Beta, Inc. general counsel. Beta, Inc.'s counsel has responded by sending the mark-up available in the Online Appendix. The general counsel of Alpha Co. asks that you to take a look at the draft and see if any further changes are made. "Don't take too long," she says. "It is only a confidentiality agreement and we start discussions later this week."

Please review and provide a mark-up of the confidentiality agreement.

CHAPTER XIV

DOCUMENTATION AND NEGOTIATION: THE MERGER AGREEMENT

■ ■ ■

A. OVERVIEW

Most M&A lawyers spend considerable amounts of their time drafting and negotiating merger agreements, and explaining the agreements to their clients. Consequently, it is extremely important to understand the landscape of a typical merger agreement. Merger agreements all have a common structure and format: the tables of contents of merger agreements are all quite similar, as are many of the "boilerplate" provisions. And the agreements, in broad brush, all have the same general coverage. But some provisions are very highly negotiated. Negotiations focus quickly and principally on these provisions. In this Chapter we will introduce you to the basic contours of a merger agreement. As we will explain, the trajectory by which the parties negotiate and agree upon the merger agreement can be understood as a means to efficiently produce information and allocate risk to the party best able to bear it. We will illustrate how the merger agreement helps achieve these objectives.

You can find sample merger agreements for two transactions, Michael Dell and Silver Lake's acquisition of Dell, and Men's Wearhouse's acquisition of Jos. A. Bank, in the Online Appendix. The general structure of a merger agreement is the same whether the target is a public or private company. But there are some significant differences. Many provisions discussed below are found principally in transactions involving publicly traded sellers. In Subsection L, we introduce you to a number of provisions that are relevant for transactions involving private company sellers.

B. LANDSCAPE OF THE MERGER AGREEMENT

As noted above, although the specifics of each merger agreement are different, sometimes in significant ways, merger agreements all share a common architecture. Merger agreements describe the transaction contemplated by the parties and the company being acquired. In the agreements, each party makes statements (representations and warranties) about its attributes and condition that are particularly important to the other party. A buyer (an acquirer) wants, for instance, to know a great deal about the financial condition of the seller (the target), its major contracts, any pending, threatened, or likely lawsuits, and many other matters. A seller wants to know about the buyer's ability to consummate the transaction. Because parties to the typical merger transaction contemplate a delay, sometimes considerable, between the signing of the merger agreement and the closing of the transaction, the merger agreement sets forth the commitments of the target with respect to its operation during this interim period. The merger agreement also sets forth commitments by both parties to work towards closing the transaction. Finally, merger agreements also set forth conditions to each party's obligation to close the transaction as well as provisions governing the circumstances in which the closing does not occur, and when the agreement terminates.

The main features of a typical merger agreement are as follows:

Recitals. The recitals describe the operative provisions of the transaction, and recount salient facts about the deal's background. Although the recitals describe the transaction, the recitals themselves are not operative and thus not formally binding on the parties.

Mechanics of the transaction. This section of the merger agreement describes the transaction contemplated by the parties as well as the consideration being offered for the target. This section also designates the surviving as well as the disappearing corporation in the merger. If shareholders of the target are to receive appraisal rights, that fact is usually indicated in this section.

Representations and warranties of the target and the acquirer. (Note that "acquirer" will include the entity which will be merging, often an acquisition subsidiary, as well as its parent.) In these sections of the agreement, the parties each make statements about themselves. These statements serve both to convey information to the other party and to allocate risk. The statements are made at the time the agreement is signed. If a representation about the condition of the target is not also true at the time of closing (these are "closing conditions"), the acquirer may not be obligated to close the transaction. Representations and warranties often contain "materiality qualifiers"—that the representation is true "in all material respects" or some such formulation. Closing conditions, too, may be qualified by "materiality"—for instance, the acquirer may be required to close so long as the target's representations are true in all material respects. We will discuss these sorts of "qualifiers" in greater detail below.

Covenants and agreements of the target and the acquirer. In transactions where the signing and closing are separated by some period of time, the target agrees (covenants) to operate in a manner largely consistent with its previous practice to preserve its assets, until such time as the transaction is completed and the acquirer can take control. The parties also make certain agreements with respect to their own efforts to work towards closing the transaction, including as to seeking necessary regulatory approvals. "Qualifiers" with respect to the efforts the parties have to expend-reasonable efforts, or best efforts—are common. We discuss these qualifiers in greater detail below. In addition the target will often agree to limits on its ability to seek out or even hold discussions with other potential acquirers.

Conditions to closing of the merger agreement. Merger agreements are conditional contracts. Each party to the agreement agrees to close the transaction, but only if the conditions precedent to its obligation to close are met. Some conditions in the contract, such as regulatory and shareholder approvals, apply to both parties. Other conditions, for example, that the target's representations and warranties in the agreement remain true (perhaps, in all material respects) at the time of the closing, apply only to one party--in this example, the acquirer.

Termination provisions. Merger agreements may be terminated pursuant to their terms under certain conditions. The most common reason merger agreements are terminated is that the target receives a better bid (a superior proposal) during the period between the signing of the agreement and the closing. Most merger agreements include a fiduciary termination right, also known as a "fiduciary out," a right to terminate the agreement if the target board's fiduciary duties so require, a right that is triggered in the event that the seller receives or perhaps accepts an alternate superior offer during the interim period. Another common termination right is triggered if the deal does not receive the required regulatory approvals. Merger agreements often provide for termination fees (which are akin to liquidated damages) to be paid by the party seeking to terminate the agreement. Different fees may be payable depending on the reason why (and the provision under which) the agreement was terminated.

Indemnification provisions. Indemnification provisions provide for payments by the seller's shareholders if, post-closing, the seller's representations and warranties turn out to be false. Indemnification provisions are typically only included in transactions involving a private company seller. By contrast, public company representations and warranties typically "die at the closing." Think about why: private company shareholders selling their shares are not infrequently involved in running their companies and may therefore know quite a bit about those companies. The same is not true of most public company shareholders: large companies may have many, even millions of, quite passive shareholders. In addition to providing for liability for incorrect representations and warranties and for other matters, indemnification provisions also lay out procedures for dealing with potential liabilities for which indemnification could be sought. (Note that there is another sort of indemnification provision, one in which the buyer promises to have the company surviving the merger indemnify the seller's directors and officers for a specified period of time. That provision would typically be in the Covenants and Agreements portion of the merger agreement.)

Boilerplate provisions. Every merger agreement includes a number of "boilerplate" provisions. Most of these are typically in the last section of the agreement. Some of these provisions are "boilerplate" in the sense of truly being unimportant and not negotiated (for instance, that captions of a provision are not part of the provision, or that references to one gender are for convenience and do not exclude the other gender). But many provisions which are sometimes referred to as boilerplate can be quite important, and should not be ignored. Some such provisions may be negotiated, at times quite vigorously. These include provisions governing remedies, and choice of forum and choice of law.

Disclosure Schedule. The representations and warranties provisions will refer to an accompanying disclosure schedule, and therefore are to be read in conjunction with that schedule. The schedule modifies or limits statements made in each of the representations and warranties. Statements that might appear "unqualified" in the merger agreement may in fact be qualified by an exception listed on the disclosure schedule. As discussed below, a "qualification" is an exception to a representation. An "unqualified" representation might be "We are not party to any litigation." The "qualification" would be "except as set forth in Schedule 1." The disclosure schedule is therefore an integral part of the merger agreement.

Merger agreement provisions cannot be read in isolation from one another. They often explicitly refer to one another. Indeed, many of a merger agreement's provisions are expressly tied to other provisions in the agreement. For instance, a seller's representations and warranties made at the time the agreement is signed must be true (or materially true) at the closing or the buyer will not have an obligation to close. Representations and warranties are thus tied to closing conditions; as we will see, closing conditions are also tied to termination provisions. The same is true of post-signing covenants by the target. Covenants are tied to closing conditions, as well as termination provisions. In the case of a private company seller, representations and warranties and covenants can also be tied to indemnification provisions.

There are many "defined terms"—terms that are capitalized, signaling a specialized use set forth expressly as a definition in the agreement. When we review the sections of the merger agreement below, we often do not include the definitions, since they may be quite technical and the general understanding of the word suffices for purposes of our discussion; know, however that the definitions will be contained in the agreement and may be quite important.

Finally, even apart from use of an explicit reference or defined term, the agreement is to be read as a whole: the merger agreement is an "integrated" document.

C. PRICING FORMULAS, COLLARS, AND RISK ALLOCATION

When parties are using cash as consideration, as was the case in the Dell transaction, the pricing formula is usually fairly straightforward. Below is the relevant portion of the pricing provision in the Dell merger agreement:

> Conversion of Common Stock. Each Share [other than shares held by those who would continue to own shares in the private Dell, and Dissenting Shares] issued and outstanding immediately prior to the Effective Time shall be converted automatically into the right to receive $13.65 in cash [later increased to $13.75 per share plus a dividend of $.13/share], without interest.

By contrast, when the consideration used is stock, pricing formulas get more complicated. The buyer and seller shareholders are both continuing as shareholders in the merged company; the value of their respective interests in the merged company will differ depending on the formula used.[1] The buyer's stock could increase or decrease in value in the period between the time the transaction is agreed to and when it closes. The risk of price changes during the interim period between signing and closing can be allocated between the parties; the most common way of doing so is by use of a pricing "collar," discussed below. Unless an adjustment is made, the change in the buyer's stock price will allocate the risk exclusively to one party.

Most transactions where the consideration used is buyer stock rely on fixed exchange ratio formulas to determine the amount of stock to be issued at closing. Such a formula specifies a fixed amount of buyer stock in exchange for target stock—for instance, 1:1 or 2:1. The buyer knows how many shares it will have to issue at the closing. But the value of its stock may change, in either direction. Consequently, sellers take a risk that a transaction in which they would have gotten $1 billion worth of buyer stock had it closed when the merger agreement was entered into will only yield buyer stock worth some lesser amount, say, $800 million, by the time the buyer is required to issue shares, if the value of the

---

[1]   There are also deals where the consideration is both stock and cash.

buyer's shares goes down. Buyers take a risk that the value of the consideration they are offering for the target will go up in the event their share value rises between signing and closing.

The following figure illustrates how a fixed exchange ratio works in practice. In this example, the exchange ratio is one buyer share for every two target shares. There are 1,000,000 shares of the target outstanding, meaning that in all cases, the buyer is issuing 500,000 shares. Buyer's stock price upon announcement is $20 per share, so that the total value of the consideration upon announcement is $10,000,000. However, depending upon buyer's stock price at closing, the total value can increase or decrease.

Figure 1: Fixed Exchange Ratio Contracts.

Exchange Ratio, 1:2
(i.e., one share of Buyer for 2 shares of Seller)

Buyer Stock Price at Announcement	Shares of Seller	Value of Consideration at Announcement	Buyer Stock Price at Closing	Value of Consideration at Closing	Exchange Ratio
$20	1,000,000	$10,000,000	$25	$12,500,000	1:2
$20	1,000,000	$10,000,000	$24	$12,000,000	1:2
$20	1,000,000	$10,000,000	$23	$11,500,000	1:2
$20	1,000,000	$10,000,000	$22	$11,000,000	1:2
$20	1,000,000	$10,000,000	$21	$10,500,000	1:2
$20	1,000,000	$10,000,000	$20	$10,000,000	1:2
$20	1,000,000	$10,000,000	$19	$ 9,500,000	1:2
$20	1,000,000	$10,000,000	$18	$ 9,000,000	1:2
$20	1,000,000	$10,000,000	$17	$ 8,500,000	1:2
$20	1,000,000	$10,000,000	$16	$ 8,000,000	1:2
$20	1,000,000	$10,000,000	$15	$ 7,500,000	1:2

The following chart illustrates how the number of shares stays fixed while total value to target shareholders fluctuates as the stock price of the buyer fluctuates between signing and closing:

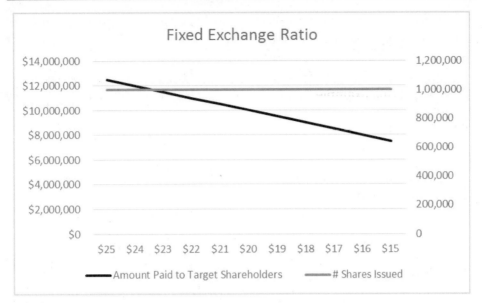

A fixed value formula provides an alternative to fixed exchange ratio formula. Consideration is also in the form of buyer stock, but the amount of stock to be issued will be determined immediately prior to closing based on a formula the parties negotiate and include in the agreement.

The next figure illustrates this formula. In this scenario, the target shareholders are to be paid $10 worth of buyer stock, valued at the time of the closing (or the average of its price for some period, such as 10 days, beforehand) for every share of seller stock. A buyer whose stock price declines will have to issue more shares than it would have had to issue had the transaction closed immediately upon signing; a buyer whose stock price increases will have to issue fewer shares. This is illustrated by the column "# of shares of Buyer at Closing," which is the number of shares the buyer must issue depending upon its stock price at closing. Note that in all cases, the total consideration (and per share consideration) paid to target shareholders does not change.

Figure 2: Fixed Value Formula.

Value Ratio, $10:1

(i.e., $10 of Buyer stock for 1 share of Seller)

Buyer Stock Price at Announcement	Value Per Share of Seller	Shares of Seller	#of Shares of Buyer at Announcement	Buyer Stock Price at Closing	#of shares of Buyer at Closing	Value of Consideration at Closing	Exchange Ratio
$20	$10	1,000,000	500,000	$25	400,000	$10,000,000	0.8:1
$20	$10	1,000,000	500,000	$24	416,666.67	$10,000,000	0.83:1
$20	$10	1,000,000	500,000	$23	434,782.61	$10,000,000	0.8:1

$20	$10	1,000,000	500,000	$22	454,545.45	$10,000,000	.91:1
$20	$10	1,000,000	500,000	$21	476,190.48	$10,000,000	.95:1
$20	$10	1,000,000	500,000	$20	500,000.00	$10,000,000	1:1
$20	$10	1,000,000	500,000	$19	526,315.79	$10,000,000	1.05:1
$20	$10	1,000,000	500,000	$18	555,555.56	$10,000,000	1.11:1
$20	$10	1,000,000	500,000	$17	588,235.29	$10,000,000	1.18:1
$20	$10	1,000,000	500,000	$16	625,000.00	$10,000,000	1.25:1
$20	$10	1,000,000	500,000	$15	666,666.67	$10,000,000	1.33:1

The following chart illustrates how the number of shares fluctuates while total value to target shareholders remains fixed as the stock price of the buyer fluctuates between signing and closing:

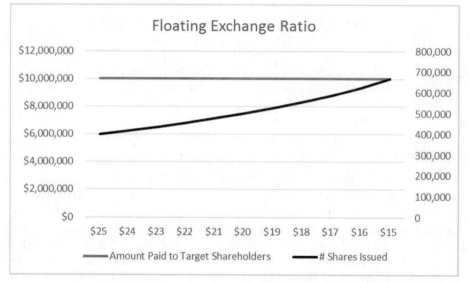

The result of using simple fixed ratios, whether exchange or value, is that the risk of each type of price movement is allocated to one party; the parties do not share the risk. Each party's risk can be mitigated by "collars." These are mechanisms that adjust the amount of buyer stock to be given in the event of changes in the buyer's stock value, or, in the case of extreme price movements, allow some portion of the consideration to be given as cash, (or even, in some circumstances, allow a party to walk away from the transaction). The structuring can be exceedingly complex; below, we discuss a few simple collars.

For a fixed exchange ratio, a collar can specify a price range within which the exchange ratio does not change. For instance, a share of seller stock becomes a share of buyer stock so long as buyer stock's market price over the ten days preceding the closing is between $45 and $75; if the price is higher or lower, then certain specified adjustments are made. More generally, a collar can further specify that if buyer's stock is no longer within that range, the ratio changes, some of the consideration is paid in cash, or perhaps, a party can walk away from the deal. It can specify a maximum and minimum number of shares to be issued. A fixed value ratio also can specify a minimum and maximum number of shares to be issued.[2]

The chart below shows the effect of a collar. The exchange ratio is set at 1 share of buyer's stock for 2 shares of the seller's stock, subject to a collar that sets a limit on the total value available to sellers in the event the price of the buyer's stock exceeds $75 per share. In the event the buyer's stock price exceeds $75, then each share of the seller will be converted for only $75 worth of the buyer's stock. At the same time, the formula sets a floor on the value available: in the event the buyer's stock falls below $45, each share of the seller's stock will be converted for $45. The collar, in this case, permits some variation around an expected trading range for the buyer's stock, but protects both the buyer and the seller from extreme movements in the price of the buyer's stock.

Figure 3: Fixed Exchange Ratio with a Value Collar

Exchange Ratio, 1:2 (with value collar)

Buyer Stock Price at Announcement	Shares of Seller	Value at Announcement	Buyer Stock Price at Closing	Value of Consideration at Closing	# Shares of Buyer at Closing	Exchange Ratio
$60	1,000,000	$30,000,000	$85	$37,500,000	441,176.5	.88:2
$60	1,000,000	$30,000,000	$80	$37,500,000	468,750	.94:2
$60	1,000,000	$30,000,000	$75	$37,500,000	500,000	1:2
$60	1,000,000	$30,000,000	$70	$35,000,000	500,000	1:2
$60	1,000,000	$30,000,000	$65	$32,500,000	500,000	1:2
$60	1,000,000	$30,000,000	$60	$30,000,000	500,000	1:2
$60	1,000,000	$30,000,000	$55	$27,500,000	500,000	1:2
$60	1,000,000	$30,000,000	$50	$25,000,000	500,000	1:2
$60	1,000,000	$30,000,000	$45	$22,500,000	500,000	1:2
$60	1,000,000	$30,000,000	$40	$22,500,000	562,500	1.13:2
$60	1,000,000	$30,000,000	$35	$22,500,000	642,857.1	1.29:2

---

[2] The buyer would certainly want to limit the number of shares it issued to an amount below that which would trigger voting requirements under the NYSE or NASDAQ rules.

The following chart illustrates how the number of shares fluctuates while total value to target shareholders also fluctuates within the collar as the stock price of the buyer fluctuates between signing and closing:

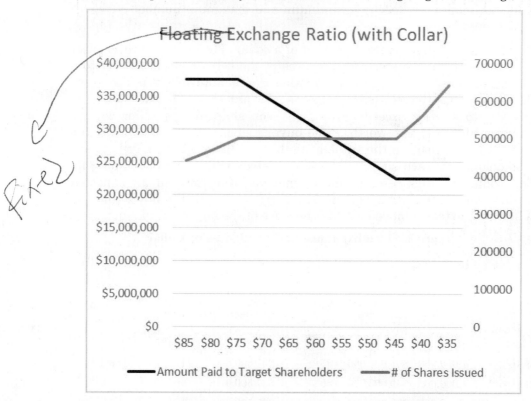

A collar can also be used for a floating exchange ratio. In such a situation, the protection is to the buyer. Within the collar, the number of shares paid to the target shareholders fluctuates while the value paid to the target shareholders remains fixed. Above and below the collar (in the example below, $75 and $45, respectively), the number of shares issued by the buyer remains fixed. In such a circumstance, the target shareholders then bear the risk that the buyer's stock price will go below $45 per share. In exchange for bearing this risk, though, a target will often negotiate an upside collar. The number of shares issued by the buyer will not be reduced above a certain $ per share price of the buyer.

Buyer Stock Price at Announcement	Shares of Seller	Value at Announcement	Buyer Stock Price at Closing	Value of Consideration at Closing	# Shares of Buyer at Closing	Exchange Ratio
$60	1,000,000	$30,000,000	$85	$34,000,000	400,000	.8:2
$60	1,000,000	$30,000,000	$80	$32,000,000	400,000	.8:2
$60	1,000,000	$30,000,000	$75	$30,000,000	400,000	.8:2
$60	1,000,000	$30,000,000	$70	$30,000,000	428,571	.86:2
$60	1,000,000	$30,000,000	$65	$30,000,000	461,538	.92:2
$60	1,000,000	$30,000,000	$60	$30,000,000	500,000	1:2
$60	1,000,000	$30,000,000	$55	$30,000,000	545,455	1.09:2
$60	1,000,000	$30,000,000	$50	$30,000,000	600,000	1.2:2
$60	1,000,000	$30,000,000	$45	$27,000,000	600,000	1.2:2
$60	1,000,000	$30,000,000	$40	$24,000,000	600,000	1.2:2
$60	1,000,000	$30,000,000	$35	$21,000,000	600,000	1.2:2

The following chart illustrates how the number of shares fluctuates while total value to target shareholders remains fixed within the collar as the stock price of the buyer fluctuates between signing and closing:

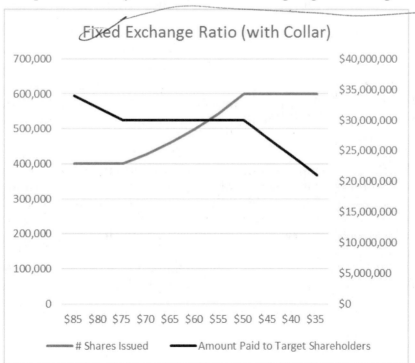

D. EARNOUTS

An earnout provision creates a contingent payment obligation for the buyer.[3] Stated differently, an earnout is a promise by the buyer to pay to the seller an additional amount if after the closing, the business performs at or above a certain level or meets or exceeds certain milestones. An earnout helps overcome significant valuation differences the parties may have which could prevent them from agreeing to a deal. As we have discussed in Chapter X, in virtually all cases, a business is worth what it will earn in the future. Sometimes the parties simply cannot agree on what the business will earn in the future. The seller will presumably think the business will earn more, while the buyer thinks it will earn less. An earnout can bridge this gap: the parties agree to defer the ultimate valuation question until the uncertainties with respect to valuation have been resolved, thereby allocating the risk of a mistaken valuation to the seller rather than the buyer.

Why might agreeing on a business's future earnings be difficult? Corporate acquisitions are highly complex transactions that often involve large amounts of private information. This private information may relate to the future prospects of the seller or status of the seller's product that may be known only to the seller. Although buyers engage in significant due diligence, it may be impossible, without great effort, for a buyer to uncover all of the private information that a seller may possess. To the extent the seller's private information is negative, a seller may have an incentive to shade it or downplay its importance. Sellers may also find conveying positive information to the buyer in a way that is credible to be difficult. In addition to information problems, there may also be fundamental disagreements about the future of the seller or the seller's industry that can negatively affect the acquirer's valuation of the seller. These fundamental disagreements often reflect the high degree of uncertainty present in a complex merger transaction. Especially in sales of private companies, sellers will often be more optimistic than buyers about their business's prospects. Consequently, buyers and sellers may find themselves unable to agree on an appropriate valuation for the seller. By providing parties with an ex post opportunity to settle up, the earnout provision helps fill the valuation gap between buyers and sellers generated either by information asymmetries, uncertainty—that is, differing expectations about the cash flows the business will generate in the future. The price is only set after the closing, and sometimes significantly after the closing, when the buyer has had an opportunity to learn the seller's private information or after uncertainties affecting

---

[3] Portions of this subsection are adapted from Brian JM Quinn, *Putting Your Money Where Your Mouth Is: The Performance of Earnouts in Corporate Acquisitions*, 81 CINC. L. REV. 127 (2013).

valuation have been resolved.[4] Typically, some amount is paid at the closing, with the remainder subject to the earnout.

Earnout provisions are more common in private transactions, but they are also used in some public transactions, especially in deals involving life sciences or medical device companies. In public transactions, the valuation difference may be less specifically and directly about what the business will earn in the future than what regulatory approvals the company will receive, although of course, the matter ultimately at issue is the seller's higher earnings that would result from the approval.

Earnout provisions all have the same general structure, but differ significantly in the specifics. First, they tie the payment of additional merger consideration to the seller's accomplishment of certain specified targets or milestones during the post-closing period. Earnout targets fall into one of two general categories: financial or non-financial targets. Financial targets may include some measure of gross revenues, cash flow, EBITDA, profitability, or other costs that relates to the financial performance of the seller. Non-financial targets may include some non-financial proxy for revenue—for example, unit sales or licenses. Alternatively, non-financial targets may include market share targets, or specific customer-oriented goals. Non-financial targets may also include certain technological achievements or regulatory approvals, such as FDA approval for medical devices and pharmaceutical products.

Second, there will be triggers for the payment, but these will take different forms: sliding scale, which, as the name suggests, provide for payments for intermediate albeit specified outcomes, or cliffs or binary triggers. Binary triggers are common and relatively easy to administer. Binary triggers authorize payment of the earnout once the specified milestone is achieved. Non-financial targets, like regulatory approval, are amenable to binary payment milestones. A product either receives regulatory approval or it does not. Why is regulatory approval a trigger? The uncertainty about the prospect of receiving regulatory approval can have a material effect on the acquirer's valuation of the seller, and the parties may not be able to agree on the likelihood of approval. The seller may, for instance, have had information about the likelihood of receiving government approval that it was unable to credibly convey to the acquirer. Or both parties may not have had sufficient information to make an assessment about which they were confident.

When Genzyme was acquired by Sanofi in 2011, the parties agreed to an earnout in the form of a "contingent value right" (CVR), a registered security. Payment triggers in the Genzyme earnout were related to FDA

---

[4] A seminal discussion of the function of earnouts is in Ronald J. Gilson, *Value Creation by Business Lawyers: Legal Skills and Asset Pricing,* 94 YALE L. J. 239 (1984).

approval of a new drug in the Genzyme pipeline as well as production and revenue targets. Sanofi contracted to make payments to security-holders contingent upon the following milestones:

1. $1/CVR if specified Cerezyme and Fabrazyme production thresholds are met for 2011;

2. $1/CVR upon final FDA approval of Lemtrada;

3. $2/CVR if global net sales revenue total $400 million;

4. $3/CVR if global net sales revenue total $1.8 billion;

5. $4/CVR if global net sales revenue total $2.3 billion; and

6. $3/CVR if global net sales revenue total $2.8 billion.[5]

Third, the length of earnouts typically varies anywhere between one and five years. In general, the term of the earnout provision should (and generally will) be long enough to resolve the uncertainty that caused the fundamental disagreement over valuation. Fourth, the size of an earnout relative to the total consideration in the transaction also varies. In general, the size typically reflects the degree of uncertainty between the parties with respect to the seller's value. To the extent the duration and the size of the earnout are long and large enough to overcome the uncertainty that gives rise to the valuation differences between the parties, the earnout mechanism is an appropriate device to address valuation disagreements.

In addition to questions of size and duration of the earnout, the degree of autonomy and control over the seller's business during the post-closing period is often central to the negotiation of the provision. Control and autonomy are important because the likelihood that the seller's shareholders will receive any contingent payments is tied to the ability of continuing employees to take actions that will maximize the seller's value with respect to the earnout targets. To the extent selling shareholders will not continue their involvement with the seller post-closing and to the degree buyers do not keep the seller apart from the parent, buyers may face incentives to undermine the implementation of the earnout in an effort to reduce their payment obligations.

The clauses below, typically included in an earnout provision, address some of these issues:

a) Unless otherwise provided herein, Buyer shall manage the Company during the Earn-Out Period as a distinct business entity substantially in accordance with the strategic business plan outlined in Schedule 4 hereto (the "Strategic

---

[5] See Description of the CVRs, in Amendment No. 2 to Sanofi-Aventis's Registration Statement on Form F–4, available at http://www.sec.gov/Archives/edgar/data/1121404/00011 9312511076085/df4a.htm#rom153596_51.

Business Plan"), provided, however, that Buyer shall be free to deviate therefrom, after consulting with Seller, if (i) in its good faith opinion, this is desirable and necessary to deal with major changes in economic or market conditions or to improve the Company's position or results, or (ii) the Pre-Tax Profit (Loss) of the Company for any calendar year is less than 50% of the amount projected pursuant to the annual budget established for such year.

b) Notwithstanding the provisions of (a), Buyer shall not be required to continue the business operations of the Company in the form then being conducted, and shall be entitled to restructure such business operations, if, due to major changes in the industry or the economy as a whole, the Company has suffered losses (before taxes but exclusive of extraordinary losses) of more than $2 million cumulatively as of the end of any Period during the Earn-Out Period, and Buyer in good faith sees little prospect to restore the Company to profitability at a cost and within a period of time which it considers reasonable in the light of the result likely to be produced thereby.

Beyond the issue of who makes decisions with respect to the business, the computation of earnings can be a subject of significant negotiation. Which, if any, non-recurring "extraordinary" items should be excluded? How is overhead allocated? The seller has now become part of a new enterprise that has expenses such as, perhaps, legal staff, a more extensive "back office" and so on. How is goodwill taken into account? What happens if the buyer would like to sell the business or merge or otherwise reorganize it, or shut part of it down? What happens if the seller contests the buyer's computation? If the earnout would have been negative in one year, do those results carry over to reduce the amount of the next year's earnout? What happens if the buyer's financial statements are later restated? (Financial statements are "restated" when they are, roughly speaking, inaccurate; this may occur several years after the time period covered by the statement.) Again, as with many matters we discuss, there are significant technical issues in determining appropriate terms, but each party is also on its guard against ways the other party could take advantage. For instance, the seller might fear a too-large allocation of buyer overhead that would reduce what it viewed as the earnings of the business it sold to the buyer.

Following is a clause that addresses some of these issues. Note that "Pre-Tax Profit (Loss) is the defined term on the basis of which the earnout is computed:

"Pre-Tax Profit (Loss)" shall mean, for any Period, the earnings (or losses, as the case may be) of the Company for such Period before payment or provision for any required taxes, as determined in accordance with generally accepted accounting principles applied on a basis consistent with the accounting policies of the Buyer, except that such earnings or losses shall be modified by the following:

(i)   There shall be charged to the Company all reasonable and appropriate fees and expenses of third parties incurred by or on behalf of the Company in the operation of its business, including the fees and expenses of the Company's Accountants for audit review and other services rendered to or for the Company pursuant to the terms of this Agreement; provided, however, that any material fees and expenses of third parties shall not be charged to the Company unless necessary in Buyer's reasonable judgment for the prudent conduct of the Company's business;

(ii) If, after the Closing Date, Buyer or an Affiliate of Buyer advances funds to the Company, then the Company shall be charged interest thereon [at a specified rate];

(iii) If, after the Closing Date, Buyer shall increase or make a contribution to the Company's capital, such increase or contribution shall be treated as an advance of funds to the Company in accordance with the immediately preceding clause (ii);

(iv) No charge shall be made for amortization of goodwill, except (A) with respect to goodwill shown on the Closing Balance Sheet, and (B) with respect to any future acquisition or similar transaction made by the Company;

(v)   No charge shall be made for R&D Expenses, as that term is defined in [Section x].

(vi) The amount of any extraordinary items of income, gain, loss or expense determined under GAAP, consistently applied and as in effect on the Closing Date, shall be excluded in determining Pre-Tax Profit (Loss);

(vii) Any management fee or other corporate overhead item charged by Buyer to its operating units, including the Company, shall not be deemed an expense in determining Pre-Tax Profit (Loss); and

(viii) The costs and expenses incurred by the Buyer which relate to the negotiation and preparation of this Agreement and the consummation of the transactions contemplated hereby, including any expenses incurred in the conduct of due diligence and any legal fees, shall be excluded in determining Pre-Tax Income (Loss).

Note the detail with which the manner of making the computation is specified. These agreements also may contain a provision giving the seller the rights to review the computation and a procedure by which any disputes between the seller and the buyer as to the computation can be resolved.

In private transactions, the parties sometimes agree that if a seller would otherwise have received an earnout but owes the buyer indemnification, then the buyer can offset the earnout against the indemnification. Whether the buyer has this right and if so, the terms under which it can be exercised, is subject to considerable negotiation.

Especially if the size of the earnout is large, its implementation can be challenging, not infrequently leading to litigation when disputes arise. Earnout provisions will typically direct post-closing disputes over payments to arbitration or other alternate dispute resolution mechanism. Indeed, the propensity for earnouts to lead to post-closing disputes is an important reason earnouts are often frowned up by experienced deal makers. Take for example this not uncommon scenario: a large technology company acquires a small start-up with promising technology and talented engineers. Because the start-up is still years away from profitability, the parties agree to an earnout. After some years, the start-up may have failed to meet the earnout milestones for one reason or another. At that point, the acquirer faces a difficult question, whether to pay or not. If the acquirer does not pay, then it faces the prospect of litigation from disgruntled employees who may be talented and valuable engineers. Or, it could pay the earnout and buy peace. More than a few acquirers opt for the latter strategy. Because of this and other implementation issues with earnouts, some practitioners, especially those doing larger deals, prefer not to use them. Indeed, a lawsuit has been brought relating to the CVRs discussed earlier in this subsection, those given in Sanofi's acquisition of Genzyme. According to the plaintiff's complaint, Sanofi violated the agreement's requirement that it would use its "Diligent Efforts" to meet the relevant milestones and instead "embarked on a slow path to FDA approval and departed from its own drug commercialization patterns and those of others in the industry" "[a]s a result [of which] it[ ] Sanofi missed the contractual milestones and skirted its payment obligations of at least $708 million."

E. INFORMATION PRODUCTION AND RISK ALLOCATION: REPRESENTATIONS AND WARRANTIES

Although buyers can learn a great deal about the seller by conducting due diligence, due diligence can be an expensive and long process. The process of negotiating the merger agreement, particularly the representations and warranties, can play an important role in producing credible information about the seller. In the representations and warranties, the seller describes itself to the buyer, and represents and warrants that it is being truthful. If the seller is not being truthful, it takes the risk that the buyer will not be obligated to close the transaction, and, in a private transaction, if the buyer does close the transaction, that the buyer will be able to get indemnification from the selling shareholders.

The process by which representations and warranties are negotiated helps the parties describe what is being conveyed in the transaction. The buyer will request more expansive representations, and the seller will respond by saying what (more limited) representation it is willing to make, triggering a buyer response, and so on, until the parties agree.

Representations and warranties also allocate risks associated with the description not being accurate, whether as a result of a party not being truthful or not having the information at issue. For example, consider a representation in a merger agreement that addresses the presence or absence of litigation. The following "absence of litigation representation" states that there is no litigation against the seller (the Company) at the time of the merger agreement:

> Absence of Litigation. As of the date hereof, there is no claim, action, proceeding, or investigation pending or threatened against the Company or any of its respective affiliates or any of its respective properties or assets at law or in equity, and there are no Orders by or before any arbitrator or Governmental Authority. [*Editor: Note that the capitalized terms—Orders and Governmental Authority—will be defined in the agreement.*]

This is a very broad statement; many sellers will not know whether it is true, and indeed, it may not be true. Someone might be threatening litigation against the company, but that news has not yet reached the company's management. If this statement is left "unqualified," that threatened litigation could subsequently give the buyer the right not to complete the transaction. Consequently, this statement is commonly qualified in the following way:

> Absence of Litigation. As of the date hereof, there is no claim, action, proceeding, or investigation pending or, *to the knowledge*

of the Company, threatened against the Company or any of its respective affiliates or any of its respective properties or assets at law or in equity, and there are no Orders by or before any arbitrator or Governmental Authority.

What counts as knowledge—only "actual" knowledge, or "constructive" knowledge? And whose knowledge counts? Agreements often give specifics on both these matters. As to whose knowledge counts, certain individuals may be named, and/or certain titles or positions in the corporate hierarchy may be specified. For instance, the Dell merger agreement defines "Knowledge" specifically as the actual knowledge of certain named individuals.

The Absence of Litigation representation, even when qualified in this way, is still extremely broad: only part of the representation is qualified by knowledge. Part of it is unqualified: the representation states that there are no existing, pending or threatened claims or actions against the company. Existing litigation would be the easiest for a company to know about. But even existing litigation might escape broad notice within the company if it is not major or is at a very early stage, especially if it relates to far-flung operations the company may have, such that only low-level people in the company may be aware of it. The company might know about pending or threatened litigation, but it also might not. Maybe the "threat" was not taken seriously, but will in fact turn into a serious lawsuit.

Another way to qualify the representation is by reference to "materiality:"

> Absence of Litigation. As of the date hereof, there is no *material* claim, action, proceeding, or investigation pending or, to the knowledge of Company, threatened against the Company or any of its respective affiliates or any of its respective properties or assets at law or in equity, and there are no Orders by or before any arbitrator or Governmental Authority.

A merger agreement may define the term "material." If the term is not specifically defined, "material" is generally considered to have the same definition ascribed to it in *TSC Industries v. Northway*, 426 US 438 (1976): a fact is material if there is a substantial likelihood that a reasonable shareholder would consider it important in deciding how to vote or invest. A materiality qualifier gets at what a buyer presumably most cares about: material claims. There may in fact be claims against the company that are not disclosed here, but the representation will be breached if they are material to the operation of the seller's business.

What if the seller has litigation against it, or litigation is pending or threatened? To make an accurate representation, the seller can disclose what it knows, in the following manner:

> Absence of Litigation. *Except as disclosed in the Disclosure Schedule*, as of the date hereof, there is no material claim, action, proceeding, or investigation pending or, to the knowledge of Company, threatened against the Company or any of its respective affiliates or any of its respective properties or assets at law or in equity, and there are no Orders by or before any arbitrator or Governmental Authority.

This statement will still be true even if the seller has a material claim against it, provided the seller disclosed the existence of the litigation on its disclosure schedule. There will be no breach of representation or of the related closing condition—the litigation will not give the buyer grounds not to close the transaction.

Both parties benefit if the buyer can get the information about the litigation more cheaply and take the information into account in the terms on which it agrees to be bound to close the transaction. Indeed, the whole process of negotiating a merger agreement is not as adversarial as you might initially think. The seller wants as high a price as it can get, and thus it has to convince the buyer that it is of good quality. The buyer's baseline assumption is not going to be, for instance, that the seller has no litigation; rather, the buyer will be uncertain, thinking that there may be litigation, and that some of it may be material. Both parties benefit when the process of eliciting information can be done as cheaply as possible. Both parties also benefit if risks are allocated to the party best situated to bear them. What determines whether a party is better able to bear a risk? This may be a function of information—if a seller is not able to credibly convey to the buyer that a bad event is less likely than the buyer thinks, the seller may be best off retaining the risk that the event occurs. Putting this another way, the better situated party is in a better position to prevent the risk. The seller is almost certainly better situated to bear the risk of litigation against it between signing and closing than the buyer is.

In the context of public companies, which are subject to disclosure obligations under the federal securities laws, market practice is now to use qualifiers like the one below:

> Absence of Litigation. As of the date hereof, there is no claim, action, proceeding, or investigation pending or, to the knowledge of Company, threatened against the Company or any of its respective affiliates or any of its respective properties or assets at law or in equity, and there are no Orders by or before any arbitrator or Governmental Authority, *in each case as would have, individually or in the aggregate, a Company Material Adverse Effect.*

What does it mean when a representation is qualified by a statement that the litigation not disclosed to the buyer would not individually or in the aggregate amount to a material adverse effect? As you will see below, qualifying a representation with a material adverse effect clause means that a good deal of material litigation will not need to be disclosed.

F. REPRESENTATIONS AND WARRANTIES GENERALLY

The Representations and Warranties sections of merger agreements look quite similar to one another, as is the case for many of the sections in merger agreements. The landscape of the Representations and Warranties section is critical to understanding the functioning of the rest of the agreement. The merger agreements in the Online Appendix contain typical Representations and Warranties sections.

Preamble: It is customary for the representations and warranties section to open with a statement that the representations that follow are qualified by an accompanying disclosure schedule. Although thought to be boilerplate, how this preamble language is negotiated can be important. The preamble makes it clear that each representation is qualified by the contents of a disclosure schedule, or a disclosure letter, that accompanies the merger agreement. In a public deal, the representations and warranties are also typically qualified by any information contained in the target's public filings. Below you will find the preamble to the representations and warranties section of the Dell merger agreement.

> The Company represents and warrants to Parent and Merger Sub as set forth in this Article III; _provided_ that such representations and warranties by the Company are qualified in their entirety by reference to the disclosure (i) in the Company SEC Documents filed or furnished with the SEC prior to the date hereof . . . or (ii) set forth in the disclosure schedule delivered by the Company to Parent immediately prior to the execution of this Agreement (the "Company Disclosure Letter"), it being understood and agreed that each disclosure set forth in the Company Disclosure Letter or such Company SEC Documents shall qualify or modify each of the representations and warranties set forth in this Article III . . . to the extent the applicability of the disclosure to such representation and warranty is reasonably apparent from the text of the disclosure made.

Organization and Qualification Representation: Almost without exception, the first representation made by a seller is the organization and qualification representation. This representation states without qualification that the seller is a corporation in good standing wherever required. To the extent the representation is not true, failure to comply may cause administrative difficulties in closing the transaction. Luckily, good standing problems are typically easy to cure prior to closing. This representation also requires the seller to provide the buyer with copies of all corporate documents, including certificates of incorporation and bylaws, as well as set forth a list of all material subsidiaries of the seller in the accompanying disclosure schedule. Below you will find Dell's organization and qualification representation:

> The Company is a corporation duly incorporated, validly existing and in good standing under the Laws of the State of Delaware. The Company has all requisite corporate power and authority to own, lease and operate its properties and assets and to carry on its business as presently conducted and is qualified to do business and is in good standing as a foreign corporation or other relevant legal entity in each jurisdiction where the ownership, leasing or operation of its assets or properties or conduct of its business requires such qualification, except where any such failure to be so qualified or in good standing would not, individually or in the aggregate, constitute a Company Material Adverse Effect. . . . The Company has made available to Parent prior to the date hereof true, complete and correct copies of the certificate of incorporation and bylaws (or equivalent organizational and governing documents) of the Company . . .

> Section 3.1(b) of the Company Disclosure Letter sets forth a true and complete list of each Significant Subsidiary of the Company as of the date hereof, each such Significant Subsidiary's jurisdiction of organization and its authorized, issued and outstanding equity interests . . .

Capitalization: The Capitalization representation is perhaps one of the most important representations a seller can make. Like the organization and qualification representation, it is also typically an unqualified representation. This is because all the information with respect to the seller's capitalization is knowable and it is, or should be, known by the seller. In the context of a seasoned public company, this representation is usually an easy one to make. On the other hand, where the target is a private company, this representation can involve some risk, depending on the quality of corporate governance practices in the target. It is not unusual for start-up companies to compensate employees or even landlords with stock options or grants of stock. Thus, smaller private firms often have difficulty making this representation. To the extent price is calculated on a per share basis, getting this representation wrong can be extremely expensive to remedy. Consequently, a good deal of work is done by lawyers in making sure the representations here are correct. To the extent the seller has issued options, warrants, or restricted stock, these issuances are listed on the accompanying disclosure schedule. Below you will find Dell's capitalization representation:

The authorized share capital of the Company consists of 7,000,000,000 shares of Common Stock and 5,000,000 shares of preferred stock, par value $0.01 per share (the "Preferred Stock"). As of February 3, 2013, there were (i) 1,738,600,597 shares of Common Stock issued and outstanding (15,000 of which were Company Restricted Shares), (ii) no shares of Preferred Stock issued and outstanding, (iii) 1,675,670,553 shares of Common Stock issued and held in the treasury of the Company, (iv) 117,417,732 shares of Common Stock subject to outstanding Company Options . . . , (v) 41,785,565 shares of Common Stock underlying Company RSU Awards . . . , and (vi) no more than 98,620,451 shares of Common Stock reserved for issuance under the Company Stock Plans. Since February 3, 2013, the Company has not issued any shares of its capital stock or other rights or securities exercisable, convertible into or exchangeable for shares in its capital, other than or pursuant to any equity awards or interests referred to above that were issued pursuant to the Company Stock Plans and that were outstanding on February 3, 2013, or as expressly permitted by Section 5.1(b) [the section that governs what Dell can do between signing and closing]. All outstanding Shares are duly authorized, validly issued, fully paid and nonassessable, and are not subject to and were not issued in violation of any preemptive or similar right, purchase option, call or right of first refusal or similar right. No Subsidiary of the Company owns any shares of capital stock of the Company. . . .

Section 3.2(c) of the Company Disclosure Letter sets forth a correct and complete list, as of February 3, 2013, of (i) each outstanding Company Option, including the number of shares of Common Stock issuable upon exercise of such Company Stock Option, the exercise price with respect thereto, the applicable grant date thereof and the applicable Company Stock Plan governing such Company Option, (ii) each outstanding Company RSU Award, including the target and maximum number of shares of Common Stock underlying such Company RSU Award [an award of certain restricted stock units], the applicable grant date thereof and the applicable Company Stock Plan governing such Company RSU Award, and (iii) each award of Company Restricted Shares, including the number of Company Restricted Shares subject to such award, the applicable grant date thereof and the applicable Company Stock Plan governing such award of Company Restricted Shares. . . .

Corporate Authority: Parties will normally make a representation with respect to authority. This is an unqualified statement that attempts to assure that the parties acting as agents for the seller in fact have the power to commit the seller in contract. The representation may also include certain statements of fact to the effect that the board of the seller has recommended the merger agreement to its shareholders. This statement is not a commitment to act; rather, it is simply a statement of fact. If the seller's board ultimately does not recommend the merger to shareholders, then the representation will not be true and the buyer will not have an obligation to close the merger. Below you will find Dell's corporate authority representation:

> The Company has the requisite corporate power and authority to enter into and deliver this Agreement and, subject to receipt of the Company Stockholder Approvals, to perform its obligations hereunder and to consummate the transactions contemplated herein. The execution and delivery of this Agreement by the Company and the consummation by the Company of the Merger and the other transactions contemplated by this Agreement have been duly and validly authorized by the Company Board and no other corporate action on the part of the Company, pursuant to the DGCL or otherwise, is necessary to authorize this Agreement or to consummate the transactions contemplated herein, subject, in the case of the Merger, to the Company Stockholder Approvals and the filing of the Certificate of Merger. This Agreement has been duly and validly executed and delivered by the Company and, assuming due and valid authorization, execution and delivery hereof by each of the Parent Parties, is a valid and binding obligation of the Company, enforceable against the Company in accordance with its terms . . .

Approval of the Merger Agreement: The target will make an unqualified representation that it has approved the transaction and resolved to recommend it to shareholders. As discussed below, in Change of Board Recommendation, its obligation to recommend the transaction is not absolute. This is the relevant language from Dell's merger agreement.

> The Company Board (upon the unanimous recommendation of the Special Committee) at a duly held meeting unanimously (other than Michael S. Dell) has (i) determined that the transactions contemplated by this Agreement, including the Merger, are fair to, and in the best interests of, the Company's stockholders (other than the MD Investors), (ii) approved and declared advisable the execution, delivery and performance of this Agreement and the consummation of the transactions contemplated herein, including the Merger, and (iii) resolved, . . . to recommend that the stockholders of the Company adopt this

Agreement . . . and directed that such matter be submitted for consideration of the stockholders of the Company at the Company Meeting.

No Conflict: The conflicts representation lists the foreseeable governmental approvals required, and represents that there are no other material regulatory approvals required. It also requires the seller to represent that the merger will not cause a default on any contracts of the seller, or if so to list such possible defaults on the accompanying disclosure schedule. Unlike the representations we discussed above, the conflicts representation generally contains a materiality qualifier. This representation can be quite important: the types of conflicts that may exist and would be disclosed often relate to change of control issues in contracts, or with regulatory authorities, either of which may impair the value of the target if acquired. Below you will find Dell's no conflicts representation.

> The execution, delivery and performance by the Company of this Agreement and the consummation by the Company of the Merger and the other transactions contemplated herein do not and will not require any consent, approval, authorization or permit of, action by, filing with or notification to any Governmental Entity, other than (i) the filing of the Certificate of Merger, (ii) the filing of the pre-merger notification report under the Hart-Scott-Rodino Antitrust Improvements Act of 1976 . . . , the filing with the European Commission of a merger notification . . . , and such other filings as may be required under any other Regulatory Laws (and any actions or nonactions, waivers, consents, clearances or approvals by a Governmental Entity, or expirations or terminations of waiting periods, required in connection with the foregoing), (iii) compliance with the applicable requirements of the Exchange Act, including the filing of the Proxy Statement and the Schedule 13E–3 with the SEC, . . . , (vi) compliance with the rules and regulations of NASDAQ, . . . and other than any consent, approval, authorization, permit, action, filing or notification the failure of which to make or obtain would not, individually or in the aggregate, constitute a Company Material Adverse Effect.

> Assuming receipt of the Company Approvals and the receipt of the Company Stockholder Approvals, the execution, delivery and performance by the Company of this Agreement and the consummation by the Company of the Merger and the other transactions contemplated herein do not and will not (i) conflict with, or breach any provision of, the organizational or governing documents of the Company or any of its Significant Subsidiaries, (ii) violate any Law binding upon or applicable to the Company

or any of its Subsidiaries or any of their respective properties or assets, or (iii) result in any violation of, or default . . . under, or give rise to a right of termination, cancellation or acceleration of any obligation or to the loss of a benefit under any loan, guarantee of indebtedness or credit agreement, note, bond, debenture, mortgage, indenture, lease, agreement or other contract (collectively, "Contracts") binding upon the Company or any of its Subsidiaries or result in the creation of any Lien . . . upon any of the properties or assets of the Company or any of its Subsidiaries, other than, in the case of clauses (ii) and (iii), any such violation, conflict, default, termination, cancellation, acceleration, right, loss or Lien that would not, individually or in the aggregate, constitute a Company Material Adverse Effect . . .

Financial Reports: Sellers will usually make a representation about their financial statements. This representation typically states that the financial statements of the seller were prepared in conformity with GAAP in all material respects and that they fairly present the financial position of the company. Notice that unlike the capitalization representation, this representation is qualified. Because GAAP itself includes materiality standards, the financial reports representation can often fall victim to the problem of "double materiality" discussed further below. Below you will find Dell's financial reports representation.

The consolidated financial statements . . . of the Company included in the Company SEC Documents, and including all Company SEC Documents filed after the date hereof, fairly presented, or if not yet filed, will fairly present, in all material respects the consolidated financial position of the Company and its consolidated Subsidiaries, as at the respective dates thereof, and the consolidated results of their operations, their consolidated cash flows and changes in stockholders' equity for the respective periods then ended (subject, in the case of the unaudited statements, to normal year-end adjustments and to any other adjustments described therein, including the notes thereto) and were prepared . . . in all material respects in conformity with GAAP (except, in the case of the unaudited financial statements, as permitted by the SEC) applied on a consistent basis during the periods referred to therein (except as may be indicated therein or in the notes thereto).

No Undisclosed Liabilities: This is another important representation. This representation states that except as set forth in the financial statements of the company and for certain other specified types of liabilities including those incurred in the ordinary course, the company has no liabilities. This representation provides assurances to the buyer that it knows what liabilities the seller has, and that such liabilities are either disclosed in the disclosure schedule or in the seller's financial statements. This representation is typically qualified by material adverse effect (discussed below) so that only the significant liabilities which might substantially affect pricing are encompassed. The following is the No Undisclosed Liabilities representation from the Dell merger agreement:

> **No Undisclosed Liabilities.** Except (a) as disclosed, reflected or reserved against in the consolidated balance sheet of the Company and its Subsidiaries as of November 2, 2012 (or the notes thereto), (b) for liabilities and obligations incurred under or in accordance with this Agreement or in connection with the transactions contemplated herein, (c) for liabilities and obligations incurred under any contract or other agreement or arising under any applicable Law (other than liabilities or obligations due to breaches thereunder or violations thereof), in each case, in the ordinary course of business since November 2, 2012, (d) for liabilities and obligations incurred in the ordinary course of business since November 2, 2012 and (e) for liabilities or obligations that have been discharged or paid in full, neither the Company nor any Subsidiary of the Company has any liabilities or obligations of any nature, whether or not accrued, contingent or otherwise, that would be required by GAAP to be reflected on a consolidated balance sheet (or the notes thereto) of the Company and its Subsidiaries, other than as does not constitute, individually or in the aggregate, a Company Material Adverse Effect.

10b–5 Representation: The 10b–5 representation is a relatively common representation given by sellers in public transactions. In such a 10b–5 representation, the seller uses the language of Rule 10b–5 under the '34 Act to state that all of its filings with the SEC are accurate, and specifically, that the seller's filings do not contain any untrue statement of a material fact or omit to state any material fact required to make the statements therein not misleading. Notice that although it tracks the language of 10b–5, it is more stringent than 10b–5. As you may have learned in your Business Associations or Securities Regulation classes, under 10b–5, a plaintiff must prove scienter as an element of a 10b–5 claim. By contrast, here, the buyer need not prove scienter before invoking a violation of this representation as a reason to refuse to close, or even terminate the transaction. Because this representation references documents the seller has filed with the SEC, it is made only by publicly traded companies. Private companies that do not file with the SEC are unable to make this representation. In private deals, the buyer may ask the seller to make a similar representation as to the representations and warranties—that they disclose all material information. A seller will generally resist this request because of its breadth, perhaps agreeing to a highly qualified representation. Below you will find Dell's 10b–5 representation.

> The Company has filed or furnished all forms, documents and reports required to be filed or furnished by it with the SEC on a timely basis since January 28, 2011. . . . Each of the Company SEC Documents, including all Company SEC Documents filed or furnished after the date hereof, complied . . . as to form in all material respects with the applicable requirements of the Securities Act, the Exchange Act and the Sarbanes-Oxley Act. As of the date filed or furnished with the SEC, none of the Company SEC Documents, including all Company SEC Documents filed . . . contained . . . any untrue statement of a material fact or omitted . . . to state any material fact required to make the statements . . . not misleading. As of the date hereof, there are no material outstanding or unresolved comments received from the SEC with respect to any of the Company SEC Filings.

Absence of changes (MAC): The material adverse effect or material adverse change clause makes its appearance in the representations and warranties most directly through the absence of changes representation. The absence of changes representation provides that in the interim period between, typically, the date of the target's last financial statements and closing, no event has occurred which would constitute a material adverse change. Because this statement is prospective, if there is a material adverse change between signing and closing, the buyer does not have an obligation to close. See Subsection E below, discussing Material Adverse Effect. The representation will also state that since a particular date (typically, the date of the target's last financial statements) the business of the target has been run in the ordinary course. Taken together, these representations help assure the buyer that there has been no substantial change to the target. Below you will find the absence of changes representation from the Dell merger agreement.

> Since November 2, 2012 through the date hereof, the Company has conducted its business in all material respects in the ordinary course, except in connection with this Agreement and the transactions contemplated herein.

> Since November 2, 2012, there has not occurred any facts, circumstances, changes, events, occurrences or effects that, individually or in the aggregate, constitute a Company Material Adverse Effect.

In addition to the representations discussed above, a number of other representations are typically made in merger agreements, including representations with respect to: the seller's compliance with all applicable laws and regulations; the seller's compliance with environmental and labor laws; the seller's compliance with tax laws; the seller's access to and ownership of the intellectual property required to run the seller's business; the seller's ownership of any real property (it purports to own); the shareholder approvals required to approve the merger; and the non-applicability of state anti-takeover laws (discussed in Chapter XV) to the merger. Finally, the seller will usually make a representation that all of its material contracts are listed on the accompanying disclosure schedule. While agreements tend to contain representations that cover similar areas, and there are some conventions with respect to the use of qualifiers, representations and warranties are heavily negotiated, and there can be very significant differences between agreements.

Until now we have focused on the representations given by a seller to a buyer. But in every merger agreement, buyers also give representations to the seller. Where the consideration in the transaction is cash, a buyer's representations are usually quite brief: that the buyer has the corporate power and authority to act and that the buyer has sufficient cash to complete the transaction. Think about why this is so: shareholders are getting cash, and so long as they can do so, they do not need to be concerned about other aspects of the buyer. By contrast, where consideration in the transaction is stock of the buyer, the buyer's representations are much longer, usually on par with the representations given by the seller. This is because when a seller is accepting stock of the buyer as consideration in a merger, the seller is asking its shareholders to make a decision to invest in the buyer. Consequently, the seller and its shareholders are interested in the quality of the buyer and the value of the stock being offered in the transaction. In the merger agreements in the Online Appendix, notice the number and length of representations given to the seller by the buyer when the buyer is paying cash as contrasted with when the buyer is paying in whole or in part in buyer stock.

Special Issue: Filing the Disclosure Schedule

As discussed above, many representations are qualified by statements in an accompanying disclosure schedule. A representation might state "there is no material litigation except as set forth in the disclosure schedule." The representation is, again, not that there is no material litigation. The representation is that all such litigation is disclosed on the disclosure schedule.

While merger agreements involving public companies are generally required to be filed with the SEC, the SEC does not require the filing of disclosure schedules. Item 601 of Regulation S–K requires the filing of merger agreements. However, it also states that accompanying schedules, including the disclosure schedule, "shall not be filed unless such schedules contain information which is material to an investment decision and which is not otherwise disclosed in the agreement or the disclosure document."

In many cases, the reason why parties would not want to disclose much of the information on the schedules is understandable. In addition to sensitive commercial information, the disclosure schedule may contain confidential information of the type that might be embarrassing to the corporation. It is no surprise, as James Freund noted, that nondisclosure "serves the incidental purpose of enabling the parties to avoid baring their souls in public."[6] Of course, information about the company that is embarrassing may also be material. When it is, transaction lawyers face an important decision: whether to file at least portions of the disclosure schedule along with the merger agreement.

This question, whether filing the disclosure schedule accompanying a merger agreement is required, was brought into sharp relief by a case brought by the SEC against the Bank of America in the wake of the 2008 financial crisis. At the height of the financial crisis, the US government brokered a merger between Bank of America and Merrill Lynch in order to help prop up the country's financial system. Following the merger, the SEC sued Bank of America, asserting that Bank of America had violated the proxy disclosure rules when it neglected to file the disclosure schedule along with the Merrill Lynch merger agreement.

The Bank of America-Merrill Lynch merger agreement included the following covenant:

> 5.2 <u>Covenant Forbearances</u>. During the period from the date of this Agreement to the Effective Time, except as set forth in this Section 5.2 of the Company Disclosure Schedule or except as expressly contemplated or permitted by this Agreement, Company shall not, and shall not permit any of its Subsidiaries to, without the prior written consent of Parent: . . . (c) except as required under applicable law or the terms of any Company Benefit Plan existing as of the date hereof . . . (ii) pay any amounts to Employees not required by any current plan or agreement (other than base salary in the ordinary course of business)[7]

Bank of America had actually agreed to allow Merrill to pay up to $5.8 billion in discretionary bonuses before the merger.

> The agreement to allow Merrill to pay these discretionary bonuses was memorialized in a separate schedule that was

---

[6] JAMES C. FREUND, ANATOMY OF A MERGER: STRATEGIES AND TECHNIQUES FOR NEGOTIATING CORPORATE ACQUISITIONS 235 (1975).

[7] The joint proxy statement prospectus containing the merger agreement is available at http://www.sec.gov/Archives/edgar/data/65100/000095012308014246/g15211mldefm14a.htm.

omitted from the proxy statement and whose contents were never disclosed before the shareholders' vote on the merger . . . The omission of Bank of America's agreement authorizing Merrill to pay discretionary year-end bonuses made the statements to the contrary in the joint proxy statement and its several subsequent amendments materially false and misleading. Bank of America's representations that Merrill was prohibited from making such payments were materially false and misleading because the contractual prohibition on such payments was nullified by the undisclosed contractual provision expressly permitting them.[8]

The covenant above, about which the SEC made its allegation, is what is known as a negative covenant. Merrill agreed in the merger agreement *not* to take certain actions while the merger was pending. (A typical negative covenant in a loan agreement would be a borrower's promise not to take on more debt or grant liens on its assets.) One of those actions Merrill agreed not to take was paying bonuses except as set forth on the disclosure schedule. The SEC argued that this piece of information would have been material and should have been disclosed in Bank of America's 225-page proxy statement asking its shareholders to approve the transaction. The dispute between the SEC and Bank of America over this disclosure question ultimately resulted in a settlement. Although custom, practice, and rules dictate that disclosure schedules are not typically publicly filed, a careful lawyer will be attentive to situations that might prove the exception.

G. RISK ALLOCATION AND THE MATERIAL ADVERSE CHANGE CLAUSE

As discussed in the previous Subsection, in addition to the information production function, merger agreements also act to allocate risk. A seller who represents that there is no litigation against it bears the consequences of breach (most importantly, that the buyer need not close the transaction) even if, unbeknown to it, there is litigation against it, as does a seller who represents that it has all permits it needs to conduct its business even if, unbeknown to it, it is missing one or more permits.

Who bears the risk that the seller's business declines significantly between contract signing and closing? Many specific types of decline will be covered in the agreement. The seller will make a representation as of the date of contract signing that must be true (or true in all material respects) as of the date the transaction is to close, in order for the buyer

---

[8] The SEC's complaint is available at https://www.sec.gov/litigation/complaints/2009/comp21164–amended.pdf. The quoted text is from page 2 of the complaint.

to be obligated to close. But what about matters not addressed specifically? Who bears the residual risk?

A material adverse effect (MAE) or material adverse change (MAC) clause (we will use the terms synonymously) addresses and allocates the residual risk—that is, the risks other than those covered in the other provisions addressing and allocating risk. In general terms, the structure of the clause, subject to certain significant carve-outs, allocates residual risk to the seller, providing the buyer the ability to not close the transaction in the event of a material adverse change. The clause can take the form of a representation "brought down" in a closing condition, or it can simply be a closing condition. In the Dell merger agreement, the relevant section of which is set forth below, it takes the form of a representation:

> Section 3.8 . . . (b) Since November 2, 2012 [the date of Dell's most recent financial statements prior to the date the merger agreement was signed], there has not occurred any facts, circumstances, changes, events, occurrences or effects that, individually or in the aggregate, constitute a Company Material Adverse Effect.

Company Material Adverse Effect is defined as follows:

> "Company Material Adverse Effect" means any fact, circumstance, change, event, occurrence or effect that would, or would reasonably be expected to, (1) have a material adverse effect on the financial condition, business, properties, assets, liabilities or results of operations of the Company and its Subsidiaries taken as a whole; provided that for purposes of this clause (1), none of the following, and no fact, circumstance, change, event, occurrence or effect to the extent arising out of or relating to the following, shall constitute or be taken into account in determining whether a "Company Material Adverse Effect" has occurred or may, would or could occur: (i) any facts, circumstances, changes, events, occurrences or effects generally affecting (A) any of the industries in which the Company and its Subsidiaries operate or (B) the economy, credit or financial or capital markets in the United States or elsewhere in the world, including changes in interest or exchange rates (except, for purposes of this clause (i)(B) only, to the extent that such fact, circumstance, change, event or occurrence adversely affects the Company and its Subsidiaries, taken as a whole, in a materially disproportionate manner relative to other companies operating in any of the industries in which the Company and its Subsidiaries primarily operate), or (ii) any facts, circumstances, changes, events, occurrences or effects arising out of, resulting

from or attributable to (A) changes or prospective changes in Law, applicable regulations of any Governmental Entity, generally accepted accounting principles or accounting standards, or any changes or prospective changes in, or issuance of any administrative or judicial notice, decision or other guidance with respect to, the interpretation or enforcement of any of the foregoing, (B) the negotiation, execution, announcement, pendency or performance of this Agreement or the consummation of the Merger or the other transactions contemplated by this Agreement (other than compliance with Section 5.1(a) [requiring the Company to act to preserve its business until the Effective Time]), including the impact thereof on relationships, contractual or otherwise, with customers, suppliers, distributors, partners, employees or regulators, or any litigation relating to this Agreement, the Merger or the other transactions contemplated by this Agreement or compliance by the Company with the terms of this Agreement, except that this clause (ii)(B) shall not apply in the determination of a breach or violation of the representations and warranties contained in Sections 3.4 [relating to conflicts and approvals] and 3.11(e) [relating to entitlement to severance or unemployment pay] (C) acts of war (whether or not declared), sabotage or terrorism, or any escalation or worsening of any such acts of war (whether or not declared), sabotage or terrorism, (D) pandemics, earthquakes, hurricanes, tornados or other natural disasters, (E) any change or announcement of a potential change in the credit ratings in respect of the Company or any indebtedness of the Company or its Subsidiaries, (F) any change to the extent resulting or arising from the identity of, or any facts or circumstances relating to, the Parent Parties or their respective Affiliates (but excluding Michael S. Dell other than in his capacity as a MD Investor), (G) any decline in the market price, or change in trading volume, of any capital stock of the Company or (H) any failure to meet any internal or public projections, forecasts or estimates of revenue, earnings, cash flow, cash position or other financial measures; provided that the underlying cause of any decline, change or failure referred to in clause (ii)(E), (ii)(G) or (ii)(H) (if not otherwise falling within any of clause (i) or clauses (ii)(A) through (H) above) may be taken into account in determining whether there is a "Company Material Adverse Effect"; or (2) prevent the ability of the Company to perform its obligations under this Agreement in any material respect.

This lengthy definition is best understood by breaking down the language. First, let us consider the provision without its lengthy exclusions. The first part of the definition provides the buyer with what might seem like fairly broad protection against residual risks:

> **Company Material Adverse Effect** means any fact, circumstance, change, event, occurrence or effect that would, or would reasonably be expected to, (1) have a material adverse effect on the financial condition, business, properties, assets, liabilities or results of operations of the Company and its Subsidiaries taken as a whole ... or (2) prevent the ability of the Company to perform its obligations under this Agreement in any material respect.

This qualitative definition of an MAE is intentionally vague because it is meant to cover all types of residual risks related to the "financial condition, business, properties, assets, liabilities or results of operations" that the parties may not have contemplated, and assign those risks to the seller. Any material negative change in any of those vaguely defined areas can generate an MAE and thus trigger rights by the buyer not to close the merger. In private transactions, it is not uncommon for the buyer to also negotiate to include "prospects," an inclusion the seller will resist. "This term is not typically included in public acquisitions, because it is considered to significantly broaden the MAC to include events that adversely affect the future performance of the company. There is not much, if any, case law interpreting what the term 'prospects' actually means and what future events it is meant to cover, but it is generally thought to at least cover adverse changes in earnings projections."[9]

The MAE language is intended to cover any residual risks that the parties have not identified and assign them to the seller: as between the buyer and the seller, the seller is likely in a better position to identify and anticipate residual risks in its own business. Recall that "assigning them to the seller" means that the buyer gets to not close the deal if the risk comes to pass. But there are many residual risks that the MAE section effectively assigns to the buyer, by excluding them from the definition of MAE. These specific exclusions, or carveouts, from the MAE definition can be found in the clauses following the "provided that" clause after the broad definition of the MAE:

> ... **provided** that for purposes of this clause (1), none of the following, and no fact, circumstance, change, event, occurrence or effect to the extent arising out of or relating to the following, shall constitute or be taken into account in determining whether a "Company Material Adverse Effect" has occurred...

[9] Steven M. Davidoff, *The MAC Is Back, But Does It Kill a Deal?*, N.Y. TIMES, August 23, 2011, available at http://dealbook.nytimes.com/2011/08/23/the-big-mac-is-back-but-does-it-kill-a-deal/.

Following this is a lengthy list of exclusions from the MAE definition. Should any adverse effect arise in connection with, among many other things, changes in the economy generally, in the industry in which the target operates, or in the law, it will not constitute an MAE for purposes of the merger agreement. Through these exclusions, the risk of any of the preceding events occurring during the interim period is assigned to the buyer. These exclusions, like the impact of general economic conditions on the business of the seller, are generally out of the seller's control. Whether or not they are out of the seller's control, the buyer has agreed to accept those risks. The effect of modern MAEs with their large number of exclusions is that most residual risks are assigned to the buyer. What is left with the seller are unidentified idiosyncratic risks—unknown risks which particularly affect the seller.[10]

The MAE may be drafted as a representation and warranty that no MAE has occurred, as is the case with the Dell provision. In Dell, the representation and warranty is made by the seller, since the buyer is paying cash for Dell. In this form, the representations and warranties are tested again at the time of closing, or "brought down" to closing. Alternatively, an MAE may simply be a closing condition, as is the case in *Hexion Specialty Chemicals v. Huntsman Corp,* discussed below. In *Huntsman,* the MAE representation only covered the period between the date of the most recent financial statements prior to the agreement, and the date of the agreement. The clause governing MAEs between the time of the signing of the agreement and the closing was instead a closing condition providing that the buyer's obligation to close was conditioned on there not having occurred "after the date of this Agreement any event, change, effect or development that has had or is reasonably expected to have, individually or in the aggregate, a Company Material Adverse Effect."[11]

As a practical matter, whether an MAE is structured as a representation that must be made as of the closing, or simply as a closing condition, makes no substantive difference. But understanding the mechanical difference is important. In the former case, the representation will likely be qualified by the seller's disclosure schedules and publicly available information or information otherwise known to the seller. In the latter case, this qualification may be in the actual MAE definition.

The MAE clause is thus the key element of the merger agreement dictating when and if a buyer has a right to refuse to close the transaction. However, a buyer invoking an MAE clause in an agreement is almost always uncertain of the ultimate validity of its claim. This is so

---

[10] Ronald J. Gilson & Alan Schwartz, *Understanding MACs: Moral Hazard in Acquisitions,* 21 J. L. ECON. & ORG. 330 (2005).

[11] http://www.sec.gov/Archives/edgar/data/1307954/000110465907053855/a07–18690_3ex2d1.htm.

for two reasons. First, MAE clauses are typically defined in qualitative terms rather than quantitative terms. More specifically, they do not put dollar amounts on what constitutes an MAE, but rather simple say that an event fulfilling the clause is "materially adverse," leaving the matter to a court to determine. Second, while the court is left to decide what constitutes an MAE, there have been few cases on the subject; there is very little guidance on what constitutes an MAE.

IBP v. Tyson, 789 A.2d 14 (Del. Ch. 2001) is the leading case on the issue. In *IBP*, IBP and Tyson entered into a merger agreement pursuant to which Tyson would acquire IBP. During the interim period between signing and closing, both IBP and Tyson suffered economic downturns. Suffering from buyer's remorse, Tyson sought to terminate the merger agreement. Tyson claimed that it was entitled to terminate the agreement because IBP had suffered a material adverse effect. The agreement defines material adverse effect as "any event, occurrence or development of a state of circumstances or facts which has had or reasonably could be expected to have a Material Adverse Effect" . . . "on the condition (financial or otherwise), business, assets, liabilities or results of operations of [IBP] and [its] Subsidiaries taken as whole."[12]

The provision at issue was section 5.10 of the merger agreement, a "representation and warranty that IBP had not suffered a material adverse effect since the "Balance Sheet Date" of December 25, 1999, except as set forth in the Warranted Financials or Schedule 5.10 of the Agreement."

> The application of those words is dauntingly complex. On its face, § 5.10 is a capacious clause that puts IBP at risk for a variety of uncontrollable factors that might materially affect its overall business or results of operation as a whole. Although many merger contracts contain specific exclusions from MAE clauses that cover declines in the overall economy or the relevant industry sector, or adverse weather or market conditions, § 5.10 is unqualified by such express exclusions.

But the court nevertheless ruled for IBP, ordering that Tyson specifically perform its merger agreement and acquire IBP:

> Tyson has not persuaded me that IBP has suffered a Material Adverse Effect. By its own arguments, Tyson has evinced more confidence in stock market analysts than I personally harbor. . . . [The analysts' predicted range of performance] suggests that no Material Adverse Effect has occurred. Rather, the analyst views support the conclusion that IBP remains what the baseline evidence suggests it was—a consistently but erratically

---

[12]   *Id.* at 65.

profitable company struggling to implement a strategy that will reduce the cyclicality of its earnings. Although IBP may not be performing as well as it and Tyson had hoped, IBP's business appears to be in sound enough shape to deliver results of operations in line with the company's recent historical performance. Tyson's own investment banker still believes IBP is fairly priced at $30 per share. The fact that Foodbrands [an important unit housed in a subsidiary of IBP's that had had issues with accounting fraud] is not yet delivering on the promise of even better performance for IBP during beef troughs is unavailing to Tyson, since § 5.10 focuses on IBP as a whole and IBP's performance as an entire company is in keeping with its baseline condition. Therefore, I conclude that Tyson has not demonstrated a breach of § 5.10. I admit to reaching this conclusion with less than the optimal amount of confidence. The record evidence is not of the type that permits certainty.

The paucity of caselaw reflects that most disputes over MAEs are settled long before a court is required to determine whether an MAE has actually occurred. A buyer may claim that an MAE has occurred simply because it does not want to go through with the transaction on the agreed-upon terms. It may not want to go through with the transaction on any plausible terms. But it also might be willing to proceed with the transaction at a much lower price. Thus, it might invoke an MAE in order to force a price renegotiation. The seller may not want to risk the uncertainty of litigation and an adverse decision that would leave its shareholders with no acquisition or premium for their shares. Consequently, when a buyer invokes an MAE, although the buyer's legal claim that there is an MAE might not be strong, a seller might nevertheless be willing to renegotiate and accept a lower price. Claiming that there has been an MAE thus can allow a buyer to drive the price of an acquisition down by taking advantage of either changed market conditions or adverse events affecting the seller. This is so, again, even if the buyer's claim is weak. But the more expansive the carveouts to an MAE—that is, the more residual risks are allocated to the buyer—the better a position a seller should be in to resist a buyer's renegotiation based on a claimed MAE.

In *Hexion Specialty Chemicals v. Huntsman Corp,* Hexion sought to invoke an MAE in order to avoid performance of its merger agreement with Huntsman; the transaction had been scheduled to close at the height of the financial crisis.

HEXION SPECIALTY CHEMICALS, INC. V. HUNTSMAN CORP.

Delaware Court of Chancery
965 A.2d 715 (2008)

LAMB, VICE CHANCELLOR.

* * *

A. The Parties

The plaintiffs and counterclaim defendants in this action are Hexion Specialty Chemicals, Inc., Apollo Global Management, LLC, and various entities through which Apollo Global Management conducts its business (Apollo Global Management and its related entities are collectively referred to as "Apollo"). Hexion, a New Jersey corporation, is the world's largest producer of binder, adhesive, and ink resins for industrial applications. Apollo Global Management, a Delaware limited liability company, is an asset manager focusing on private equity transactions. Through its ownership in Hexion's holding company, Apollo owns approximately 92% of Hexion.

The defendant and counterclaim plaintiff in this action is Huntsman Corporation, a Delaware corporation. Huntsman, a global manufacturer and marketer chemical products, operates five primary lines of business: Polyurethanes, Advanced Materials, Textile Effects, Performance Products and Pigments.

B. Procedural History

On July 12, 2007, Hexion and Huntsman signed a merger agreement whereby Hexion agreed to pay $28 per share in cash for 100% of Huntsman's stock. The total transaction value of the deal was approximately $10.6 billion, including assumed debt. The plaintiffs filed suit in this court on June 18, 2008 seeking declaratory judgment on three claims: (1) Hexion is not obligated to close if the combined company would be insolvent and its liability to Huntsman for failing to close is limited to no more than $325 million; (2) Huntsman has suffered a Company Material Adverse Effect ("MAE"); and (3) Apollo has no liability to Huntsman in connection with the merger agreement. On July 2, 2008, Huntsman filed its answer and counterclaims requesting declaratory judgment that: (1) Hexion knowingly and intentionally breached the merger agreement; (2) Huntsman has not suffered an MAE; and (3) Hexion has no right to terminate the merger agreement. Also, Huntsman's counterclaims seek an order that Hexion specifically perform its obligations under various sections of the merger agreement, or, alternatively, and in the event Hexion fails to perform, the award of full contract damages. . . .

Beginning on September 8, 2008, a six-day trial was held on Huntsman's counterclaims and counts I (damages limited to $325 million), II (material adverse effect), and IV (invalid extension of termination date) of Hexion's amended complaint.

C.   Negotiations Between The Parties In 2005 And 2006

In late 2005 and early 2006, Apollo and Hexion entered negotiations with Huntsman concerning a proposed transaction whereby Hexion would merge with Huntsman's specialty chemical business and Huntsman's commodity business would be spun out and acquired by Apollo. Hexion and Apollo performed substantial due diligence on Huntsman, but the deal died when Huntsman missed earnings targets and Apollo advised Huntsman that it could no longer justify the $25 per share price then being discussed.

D.   2007 Negotiations Leading To July 12, 2007 Merger Agreement

In May 2007, Huntsman, through its financial advisor Merrill Lynch & Co., Inc., began to solicit bids for the company. Apollo (through Hexion) and Basell, the world's largest polypropylene maker, emerged among the potential buyers. Huntsman signed confidentiality agreements and began to negotiate merger agreements with both Hexion and Basell. On June 25, 2007, Huntsman rejected Hexion's offer of $26 per share and executed a merger agreement with Basell for $25.25 per share. The same day, but after the agreement was signed, Hexion raised its bid to $27 per share. Basell refused to raise its bid, stating that its deal remained superior because it was more certain to close. On June 29, 2007, Huntsman reentered negotiations with Hexion after Hexion further increased its bid to $27.25 per share. On July 12, 2007, Huntsman terminated its deal with Basell and signed an all cash deal at $28 per share with Hexion.

E.   The Financing

One day before the signing of the merger agreement, Hexion signed a commitment letter with affiliates of Credit Suisse and Deutsche Bank (the "lending banks") to secure financing for the deal. In section 3.2(e) of the merger agreement, Hexion represented that the "aggregate proceeds contemplated to be provided by the Commitment Letter will be sufficient . . . to pay the aggregate Merger Consideration." The commitment letter required a "customary and reasonably satisfactory" solvency certificate from the Chief Financial Officer of Hexion, the Chief Financial Officer of Huntsman, or a reputable valuation firm as a condition precedent to the lending banks obligation to provide financing.

F.   July 12, 2007 Merger Agreement

Due to the existence of a signed agreement with Basell and Apollo's admittedly intense desire for the deal, Huntsman had significant negotiating leverage. As a result, the merger agreement is more than usually favorable to Huntsman. For example, it contains no financing contingency and requires Hexion to use its "reasonable best efforts" to consummate the financing. In addition, the agreement expressly provides for uncapped [*Editor: unlimited*] damages in the case of a "knowing and intentional breach of any covenant" by Hexion and for liquidated damages of $325 million in cases of other enumerated breaches. The narrowly tailored MAE clause is one of the few ways the merger agreement allows Hexion to walk away from the deal without paying Huntsman at least $325 million in liquidated damages.

G.   April 22, 2008: Huntsman Reports Poor First Quarter Of 2008

Initially, Hexion and Apollo were extremely excited about the deal with Huntsman. Apollo partner Jordan Zaken testified at trial that Apollo really wanted the deal and that "the industrial logic was very strong." Indeed, Hexion's April 2007 presentation materials regarding the potential transaction with Huntsman reflect that the Hexion/Huntsman combination would create the largest specialty chemical company in the world. While Huntsman's Pigments business had been slowing since shortly after signing, Hexion and Apollo's view of the deal did not seem to change dramatically until after receipt of Huntsman's disappointing first quarter numbers on April 22, 2008. Following receipt of these numbers, Apollo revised its deal model and concluded that the transaction would produce returns much lower than expected. At this time, Apollo also questioned whether Huntsman had experienced an MAE as defined in the merger agreement. . . .

The May 9 models, while showing unfavorable returns for Apollo and tight liquidity, do not clearly show insolvency.

After its May 9, 2008 meeting with counsel, perhaps realizing that the MAE argument was not strong, Apollo and its counsel began focusing on insolvency. However, under the merger agreement, Hexion had no right to terminate the agreement based on potential insolvency of the combined company or due to lack of financing. Also, Hexion would be subject to full contract damages if it "knowingly and intentionally" breached any of its covenants. Therefore, it appears that after May 9, 2008, Apollo and its counsel began to follow a carefully designed plan to obtain an insolvency opinion, publish that opinion (which it knew, or reasonably should have known, would frustrate the financing), and claim Hexion did not "knowingly and intentionally" breach its contractual obligations to close (due to the impossibility of obtaining financing without a solvency certificate).

I.   Duff & Phelps Is Hired To Support Apollo's Insolvency Theory

Watchell, Lipton, Rosen & Katz, Apollo's counsel, hired Duff & Phelps, LLC to support potential litigation, and Duff & Phelps personnel knew they were being hired for that purpose. . . .

. . .

L.   The Duff & Phelps Insolvency Opinion Is Unreliable

Duff & Phelps's June 18, 2008 insolvency opinion was produced with the knowledge that the opinion would potentially be used in litigation, was based on skewed numbers provided by Apollo, and was produced without any consultation with Huntsman management. These factors, taken together, render the Duff & Phelps opinion unreliable.

. . .

M.   The June 18, 2008 Lawsuit

After obtaining the Duff & Phelps insolvency opinion, Hexion, without notice to Huntsman, published that opinion as part of this lawsuit, very likely prejudicing the lending banks, the pension boards, and the FTC. Malcolm Price, a managing director at Credit Suisse, testified that, until the filing of the lawsuit, the bank had not questioned the solvency of the combined company or whether an MAE had occurred, although it had recorded large mark-to-market losses. Following publication of the insolvency opinion, Credit Suisse began to study the potential insolvency of the company. On September 5, Credit Suisse finished its own insolvency analysis, largely based on the deal model used by Duff & Phelps, and sharply reduced its expected losses on the financing. The Credit Suisse analysis showed insolvency under all three tests, by an even greater margin than the Duff & Phelps report. Currently, both lending banks have stated that they would be willing to meet their obligations to provide financing *if* a customary and reasonably satisfactory solvency certificate could be provided. At trial however, Hexion's CEO, Craig Morrison, agreed that publication of the Duff & Phelps opinion and the filing of the lawsuit "effectively kill[ed] the financing" and "make it virtually impossible for [the lending banks] to go forward with the financing." Nonetheless, Hexion still made the deliberate decision not to consult with Huntsman regarding the analysis prior to filing the lawsuit. Price admitted that it would be premature to draw a definite conclusion about solvency before closing. However, he also testified that he could not think of anything plausible that would change his view on solvency in the very near future and admitted that it would be financially advantageous to Credit Suisse if it did not have to honor its commitment letter. . . .

P.   The Huntsman Projections

. . .

[Huntsman produces higher estimates]

Just as Apollo's estimates for Huntsman's July 25, 2008 projections for EBITDA appear artificially depressed, Huntsman's EBITDA projections appear somewhat optimistic. Both sets of projections have been influenced by the potential or the reality of litigation. . . . However, the Duff & Phelps report and Hexion's projections of Huntsman EBITDA surely have affected the expectations of the analysts. . . .

Q. Huntsman's Solvency Analysis

Huntsman hired David Resnick, an expert on valuation and solvency, to review the Duff & Phelps report for errors. Resnick is the head of global restructuring and the co-head of investment banking in North America for Rothschild, Inc. Duff & Phelps in its June 18 report found a funding deficit of $858 million. Resnick's report finds a surplus of $124 million. The majority of the difference is made up of U.S. and U.K. pension liability, costs related to refinancing the Huntsman debt, the Apollo fee, and timing of divestiture proceeds. [The court discusses the expert's testimony; the expert used the language we have seen in the Valuation section, including the comparables analysis and DCF]. . .

II.

Hexion argues that its obligation to close is excused as a result of a Company Material Adverse Effect in the business of Huntsman. For the reasons detailed below, Hexion's argument fails.

A. The "Chemical Industry" Carve-Outs are Inapplicable

Section 6.2(e) of the merger agreement states that Hexion's obligation to close is conditioned on the absence of "any event, change, effect or development that has had or is reasonably expected to have, individually or in the aggregate," an MAE. MAE is defined in section 3.1(a)(ii) as:

> any occurrence, condition, change, event or effect that is materially adverse to the financial condition, business, or results of operations of the Company and its Subsidiaries, taken as a whole; *provided, however,* that in no event shall any of the following constitute a Company Material Adverse Effect: (A) any occurrence, condition, change, event or effect resulting from or relating to changes in general economic or financial market conditions, except in the event, and only to the extent, that such occurrence, condition, change, event or effect has had a disproportionate effect on the Company and its Subsidiaries, taken as a whole, as compared to other Persons engaged in the chemical industry; (B) any occurrence, condition, change, event or effect that affects the chemical industry generally (including changes in commodity prices, general market prices and regulatory changes affecting the chemical industry generally) except in the event, and only to the extent, that such occurrence, condition, change, event or effect has had a disproportionate

effect on the Company and its Subsidiaries, taken as a whole, as compared to other Persons engaged in the chemical industry. . . .

The parties disagree as to the proper reading of this definition. Hexion argues that the relevant standard to apply in judging whether an MAE has occurred is to compare Huntsman's performance since the signing of the merger agreement and its expected future performance to the rest of the chemical industry. Huntsman, for its part, argues that in determining whether an MAE has occurred the court need reach the issue of comparing Huntsman to its peers if and only if it has first determined that there has been an "occurrence, condition, change, event or effect that is materially adverse to the financial condition, business, or results of operations of the Company and its Subsidiaries, taken as a whole. . . ." Huntsman here has the better argument. The plain meaning of the carve-outs found in the proviso is to prevent certain occurrences which would *otherwise* be MAE's being found to be so. If a catastrophe were to befall the chemical industry and cause a material adverse effect in Huntsman's business, the carve-outs would prevent this from qualifying as an MAE under the Agreement. But the converse is not true—Huntsman's performance being disproportionately worse than the chemical industry in general does not, in itself, constitute an MAE. Thus, unless the court concludes that the company has suffered an MAE as defined in the language coming before the proviso, the court need not consider the application of the chemical industry carve-outs.

Hexion bases its argument that Huntsman has suffered an MAE principally on a comparison between Huntsman and other chemical industry firms. Hexion's expert witness, Telly Zachariades of The Valence Group, largely focused on this at trial. Zachariades testified regarding a comparison of the performance of Huntsman during the second half of 2007 and first half of 2008, relative to two sets of benchmark companies which he chose as representative of the industry—the Bloomberg World Chemical Index and the Chemical Week 75 Index. Zachariades compared Huntsman to these two benchmarks in a variety of different areas, both backward and forward-looking, and, in each, found Huntsman significantly worse than the mean, and, in most, in the bottom decile. This potentially would be compelling evidence if it was necessary to reach the carve-outs, although Huntsman's expert, Mark Zmijewski, managed to cast doubt on Zachariades's analysis. However, because, as discussed below, Huntsman has not suffered an MAE, the court need not reach the question of whether Huntsman's performance has been disproportionately worse than the chemical industry taken as a whole.

B.   Huntsman Has Not Suffered An MAE

For the purpose of determining whether an MAE has occurred, changes in corporate fortune must be examined in the context in which the parties were transacting. In the absence of evidence to the contrary, a corporate acquirer may be assumed to be purchasing the target as part of a long-term strategy. The important consideration therefore is whether there has been an adverse change in the target's business that is consequential to the company's long-term earnings power over a commercially reasonable period, which one would expect to be measured in years rather than months. A buyer faces a heavy burden when it attempts to invoke a material adverse effect clause in order to avoid its obligation to close. Many commentators have noted that Delaware courts have never found a material adverse effect to have occurred in the context of a merger agreement. This is not a coincidence. The ubiquitous material adverse effect clause should be seen as providing a "backstop protecting the acquirer from the occurrence of unknown events that substantially threaten the overall earnings potential of the target in a durationally-significant manner. A short-term hiccup in earnings should not suffice; rather [an adverse change] should be material when viewed from the longer-term perspective of a reasonable acquirer." This, of course, is not to say that evidence of a significant decline in earnings by the target corporation during the period after signing but prior to the time appointed for closing is irrelevant. Rather, it means that for such a decline to constitute a material adverse effect, poor earnings results must be expected to persist significantly into the future.

Hexion protests being shouldered with the burden of proof here, urging the court that Huntsman bears the burden of showing the absence of an MAE, because that is a condition precedent to closing. . . . Hexion argues that *IBP*, in placing the burden to prove a material adverse effect on the buyer, is distinguishable because in *IBP* the material adverse effect clause was drafted in the form of a representation and warranty that no material adverse effect had occurred. But material adverse effect clauses are strange animals, *sui generis* among their contract clause brethren. It is by no means clear to this court that the form in which a material adverse effect clause is drafted (i.e., as a representation, or warranty, or a condition to closing), absent more specific evidence regarding the intention of the parties, should be dispositive on the allocation of the burden of proof. Typically, conditions precedent are easily ascertainable objective facts, generally that a party performed some particular act or that some independent event has occurred. A material adverse effect clause does not easily fit into such a mold, and it is not at all clear that it ought to be treated the same for this purpose. Rather, for the same practical reasons that the court in *IBP* cites, it seems the preferable view, and the one the court adopts, that absent clear language to the contrary, the burden of proof with respect to a material adverse effect rests on the party seeking to excuse its performance under the contract. . . . [A]s the parties jointly stipulate, the question is "[w]hether Hexion has established that a 'Company Material Adverse

Effect,' as defined in the Merger Agreement, has occurred." This again places the burden to show the existence of an MAE squarely on Hexion.

. . .

[The court concludes that EBITDA is a better measure than earnings per share given that earnings per share is "very much a function of the capital structure of the company, reflecting the effects of leverage."]

Hexion focuses its argument that Huntsman has suffered an MAE along several lines: (1) disappointing results in Huntsman's earnings performance over the period from July 2007 through the present; (2) Huntsman's increase in net debt since signing, contrary to the expectations of the parties; and (3) underperformance in Huntsman's Textile Effects and Pigments lines of business.

1. Huntsman Has A Difficult Year After The Signing Of The Merger Agreement

There is no question that Huntsman's results from the time of signing in July 2007 until the end of the first half of 2008 have been disappointing. Huntsman's first-half 2008 EBITDA was down 19.9% year-over-year from its first-half 2007 EBITDA. And its second-half 2007 EBITDA was 22% below the projections Huntsman presented to bidders in June 2007 for the rest of the year.

Realizing, however, that these results, while disappointing, were not compelling as a basis to claim an MAE, Hexion focused its arguments on Huntsman's repeated misses from its forecasts. In its "Project Nimbus" forecasts, Huntsman management projected 2008 consolidated EBITDA of $1.289 billion. As of August 1, 2008, Huntsman management projected EBITDA for 2008 was $879 million, a 32% decrease from the forecast the year before. Hexion points to these shortfalls from the 2007 projections and claims that Huntsman's failure to live up to its projections are key to the MAE analysis.

But this cannot be so. Section 5.11(b) of the merger agreement explicitly disclaims any representation or warranty by Huntsman with respect to "any projections, forecasts or other estimates, plans or budgets of future revenues, expenses or expenditures, future results of operations . . . , future cash flows . . . or future financial condition . . . of [Huntsman] or any of its Subsidiaries . . . heretofore or hereafter delivered to or made available to [Hexion or its affiliates]. . . ." The parties specifically allocated the risk to Hexion that Huntsman's performance would not live up to management's expectations at the time. If Hexion wanted the short-term forecasts of Huntsman warranted by Huntsman, it could have negotiated for that. It could have tried to negotiate a lower base price and something akin to an earn-out, based not on Huntsman's post-closing performance but on its performance between signing and closing.

Creative investment bankers and deal lawyers could have structured, at the agreement of the parties, any number of potential terms to shift to Huntsman some or all of the risk that Huntsman would fail to hit its forecast targets. But none of those things happened. Instead, Hexion agreed that the contract contained no representation or warranty with respect to Huntsman's forecasts. To now allow the MAE analysis to hinge on Huntsman's failure to hit its forecast targets during the period leading up to closing would eviscerate, if not render altogether void, the meaning of section 5.11(b). It is a maxim of contract law that, given ambiguity between potentially conflicting terms, a contract should be read so as not to render any term meaningless. Thus, the correct interpretation cannot be that section 6.2(e) voids section 5.11(b), making it a condition precedent to Hexion's obligation to consummate the merger that Huntsman substantially meet its forecast targets. Rather, the correct analysis is that Huntsman's failure to hit its forecasts cannot be a predicate to the determination of an MAE in Huntsman's business. Moreover, at trial Jordan Zaken, one of the Apollo partners involved in negotiating the Huntsman deal on behalf of Hexion, admitted on cross-examination that Hexion and Apollo never fully believed Huntsman's forecasts. Those forecasts, therefore, cannot be the basis of a claim of an MAE, since they never formed part of the expectations of the parties (in a strict contractual sense) to begin with.

Rather, as Huntsman's expert Zmijewski testified at trial, the terms "financial condition, business, or results of operations" are terms of art, to be understood with reference to their meaning in Regulation S–K and Item 7, the "Management's Discussion and Analysis of Financial Condition and Results of Operations" section of the financial statements public companies are required to file with the SEC. In this section, a company is required to disclose its financial result for the period being reported, along with its pro forma financial results for the same time period for each of the previous two years. Zmijewski testified at trial that these results are analyzed by comparing the results in each period with the results in the same period for the prior year (i.e., year-end 2007 results to year-end 2006 results, first-quarter 2005 results to first-quarter 2004 results, and so forth). The proper benchmark then for analyzing these changes with respect to an MAE, according to Zmijewski (and the analysis the court adopts here), is to examine each year and quarter and compare it to the prior year's equivalent period. Through this lens, it becomes clear that no MAE has occurred. Huntsman's 2007 EBITDA was only 3% below its 2006 EBITDA, and, according to Huntsman management forecasts, 2008 EBITDA will only be 7% below 2007 EBITDA. Even using Hexion's much lower estimate of Huntsman's 2008 EBITDA, Huntsman's 2008 EBITDA would still be only 11% below its 2007 EBITDA. And although Huntsman's fourth quarter 2007 EBITDA was 19% below its third quarter 2007 results, which were in turn 3%

below its second quarter 2007 results, Huntsman has historically been down on a quarter-over-quarter basis in each of the third and fourth quarters of the year. Moreover, comparing the trailing-twelve-months EBITDA for second quarter 2007 to second quarter 2008, the 2008 result is only down 6% from 2007.

Of course, the expected future performance of the target company is also relevant to a material adverse effect analysis. Hexion, on the basis of its estimates of Huntsman's future profitability, urges that Huntsman has or is expected to suffer an MAE. Hexion estimates that Huntsman will earn only $817 million in 2008, and that its earnings will contract further in 2009, to $809 million.

Huntsman responds with its own projections, that it will generate $878 million of EBITDA in 2008, and $1.12 billion of EBITDA in 2009. To support its projections, Huntsman offered testimony at trial by [various high-level officials] . . . While the court recognizes that management's expectations for a company's business often skew towards the overly optimistic, especially in the presence of litigation, the court ultimately concludes that Hexion's projections reflect an overly pessimistic view of Huntsman's future earnings.

The fact that Hexion offered little detail as to how it arrived at its projections for Huntsman's business also diminishes the weight its projections deserve. Ultimately, the likely outcome for Huntsman's 2009 EBITDA is somewhere in the middle. This proposition is confirmed by current analyst estimates for Huntsman 2009 EBITDA, which average around $924 million. This would represent a mere 3.6% decrease in EBITDA from 2006 to 2009, and a result essentially flat from 2007 to 2009. The court also notes that in two of the four original deal models Apollo produced in June of 2007 to justify its $28 per share offer, Huntsman's projected 2009 EBITDA was significantly below this estimate, at $833 million in the "Hexion Management Flat Case," and at a mere $364 million in its recession case. . . . Thus in only one of Hexion's three views of future operating performance of Huntsman at the time of signing did Huntsman perform better in 2009 than it is presently expected to by analysts.

These results do not add up to an MAE, particularly in the face of the macroeconomic challenges Huntsman has faced since the middle of 2007 as a result of rapidly increased crude oil and natural gas prices and unfavorable foreign exchange rate changes. Ultimately, the burden is on Hexion to demonstrate the existence of an MAE in order to negate its obligation to close, and that is a burden it cannot meet here.

2.   Huntsman's Net Debt Expands During The Same Period

Hexion urges that Huntsman's results of operations cannot be viewed in isolation, but should be examined in conjunction with Huntsman's increase in net debt. . . . [Contrary to its forecast,] rather than shrinking by a billion dollars, Huntsman's net debt since signing has expanded by over a quarter of a billion dollars.

Hexion points to this debt expansion as further evidence (when combined with the results of operations discussed above) of an MAE based on changes in the financial condition of Huntsman. Huntsman, of course, points out that this increase in net debt from signing until the present is only on the order of 5% or 6% (depending upon which date one chooses to measure Huntsman's debt, since weekly changes in the total debt as a result of working capital fluctuations can be as much as plus or minus $100 million), a far cry from an MAE based on financial condition. Hexion responds that this view ignores the fact that "post-signing Huntsman received $794 million in cash proceeds from divestitures that were to have been used to repay debt. The assets were sold along with their revenue generating capacity. An apples-to-apples comparison (adjusting to eliminate the divestiture proceeds) would show an increase in net debt of 32%." This argument initially appears attractive, but examination of Apollo's initial deal-model negates any persuasive power it might have initially held. In all four of the cases which Apollo modeled, Huntsman's net debt at closing is assumed to be $4.1 billion. All of Hexion's assumptions about the value of the deal were predicated on Huntsman net debt levels on that order-the projected decrease in Huntsman's net debt of a billion dollars was simply an added attraction. Hexion cannot now claim that a 5% increase in net debt from its expectations in valuing the deal, even combined with the reduced earnings, should excuse it from its obligation to perform on the merger agreement.

3.   Challenging Times At Textile Effects And Pigments

Both in its pretrial brief and at trial, Hexion focused most of its attention on two Huntsman divisions which have been particularly troubled since the signing of the merger agreement-Pigments and Textile Effects. These two divisions were expected to compose only 25% of Huntsman's adjusted EBITDA in 2008–14% coming from Pigments, and 11% coming from Textile Effects. Little space need be spent on this argument as it falls under its own weight.

First, as already discussed, under the terms of the merger agreement, an MAE is to be determined based on an examination of Huntsman taken as a whole. A close examination of two divisions anticipated to generate at most a fourth of Huntsman's EBITDA is therefore only tangentially related to the issue. Although the results in each of these two divisions, if standing alone, might be materially impaired, as already illustrated above, Huntsman as a whole is not materially impaired by their results. If it is unconvincing to say

Huntsman's business as a whole has been materially changed for the worse, it is even more unconvincing to claim that 75% of Huntsman's business is fine, but that troubles in the other 25% materially changes the business as a whole.

Additionally, there is reason to believe that much of Huntsman's troubles in each of these divisions are short-term in nature. . . . [The court gives reasons, including inherited problems which are being addressed, and a "perfect storm" of macroeconomic challenges.] In addition, Huntsman has been able to develop some traction in passing price increases into the market since July 2008.

As for Pigments, titanium dioxide is a notoriously cyclical business, which Apollo well knew at the time of bidding. During an initial presentation meeting with the management of Huntsman, Josh Harris of Apollo expressed to Peter Huntsman that Apollo knew as much about the titanium dioxide business as Huntsman did. . . . Hexion focuses its argument on Huntsman's use predominantly of the sulfate process, while the majority of its competitors use the chlorine process for manufacturing titanium dioxide. As a result of a recent run-up in the price of sulfuric acid, a key input to the sulfate process, Huntsman has thus faced increased input costs that its competitors have not shared. Nevertheless, Tronox, one of Huntsman's major competitors in the pigments business and a user of the chlorine process, is itself facing financial distress, partly as a result of its own cost increases, illustrating that the present pain in the pigments business is not restricted to those manufacturers using the sulfate process.

IV.

Hexion strenuously argues, and urges the court to declare, that on a pro forma basis (assuming the merger closes on the financing terms contemplated in the commitment letter), the combined entity will be insolvent. In support of its contention, Hexion offers the opinion it obtained from Duff & Phelps, based on Hexion's gloomy projections of Huntsman's future performance. It also points to a rudimentary solvency analysis done by a Merrill Lynch analyst in May 2008.

Huntsman argues, in opposition, that solvency is not even an issue under the merger agreement and, thus, is not a proper subject for declaratory relief at this time. Huntsman also contends that the combined entity (1) will be solvent; (2) to the extent that it is not solvent, that would come as a result of Hexion's knowing and intentional breach of contract, and (3) Hexion is, in any event, obligated to put in whatever equity is necessary to close the transaction and make the combined entity solvent. To support its argument regarding solvency, Huntsman relies on Resnick's expert valuation opinion, based on Huntsman's revised July 2008 projections. In addition, at trial Huntsman introduced evidence suggesting that American Appraisal Associates, Inc. has determined that, if engaged for that purpose, it expected to be able to deliver a favorable solvency opinion. Even more recently, Huntsman filed a Form 8–K stating that it has engaged American Appraisal for this purpose, and asks the court to take judicial notice of that fact.

The court thus finds itself asked to referee a battle of the experts in which there is no clear answer and no possibility of splitting the difference. For the reasons briefly discussed below, the court determines not to reach the issue of solvency at this time because that issue will not arise unless and until a solvency letter or opinion is delivered to the lending banks and those banks then either fund or refuse to fund the transaction.

To begin with, Huntsman is correct that the solvency of the combined entity is not a condition precedent to Hexion's obligations under the merger agreement. In fact, looking only at terms of the merger agreement, Hexion's avowed inability to deliver a suitable solvency opinion does not negate its obligation to close: rather, the receipt of such an opinion is merely a condition precedent to Huntsman's duty to close, protects Huntsman (and its shareholders), and is, therefore, waivable by Huntsman. To put it differently, Hexion's fear that it has agreed to pay too high a price for Huntsman does not provide a basis for it to get out of the transaction.

The issue of solvency is only relevant to the obligation of the lending banks to fund when the time comes for them to do so. Paragraph 6 of exhibit D to the commitment letter makes it a condition precedent to funding that the lending banks receive a reasonably satisfactory solvency letter in such form and substance as has been customary in prior Apollo transaction. But Huntsman, in order to avoid or ameliorate the very situation it now finds itself in, specifically bargained for and obtained the right to have its CFO provide such a letter. Esplin, Huntsman's CFO, testified that he was prepared to provide the required letter. Moreover, it now appears that Huntsman has retained American Appraisal to furnish a back up opinion to support such a letter.

Thus, there is only one point in time at which it is necessary to make a determination of solvency—at (or as of) closing. For the reasons discussed elsewhere in this opinion, the court is issuing a judgment and order that will require Hexion to specifically perform its covenants and obligations under the merger agreement (other than its obligation to close). Thus, if the other conditions to closing are met, Hexion will be obligated to call upon the lending banks to perform on their funding obligations. In that circumstance, the banks will then have to choose whether to fund on the basis of the solvency letter delivered by Huntsman or, instead, reject that letter as unsatisfactory and refuse to fund. If the lending banks refuse to fund, they will, of course, be opening themselves to the potential for litigation, including a claim for damages for breach of contract. In such litigation, the prospective insolvency of the combined entity would likely be an important issue.

If the banks agree to fund, Hexion will then have to determine whether it considers it in its best interests to close the transaction, or instead refuse to close, subjecting itself to the possibility of an additional finding of knowing and intentional breach of contract and uncapped contract damages. If Hexion chooses to close, the issue will be moot. If it does not, the posture of the matter, and the decision presented to the court, will be far more concrete and capable of judicial resolution than the issue now framed by the parties.

[T]he question of whether the combined entity would be solvent or not. . . . may arise in the future in the course of this litigation or some related action, but it is not now . . . ripe for a judicial determination.

V.

Huntsman asks the court to enter a judgment ordering Hexion and its merger subsidiary, Nimbus, to specifically perform their covenants and obligations under the merger agreement. . . . [T]he court finds that, under the agreement, Huntsman cannot force Hexion to consummate the merger, but that Huntsman is entitled to a judgment ordering Hexion to specifically perform its other covenants and obligations."

H. COVENANTS AND ADDITIONAL AGREEMENTS

The Covenants and Additional Agreements section of the merger agreement deals with actions of the buyer and the seller during the interim period between signing and closing. Some contract drafters will separate Covenants from Additional Agreements. The reason for separating the two is relatively straightforward. Covenants are typically commitments by a seller, and sometimes a buyer with respect to the operation of the seller or the buyer's business during the interim period. Additional Agreements are a series of commitments made by both parties to each other regarding the actions required to complete the merger transaction.

1. COVENANTS

The most common covenant that a seller will give to a buyer is a conduct of business covenant. One of the biggest risks a buyer faces during the interim period is that a seller, who still has control over the operations of the business, will operate it in such a way as to extract value. Especially if the interim period is lengthy, the risk that the seller might manage the business in a manner detrimental to the buyer can be significant, and the value diminution can be significant as well. For example, if the seller has large cash balances, the seller can declare a cash dividend and thereby appropriate the company's cash before the transaction closes. Alternatively, the seller may attempt to sell a valuable subsidiary or other line of business and perhaps distribute the proceeds as a dividend. Or, the seller may make large, perhaps value reducing, capital investments without the approval of the buyer, or make loans to its executives. Hence, conduct of business covenants addressing and limiting what the seller can do during the interim period are an extremely important part of the merger agreement. Below you will find relevant portions of the conduct of business covenant given by Dell:

> From and after the date hereof and prior to the Effective Time . . . the Company shall, and shall cause each of its Subsidiaries to, conduct its business in the ordinary course of business and use its commercially reasonable efforts to preserve in all material respects its business organization and maintain in all material respects existing relations and goodwill with Governmental Authorities, customers, suppliers, creditors, lessors and other Persons having material business relationships with the Company or any of its Subsidiaries.

The covenant also specifically prohibits Dell from undertaking any of the following actions without the express prior permission of the buyer: amending its certificate of incorporation or bylaws; undertaking a stock split or other reclassification of its capital stock; issuing any additional stock or other equity interests, including stock options; issuing any quarterly cash dividends in excess of $0.08/share; repurchasing or redeeming any capital stock of the company; making any corporate acquisition in excess of $150 million; making any loans or capital contributions in excess of $75 million; incurring any indebtedness in excess of $25 million; or settling any litigation against the company in excess of $300 million.

The conduct of business covenant is a recognition that during the interim period, the seller's and buyer's incentives diverge in some important respects. An analogy is to a homeowner who has contracted to sell her house. She might not do maintenance that she would do were she continuing to own the house; she might antagonize the neighbors rather than being solicitous to them, given that she will soon not have to deal with them. The buyer would inherit these problems. (Another helpful analogy is to renting a car. Compare how people drive a short-term rental to how they drive their own cars.)

An overly constraining covenant could, however, cause damage to the business. It may even be deemed by the federal government to give too much control to the buyer before antitrust clearance has been given, constituting a violation of the antitrust laws. Consequently, this covenant as usually negotiated permits the seller to continue to conduct its business in the normal course while deferring, or at least seeking the permission of the buyer for, non-ordinary course expenditures or decisions.

2. ADDITIONAL AGREEMENTS

In the additional agreements section, both the buyer and the seller make certain commitments regarding the steps needed for the transaction to close. Most mergers require some sort of government or regulatory approval prior to closing; filings will need to be made, such as filings with antitrust authorities and the SEC. (These filings are discussed in Chapters V–VIII). The seller will need to hold a shareholder meeting; the buyer may need to do so as well. The relevant portion of Dell's agreement to call a shareholder meeting for the purpose of approving the merger is below:

> Stockholders Meeting. . . . [T]he Company shall take all action necessary in accordance with the DGCL and its certificate of incorporation and bylaws to duly call, give notice of, convene and hold a meeting of its stockholders as promptly as practicable after the Proxy Statement is cleared by the SEC for mailing to the Company's shareholders, subject to compliance with the DGCL and the Exchange Act, for the purpose of obtaining the Company Stockholder Approvals . . .

When parties want the deal to proceed as scheduled, they will diligently work towards that goal. However, if, after the parties sign a merger agreement, one side becomes less enthusiastic about the deal, that side may lack the motivation to take the actions required to move towards closing, and may even attempt to prevent the conditions to closing from being met, as seems to have happened in *Hunstman*, discussed above. (A consumer-focused example is of a buyer who contracts to buy a house but only if she can obtain financing, but then does not do enough to get the financing. Home purchase contracts deal with this problem by specifying what a buyer has to do—for instance, approach some number of lending institutions and provide them with the requested information, and accept market-rate financing that is offered.) Consequently, the additional agreements section specifies the actions required to move the deal forward towards closing, and attempts to specify the level of effort that both sides are required to expend. In the provision above, the parties sought to ensure compliance by requiring that Dell call a shareholder meeting ("The Company shall take all action necessary. . ."). At times, parties may want to dictate even higher levels of commitment to accomplishing the deal. Consider the recent acquisition of

Family Dollar by Dollar Tree. Dollar Tree committed to divest itself of any and all retail stores required in order to secure antitrust approval for the transaction, a so-called "hell or high water" provision:

> ... Parent shall, solely to the extent necessary ... so as to permit the Closing to occur by the End Date, propose, negotiate, effect, become subject to, and agree to conduct remedies and the sale, divestiture, license, holding separate, and other disposition of, changes to, and restriction and limitation on, any and all retail stores and any and all assets, properties and rights in or about the retail store premises (including the arrangement for all such sales and divestitures in a timely manner sufficiently in advance of the End Date ... and take all such action and actions that would in the aggregate have a similar effect ...[13]

Only the most motivated buyers will agree to this provision. Indeed, such a provision may act as an invitation for antitrust authorities to order a divestiture, or a greater divestiture than they might otherwise have ordered. Most acquirers would probably not agree to such an expansive provision, instead agreeing to some lesser, albeit considerable, obligation, such as the use of their "best efforts," "reasonable best efforts," or "reasonable efforts."

What does "best efforts" mean? Courts are often asked to weigh in on this question. Even if the agreement specifies the use of "best efforts," courts generally read a reasonableness qualifier into the obligation. In *Bloor v. Falstaff* Judge Friendly noted that a promise to use "best efforts" does not strip the party making the promise of its "right to give reasonable consideration to its own interests."[14] A Massachusetts case, *Macksey v. Egan* noted with apparent approval authority to the effect that "best efforts" in the natural sense of the words [requires (only)] ... that the party put its muscles to work to perform with full energy and fairness the relevant express promises and reasonable implications therefrom." "[B]est efforts" did not entail a duty to make an investment that would be significantly different in kind from that contemplated by the Agreement, involving additional outlay or alteration of the business risks."[15] Notwithstanding the language in these cases, practitioners generally regard "best efforts" as requiring all efforts short of bankruptcy, an example of where practitioner "lore" seems at odds with the actual law. Thus, parties are more apt to use formulations such as "reasonable best efforts," "commercially reasonable efforts" or "reasonable efforts." At

---

[13] http://www.sec.gov/Archives/edgar/data/935703/000093570314000064/a8k090514 amendedmergeragreem.pdf.

[14] *Bloor v. Falstaff Brewing Corporation*, 601 F.2d 609, 614 (2d Cir.1979).

[15] *Macksey v. Egan*, 36 Mass. App. Ct. 463, 472, 633 N.E 2d 408, 414, (1994).

least one commentator has remarked that in practice these (including "best efforts") all appear to require the same level of "effort."[16]

What "best efforts," including "reasonable" such efforts, require is not completely clear, but further clarification is either impossible or inadvisable. Parties are usually reluctant, for good reason, to specify in advance the level of effort they will expend, or the precise steps they will take, to move forward towards closing a deal. By requiring a particular level of effort, parties are committed to a baseline level of effort, but not beyond a point where efforts no longer make commercial sense.

3. NO-SHOP PROVISIONS

Agreements to acquire public companies typically include provisions that "protect" the deal. Common types of deal protection provisions include "exclusivity" provisions, which limit the seller's dealings with other potential buyers. These may take the form of no-shop or even no-talk provisions. No-shop provisions restrict sellers and their agents from actively seeking an alternative buyer. Typically, no-shop provisions allow a seller to respond to an unsolicited bid but do not allow a seller to initiate discussions with a potential bidder or use a signed agreement to actively shop a target. A term used is "window shop"—the target is "in the window," available to be considered for purchase. A variant on the no-shop, the "no-talk" provisions goes further by prohibiting sellers from sharing proprietary and non-public information or engaging in any discussions with a potential subsequent bidder, even an unsolicited bidder. In preventing sellers from sharing any non-public information or speaking with subsequent bidders, no-talk provisions can shut down a potential bid by denying a subsequent bidder the information it would require to be willing to generate a competitive bid. Courts have held that strict no-talk provisions are troubling because they "prevent a board from meeting its duty to make an informed judgment with respect to even considering whether to negotiate with a third party."[17] No-shop provisions, too, are highly scrutinized by courts (albeit less so than no-talk provisions) especially if a target has several bidders or is subject to *Revlon* duties or both, something we discuss further in Chapter XVIII.

The following discusses the proper scope of a no-shop and no-talk provision:

> Virtually every public merger agreement includes covenants, often referred to as "no-shop covenants," restricting the target's ability to negotiate with an alternative bidder. Sometimes the no-shop covenants take effect immediately upon signing the

---

[16] *See* Kenneth A. Adams, *Understanding 'Best Efforts' and Its Variants (Including Drafting Recommendations)*, 50 PRAC. LAW. 11 (2004).

[17] *Phelps Dodge Corporation v. Cyprus Amax Minerals Company*, No. CIV.A. 17383, 1999 WL 1054255, *1 (Del. Ch. 1999).

merger agreement, while other times they spring into effect after a period of time during which the target is permitted to actively solicit competing offers.

Typically, the no-shop covenants require the target to terminate any existing negotiations with respect to "acquisition proposals" and not to initiate, solicit or otherwise facilitate any new negotiations with respect to an "acquisition proposal." Because the no-shop covenants do not apply to all transactions—only acquisition proposals—the definition of "acquisition proposal" is a key point of negotiation.... [T]ypically an "acquisition proposal" is defined as a transaction involving at least 15% or 20% of the target's equity or assets....

No-shop covenants are rarely absolute. That is, notwithstanding the no-shop covenants, a target will almost always be permitted to engage in negotiations with respect to an acquisition proposal if certain requirements are satisfied. In some merger agreements, one of those requirements is that the target's board of directors determines that its fiduciary duties necessitate engaging in such negotiations. However, not all merger agreements contain this requirement ... and those that do contain this requirement are not uniform in their formulation of the determination to be made by the target's board of directors. For example, a more buyer-friendly formulation may require that the target's board determine that not engaging in negotiations "would be a breach of its fiduciary duties," whereas a more seller-friendly formulation may require a determination that not engaging in negotiations "would be reasonably likely to be inconsistent with its fiduciary duties."[18]

As the foregoing suggests, no-shop provisions are heavily negotiated, with the most pro-buyer ones restricting the seller's conduct the most, and the most pro-seller ones containing fewer restrictions.

Below you will find the no-shop provision for Valeant's acquisition of another pharmaceutical company, Salix.

> 5.4 No Solicitation of Transactions. (a) Subject to Section 5.4(b), from and after the date of this Agreement until the Effective Time ... the Company shall not, and shall cause the Company Subsidiaries and the Company Representatives not to, directly or indirectly: (i) initiate, solicit or knowingly encourage (including by way of providing information) or facilitate the submission of any inquiries, proposals or offers or any other

---

[18] Robert Little et al, *No-Shops and Fiduciary Outs: A Survey of 2012 Public Merger Agreements*, GIBSON DUNN M&A REPORT Winter 2013, available at http://www.gibsondunn.com/publications/Documents/MAReport–Winter2013.pdf.

efforts or attempts that constitute, or would reasonably be expected to lead to, any Acquisition Proposal or engage in any discussions or negotiations or otherwise cooperate with or assist or participate in or facilitate any such inquiries, proposals, offers, discussions or negotiations, (ii) furnish to any Person any nonpublic information in connection with an Acquisition Proposal or any inquiry, proposal or offer that would reasonably be expected to lead to an Acquisition Proposal, [(iii) and (iv) effect a Change of Board Recommendation, as defined in the agreement and discussed in the next subsection below], (v) enter into any . . . agreement . . . relating to an Acquisition Proposal or . . . requiring the Company to abandon, terminate or fail to consummate the transactions contemplated hereby or breach its obligations hereunder. . . , or (vi) resolve, propose or agree to do any of the foregoing. The Company shall immediately cease and cause to be terminated any activities, discussion or negotiation with any Persons conducted theretofore by the Company, the Company Subsidiaries or any Company Representatives with respect to any Acquisition Proposal and request to be returned or destroyed all confidential information provided by or on behalf of the Company or any Company Subsidiary to such Person.

Notice the breadth of the prohibition above. Notice, also, however, that there are carveouts, or exceptions, described below. As you have seen and will continue to see, the structure of a broad prohibition with exceptions is a common one.

(b) Notwithstanding anything to the contrary contained in Section 5.4(a), if at any time following the date of this Agreement and prior to the Acceptance Time (i) the Company has received an unsolicited bona fide written Acquisition Proposal from a third party, (ii)(A) such Acquisition Proposal . . . did not result from a breach of this Section 5.4 and the Company has complied with the terms of this Section 5.4 in all respects with respect to such Acquisition Proposal . . . and (B) the Company has not breached this Section 5.4 in any material respect, (iii) the Company Board determines in good faith, after consultation with its financial advisors of nationally recognized reputation . . . and outside counsel, that such Acquisition Proposal constitutes or could reasonably be expected to result in a Superior Proposal and (iv) after consultation with its outside counsel, the Company Board determines in good faith that failure to take such action would be inconsistent with its fiduciary duties to the stockholders of the Company under applicable Law, then the Company . . . may (A) furnish information with respect to the Company . . . to the Person making such Acquisition Proposal and (B) participate in discussions or negotiations with the Person making such Acquisition Proposal regarding such Acquisition Proposal; provided that the Company (x) will not . . . disclose any nonpublic information to such Person without first entering into an Acceptable Confidentiality Agreement and (y) will promptly (and in no event later than 24 hours after providing such information) provide to Parent any information concerning the Company or the Company Subsidiaries provided to such other Person not previously provided to Parent.

Recall the memo quoted above concerning the proper scope of no-shop provisions. Note that the Company is permitted to take certain actions in furtherance of a possible alternative transaction with another party, including the provision of information to, and participation in negotiations with, the other party, if "the Company Board determines in good faith that failure to take such action would be inconsistent with its fiduciary duties to the stockholders of the Company under applicable Law." Note that the acquirer, Parent, is to be given any information concerning the Company or its subsidiaries given to the other party.

(c) The Company shall promptly (and in any event within 24 hours) notify Parent in the event that the Company, any Company Subsidiary or any Company Representative receives (i) any Acquisition Proposal or indication by any Person that it is considering making an Acquisition Proposal, (ii) any request for non-public information relating to the Company . . . other than requests for information unrelated to an Acquisition Proposal or (iii) any inquiry or request for discussions or negotiations regarding any Acquisition Proposal. The Company shall notify Parent promptly (and in any event within 24 hours) of the identity of such Person and provide Parent a copy of such Acquisition Proposal, indication, inquiry or request (or, where no such copy is available, a reasonably detailed description of such Acquisition Proposal, indication, inquiry or request), including any modifications thereto. The Company shall keep Parent reasonably informed on a current basis (and in any event at Parent's request and otherwise no later than 24 hours after the occurrence of any changes, developments, discussions or negotiations) of the status of any Acquisition Proposal, indication, inquiry or request (including the terms and conditions thereof and of any modification thereto), and any material developments, discussions and negotiations. Without limiting the foregoing, the Company shall promptly (and in any event within 24 hours) notify Parent orally and in writing if it determines to begin providing information or to engage in discussions or negotiations concerning an Acquisition Proposal pursuant to Section 5.4(b).

Note that the Company is required to give the Parent complete information on a possible alternative Acquisition Proposal. The next provision sets forth the conditions under which the Company can accept such a proposal. One condition is that the Parent has first been allowed to match the offer. This is discussed further in the next Subsection, on Change of Board Recommendation.

(d) Notwithstanding anything to the contrary contained in Section 5.4(a), but subject to Section 5.4(f) [relating to the Parent's right to match another acquisition proposal], if the Company receives an unsolicited Acquisition Proposal which the Company Board concludes in good faith, after consultation with outside counsel and its financial advisors, constitutes a Superior Proposal [*Editor: A Superior Proposal is defined as "an unsolicited written bona fide proposal or offer constituting an Acquisition Proposal . . . , and which, in the good faith judgment of the Company Board (after consultation with its financial advisors of nationally recognized reputation . . . and outside counsel), taking into account the various legal, financial and regulatory aspects of the proposal, including . . . , and the Person making such proposal (a) if accepted, is reasonably likely to be consummated in accordance with its terms, and (b) if consummated would result in a transaction that is more favorable to the Company's stockholders, from a financial point of view, than the Offer and the Merger"*] . . . , and so long as (A) [there has been no breach (or material breach by the Company) of Section 5.4], the Company Board may at any time prior to the Acceptance Time, if it determines in good faith, after consultation with outside counsel, that failure to take such action would be inconsistent with its fiduciary duties to the stockholders of the Company under applicable Law, (x) effect a Change of Board Recommendation [*Editor: Changes of Board Recommendation are discussed in the next Subsection*] with respect to such Superior Proposal and/or (y) terminate this Agreement to enter into a definitive agreement with respect to such Superior Proposal . . . [so long as] in advance of or concurrently with such termination the Company pays or causes to be paid to Parent the Termination Fee and otherwise complies with the provisions of Section 7.1(e) [that the Company determines to accept the Superior Proposal, and that its doing so does not breach this agreement] . . .

(i) Nothing contained in this Section 5.4 or elsewhere in this Agreement shall prohibit the Company from responding to any unsolicited proposal or inquiry solely by (i) advising the Person making such proposal or inquiry of the terms of this Section 5.4 or (ii) seeking to clarify the terms and conditions thereof.

4. CHANGE OF BOARD RECOMMENDATION

The seller provides the buyer in a public company transaction with a representation that the seller's board has recommended the merger to the shareholders or a covenant that the board will do so. The board recommendation, either as a representation or a covenant, is critical to any merger transaction. As you may recall, statutory mergers require action by the board, in the form of a resolution that the merger is advisable and in the best interests of the corporation, prior to any vote of the shareholders. It had been common practice for seller boards to represent or covenant that they would recommend the transaction to the shareholders.

But what would happen if the board later concluded that the transaction was not in the best interests of the shareholders? Their fiduciary duty would then require them to withdraw any such recommendation. Courts confronted with the issue were unwilling to say that boards could contract away their obligations to abide by their fiduciary duty. Thus, parties include "fiduciary outs" in their agreements, allowing boards to change their recommendations under certain circumstances. The specifics of such provisions are heavily negotiated, as you shall see when you read the *Ace Limited* case, discussed in Chapter XVI.D. But the scenario where a board changes its view as to the advisability of a merger used to present another problem.

How could a board present a merger to be voted on by its shareholders if it no longer recommended the merger? In *Smith v. Van Gorkom,* the court articulated the law at the time:

> [u]nder § 251(b), the Board had but two options: (1) to proceed with the merger and the stockholder meeting, with the Board's recommendation of approval; or (2) to rescind its agreement with Pritzker, withdraw its approval of the merger, and notify its stockholders that the proposed shareholder meeting was cancelled.[19]

In 2003, the Delaware legislature adopted § 146, which permits a board to submit a merger agreement to its shareholders notwithstanding the fact that it no longer recommends the transaction. Section 146 permits a board, when faced with new facts following the signing of a merger agreement, to change its view with respect to the advisability of a merger, but still permit shareholders to vote on whether to accept it.

---

[19] *Smith v. Van Gorkom* at 888.

When a change of recommendation is combined with a restriction that the merger agreement may not be terminated until after a shareholder vote, then parties have effectively "forced the vote" on the merger. Such structures, post § 146, are permissible. Alternatively, parties may negotiate to permit a change in the board's recommendation to trigger rights to terminate the merger agreement immediately (see Termination Rights below).

A board not infrequently may be permitted under the terms of the merger agreement to change its recommendation when faced with new information or a superior alternative bid. But the provision may not allow for an immediate or automatic change. Instead, the buyer may have matching rights. These matching rights can be explicit or implicit. In the case of the typical matching right in the recommendation provision, such a matching right will usually require that the seller's board give the buyer an opportunity to renegotiate their offer prior to a recommendation change.

Following is the provision from the Valeant/Salix merger agreement setting forth the terms on which the Salix board can change its recommendation of the Valeant/Salix merger.

> (e) Notwithstanding anything to the contrary contained in Section 5.4(a) but subject to Section 5.4(f) [set forth below], the Company Board may, at any time prior to the Acceptance Time, effect a Change of Board Recommendation for a reason unrelated to an Acquisition Proposal if the Company Board has determined in good faith, after consultation with its outside counsel, that, in light of material facts, events or circumstances that have arisen or occurred after the date of this Agreement that were not known by or reasonably foreseeable to the Company or the Company Board prior to the date hereof, other than (i) changes in the market price or trading volume of the Shares . . . , (ii) the timing of any consents . . . [required in connection with the transaction], (iii) an Acquisition Proposal, or an inquiry, proposal or offer that could reasonably be expected to lead to an Acquisition Proposal . . . , (iv) [the Company exceeds revenue or earnings projections] . . . or (v) events set forth on Section 5.4(e) of the Company Disclosure Schedule (an "Intervening Event"), failure to take such action would be inconsistent with its fiduciary duties to the stockholders of the Company under applicable Law.

> (f) The Company Board may not withdraw, modify or amend the Company Board Recommendation in a manner adverse to Parent pursuant to clause (x) of Section 5.4(d) or Section 5.4(e) or terminate this Agreement pursuant to clause (y) of Section 5.4(d) unless (A) in the case of actions taken in relation to a Superior

Proposal, (1) such Superior Proposal ... did not result from a breach of this Section 5.4 and the Company has complied with the terms of this Section 5.4 in all respects with respect to such Superior Proposal ... and (2) the Company has not breached this Section 5.4 in any material respect, and (B) whether or not such action relates to a Superior Proposal:

(i) the Company shall have provided prior written notice to Parent, at least four Business Days in advance (the "Notice Period"), of its intention to take such action, which notice shall specify (A) if such action is to be taken in relation to a Superior Proposal, the material terms and conditions of such Superior Proposal (including the identity of the party making such Superior Proposal), and shall have contemporaneously provided a copy of the relevant proposed transaction agreements with the party making such Superior Proposal and other material documents, including the definitive agreement with respect to such Superior Proposal (the "Alternative Acquisition Agreement") or (B) if such action is to be taken in relation to an Intervening Event, a reasonably detailed description of the underlying facts giving rise to, and the reasons for taking, such action; and

(ii) prior to effecting such Change of Board Recommendation or terminating this Agreement to enter into a definitive agreement with respect to a Superior Proposal, the Company shall ... during the Notice Period, negotiate with Parent in good faith (to the extent Parent desires to negotiate) to make such adjustments to the terms and conditions of this Agreement so that (A) if such action is to be taken in relation to a Superior Proposal, the Acquisition Proposal ceases to constitute a Superior Proposal or (B) if such action is to be taken in relation to an Intervening Event, the need for making a Change of Board Recommendation is obviated.

As discussed above, acquirers sometimes get, and this acquirer in this transaction got matching rights. We quoted in the preceding Subsection the provision under which the Company's right to accept a Superior Proposal was subject to the Parent's right to match the proposal. The Company's right to change its recommendation in connection with accepting such a proposal is also subject to the Parent's match right. The board is required to negotiate in good faith with the buyer for four business days. This four-day negotiating requirement, in combination with the previously discussed information rights, makes clear that if the seller wishes to pursue a superior offer from a second bidder, the buyer will have ample opportunity to be kept apprised, and match any competing bid. In combination, information rights and matching rights put the initial bidder in a very good position in any post-signing bidding contest. (The matching rights here are explicit; matching rights can also be implicit. To the extent parties draft delays in the ability of the seller's board to change their board recommendation those delays combined with contractual rights to receive information about subsequent offers create implicit matching rights.) The provision also describes other circumstances under which there can be a Change of Board Recommendation.

5. GO-SHOP PROVISIONS

As we saw earlier, while no-shop provisions restrict the extent to which targets can look for or even consider bids from parties other than the one with which they have signed an agreement, go-shops are precisely the opposite: for a limited period of time, targets are supposed to look for other bidders, using the existence of the first agreement to generate an active auction. As we discuss further in Chapter XVIII, a target will request a go-shop in order to adhere to its board fiduciary duties to obtain the highest price reasonably available when there is a sale or change of control of the company. Professor Christina M. Sautter describes how this works in her article on the subject:

> [D]ealmakers have relied primarily on pre-signing public auctions or targeted market canvasses in an effort to obtain the highest possible price for shareholders. Because these sale methods are completed presigning, M&A agreements generally include a "fiduciary out" that enables the target board to consider unsolicited third party offers received between signing and receipt of shareholder approval. However, the board may only consider the third party offer if it is, or may become, a superior offer. Thus, in the typical deal, a target is "closed for business" and must ignore advances from third parties unless an unsolicited superior proposal is received. By contrast, go-shop provisions effectively allow a target to extend its typical "store hours" and actively seek a better deal during the time in which it otherwise would have been officially closed for business.[20]

Below you will find relevant portions of Dell's go-shop provision, which, as is common, is incorporated within a no-shop provision. For some period of time after the transaction is entered into, the target can shop itself; when that time period ends, the target agrees no longer to shop itself.

---

[20] Christina M. Sautter, *Shopping During Extended Store Hours: From No Shops to Go-Shops—The Development, Effectiveness, and Implications of Go-Shop Provisions in Change of Control Transactions,* 73 BROOK. L. REV. 525, 529–30 (2008).

<u>Acquisition Proposals</u> (a) Notwithstanding anything to the contrary contained in this Agreement, during the period beginning on the date of this Agreement and continuing until 12:01 a.m. (New York time) on the 46th calendar day after the date of this Agreement (the "<u>No-Shop Period Start Date</u>"), the Company and its Subsidiaries and their respective directors, officers, employees, investment bankers, attorneys, accountants and other advisors or representatives (collectively, "<u>Representatives</u>") shall have the right to (i) initiate, solicit and encourage any inquiry or the making of any proposal or offer that constitutes an Acquisition Proposal, including by providing information (including non-public information and data) regarding, and affording access to the business, properties, assets, books, records and personnel of, the Company and its Subsidiaries to any Person pursuant to (x) a confidentiality agreement entered into by such Person containing confidentiality terms that are no more favorable in the aggregate to such Person than those contained in the SLP Confidentiality Agreement [the confidentiality agreement with Silver Lake Partners, an entity that was part of Michael Dell's buyout group] . . . <u>provided</u> that the Company shall promptly (and in any event within 48 hours) make available to the Parent Parties any non-public information concerning the Company or its Subsidiaries that is provided to any Person given such access that was not previously made available to the Parent Parties, and (ii) engage in, enter into, continue or otherwise participate in any discussions or negotiations with any Persons or group of Persons with respect to any Acquisition Proposals and cooperate with or assist or participate in or facilitate any such inquiries, proposals, discussions or negotiations or any effort or attempt to make any Acquisition Proposals. No later than two (2) Business Days after the No-Shop Period Start Date, the Company shall notify Parent in writing of the identity of each Person or group of Persons from whom the Company received a written Acquisition Proposal after the execution of this Agreement and prior to the No-Shop Period Start Date and provide to Parent (x) a copy of any Acquisition Proposal made in writing and any other written terms or proposals provided (including financing commitments) to the Company or any of its Subsidiaries and (y) a written summary of the material terms of any Acquisition Proposal not made in writing (including any terms proposed orally or supplementally).

In Dell's go-shop, the board of Dell is permitted to seek out better bids for a period of 45 days from the date of signing and may freely negotiate with anyone during that period. In the words of then-Vice Chancellor Strine, the go-shop permits Dell "to shop like Paris Hilton" during the go-shop period.[21] Go-shop provisions are relatively common in private equity financed transactions. As we noted in Chapter XI.B.3, private equity buyers do not like to participate in auctions, limiting the information available to the company as to its value. In order to abide by their fiduciary duties, boards agreeing to sell their companies to such buyers will want to do some sort of market check. In Chapter XVIII, we review the fiduciary obligations of directors in change of control transactions; the motivation for using go-shop provisions in merger agreements will become more obvious.

I. CLOSING CONDITIONS

Merger agreements almost always contemplate a "delayed" closing. The parties will complete the merger at some point in time after the merger agreement is signed. As previously discussed, the reasons for a delayed closing often relate to regulatory and other required approvals. Such approvals must be obtained before the transaction can close; financing may also be needed. Especially in transactions involving private company targets, the acquirer may need the opportunity to do extensive due diligence given the absence of publicly available information about such targets.

Many things will necessarily change given the passage of time; some things, it is hoped, will not change, at least not for the worse, such as the target's financial condition. Consequently, the merger agreement will contain a number of conditions to each party's obligation to close the transaction.

1. "BRING DOWN" CONDITION

The condition that the target's representations and warranties made at the date of the signing of the agreement remain true and correct as of the date of the closing is one of the most important closing conditions. This condition requires that the representations and warranties made by the parties at the time of signing are tested again at the time of closing, or are "brought down to closing." If anything has occurred during the interim period such that the seller's representations are no longer true and correct as of the closing date, the buyer will not have an obligation to close the transaction. The buyer may walk away from the deal. The bring-down condition plays an important risk allocation function. By testing the representations and warranties twice, the bring-down condition allocates to the seller the risk of an adverse change in the seller's representations between the time the agreement is signed and the time the transaction closes.

---

[21] *In re Topps Shareholder Litigation*, 926 A.2d 58, 86 (2007).

Note the different levels of qualifications for different representations and warranties. Some must be true and correct except for *de minimis* deviations, some must be true and correct in all material respects, and some must be true and correct except where the failure to be so does not individually or in the aggregate constitute an MAE.

Some matters are more within a party's knowledge, control, or both; deviations from representations relating to such matters may have fewer qualifications to encourage appropriate information-production and behavior by the better-situated party. By contrast, where a matter is less within a party's knowledge or control, the issue is more one of risk allocation; who is the best-situated party to bear a particular risk is less evident. As you review the provision below, note which types of conditions have more qualifications, and which have fewer qualifications. Consider the matters in (i) that must be true but for *de minimis* exceptions. One is the capitalization representation, which is both critical to the buyer, and very much something the seller is far better situated to know than the buyer. Buyers typically get such representations, made and also brought down in the closing condition; the representations are either unqualified or are qualified only by *de minimis* exceptions. Below you will find the target's bring-down condition from the Dell merger agreement.

a) Representations and Warranties.

(i)   The representations and warranties of the Company set forth in Sections 3.2(a) [describing the Company's capitalization], 3.2(b) [that there is no stock or related instrument other than what is set forth in Section 3.2(a) or disclosed in a schedule], 3.2(g) [there are no declared unpaid dividends], 3.8(b) [there has been no Company Material Adverse Effect], 3.20 [no broker fee is due] and 3.22 [DGCL Section 203, the antitakeover section, to be discussed in Chapter XV, doesn't apply; the Company does not have a poison pill] shall be true and correct (except for such inaccuracies as are *de minimis* in the case of (x) Sections 3.2(a) and 3.2(b) taken as a whole, (y) Section 3.2(g) and (z) Section 3.20), both when made and at and as of the Closing Date, as if made at and as of such time (except to the extent expressly made as of a specified date, in which case as of such date),

(ii)   the representations and warranties of the Company set forth in Sections 3.1(b) [there is no significant subsidiary other than those disclosed on the list of subsidiaries], 3.3(a) [the Company has the power and authority to enter into agreement] and 3.2(h) [describing the debt the Company has and has not, incurred] shall be true and correct in all material respects, both when made and at and as of the Closing Date, as if made at and as of such time (except to the extent expressly made as of an earlier date, in which case as of such date), and

(iii) all other representations and warranties of the Company set forth in Article III [including, among other things, representations about internal controls, other liabilities, employee benefit plans, environmental matters, real property owned and leased and material contracts,] shall be true and correct both when made and at and as of the Closing Date, as if made at and as of such time (except to the extent expressly made as of an earlier date, in which case as of such date), except with respect to this clause (iii) where the failure of such representations and warranties to be so true and correct (without regard to any qualifications or exceptions as to materiality or Company Material Adverse Effect contained in such representations and warranties), individually or in the aggregate, does not constitute a Company Material Adverse Effect.

Clearly, it will be easiest for the buyer to be excused from closing if the buyer's obligation is conditioned only on there being no breach, or only a *de minimis* breach, of the representations. The more that is required to constitute a breach—that the seller's representation need not be true so long as it is true "in all material respects"—the harder it will be for a buyer to avoid her obligation to close a transaction in the event a representation is no longer true at the time of closing. The buyer will have the most difficulty being excused from closing if what is required is that the breach, together with other breaches, constitutes a material adverse effect.[22]

Qualifying the bring-down condition with materiality, especially MAE, presents the problem of "double materiality." To the extent each of the underlying representations is already qualified by materiality or by a material adverse effect clause, there may be a series of immaterial inaccuracies that in the aggregate result in a material adverse effect. However, individually none of the qualified representations would of themselves be inaccurate as of the closing because of the materiality qualifiers. Consequently the buyer would not be permitted to avoid closing notwithstanding the inaccuracies. To get around this double materiality problem, at closing, each of the individual representations is

---

[22] Recall from subsection G above that while MAE provisions sometimes take the form of representations which are brought down in and by a closing condition, sometimes, as in the transaction discussed in the Hexion case included in that subsection, they are simply independent closing conditions: the buyer is not required to close if the seller has experienced an MAE.

read "without regard to any qualifications or exceptions as to materiality or Company Material Adverse Effect." The condition is not met if, individually or in the aggregate, any inaccuracies in the representations (read as though they were unqualified) at the time of closing constitute a material adverse effect. Read in this way, inaccuracies in the representations get the benefit of a materiality qualifier only once and there is no potential problem with double materiality.

How does this work in practice? Let's look at another example. In the Complete Genomics Merger Agreement the representation made concerning litigation is qualified by "Material Adverse Effect" as follows:

> 3.15 <u>Litigation</u>.
>
> (a) There is no suit, claim, action, or proceeding pending or, to the knowledge of the Company, threatened against the Company or any Company Subsidiary, <u>that, individually or in the aggregate, if determined adversely to the Company or any Company Subsidiary would reasonably be expected to have a Company Material Adverse Effect.</u> As of the date of this Agreement, <u>Section 3.15</u> of the Company Disclosure Schedule sets forth a description of each current Action pending or, to the Knowledge of the Company, threatened against or affecting the Company or any Company Subsidiary (including by virtue of indemnification or otherwise) or their respective assets or properties, or any executive officer or director of the Company or any Company Subsidiary.

The buyer in the Complete Genomics transaction acquired Complete Genomics pursuant to a tender offer followed by a back-end merger. In such a situation, the closing conditions become conditions to the completion of the tender offer: the "Absence of Litigation" representation and warranty needs to be true and correct (in the applicable degree of materiality) for the buyer to be required to complete its tender offer. For the tender offer to close, the following condition must be fulfilled:

> (B) <u>any other representation or warranty of the Company</u> contained in the Merger Agreement <u>(without giving effect to any references to any Company Material Adverse Effect or materiality qualifications and other qualifications based upon the concept of materiality or similar phrases contained therein)</u> shall fail to be true and correct in any respect as of the date of the Merger Agreement or as of the Expiration Date with the same force and effect as if made on and as of such date, except for representations and warranties that relate to a specific date or time (which need only be true and correct as of such date or time), <u>except as has not had and would not reasonably be expected to have, individually or in the aggregate with all other</u>

failures to be true or correct, a Company Material Adverse
Effect;

Think how this applies to the Absence of Litigation representation
above. If we didn't have the double underlined language, the bring-down
closing condition for the representation would effectively be as follows
(this is our wording):

> The Absence of Litigation representation shall fail to be true
> and correct in any respect as of the date of the Merger
> Agreement, except as has not had and would not reasonably be
> expected to have, individually or in the aggregate with all other
> failures to be true or correct, a Company Material Adverse
> Effect;

But the Absence of Litigation representation already has a qualifier
about Material Adverse Effect! For the condition not to be met—for buyer
to be able not to close—the representation would have to be sufficiently
untrue as to arise to a Material Adverse Effect, and, in addition, the
breached representation itself would have to arise to a Material Adverse
Effect. This is two Material Adverse Effects—and one more than was
intended. To deal with this issue, the drafters add the words above with
double underlining. Thus, for purposes of the condition to closing, the
Absence of Litigation representation reads as follows:

> 3.15 Litigation.

> (a) There is no suit, claim, action, or proceeding pending or,
> to the knowledge of the Company, threatened against the
> Company or any Company Subsidiary, ~~that, individually or in
> the aggregate, if determined adversely to the Company or any
> Company Subsidiary would reasonably be expected to have a
> Company Material Adverse Effect.~~ As of the date of this
> Agreement, Section 3.15 of the Company Disclosure Schedule
> sets forth a description of each current Action pending or, to the
> Knowledge of the Company, threatened against or affecting the
> Company or any Company Subsidiary (including by virtue of
> indemnification or otherwise) or their respective assets or
> properties, or any executive officer or director of the Company or
> any Company Subsidiary.

This formulation works: the condition to close still contains a
Material Adverse Effect qualifier.

2. OTHER CONDITIONS

While some conditions to closing apply only to the buyer or the seller,
a number of other conditions apply to both the buyer and the seller.
Common conditions applicable to both parties include the obtaining of

legally required approvals from regulators and a successful shareholder vote. While approval by the statutorily required percentage of shareholders is a condition to the parties' obligation to close, there may be circumstances, such as in transactions potentially involving a conflict of interest, where parties may want a higher percentage than the statute requires. A common requirement for a transaction with a controlling shareholder is that it be approved by a majority of the unaffiliated (or, if the controlling shareholder is a majority shareholder, the minority) shareholders, something we discuss further in Chapter XIX.

Regulatory approval is another common condition to parties' obligations to close. In most cases, the merger will be subject to the Hart-Scott-Rodino premerger notification regime. Closing of the transaction is usually conditioned on there being no judicial action by any regulator, such as the DOJ or the FTC, which would prevent the transaction from closing. Failure to secure regulatory approval can thus halt a transaction and prevent the parties from meeting the conditions to closing.

Other conditions typically covered include a performance of obligations condition. This condition requires each of the parties comply in all material respects with the covenants in the merger agreement. To the extent one party deviates from her covenants with respect to the operation of the business during the period between signing and closing, the other party may be able to refuse to close the merger for failure of this condition. Of course, parties are not excused from closing if their own conduct causes a closing condition not to occur.

J. TERMINATION PROVISIONS

Every merger agreement includes provisions pursuant to which one or both parties can terminate the merger agreement. As with closing conditions, some provisions allow either party to terminate, and some allow a specified party to terminate. First, parties can terminate the agreement by mutual consent. Second, typically, either party can terminate the agreement if needed regulatory approvals cannot be obtained, or if the seller cannot obtain the required shareholder vote to approve the transaction. Third, the seller may usually terminate the agreement: to pursue a higher subsequent bid or, following an unsuccessful shareholder vote, in order to pursue a higher bid (the fiduciary out); if the buyer's representations and warranties are no longer true and correct or the buyer has failed to perform any of its covenants; or if the buyer's financing is not available. Fourth, the buyer may typically terminate the agreement in the event the seller's representations and warranties are no longer true and correct, or the seller has failed to perform any of its covenants. These provisions are explained at greater length below.

Note the relationship between the representations, the closing conditions, and the termination provisions. If, subject to any materiality qualifications, representations made about the seller are no longer true as of the closing date, the buyer may not only not be required to complete the transaction, but may also be able to terminate the agreement. Thus, failure by the seller to make truthful representations at the outset, or to exert sufficient efforts following the signing of the agreement to abide by its covenants and agreements, may give the buyer the right to refuse to close the merger and to terminate the agreement.

The interim period between signing and closing is not intended to be open ended. At the time of signing, both the acquirer and the target ostensibly wish to accomplish the transaction in the fastest time reasonably possible. But "unexpected" issues always arise, some of which may cause significant delays in the completion of the merger. Most, if not all, of these delays are related to government approvals. To guard against the possibility of extremely long delays, parties typically include an "outside date" or a "drop dead date" in merger agreements. If, by the merger agreement's "outside date" or "drop dead date," the parties, notwithstanding their efforts, have failed to secure the regulatory approvals required to complete the transaction, either party may terminate the merger agreement.

A "fiduciary termination right" may allow the seller to terminate the agreement. If, after the agreement has been signed, a superior competing bid is made for the seller, the seller's board may terminate the merger agreement in order to comply with its fiduciary obligations to consider and perhaps accept the competing bid. Issues with respect to when and under what circumstances a target board's fiduciary obligations might require it to terminate a transaction in order to pursue a competing bid will be discussed in Chapter XVIII.

If a party is entitled to terminate a merger agreement, and does so, there is no breach. Remedies for breach will not be available; instead, the parties will have agreed upon different remedies depending on why the agreement was terminated. A common remedy is a termination fee, as explained in the next Section. If termination is not permitted pursuant to the terms of the agreement, remedies for breach are available. The agreement may, and usually does, specify that such remedies are limited to specific performance. If not, then the remedy for breach of contract is expectation damages, the traditional measure for damages in any contract case. In the case of a merger transaction, expectation damages can potentially be extremely large if a court decides that they include the premium to be paid by the buyer to the seller's shareholders.[23]

---

[23] Caselaw to date, however, does not support this position. In *Consolidated Edison v. Northeast Utilities*, 426 F.3d 524 (2d Cir. 2005), the Second Circuit held that under New York law a buyer could not be liable to a seller's shareholders for the lost premium (in the amount of

Below you will find relevant portions of Dell's termination provision:

> **Section 7.1 Termination.** Notwithstanding anything in this Agreement to the contrary, this Agreement may be terminated and abandoned at any time prior to the Effective Time except with respect to Section 7.1(c)(ii) below, whether before or after the adoption of this Agreement by stockholders of the Company and the sole stockholder of Merger Sub [that is, the intermediate corporation owned by the Parent, Denali, which in turn is owned by Michael Dell, Silver Lake Partners and others]:
>
> (a) by the mutual written consent of the Company and Parent;
>
> (b) by either the Company or Parent if:
>
>> (i)   the Effective Time shall not have occurred on or before November 5, 2013 (the "Outside Date"); provided that the party seeking to terminate this Agreement pursuant to this Section 7.1(b)(i) shall not have breached in any material respect its obligations under this Agreement in any manner that shall have been the primary cause of the failure to consummate the Merger on or before such date;
>
>> (ii) any Governmental Entity ... shall have issued or entered an injunction or similar order permanently enjoining or otherwise prohibiting the consummation of the Merger and such injunction or order shall have become final and non-appealable; provided that the party seeking to terminate this Agreement pursuant to this Section 7.1(b)(ii) shall have used such efforts as may be required by Section 5.7 [the agreement by the parties to use reasonable best efforts to obtain required approvals] to prevent oppose and remove such injunction; or
>
>> (iii) the Company Meeting ... shall have concluded and the Company Stockholder Approvals shall not have been obtained;
>
> (c) by the Company, if:
>
>> (i)   the Parent Parties shall have breached or failed to perform in any material respect any of their representations, warranties, [or] covenants ... provided that the Company is not then in material breach of any

---

$1.2 billion) when those shareholders were not third party beneficiaries of the merger agreement. This decision has been viewed as limiting the potential damages a seller can obtain due to a buyer's breach of a merger agreement to out of pocket and other expenses. This issue has yet to be considered by the Delaware courts. It is also not uncommon for a merger agreement to specifically state that damages related to the share premium are unavailable in the case of breach.

representation, warranty, agreement or covenant contained in this Agreement;

(ii) at any time prior to the time the Company Stockholder Approvals are obtained, the Company Board shall have authorized the Company to enter into an Alternative Acquisition Agreement with respect to a Superior Proposal; provided that substantially concurrently with such termination, the Company enters into such Alternative Acquisition Agreement and pays to Parent (or one or more of its designees) the applicable Company Termination Payment in accordance with Section 7.3 [specifying who can get termination payments and under what circumstances]; or

(iii)(A) all of the conditions set forth in Sections 6.1 [conditions to both parties' obligations to close] and 6.3 [conditions to the Parent Parties' obligations to close] have been satisfied (other than those conditions that by their nature are to be satisfied at the Closing, but each of which was at the time of termination capable of being satisfied as if such time were the Closing), (B) the Company has irrevocably notified Parent in writing (x) that all of the conditions set forth in Section 6.2 [conditions to the Company's obligation to close] have been satisfied (other than those conditions that by their nature are to be satisfied at the Closing, but each of which was at the time of termination capable of being satisfied or waived at the Closing) or that it is willing to waive any unsatisfied conditions in Section 6.2 for the purpose of consummating the Closing and (y) it is ready, willing and able to consummate the Closing; (C) the Parent Parties fail to complete the Closing within three (3) Business Days following the date the Closing was required by Section 1.2; and (D) the Company stood ready, willing and able to consummate the Closing during such three (3) Business Day period.

(d) by Parent, if:

(i) the Company shall have breached or failed to perform in any material respect any of its representations, warranties, [or] covenants . . . provided that the Parent Parties are not then in material breach of any representation, warranty, agreement or covenant contained in this Agreement; or

(ii) the Company Board or any committee thereof (including the Special Committee) shall have made a Change of Recommendation, provided that Parent's right to terminate this Agreement pursuant to this Section 7.1(d)(ii) shall expire at 5:00 p.m. (New York City time) on the 30th calendar day following the date on which such Change of Recommendation occurs; or

(iii) . . .[effectively, affiliates of the parent will not get the favorable tax treatment they contemplated on their equity contribution in connection with the transaction, or there is a change in law that otherwise adversely affects the liquidation of certain securities by, or the transfer of amounts from the Company's subsidiaries into the Company] or (C) the amount of Cash on Hand is less than the Target Amount . . . as of the beginning of the [date the transaction was required to close] . . .

As with all merger agreements, this agreement contains some combination of typical provisions and provisions that reflect specifics of the particular transaction. An example of the latter is the buyer's termination right in the event Dell's cash on hand on the closing date is less than the "Target Amount" of $7.4 billion. An issue identified by the parties in the transaction was that much of Dell's cash was in its overseas subsidiaries. In the agreement, Dell covenanted to do various things, including repatriating some of these funds from its overseas subsidiaries prior to closing. The Target Amount was to be available to the buyer to immediately pay down some of the debt incurred to accomplish the acquisition, and its availability was structured as a condition to the buyer's obligation to close. The merger agreement gave the buyer the right to terminate the merger agreement in the event the Company did not meet the Target Amount condition on the date the merger is to close.

K. TERMINATION FEES

A valid termination has two effects. First, the parties are no longer under any obligation to pursue the transaction. Second, in certain circumstances, a termination triggers an obligation by either the seller or the buyer to pay a termination fee to the other.

If the seller exercises its fiduciary termination right (i.e., its right to terminate the merger agreement to accept a superior offer), such a termination will usually trigger an obligation to pay a termination fee to the buyer. If the buyer exercises its regulatory termination right, doing so may trigger an obligation to pay a termination fee to the seller. In addition to the termination fee, which is the functional equivalent of liquidated damages, the seller may also be under an obligation to compensate the buyer for its reasonable actual expenses as specified in the agreement. Below you will find relevant portions of Dell's termination fee language from the merger agreement.

Section 7.3. Termination Payments

(a) In the event that:

> (i)(x) this Agreement is terminated ... by the Company pursuant to Section 7.1(b)(i) ... (y) the Company or any other Person shall have publicly disclosed or announced an Acquisition Proposal on or after the date of this Agreement but prior to the Company Meeting, and (z) within twelve months of such termination the Company shall have entered into a definitive agreement with respect to an Acquisition Proposal or an Acquisition Proposal is consummated ... or

> (ii) this Agreement is terminated by the Company pursuant to Section 7.1(c)(ii); or

> (iii) this Agreement is terminated by Parent pursuant to Section 7.1(d)(ii),

then, the Company shall, (A) in the case of clause (i) above, no later than the earlier of (x) the date the Company enters into a definitive agreement with respect to an Acquisition Proposal or (y) the date on which the Company consummates such Acquisition Proposal, (B) in the case of clause (ii) above, prior to or substantially concurrently with such termination (and any purported termination pursuant to Section 7.1(c)(ii) shall be void and of no force and effect unless and until the Company shall have made such payment), and (C) in the case of clause (iii) above, no later than three (3) Business Days after the date of such termination, pay Parent (or one or more of its designees) the applicable Company Termination Payment [defined below], by wire transfer of same day funds to one or more accounts designated by Parent (or one or more of its designees); it being understood that in no event shall the Company be required to pay the Company Termination Payment on more than one occasion. Following receipt by Parent (or one or more of its designees) of the Company Termination Payment in accordance with this Section 7.3, the Company shall have no further liability with respect to this Agreement or the transactions contemplated herein to the Parent Parties, except in the event of a willful and material breach by the Company of Section 5.3 [the no-shop provision].

[*Note: in the definitions section, Company Termination Payment is defined as follows*:

" "Company Termination Payment" means (i) if payable in connection with a termination of this Agreement by (x) the Company pursuant to Section 7.1(c)(ii) with respect to the Company entering into an Alternative Acquisition Agreement with a Person or group that is an Excluded Party [*Editor: Recall that Excluded Parties include those making offers during the go-shop period*] at the time of such termination; (y) Parent pursuant to Section 7.1(d)(ii) [*Editor: Because the Board has changed its recommendation, and is no longer recommending the transaction*] and the event giving rise to such termination is the submission of an Acquisition Proposal by a Person or group that is an Excluded Party at the time of such termination; or (z) by the Company or Parent pursuant to Section 7.1(b)(iii), [*Editor: Shareholder approval of the transaction has not occurred at the shareholder meeting*] and within twelve months of such termination the Company shall have entered into a definitive agreement with respect to any recapitalization, or any extraordinary dividend or share repurchase, or a recapitalization, or an extraordinary dividend or share repurchase, is consummated that, together with any related transactions, would not result in any Person or group beneficially owning 50% or more of any class of equity securities of the Company [unless during such time the Company agrees to consummate, or consummates, certain types of acquisition and other transactions, not including those described in (x), (y) or (z)] then, in the case of each clause (x), (y) or (z) of this definition, $180,000,000, and (ii) if payable in any other circumstance, an amount equal to $450,000,000."]

(b) In the event that this Agreement is terminated by Parent pursuant to (x) Section 7.1(d)(iii)(A) or (B) or (y) Section 7.1(d)(iii)(C) (but only if Cash on Hand would not have been less than the Target Amount but for a Legal Impediment or Charge, assuming all Cash Transfers that could have been made but for such Legal Impediment or Charge were in fact made), then Parent shall pay, or cause to be paid, to the Company an amount equal to $250,000,000 (the "Cash Shortfall Fee"), such payment to be made by wire transfer of immediately available funds within three Business Days following such termination.

(c) In the event that this Agreement is terminated (i) by the Company pursuant to Section 7.1(c)(i) or Section 7.1(c)(iii) or (ii) by the Company or Parent pursuant to Section 7.1(b)(i) if, at the time of or prior to such termination, the Company would have been entitled to terminate this Agreement pursuant to Section 7.1(c)(iii), then Parent shall pay, or cause to be paid, to the

Company an amount equal to $750,000,000 (such amount, the "Parent Termination Fee") to be made by wire transfer of immediately available funds within three Business Days following such termination. . . .

(e) Without limiting or otherwise affecting any way the remedies available to Parent, in the event of termination of this Agreement pursuant to Section 7.1(b)(iii), then the Company shall promptly, but in no event later than three (3) Business Days after such termination, pay Parent (or one or more of its designees) the documented out-of-pocket expenses incurred by the Parent Parties and their respective Affiliates in connection with this Agreement and the Finances and the transactions contemplated hereby and thereby up to a maximum amount of $15,000,000, by wire transfer of same day funds, which amount shall be credited against any Company Termination Payment payable to any Parent Party.

(f) Notwithstanding anything in this Agreement to the contrary, but without limiting the Parent Parties' rights under Section 8.5 [relating to specific performance], in no event shall the Company have any liability, whether at law or equity, in contract, in tort or otherwise, related to or arising out of this Agreement to any of the Parent Parties or any other Person in excess of $750,000,000, in the aggregate.

Note that there are four different possible fees payable: $180 million; $250 million, $450 million and $750 million. The $250 million, called a "Cash Shortfall Fee," is payable by the seller to the buyer if, principally, the seller does not have the Target Amount on hand when the transaction would otherwise have closed. The $180 million and $450 million are payable if the termination relates to the Company's consideration of or entry into another transaction.[24] The lower amount, the $180 million, is payable in the event of a transaction with an Excluded Party, a termination of the agreement to pursue a possible superior transaction with an Excluded Party, or, if the agreement is terminated because the shareholders did not approve the transaction at the shareholder meeting, within twelve months the Company enters into a transaction which would result in any Person or group beneficially owning more than 50% of the Company. These fees are all payable by the seller.

The $750 million would be payable by the buyer, principally if the Parent Parties breach the agreement or refuse to close the transaction. Also, if the agreement is terminated because the meeting at which shareholder approval was to have been obtained finishes without

---

[24] The original agreement called for a higher termination fee, but the fee was lowered when the consideration in the transaction was raised.

shareholder approval, Dell will have to pay Parent Parties' documented out of pocket expenses, up to $15 million. The amount will be credited against any termination fee payable by Dell to any Parent Party.

Termination fees are often scrutinized by courts. They are essentially liquidated damages; you may recall from contract law that liquidated damages must be a reasonable estimate of the parties' damages. In general, when the termination relates to a target's acceptance of a competing bid, the termination fee that the target pays to the original buyer is three to four percent of the transaction value. Caselaw has examined whether a termination fee above this range payable by a target to a bidder with which the target had previously signed a merger agreement might be an impermissible defensive measure. This subject is discussed at greater length in Chapter XVI.G.

Note that the Dell transaction also included a "reverse termination fee." A reverse termination fee is payable by the buyer to the seller in order to facilitate the buyer's termination of the merger agreement. While the termination fee is typically tied to a fiduciary termination right, the reverse termination fee is more typically tied to terminations by the buyer where the transaction is held up by government or other regulatory hurdles and the buyer is not able, willing or required under the merger agreement to do what the regulator would require to grant its approval. Recall in this regard our previous discussion of the "best efforts" language and the limits of a buyer's requirement to take actions to close the transaction. In the event the buyer decides to terminate the merger agreement rather than comply with government requests (usually, for divestitures, but sometimes for other matters) that require it to do more than it otherwise is required to do under the merger agreement, this payment would be required. The parties can negotiate for sellers to get reverse termination fees for other reasons. In private equity transactions, the buyer is typically allowed to terminate the agreement if financing becomes unavailable. In connection with such a termination, the buyer will be required to pay a reverse termination fee to compensate the seller.

Buyers will also sometimes agree to pay a reverse termination fee if a shareholder vote is required by the buyer to issue securities in the transaction, and the buyer's shareholders fail to approve the issuance.

If a regulator is demanding divestitures or other remedies whose value is below the value of the reverse termination fee, then the buyer is economically incentivized to agree to these remedies. Once the cost of the remedies exceeds the fee, it may be more economical to simply pay the fee and exit the transaction if the merger agreement so permits. Reverse termination fees can be quite large, particularly when they are designed to compensate a target for a deal that fails due to the failure to obtain regulatory clearances. AT&T paid a $4.8 billion reverse termination fee to T-Mobile when the transaction was blocked by the antitrust authorities.

L. ALLOCATING RISK IN THE PRIVATE COMPANY SALE: ESCROW AND INDEMNIFICATION

Merger agreements in private company transactions may also include provisions by which the selling shareholders indemnify the buyer. They sometimes also include escrow arrangements under which some portion of the sales proceeds are placed in escrow, available to be paid to the buyer under certain circumstances. These provisions provide the buyer with a mechanism for ex post settling up against the seller's shareholders in the event that their representations and warranties made about the condition of the seller turn out after the closing to be incorrect.

By contrast, in public company transactions, the representations and warranties do not survive the closing. It would not be feasible or desirable for the buyer to pursue millions of public company shareholders; in any event such shareholders almost certainly do not have information about the condition of the company being acquired that is not already known by the buyer, especially given that a great deal of information about such companies is publicly available, vouched for by the respective companies, who would be subject to legal penalties if the information were false. There are also always third parties with significant reputational stakes involved in a public company's provision of information—the company's accounting firm, for instance, is named in its public filings, and has legal obligations itself. Thus, shareholders of publicly-traded companies are not asked to bear the costs associated with any inaccurate statements made about their companies in the merger agreements. If those statements are inaccurate, a breach can excuse the buyer from closing the transaction, but the breach will have few if any consequences once the acquisition closes. The buyer is therefore motivated to find out as much as it can before it takes over, even though doing so might be more expensive, and will surely be less thorough, than being able to find out at leisure after the closing if what it bought was as represented.[25]

The situation is quite different in transactions where a private company is being acquired. Private companies may have only a small number of shareholders; such shareholders may know a great deal about the business and indeed, may be involved in running it. Unlike public companies, information about the company will be harder to obtain, with the shareholders being an important source, and there may be fewer third parties with strong reputational stakes involved, both on an ongoing basis

---

[25] There have been rare instances in public transactions where post-closing indemnification is provided for, principally for certain tax issues. This indemnification has been either provided by a principal shareholder or through an escrow mechanism.

and in the transaction. Therefore, it makes sense for at least some private company shareholders to be liable if, after the closing, the representations and warranties turn out not to be accurate. When selling shareholders stand behind the representations and warranties they give about the company being sold, the buyer should be willing to pay a higher price.

Thus, in private company deals, the seller's representations and warranties will survive for some period beyond the closing. The seller may also provide an escrow of some portion of the merger proceeds. The seller will often indemnify the buyer for breaches of the representations and warranties, and may also indemnify the buyer as to some matters not covered in the representations, such as the seller's nonperformance of a covenant. Because of the indemnification for breaches of representations and warranties, the negotiation of the representations and warranties is much more vigorous, since their scope can determine if there is later liability for any breach. In contrast, in public transactions, representation and warranties are qualified by the MAE condition and there is no indemnification for breach. Thus the negotiation of the representations and warranties is not as significant, and the focus is more on the MAE clause.

Indemnification provisions included in the merger agreement or in a separate indemnification agreement will specify procedures the parties are to follow regarding notice, timing, and other matter. There will also not infrequently be "caps"—maximums for buyer liability for particular breaches or for breaches or other indemnifiable events in the aggregate— and "baskets"—minimum amounts of claims a buyer needs in order to make a claim against the seller(s) at all to limit *de minimis* claims. There will often be provisions specifying how a claim made by a third party against the buyer for which the seller(s) are indemnifying the buyer will be dealt with. If there is an escrow, the conditions under which the escrow can be drawn upon will be specified.

Below you will find relevant portions of an indemnification provision from Facebook's acquisition of WhatsApp in which the seller shareholders indemnify the buyer.[26] As part of that agreement, the seller and its shareholders agreed to indemnify the buyer for certain losses post-closing in the event the buyer sustained any damages as a result of inaccuracies in the seller's representations and warranties and various other inaccuracies in other documents, as well as certain third party claims. You can find the complete provision in the Online Appendix.

---

[26] Note that the actual provision is not only an indemnification of the buyer, but also indemnifies the seller shareholders for certain breaches by the buyer; those portions are omitted from this excerpt.

8.2 Indemnification.

(a) Subject to the limitations set forth in this Article 8, from and after the Closing, the Converting Holders shall, severally (according to their respective Pro Rata Shares) but not jointly, indemnify and hold harmless Parent, Acquirer, Merger Sub, the Company, the First Step Surviving Corporation, the Final Surviving Corporation [*Editor: Note that this transaction is being done in two steps, with two mergers; see the footnote for a roadmap of how this will work*[27]] and their respective officers, directors, agents and employees . . . (each of the foregoing being referred to individually as an "***Parent Indemnified Person***" and collectively as "***Parent Indemnified Persons***") from and against, and shall compensate and reimburse each Indemnified Person for, any and all Indemnifiable Damages directly or indirectly, whether or not due to a Third-Party Claim, arising out of, resulting from or in connection with the following (the "***Parent Indemnifiable Matters***"):

This provision sets forth who is getting the benefit of the indemnification, and from whom.

(i) any failure of any representation or warranty made by the Company herein or in the Company Disclosure Letter · (including any exhibit or schedule of the Company Disclosure Letter . . .) to be true and correct (A) as of the Agreement Date [or the dates specified therein] or (B) as of the Closing Date as though such representation or warranty were made as of the Closing Date [or the dates specified therein] (in the case of each of clauses "(A)" and "(B)", without giving effect to . . . any materiality, "Material Adverse Effect" or similar standards or qualifications limiting the scope of such representation or warranty);

(ii) any failure of any certification, representation or warranty made by the Company in the Company Closing Certificate delivered to Parent or Acquirer to be true and correct as of the date such certificate is delivered to Parent or Acquirer;

---

[27] "Parent, Acquirer, Merger Sub and the Company intend to effect a merger of Merger Sub with and into the Company in accordance with this Agreement and Delaware Law (the "***First Merger***"). Upon consummation of the First Merger, Merger Sub will cease to exist, and the Company will become a wholly owned subsidiary of Acquirer. Parent, Acquirer and the Company intend to effect, following the consummation of the First Merger, the merger of the First Step Surviving Corporation with and into Acquirer in accordance with this Agreement and Delaware Law (the "***Second Merger***" and together or *in seriatim* with the First Merger, as appropriate, the "***Mergers***"). Upon consummation of the Second Merger, the First Step Surviving Corporation will cease to exist, and Acquirer will continue to exist as a wholly owned (in part directly and in part indirectly) subsidiary of Parent."

(iii) regardless of the disclosure of any matter set forth in the Company Disclosure Letter, any breach of, or default in connection with, any of the covenants, agreements or obligations made by the Company herein; [or]

(iv) regardless of the disclosure of any matter set forth in the Company Disclosure Letter, any inaccuracies in the Spreadsheet; . . .

This provision sets forth minimum thresholds for when indemnification is payable.

8.3 Indemnifiable Damage Threshold; Other Limitations.

(a) Notwithstanding anything to the contrary contained herein, no Parent Indemnified Person may make a claim against the Escrow Fund in respect of any claim for Indemnifiable Damages arising out of, resulting from or in connection with the matters listed in clauses "(i)" and "(ii)" of Section 8.2(a) (other than any failure of any of the Company Special Representations to be true and correct as aforesaid) unless and until a Claim Certificate (together with any other delivered Claim Certificates) describing Indemnifiable Damages in an aggregate amount greater than $10,000,000 (the "*Aggregate Deductible*") has been delivered, in which case the Parent Indemnified Person may make claims for indemnification, compensation and reimbursement and may recover all Indemnifiable Damages in excess of the amount of the Aggregate Deductible. . . . The Aggregate Deductible shall not apply to any other Indemnifiable Damages.

Note that there is a deductible of $10,000,000; claims are not payable until the deductible is reached, and once it has been reached, only claims in excess of the deductible are payable. (In some deals, claims from the first dollar are payable once the deductible has been reached. This is known as a basket). Note that the deductible does not apply to the whole indemnification obligation; some damages are not encompassed, and are hence not subject to the deductible. In addition, some agreements contain a *de minimis* requirement—that any claim must exceed a minimum amount before a claim can be made for indemnification. The WhatsApp merger agreement did not contain a *de minimis requirement*, but it did contain specific provisions setting forth how indemnification would be paid:

(b) Subject to Section 8.3(c), if the First Merger is consummated, recovery from the Escrow Fund shall constitute the sole and exclusive remedy for the indemnity obligations of each Converting Holder under this Agreement for Indemnifiable Damages arising out, resulting from or in connection with of any of the matters listed in: (i) clause "(i)" or clause "(ii)" of Section

8.2(a) (except (A) in the case of intentional fraud by or on behalf of the Company under this Agreement and (B) any failure of any of the representations and warranties contained in Section 2.2 (Capital Structure) or Section 2.3(a) (Authority) or the representations and warranties of the Company contained in any Closing Certificate delivered to Parent or Acquirer that are within the scope of those covered in Section 2.2 or Section 2.3(a) (collectively, the *"Company Special Representations"*) to be true and correct as aforesaid), (ii) clause "(iii)" of Section 8.2(a) (other than with respect to any intentional breach or default), and (iii) clause "(vi)" of Section 8.2(a). In the case of claims for Indemnifiable Damages arising out of, resulting from or in connection with (i) intentional fraud by or on behalf of the Company under this Agreement, (ii) any failure of any of the Special Representations to be true and correct as aforesaid, (iii) any of the matters set forth in clause "(iii)" (solely with respect to any intentional breach or default), clause "(iv)" or clause "(v)" of Section 8.2(a) (collectively, *"Fundamental Matters"*), after Indemnified Persons have exhausted or made claims upon all amounts of cash or all shares of Parent Common Stock held in the Escrow Fund (after taking into account all other claims for indemnification, compensation or reimbursement from the Escrow Fund made by Indemnified Persons) (it being understood that recovery for all Company Indemnifiable Matters shall first be sought from the Escrow Fund), each Converting Holder shall have Liability for such Converting Holder's Pro Rata Share of the amount of any Indemnifiable Damages resulting therefrom; <u>provided</u> that such liability shall be limited to an amount equal to such Converting Holder's Pro Rata Share of the aggregate value of the Merger Consideration (inclusive of such Converting Holder's Pro Rata Share of the aggregate value of the Escrow Fund) . . . ; <u>provided, further</u>, that such limitation of liability shall not apply to a Converting Holder in the case of (x) intentional fraud by or on behalf of such Converting Holder or (y) intentional fraud by or on behalf of the Company in which such Converting Holder participated or had actual knowledge. . . .

(c)   The amounts that an Indemnified Person recovers from the Escrow Fund pursuant to Fundamental Matters shall not reduce the amount that an Indemnified Person may recover with respect to claims that are not Fundamental Matters. By way of illustration and not limitation, assuming there are no other claims for indemnification, in the event that Indemnifiable Damages resulting from a Fundamental Matter are first satisfied from the Escrow Fund and such recovery fully depletes the Escrow Fund, the maximum amount recoverable by an Indemnified Person pursuant to a subsequent claim that is not a Fundamental Matter shall continue to be $600,000,000 irrespective of the fact that the Escrow Fund was used to satisfy such Fundamental Matter, such that the amount recoverable for such two claims would be the same regardless of the chronological order in which they were made.

     . . .

(g) Following the Closing, except in the event of intentional fraud (other than intentional fraud to the extent such intentional fraud is by or on behalf of the Company under this Agreement) (i) this <u>Article 8</u> shall constitute the sole and exclusive remedy for recovery of monetary Indemnifiable Damages by the Parent Indemnified Persons . . . for all Company Indemnifiable Matters . . . under this Agreement (which means, for example, that the survival periods and liability limits set forth in this <u>Article 8</u> shall control . . .), and (ii) all applicable statutes of limitations or other claims periods with respect to claims for Indemnifiable Damages shall be shortened to the applicable claims periods and survival periods set forth herein; <u>provided</u>, <u>however</u>, that for clarity, nothing in this Agreement shall limit the rights or remedies of Indemnified Person in connection with any claims seeking injunctive relief or specific performance.

These sections define indemnification obligations that are treated differently from one another. Some are limited to the amount in escrow, which is approximately $600,000,000 (in a transaction valued at $19 billion), but some, special representations and fundamental matters, as defined, are not.[28] Note also that this provision requires that indemnification be pro rata, from each WhatsApp shareholder in proportion to his or her ownership of shares, and that it is the sole mechanism for indemnification except in cases of intentional fraud.

In addition to limitations on the maximum amount of indemnification which is to be provided, the parties typically put a time limit on the assertion of indemnification claims, a provision included in the WhatsApp merger agreement:

---

[28] Typically, putting aside the seller's liability for intentional fraud, the maximum indemnification for breach of the representation and warranties is 10% to 15% of the purchase price. This equivalent amount is then taken from the purchase price and held in escrow until the survival period is over. The amount will then be used to fund the seller's indemnification obligation. Issues arising as to escrows include the length of time the amounts are escrowed, and the procedure by which amounts are released from escrow during the escrow period, more specifically how does the buyer demonstrate its entitlement to the money? *See generally* Sanjai Bhagat, Sandy Klasa, and Lubomir P. Litov, *The Use of Escrow Contracts in Acquisition Agreements* (2015), available at http://papers.ssrn.com/sol3/papers.cfm?abstract_id=2271394.

8.4 <u>Period for Claims</u>. Except as otherwise set forth in this Section 8.4 and in the case of claims alleging intentional fraud by or on behalf of the Company under this Agreement, the period during which claims for Indemnifiable Damages may be made (the *"Claims Period"*) against the Escrow Fund for Indemnifiable Damages arising out of, resulting from or in connection with the matters listed in clauses "(i)" and "(ii)" and "(iii)" (as to non-intentional breaches or defaults) of Section 8.2(a) (other than with respect to any of the Special Representations) shall commence at the Closing and terminate at 11:59 p.m. Pacific time on the Escrow Release Date [*This is one year after the completion of the acquisition*]. The Claims Period for Indemnifiable Damages arising out of, resulting from or in connection with the other matters listed in Section 8.2(a), consisting of claims alleging (i) intentional fraud by or on behalf of the Company under this Agreement, and (ii) any failure of any of the Company Special Representations to be true and correct, shall commence at the Closing and terminate at 11:59 p.m. Pacific time on the date that is 30 days following the expiration of the applicable statute of limitations. . . .

Note that different sorts of claims have different sorts of timing obligations and restrictions. In this case, the principal period for the assertion of an indemnification claim is one year. This means that for any breach of a representation and warranty, Facebook has one year to discover and assert the claim. This one-year survival period is typical, and is designed to encompass one full audit period. Matters involving intentional fraud or some "special" representations have a longer survival period, namely the statute of limitations.

The merger agreement in a private transaction will also set forth the procedures for the assertion of indemnification:

8.5 <u>Claims</u>.

(a) From time to time during the Claims Period, Acquirer or the Stockholders' Agent, as applicable, may deliver to the Stockholders' Agent or Acquirer, as applicable, one or more certificates signed by any officer of Acquirer or by the Stockholders' Agent (each, a *"Claim Certificate"*): . . . [*Editor: specifics of certificate contents omitted.*]

8.6 <u>Resolution of Objections to Claims</u>.

[*This Section addresses the procedure to pay claims; first non-contested claims, and then contested claims, providing for attempts to reach agreement and eventual recourse to arbitration.*]

8.8 Third-Party Claims.

In the event Acquirer becomes aware of a claim by a third party that Acquirer in good faith believes may result in Indemnifiable Damages (a *"Third-Party Claim"*), Acquirer shall have the right in its sole discretion to conduct the defense of and to settle or resolve any such Third-Party Claim (and, for the avoidance of doubt, the costs and expenses incurred by Acquirer in connection with conducting such defense, settlement or resolution (including reasonable attorneys' fees, other professionals' and experts' fees and court or arbitration costs) shall be included in the Indemnifiable Damages for which Acquirer may seek indemnification pursuant to a claim made hereunder, if any (provided that for clarity such costs and expenses shall constitute Indemnifiable Damages if and solely to the extent that Acquirer is entitled to indemnification for the matter underlying such Third-Party Claim). The Stockholders' Agent shall have the right to receive copies of all pleadings, notices and communications with respect to such Third-Party Claim to the extent that receipt of such documents does not affect any privilege relating to any Indemnified Person, subject to execution by the Stockholders' Agent of Acquirer's (and, if required, such third party's) standard non-disclosure agreement to the extent that such materials contain confidential or propriety information. However, Acquirer shall have the right in its sole discretion to determine and conduct the defense of any Third-Party Claim and the settlement, adjustment or compromise of such Third-Party Claim. Unless otherwise consented to in writing in advance by Acquirer in its sole discretion, the Stockholders' Agent and its Affiliates may not participate in any Third-Party Claim or any action related to such Third-Party Claim (including any discussions or negotiations in connection with the settlement, adjustment or compromise thereof). Except with the consent of the Stockholders' Agent, which consent shall be deemed to have been given unless the Stockholders' Agent shall have objected within 30 days after a written request for such consent by Acquirer, no settlement or resolution by Acquirer of any such Third-Party Claim shall be determinative of the existence of or amount of Indemnifiable Damages relating to such matter. In the event that the Stockholders' Agent has consented to any such settlement or resolution, neither the Stockholders' Agent nor any Converting Holder shall have any power or authority to object under Section 8.6 or any other provision of this Article 8 to the amount of any claim by or on behalf of any Indemnified Person against the Escrow Fund for indemnity with respect to such settlement or resolution.

Acquirer shall give the Stockholders' Agent prompt notice of the commencement of any legal proceeding against Acquirer, the First Surviving Corporation or the Final Surviving Corporation in connection with any Third-Party Claim; provided, that any failure on the part of Acquirer to so notify the Stockholders' Agent shall not limit any of the obligations of any Converting Holder under the Article 8 (except to the extent that such failure materially prejudices the Converting Holder in terms of the amount of Indemnifiable Damages such holder is liable to indemnify the Indemnified Person for).

To understand this provision, consider a simple situation where a seller warrants that there are no lawsuits pending against it, and after the closing, a lawsuit is soon brought. If the buyer could make all decisions about the lawsuit and simply get indemnified by the seller, the buyer would have an incentive to settle quickly, spending as little of its time as it could without regard to how much of the seller's money was required. By contrast, if the seller gets to make decisions about the lawsuit, it wants to spend a great deal of the buyer's time, while spending as little of its money as it can. Not surprisingly, the parties therefore agree on some allocation of responsibilities and some mechanism for each to have input on how such matters are handled. Notice how Section 8.8 addresses each of these matters: it gives the Acquirer (the indemnified party) the right to conduct and settle Third Party Claims "in its sole discretion," requiring only notice to Stockholders' Agent (the agent for the indemnifying party). By contrast, in some other transactions, the indemnifying party might have more rights. Here is an example of a provision giving the seller more rights to be involved in the process by which Third Party Claims are handled:

If any claim shall arise for indemnification under Section [x] [relating to third-party claims], the Indemnified Party shall promptly provide Notice of such claim to the Indemnifying Party. The Indemnifying Party, at its sole cost and expense and upon written notice to the Indemnified Party, may assume the defense of any such Action with its own counsel, and the Indemnified Party shall cooperate in good faith in such defense. [*Alternatively, Indemnifying Party's choice of counsel could be subject to the reasonable satisfaction of the Indemnified Party.*] The Indemnified Party shall be entitled to participate in the defense of any such Action, with its counsel and at its own cost and expense. If the Indemnifying Party does not assume the defense of any such Action, the Indemnified Party may, but shall not be obligated to, defend against such Action in such manner as it may deem appropriate, including, but not limited to, settling such Action, after giving notice of it to the Indemnifying

Party, on such terms as the Indemnified Party may deem appropriate and no action taken by the Indemnified Party in accordance with such defense and settlement shall relieve the Indemnifying Party of its indemnification obligations herein provided with respect to any damages resulting therefrom. The Indemnifying Party shall not settle any Action without the Indemnified Party's prior written consent (which consent shall not be unreasonably withheld or delayed).

M. A RETURN TO CONTRACT PRINCIPLES: DRAFTING AND NEGOTIATING THE MERGER AGREEMENT

As you have seen from the provisions quoted above, merger agreements contain many provisions that are intricately crafted with references to other provisions. A termination for reasons specified in section X yields $A damages, a termination for reasons specified in section Y yields $B damages, and so on. To aid the exposition, and to introduce you more gradually to agreements, we have thus far spared you some of the most intricate cross-references. You will see many such cross-references in the case described below. Cross-references are particularly tricky when they are negative: "notwithstanding anything in Section X" or "anything in Section Y to the contrary notwithstanding." Because of the genesis of agreements and the pace of negotiations and drafting, agreements can have warring "notwithstandings." Some notwithstanding clauses do not reference another provision specifically—rather, they might say "Anything else in this agreement to the contrary notwithstanding." Or there may be implicit notwithstandings, such as provisions saying that something is the "exclusive" remedy—if there is another remedy set forth elsewhere in the agreement, how are the two provisions reconciled? The case described below involved precisely such issues. More generally, it illustrates the perils of time-pressured back-and-forth negotiations of highly complex and adversarial matters.

The judge concluded that both parties' readings of the agreement were reasonable, but made his decision based on the venerable contract interpretation principle (that the court refers to as the "forthright negotiator principle") that where Party 1 knows of Party 2's meaning, but Party 2 does not know of Party 1's meaning, Party 2's meaning prevails.

Cerberus Capital and United Rentals ("URI") agreed to a merger at the height of the recent credit bubble. When the financial crisis of 2008 froze capital markets, Cerberus was unable to move forward with the deal. Cerberus took the position that it could be relieved of its obligations under the agreement by paying a termination fee.

RAM Holdings and RAM Acquisitions (collectively, "RAM"), corporations controlled by Cerberus Capital Management, L.P., a major private equity firm, were formed to acquire URI. URI, RAM, and for some purposes, another affiliate of Cerberus entered into a merger agreement governing the terms by which URI would be acquired. At some point after entry into the merger agreement, Cerberus (and therefore RAM) decided it didn't want to acquire URI, and RAM informed URI that it would not be proceeding with the acquisition. RAM took the position that under the Merger Agreement, it could terminate its obligations by paying a termination fee of $100 million. The Merger Agreement indeed provided that RAM could satisfy its obligations by paying such a fee. However, the merger agreement also contained a conflicting provision: that URI could obtain specific performance. Not surprisingly, URI took the position that it could require RAM to consummate the transaction, and sued RAM. RAM counter-claimed that the other provision allowing it to pay $100 million and terminate the agreement applied.

The court was called upon to determine which provision, the termination fee provision and the specific performance provision, trumped. The termination fee provision, Section 8.2(e), had a "notwithstanding" clause:

> Notwithstanding anything to the contrary in this Agreement, including with respect to Sections 7.4 and 9.10 [the specific performance provision], (i) the Company's right to terminate this Agreement in compliance with the provisions of Sections 8.1(d)(i) and (ii) and its right to receive the Parent Termination Fee pursuant to Section 8.2(c) or the guarantee thereof pursuant to the Guarantee, and (ii) [RAM Holdings]'s right to terminate this Agreement pursuant to Section 8.1(e)(i) and (ii) and its right to receive the Company Termination Fee pursuant to Section 8.2(b) shall, in each case, be the sole and exclusive remedy, including on account of punitive damages, of (in the case of clause (i)) the Company and its subsidiaries against [RAM Holdings], [RAM Acquisition], [Cerberus Partners] or any of their respective affiliates, shareholders, general partners, limited partners, members, managers, directors, officers, employees or agents (collectively "Parent Related Parties") and (in the case of clause (ii)) [RAM Holdings] and [RAM Acquisition] against the Company or its subsidiaries, affiliates, shareholders, directors, officers, employees or agents (collectively "Company Related Parties"), for any and all loss or damage suffered as a result thereof, and upon any termination specified in clause (i) or (ii) of this Section 8.2(e) and payment of the Parent Termination Fee or Company Termination Fee, as the case may be, none of [RAM Holdings], [RAM Acquisition], [Cerberus Partners] or any of

their respective Parent Related Parties or the Company or any of the Company Related Parties shall have any further liability or obligation of any kind or nature relating to or arising out of this Agreement or the transactions contemplated by this Agreement as a result of such termination.

Another part of Section 8.2(e) provided that:

In no event, whether or not this Agreement has been terminated pursuant to any provision hereof, shall [RAM Holdings], [RAM Acquisition], [Cerberus Partners] or the Parent Related Parties, either individually or in the aggregate, be subject to any liability in excess of the Parent Termination Fee for any or all losses or damages relating to or arising out of this Agreement or the transactions contemplated by this Agreement, including breaches by [RAM Holdings] or [RAM Acquisition] of any representations, warranties, covenants or agreements contained in this Agreement, and in no event shall the Company seek equitable relief or seek to recover any money damages in excess of such amount from [RAM Holdings], [RAM Acquisition], [Cerberus Partners] or any Parent Related Party or any of their respective Representatives.

The last sentence of Section 8.2(a) provided that:

The parties acknowledge and agree that, subject to Section 8.2(e), nothing in this Section 8.2 shall be deemed to affect their right to specific performance under Section 9.10

URI claimed that they were entitled to specific performance under the Merger Agreement; RAM claimed that URI was not. In other words, the parties explicitly acknowledged that their lawyers had drafted conflicting termination provisions, provisions which appeared irreconcilable.

The court concluded that there was no "single, shared understanding with respect to the availability of specific performance under the Merger Agreement." It deemed both interpretations reasonable and looked to extrinsic evidence. It ruled for RAM, on grounds that URI didn't communicate its understanding that specific performance was available to RAM, but RAM did communicate to URI its understanding that specific performance was not available (in other words, that URI knew of the conflicting wording but didn't alert RAM to the conflict). URI therefore didn't meet its burden of persuasion. RAM consequently terminated the agreement and paid $100 million to URI. In the wake of the termination URI's market capitalization declined by about $3 billion.

Ultimately, the battle between URI and RAM was a "there but for the grace of god" moment for M&A lawyers. In the heat of negotiation, the lawyers had negotiated directly conflicting provisions—and one side had apparently not noticed the conflict. The difference led URI to lose over $3 billion in market capitalization and a buy-out at this higher price.[29]

QUESTIONS

1.   Under what circumstances might one want to use a "collar" in a merger agreement's price term?

2.   In deciding whether or not a seller should offer a qualified representation, what kinds of considerations might be important?

3.   How might the qualification of "knowledge" affect a representation about a seller's liabilities?

4.   What is a "bring-down" condition and how does it work together with the representations and warranties?

5.   Courts have regularly held that strict "no-talk" provisions are illegal. Why do you think that is the case?

6.   Consider the "taxonomy" of deal protection measures. Can you think of new deal protection measures that might be equally effective as the ones commonly deployed in merger agreements?

7.   Find the definition of an MAE in the Men's Wearhouse merger agreement (located in the Online Appendix). If, between signing and closing, there was a financial crisis that made it impossible for Men's Wearhouse to access any commercial credit thereby crippled its business, would that constitute an MAE under the definition?

8.   How does an indemnification provision in a private company deal ensure the buyer gets the benefit of her bargain?

9.   Why is there indemnification in a private transaction but not a public one?

PROBLEMS

1.   Write a memo explaining the Dell termination fee provisions to a client. How are the events triggering a $180 million termination fee different from those triggering the $450 million fee? What is the reason for the difference?

2.   Draft an earnout provision for a seller of a small manufacturing company who has sold his business to a diversified conglomerate. Address the following issues:

- How should the earnout be computed? If the business will be part of a broader company, how much "overhead" can be allocated to the business?

---

[29] Adapted from Claire A. Hill, *Bargaining In The Shadow Of The Lawsuit*, 34 DEL J. CORP. L. 191, 201–3 (2009).

- How will decisions regarding matters that might affect the earnout be decided? For instance, what about the acquisition of equipment, or the decision to hire or fire employees or change the terms of their employment?

- How will reorganizations involving the acquired business be treated for purposes of the earnout? Will the person getting the earnout have any say on whether the deal is done and on what terms?

- Who gets to do the earnout computation? What happens if there is disagreement on the results of the computation?

- Can amounts owing under the earnout be offset against other obligations, such as indemnification obligations, that the seller might owe to the buyer?

3. Go to SSRN and download: Steven M. Davidoff & Kristen Baiardi, Accredited Home Lenders v. Lone Star Funds: A MAC Case Study (Draft dated, Feb. 11, 2008), available at http://papers.ssrn.com/sol3/papers.cfm?abstract_id=1092115. Please review the MAC case study and do the assignment contained therein.

CHAPTER XV

RESISTING A HOSTILE OFFER

■ ■ ■

In this Chapter we discuss a target company's defenses to an attempted hostile takeover. A target company can have many reasons for wishing to defend itself against a takeover attempt. The target's board may believe that the company's long term prospects are better if it remains independent, or that the particular acquirer is undesirable because of antitrust or other regulatory concerns. The acquirer who is refused is faced with a choice: go away or "go hostile." "Going hostile" means trying to cause the target's board to agree to the transaction, or making a tender offer to the shareholders against the will of the board.

In this Section, we will introduce you to much of the vocabulary necessary to understand hostile, as well as friendly, deals. In the following Chapters we discuss the fiduciary duties of a board in deciding to resist a hostile takeover, as well its duties when it accepts an offer to be acquired.

A. THE MARKET FOR CORPORATE CONTROL

Henry Manne is credited with the idea that there is a market for corporate control. The following excerpt describes the intellectual history behind the market for corporate control and the role the hostile tender offer plays.

TAKEOVER THEORY AND THE LAW AND ECONOMICS MOVEMENT

Steven M. Davidoff
in CLAIRE HILL & BRETT MCDONNELL (EDS), RESEARCH HANDBOOK
ON THE ECONOMICS OF CORPORATION LAW 216, 219–221 (2012)

In his . . . ten-page article *Mergers and the Market for Corporate Control [1965]*, Manne set forth a theory of the market for corporate control. The takeover market serves as a monitor for managers in public corporate entities. If these managers fail to efficiently run the corporate enterprise or otherwise seek their own private benefits to the detriment of the corporation, the takeover market serves as a monitor. The value of the corporate enterprise will decline relative to shares in similarly situated corporations. This will attract third parties to bid for control of the company, actors who will otherwise operate it more efficiently and without such detriment. . .

Manne's article was an implicit endorsement of an unconstrained takeover market; one where acquirers could freely bid for companies. This would produce net social gains by allocating resources more efficiently; it would also force managers to operate their companies more capably or otherwise be replaced, itself a net social gain.

. . .

The 1980s takeover wave transformed the capital markets and was marked by a surge in hostile and unsolicited takeover offers. It spurred a heated legislative, judicial and academic debate over the proper regulation of these offers. The academic debate was heavily influenced by three law and economics articles written in the early 1980s. While these articles continue to shape takeover theory through today, their influence on courts and legislatures has been less significant.

The first of these papers was published by Frank Easterbrook and Daniel Fischel in the *Harvard Law Review* in 1981; it was entitled 'The Proper Role of a Target's Management in Responding to a Takeover.' In this article, Easterbrook and Fischel argued that a defensive response by management to a hostile takeover offer decreases shareholder welfare. This conclusion was predicated on the efficiency of the stock market and the influence of the market on any takeover bid premium, making any bid that was above the stock price a wealth maximizing one for shareholders. Easterbrook and Fischel stated:

> [w]e can conclude . . . that a tender offer at a price higher than the prevailing one also exceeds the value of the stock. True, the target's managers may know something about the firm's prospects not yet incorporated into the price of the shares. But the disparity between price and worth could not last long. If a bidder tried to steal the target by capitalizing on its special information, the target's managers could defeat the offer by disclosing the information to the public. The price would adjust to reflect the new information, and the offer would succeed only if it were higher than the new price. Tender offers at a premium thus must benefit the target's shareholders.

Since any premium would benefit the stockholders and the price was self-adjusting, the proper response of a target board was passivity. Any target board defense would only forestall social welfare enhancing bids and chill takeover activity, such bids and takeover activity being desirable as encouraging the market for corporate control. As a corollary to this conclusion, Easterbrook and Fischel posited that bidding competitions for targets should be discouraged as they would diminish search returns and reduce takeover activity.

Lucian Bebchuk, then still a graduate student at Harvard Law School, responded in an article a year later entitled 'The Case for Facilitating Competing Tender Offers' (1982). Bebchuk noted that there were 'strong reasons' to restrict defensive tactics since they would entrench management as well as remove shareholders as the primary decision-maker in the takeover decision. However, in contrast to Easterbrook and Fischel, Bebchuk argued for an auctioneering rule: boards should be allowed to adopt defensive tactics in order to facilitate auctions. He concluded that bidders for a company were driven by the prospect of synergies and improved management; to the extent they were successful these transactions should increase social welfare. In response to Easterbrook and Fischel, Bebchuk also argued that auctions would not increase search costs unduly, as significant motivational forces would remain which would still incentivize bidders to make an offer. An auctioneering rule would increase premiums to, and maximize economic welfare for, target shareholders, without decreasing bidding rates.

In between the publication of these two articles, Ronald Gilson published 'A Structural Approach to Corporations: The Case Against Defensive Tactics in Tender Offers' (1981). Gilson examined the structure of the corporation and the role of management in light of Michael Jensen and William Meckling's theory of the firm. Like Manne, Gilson posited that management was likely to rent-seek to its own benefit. Gilson argued that 'the tender offer is centrally important to the structure of the corporation because it is the key displacement mechanism through which the market for corporate control constrains management behavior and because it is a critical safety valve against management's misuse of its controlling role in all other displacement mechanisms.' According to Gilson, the tender offer was the key to the market for corporate control; the structure of the corporation necessitated barring defensive tactics by corporate boards and placing the corporate control decision with shareholders. A rule forbidding management from interfering with shareholder ability to accept offers was appropriate.

Though the details and rationale were different, each of the three articles placed the decision to accept or decline a tender offer with shareholders. This would enable the market for corporate control to effectively function in the manner Manne theorized. There were detractors: Marty Lipton argued that directors were best positioned to make the takeover decision and that takeover defenses were appropriate. Louis Lowenstein famously argued that the stock market was too inefficient for the disciplining force of the market for corporate control to work. But the words of John Coffee in 1984 highlighted the continuing influence of Manne's theory. Coffee wrote that 'the claim that hostile takeovers generate a disciplinary force that constrains managerial behavior cannot seriously be disputed'. This idea (and these articles) would shape the takeover debate through the 1980s and 1990s. 1970s notions of fairness no longer came to the fore; instead, economics and Manne's theory were the start of any takeover regulation analysis.

As the 1980s progressed, this debate would become more complex as others built upon the theories put forth in these three articles. Coffee was notable in expanding the framework of this debate and noting its limitations. In that same 1984 article referred to above, Coffee asserted that 'this view both overstates the potential of the market for control and understates the potential efficacy of other modes of corporate accountability—such as independent boards or intra-corporate litigation'. Coffee postulated that other mechanisms might increase social welfare more than the market for corporate control. Coffee was arguing that these issues were far more complicated than the early literature suggested and that caution was therefore necessary.

While the academic battle raged, the political and judicial one also continued. The battle over the proper regulation of targets and takeovers took place in Congress, the state legislatures and the Delaware judiciary. In all three instances, the advocates of a free market for corporate control eventually lost. Second generation state anti-takeover laws were struck down by the Supreme Court in *Edgar v. Mite* but the states proceeded to enact third generation laws which the Supreme Court upheld in *CTS Corp. v. Dynamics Corp.* In the wake of *CTS*, even Delaware passed a mild form of business combination statute. Congress, despite a number of proposed bills, largely failed to act other than to limit golden parachutes and greenmail.

The Delaware judiciary itself in *Unocal v. Mesa Petroleum* set forth a standard of review for a board decision to adopt takeover defenses. A year after *Unocal*, the Delaware Supreme Court in *Revlon, Inc. v. MacAndrews & Forbes Holdings, Inc.* also adopted a rule requiring that a target board accept the highest price reasonably available upon a decision to sell the company. The *Unocal* and *Revlon* decisions were notable for restricting the use of takeover and transaction defenses, and for doing so on the basis of the inherent conflict between management and shareholders in the takeover context. These decisions posited a judicial review function to ensure that this conflict was mitigated in the market for corporate control. However, in later decisions such as *Paramount Communications, Inc. v. Time, Inc.* the Delaware Supreme Court took a more restrictive view of the scope of both the *Unocal* and *Revlon* standards, significantly cutting back their potential impact on the market for corporate control. None of these decisions relied on the law and economics literature as the basis for their rulings.

As the excerpt highlights, Manne's idea, and subsequent scholarship based on his thesis, proved quite influential in promoting the hostile takeover in academic circles, but failed to substantially influence legal doctrine. Instead, states responded to pressure by managers and others by passing anti-takeover laws. Meanwhile, Delaware, in particular, developed a jurisprudence which rejected the idea of an unconstrained takeover market. In this Chapter and what follows, we discuss these responses as well as the fiduciary duties of boards in hostile and friendly takeovers.

B. THE INITIAL APPROACH

A potential acquirer begins the process of an acquisition by making private entreaties to the target's board. In some cases, this will result in negotiations, and ultimately, a deal. In other cases, the acquirer's approaches will be rebuffed, possibly after substantial negotiations, and the potential acquirer will abandon its pursuit of the target. In still other cases, the acquirer will be unable to reach a deal with the target, but may still wish to acquire the company. This last scenario sets the stage for the hostile offer.

1. THE BEAR HUG

The acquirer's first step in a hostile acquisition may not be to launch a fully hostile offer. Instead, it may decide to send a "bear hug" letter to the target's board. The "hug' is the offer to acquire the target. The "bear" has claws—the implicit threat to launch a hostile offer if the friendly offer is not accepted. At the same time that the letter is sent to the board, it is made public, alerting shareholders of the possible bid. In his book *Big Deal*, Bruce Wasserstein dated the practice to 1982, to T. Boone Pickens's bear hug letter sent to the CEO of Cities Services and simultaneously announced to the public. Mr. Wasserstein wrote that the chance of the offer being accepted was "slim," but "that wasn't the point. Pickens just wanted to build public pressure on Cities' incumbent managers and board of directors."[1]

If the bear hug letter is sent privately and not made public, then it is called a "teddy bear" hug. This softer form of letter is designed to apply less pressure to the board, letting them know that even though a hostile offer lurks in the background, for a time the acquirer is willing to keep any negotiations confidential.

Following is an example of a bear hug letter. This bear hug letter was sent by CEO of Valeant J. Michael Pierson to the CEO of Allergan, David

---

[1] BRUCE WASSERSTEIN, BIG DEAL: MERGERS AND ACQUISITIONS IN THE DIGITAL AGE, 173 (3d ed. 1998).

Pyott. The letter, which was publicly filed with the SEC, disclosed previous private approaches by Valeant to Allergan.

Mr. David Pyott
Chairman & CEO Allergan
Allergan, Inc.
2525 Dupont Drive
Irvine, California 92612

Dear Mr. Pyott,

Valeant is pleased to provide Allergan shareholders with the opportunity to consider a strategically compelling and enormously value-creating opportunity to merge with Valeant. Our merger offer is comprised of $48.30 in cash and 0.83 of a Valeant share for each Allergan share based on the fully diluted number of Allergan shares outstanding. Shareholders will be able to elect their mix of cash and shares, subject to proration, in the combined company hereafter referred to as the "New Company." Allergan shareholders will receive a substantial premium over Allergan's April 10, 2014, unaffected stock price of $116.63 and will own 43% of the New Company.

We firmly believe that applying Valeant's operating philosophy, strategy, and financial discipline to a broader set of superb assets will create extraordinary returns for shareholders over the short, intermediate, and long term.

A Highly Strategic Combination

The New Company will be extremely well positioned in the markets it serves. Our portfolios are extremely complementary—the New Company will be a leader in ophthalmology, dermatology, aesthetics, dental products, and the emerging markets—healthcare segments that are forecasted to grow well above overall industry growth rates over the next decade. In light of the markets served and the marketing efficiencies created by the combination, we are confident that New Company will generate high single-digit organic growth rates for the foreseeable future.

The New Company will generate stable and recurring cash flows: approximately 75% of its revenue will come from durable products, 90% of the New Company's combined revenue is not expected to face any significant patent cliffs over the next decade, and 70% of the New Company's business is expected to be cash-pay or third-party reimbursed, with only 30% exposed to government reimbursement. With this transaction, we expect 25–30% pro forma 2014 Cash EPS accretion assuming the transaction closed and full synergies realized on January 1, 2014. We expect Cash EPS in year 2 and beyond to grow 15–20% plus, depending upon the deployment of free cash flow.

No Material Social Issues

We would have preferred to negotiate this transaction in a confidential manner, but given that Allergan has not been receptive to our overtures for over eighteen months and has made it clear both privately and publicly that it is not interested in a deal with us, we chose to present this proposal to Allergan shareholders directly. We are open to discussing and addressing social issues such as board composition, senior management team composition, U.S. headquarters location and other concerns that you may have. Shareholder value is our primary consideration.

We encourage Allergan to enter into discussions with us promptly so that we can consummate this mutually beneficial transaction in a timely manner. We look forward to hearing from you.

Sincerely,
J. Michael Pearson
cc: Allergan, Inc. Board of Directors

———————————

A bear hug letter puts the market on notice that a company may be subject to a hostile offer. A company which attracts one or more suitors, including as a result of a bear hug letter, is referred to as being "in play." When a company is in play, market reactions include purchases of the company's stock by merger arbitrageurs and others who want to bet that the company may be sold in the near future, perhaps after a bidding war. The stock price of the potential target may rise to close to a bear hug letter's offer price following the release of the letter, as shareholders at the time the offer becomes public sell for immediate gain. The shares are bought by new shareholders who expect the price to rise even further, from one or more bidders' interest in the company and a possible sale at a price higher than the initial offer price. If enough shares are sold, the target may come to be dominated by new shareholders seeking gains from a takeover transaction, pressuring the company towards a sale. The bear hug letter thus carries significant consequences for a target company.

2. THE HOSTILE TENDER OFFER

As noted previously, acquisition transactions can take a variety of forms, including mergers, tender offers, and asset sales. The hostile transaction, however, can only take one form: a tender offer. Statutory mergers and asset sales require board action. Whatever one or more shareholders may think of an acquirer's offer, they cannot act for the company. Only the board may initiate a statutory transaction like a merger or an asset sale. Consequently, when potential acquirers wish to conduct an acquisition over the objections of the incumbent board of directors, they must make a tender offer. A tender offer is effective for this purpose since it is made directly to shareholders; there is no statutory role for the board.

Modern-day tender offers typically are made for all of the outstanding shares of the company. Contrast this with the "two-tier front-loaded' tender offer common in the 1980s. The first "tier" was the cash tender offer for 51% of the company. In the second tier, shareholders who had not tendered in the first tier would be "squeezed out," getting high-yield bonds, also known as junk bonds, which the acquirers said were worth the same amount as the cash for their shares. Many were skeptical that the bonds really were worth the same as the cash. The *Unocal* case, *Unocal v. Mesa*, 493 A.2d 946 (Del. 1985), discussed in Chapter XVI, concerns a two-tier front-loaded tender offer initiated by Mesa Petroleum for Unocal. The front tier was cash in the amount of $54 per share, while the back end (second tier) was debt securities which Mesa asserted were also worth $54. The court's skepticism about this assertion was clear: the court noted that "Unocal has rather aptly termed such securities 'junk bonds.'"

Are "junk bonds" really junk? As the famous investment banker Bruce Wasserstein was known to say, "cash is king." This is not to say that an offer of stock or debt securities rather than cash is somehow coercive or defective. But the value of cash is certain, while securities always present a valuation issue. The highest quality securities, such as those issued by the U.S. government and backed by its full faith and credit, are cash equivalents and due to the low risk have lower yields. Securities issued by a debt-laden company, and especially highly subordinated securities issued by such a company, may be quite difficult to value due to the high risk of default and commensurate higher interest rate. These riskier securities may—or may not—be worth what the hostile bidder is saying they are worth.[2].

In the 1980s, a company whose shareholders were receiving such a two-tiered offer was justly concerned that the shareholders might feel pressured to tender into the front end in order to avoid getting the back-end consideration, debt securities which might be of very low quality. Thus, even an offer that was, or was thought by shareholders to be,

---

[2] Of course, it is not as though the hostile bidder can simply assign a high value to the junk bonds—it will have to have some justification for its valuation. But, again, debt is not cash, and risky debt may be particularly hard to value with precision.

inadequate might succeed. Success would simply require more than 50% of the shareholders to accept, either because they found the offer to be attractive, or because they feared getting the back-end consideration. A shareholder deciding whether to tender would assess what the other shareholders were likely to do, and if she concluded enough of them were likely to accept, she would as well.

Today, two-tiered front-loaded cash tender offers are no longer made, primarily because of the advent of the poison pill (discussed below), which provided companies with an effective defense. Rather, as noted below, tender offers today are generally for any and all shares. Such offers are not coercive in the way two-tiered offers of the sort described above were, but they may present other issues. For example, a tender offer may be timed to take advantage of a price drop below what the board in good faith believes to be the corporation's intrinsic or fundamental value. There may be a setback which the board believes is temporary, and to which the board believes the market is overreacting. Or there may be a general "bearish" sentiment that causes many stock prices to decline. An offeror can offer shareholders more than the then-current market price, but, in the board's view, still be offering less than the corporation's fundamental long term value.

Targets are also concerned when the consideration offered is stock, as was the case in Allergan's bid for Valeant. To assess the value of the bidder's offer, the target will be required to assess the value of the bidder's stock. Not surprisingly, Valeant's bear hug letter extolled the value of its own stock. The target might understandably be more skeptical. It might think the acquirer's stock is overvalued, such that the price being offered is insufficient. Indeed, one of Allergan's defenses against Valeant's offer was to argue that Valeant stock was overpriced.

A hostile offer also can be subject to contingencies that make its completion uncertain. Typical conditions might include a minimum tender condition, a financing condition, or a diligence condition. That an offer is highly contingent can motivate a company to defend itself. Such an offer can put a target company in play without the bidder making any real commitment to actually complete the transaction. Being in play can be quite damaging to a target, as employees may seek other employment, and those dealing with the company as buyers or sellers may seek transacting parties offering more certainty. Shareholders, too, may sell their shares, and the buyers are apt to be those interested in quick price increases. As a consequence, the highly contingent offer can be perceived as a threat to the corporation. Note that in the Valeant bear hug letter included above, Valeant stresses that antitrust and financing should not present obstacles to the consummation of its offer, thus attempting to limit Allergan's ability to characterize the offer as "highly contingent."

3. A NOTE ABOUT TOEHOLDS

Valeant's offer was buttressed by the 9.7% stake that Pershing Square and Valeant took in Allergan. A position of this type can be valuable because it gives the hostile bidder an advantage in any future proxy contest. The shares they own will be voted in favor of their transaction, and not in favor of another bid. Such a stake also allows the bidder to pay less than other bidders are likely to have to pay. The bidder will purchase the shares before its offer is disclosed, and therefore (almost certainly) at a lower price than the offer price. A toehold also allows a bidder to profit if the target subsequently is sold to a third party, compensating the bidder if its offer fails.

Despite the value of a toehold, bidders rarely take such positions. As discussed in Chapter VIII.A, HSR filing requirements require a hostile bidder to make a filing, and obtain pre-clearance, for transactions exceeding a certain size. Toeholds themselves can thus sometimes require a filing. While the filing is not disclosed to the public, the target will be notified and required to also make a filing. The target will therefore be alerted the target of the possibility of a hostile bid. The effect has been to deter bidders from taking toeholds in order to avoid premature disclosure of a transaction. This is why Valeant's co-bid with Pershing Square was so novel. But the co-bid was structured so that a filing would not be required: Pershing Square structured its bid not through acquisition of equity, which would have triggered an immediate HSR filing, but through acquisition of equity options and forward contracts that could be exercised after HSR clearance. The filing could thus be made after the announcement of the derivative position, a position that could be promptly converted to Allergan shares after HSR clearance.

There is another reason why toeholds are rare. Once the bidder announces its offer, it is typically prevented from additional purchases by Rule 14e–5, the Williams Act rule which prevents outside purchases once an offer is announced. Even if the bidder does not plan to commence a tender offer at the time of the announcement, concerns over losing flexibility to change course and launch a tender offer later will cause it to avoid purchases even if HSR clearance is obtained.

C. THE TARGET RESPONSE

The twenty business day period that a tender offer must remain open under the Williams Act provides a company with an initial period of time to react to the hostile offer. A company's response will typically consist of two components: the company's strategic response to the offer, and the defenses it adopts against being taken over. We first discuss the strategic response, the company's justification for its unwillingness to accept the offer, and then turn to its adoption of takeover defenses. One sort of defense is "responsive"—that is, it responds to an unwanted offer. Another sort is "structural"—it is put in place, ready to discourage unwanted offers from being made or from progressing. In the succeeding Chapter, we discuss how boards' fiduciary duties have affected their uses of these defenses.

1.   JUST SAY NO

The *"just say no"* defense takes its name from an anti-drug campaign started by First Lady Nancy Reagan in the 1980s. In a just say no defense, a company's board will reject an offer made by a hostile acquirer and take the position that shareholders should not accept the offer. The typical grounds for a "just say no" defense are that the offer "grossly undervalues" the company based on the board's long term perspective of the company's value. In its most extreme form, a board asserting a "just say no" defense takes the position that the company is not for sale at any price. Of course, simply saying no to an unwanted transaction is hardly a defense. If a board refuses to negotiate a merger agreement, an unwanted bidder is free to pursue a tender offer, since doing so does not involve the board. For the "just say no" defense to have any bite, it must be combined with other defenses. The cornerstone of a formidable "just say no" defense is a combination of a staggered board and a poison pill, something we discuss further in Chapter XVI. This combination permits a board to "just say no" and rely on its defenses, while forcing an unwanted bidder to rely on a length proxy contest (which will last for two election cycles given the typical staggered board) in order to unseat a majority of the board and dismantle the defenses.

A "just say no" defense often leads to an argument over whether shareholders will do better by accepting the immediate and certain payment offered by the hostile bidder or, as the company advocates and points to as a justification for the defense, retaining their shares as the target board continues with or puts into place its longer-term plan. As discussed above, the announcement of a hostile bid may lead many target shareholders to sell to merger arbitrage firms who may not be persuaded by the board's having said no. These shareholders will be inclined to favor a takeover. Thus, in the absence of any other takeover defenses, "just say no" can be a weak defense against an unwanted offer because a hostile bidder is still free to make a tender offer directly to shareholders. Consequently, it is common for boards to adopt additional defenses along with the "just say no" defense.

Allergan adopted a "just say no" defense upon receipt of the Valeant bear hug letter, and a subsequent revision of Valeant's offer:

June 10, 2014
Mr. Michael Pearson
Chairman & Chief Executive Officer
Valeant Pharmaceuticals International, Inc.

Dear Michael:

The Board of Directors of Allergan (the "Allergan Board") has received your letter dated May 30, 2014 in which Pershing Square and Valeant made a second revised, unsolicited proposal to acquire all of the outstanding shares of Allergan for a combination of 0.83 of Valeant common shares, $72.00 in cash per share of common stock of the Company, and a Contingent Value Right (CVR) related to DARPin® sales. With the assistance of its financial advisors and legal counsel, the Allergan Board carefully reviewed the revised proposal as well as your recent presentations.

After thorough consideration, the Allergan Board has unanimously determined that your second revised proposal substantially undervalues Allergan, creates significant risks and uncertainties for the stockholders of Allergan, and is not in the best interests of Allergan and its stockholders. In addition, we do not believe your latest proposal offers sufficient or certain value to warrant discussions between Allergan and Valeant.

As we have indicated previously, the Allergan Board has serious concerns about the large stock component of your proposal, and the recent presentations by both you and Pershing Square did nothing to address the issues we previously raised. The Allergan Board must seriously consider the many questions around the sustainability of Valeant's business model as they directly impact the total future consideration for our stockholders.

Allergan has a track record of delivering consistently robust results and value for its stockholders, and we have strong momentum in our business. The Allergan Board believes that through continued innovation and marketing excellence, the Company will extend its track record of substantial, long-term organic growth. This is reflected in Allergan's premium trading multiple, which significantly exceeds Valeant's lagging multiple, as well as the revised expectations from the investment community for a standalone Allergan.

We expect that our plan will generate double digit sales growth and earnings per share compounded annual growth of 20 percent, as well as approximately $14 billion in additional free cash flow over the next five years. This provides Allergan with financial flexibility, and the Allergan Board is confident that Allergan will create significantly more value for stockholders than Valeant's proposal.

On behalf of the Board of Directors,
/s/
David E.I. Pyott, CBE
Chairman & Chief Executive Officer

Allergan's response to Valeant's hostile offer had three components. First, Allergan's board argued that Valeant's offer undervalued the company. Second, Allergan's board argued that the Allergan's strategic plan was superior to Valeant's offer, and able to provide superior value in the long term. Third, Allergan's board argued that there were significant risks to taking Valeant stock, justifying a rejection of Valeant's offer. All three of these types of arguments are typically made in a just say no defense where the consideration offered is stock; the first two are typically made if the consideration offered is cash.

2. WHITE KNIGHT AND WHITE SQUIRE DEFENSES

In the *White Knight* defense, target management seeks out a friendly acquirer to whom it sells the corporation. In this friendly sale, managers hope to ensure the continuation of their strategy and perhaps their own employment as well. *Revlon*, discussed in Chapter XVIII, was a case in which the target pursued a White Knight, Forstmann Little & Co., entering into an agreement with them, rather than succumb to an unwanted acquirer, Pantry Pride. As the board of Revlon discovered, the White Knight defense can be problematic. Not only is it almost impossible for a board (or management) to guarantee that they will be able to maintain their positions post-transaction, a White Knight transaction may effectively put the company up for sale, providing an opening that would require the board to accept a subsequent higher offer from the hostile bidder.

A White Knight sale may also be a recognition that a hostile offer would otherwise be likely to succeed, and that the board is willing to sell at a high (enough) price. Valeant's hostile offer for Allergan ultimately ended in a white knight defense, with Allergan agreeing to be acquired by Actavis for $219 a share in cash and stock, substantially above Valeant's initial bid of about $160 per share. Upon announcement of the Actavis purchase, Valeant's chief executive, J. Michael Pearson, said, "While we will review any such agreement in determining our course of action, Valeant cannot justify to its own shareholders paying a price of $219 or more per share for Allergan." Valeant then withdrew its offer.

As discussed in Chapter XVIII, the agreement Revlon entered into with Forstmann Little included an "asset lock-up," a sale of certain assets at less than fair market value to Forstmann if Revlon did a deal with another acquirer (that is, if another acquirer got 40% of Revlon's shares), and a termination fee, also payable to Forstmann if Revlon did a deal with another acquirer (that is, if the merger agreement terminated or another acquirer got more than 19.9% of Revlon's stock). Both the lock-up and termination fee were invalidated by the court. Asset lock-ups, for a time less used, may be having somewhat of a renaissance.[3] Termination fees, by contrast, are common. There are also other types of lock-ups-which we also refer to as deal protections—discussed in Chapter XVI.G.[4]

A related defense is the *White Squire* defense. In this defense, the target board places (sells) a block of stock with a friendly shareholder in an attempt to make it difficult or impossible for an unwanted bidder to acquire a controlling share of the target. In a well-known 1980s Williams Act case, *SEC v. Carter Hawley Hale Stores,* 760 F.2d 94 (9th Cir. 1985), Carter Hawley Hale Stores attempted to thwart an unwanted acquisition by The Limited by relying on a White Squire defense:

> On April 4, 1984 Limited commenced a cash tender offer for 20.3 million shares of CHH common stock, representing approximately 55% of the total shares outstanding, at $30 per share. Prior to the announced offer, CHH stock was trading at approximately $23.78 per share (pre-tender offer price). Limited disclosed that if its offer succeeded, it would exchange the remaining CHH shares for a fixed amount of Limited shares in a second-step merger. . .

> On April 16, 1984 CHH responded to Limited's offer. CHH issued a press release announcing its opposition to the offer because it was "inadequate and not in the best interests of CHH or its shareholders." CHH also publicly announced an agreement with General Cinema Corporation ("General Cinema"). CHH sold one million shares of convertible preferred stock to General Cinema for $300 million. The preferred shares possessed a vote equivalent to 22% of voting shares outstanding. General Cinema's shares were to be voted pursuant to CHH's Board of Directors recommendations. General Cinema was also granted an option to purchase Walden Book Company, Inc., a profitable CHH subsidiary, for approximately $285 million. Finally, CHH announced a plan to repurchase up to 15 million shares of its own common stock for an amount not to exceed $500 million. If

---

[3]   Daniel E. Wolf et al.,*Update: Crown Jewels—Restoring the Luster to Creative Deal Lock-ups?*, KIRKLAND & ELLIS, Feb. 14, 2013, http://www.kirkland.com/files/MA Update/021413.pdf.

[4]   *See generally* Steven M. Davidoff & Christina M. Stautter, *Lock-Up Creep*, 38 J. CORP. L. 681 (2013).

all 15 million shares were purchased, General Cinema's shares would represent 33% of CHH's outstanding voting shares.

As described above, General Cinema, the White Squire, bought shares in Carter Hawley with 22% of Carter's voting power. General Cinema agreed to vote those shares in the manner recommended by the Carter board, and was granted an option to buy a Carter subsidiary. Carter also engaged in a transaction, a share repurchase from other shareholders, in order to enable General to block a squeeze-out merger under New York's corporate law at the time.

3. PAC MAN

A less common defense is the *Pac Man* defense. In the *Pac Man* defense, the target board responds to a bear hug by making an offer to acquire the bidder, in a manner reminiscent of the 1980s arcade game of the same name. The strategy was first used in the battle between Martin Marietta and Bendix.[5] A recent example is the Men's Wearhouse (MW)/Jos. A. Bank (JOSB) transaction. JOSB made an unsolicited offer for MW. Rather than accept the offer, MW responded by making its own offer to acquire JOSB. Below you will find a copy of the Pac Man offer sent by the board of MW to the independent directors of JOSB.

January 30, 2014
Jos. A. Bank Clothiers, Inc.
500 Hanover Pike
Hampstead, MD 21074

Dear Independent Directors:

We are writing to you, the independent directors of Jos. A. Bank Clothiers, Inc. ("JOSB" or the "Company"), regarding our all-cash $57.50 per share offer to acquire the Company. As we have made clear, our strong preference is to work collaboratively with the JOSB Board and management to realize the benefits of this combination. Our offer would provide your shareholders with a substantial premium and immediate and certain value.

As independent directors, each of you has a heightened responsibility to serve the best interests of shareholders, without regard to conflicting personal interests. As you are no doubt aware, on October 18, 2013, when JOSB proposed to acquire Men's Wearhouse, Mr. Wildrick articulated a compelling rationale for combining our two companies: "We believe that Men's Wearhouse and Jos. A. Bank are ideal partners. . . . By combining our two companies, we can together create the best

---

[5] *See generally* ALLAN SLOAN, THREE PLUS ONE EQUALS BILLIONS: THE BENDIX-MARTIN MARIETTA WAR (1983).

men's apparel and sportswear designer, manufacturer and retailer in the U.S." At that time, the Company was proposing to acquire Men's Wearhouse, and Mr. Wildrick was slated to lead the combined business.

Now, when Men's Wearhouse is proposing to acquire JOSB, and Mr. Wildrick will not be CEO of the combined business, JOSB, rather than engaging in discussions that might lead to that "ideal" combination, is pursuing an alternative transaction, including a material acquisition. Obviously, in considering Men's Wearhouse's offer to acquire the Company, Mr. Wildrick has a conflict of interest that might naturally make him prefer some other strategic alternative. Accordingly, we urge you to form a special committee of <u>independent</u> directors to re-consider Men's Wearhouse's offer and the JOSB Board's decision to reject it (without any discussion whatsoever with Men's Wearhouse).

We are confident that the Men's Wearhouse offer to acquire the Company delivers significant value to the Company's shareholders that is superior to what we believe you can reasonably expect to create as a standalone company. Our offer represents a 52% premium over JOSB's unaffected enterprise value and a 38% premium over the closing share price on October 8, 2013, the day prior to the Company's public announcement of its proposal to acquire Men's Wearhouse. Further, the transaction represents a 9.4x enterprise value to last twelve months ("LTM") Adjusted EBITDA multiple (assuming $135 million of LTM Adjusted EBITDA as of November 2, 2013), which is (i) a significant premium to Jos. A. Bank's proposal to acquire Men's Wearhouse, (ii) in excess of Jos. A. Bank's historical average trading multiple and (iii) near the upper end of recent precedent apparel retail transactions. Moreover, we are prepared to increase our offer price if you can demonstrate or we can discover additional value through discussions or limited due diligence. . . .

With this compelling offer on the table and our mutual belief in the strategic and financial value of combining our companies, we urge you to do what is right for your shareholders and form a special committee of independent directors and enter constructive negotiations with us immediately.

On Behalf of the Board of Directors of The Men's Wearhouse, Inc.,
Douglas S. Ewert
President, Chief Executive Officer and Director

In the context of a Pac Man defense, the question is not whether the two companies should be combined, but which of the two companies is the more appropriate acquirer and perhaps more importantly, which group of managers should lead the combined company. MW ultimately won the argument, and the combined MW/JOSB is now led by managers of MW, which was initially the target in the transaction.

While managers may like the Pac Man defense, target *shareholders* dislike it because if it succeeds, the result is that their company becomes the acquirer, paying a premium to the target, rather than being the one acquired at a premium. It is thus a defense (and offense) that shareholders are particularly skeptical of.

4. LEVERAGED (DIVIDEND) RECAPITALIZATION

In a *leveraged recapitalization*, the target uses its own cash and also borrows heavily to finance a special dividend to current shareholders. The effect of the leveraged recapitalization is, first, to deter any current shareholders from tendering their shares to the bidder, since they will want to get the dividend. Second, the leveraged recapitalization reduces the target firm's equity cushion and its future ability to borrow, making it more difficult for a leveraged acquirer to use the assets the firm (including its cash flows) to finance the acquisition.[6] With the rise of the poison pill, target firms now rarely rely on leveraged recapitalizations.

One recent example of a company considering a leveraged recapitalization is PetSmart. After Jana Partners, a well-known hedge fund, filed a Schedule 13D in July of 2014 announcing a stake in PetSmart, PetSmart considered a leveraged dividend recapitalization, planning to borrow money to return cash through a dividend to its shareholders. But it did not maintain a defensive posture for any appreciable time—it quickly began exploring many alternatives, including a sale, favored by Jana, and agreed in December of 2014 to sell itself to BC Partners, a private equity group.[7]

Some activist shareholders have pushed for leveraged recapitalizations as ways of obtaining quick and high returns on their shareholdings. For instance, during the recent contest in which Dell was

---

[6]   This Section considers leveraged recapitalization as a takeover defense. Companies may have other reasons for engaging in such transactions beyond the context of M&A; these are beyond the scope of this book.

[7]   *See* Beth Jinks, *Jana Urges PetSmart to Pursue Sale Instead of Taking On Debt*, BLOOMBERG BUSINESS, Jul. 29, 2014, available at http://www.bloomberg.com/news/articles/2014–07–29/jana-urges-petsmart-to-consider-sale-before-recapitalization; Michael J. De La Merced, *PetSmart Accepts $8.7 Billion Buyout*, N.Y. TIMES, Dec. 14, 2014, available at http://dealbook.nytimes.com/2014/12/14/petsmart-to-sell-itself-to-investor-group-for–8–7–billion/.

eventually taken private, Carl Icahn urged Dell to engage in such a transaction in lieu of the going-private transaction.

5. STOCK REPURCHASE

The *stock repurchase* is another common takeover defense. Many acquirers, particularly financial buyers, will rely on the assets of the target to finance their bids. These assets include cash on hand as well as the capacity to borrow. The stock repurchase takes away at least one and sometimes both of these assets. By using corporate cash to engage in a repurchase, managers can provide current shareholders who may wish to sell with an immediate return at a premium to market while reducing cash on hand—cash that will no longer be available for acquirers to use to fund an acquisition. Managers can even borrow to finance a stock repurchase and in that way reduce the firm's borrowing capacity further, degrading the value of the firm as a target. Because managers typically do not participate in the repurchase, the repurchase increases their relative stake in the target. In target companies where managers have a relatively large stake to begin with, a stock repurchase can be an effective deterrent to an unwanted bidder.

A leveraged recapitalization often includes a stock repurchase. Cases in which companies effectively borrowed to fund repurchases of their stock include *Unocal*, discussed in Chapter XVI of this book, and *Revlon*, discussed in Chapter XVIII. In both instances, the companies defended against a hostile acquirer by offering to exchange debt for some of their shares. In both instances, the exchanges were on terms that were very attractive to shareholders. After the exchange offers, the targets were far more leveraged than they previously had been. In *Unocal*, the acquirer was defeated. Revlon was taken over by the hostile acquirer.

6. DEFENSIVE ACQUISITIONS AND SALES

Another technique similar to share repurchases is a *defensive acquisition*. In a defensive acquisition, a target corporation acquires another company, in order to reduce its cash on hand, its borrowing capacity, or both, thus making itself less attractive to a hostile acquirer or improving its bargaining leverage. For example, in response to MW's Pac Man offer to acquire Jos A. Banks, Jos A. Banks entered into an agreement to acquire Eddie Bauer for $825 million.[8] Jos A. Banks used the agreement as leverage to negotiate additional consideration from Men's Wearhouse, abandoning the Bauer deal when it agreed to be acquired by Men's Wearhouse. A target can also make an acquisition that will cause antitrust complications for the hostile bidder.

---

[8]   *Jos. A. Bank Buys Eddie Bauer Brand in $825M Deal*, BLOOMBERG NEWS, Feb. 14, 2014, available at http://www.bloomberg.com/news/videos/b/b5b36ad3–b623–4070–8ac0–eed1b97e2ebc.

These are all "strategic responses," in the sense that they make the case that the target's business plan is better than the acquirer's, or change the target's capital structure or business. Targets also typically adopt "defenses" against a hostile offer that are expressly mechanisms to defeat the offer. The main defense adopted by companies today is the shareholder rights plan, also known as a poison pill, discussed in Subsection D below.

7.   GOLDEN AND TIN PARACHUTES

When describing the array of takeover defenses any corporation has in place, commentators will often refer to *golden parachutes* as a takeover defense. Golden parachutes are payments made to certain executives of the target company in the event they are laid off following an acquisition. Although commonly thought of as part of the array of takeover defenses, strictly speaking they are not. The justification for golden parachutes is that these payments change the incentives of executives and make them more willing to consider a valuable acquisition offer, even if that offer would result in the executives losing their jobs.

In the context of an acquisition, golden parachutes for executives often generate a lot of attention and public anger. The amount executives are paid just by way of normal compensation is a subject of visceral populist anger. When executives are getting paid what seem like large lump sums to "parachute" away from the company, the reaction is magnified. Many mainstream commentators suggest that given the levels of compensation the executives are already getting, they should not need more to do what their jobs already require them to do. "Should" is the operative word in this construction. If, for conscious, or even unconscious reasons, the executive in fact is influenced by his own prospects in deciding how his company should react to the merger, the corporation may be best served by using golden parachutes.

Another defensive measure is the *tin parachute*. While the golden parachute provides exit payments only to senior managers in the event of an acquisition, the tin parachute vests a much larger swath of employees with benefits. The rationale for tin parachutes is quite different than the rationale for golden parachutes. The tin parachute is intended to be a poison pill. By raising the costs of terminating large numbers of employees, the tin parachute increases the costs of the acquisition, hopefully high enough to dissuade an unwanted acquirer from proceeding.

In 2008, when Yahoo was attempting to stave off unwanted interest from Microsoft, Yahoo adopted a tin parachute program which provided change of control payments to all of Yahoo's employees. In the event of an acquisition of Yahoo by Microsoft that entailed the termination of Yahoo's employees, Microsoft could find itself on the hook for as much as $2.4 billion in termination payments. Ultimately, Microsoft did not move forward with its acquisition of Yahoo. Following is an excerpt from a letter to the board of Yahoo from investor Carl Icahn complaining about the defensive effect of the tin parachutes.

ICAHN CAPITAL LP
767 Fifth Avenue, 47th Floor
New York, NY 10153

June 6, 2008

Roy Bostock
Chairman
Yahoo! Inc.
701 First Avenue
Sunnyvale, CA 94089

Dear Roy:

While you may take issue with the content of my letter, I take issue with your oversight of Yahoo! Again, I stand by my characterization of your "poison pill" severance plan and I find it humorous to see you attempt to defend it.

Roy, it is you who "misrepresents and misstates the details" of the plan. Much like the rhetoric in many well known political campaigns, you keep repeating misstatements in the hopes that by repeating misstatements enough times it will convince your shareholders that these misstatements are valid. For example, you repeated, "the plan was fully disclosed at the time of its adoption and should be no surprise to anyone at this point."

This is simply not true. The egregious magnitude of the dollar amount cost of the plan was never fully disclosed, nor was the email from your compensation advisor calling the plan "nuts." While you keep repeating that the severance plan was in the "best interests of shareholders", you neglect to mention that the financial cost of the plan could be immense. The documents obtained during discovery and released in the shareholder complaint show that Yahoo! estimates the maximum change in control severance expenses to be a staggering $2.4 billion if Microsoft bids $35 per share for Yahoo! You neglected to mention that the true cost to an acquirer may be even higher as the perverse change in control severance incentives may diminish the work effort of Yahoo! employees. In case you do not understand the plan, in addition to the $2.4 billion of severance expenses, I believe the plan will negatively impact employee behavior and degrade the ability of an acquirer to successfully integrate the acquisition. In the event of a change of control, the employee may decide not to work as hard in the hopes of cashing in on a robust severance package that awards up to two years salary and benefits, $15,000 of outplacement expenses, and accelerated vesting of stock options and restricted stock units. To make matters worse, it is not just the acquirer firing the employee that can trigger the severance package but the employee who may decide on his or her own to resign for "good reason" at any point within two years of a change in control. It is quite obvious to me that this plan impacts the price an acquirer would pay. Is it any wonder than an acquirer, once fully comprehending this plan, might not wish to negotiate any further? I again call upon you to honor your fiduciary duty to your shareholders and rescind this "poison pill" severance plan. . . .

Sincerely yours,
CARL C. ICAHN

D. THE TARGET DEFENSE: THE POISON PILL

The invention in 1982 of the poison pill as a takeover defense changed everything. It provided targets with an effective defense to hostile takeovers, one that required hostile bidders to bargain with a target's board or have their tender offers blocked. The power of the poison pill to force acquirers to negotiate with the target board reallocated authority for "who decides" in a hostile takeover from shareholders to the target board. The poison pill reallocates authority in a tender offer by making the bidder's acquisition of more than a threshold amount of shares prohibitively expensive if not impossible unless the bidder secures the target board's approval.

1. THE INVENTION OF THE POISON PILL

The poison pill was first developed by Martin Lipton and his colleagues at Wachtell Lipton Rosen & Katz in 1982.

The first generation of the poison pill was the so-called "flip-over" pills, which were intended to raise the costs associated with the second step merger in a two-step transaction. In such a merger, the pill gave the target shareholders the right to obtain the acquirer's stock at a significant discount unless the target board redeemed the pill. This right only arose (indeed, it could only arise) in conjunction with a second step merger after the initial hostile tender offer was completed. Ultimately, determined acquirers were not deterred by Lipton's flip-over pill. For example, Sir James Goldsmith acquirer majority control of Crown Zellerbach in 1985, notwithstanding the fact that Crown had a flip-over pill in place. He simply did not proceed with the second-step merger.[9]

The second generation pills are known as "flip-in" pills. The flip-in pill is triggered upon a person acquiring more than a set percentage of the target's shares (typically 10–20%). Once the flip-in pill is triggered, all of the shareholders except the person triggering the pill get the right to buy target shares at less than market price. As a result, the acquirer's position is significantly diluted and the acquirer is left, like Sisyphus of ancient Greek mythology, futilely pushing a rock up a hill only to see it roll back down every time the acquirer hits the triggering percentage. The mechanics of the flip-in pill is explained further below.

Initially, the validity of the poison pill was uncertain. A few state courts, including in New York and New Jersey, held that a poison pill was an invalid exercise of board authority. However, in 1986, the Delaware Supreme Court upheld the poison pill in *Moran v. Household International*, 500 A.2d 1346 (1985) (discussed in the next Chapter.) Simultaneously, corporations lobbied state legislatures to enact statutes validating poison pills. Thirty seven states have done so to date, including both New York and New Jersey.[10] With Delaware and state legislatures acting, courts followed suit, and the last significant challenge to a poison pill was rejected in the 1990 case *Georgia-Pacific Corp. v. Great Northern Nekoosa Corp.*, 731 F. Supp. 38 (D. Me. 1990), litigated under the laws of the state of Maine. Today the validity of the poison pill is unquestioned, and it is the primary tool used by targets to fight off hostile bidders.

2. THE MECHANICS OF THE POISON PILL

The poison pill can be adopted by the target board of directors without shareholder approval. According to FactSet Shark Repellent, only six percent of the S&P 1,500 had a poison pill in effect as of December 20, 2015.[11] However, this figure makes poison pills seem far less important than they are: almost every public company board has the ability to adopt

---

[9] *See* Eric N. Berg, *Crown Defeat Casts Pall On Poison Pill Defense*, N.Y. TIMES, July 27, 1985, available at http://www.nytimes.com/1985/07/27/business/crown-defeat-casts-pall-on-poison-pill-defense.html.

[10] See Matthew D. Cain, Stephen B. McKeon, & Steven Davidoff Solomon, *Do Takeover Laws Matter? Evidence from Five Decades of Hostile Takeovers* (2015), available at http://ssrn.com/abstract=2517513.

[11] One reason why the percentage is low is because of pressure by "governance activists" to persuade companies to put up fewer obstacles to being taken over—many companies were persuaded to remove their poison pills. We discuss shareholder activism in Chapter XX; while we mostly focus on activists such as Pershing Square and other "economic activists" who are attempting to change the business direction of particular companies, we touch on the governance activists, such as Harvard Law School Professor Lucian Bebchuk, who have pushed for governance changes which reduce companies' defenses to being taken over.

a poison pill without shareholder approval in a day or two.[12] This means that every such company has a "shadow" poison pill which can be quickly implemented.

A poison pill is implemented by resolution of the board. Pursuant to a resolution, the board of directors issues "Rights." These Rights attach to all shares. The poison pill's terms are specified in two documents: A certificate of designation to the target's certificate of incorporation which sets forth the basic terms of the Rights, and an indenture agreement between the target and a bank trustee which sets forth the terms applicable when the Rights are triggered. When we refer to a poison pill we are referring to these two documents.

The Rights give shareholders the ability to purchase shares or fractions of shares of preferred stock of the issuer. The exercise price for these Rights is deliberately set at a price well above the current or expected market price for the issuer. For example, Allergan's shareholder rights plan provides that initially each Right can be exercised for $500.00 for one share of Allergan Common Stock. (A copy of Allergan's poison pill (the certificate of designation and the indenture agreement), as well as Allergan's Form 8–K filing which explains the pill, is included in the Online Appendix.) At this price, the Rights are in effect "out of the money" options, and there is no economic incentive for any shareholder to exercise the Rights. ("Out of the money" is to be contrasted with "at the money," which in this context would mean that the rights were priced at the market price, and "in the money," which means that the rights were priced below the market price.). Consequently, the Rights remain unused until they are triggered.

The Rights are triggered when an acquirer obtains a specified amount of stock in the target, typically somewhere between 10% and 20%. When the Rights Plan is triggered, each of the Rights are re-priced such that they become "in the money" options. At this point, shareholders have an economic incentive to exercise the rights. But not all shareholders can do so, as we explain below.

The language below from the Allergan rights plan is typical of the language used to re-price rights:

> [Upon a triggering event,] each holder of a Right, other than Rights that are or were acquired or beneficially owned by the Acquiring Person [the person acquiring more than a specified percentage of Allergan stock] (which Rights will thereafter be void), will thereafter have the right to receive upon exercise that number of shares of Common Stock having a market value of two times the then current Purchase Price of one Right.

[12] See John C. Coates IV, *Takeover Defenses in the Shadow of the Pill: A Critique of the Scientific Evidence*, 79 TEX. L. REV. 271 (2000).

Assuming the Common Stock of the issuer is trading for $50/share, the formula above looks like this:

(Purchase Price of Right * 2)/Current Price of Allergan Common Stock =
Number of Shares of Allergan Stock Purchasable

or

($500 * 2) / $50 = 20 shares of Allergan

Prior to the triggering event, a shareholder could purchase ten shares of Allergan common stock for $500. At that price, the Right is worthless. Following the triggering event, a shareholder can purchase 20 shares of Allergan common stock for $500. The Right thus becomes valuable and shareholders have an incentive to exercise it. If all shareholders exercise their Rights, each of the shareholders' relative positions would be unchanged. But the Rights are not exercisable by all shareholders. The rights plan is typically triggered when any person becomes an "Acquiring Person" by acquiring a pre-specified proportion of the issuer's stock. Once the rights plan is triggered, Acquiring Persons are not permitted to exercise the rights. As a result, when shareholders other than the Acquiring Person exercise their rights, the Acquiring Person's stockholding is dramatically diluted. Under most Rights Plans, a person becomes an Acquiring Person once that person acquires more than 10% (or 15% or 20%) of the issuer's stock.

The board of directors retains the right prior to a triggering event to redeem the Rights for only a nominal price. The board of directors also retains the right to declare certain persons not to be Acquiring Persons notwithstanding an increase in their stockholding position. Consequently, a Rights Plan creates a natural incentive for potential acquirers to engage directly with the board in a friendly fashion rather than attempt to engage in an expensive, and possibly fruitless, hostile tender offer.

3. THE EFFECT OF A POISON PILL

The poison pill makes far more costly, and thus effectively prevents, the hostile acquirer's acquisition of shares above the amount triggering the poison pill. No rational acquirer will want to have the value of its holding massively diminished. In the Allergan example above, a person buying 11% of Allergan's stock would have its interest diluted to as low as 0.6% of the company's stock.

Since they were invented and began to be used, poison pills have only been triggered twice. The first time involved Crown Zellerbach, mentioned at the beginning of this Subsection D. The pill in question was a "flip-over" pill; the hostile acquirer simply did not undertake a back-end squeezeout merger, thus effectively denuding the pill of its power. The second triggering of a pill occurred in 2010, when Versata Enterprises deliberately triggered a "flip-in" pill put in place by Selectica. Versata subsequently challenged the decision of the Selectica board to allow the pill to be triggered, but the board's decision was upheld by the Delaware Supreme Court.[13]

4. DEAD HAND AND SLOW HAND POISON PILLS

In the 1990s, practitioners developed new and more powerful variants of the poison pill. The first of these was the dead-hand pill. The dead-hand pill prevents any directors of the target, except those who were in office as of the date of the pill's adoption or their designated successors, from redeeming the pill. The dead-hand pill strikes at the heart of the modern day form of hostile takeover by eliminating a proxy contest as a useful way for a hostile acquirer to gain control. Even if the acquirer wins the proxy contest, its newly-elected director representatives do not have the power to redeem the pill and must wait for it to expire, which may take as long as 10 years. The dead-hand pill was struck down in Delaware and a number of other states precisely because it makes a proxy contest "prohibitively expensive and effectively impossible."[14] It also coerces shareholders, effectively forcing them "to vote for incumbent directors or their designees if shareholders want to be represented by a board entitled to" redeem the poison pill.[15]

Around the same time dead-hand pills were invalidated, slow-hand pills were developed. Newly-elected directors can redeem the pill, but not for a period of time (typically six months) after taking office, if the purpose or effect of the proposed redemption would be to facilitate a transaction with the acquirer. Even subsequent to a successful proxy contest where a majority of shareholders replaced the incumbent board with a board that was in favor of the tender offer, that board would not have the power to redeem the pill for the specified period of time. This technique is not allowed in some jurisdictions, including Delaware, because it impermissibly ties directors' hands, preventing the board from managing the corporation.[16]

E.   THE ACQUIRER RESPONSE: THE PROXY CONTEST

The advent of the poison pill in the mid-1980s transformed the nature of a hostile transaction, making previous defenses obsolete. A poison pill effectively prevents a corporation from being acquired without

---

[13] *Versata Enterprises Inc. v. Selectica, Inc.*, 5 A.3d 586 (Del. 2010).

[14] A dead hand pill, has however, been validated in Georgia under its state corporate law code. *See Invacare Corp, v. Healthdyne Technologies, Inc.*, 968 F. Supp. 1578 (N.D. Ga. 1997).

[15] *Carmody v. Toll Brothers*, 723 A.2d 1180 (Del. Ch. 1998).

[16] *See Mentor Graphics v. Quickturn*, 728 A.2d 25 (Del. Ch. 1998), affirmed by *Quickturn Design Systems, Inc. v. Shapiro*, 721 A.2d 1181 (Del. 1998).

the consent of the target's board of directors since only the target board's directors can redeem the pill and allow an acquisition to proceed. The poison pill thus placed the board at the center of the hostile tender offer process. Acquirers responded by adopting strategies to overcome the pill and a resistant board—in particular, to complement their hostile bids with a proxy contest to remove the target's directors and replace them with the bidder's chosen directors. When elected, these new directors would then presumably vote to remove the poison pill and agree to a transaction with the bidder.

The need to complement a hostile bid with a proxy contest drives the timing of hostile offers. It effectively means that a hostile offer must come at a time when a company's directors can be replaced. Opportunities to replace the board of directors can come at an annual meeting of the shareholders, a special meeting of the shareholders called for that purpose, or outside the annual or special meeting by action by written consent of the shareholders. The timing is dependent upon the company's certificate of incorporation and bylaws, including whether they permit special meetings to be called by shareholders, or shareholder action by written consent. Because of the opening it provides to attempt to side-step the poison pill, some companies have restricted the ability of shareholders to act by written consent or call a special meeting. A recent survey by the law firm Shearman & Sterling found that of the top 100 public companies, 24 do not permit shareholders to hold a special meeting, and 64 companies do not permit shareholder action by less than unanimous written consent. (The survey also stated that "[o]f the 76 Top 100 Companies that permit shareholders to call special meetings, 25% is the most common voting threshold required to call a meeting (34 companies). The second most common voting threshold is 10% (12 companies), followed by 20% (11 companies).")[17]

In companies that prohibit shareholders from calling special meetings or acting by written consent, shareholders can remove directors only at the company's annual meeting. The annual meeting has its name because it happens only once a year. Thus, in such a circumstance, a hostile bidder must time its bid (and, of course, proxy contest) to coincide with this meeting. In an influential article, Professor Grundfest, who is also a former SEC commissioner, described a hostile bid as being like a tulip, able to blossom once a year.[18] Of course, targets know of this timing, and have the remainder of the year to plan for any impending proxy contest and hostile offer.

---

[17] The text continues: "This does not include companies that have different thresholds for a single shareholder and group of shareholders." Shearman & Sterling 2014 Corporate Governance Survey 49, available at http://digital.shearman.com/i/387079.

[18] Joseph A. Grundfest, *Just Vote No: A Minimalist Strategy for Dealing with Barbarians Inside the Gates*, 45 STAN. L. REV. 857, 860 n.6 (1993).

In the case of Valeant's bid for Allergan, Valeant had an ally, Pershing Square, who launched a proxy contest in the following news release:

> Pershing Square Capital Management, L.P. ("Pershing Square") today announced a slate of six highly experienced, independent directors for the board of directors of Allergan, Inc. ("Allergan"). The six members of the slate are: Betsy Atkins, Cathleen P. Black, Fredric N. Eshelman, Steven J. Shulman, David A. Wilson and John J. Zillmer.

> "Each member of our slate of nominees is an independent, skilled leader with relevant domain, industry and/or executive management experience. By supporting this slate, Allergan shareholders can ensure that the interests of shareholders will be well represented on the board of Allergan."

> As previously announced, Pershing Square is seeking to call a special meeting of Allergan shareholders. At this special meeting, Allergan shareholders will be able to voice their support for a number of critical matters, including the removal of six incumbent members of the Allergan board, the appointment of the independent Pershing Square slate and certain other actions to improve the corporate governance of Allergan. To that end, Pershing Square will file today revised preliminary solicitation materials with the Securities and Exchange Commission.

> Commenting on the decision to offer a slate of seasoned business executives for the Allergan board, Pershing Square CEO Bill Ackman said, "Each member of our slate of nominees is an independent, skilled leader with relevant domain, industry and/or executive management experience. By supporting this slate, Allergan shareholders can ensure that the interests of shareholders will be well represented on the board of Allergan."

> The business executives on the slate bring a wealth of experience leading important enterprises as well as serving as directors of prominent public companies and leading not-for-profit organizations. Each of these executives is also independent of Pershing Square and Valeant Pharmaceuticals International, Inc.

Note that Allergan had a "hole" in its defenses: shareholders had the ability to call a special meeting with the agreement of 25% of its shareholders. Pershing Square had previously sought to obtain the consent of shareholders to hold a special meeting to nominate the above directors, and succeeded, at which point Pershing Square took the next step, nominating the directors.

A proxy contest is also called a proxy "fight," and for good reason. The hostile bidder and the target engage in a battle to elect their directors. The outcome of this proxy contest dictates the future of the target. Most proxy battles do not continue until the date of the election. In the period leading up to the election, if the target's directors seem apt to lose, the target's board will either seek to negotiate with the hostile bidder or will seek a white knight transaction. Indeed, Allergan's decision to be acquired by Actavis was no doubt driven by signals from shareholders that it was about to lose the proxy contest initiated by Pershing Square.

F. STRUCTURAL DEFENSES

In addition to the responsive defenses, boards can deploy structural defenses, also known as shark repellents, against an unwanted offer. These structural defenses differ from responsive defenses in that they can only be deployed well in advance of any offer. These defenses work by deterring unwanted offers. Because they are embedded in corporate charters and, when approved by shareholders, in bylaws as well, they are difficult to remove. Boards' use of structural defenses is generally accorded business judgment deference.

The most common structural defense is the classified, or staggered, board. A staggered board has directors whose terms do not all expire at the same time. A typical term is three years, and one-third of the directors will be up for election in any given year. In recent years, however, the classified board has come under attack by shareholder rights advocates. Such advocates now regularly sponsor declassification proposals at publicly traded corporations. According to the Shareholder Rights Project at Harvard Law School, during the 2012–2014 proxy seasons, 98 S&P 500 companies declassified their boards.[19] According to FactSet SharkRepellent, in 2002 60% of the S&P 500 had a staggered board, a figure which declined to 10.21% in 2015. However, outside the S&P 500, staggered boards are more common; according to FactSet SharkRepellent, in 2015, 42.56% of the Russell 3000 had a staggered board.[20]

The staggered board is particularly powerful when combined with the poison pill. For a typical staggered board where the board members' terms last three years, the net effect is that replacing a majority of the board with directors presumably more inclined to redeem the pill will take an acquirer two years. In the fast-paced world of deal-making, two years is an extremely long time. The staggered board/poison pill

---

[19] *See* HARVARD SHAREHOLDER RIGHTS PROJECT at http://srp.law.harvard.edu/declassifications.shtml.

[20] "The S&P 500 is an index of the 500 largest listed companies. The Russell 3000 is an index of the 3000 largest publicly held companies, " 'representing approximately 98% of the investable U.S. equity market.' "

combination therefore serves as a significant deterrent to hostile offers being made. A study by Professors Bebchuk, Coates, and Subramanian found the combination to be a "powerful" anti-takeover defense if the target board refuses to agree to a takeover.[21]

Even though the defense is very effective, it has nevertheless been upheld by the Delaware Supreme Court on grounds that it could be overcome by a determined acquirer: "[B]ecause only one third of a classified board would stand for election each year, a classified board would *delay—but not prevent—a hostile acquiror from obtaining control of the board*, since a determined acquiror could wage a proxy contest and obtain control of two thirds of the target board over a two year period, as opposed to seizing control in a single election."[22]

Other commonly used shark repellents include:

1. DUAL CLASS STOCK

In recent years since the IPO of Google, *dual-class stock* has made a comeback as a structural defense against unwanted offers. In its most common incarnation, it is used by entrepreneurial tech firms, who now go public with dual class stock. Google, Facebook, Groupon, and Zynga, among many others, are examples of firms taken public by entrepreneurs who held on to high vote shares while the corporations issued low vote shares to the public. As a result, the entrepreneurs now own less than a majority of the outstanding equity while retaining voting control of the corporation. Where a controlling shareholder controls the corporation via his ownership of high vote stock, a hostile tender offer will never succeed unless the controlling shareholder acquiesces.

2. ADVANCE NOTICE BYLAW PROVISIONS

Advance notice provisions in corporate charters, or more commonly, in corporate bylaws, are another structural defense. *Advance notice bylaws* require a shareholder who wishes to bring a particular item of business, or one or more director nominations, to be acted upon at a meeting of the shareholders to provide the board with advance notice, typically a specific number of days (not less than 90 days and not more than 120 days is common) before the first anniversary of the previous year's shareholder meeting date. While advance notice bylaws ostensibly exist to "help organize what could otherwise be a chaotic shareholder

---

[21] Lucian Arye Bebchuk, John C. Coates IV & Guhan Subramanian, *The Powerful Antitakeover Force of Staggered Boards: Theory, Evidence, and Policy*, 54 STAN. L. REV. 887 (2002).

[22] *Versata v. Selectica*, 5 A.3d 586, 604 (Del. 2010). The court's preference for proxy contests over the more direct route of simply permitting the tender offer to proceed reflects a choice among alternatives by the courts and not necessarily an optimal policy. Other jurisdictions, like the U.K., opt for a different approach as regards permitting boards to step between an offeror and the shareholders without negative consequences.

meeting,"[23] they also have a "side benefit" as a defensive measure. The smaller the window for getting business and nominations before the shareholders, the harder it is for an insurgent shareholder or unwanted bidder to run a successful proxy contest. We discuss these provisions further in Chapter XX.

3.   FAIR PRICE PROVISIONS

Another common structural defense is a *fair price* provision. The provision, included in a corporation's charter, gives shareholders the right to receive a minimum price for their stock in the event of a back-end merger following a tender offer. Typically, that minimum price is either the tender offer price or some other formula deriving the fair price. These provisions are designed to mimic state anti-takeover fair price statutes discussed below. Structurally coercive tender offers of the type that gave rise to the fair price provision are no longer common. As a consequence the fair price provision seldom comes into play.

4.   POISON PUT

The *poison put* falls into a category of defenses termed "embedded defenses."[24] Embedded defenses are found in contracts entered into with third parties in the ordinary course of business. These contracts include default provisions or termination provisions that are triggered upon a change of control. Embedded defenses work by raising the costs of post-merger integration sufficiently high—by terminating a key contract or causing a penalty to be paid—as to dissuade an unwanted bidder from pursuing a target. A poison put might, for instance, require a company's debt to be repaid in full upon a change in control; such a provision is included as part of a loan or other debt agreement. The ostensible reason for the put arrangement is to provide lenders with a certain degree of stability over the course of the borrowing. Indeed, the genesis of such provisions was protection of lenders. Afraid that leveraged buyers might acquire a corporation, add more debt and then cause the company to default, lenders began to add such provisions to their lending documents. However, nowadays, such provisions are as likely to be included at the behest of borrowers as they are lenders. In 2009, NRG used a poison put to good effect in rebuffing an unwanted bid from rival Exelon. Had Exelon succeeded in acquiring control of NRG, $8.4 billion in debt would immediately have become due. Similarly, in 2010, Casey's General Stores was faced with a hostile takeover offer from Canadian convenience store operator Couche-Tard (the translation of which is "goes to bed late" or night owl). While the offer was pending, Casey's negotiated a put in a

---

[23] *Boilermakers Local 154 Ret. Fund v. Chevron*, 73 A.3d 934, 952 (Del. Ch. 2013).

[24] This term was coined by Jennifer Arlen and Eric Talley in their paper, *Unregulable Defenses and the Perils of Shareholder Choice*, 152 U. PENN. L. REV. 577 (2003).

provision in its debt under which, as described in Couche-Tard's press release, "Casey's is required to pay the noteholders approximately $95 million in penalties based on current treasury rates, in addition to the outstanding principal amount and accrued interest on the notes, if any party acquires 35% or more of the outstanding shares of Casey's." "The terms of the notes would also require Casey's to pay the noteholders approximately $95 million in penalties if the Casey's shareholders decide to replace a majority of the Casey's Board."[25] Couche-Tard eventually withdrew its offer. We discuss poison puts further in Chapter XX.

G. STATE ANTI-TAKEOVER STATUTES

State anti-takeover statutes are, as the name suggests, statutes enacted by states as part of their corporate law that make taking over companies more difficult. These statutes are essentially political products, enacted by state legislatures to protect domestic corporations without regard to their economic effect. As such, they are very much a product of the hostile takeover boom of the 1980s.

1. THE HISTORY OF STATE ANTI-TAKEOVER STATUTES

The recent history of state anti-takeover statutes begins with the passage of the Williams Act of 1968, discussed at length in Chapter IV. The Williams Act was adopted in response to perceived abuses by hostile acquirers. It was intended to, and did, have the effect of slowing down and reducing the number of tender offers.

In the 1970s, companies began to approach the legislatures in the states in which they were incorporated, requesting protection against hostile acquirers; the result was that many states began adopting anti-takeover statutes. An article recounts the history:

IS DELAWARE'S ANTITAKEOVER STATUTE UNCONSTITUTIONAL? EVIDENCE FROM 1988–2008
Guhan Subramanian, Steven Herscovici and Brian Barbetta
65 BUS. LAW. 685, 688–94 (2010)

When the Williams Act was passed in July 1968, only one state (Virginia) regulated tender offers, and even the Virginia statute had been passed just four months earlier. Perhaps as a result, there is no evidence from the lengthy hearings and extended debates that Congress considered the extent to which the Williams Act should preempt state antitakeover laws. The Williams Act itself is silent on the question of preemption. . . .

---

[25] Press Release, Alimentation Couche-Tard Issues Statement In Response To Casey's General Stores' Private Placement, August 12, 2010, available at http://www.sec.gov/Archives/edgar/containers/fix170/1081825/000119312510187441/dex99a5m.htm.

[T]he main constraints on the states' ability to regulate takeovers come from the Supremacy Clause and the Commerce Clause of the U.S. Constitution. Under the Supremacy Clause, federal law implicitly preempts a state statute if (a) compliance with both the federal law and the state law is impossible; or (b) the state statute frustrates the purposes of the federal law. Under the so-called "dormant" Commerce Clause, a state may regulate interstate commerce only if the state's interest in regulating the commerce outweighs any adverse impact on interstate commerce.

Between 1968 and 1982, thirty-seven U.S. states passed antitakeover statutes that tested the contours of the Supremacy Clause and dormant Commerce Clause doctrine as applied to the Williams Act. Delaware joined the party in May 1976 with the Delaware Tender Offer Act, codified in Section 203 of the Delaware corporate code. Following a common blueprint among these "first generation" antitakeover statutes, Section 203 imposed waiting periods on the bidder before and after a tender offer was launched.

. . .

Inconsistency reigned as the same law that was upheld by one court was overturned by another. Neither bidder nor target could confidently predict the outcome of any case." In perhaps the most sweeping pronouncement during this era, the U.S. Court of Appeals for the Fifth Circuit struck down the Idaho Tender Offer Act, and in doing so held that all state statutes regulating tender offers were unconstitutional under the Supremacy Clause. Each subsequent case seemed only to muddy, rather than clarify, the contours of the arena that the Williams Act and the dormant Commerce Clause had left to the states.

In 1982, the U.S. Supreme Court intervened. The statute at issue was the Illinois Business Takeover Act, which imposed a twenty-day pre-offer notification period like the Delaware Act, but also required the bidder to register its offer with the Illinois Secretary of State. During the twenty-day waiting period, the secretary could call a hearing to adjudicate the substantive fairness of the offer, in which registration would be denied if a tender offer failed to "provide full and fair disclosure" or was "inequitable or would work or tend to work a fraud or deceit upon the offerees."

In *Edgar v. MITE Corp.*, the U.S. Supreme Court invalidated the Illinois Act as a violation of the Commerce Clause and (likely) the Supremacy Clause. Writing for a five-Justice majority, Justice White held that the Illinois Act violated the Commerce Clause because it failed the *Pike v. Bruce Church* balancing test. The Court acknowledged that Illinois might have an interest in regulating tender offers, but also noted the substantial burdens that the Act imposed on interstate commerce.

"While protecting local investors is plainly a legitimate state objective, the State has no legitimate interest in protecting nonresident shareholders." Writing for a three-Justice plurality, Justice White also found that the Illinois Act violated the Supremacy Clause. "[I]t is . . . crystal clear that a major aspect of the effort to protect the investor [in the Williams Act] was to avoid favoring either management or the takeover bidder." The Illinois Act upset this balance: "[B]y providing the target company with additional time within which to take steps to combat the offer, the precommencement notification provisions furnish incumbent management with a powerful tool to combat tender offers. . . ."

Although the Illinois Business Takeover Act went further than first-generation statutes in most other states, state legislatures read the tea leaves of the MITE decision and slowly took their pre-bid disclosure laws off the books. By far the most important retrenchment of this kind occurred in Delaware. Even though Section 203 did not include the same registration process and substantive scrutiny as the Illinois Act, the Delaware legislature repealed Section 203 in July 1987 on the "generally accepted" view that Section 203 was unconstitutional.

But because of the lack of explicit preemption in the Williams Act and the fractured opinion in *MITE*, state legislatures cautiously climbed back into the ring. Between 1982 and 1987, twenty-one states, though not Delaware, adopted "second generation" antitakeover statutes. Unlike the first generation statutes, which generally focused on pre-bid disclosure of the offer, the second generation statutes were designed to survive constitutional scrutiny by regulating collateral issues around the tender offer rather than the tender offer itself.

Indiana's Control Share Acquisition Act, signed into law in March 1986, was one such second generation statute. The Indiana Act provided that anyone who acquires 20%, 33.33%, or 50% of an Indiana corporation's shares must win the approval of a majority of the disinterested shares, at the next shareholder's meeting, in order to be able to vote the shares that it owned. In the paradigmatic case where the bidder launched an any-and-all tender offer and acquired more than 50% of the shares, it would then have to obtain majority approval from the remaining shareholders, all of whom by definition did not tender into the offer, before it could vote its shares. The Indiana Act clearly tilted the balance between bidders and targets by making it more difficult for a bidder to gain board control. However, unlike the first generation statutes, the Indiana Act and other "control share acquisition" statutes did not impede the tender offer process itself.

Notwithstanding the plausible point of distinction from the first generation statutes, federal district and appellate courts applied the Supreme Court's holding in *MITE* to invalidate the control share acquisition statutes in Hawaii, Minnesota, Missouri, and Ohio between 1982 and 1986. In 1987, the U.S. Supreme Court granted certiorari after the federal district court and U.S. Court of Appeals for the Seventh Circuit similarly invalidated the Indiana Act. Surprising many commentators, the Supreme Court upheld the Indiana Act against Supremacy Clause and Commerce Clause challenges. In *CTS Corp v. Dynamics Corp. of America*, the Court distinguished the Indiana Act from the Illinois Act that was struck down in *MITE*:

> [T]he overriding concern of the *MITE* plurality was that the Illinois statute considered in that case operated to favor management against offerors, to the detriment of shareholders. By contrast, the statute now before the Court protects the independent shareholder against the contending parties. Thus, the Act furthers a basic purpose of the Williams Act, "plac[ing] investors on an equal footing with the takeover bidder."

Writing for a six-Justice majority, Justice Powell concluded that the Indiana Act "furthers the federal policy of investor protection" and therefore did not frustrate the objectives of the Williams Act. The Court also found that the Indiana Act did not discriminate against interstate commerce because it applied equally to both interstate and local businesses, and that any burden on interstate commerce was outweighed by Indiana's compelling interest in defining the voting rights of shares of Indiana corporations. The majority therefore held that the Indiana Act was valid under the Supremacy Clause and the Commerce Clause."

In the wake of *Edgar v. MITE*, states felt free to adopt anti-takeover statutes. Again, they were egged on by domestic companies, as recounted by Professor Macey:

> In a pioneering article, Roberta Romano argued that the state of Connecticut enacted an anti-takeover statute at the behest of a single politically powerful corporation, rather than through the interplay of a number of competing interest groups. The corporation, the Aetna Life and Casualty Company, persuaded the Connecticut legislature to pass the statute despite the strong possibility that the firm's own shareholders would have declined to support a similar measure if the matter had been put to them for a vote. Romano observed that several other state statutes were apparently passed at the behest of particular firms. Specifically, she noted that Maine, Pennsylvania, Illinois and Missouri had passed statutes to benefit individual firms that were threatened with outsider takeovers.

Other state anti-takeover measures also appear to reflect the lobbying of a single-minded political group of individual firms rather than a broader political consensus. The action of the legislature that Romano observed in Connecticut appears to be repeating itself across the country. In North Carolina, for example, Burlington Industries persuaded the legislature to adopt an anti-takeover statute in order to thwart a hostile takeover by Asher Edelman and Dominion Textile Corporation. Indiana enacted a control-share acquisition statute and a freeze-out fair-price statute in response to the threatened takeover of Arvin Industries by the Belzberg family.

Similarly, the threatened takeover of Goodyear Tire and Rubber Company "galvanized the Ohio legislature to pass a new [anti-takeover] law." And it is well known that Washington's anti-takeover statute was passed at the behest of Boeing Industries. The list goes on. In perhaps the most shameless transfer of wealth from shareholders to incumbent management, Dayton Hudson Corporation prevailed upon the Governor of Minnesota to call a special legislative session so that a law could be passed to protect the firm from takeover by Dart Group, Inc. In Massachusetts, to relieve any lingering doubts about the special-interest basis of that state's anti-takeover statute, the Governor appeared at a Gillette Company plant to sign the statute into effect. Gillette had been the subject of a takeover attempt by Revlon. In Wisconsin, when the G. Heileman Brewing Company of LaCrosse came under attack from Bond Holdings Corporation, Heileman persuaded Governor Tommy Thompson to convene a special legislative session at which a particularly draconian anti-takeover measure was enacted into law.

Companies favored the state adoption of anti-takeover laws rather than adopting their own defenses, through shark repellents, because these laws avoided the need to obtain any necessary shareholder approval. The thirst for anti-takeover statues was particularly high in the "rust belt," Midwestern states which experienced significant economic decline during the 1980s due to the shift of industry out of the region. These states did not want to lose any more companies to other states. Moreover, convincing the state to adopt the statute allowed a company to blame the state for diminished takeover prospects, shifting blame away from itself. The result is that as of today, 43 states have some sort of anti-takeover law.[26] To be sure, many of these statutes contained opt-out

----

[26] Cain, McKeon & Solomon, *supra* note 10. There are many different types of anti-takeover laws, as the material in the text indicates. Different states have different types of such laws. Moreover, what counts as an anti-takeover law is a matter of some dispute. In particular, "other constituency" laws (sometimes called director discretion laws), allowing directors to take into account the interests of constituencies other than shareholders, are sometimes considered to be

provisions (a small number were opt-ins), but companies seldom opted out except in extreme circumstances.

2. SECOND GENERATION ANTI-TAKEOVER STATUTES AND BEYOND

The initial state anti-takeover laws, mostly passed in the 1970s and known as first generation laws, were directed to the tender offer process. They required that hostile bidders file their tender offer documents with the secretary of state of the target's company's state of incorporation. The secretary of state would then review and make a determination on the offer within a fixed period of time. Many of these statutes allowed the secretary of state to reject these offers. These laws were struck down in *Edgar v. MITE* on constitutional grounds, including that they were preempted by the Williams Act.

In the wake of *Edgar v. MITE*, states adopted second generation statutes designed to comport with the requirements of the *Edgar* opinion. The three primary types of state anti-takeover statutes adopted were:

Business Combination Statute. Also known as "freeze-out" statutes, these statutes prohibit bidders from engaging in a business combination (i.e., a merger) with a target for a specified period, typically three to five years, upon the bidder's acquisition of, typically, 15% to 20% or more of the target's equity, unless the purchase is pre-approved by the target's board or a specified percentage of disinterested target shareholders, or the bidder achieves a breakthrough acquisition (i.e., it acquires greater than 85% of the company in the tender offer). The net effect of this law is to require a hostile bidder who completes a tender offer to wait a specified period of years before completing the back-end merger. This can be problematic if the bidder needs to finance the acquisition and use the target company's assets for collateral. In addition, the minority shareholders will share in any gains in the target's value that occur during this waiting period. Delaware's anti-takeover statute, DGCL Section 203, is an example of a business combination statute.

Fair Price Statute. The fair price statute is directed at the two-tiered tender offer. It requires the same price and type of consideration to be paid in a second step merger as in a tender offer unless one of the exceptions is met. The requirement is not applicable if the acquirer obtains disinterested board approval or a supermajority vote of shareholders (usually 80%).

---

anti-takeover laws because these laws would, for instance, allow directors to reject an offer at a high price because the offeror proposed to reduce the size of the company's workforce. But whatever definition one uses, the number of states with anti-takeover laws is a significant majority. *See generally* B. Jeffrey Bell, *The Acquisition of Control of a United States Public Company*, 2014 Edition, MORRISON & FOERSTER, available at http://media.mofo.com/files/Uploads/Images/1302–The–Acquisition-of-Control-of-a-United–States–Public–Company.pdf.

Control Share Acquisition Statute. Any target shares acquired by a bidder in excess of a specified threshold cannot be voted by the bidder unless approval is granted by a majority or supermajority of disinterested target shareholders. A typical control share acquisition statute will have thresholds of 20%, 30% and 50%, requiring shareholder approval at each threshold. The net effect of this statute is to force the acquirer to obtain a shareholder vote before completing a tender offer. Otherwise, the shares the bidder acquires in the tender offer will have no votes, and the bidder will be unable to wield control over the target or vote to effectuate a back-end merger.

States did not stop with these three types of statutes. In addition to the main types of anti-takeover statutes there are a variety of other less common statutes:

Control Share Cash-Out. Dissident target shareholders gain the right to "cash-out" or sell their shares to the bidder at the highest acquiring price paid during the acquisition period.

Disgorgement. This type of statute allows a target to recover any potential profits obtained by a person or group who held more than 20% of the issuer in an eighteen month period prior to the takeover.

Mandatory Staggered Board. These statutes require all publicly-traded companies incorporated in their state to have a staggered board. Only a few states, including Oklahoma, Indiana, Iowa and Massachusetts, have adopted such statutes; Oklahoma subsequently repealed its statute. Maryland—where many publicly traded real estate investment trusts are incorporated—recently adopted a similar statute which permits companies incorporated there to opt into a staggered board at any time by board vote and without shareholder approval. The provision was recently used by Macerich to deter a $16.8 billion unsolicited offer from Simon Property Group.[27]

Illinois's business combination and fair price statutes were upheld by the Supreme in *CTS v. Dynamics Corp. of America*, 481 U.S. 69 (1987). After that time, courts have largely upheld the constitutional validity of state anti-takeover statutes despite criticisms, notably including the issues raised by Professor Subramanian and his co-authors in the excerpt above.

3. ANTI-TAKEOVER STATUTES IN ACTION

In practice, the existence of the poison pill means that state anti-takeover statutes seldom play a significant role in takeovers. These statutes are generally aimed at forcing an acquirer to bargain with a

---

[27] George Stahl, *Macerich Rejects Simon Property's $16.8 Billion Takeover Bid,* WALL ST. J., April 1, 2015, available at http://www.wsj.com/articles/macerich-rejects-simon-propertys-takeover-bid–1427863593.

target board and enter into a friendly takeover, something the poison pill also does. Thus, while these statutes could conceivably affect a particular takeover contest, in many cases they do not play a role.

Perhaps the most important anti-takeover statute is Delaware's business combination statute, § 203. The statute is also a good example of how a business combination statute works.

Delaware passed its business combination statute in 1988. It was quite controversial; among those opposed were the SEC. Perhaps (indeed, probably) for self-serving reasons, Delaware corporations very much wanted the statute, and the Delaware Secretary of State wanted the franchise tax revenues such corporations were providing; this argument won the day.[28] While the rust belt states rushed headlong to adopt anti-takeover statutes, with Pennsylvania adopting six, Delaware adopted only this one, and not in a particularly extreme form.

Section 203 provides that a Delaware target may not engage in a "business combination," which includes a back-end merger and comparable transactions, for a period of three years with an "interested shareholder, which includes any "owner" of 15% or more of the target's outstanding shares, unless:

- The corporation has elected to opt out of § 203's requirements in its original certificate of incorporation;

- Prior to the date on which the would-be acquirer crosses the 15% threshold, the business combination or the triggering acquisition is approved by the target's board of directors;

- The would-be acquirer, in a single transaction, goes from less than 15% to more than 85% of the target's voting stock (not counting shares owned by inside directors or by employee stock plans);

- During the three year freeze period, the transaction is approved by the board of directors and by the two-thirds of the outstanding shares not owned by the would-be acquirer; or

- The target's board of directors approves a "white knight" transaction.

Section 203 thus creates incentives for a hostile bidder to deal directly with the board. If the board approves, the bidder need not wait three years before being able to complete a back-end merger.

---

[28] See Dale Oesterle, *Delaware's Takeover Statute: Of Chills, Pills, Standstills, And Who Gets Iced*, 13 DEL. J. CORP. L. 879, 891–2 (1988).

4.   DGCL 203 IN APPLICATION: *DIGEX, INC. SHAREHOLDERS LITIGATION*

As noted above, the poison pill has effectively made the issue of state anti-takeover laws recede to the background. However, this does not mean that § 203 is never an issue, as the following case highlights:

IN RE DIGEX, INC. SHAREHOLDERS LITIGATION

Supreme Court of Delaware
789 A.2d 1176 (2000)

CHANDLER, CHANCELLOR.

This is my decision on plaintiffs' motion to preliminarily enjoin the proposed merger between defendants WorldCom, Inc. ("WorldCom") and Intermedia Communications, Inc. ("Intermedia"), the controlling shareholder of Digex, Inc. ("Digex"). Plaintiffs, minority shareholders of Digex, seek either of two alternative forms of relief: (1) an order enjoining the defendants from consummating the Agreement and Plan of Merger dated September 1, 2000, (the "merger"), or (2) an order enjoining the Digex board's waiver of 8 Del. C. § 203. Intermedia's shareholders are tentatively scheduled to vote on the proposed merger on December 18, 2000.

Plaintiffs' . . . theory is that the Digex board, more specifically the four interested Digex directors, breached a fiduciary duty when they voted to waive the protections afforded Digex by § 203 of the Delaware General Corporate Law ("DGCL").

For the reasons discussed more fully below, the plaintiffs. . . have shown a likelihood of success on the merits of their § 203 claim. . . .

IV. SECTION 203 CLAIM

[T]he plaintiffs argue that the interested Digex directors breached their fiduciary duties by causing Digex to improperly waive § 203 of the DGCL. Specifically, the plaintiffs assert that because the waiver was accomplished by the vote of the four Intermedia-affiliated Digex directors, and against the vote and advice of the three independent Digex directors, the vote must be judged under the entire fairness standard. Plaintiffs contend that the defendants have failed to meet this standard. . . .

The defendants [argue] . . . that the § 203 waiver did not constitute a breach of fiduciary duty and therefore will not support preliminary injunctive relief. First, defendants contend that § 203 will not prohibit a future business combination between Digex and WorldCom because even if the waiver was invalid, WorldCom still is exempt from § 203 because it will possess over 85% of the Digex voting power. . . . [*Second argument omitted.*] Third, the defendants argue that the § 203 waiver was, in any case, entirely fair to the Digex shareholders.

A.   Does the 85% exemption apply to WorldCom?

The facts are undisputed by either party that upon the completion of the merger, WorldCom will possess well over 85% of the voting power of Digex but well under 85% of the number of outstanding voting shares of Digex. The three year waiting period imposed by § 203, the Delaware anti-takeover statute, does not apply where "upon consummation of the transaction which resulted in the shareholder becoming an interested shareholder, the interested shareholder owned at least 85% of the voting stock of the corporation outstanding at the time that the transaction commenced" excluding certain shares for the purposes of determining the number of shares outstanding. The interpretation of the term "voting stock," therefore, lays directly at the center of this dispute whether § 203 limitations would apply to WorldCom absent the waiver. Simply put, if "85% of the voting stock" refers to voting power, WorldCom would be exempt from § 203. If "85% of the voting stock" refers to the number of shares held in the corporation as a percentage of its outstanding number of shares, then WorldCom would need to rely on the vote of the Digex board to waive its § 203 protections. . . .

The legislative history of § 203(a)(2), although ultimately unclear, strongly suggests that those contemplating the adoption of the statute believed they were talking about an economic equity percentage, not a voting power percentage. Section 203 received an unprecedented amount of scrutiny before its adoption. . . .

The intense debate over § 203 in part centered on § 203(a)(2). Specifically, the 85% shareholder exemption was one of the most disputed provisions in the entire statute and received a tremendous amount of scrutiny. Among the most vociferous opponents of the 85% shareholder exemption (originally set at 90%) was then-SEC Commissioner Joseph Grundfest. In a series of letters and testimony before the Delaware Legislature, Commissioner Grundfest objected to the 85% exemption because of the unreasonably onerous burden he believed this requirement would place on tender offers. According to Grundfest, after an investigation by the SEC's Office of the Chief Economist, he was "aware of no case in which a tender offer obtained more than 90% of the target's shares despite management opposition." In a subsequent letter, Grundfest argued to lower the then 90% threshold based on a table consisting of data showing "the number of shares tendered as a percentage of the shares not already owned by the bidder." On the other side in this debate, Martin Lipton of the firm Wachtell, Lipton, Rosen & Katz, argued that even the 90% exemption level would create a "barn-door size exception" to § 203 and that it would "be a rare situation where a tender offer will not attract 85% of the target's non-management stock." Apparently in response to the concerns expressed by Grundfest and others, the recommended bill ultimately lowered the percentage exemption from 90% to 85%.

As this debate over the 85% threshold exception evidences, § 203(a)(2) was crafted with the procedures of tender offers in mind. The primary policy motivation behind this statute was to deter potential acquirers from using two-tiered highly leveraged tender offers. The main argument in support of any percentage exemption was that if an offer successfully attracted such a significant percentage of the voting shareholders of a corporation, then the tender offer must be a good one. In conducting a tender offer, the number of votes a given share possesses at the time of the decision to tender does not figure into the percentage of shares that have decided to tender although the number of votes may determine an acquirer's ability to elect directors and direct corporate policy. The primary policy reason to provide the 85% exemption was to allow tender offerors an exemption from § 203 if their offer was sufficiently attractive to such a high percentage of the outstanding shares of the corporation. The situation presented here defeats that intent. . . .

Given the difficulty and complexity of this legal issue, there is no question that the § 203 waiver had redundant value to WorldCom. WorldCom, as well as Intermedia and Digex, were all advised by able legal counsel regarding the applicability of § 203 and these attorneys disagreed on the proper interpretation. Perhaps more importantly, based on this disagreement, as well as the recognition of each lawyer in this matter who advised any of the parties on the applicability of § 203, there was no way to definitively know at the time of the waiver vote whether WorldCom actually would qualify for the 85% exception. This alone is enough for this Court to conclude that the waiver had value and granted some degree of bargaining leverage to Digex. The directors of the Digex board, regardless of the ultimate applicability of § 203 to WorldCom after the completion of this merger, had a fiduciary obligation that fully applied to them during the vote to grant WorldCom a waiver of the prohibitions contained in § 203.

In concluding this analysis of entire fairness, it appears that the only entity that really stood to lose should the Digex board decide to further analyze § 203 and vote to at least delay the grant of the waiver by a day or two was Intermedia, not Digex. The behavior of the interested directors in controlling both the negotiations and vote over the § 203 waiver surely demonstrates, in a compelling fashion, that the waiver really did present Digex with bargaining leverage against Intermedia and WorldCom. This leverage simply was not used– could not be used—because of the decision of the interested directors. In the unique circumstances here, this conduct by directors acting with a clear conflict of interest is difficult to justify and would not seem appropriate. I conclude preliminarily that the defendants are not reasonably likely to meet their burden as to the entire fairness of the Digex board's decision to waive Digex's § 203 protections and, therefore, that plaintiffs have demonstrated a reasonable probability of success on the merits of their § 203 claim.

The problem presented in *Digex* was that an acquirer—Worldcom— was purchasing the parent of a publicly-traded company which had a controlling interest in a publicly traded subsidiary which had not opted out of DGCL § 203. Worldcom wanted to preserve the flexibility of being able to acquire the remaining interest in the subsidiary without the restrictions of § 203. The issue in *Digex* was therefore whether the waiver from § 203 granted to Worldcom was appropriate. The *Digex* case stands for the proposition that the board's fiduciary duties require it to carefully consider whether it is appropriate to give a waiver from § 203 to an acquirer of a controlling but not a complete interest.

5. EMPIRICAL STUDIES OF ANTI-TAKEOVER STATUTES

What effect do anti-takeover statutes have? If Professor Manne's thesis that the takeover market disciplines managers is true, adoption of anti-takeover statutes should be seen as entrenching boards, and should reduce firms' value. Studies on the wealth effects of state anti-takeover laws have largely borne this thesis out—the adoption of state anti-takeover statutes, particularly business combination laws, resulted in reduced share prices and bond values.[29] However, recent studies have called these findings into question. These studies were primarily event studies around stock price reactions to news reports or the enactment of these statutes. With the exception of Cain, McKeon and Solomon, they did not analyze the longer term wealth effects of these takeover laws, a gap highlighted in a 2001 paper by John Coates; in that paper, Coates notes that the impact of these laws varies over time as capital markets shift.[30] In addition, a recent paper by Marcel Kahan and Emiliano Catan[31] questions the validity of these studies, finding that there is substantial miscoding, and also questioning the long term effects of these statutes due to the presence of the poison pill as the primary takeover defense. Picking up this point, Cain, McKeon and Solomon also find that over a

---

[29] *See generally* Cain, McKeon & Solomon, *supra* note 10, which also provides an extensive discussion of the literature.

[30] *See* John C. Coates, IV, *Explaining Variation in Takeover Defenses: Blame the Lawyers*, 89 CAL. L. REV. 1301 (2001)

[31] Emiliano Catan & Marcel Kahan, *The Law and Finance of Anti-Takeover Statutes*, forthcoming, 68 STAN. L. REV. (2016), available at http://papers.ssrn.com/sol3/papers.cfm?abstract_id=2517594.

longer period, certain anti-takeover laws such as business combination statutes have no wealth impact, though the authors do find indications that these laws reduce shareholder wealth, a reduction that is counter-balanced by the increased bargaining power boards have to negotiate a higher price. The matter is thus not settled: we await further studies building off the findings of Kahan and Catan and Cain, McKeon and Solomon.

QUESTIONS

1.   What is the "market for corporate control"? How might an efficient market for corporate control improve the operating efficiencies of companies generally?

2.   Why is the tender offer the structure of choice for the hostile offer? Why don't hostile acquirers rely on statutory mergers?

3.   How does a "just say no" defense work? Is it always effective? Under what circumstances might it be a weak defense?

4.   Dual-class stock is often considered a takeover defense. Why is that so?

5.   How does the poison pill work? Is it always an insurmountable defense against a hostile bid?

6.   Consider the § 203 state anti-takeover defense. How does it create a role for a target board in a hostile tender offer?

7.   Consider the facts of *Digex*. If a similar case arose after the *Digex* decision, would you advise your client to seek a § 203 waiver from the controlled subsidiary? Why or why not?

PROBLEMS

1.   Beta Corp is subject of a hostile offer by Alpha Co. Beta Corp has a poison pill in place. The Triggering Event in the pill is defined as the acquisition of 20% of the outstanding shares by an Acquiring Person. The exercise price of each Right prior to a Triggering Event is $500/Right. While Alpha Co. has been attempting to convince Beta Corp's board to accept the offer, it has also been acquiring stock of Beta Corp through a series of open market purchases. Yesterday, Alpha Co. purchased sufficient stock in the open market for its position in Beta Corp to equal 20%. The stock price on the day of the Triggering Event was $25/share. The language below is from Beta Corp's poison pill:

> Upon a Triggering Event, each holder of a Right, other than Rights that are or were acquired or beneficially owned by the Acquiring Person [the person acquiring more than a specified percentage of Beta Corp stock] (which Rights will thereafter be void), will thereafter have the right to receive upon exercise that number of

shares of Common Stock having a market value of two times the then current Purchase Price of one Right.

On the day, Alpha Co. triggered the poison pill there were 100 million shares of Beta Corp outstanding. If all of the Rights are exercised upon the Triggering Event, what percentage of Beta Corp's stock does Alpha Co. own?

2.   You represent the board of Delta Co. Delta is governed by § 203 and has a poison pill in place. Delta Co. has successfully fended off a hostile offer from Epsilon, Inc., following which Epsilon approached Delta's board with an attractive offer that it would now like to accept. The parties then agree to a transaction structured as a friendly tender offer with a back-end squeeze-out merger. The board has asked you to draft board resolutions to waive applicability of both § 203 as well as the poison pill with respect to Epsilon.

PART IV

FIDUCIARY DUTIES

■ ■ ■

CHAPTER XVI

THE DECISION TO DEFEND THE CORPORATION

∎ ∎ ∎

A. A PRIMER ON THE VARIOUS STANDARDS OF REVIEW

In prior Chapters, we discussed the federal and state statutory law governing M&A, as well as how attorneys negotiate and draft contracts. In this Chapter we now turn to rules which are mostly from the common law. These rules govern a board's decision as to whether to sell a corporation, and the process the board must use if it does decide to sell. As you will recall from your Corporations or Business Associations class, directors and officers have fiduciary duties to the corporation and its shareholders, including duties relating to their conduct in the context of M&A.

While fiduciary duties are primarily derived from caselaw, state statutory law also plays a part. Perhaps the most important provision of the Delaware corporation law in this regard is DGCL § 141(a), which provides that, "[t]he business and affairs of every corporation . . . shall be managed by or under the direction of a board of directors." This delegation of plenary authority to the board of directors has important implications, including as to the allocation of power between shareholders and directors, and the proper role of the board of directors in the context of a potential or actual merger transaction.

Most importantly, DGCL § 141(a) contemplates that courts should give significant deference to board action and board decision-making. This deference is articulated in the business judgment rule—the presumption that "the directors of a corporation acted on an informed basis, in good faith and in the honest belief that the action taken was in the best interests of the corporation."[1] The business judgment rule "in effect provides that where a director is independent and disinterested, there can be no liability for corporate loss, unless the facts are such that no person could possibly authorize such a transaction if he or she were attempting in good faith to meet their duty."[2]

---

[1]   *Aronson v. Lewis*, 473 A.2d 805, 812 (Del. 1984).
[2]   *Gagliardi v. TriFoods International, Inc.*, 683 A.2d 1049, 1052–53 (Del. Ch. 1996).

Why is there such expansive deference? Because directors might otherwise be too cautious if they had to fear they would be second guessed if their decisions turned out badly. In *Gagliardi v. Trifoods International*, then-Chancellor Allen explained the rationale for the business judgment presumption in the following way:

> Corporate directors of public companies typically have a very small proportionate ownership interest in their corporations and little or no incentive compensation. Thus, they enjoy (as residual owners) only a very small proportion of any "upside" gains earned by the corporation on risky investment projects. If, however, corporate directors were to be found liable for a corporate loss from a risky project on the ground that the investment was too risky (foolishly risky! stupidly risky! egregiously risky!—you supply the adverb), their liability would be joint and several for the whole loss. . . . Given the scale of operation of modern public corporations, this stupefying disjunction between risk and reward for corporate directors threatens undesirable effects. Given this disjunction, only a very small probability of director liability based on "negligence," "inattention," "waste," etc., could induce a board to avoid authorizing risky investment projects to any extent! Obviously, it is in the shareholders' economic interest to offer sufficient protection to directors from liability for negligence, etc., to allow directors to conclude that, as a practical matter, there is no risk that, if they act in good faith and meet minimal proceduralist standards of attention, they can face liability as a result of a business loss.[3]

A board decision to engage in a merger or other M&A transaction, or decline an unsolicited offer to be acquired or to merge, will receive the benefit of the business judgment presumption when challenged by shareholders. But the presumption is just that—a presumption. It can be rebutted. Particularized facts that suggest the board was uninformed, or acted in bad faith, or otherwise did not act in the best interests of the corporation, perhaps in furtherance of some personal interest, will be sufficient to rebut the presumption, at least initially. And if boards take defensive actions against unwanted offers, or show a preference for one offer over another, their conduct will be subject to more scrutiny.

The shareholder challenge takes the form of an argument by the plaintiff shareholder that the board breached its fiduciary duties. The

---

[3] *Id.*

duties at issue are the duty of loyalty, which includes the duty of good faith, and the duty of care.[4]

Directors' fiduciary duty of care requires them to "inform themselves, prior to making a business decision, of all material information reasonably available to them. Having become so informed, they must then act with requisite care in the discharge of their duties."[5] But director liability "is predicated upon concepts of gross negligence,"[6] making it difficult for shareholder plaintiffs to establish a breach of the duty of care. As you may recall from your Corporations or Business Associations class, in 1986, in response to the *Smith v. Van Gorkom* case (which we discuss in Chapter XVII), the Delaware legislature adopted § 102(b)(7), permitting a corporation to include in its certificate of incorporation a provision exculpating directors from monetary liability for breaches of the duty of care. Director liability for breach of the duty of care was thus considerably narrowed. The exculpation did not extend to breaches of the duty of loyalty or acts or omissions not in good faith, a fact the importance of which will be explained below.

Where shareholders can allege a possible breach of directors' duty of loyalty in entering into or rejecting an M&A or other transaction, courts' scrutiny is far more searching. The board will lose the presumption of business judgment and will be subject to the "entire fairness" standard. Entire fairness is the most searching of the corporate law standards, requiring the board to bear the burden of proving both fair price and fair dealing. Fair price "relates to the economic and financial considerations of the proposed merger, including all relevant factors: assets, market value, earnings, future prospects, and any other elements that affect the intrinsic or inherent value of a company's stock." Fair dealing "embraces questions of when the transaction was timed, how it was initiated, structured, negotiated, disclosed to the directors, and how the approvals of the directors and the shareholders were obtained."[7] Where directors are conflicted, the board will be required to bear the burden of demonstrating entire fairness unless they have "cleansed" the transaction, typically by means of a fully-informed shareholder vote and other measures; we will discuss the law in this area in Chapter XIX. Until very recently, the law had been that board cleansing of a transaction shifted the burden to plaintiffs, who could prevail if they could demonstrate that the transaction was not fair to the corporation. But in an opinion issued just as this book is going to press, *Corwin v. KKR Financial Holdings LLC*, No. 629, 2014 (Del., Oct. 2, 2015), the Delaware

---

[4] Until *Stone v. Ritter*, 911 A.2d 362 (Del. 2006), Delaware cases sometimes referred to a "triad" of fiduciary duties, with good faith being the third part of the triad.

[5] *Aronson v. Lewis* at 812.

[6] *Id.*

[7] *Weinberger v. UOP, Inc.*, 457 A.2d 701, 711 (Del. 1983).

Supreme Court held that a transaction involving a non-controlling shareholder that is approved by a fully informed vote of the disinterested shareholders will be reviewed under the deferential business judgment standard, effectively ending the possibility of a successful challenge to board conduct in such a circumstance.

Moreover, attacking the "good faith" prong of the business judgment presumption has been a controversial, and ultimately, largely unfruitful exercise from a litigant's perspective, both in the M&A context and otherwise. Taking a cue from dicta in *Cede & Co., Inc. v. Technicolor*[8] that referred to a triad of fiduciary duties, "good faith, loyalty or due care," plaintiffs attacked board decisions to engage in or refuse to engage in M&A transactions as being in bad faith. In effect, plaintiffs attempted to couch claims that might otherwise be exculpable duty of care claims as non-exculpable violations of the directors' duty of good faith. In the context of merger decisions, the Delaware Supreme Court in *Lyondell Chemical Company v. Ryan,* 970 A.2d 235 (Del. 2009), ruling for defendants, held that where "the issue is whether the directors failed to act in good faith," "bad faith will be found" if a director "intentionally fails to act in the face of a known duty to act, demonstrating a conscious disregard for his duties."[9] The Court thus defined what the duty of good faith requires—a duty not to act in bad faith. This is an extremely high bar for plaintiffs to clear. Consequently, claims that directors have violated their duty of good faith when acting in the context of a merger are among the most difficult on which to succeed.

The importance of litigation presumptions and standards of review goes well beyond litigation strategies. Structuring transactions in order to preserve the business judgment presumption for boards informs both how parties put together a deal, and how boards engage in the sales process. For example, in order to meet their obligation to be informed, boards hire investment banks, lawyers, and accountants to provide them with information about the proposed transaction. When some directors have conflicts of interest with respect to a particular transaction, boards will constitute special committees consisting only of disinterested directors to consider that transaction. Moreover, the board's fiduciary duties will significantly influence the content of merger agreements, notably the existence and scope of provisions designed to let a company out of a transaction if the board's fiduciary duties so indicate—"fiduciary outs"— as well as the extent to which the corporation restricts its ability to look for or deal with other potential suitors—to "shop" itself. Rejecting a deal, too, must be done carefully, with due regard to what the law allows and forbids.

---

[8]   634 A.2d 345, 361 (Del. 1993).

[9]   *Lyondell Chemical Company v. Ryan*, 970 A.2d 235, 243 (Del. 2009).

In the Sections that follow, we consider the fiduciary duties of directors when going forward with, or rejecting, M&A transactions. The law in this area has been developed through the "common law"—through cases, in which courts articulate the general principles to be applied. The application to different factual settings is, of course, not mechanical, since each factual setting has its own unique attributes.

Many of the seminal cases were decided in the 1980s. Prior to that time, the case law governing M&A transactions was sparse and scattered through many jurisdictions. But the significant rise in takeover transactions, particularly hostile bids, and vigorous board resistance to these bids, forced the Delaware courts to confront the issues involved for the first time and develop case law governing takeover transactions. As you read through these cases, think about whether the doctrines are still applicable to today's takeover market and to what extent they have changed in response to changes in the market and market practices.

In this Part we will cover four areas. The first Chapter will deal with the board's fiduciary duties when it is resisting an actual takeover offer or the possibility of such an offer. The next two Chapters will cover the board's fiduciary duties in deciding to sell the company, and in the sales process. In the last Chapter, we will cover transactions involving a straightforward conflict of interest, either because the board or management is interested, or because the transaction is with a controlling shareholder.

B. DEFENDING THE CORPORATION: *UNOCAL*

One of the most important of the core takeover cases is a 1985 case, *Unocal Corp. v. Mesa Petroleum Co.*, 493 A.2d 946 (Del. 1985). To understand *Unocal*, it is important to know the context of the court's decision. The 1980s was the age of the hostile takeover. Companies were besieged by bidders seeking to take them over, sometimes using coercive techniques. One term used to describe such bidders at the time was "corporate raider." These corporate raiders at the time sought to acquire companies, sometimes some of the country's most storied corporate empires, and then break them up and profit from their sale. The prospect that these raiders might be successful terrified corporate America. Companies entered the decade with few defenses. But takeover lawyers soon became creative in inventing new defensive techniques, culminating in Marty Lipton's invention of the poison pill.

Unocal is important because of the court's articulation of what has come to be known as the *Unocal* standard, which governs how far a company can go to defend itself against a corporate takeover. This was a controversial issue at the time and remains so today. Some commentators argued that a company should not be able to defend itself against an unsolicited and unwanted tender offer. Rather, its board should remain passive and let shareholders decide whether to accept the offer. Others argued that boards should have wide latitude to defend their corporations—that corporations, and shareholders, needed protection. The ultimate issue was whether allowing takeover defenses would permit boards to entrench themselves and company management, and thereby prevent the takeover market from functioning efficiently. That debate continues today.

Unocal represented the Delaware court's first attempt in the 1980s to tackle this issue. Prior to *Unocal*, the courts lived in two distinct worlds. In one, business judgment deference was the standard. In the other, when boards engaged in conflict transactions, entire fairness was the standard. *Unocal* reflected a relatively new set of questions for the court: in defending the corporation against unwanted offers, boards were making what might seem like normal business decisions, but the boards' motivations might actually be self-serving. The challenge for the court was in deciding whether the motivations of the board in such circumstances merited the closer scrutiny of entire fairness review or the deference of business judgment. In *Unocal*, the board had adopted a number of defenses in order to thwart a hostile bidder. The standard announced by the court required, for the first time, an extensive inquiry into board motives. In deciding that the board's decision to adopt defensive measures in response to an unwanted offer were protected by the business judgment presumption, the court applied this new "intermediate" or "enhanced scrutiny" standard to ferret out the board's motives.

Unocal is often referred to as an intermediate standard applied to director conduct, but this is not exactly a correct description. The word intermediate might seem to suggest that scrutiny of director action lies somewhere on a spectrum between the business judgment presumption and the entire fairness standard. *Unocal* is not applied in that way. Rather, the *Unocal* intermediate standard is a preliminary review that inquires into the motivations of directors and the reasonableness of their actions. Depending on what the inquiry reveals, either the business judgment presumption, or the entire fairness standard, is applied. Often, the court's determination of the proper standard of review at the preliminary inquiry stage determines the outcome of the case. As a result, *Unocal*'s enhanced scrutiny standard plays an extremely important role in litigation as well as in transaction planning.

After the hostile takeover era of the 1980s passed, the Delaware courts would take a different turn with respect to the application of *Unocal*'s intermediate standard. The 1980s were characterized by management resistance against unsolicited offers, raising the specter that boards were seeking to entrench themselves, which gave rise to the need for *Unocal's* preliminary inquiry. By the 1990s, management had learned the important lesson that there was much more money to be earned by engaging with leveraged buyout firms who sought to take their companies private than there was in resisting. By the 1990s, management became active proponents of the takeover. Delaware's application of the *Unocal* standard has had to adapt to that new reality.

1. PRECURSOR TO *UNOCAL*: *CHEFF v. MATHES*

The *Unocal* case was preceded by *Cheff v. Mathes*, itself one of the first Delaware cases to address defensive actions by a corporate board. Until *Cheff*, courts typically granted the presumption of business judgment to board defensive actions. In *Cheff*, for the first time, the court began to inquire into the motives of boards prior to granting them the presumption of business judgment

CHEFF V. MATHES
Supreme Court of Delaware
199 A.2d 548 (1964)

CAREY, JUSTICE.

[*Editor: Arnold Maremont and his company, Motor Products Corporation, began accumulating shares of Holland Furnace, and then approached Holland.*]

In June of 1957, Mr. Cheff [CEO of Holland Furnace] met with Mr. Arnold H. Maremont . . . Mr. Cheff testified . . . that Maremont generally inquired about the feasibility of merger between Motor Products and Holland. Mr. Cheff testified that, in view of the difference in sales practices between the two companies, he informed Mr. Maremont that a merger did not seem feasible. In reply, Mr. Maremont stated that, in the light of Mr. Cheff's decision, he had no further interest in Holland nor did he wish to buy any of the stock of Holland.

None of the members of the board apparently connected the interest of Mr. Maremont with the increased activity of Holland stock [from a monthly trading volume in a range between 10,300 and 24,2000 shares during the first five months of June to 37,000 shares the last week of June.]. However, Mr. Trenkamp and Mr. Staal, the Treasurer of Holland, unsuccessfully made an informal investigation in order to ascertain the identity of the purchaser or purchasers. The mystery was resolved, however, when Maremont called Ames in July of 1957 to inform the latter that Maremont then owned 55,000 shares of Holland stock. At this juncture, no requests for change in corporate policy were made, and Maremont made no demand to be made a member of the board of Holland.

Ames reported the above information to the board at its July 30, 1957 meeting. Because of the position now occupied by Maremont, the board elected to investigate the financial and business history of Maremont and corporations controlled by him. Apart from the documentary evidence produced by this investigation . . . , Staal testified . . . that "leading bank officials" had indicated that Maremont "had been a participant, or had attempted to be, in the liquidation of a number of companies." Staal specifically mentioned only one individual giving such advice, the Vice President of the First National Bank of Chicago. Mr. Cheff testified . . . of Maremont's alleged participation in liquidation activities. Mr. Cheff testified that: "Throughout the whole of the Kalamazoo-Battle Creek area, and Detroit too, where I spent considerable time, he is well known and not highly regarded by any stretch." This information was communicated to the board.

On August 23, 1957, at the request of Maremont, a meeting was held between Mr. Maremont and Cheff. At this meeting, Cheff was informed that Motor Products then owned approximately 100,000 shares of Holland stock. Maremont then made a demand that he be named to the board of directors, but Cheff refused to consider it. Since considerable controversy has been generated by Maremont's alleged threat to liquidate the company or substantially alter the sales force of Holland, we believe it desirable to set forth the testimony of Cheff on this point: "Now we have 8500 men, direct employees, so the problem is entirely different. He indicated immediately that he had no interest in that type of distribution, that he didn't think it was modern, that he felt furnaces could be sold as he sold mufflers, through half a dozen salesmen in a wholesale way."

Testimony was introduced by the defendants tending to show that substantial unrest was present among the employees of Holland as a result of the threat of Maremont to seek control of Holland. Thus, Mr. Cheff testified that the field organization was considering leaving in large numbers because of a fear of the consequences of a Maremont acquisition; he further testified that approximately "25 of our key men" were lost as the result of the unrest engendered by the Maremont proposal. Staal, corroborating Cheff's version, stated that a number of branch managers approached him for reassurances that Maremont was not going to be allowed to successfully gain control. Moreover, at approximately this time, the company was furnished with a Dun and Bradstreet report, which indicated the practice of Maremont to achieve quick profits by sales or liquidations of companies acquired by him. The defendants were also supplied with an income statement of Motor Products, Inc., showing a loss of $336,121.00 for the period in 1957.

On August 30, 1957, the board was informed by Cheff of Maremont's demand to be placed upon the board and of Maremont's belief that the retail sales organization of Holland was obsolete. The board was also informed of the results of the investigation by Cheff and Staal. Predicated upon this information, the board authorized the purchase of company stock on the market with corporate funds, ostensibly for use in a stock option plan.[10]

The transaction contemplated here (and challenged in the case) is "greenmail." Greenmail is a selective purchase of the stock of a party who the board considers undesirable, and often, is threatening a takeover, at a premium price. The party sells his stock to the company and may agree to stop pursuing or pressuring the company and often not to acquire more shares of the company's stock.

Greenmail was common in the 1980s: targets would buy back stock from parties they considered to be corporate raiders, at premium prices, in exchange for promises from the raiders to cease their attempts to take over the company (hence the term "greenmail," to summon up "blackmail."). In response, Congress passed an act in 1987 imposing a 50% excise tax on the profits from greenmail.[11] Many states also adopted laws prohibiting the practice. For their part, in order to dissuade greenmailers, some firms adopted provisions in their certificates of incorporation prohibiting selective dealing with shareholders. For all these reasons, greenmail is now quite rare.[12]

Against this background, the court framed the issued thusly:

> The question then presented is whether or not defendants satisfied the burden of proof of showing reasonable grounds to believe a danger to corporate policy and effectiveness existed by the presence of the Maremont stock ownership. It is important to remember that the directors satisfy their burden by showing good faith and reasonable investigation; the directors will not be penalized for an honest mistake of judgment, if the judgment appeared reasonable at the time the decision was made . . .

> [T]he evidence presented in the court below leads inevitably to the conclusion that the board of directors, based upon direct investigation, receipt of professional advice, and personal observations of the contradictory action of Maremont and his explanation of corporate purpose, believed, with justification, that there was a reasonable threat to the continued existence of

---

[10]   *Cheff v. Mathes*, 199 A.2d 548, 551–52 (Del. 1964).

[11]   26 USC § 5881—Greenmail.

[12]   *See* David Manry & David Stangeland, *Greenmail: A Brief History*, 6 STANF. J. L. BUS. & FIN. 217 (2001).

Holland, or at least existence in its present form, by the plan of Maremont to continue building up his stock holdings.[13]

The Delaware Supreme Court determined that the board's actions in defending the corporation were motivated by the results of their inquiry into Maremont's character, and were entitled to business judgment deference. It therefore ruled that the board's purchase of Maremont's Holland shares at a premium to market value was proper.

Reading the opinion, it is hard not to view Maremont unfavorably, the threat to Holland's business plans being so obvious. But further examination suggests a different view. Maremont was apparently an exemplary citizen: a patron of the arts, a fighter against discrimination and for the poor, and an excellent businessman. By contrast, the Holland Furnace Company was being pursued by the FTC for their deceptive sales practices, a pursuit that eventually resulted in a cease and desist order. [14] Holland employees would go into people's houses, represent themselves as being from the government, and dismantle people's furnaces, pronouncing the furnaces unsafe but fixable with Holland's help. Hence Holland's need for a large workforce—the workforce Maremont would have pared down. Following its successful defense against Maremont's advances, Holland's fortunes declined, and Ted Cheff eventually went to jail.

2.   THE *UNOCAL* STANDARD: *UNOCAL v. MESA PETROLEUM CO.*

In the 1985 *Unocal* case, T. Boone Pickens's Mesa Petroleum Co. was trying to acquire Unocal. Pickens was a major figure in business even before the case, and has remained active to this day. He founded Mesa, making his fortune in the oil and gas business. One of his big early successes came in 1979, when he sold Mesa's Canadian operations to Dome Petroleum for $600 million. Pickens had developed a reputation for being a greenmailer and corporate raider. In the years prior to his approach to Unocal, Pickens had bid for, among other companies, Gulf Oil, Cities Service, and Phillips Petroleum. By the time his interest in Unocal became known, Pickens and his tactics were well known to the business community.

Pickens continued in business after *Unocal*, going after targets such as Newmont Mining, Diamond Shamrock, and Koito Mfg. Pickens eventually sold Mesa Petroleum in 1997 and, in the same year, founded BP Capital Management, an investment fund specializing in traditional energy companies and nuclear power corporations. At this writing,

13   Cheff v. Mathes at 555–6.

14   *See Holland Furnace Company v. Federal Trade Commission,* 295 F.2d 302 (7th Cir. 1961), denying Holland's petition for a review of the FTC dated July 7, 1958, which "directs Holland to cease and desist from certain practices in commerce found to be unfair and deceptive." *Id.* at 302.

Pickens, born in 1928, is, according to Forbes, worth about $950 million. He still heads and owns a significant stake in BP. In addition, he has interests in wind power developments across the United States and has become a principal benefactor of the athletic department of Oklahoma State University.

UNOCAL CORP. V. MESA PETROLEUM CO.

Supreme Court of Delaware
493 A.2d 946 (1985)

MOORE, JUSTICE.

We confront an issue of first impression in Delaware—the validity of a corporation's self-tender for its own shares which excludes from participation a stockholder making a hostile tender offer for the company's stock.

The Court of Chancery granted a preliminary injunction to the plaintiffs . . . , (collectively "Mesa"), enjoining an exchange offer of the defendant, Unocal Corporation (Unocal) for its own stock. The trial court concluded that a selective exchange offer, excluding Mesa, was legally impermissible. We cannot agree with such a blanket rule. The factual findings of the Vice Chancellor, . . . establish that Unocal's board, consisting of a majority of independent directors, acted in good faith, and after reasonable investigation found that Mesa's tender offer was both inadequate and coercive. Under the circumstances the board had both the power and duty to oppose a bid it perceived to be harmful to the corporate enterprise. On this record we are satisfied that the device Unocal adopted is reasonable in relation to the threat posed, and that the board acted in the proper exercise of sound business judgment. We will not substitute our views for those of the board if the latter's decision can be "attributed to any rational business purpose." . . . . Accordingly, we reverse the decision of the Court of Chancery and order the preliminary injunction vacated.

On April 8, 1985, Mesa, the owner of approximately 13% of Unocal's stock, commenced a two-tier "front loaded" cash tender offer for 64 million shares, or approximately 37%, of Unocal's outstanding stock at a price of $54 per share. The "back-end" was designed to eliminate the remaining publicly held shares by an exchange of securities purportedly worth $54 per share. However, pursuant to [a court] order, Mesa issued a supplemental proxy statement to Unocal's stockholders disclosing that the securities offered in the second-step merger would be highly subordinated, and that Unocal's capitalization would differ significantly from its present structure. Unocal has rather aptly termed such securities "junk bonds."

Unocal's board consists of eight independent outside directors and six insiders. It met on April 13, 1985, to consider the Mesa tender offer. Thirteen directors were present, and the meeting lasted nine and one-half hours. The directors were given no agenda or written materials prior to the session. However, detailed presentations were made by legal counsel regarding the board's obligations under both Delaware corporate law and the federal securities laws. The board then received a presentation from Peter Sachs on behalf of Goldman Sachs & Co. (Goldman Sachs) and Dillon, Read & Co. (Dillon Read) discussing the bases for their opinions that the Mesa proposal was wholly inadequate. Mr. Sachs opined that the minimum cash value that could be expected from a sale or orderly liquidation for 100% of Unocal's stock was in excess of $60 per share. In making his presentation, Mr. Sachs showed slides outlining the valuation techniques used by the financial advisors, and others, depicting recent business combinations in the oil and gas industry . . .

Mr. Sachs also presented various defensive strategies available to the board if it concluded that Mesa's two-step tender offer was inadequate and should be opposed. One of the devices outlined was a self-tender by Unocal for its own stock with a reasonable price range of $70 to $75 per share. The cost of such a proposal would cause the company to incur $6.1–6.5 billion of additional debt, and a presentation was made informing the board of Unocal's ability to handle it. The directors were told that the primary effect of this obligation would be to reduce exploratory drilling, but that the company would nonetheless remain a viable entity.

The eight outside directors, comprising a clear majority of the thirteen members present, then met separately with Unocal's financial advisors and attorneys. Thereafter, they unanimously agreed to advise the board that it should reject Mesa's tender offer as inadequate, and that Unocal should pursue a self-tender to provide the stockholders with a fairly priced alternative to the Mesa proposal. The board then reconvened and unanimously adopted a resolution rejecting as grossly inadequate Mesa's tender offer. Despite the nine and one-half hour length of the meeting, no formal decision was made on the proposed defensive self-tender.

On April 15, the board met again . . . [for] two hours. Unocal's Vice President of Finance and its Assistant General Counsel made a detailed presentation of the proposed terms of the exchange offer. A price range between $70 and $80 per share was considered, and ultimately the directors agreed upon $72. The board was also advised about the debt securities that would be issued, and the necessity of placing restrictive covenants upon certain corporate activities until the obligations were paid. [*Editor: We will be discussing covenants of this type in Chapter XVIII. For present purposes, note that if Unocal were subject to the covenants, acquiring it would become more difficult because the covenants would restrict Unocal's ability to incur additional debt, something an acquirer would likely want to do to finance its acquisition.*] The board's decisions were made in reliance on the advice of its investment bankers, including the terms and conditions upon which the securities were to be issued. Based upon this advice, and the board's own deliberations, the directors unanimously approved the exchange offer. Their resolution provided that if Mesa acquired 64 million shares of Unocal stock through its own offer (the Mesa Purchase Condition), Unocal would buy the remaining 49% outstanding for an exchange of debt securities having an aggregate par value of $72 per share. The board resolution also stated that the offer would be subject to other conditions that had been described to the board at the meeting, or which were deemed necessary by Unocal's officers, including the exclusion of Mesa from the proposal (the Mesa exclusion).

Unocal's exchange offer was commenced on April 17, 1985, and Mesa promptly challenged it by filing this suit in the Court of Chancery. On April 22, the Unocal board met again and was advised by Goldman Sachs and Dillon Read to waive the Mesa Purchase Condition as to 50 million shares. This recommendation was in response to a perceived concern of the shareholders that, if shares were tendered to Unocal, no shares would be purchased by either offeror. The directors were also advised that they should tender their own Unocal stock into the exchange offer as a mark of their confidence in it.

Another focus of the board was the Mesa exclusion. Legal counsel advised that under Delaware law Mesa could only be excluded for what the directors reasonably believed to be a valid corporate purpose. The directors' discussion centered on the objective of adequately compensating shareholders at the "back-end" of Mesa's proposal, which the latter would finance with "junk bonds." To include Mesa would defeat that goal, because under the proration aspect of the exchange offer (49%) every Mesa share accepted by Unocal would displace one held by another stockholder. Further, if Mesa were permitted to tender to Unocal, the latter would in effect be financing Mesa's own inadequate proposal.

On April 24, 1985 Unocal issued a supplement to the exchange offer describing the partial waiver of the Mesa Purchase Condition. On May 1, 1985, in another supplement, Unocal extended the withdrawal, proration and expiration dates of its exchange offer to May 17, 1985.

Meanwhile, on April 22, 1985, Mesa amended its complaint in this action to challenge the Mesa exclusion.... [O]n April 23, 1985, Mesa moved for a temporary restraining order in response to Unocal's announcement that it was partially waiving the Mesa Purchase Condition....

On April 29, 1985, the Vice Chancellor temporarily restrained Unocal from proceeding with the exchange offer unless it included Mesa. The trial court recognized that directors could oppose, and attempt to defeat, a hostile takeover which they considered adverse to the best interests of the corporation. However, the Vice Chancellor decided that in a selective purchase of the company's stock, the corporation bears the burden of showing: (1) a valid corporate purpose, and (2) that the transaction was fair to all of the stockholders, including those excluded. [*Editor: Unocal appealed the Chancery Court's ruling.*]

. . .

II.

The issues we address involve these fundamental questions: Did the Unocal board have the power and duty to oppose a takeover threat it reasonably perceived to be harmful to the corporate enterprise, and if so, is its action here entitled to the protection of the business judgment rule?

Mesa contends that the discriminatory exchange offer violates the fiduciary duties Unocal owes it. Mesa argues that because of the Mesa exclusion the business judgment rule is inapplicable, because the directors by tendering their own shares will derive a financial benefit that is not available to *all* Unocal stockholders. Thus, it is Mesa's ultimate contention that Unocal cannot establish that the exchange offer is fair to *all* shareholders, and argues that the Court of Chancery was correct in concluding that Unocal was unable to meet this burden.

Unocal answers that it does not owe a duty of "fairness" to Mesa, given the facts here. Specifically, Unocal contends that its board of directors reasonably and in good faith concluded that Mesa's $54 two-tier tender offer was coercive and inadequate, and that Mesa sought selective treatment for itself. Furthermore, Unocal argues that the board's approval of the exchange offer was made in good faith, on an informed basis, and in the exercise of due care. Under these circumstances, Unocal contends that its directors properly employed this device to protect the company and its stockholders from Mesa's harmful tactics.

III.

We begin with the basic issue of the power of a board of directors of a Delaware corporation to adopt a defensive measure of this type. [The court concludes that the Board has power, under its inherent power to manage the corporation under 8 Del.C. § 141(a) and under 8 Del.C. § 160(a), conferring broad authority upon a corporation to deal in its own stock.]

. . . [I]t is now well established that in the acquisition of its shares a Delaware corporation may deal selectively with its stockholders, provided the directors have not acted out of a sole or primary purpose to entrench themselves in office. . . .

Finally, the board's power to act derives from its fundamental duty and obligation to protect the corporate enterprise, which includes stockholders, from harm reasonably perceived, irrespective of its source. . . . Thus, we are satisfied that in the broad context of corporate governance, including issues of fundamental corporate change, a board of directors is not a passive instrumentality.

Given the foregoing principles, we turn to the standards by which director action is to be measured. . . . [T]he business judgment rule, including the standards by which director conduct is judged, is applicable in the context of a takeover. The business judgment rule is a "presumption that in making a business decision the directors of a corporation acted on an informed basis, in good faith and in the honest belief that the action taken was in the best interests of the company." . . . A hallmark of the business judgment rule is that a court will not substitute its judgment for that of the board if the latter's decision can be "attributed to any rational business purpose." [quoting Aronson] . . .

When a board addresses a pending takeover bid it has an obligation to determine whether the offer is in the best interests of the corporation and its shareholders. In that respect a board's duty is no different from any other responsibility it shoulders, and its decisions should be no less entitled to the respect they otherwise would be accorded in the realm of business judgment. . . . There are, however, certain caveats to a proper exercise of this function. Because of the omnipresent specter that a board may be acting primarily in its own interests, rather than those of the corporation and its shareholders, there is an enhanced duty which calls for judicial examination at the threshold before the protections of the business judgment rule may be conferred.

. . .

We must bear in mind the inherent danger in the purchase of shares with corporate funds to remove a threat to corporate policy when a threat to control is involved. The directors are of necessity confronted with a conflict of interest, and an objective decision is difficult. . . . In the face of this inherent conflict directors must show that they had reasonable grounds for believing that a danger to corporate policy and effectiveness existed because of another person's stock ownership. . . . However, they satisfy that burden "by showing good faith and reasonable investigation. . . ." Furthermore, such proof is materially enhanced, as here, by the approval of a board comprised of a majority of outside independent directors who have acted in accordance with the foregoing standards.

IV.

A.

In the board's exercise of corporate power to forestall a takeover bid our analysis begins with the basic principle that corporate directors have a fiduciary duty to act in the best interests of the corporation's stockholders. As we have noted, their duty of care extends to protecting the corporation and its owners from perceived harm whether a threat originates from third parties or other shareholders. But such powers are not absolute. A corporation does not have unbridled discretion to defeat any perceived threat by any Draconian means available.

The restriction placed upon a selective stock repurchase is that the directors may not have acted solely or primarily out of a desire to perpetuate themselves in office. . . . The standard of proof established in *Cheff v. Mathes* and discussed *supra*, is designed to ensure that a defensive measure to thwart or impede a takeover is indeed motivated by a good faith concern for the welfare of the corporation and its stockholders, which in all circumstances must be free of any fraud or other misconduct. However, this does not end the inquiry.

B.

A further aspect is the element of balance. If a defensive measure is to come within the ambit of the business judgment rule, it must be reasonable in relation to the threat posed. This entails an analysis by the directors of the nature of the takeover bid and its effect on the corporate enterprise. Examples of such concerns may include: inadequacy of the price offered, nature and timing of the offer, questions of illegality, the impact on "constituencies" other than shareholders (i.e., creditors, customers, employees, and perhaps even the community generally), the risk of nonconsummation, and the quality of securities being offered in the exchange. While not a controlling factor, it also seems to us that a board may reasonably consider the basic stockholder interests at stake, including those of short term speculators, whose actions may have fueled the coercive aspect of the offer at the expense of the long term investor. [*Editor: Footnote omitted, which provides some evidence that stockholders of companies that resisted or defeated hostile offers did better, but mentions the "vehement contrary view."*] Here, the threat posed was viewed by the Unocal board as a grossly inadequate two-tier coercive tender offer coupled with the threat of greenmail.

Specifically, the Unocal directors had concluded that the value of Unocal was substantially above the $54 per share offered in cash at the front end. Furthermore, they determined that the subordinated securities to be exchanged in Mesa's announced squeeze out of the remaining shareholders in the "back-end" merger were "junk bonds" worth far less than $54. It is now well recognized that such offers are a classic coercive measure designed to stampede shareholders into tendering at the first tier, even if the price is inadequate, out of fear of what they will receive at the back end of the transaction. Wholly beyond the coercive aspect of an inadequate two-tier tender offer, the threat was posed by a corporate raider with a national reputation as a "greenmailer."

In adopting the selective exchange offer, the board stated that its objective was either to defeat the inadequate Mesa offer or, should the offer still succeed, provide the 49% of its stockholders, who would otherwise be forced to accept "junk bonds," with $72 worth of senior debt. We find that both purposes are valid.

However, such efforts would have been thwarted by Mesa's participation in the exchange offer. First, if Mesa could tender its shares, Unocal would effectively be subsidizing the former's continuing effort to buy Unocal stock at $54 per share. Second, Mesa could not, by definition, fit within the class of shareholders being protected from its own coercive and inadequate tender offer.

Thus, we are satisfied that the selective exchange offer is reasonably related to the threats posed. It is consistent with the principle that "the minority stockholder shall receive the substantial equivalent in value of what he had before." . . . This concept of fairness, while stated in the merger context, is also relevant in the area of tender offer law. Thus, the board's decision to offer what it determined to be the fair value of the corporation to the 49% of its shareholders, who would otherwise be forced to accept highly subordinated "junk bonds," is reasonable and consistent with the directors' duty to ensure that the minority stockholders receive equal value for their shares.

V.

Mesa contends that it is unlawful, and the trial court agreed, for a corporation to discriminate in this fashion against one shareholder. It argues correctly that no case has ever sanctioned a device that precludes a raider from sharing in a benefit available to all other stockholders. However, as we have noted earlier, the principle of selective stock repurchases by a Delaware corporation is neither unknown nor unauthorized. The only difference is that heretofore the approved transaction was the payment of "greenmail" to a raider or dissident posing a threat to the corporate enterprise. All other stockholders were denied such favored treatment, and given Mesa's past history of greenmail, its claims here are rather ironic.

. . .

Thus, while the exchange offer is a form of selective treatment, given the nature of the threat posed here the response is neither unlawful nor unreasonable. If the board of directors is disinterested, has acted in good faith and with due care, its decision in the absence of an abuse of discretion will be upheld as a proper exercise of business judgment. [*Editor: The court rejects the argument that members of the board who are stockholders are "interested" because they can tender their own shares and Mesa can't.*]

. . .

Here, the Court of Chancery specifically found that the "directors' decision [to oppose the Mesa tender offer] was made in the good faith belief that the Mesa tender offer is inadequate." . . . [W]e are satisfied that Unocal's board has met its burden of proof.

VI.

In conclusion, there was directorial power to oppose the Mesa tender offer, and to undertake a selective stock exchange made in good faith and upon a reasonable investigation pursuant to a clear duty to protect the corporate enterprise. Further, the selective stock repurchase plan chosen by Unocal is reasonable in relation to the threat that the board rationally and reasonably believed was posed by Mesa's inadequate and coercive two-tier tender offer. Under those circumstances the board's action is entitled to be measured by the standards of the business judgment rule. Thus, unless it is shown by a preponderance of the evidence that the directors' decisions were primarily based on perpetuating themselves in office, or some other breach of fiduciary duty such as fraud, overreaching, lack of good faith, or being uninformed, a Court will not substitute its judgment for that of the board. . . .

The decision of the Court of Chancery is therefore REVERSED, and the preliminary injunction is VACATED.

---

3.   NOTE ON WILLIAMS ACT AMENDMENT

In the *Unocal* case, the Delaware Supreme Court permitted Unocal's discriminatory self-tender. But, as discussed in Chapter IV, in response to the case, the SEC adopted a rule under the Williams Act to prohibit discriminatory self-tenders. Rule 13e–4(f)(8) under the Securities and Exchange Act of 1934 provides that: "No issuer or affiliate shall make a tender offer unless: (i) The tender offer is open to all security holders of the class of securities subject to the tender offer." (The SEC also adopted a rule to prohibit discriminatory tenders made by third parties, Rule 14d–10.)

Why would the SEC take this step? At the time, as the hostile takeover market was developing, the SEC took a stand against takeover defenses, and in favor of a level playing field as between the hostile acquirer and target management. The court in *Unocal*, knowing of the SEC's stand, showed less deference to boards than they previously had shown, but apparently, more than the SEC wanted them to. The SEC countermanded the specific holding, using its rule-making authority to prohibit discriminatory tender offers.

C.   THE "POISON PILL"/SHAREHOLDER RIGHTS PLAN

Not long after the poison pill, also known as the shareholder rights plan, was developed, it was subject to a legal challenge. In *Moran v. Household International*, the Delaware Supreme Court applied its new *Unocal* standard to a board's decision to adopt this potent defensive measure. Validating the pill was not a foregone conclusion, since both the poison pill and the *Unocal* standard were so new. As you read through this case and the materials thereafter, think about alternative standards or regimes the Delaware courts could have developed for review of the poison pill.

MORAN V. HOUSEHOLD INTERNATIONAL, INC.

Supreme Court of Delaware
500 A.2d 1346 (1985)

McNEILLY, JUSTICE:

This case presents to this Court for review the most recent defensive mechanism in the arsenal of corporate takeover weaponry—the Preferred Share Purchase Rights Plan ("Rights Plan" or "Plan") . . . [T]he Court of Chancery upheld the Rights Plan as a legitimate exercise of business judgment by Household. . . . We agree, and therefore, affirm the judgment below.

I

. . . On August 14, 1984, the Board of Directors of Household International, Inc. [a diversified holding company] adopted the Rights Plan by a fourteen to two vote. The intricacies of the Rights Plan are contained in a 48-page document entitled "Rights Agreement." Basically, the Plan provides that Household common stockholders are entitled to the issuance of one Right per common share under certain triggering conditions. There are two triggering events that can activate the Rights. The first is the announcement of a tender offer for 30 percent of Household's shares ("30% trigger") and the second is the acquisition of 20 percent of Household's shares by any single entity or group ("20% trigger").

If an announcement of a tender offer for 30 percent of Household's shares is made, the Rights are issued and are immediately exercisable to purchase 1/100 share of new preferred stock for $100 and are redeemable by the Board for $.50 per Right. If 20 percent of Household's shares are acquired by anyone, the Rights are issued and become non-redeemable and are exercisable to purchase 1/100 of a share of preferred. If a Right is not exercised for preferred, and thereafter, a merger or consolidation occurs, the Rights holder can exercise each Right to purchase $200 of the common stock of the tender offeror for $100. This "flip-over" provision of the Rights Plan is at the heart of this controversy.

Household did not adopt its Rights Plan during a battle with a corporate raider, but as a preventive mechanism to ward off future advances. The Vice-Chancellor found that as early as February 1984, Household's management became concerned about the company's vulnerability as a takeover target and began considering amending its charter to render a takeover more difficult. . . .

In the meantime, appellant Moran, one of Household's own Directors and also Chairman of the Dyson-Kissner-Moran Corporation, ("D-K-M") which is the largest single stockholder of Household, began discussions concerning a possible leveraged buyout of Household by D-K-M. D-K-M's financial studies showed that Household's stock was significantly undervalued in relation to the company's break-up value. . . . Moran's suggestion of a leveraged buy-out never progressed beyond the discussion stage.

Concerned about Household's vulnerability to a raider in light of the current takeover climate, Household secured the services of Wachtell, Lipton, Rosen and Katz ("Wachtell, Lipton") and Goldman, Sachs & Co. ("Goldman, Sachs") to formulate a takeover policy for recommendation to the Household Board at its August 14 meeting. After a July 31 meeting with a Household Board member and a pre-meeting distribution of material on the potential takeover problem and the proposed Rights Plan, the Board met on August 14, 1984.

Representatives of Wachtell, Lipton and Goldman, Sachs attended the August 14 meeting. The minutes reflect that Mr. Lipton explained to the Board that his recommendation of the Plan was based on his understanding that the Board was concerned about the increasing frequency of "bust-up" takeovers, the increasing takeover activity in the financial service industry . . . , and the possible adverse effect this type of activity could have on employees and others concerned with and vital to the continuing successful operation of Household even in the absence of any actual bust-up takeover attempt. Against this factual background, the Plan was approved.

Thereafter, Moran and the company of which he is Chairman, D-K-M, filed this suit. . . .

II

The primary issue here is the applicability of the business judgment rule as the standard by which the adoption of the Rights Plan should be reviewed. Much of this issue has been decided by our recent decision in *Unocal*. In *Unocal,* we applied the business judgment rule to analyze Unocal's discriminatory self-tender. We explained:

> When a board addresses a pending takeover bid it has an obligation to determine whether the offer is in the best interests of the corporation and its shareholders. In that respect a board's duty is no different from any other responsibility it shoulders, and its decisions should be no less entitled to the respect they otherwise would be accorded in the realm of business judgment.

This case is distinguishable ... since here we have a defensive mechanism adopted to ward off possible future advances and not a mechanism adopted in reaction to a specific threat. This distinguishing factor does not result in the Directors losing the protection of the business judgment rule. To the contrary, pre-planning for the contingency of a hostile takeover might reduce the risk that, under the pressure of a takeover bid, management will fail to exercise reasonable judgment. Therefore, in reviewing a pre-planned defensive mechanism it seems even more appropriate to apply the business judgment rule.

Of course, the business judgment rule can only sustain corporate decision making or transactions that are within the power or authority of the Board. Therefore, before the business judgment rule can be applied it must be determined whether the Directors were authorized to adopt the Rights Plan.

III

Appellants vehemently contend that the Board of Directors was unauthorized to adopt the Rights Plan. First, appellants contend that no provision of the Delaware General Corporation Law authorizes the issuance of such Rights. Secondly, appellants, along with the SEC, contend that the Board is unauthorized to usurp stockholders' rights to receive hostile tender offers. Third, appellants and the SEC also contend that the Board is unauthorized to fundamentally restrict stockholders' rights to conduct a proxy contest. We address each of these contentions in turn.

A.

While appellants contend that no provision of the Delaware General Corporation Law authorizes the Rights Plan, Household contends that the Rights Plan was issued pursuant to 8 Del.C. §§ 151(g) and 157. It explains that the Rights are authorized by § 157 and the issue of preferred stock underlying the Rights is authorized by § 151. Appellants respond by making several attacks upon the authority to issue the Rights pursuant to § 157.

Appellants begin by contending that § 157 cannot authorize the Rights Plan since § 157 has never served the purpose of authorizing a takeover defense. Appellants contend that § 157 is a corporate financing statute, and that nothing in its legislative history suggests a purpose that has anything to do with corporate control or a takeover defense. Appellants are unable to demonstrate that the legislature, in its adoption of § 157, meant to limit the applicability of § 157 to only the issuance of Rights for the purposes of corporate financing. Without such affirmative evidence, we decline to impose such a limitation upon the section that the legislature has not. . . .

Secondly, appellants contend that § 157 does not authorize the issuance of sham rights such as the Rights Plan. They contend that the Rights were designed never to be exercised, and that the Plan has no economic value. . . .

Appellants' sham contention fails in both regards. As to the Rights, they can and will be exercised upon the happening of a triggering mechanism, as we have observed during the current struggle of Sir James Goldsmith to take control of Crown Zellerbach. . . .

Third, appellants contend that § 157 authorizes the issuance of Rights "entitling holders thereof to purchase from the corporation any shares of *its* capital stock of any class . . ." (emphasis added). Therefore, their contention continues, the plain language of the statute does not authorize Household to issue rights to purchase another's capital stock upon a merger or consolidation.

Household contends, *inter alia,* that the Rights Plan is analogous to "anti-destruction" or "anti-dilution" provisions which are customary features of a wide variety of corporate securities. While appellants seem to concede that "anti-destruction" provisions are valid under Delaware corporate law, they seek to distinguish the Rights Plan as not being incidental, as are most "anti-destruction" provisions, to a corporation's statutory power to finance itself. We find no merit to such a distinction. We have already rejected appellants' similar contention that § 157 could only be used for financing purposes. We also reject that distinction here.

"Anti-destruction" clauses generally ensure holders of certain securities of the protection of their right of conversion in the event of a merger by giving them the right to convert their securities into whatever securities are to replace the stock of their company. . . . The fact that the rights here have as their purpose the prevention of coercive two-tier tender offers does not invalidate them. . . .

Having concluded that sufficient authority for the Rights Plan exists in 8 Del.C. § 157, we note the inherent powers of the Board conferred by 8 Del.C. § 141(a), concerning the management of the corporation's "business and *affairs*" (emphasis added), also provides the Board additional authority upon which to enact the Rights Plan.

B.

Appellants contend that the Board is unauthorized to usurp stockholders' rights to receive tender offers by changing Household's fundamental structure. We conclude that the Rights Plan does not prevent stockholders from receiving tender offers, and that the change of Household's structure was less than that which results from the implementation of other defensive mechanisms upheld by various courts. . . .

The evidence at trial also evidenced many methods around the Plan ranging from tendering with a condition that the Board redeem the Rights, tendering with a high minimum condition of shares and Rights, tendering and soliciting consents to remove the Board and redeem the Rights, to acquiring 50% of the shares and causing Household to self-tender for the Rights. One could also form a group of up to 19.9% and solicit proxies for consents to remove the Board and redeem the Rights. These are but a few of the methods by which Household can still be acquired by a hostile tender offer.

In addition, the Rights Plan is not absolute. When the Household Board of Directors is faced with a tender offer and a request to redeem the Rights, they will not be able to arbitrarily reject the offer. They will be held to the same fiduciary standards any other board of directors would be held to in deciding to adopt a defensive mechanism, the same standard as they were held to in originally approving the Rights Plan.

In addition, appellants contend that the deterrence of tender offers will be accomplished by what they label "a fundamental transfer of power from the stockholders to the directors." They contend that this transfer of power, in itself, is unauthorized.

The Rights Plan will result in no more of a structural change than any other defensive mechanism adopted by a board of directors. The Rights Plan does not destroy the assets of the corporation. The implementation of the Plan neither results in any outflow of money from the corporation nor impairs its financial flexibility. It does not dilute earnings per share and does not have any adverse tax consequences for the corporation or its stockholders. The Plan has not adversely affected the market price of Household's stock.

Comparing the Rights Plan with other defensive mechanisms, it does less harm to the value structure of the corporation than do the other mechanisms. Other mechanisms [including the payment of greenmail and a discriminatory self-tender] result in increased debt of the corporation. . . .

There is little change in the governance structure as a result of the adoption of the Rights Plan. The Board does not now have unfettered discretion in refusing to redeem the Rights. The Board has no more discretion in refusing to redeem the Rights than it does in enacting any defensive mechanism.

The contention that the Rights Plan alters the structure more than do other defensive mechanisms because it is so effective as to make the corporation completely safe from hostile tender offers is likewise without merit. As explained above, there are numerous methods to successfully launch a hostile tender offer.

C.

Appellants' third contention is that the Board was unauthorized to fundamentally restrict stockholders' rights to conduct a proxy contest. Appellants contend that the "20% trigger" effectively prevents any stockholder from first acquiring 20% or more shares before conducting a proxy contest and further, it prevents stockholders from banding together into a group to solicit proxies if, collectively, they own 20% or more of the stock. In addition, at trial, appellants contended that read literally, the Rights Agreement triggers the Rights upon the mere acquisition of the right to vote 20% or more of the shares through a proxy solicitation, and thereby precludes any proxy contest from being waged.

Appellants seem to have conceded this last contention in light of Household's response that the receipt of a proxy does not make the recipient the "beneficial owner" of the shares involved which would trigger the Rights. In essence, the Rights Agreement provides that the Rights are triggered when someone becomes the "beneficial owner" of 20% or more of Household stock. Although a literal reading of the Rights Agreement definition of "beneficial owner" would seem to include those shares which one has the right to vote, it has long been recognized that the relationship between grantor and recipient of a proxy is one of agency, and the agency is revocable by the grantor at any time. . . Therefore, the holder of a proxy is not the "beneficial owner" of the stock. As a result, the mere acquisition of the right to vote 20% of the shares does not trigger the Rights.

The issue, then, is whether the restriction upon individuals or groups from first acquiring 20% of shares before waging a proxy contest fundamentally restricts stockholders' right to conduct a proxy contest. Regarding this issue the Court of Chancery found:

Thus, while the Rights Plan does deter the formation of proxy efforts of a certain magnitude, it does not limit the voting power of individual shares. On the evidence presented it is highly conjectural to assume that a particular effort to assert shareholder views in the election of directors or revisions of corporate policy will be frustrated by the proxy feature of the Plan. Household's witnesses, Troubh and Higgins described recent corporate takeover battles in which insurgents holding less than 10% stock ownership were able to secure corporate control through a proxy contest or the threat of one.

We conclude that there was sufficient evidence at trial to support the Vice-Chancellor's finding that the effect upon proxy contests will be minimal. Evidence at trial established that many proxy contests are won with an insurgent ownership of less than 20%, and that very large holdings are no guarantee of success. There was also testimony that the key variable in proxy contest success is the merit of an insurgent's issues, not the size of his holdings.

IV

Having concluded that the adoption of the Rights Plan was within the authority of the Directors, we now look to whether the Directors have met their burden under the business judgment rule.

The business judgment rule is a "presumption that in making a business decision the directors of a corporation acted on an informed basis, in good faith and in the honest belief that the action taken was in the best interests of the company." [citing *Aronson*]. Notwithstanding, in *Unocal* we held that when the business judgment rule applies to adoption of a defensive mechanism, the initial burden will lie with the directors. The "directors must show that they had reasonable grounds for believing that a danger to corporate policy and effectiveness existed. . . . [T]hey satisfy that burden 'by showing good faith and reasonable investigation. . . .' " [*Unocal*,] In addition, the directors must show that the defensive mechanism was "reasonable in relation to the threat posed." Moreover, that proof is materially enhanced, as we noted in *Unocal*, where, as here, a majority of the board favoring the proposal consisted of outside independent directors who have acted in accordance with the foregoing standards. [*Unocal; Aronson*]. Then, the burden shifts back to the plaintiffs who have the ultimate burden of persuasion to show a breach of the directors' fiduciary duties. [*Unocal*]

There are no allegations here of any bad faith on the part of the Directors' action in the adoption of the Rights Plan. There is no allegation that the Directors' action was taken for entrenchment purposes. Household has adequately demonstrated, as explained above, that the adoption of the Rights Plan was in reaction to what it perceived to be the threat in the market place of coercive two-tier tender offers. Appellants do contend, however, that the Board did not exercise informed business judgment in its adoption of the Plan. . . .

To determine whether a business judgment reached by a board of directors was an informed one, we determine whether the directors were grossly negligent. [*Smith v. Van Gorkom*]. Upon a review of this record, we conclude the Directors were not grossly negligent. The information supplied to the Board on August 14 provided the essentials of the Plan. The Directors were given beforehand a notebook which included a three-page summary of the Plan along with articles on the current takeover environment. The extended discussion between the Board and representatives of Wachtell, Lipton and Goldman, Sachs before approval of the Plan reflected a full and candid evaluation of the Plan. Moran's expression of his views at the meeting served to place before the Board a knowledgeable critique of the Plan. . . .

In addition, to meet their burden, the Directors must show that the defensive mechanism was "reasonable in relation to the threat posed." The record reflects a concern on the part of the Directors over the increasing frequency in the financial services industry of "boot-strap" and "bust-up" takeovers. The Directors were also concerned that such takeovers may take the form of two-tier offers. In addition, on August 14, the Household Board was aware of Moran's overture on behalf of D-K-M. In sum, the Directors reasonably believed Household was vulnerable to coercive acquisition techniques and adopted a reasonable defensive mechanism to protect itself.

V

In conclusion, the Household Directors receive the benefit of the business judgment rule in their adoption of the Rights Plan. . . .

While we conclude for present purposes that the Household Directors are protected by the business judgment rule, that does not end the matter. The ultimate response to an actual takeover bid must be judged by the Directors' actions at that time, and nothing we say here relieves them of their basic fundamental duties to the corporation and its stockholders. . . . Their use of the Plan will be evaluated when and if the issue arises.

D.   *UNITRIN*—MODIFYING THE *UNOCAL* STANDARD

In the years following *Unocal*, dealmakers and litigants alike struggled to understand the limits of *Unocal's* proportionality standard.

No one in the courts did more than Chancellor William Allen to grapple with the meaning of the decision and apply its principles to the messy facts that present themselves in the courtroom. In *AC Acquisitions Corp. v. Anderson, Clayton & Co.*, 519 A.2d 103 (Del. Ch. 1986), Chancellor Allen first applied *Unocal* to a board's defensive tactics in response to an unsolicited offer. The board of Anderson, Clayton developed an economically coercive alternative offer for shareholders in response to an unwanted offer from Bear, Stearns & Co., Inc., Gruss Petroleum Corp. and Gruss Partners (collectively, BS/G). While agreeing with the board that BS/G's offer represented a mild threat, Chancellor Allen ruled that the board's preferred response, an economically coercive alternative that would cause all rational shareholders to eschew the BS/G offer, was coercive and therefore not reasonable in response to the threat posed. The court acknowledged that:

> [t]he BS/G offer poses a "threat" of any kind (other than a threat to the incumbency of the Board) only in a special sense and on the assumption that a majority of the Company's shareholders might prefer an alternative to the BS/G offer. On this assumption, it is reasonable to create an option that would permit shareholders to keep an equity interest in the firm, but, in my opinion, it is not reasonable in relation to such a "threat" to structure such an option so as to preclude as a practical matter shareholders from accepting the BS/G offer.

Rather than provide shareholders with a choice in the face of an unsolicited offer, the board's alternative was designed to effectively take away shareholder autonomy with respect to the decision whether or not to accept the bidder's offer. For Chancellor Allen, eliminating shareholder autonomy went too far.[15]

In *AC Acquisitions*, in what would become a trademark of the Chancery Court's approach to the application of *Unocal*, the court engaged in a substantive analysis of the threat posed by the unsolicited offer and made a determination about whether the board's response was reasonable in relation to the threat. Professors Smith and Thompson observed that in these early years of *Unocal's* implementation by the Chancery Court, the *Unocal* standard exhibited a degree of plasticity that

---

[15] *AC Acquisitions Corp.* at 115. Furthermore, the court stated that: "Plaintiffs contend to the contrary that the Company Transaction was deliberately structured so that no rational shareholder can risk tendering into the BS/G offer. Plaintiffs say this for two related reasons: (1) Shareholders tendering into the BS/G offer have no assurance that BS/G will take down their stock at $56 a share since that offer is subject to conditions including a minimum number of shares tendered and abandonment of the Company Transaction; and (2) Tendering shareholders would thereby preclude themselves from participating in the "fat" front-end of the Company Transaction and risk having the value of all their shares fall very dramatically. In such circumstances, plaintiffs say, to characterize the Board's action as an attempt to preserve the ability of shareholders to choose is a charade. They claim the Company Transaction is coercive in fact and in the circumstances presented, improperly so in law." *Id.* at 114

would permit trial courts to engage in substantive review of director decisions and provide for a real threat of sanction in the event of board overreach.[16]

In *Capital City Associates v. Interco Inc.*, 551 A.2d 787 (Del. Ch. 1988), Chancellor Allen was asked to rule on whether the board's refusal to redeem a poison pill in conjunction with its adoption of an alternative restructuring transaction was reasonable in response to an unwanted bidder's all-cash offer. Chancellor Allen adopted a version of Professors Gilson and Kraakman's approach to the *Unocal* standard when he expounded on the nature of cognizable threats to the corporation under *Unocal*. In their article, *Delaware's Intermediate Standard for Defensive Tactics: Is There Substance to Proportionality Review?*,[17] Professors Gilson and Kraakman proposed a framework for thinking about *Unocal's* "threat" prong. Professors Gilson and Kraakman introduced into the Delaware lexicon the term "substantive coercion" for a type of threat. Professors Gilson and Kraakman describe substantive coercion as "the risk that shareholders will mistakenly accept an underpriced offer because they disbelieve management's representations of intrinsic value." For his part, Allen identified two threats to the corporation. The first set of threats is the threat to voluntariness of shareholder choice. Offers that reduce shareholder autonomy are structurally coercive. For example, two-tiered, front-loaded tender offers coerce shareholders to tender against their will and are thus cognizable threats. The second set of cognizable threats identified by Allen, akin to Gilson and Kraakman's concept of substantive coercion, stems from inadequate, but otherwise non-coercive, offers. The threat in such cases is not necessarily that a shareholder will make an irrational decision to tender into a low-ball offer, but that in the absence of any negotiating leverage, a target board might be unable to engage in active negotiating to refuse an initial offer and extract a higher offer or have sufficient time to generate a more valuable alternative for shareholders. In any event, where the threat is the inadequacy of price, Gilson and Kraakman, as well as Chancellor Allen, suggested that there should be limits to the use of defensive measures intended to deprive shareholders of the right to choose the offer.

As Chancellor Allen applied the new *Unocal* standard in cases before the Chancery Court, the nature of the threat determined the limits of a reasonable response. In Allen's view, courts should grant boards significant leeway in determining appropriate defenses. But in the face of milder threats, like substantive coercion, the court should be more

---

[16] D. Gordon Smith & Robert B. Thompson, *Toward a New Theory of the Shareholder Role: 'Sacred Space' in Corporate Takeovers*, 80 TEX. L. REV. 261, 283 (2001) (noting that in the years following Unocal, the court rarely applied the standard in a manner adverse to defendant boards).

[17] Ronald J. Gilson & Reinier Kraakman, *Delaware's Intermediate Standard for Defensive Tactics: Is There Substance to Proportionality Review?*, 44. BUS. LAW. 247 (1989).

measured in permitting board discretion to resist offers. For example, although the court would likely permit a shareholder rights plan in order to assist a target board to negotiate a higher price for a seller where the threat identified by the board was an inadequate offer, Chancellor Allen made it clear that relying on a rights plan to permanently foreclose shareholders from an opportunity to choose an unsolicited offer would go too far given the nature of the threat.

In his approach to *Unocal*, Chancellor Allen sought to carefully balance the board's obligation to act in the best interests of shareholders and the corporation with the interests of shareholders in being allowed to make their own choices. On the one hand, courts are appropriately hesitant to become too involved in reviewing the substance of business decisions. On the other hand, where boards act to defend the corporation against threats, the court is in a unique position to moderate the conscious and unconscious self-interest that are the essential motivators of *Unocal*. Chancellor Allen recognized that for the *Unocal* standard to function as it was intended, judges would be required to investigate and pass judgment on the substance of board decisions with respect to defensive measures. Most of the Chancery Court opinions in the years after *Unocal* followed some form of Chancellor Allen's approach to balancing these interests.[18]

The Delaware Supreme Court, however, did not agree with Chancellor Allen's approach. When, in *Paramount Communications, Inc. v. Time, Inc.,* the court was asked to rule on the appropriateness of Time's response to Paramount's unsolicited offer, it took the opportunity, in *dicta*, to reject the Chancellor's approach to the *Unocal* standard:

> Plaintiffs' position represents a fundamental misconception of our standard of review under *Unocal* principally because it would involve the court in substituting its judgment as to what is a "better" deal for that of a corporation's board of directors. To the extent that the Court of Chancery has recently done so in certain of its opinions, we hereby reject such approach as not in keeping with a proper *Unocal* analysis.[19]

Rather than limiting the scope of cognizable threats as in *Interco*, the Delaware Supreme Court adopted an approach that was highly deferential to a board's decision to identify a broader set of threats to the

---

[18] Among others, see *Grand Metro. Public Ltd. Co. v. Pillsbury Co.*, 558 A.2d 1049, 1060 (Del. Ch. 1988) (agreeing with and following Chancellor Allen's analysis in *Interco* with respect to shareholder choice); *Robert M. Bass Grp., Inc. v. Evans*, 552 A.2d 1227, 1241–42 (Del. Ch. 1988) (identifying the development of a management-sponsored alternative as a reasonable response to the threat of an inadequate price); *Shamrock Holdings, Inc. v. Polaroid Corp.*, 559 A.2d 278, 289 (Del. Ch. 1989) (observing that "where there has been sufficient time for an alternative to developed and proposed to shareholders the threat . . . to shareholders . . . seems almost without substance").

[19] *Paramount Communications, Inc. v. Time, Inc.*, 571 A.2d 1140, 1151 (Del.1989).

corporation, including inadequacy of price, shareholder mistake, uncertainty with respect to the offer, and timing of the offer. At the time, the Court defended deference to board decisions as necessary to ensure the "flexibility" of the *Unocal* standard. In adopting a deferential position with respect to board actions, the Court made it clear that the *Unocal* standard was "not intended as an abstract standard; neither [was] it a structured and mechanistic procedure of appraisal." Although the Court may not have realized it at the time, in according what it called a high degree of flexibility to boards with respect to their identification of cognizable threats to the corporation, it was ensuring that *Unocal* (or at least its first prong) would indeed be applied mechanistically. In the years since, identification of "threats" to the corporation devolved into little more than the assertion that an offer is inadequate with support from investment banker opinions. With *Paramount*, the Court began a steady move away from the substantive intermediate standard in favor a more conservative, less flexible, approach to application of the standard.

In *Unitrin*, the Delaware Supreme Court focused on questions of substantive coercion; it also provided additional guidance as to the application of *Unocal's* proportionality prong—in particular, whether a board's power to adopt defenses was limited in time and scope. *Unitrin*, like *Interco* before it, highlights the different approaches to *Unocal* used by the Chancery Court and the Supreme Court during the 1990s, when both courts were still grappling with how best to implement it.

UNITRIN, INC. V. AMERICAN GENERAL CORP.

Supreme Court of Delaware
651 A.2d 1361 (1995)

HOLLAND, JUSTICE.

The Parties

American General is the largest provider of home service insurance. On July 12, 1994, it made a merger proposal to acquire Unitrin for $2.6 billion at $50-3/8 per share. Following a public announcement of this proposal, Unitrin shareholders filed suit seeking to compel a sale of the company. American General filed suit to enjoin Unitrin's Repurchase Program. [The court granted the injunction; this appeal followed.]

Unitrin is also in the insurance business. It is the third largest provider of home service insurance. The other defendants-appellants are the members of Unitrin's seven person Board of Directors (the "Unitrin Board" or "Board"). Two directors are employees, Richard C. Vie ("Vie"), the Chief Executive Officer, and Jerrold V. Jerome ("Jerome"), Chairman of the Board. The five remaining directors are not and have never been employed by Unitrin. These directors [include significant shareholders of Unitrin. One, Singleton,] is Unitrin's largest shareholder, owning

7,242,260 shares, in excess of 14% of the outstanding stock; [another] personally owns 1,062,335 shares of Unitrin common stock, 2.26% of the outstanding stock; [and another owns more than 400,000 shares of Unitrin stock.] . . .

American General's Offer

In January 1994, James Tuerff ("Tuerff"), the President of American General, met with Richard Vie, Unitrin's Chief Executive Officer. Tuerff advised Vie that American General was considering acquiring other companies. Unitrin was apparently at or near the top of its list. . . . Vie indicated to Tuerff that Unitrin was not for sale. . . . It was unnecessary to respond to American General because no offer had been made.

On July 12, 1994, American General sent a letter to Vie proposing a consensual merger transaction in which it would "purchase all of Unitrin's 51.8 million outstanding shares of common stock for $50-3/8 per share, in cash" (the "Offer") . . . The Offer price represented a 30% premium over the market price of Unitrin's shares. In the Offer, American General stated that it "would consider offering a higher price" if "Unitrin could demonstrate additional value." . . .

Unitrin's Rejection

Upon receiving the American General Offer, the Unitrin Board's Executive Committee (Singleton [an outside director, single largest stockholder, and co-founder and top executive for many years of company from which Unitrin was spun off], Vie, and Jerome) engaged legal counsel and scheduled a telephonic Board meeting for July 18. At the July 18 special meeting, the Board reviewed the terms of the Offer. The Board was advised that the existing charter and bylaw provisions might not effectively deter all types of takeover strategies. It was suggested that the Board consider adopting a shareholder rights plan and an advance notice provision for shareholder proposals.

The Unitrin Board met next on July 25, 1994 in Los Angeles for seven hours. All directors attended the meeting. The principal purpose of the meeting was to discuss American General's Offer.

Vie reviewed Unitrin's financial condition and its ongoing business strategies. The Board also received a presentation from its investment advisor, Morgan Stanley & Co. . . . Morgan Stanley expressed its opinion that the Offer was financially inadequate. Legal counsel expressed concern that the combination of Unitrin and American General would raise antitrust complications due to the resultant decrease in competition in the home service insurance markets.

The Unitrin Board unanimously concluded that the American General merger proposal was not in the best interests of Unitrin's shareholders and voted to reject the Offer. The Board then received advice from its legal and financial advisors about a number of possible defensive measures it might adopt, including a shareholder rights plan ("poison pill") and an advance notice bylaw provision for shareholder proposals. Because the Board apparently thought that American General intended to keep its Offer private, the Board did not implement any defensive measures at that time.

On July 26, 1994, Vie faxed a letter to Tuerff, rejecting American General's Offer. That correspondence stated:

> As I told you back in January, when you first proposed acquiring our company, we are not for sale. The Board believed then, and believes even more strongly today, that the company's future as an independent enterprise is excellent and will provide greater long-term benefits to the company, our stockholders and our other constituencies than pursuing a sale transaction.

> Accordingly, we don't view a combination with you as part of our future and our Board is unanimous and unequivocal that we should not pursue it.

> The Board has specifically directed me to say that we assume you do not want to create an adversarial situation and that you agree with us it would be counterproductive to do so. But our Board is very firm in its conclusion about your offer and if our assumption about your intentions proves to be incorrect, Unitrin has, as you know, the financial capacity to pursue all avenues the Board considers appropriate.

Vie acknowledged during discovery that the latter portion of his letter referred, in part, to the Repurchase Program.

American General's Publicity

Unitrin's Initial Responses

On August 2, 1994, American General issued a press release announcing its Offer to Unitrin's Board to purchase all of Unitrin's stock for $50-3/8 per share. The press release also noted that the Board had rejected American General's Offer. After that public announcement, the trading volume and market price of Unitrin's stock increased.

At its regularly scheduled meeting on August 3, the Unitrin Board discussed the effects of American General's press release. The Board noted that the market reaction to the announcement suggested that speculative traders or arbitrageurs were acquiring Unitrin stock. The Board determined that American General's public announcement constituted a hostile act designed to coerce the sale of Unitrin at an inadequate price. The Board unanimously approved the poison pill and the proposed advance notice bylaw that it had considered previously.

Beginning on August 2 and continuing through August 12, 1994, Unitrin issued a series of press releases to inform its shareholders and the public market: first, that the Unitrin Board believed Unitrin's stock was worth more than the $50-3/8 American General offered; second, that the Board felt that the price of American General's Offer did not reflect Unitrin's long term business prospects as an independent company; third, that "the true value of Unitrin [was] not reflected in the [then] current market price of its common stock," and that because of its strong financial position, Unitrin was well positioned "to pursue strategic and financial opportunities;" fourth, that the Board believed a merger with American General would have anticompetitive effects and might violate antitrust laws and various state regulatory statutes; and fifth, that the Board had adopted a shareholder rights plan (poison pill) to guard against undesirable takeover efforts.

Unitrin's Repurchase Program

The Unitrin Board met again on August 11, 1994 . . . Morgan Stanley recommended that the Board implement an open market stock repurchase. The Board voted to authorize the Repurchase Program for up to ten million shares of its outstanding stock.

On August 12, Unitrin publicly announced the Repurchase Program. The Unitrin Board expressed its belief that "Unitrin's stock is undervalued in the market and that the expanded program will tend to increase the value of the shares that remain outstanding." The announcement also stated that the director stockholders were not participating in the Repurchase Program, and that the repurchases "will increase the percentage ownership of those stockholders who choose not to sell."

Unitrin's August 12 press release also stated that the directors owned 23% of Unitrin's stock, that the Repurchase Program would cause that percentage to increase, and that Unitrin's certificate of incorporation included a supermajority voting provision. The following language from a July 22 draft press release revealing the antitakeover effects of the Repurchase Program was omitted from the final press release.

Under the [supermajority provision], the consummation of the expanded repurchase program would enhance the ability of non-selling stockholders, including the directors, to prevent a merger with a greater-than-15% stockholder if they did not favor the transaction.

Unitrin sent a letter to its stockholders on August 17 regarding the Repurchase Program which stated:

Your Board of Directors has authorized the Company to repurchase, in the open market or in private transactions, up to 10 million of Unitrin's 51.8 million outstanding common shares.

This authorization is intended to provide an additional measure of liquidity to the Company's shareholders in light of the unsettled market conditions resulting from American General's unsolicited acquisition proposal. The Board believes that the Company's stock is undervalued and that this program will tend to increase the value of the shares that remain outstanding.

Between August 12 and noon on August 24, Morgan Stanley purchased nearly 5 million of Unitrin's shares on Unitrin's behalf. The average price paid was slightly above American General's Offer price. . . .

Unocal's Standard

Business Judgment Rule

Enhanced Judicial Scrutiny

. . . In *Unocal,* this Court reaffirmed "the application of the business judgment rule in the context of a hostile battle for control of a Delaware corporation where board action is taken to the exclusion of, or in limitation upon, a valid stockholder vote." This Court has recognized that directors are often confronted with an " 'inherent conflict of interest' during contests for corporate control '[b]ecause of the omnipresent specter that a board may be acting primarily in its own interests, rather than those of the corporation and its shareholders.' " . . . Consequently, in such situations, before the board is accorded the protection of the business judgment rule, and that rule's concomitant placement of the burden to rebut its presumption on the plaintiff, the board must carry its own initial two-part burden:

First, a *reasonableness test,* which is satisfied by a demonstration that the board of directors had reasonable grounds for believing that a danger to corporate policy and effectiveness existed, and

Second, a *proportionality test,* which is satisfied by a demonstration that the board of directors' defensive response was reasonable in relation to the threat posed. . . .

Parties' Burdens Shift

Judicial Review Standards Differ

Business Judgment Rule and Unocal

. . . The ultimate question in applying the *Unocal* standard is: what deference should the reviewing court give "to the decisions of directors in defending against a takeover?" . . .

The business judgment rule has traditionally operated to shield directors from personal liability arising out of completed actions involving operational issues. . . . When the business judgment rule is applied to defend directors against personal liability, as in a derivative suit, the plaintiff has the initial burden of proof and the ultimate burden of persuasion. . . . In such cases, the business judgment rule shields directors from personal liability if, upon review, the court concludes the directors' decision can be attributed to any rational business purpose. . . .

Conversely, in transactional justification cases involving the adoption of defenses to takeovers, the director's actions invariably implicate issues affecting stockholder rights. . . . In transactional justification cases, the directors' decision is reviewed judicially and the burden of going forward is placed on the directors. . . . If the directors' actions withstand *Unocal's* reasonableness and proportionality review, the traditional business judgment rule is applied to shield the directors' defensive decision rather than the directors themselves.

The litigation between Unitrin, American General, and the Unitrin shareholders in the Court of Chancery is a classic example of a transactional justification case. . . .

American General Threat

Reasonableness Burden Sustained

The first aspect of the *Unocal* burden, the reasonableness test, required the Unitrin Board to demonstrate that, after a reasonable investigation, it determined in good faith, that American General's Offer presented a threat to Unitrin that warranted a defensive response. This Court has held that the presence of a majority of outside independent directors will materially enhance such evidence. . . . An "outside" director has been defined as a non-employee and non-management director, (*e.g.,* Unitrin argues, five members of its seven-person Board). . . . Independence "means that a director's decision is based on the corporate merits of the subject before the board rather than extraneous considerations or influences." . . .

The Unitrin Board identified two dangers it perceived the American General Offer posed: inadequate price and antitrust complications. The Court of Chancery characterized the Board's concern that American General's proposed transaction could never be consummated because it may violate antitrust laws and state insurance regulations as a "makeweight excuse" for the defensive measure. It determined, however, that the Board reasonably believed that the American General Offer was inadequate and also reasonably concluded that the offer was a threat to Unitrin's uninformed stockholders.

The Court of Chancery held that the Board's evidence satisfied the first aspect or reasonableness test under *Unocal.* The Court of Chancery then noted, however, that the threat to the Unitrin stockholders from American General's inadequate opening bid was "mild," because the Offer was negotiable both in price and structure. . . .

Proportionality Burden

Chancery Approves Poison Pill

The second aspect or proportionality test of the initial *Unocal* burden required the Unitrin Board to demonstrate the proportionality of its response to the threat American General's Offer posed. The record reflects that the Unitrin Board considered three options as defensive measures: the poison pill, the advance notice bylaw, and the Repurchase Program. The Unitrin Board did not act on any of these options on July 25.

On August 2, American General made a public announcement of its offer to buy all the shares of Unitrin for $2.6 billion at $50–3/8 per share. The Unitrin Board had already concluded that the American General offer was inadequate. It also apparently feared that its stockholders did not realize that the long term value of Unitrin was not reflected in the market price of its stock.

On August 3 ... [t]he Unitrin Board decided to adopt defensive measures to protect Unitrin's stockholders from the inadequate American General Offer in two stages: first, it passed the poison pill and the advance notice bylaw; and, a week later, it implemented the Repurchase Program.

With regard to the second aspect or proportionality test of the initial *Unocal* burden, the Court of Chancery analyzed each stage of the Unitrin Board's defensive responses separately. Although the Court of Chancery characterized Unitrin's antitrust concerns as "makeweight," it acknowledged that the directors of a Delaware corporation have the prerogative to determine that the market undervalues its stock and to protect its stockholders from offers that do not reflect the long term value of the corporation under its present management plan.... The Court of Chancery concluded that Unitrin's Board believed in good faith that the American General Offer was inadequate and properly employed a poison pill as a proportionate defensive response to protect its stockholders from a "low ball" bid....

Proportionality Burden

Chancery Enjoins Repurchase Program

The Court of Chancery did not view either its conclusion that American General's Offer constituted a threat, or its conclusion that the poison pill was a reasonable response to that threat, as requiring it, *a fortiori*, to conclude that the Repurchase Program was also an appropriate response. The Court of Chancery then made two factual findings: first, the Repurchase Program went beyond what was "necessary" to protect the Unitrin stockholders from a "low ball" negotiating strategy; and second, it was designed to keep the decision to combine with American General within the control of the members of the Unitrin Board, as stockholders, under virtually all circumstances. Consequently, the Court of Chancery held that the Unitrin Board failed to demonstrate that the Repurchase Program met the second aspect or proportionality requirement of the initial burden *Unocal* ascribes to a board of directors. . . .

Before the Repurchase Program began, Unitrin's directors collectively held approximately 23% of Unitrin's outstanding shares. Unitrin's certificate of incorporation already included a "shark-repellent" provision barring any business combination with a more than—15% stockholder unless approved by a majority of continuing directors or by a 75% stockholder vote ("Supermajority Vote"). Unitrin's shareholder directors announced publicly that they would not participate in the Repurchase Program and that this would result in a percentage increase of ownership for them, as well as for any other shareholder who did not participate.

The Court of Chancery found that by not participating in the Repurchase Program, the Board "expected to create a 28% voting block to support the Board's decision to reject [a future] offer by American General." From this underlying factual finding, the Court of Chancery concluded that American General might be "chilled" in its pursuit of Unitrin:

> Increasing the board members' percentage of stock ownership, combined with the supermajority merger provision, does more than protect uninformed stockholders from an inadequate offer, it chills any unsolicited acquiror from making an offer.

The parties are in substantial disagreement with respect to the Court of Chancery's ultimate factual finding that the Repurchase Program was a disproportionate response under *Unocal*. Unitrin argues that American General or another potential acquiror can theoretically prevail in an effort to obtain control of Unitrin through a proxy contest. American General argues that the record supports the Court of Chancery's factual determination that the adoption of the Repurchase Program violated the principles of *Unocal*, even though American General acknowledges that the option of a proxy contest for obtaining control of Unitrin remained theoretically available. The stockholder-plaintiffs argue that even if it can be said, as a matter of law, that it is acceptable under certain circumstances to leave potential bidders with a proxy battle as the sole avenue for acquiring an entity, the Court of Chancery correctly determined, as a factual matter, that the Repurchase Program was disproportionate to the threat American General's Offer posed. . . .

Takeover Strategy

Tender Offer/Proxy Contest

We begin our examination of Unitrin's Repurchase Program mindful of the special import of protecting the shareholder's franchise within *Unocal's* requirement that a defensive response be reasonable and proportionate. . . .

The Court of Chancery concluded that Unitrin's adoption of a poison pill was a proportionate response to the threat its Board reasonably perceived from American General's Offer. Nonetheless, the Court of Chancery enjoined the additional defense of the Repurchase Program as disproportionate and "unnecessary."

The record reflects that the Court of Chancery's decision to enjoin the Repurchase Program is attributable to a continuing misunderstanding, i.e., that in conjunction with the longstanding Supermajority Vote provision in the Unitrin charter, the Repurchase Program would operate to provide the director shareholders with a "veto" to preclude a successful proxy contest by American General. The origins of that misunderstanding are three premises that are each without record support. Two of those premises are objective misconceptions and the other is subjective.

Directors' Motives

"Prestige and Perquisites"

Subjective Determination

The subjective premise was the Court of Chancery's *sua sponte* determination that Unitrin's outside directors, who are also substantial stockholders, would not vote like other stockholders in a proxy contest, *i.e.*, in their own best economic interests. At American General's Offer price, the outside directors held Unitrin shares worth more than $450 million. Consequently, Unitrin argues the stockholder directors had the same interest as other Unitrin stockholders generally, when voting in a proxy contest, to wit: the maximization of the value of their investments.

In rejecting Unitrin's argument, the Court of Chancery stated that the stockholder directors would be "subconsciously" motivated in a proxy contest to vote against otherwise excellent offers which did not include a "price parameter" to compensate them for the loss of the "prestige and perquisites" of membership on Unitrin's Board. The Court of Chancery's subjective determination that the *stockholder directors* of Unitrin would reject an "excellent offer," unless it compensated them for giving up the "prestige and perquisites" of directorship, appears to be subjective and without record support. It cannot be presumed. . . [but must instead] be the subject of proof. . . . Even the shareholder-plaintiffs in this case agree with the legal proposition Unitrin advocates on appeal: stockholders are presumed to act in their own best economic interests when they vote in a proxy contest.

Without Repurchase Program

Actual Voting Power Exceeds 25%

The first objective premise relied upon by the Court of Chancery, unsupported by the record, is that the shareholder directors needed to implement the Repurchase Program to attain voting power in a proxy contest equal to 25%. . . . [But even]*without* the Repurchase Program, the director shareholders' absolute voting power of 23% would already constitute *actual voting power greater than* 25% in a proxy contest with normal shareholder participation below 100%. . . .

Supermajority Vote

No Realistic Deterrent

The second objective premise relied upon by the Court of Chancery, unsupported by the record, is that American General's ability to succeed in a proxy contest depended on the Repurchase Program being enjoined because of the Supermajority Vote provision in Unitrin's charter. Without the approval of a target's board, the danger of activating a poison pill renders it irrational for bidders to pursue stock acquisitions above the triggering level. Instead, "bidders intent on working around a poison pill must launch and win proxy contests to elect new directors who are willing to redeem the target's poison pill." . . .

As American General acknowledges, a less than 15% stockholder bidder need not proceed with acquiring shares to the extent that it would ever implicate the Supermajority Vote provision. In fact, it would be illogical for American General or any other bidder to acquire more than 15% of Unitrin's stock because that would not only trigger the poison pill, but also the constraints of 8 Del.C. § 203. If American General were to initiate a proxy contest *before* acquiring 15% of Unitrin's stock, it would need to amass only 45.1% of the votes assuming a 90% voter turnout. If it commenced a tender offer at an attractive price contemporaneously with its proxy contest, it could seek to acquire 50.1% of the outstanding voting stock.

The record reflects that institutional investors own 42% of Unitrin's shares. Twenty institutions own 33% of Unitrin's shares. It is generally accepted that proxy contests have re-emerged with renewed significance as a method of acquiring corporate control because "the growth in institutional investment has reduced the dispersion of share ownership." . . . "Institutions are more likely than other shareholders to vote at all, more likely to vote against manager proposals, and more likely to vote for proposals by other shareholders."

With Supermajority Vote

After Repurchase Program

Proxy Contest Appears Viable

The assumptions and conclusions American General sets forth in this appeal for a different purpose are particularly probative with regard to the effect of the institutional holdings in Unitrin's stock. American General's two predicate assumptions are a 90% stockholder turnout in a proxy contest and a bidder with 14.9% holdings, i.e., the maximum the bidder could own to avoid triggering the poison pill and the Supermajority Vote provision. American General also calculated the votes available to the Board or the bidder with and without the Repurchase Program:

> Assuming no Repurchase [Program], the [shareholder directors] would hold 23%, the percentage collectively held by the [directors] and the bidder would be 37.9%, and the percentage of additional votes available to either side would be 52.1%.

> Assuming the Repurchase [Program] is fully consummated, the [shareholder directors] would hold 28%, the percentage collectively held by the bidder and the [directors] would be 42.9%, and the percentage of additional votes available to either side would be 47.1%.

American General then applied these assumptions to reach conclusions regarding the votes needed for the 14.9% stockholder bidder to prevail: first, in an election of directors; and second, in the subsequent vote on a merger. With regard to the election of directors, American General made the following calculations:

> Assume 90% stockholder turnout. To elect directors, a plurality must be obtained; assuming no abstentions and only two competing slates, one must obtain the votes of 45.1% of the shares.

The percentage of additional votes the bidder needs to win is: 45.1% − 14.9% (maximum the bidder could own and avoid the poison pill, § 203 and supermajority) = 30.2%. A merger requires approval of a majority of outstanding shares, 8 Del.C. § 251, not just a plurality. In that regard, American General made the following calculations:

> Assume 90% stockholder turnout. To approve a merger, one must obtain the favorable vote of 50.1% of the shares.

> The percentage of additional votes the bidder needs to win is 50.1 − 14.9% = 35.2%.

Consequently, to prevail in a proxy contest with a 90% turnout, the percentage of additional shareholder votes a 14.9% shareholder bidder needs to prevail is 30.2% for directors and 35.2% in a subsequent merger.

The record reflects that institutional investors held 42% of Unitrin's stock and 20 institutions held 33% of the stock. Thus, American General's own assumptions and calculations in the record support the Unitrin Board's argument that "it is hard to imagine a company more readily susceptible to a proxy contest concerning a pure issue of dollars."

The conclusion of the Court of Chancery that the Repurchase Program would make a proxy contest for Unitrin a "theoretical" possibility that American General could not realistically pursue may be erroneous and appears to be inconsistent with its own earlier determination that the "repurchase program strengthens the position of the Board of Directors to defend against a hostile bidder, but will not deprive the public stockholders of the 'power to influence corporate direction through the ballot.'" Even a complete implementation of the Repurchase Program, in combination with the pre-existing Supermajority Vote provision, would not appear to have a preclusive effect upon American General's ability successfully to marshal enough shareholder votes to win a proxy contest.... A proper understanding of the record reflects that American General or any other 14.9% shareholder bidder could apparently win a proxy contest with a 90% turnout.

The key variable in a proxy contest would be the merit of American General's issues, not the size of its stockholdings.... If American General presented an attractive price as the cornerstone of a proxy contest, it could prevail, irrespective of whether the shareholder directors' absolute voting power was 23% or 28%. In that regard, the following passage from the Court of Chancery's Opinion is poignant:

> Harold Hook, the Chairman of American General, admitted in his deposition that the repurchase program is not a "show stopper" because the directors that own stock will act in their own best interest if the price is high enough....

Consequently, a proxy contest apparently remained a viable alternative for American General to pursue notwithstanding Unitrin's poison pill, Supermajority Vote provision, and a fully implemented Repurchase Program.

Substantive Coercion

American General's Threat

This Court has recognized "the prerogative of a board of directors to resist a third party's unsolicited acquisition proposal or offer.", . . . [T]he purpose of enhanced judicial scrutiny is to determine whether the Board acted reasonably in "relation . . . to the threat which a particular bid allegedly poses to stockholder interests." . . .

"The obvious requisite to determining the reasonableness of a defensive action is a clear identification of the nature of the threat." . . .

Courts, commentators and litigators have attempted to catalogue the threats posed by hostile tender offers. . . . Commentators have categorized three types of threats:

> (i) *opportunity loss* . . . [where] a hostile offer might deprive target shareholders of the opportunity to select a superior alternative offered by target management [or, we would add, offered by another bidder]; (ii) *structural coercion*, . . . the risk that disparate treatment of non-tendering shareholders might distort shareholders' tender decisions; and (iii) *substantive coercion*, . . . the risk that shareholders will mistakenly accept an underpriced offer because they disbelieve management's representations of intrinsic value. . . .

This Court has held that the "inadequate value" of an all cash for all shares offer is a "legally cognizable threat." In addition, this Court has specifically concluded that inadequacy of value is *not* the only legally cognizable threat from "an all-shares, all-cash offer at a price below what a target board in good faith deems to be the present value of its shares." . . . In making that determination, this Court held that the Time board of directors had reasonably determined that inadequate value was not the only threat that Paramount's all cash for all shares offer presented, but was *also* reasonably concerned that the Time stockholders might tender to Paramount in ignorance or based upon a mistaken belief, *i.e.*, yield to substantive coercion.

The record reflects that the Unitrin Board perceived the threat from American General's Offer to be a form of substantive coercion. The Board noted that Unitrin's stock price had moved up, on higher than normal trading volume, to a level slightly below the price in American General's Offer. The Board also noted that some Unitrin shareholders had publicly expressed interest in selling at or near the price in the Offer. The Board determined that Unitrin's stock was undervalued by the market at current levels and that the Board considered Unitrin's stock to be a good long-term investment. The Board also discussed the speculative and unsettled market conditions for Unitrin stock caused by American General's public disclosure. The Board concluded that a Repurchase Program would provide additional liquidity to those stockholders who wished to realize short-term gain, and would provide enhanced value to those stockholders who wished to maintain a long-term investment. Accordingly, the Board voted to authorize the Repurchase Program for up to ten million shares of its outstanding stock on the open market.

In *Unocal*, this Court noted that, pursuant to Delaware corporate law, a board of directors' duty of care required it to respond actively to protect the corporation and its shareholders from perceived harm. . . . In *Unocal*, when describing the proportionality test, this Court listed several examples of concerns that boards of directors should consider in evaluating and responding to perceived threats. Unitrin's Board deemed three of the concerns exemplified in *Unocal* relevant in deciding to authorize the Repurchase Program: first, the inadequacy of the price offered; second, the nature and timing of American General's Offer; and third, the basic stockholder interests at stake, including those of short-term speculators whose actions may have fueled the coercive aspect of the Offer at the expense of the long-term investor. . . .

The record appears to support Unitrin's argument that the Board's justification for adopting the Repurchase Program was its reasonably perceived risk of substantive coercion, *i.e.*, that Unitrin's shareholders might accept American General's inadequate Offer because of "ignorance or mistaken belief" regarding the Board's assessment of the long-term value of Unitrin's stock. . . . In this case, the Unitrin Board's letter to its shareholders specifically reflected those concerns in describing its perception of the threat from American General's Offer. The adoption of the Repurchase Program also appears to be consistent with this Court's holding that economic inadequacy is not the only threat presented by an all cash for all shares hostile bid, because the threat of such a hostile bid could be exacerbated by shareholder "ignorance or . . . mistaken belief." . . .

Range of Reasonableness
Proper Proportionality Burden

The Court of Chancery's legal conclusions are subject to *de novo* review by this Court. . . . The Court of Chancery's factual findings will be accepted if "they are sufficiently supported by the record and are the product of an orderly and logical deductive process." . . .

We have already noted that the Court of Chancery made a factual finding unsupported by the record . . . The Court of Chancery applied an incorrect legal standard when it ruled that the Unitrin decision to authorize the Repurchase Program was disproportionate because it was "unnecessary." The Court of Chancery stated:

> Given that the Board had already implemented the poison pill and the advance notice provision, the repurchase program was unnecessary to protect Unitrin from an inadequate bid.

In *QVC*, this Court recently elaborated upon the judicial function in applying enhanced scrutiny, citing *Unocal* as authority, albeit in the context of a sale of control and the target board's consideration of one of several reasonable alternatives. That teaching is nevertheless applicable here:

> a court applying enhanced judicial scrutiny should be deciding whether the directors made *a reasonable* decision, not *a perfect*

decision. . . . , courts will not substitute their business judgment for that of the directors, but will determine if the directors' decision was, on balance, within a range of reasonableness . . .

The Court of Chancery did not determine whether the Unitrin Board's decision to implement the Repurchase Program fell within a "range of reasonableness."

The record reflects that the Unitrin Board's adoption of the Repurchase Program was an apparent recognition on its part that all shareholders are not alike. This Court has stated that distinctions among types of shareholders are neither inappropriate nor irrelevant for a board of directors to make, *e.g.*, distinctions between long-term shareholders and short-term profit-takers, such as arbitrageurs, and their stockholding objectives. . . . In *Unocal* itself, we expressly acknowledged that "a board may reasonably consider the basic stockholder interests at stake, including those of short term speculators, whose actions may have fueled the coercive aspect of the offer at the expense of the long term investor.".

The Court of Chancery's determination that the Unitrin Board's adoption of the Repurchase Program was unnecessary constituted a substitution of its business judgment for that of the Board, contrary to this Court's "range of reasonableness" holding in [*Paramount v. QVC*, discussed in the Chapter XVIII of this textbook] Its decision to enjoin the Repurchase Program as an "unnecessary" *addition* to other complementary defensive mechanisms is also inconsistent with a similar analysis in [another case that also included a repurchase plan].

Draconian Defenses

Coercive or Preclusive

Range of Reasonableness

In assessing a challenge to defensive actions by a target corporation's board of directors in a takeover context, this Court has held that the Court of Chancery should evaluate the board's overall response, including the justification for each contested defensive measure, and the results achieved thereby. Where all of the target board's defensive actions are inextricably related, the principles of *Unocal* require that such actions be scrutinized collectively as a unitary response to the perceived threat. . . . Thus, the Unitrin Board's adoption of the Repurchase Program, in addition to the poison pill, must withstand *Unocal*'s proportionality review. . . .

In *Unocal*, . . . this Court held that the board "does not have unbridled discretion to defeat any perceived threat by any Draconian means available." . . . Immediately following those observations in *Unocal*, when exemplifying the parameters of a board's authority in adopting a restrictive stock repurchase, this Court held that "the directors may not have acted *solely* or *primarily* out of a desire to perpetuate themselves in office" (preclusion of the stockholders' corporate franchise right to vote) and, further, that the stock repurchase plan must not be inequitable.

An examination of the cases applying *Unocal* reveals a direct correlation between findings of proportionality or disproportionality and the judicial determination of whether a defensive response was draconian because it was either coercive or preclusive in character. In *Time*, for example, this Court concluded that the Time board's defensive response was reasonable and proportionate since it was not aimed at "cramming down" on its shareholders a management-sponsored alternative, *i.e.*, was not coercive, and because it did not preclude Paramount from making an offer for the combined Time-Warner company, *i.e.*, was not preclusive.

This Court also applied *Unocal's* proportionality test to the board's adoption of a "poison pill" shareholders' rights plan in [*Moran v. Household Int'l*]. After acknowledging that the adoption of the rights plan was within the directors' statutory authority, this Court determined that the implementation of the rights plan was a proportionate response to the theoretical threat of a hostile takeover, in part, because it did not "strip" the stockholders of their right to receive tender offers *and* did not fundamentally restrict proxy contests, *i.e.,* was not preclusive. . . .

In the modern takeover lexicon, it is now clear that since *Unocal*, this Court has consistently recognized that defensive measures which are either preclusive or coercive are included within the common law definition of draconian.

If a defensive measure is not draconian, however, because it is not either coercive or preclusive, the *Unocal* proportionality test requires the focus of enhanced judicial scrutiny to shift to "the range of reasonableness." Proper and proportionate defensive responses are intended and permitted to thwart perceived threats. When a corporation is not for sale, the board of directors is the defender of the metaphorical medieval corporate bastion and the protector of the corporation's shareholders. The fact that a defensive action must not be coercive or preclusive does not prevent a board from responding defensively before a bidder is at the corporate bastion's gate.

The *ratio decidendi* for the "range of reasonableness" standard is a need of the board of directors for latitude in discharging its fiduciary duties to the corporation and its shareholders when defending against perceived threats. The concomitant requirement is for judicial restraint. Consequently, if the board of directors' defensive response is not draconian (preclusive or coercive) and is within a "range of reasonableness," a court must not substitute its judgment for the board's . . .

This Case

Repurchase Program

Proportionate With Poison Pill

In this case, the initial focus of enhanced judicial scrutiny for proportionality requires a determination regarding the defensive responses by the Unitrin Board to American General's offer. We begin, therefore, by ascertaining whether the Repurchase Program, as an addition to the poison pill, was draconian by being either coercive or preclusive.

A limited nondiscriminatory self-tender, like some other defensive measures, may thwart a current hostile bid, but is not inherently coercive. Moreover, it does not necessarily preclude future bids or proxy contests by stockholders who decline to participate in the repurchase. . . . A selective repurchase of shares in a public corporation on the market, such as Unitrin's Repurchase Program, generally does not discriminate because all shareholders can voluntarily realize the same benefit by selling. . . . Here, there is no showing on this record that the Repurchase Program was coercive.

We have already determined that the record in this case appears to reflect that a proxy contest remained a viable (if more problematic) alternative for American General even if the Repurchase Program were to be completed in its entirety. Nevertheless, the Court of Chancery must determine whether Unitrin's Repurchase Program would only inhibit American General's ability to wage a proxy fight and institute a merger or whether it was, in fact, preclusive because American General's success would either be mathematically impossible or realistically unattainable. If the Court of Chancery concludes that the Unitrin Repurchase Program was not draconian because it was not preclusive, one question will remain to be answered in its proportionality review: whether the Repurchase Program was within a range of reasonableness?

The Court of Chancery found that the Unitrin Board reasonably believed that American General's Offer was inadequate and that the adoption of a poison pill was a proportionate defensive response. Upon remand, in applying the correct legal standard to the factual circumstances of this case, the Court of Chancery may conclude that the implementation of the limited Repurchase Program was also within a range of reasonable additional defensive responses available to the Unitrin Board. In considering whether the Repurchase Program was within a range of reasonableness the Court of Chancery should take into consideration whether: (1) it is a statutorily authorized form of business decision which a board of directors may routinely make in a non-takeover context; (2) as a defensive response to American General's Offer it was limited and corresponded in degree or magnitude to the degree or magnitude of the threat, (*i.e.*, assuming the threat was relatively "mild," was the response relatively "mild?"); (3) with the Repurchase Program, the Unitrin Board properly recognized that all shareholders are not alike, and provided immediate liquidity to those shareholders who wanted it.

The Court of Chancery's holding in *Shamrock*, cited with approval by this Court in *Time*, appears to be persuasive support for the proportionality of the multiple defenses Unitrin's Board adopted. In *Shamrock*, the Court of Chancery concluded that the Polaroid board had "a valid basis for concern that the Polaroid stockholders [like Unitrin's stockholders] will be unable to reach an accurate judgment as to the intrinsic value of their stock.". The Court of Chancery also observed, "the likely shift in the stockholder profile in favor of Polaroid" as a result of the repurchase plan "appears to be minimal." Consequently, the Court of Chancery concluded that Polaroid's defensive response as a whole—the ESOP [Employee Stock Ownership Plan, sometimes used as a defensive measure given that employees are less likely to tender their shares than other shareholders], the issuance of stock to a friendly third party and the stock repurchase plan—was not disproportionate to the Shamrock threat or improperly motivated, and "individually or collectively will [not] preclude the successful completion of Shamrock's tender offer."

American General argues that the all cash for all shares offer in *Shamrock* is distinguishable because *Shamrock* involved a hostile tender offer, whereas this case involves a fully negotiable Offer to enter into a consensual merger transaction. Nevertheless, American General acknowledges that a determinative factor in *Shamrock* was a finding that the defensive responses had only an incidental effect on the stockholder profile for the purpose of a proxy contest, *i.e.*, was not preclusive. In *Shamrock*, the Court of Chancery's proportionality holding was also an implicit determination that the series of multiple defensive responses were within a "range of reasonableness."

We hold that the Court of Chancery correctly determined that the *Unocal* standard of enhanced judicial scrutiny applied to the defensive actions of the Unitrin defendants in establishing the poison pill and implementing the Repurchase Program. The Court of Chancery's finding, that the Repurchase Program was a disproportionate defensive response, was based on faulty factual predicates, unsupported by the record. This error was exacerbated by its application of an erroneous legal standard of "necessity" to the Repurchase Program as a defensive response.

The interlocutory judgment of the Court of Chancery, in favor of American General, is REVERSED. This matter is REMANDED for further proceedings in accordance with this opinion.

————————

E. *UNOCAL* IN THE MODERN DAY

Post-*Unitrin*, the courts developed a bifurcated analysis for the application of *Unocal*. Courts first require boards to demonstrate that they had "reasonable grounds for believing that a danger to corporate policy and effectiveness existed." Next, courts examine whether the "defensive response was reasonable in relation to the threat posed." A response is unreasonable when it is either "preclusive or coercive" or otherwise outside the range of reasonableness.

In practice, as this next excerpt discusses, *Unocal* has been reduced to a single prong test, as the "threat" part of the analysis has been largely ignored or simply readily satisfied by a "mere incantation" of inadequate value.[20] The importance of the second prong, the reasonableness review, has been paramount. And it, too, has been readily satisfied. *Unocal* review has seldom resulted in a defensive action being struck down:

> Between the issuance of *Unocal* in 1985 and the end of 2000, a Westlaw search shows that the Delaware Court of Chancery issued 141 opinions citing *Unocal* and that the Delaware Supreme Court issued 33 opinions citing *Unocal*. Very few cases are decided exclusively on the first prong of *Unocal*. In almost every case raising this issue, the courts find a cognizable threat.
>
> The most dramatic evidence of *Unocal*'s feebleness is revealed in the outcomes of proportionality review, the second prong of *Unocal* analysis. Since *Unocal* was decided in 1985, the Delaware Supreme Court has not found defensive tactics to be disproportionate outside of a *Revlon* context. The Court of Chancery has been more aggressive in finding disproportionality, but in every such case that has reached the Delaware Supreme Court, the finding of disproportionality has been reversed or pushed to the side.
>
> What effect has the inhospitable reception given to *Unocal* claims by the Delaware Supreme Court had on the takeover market? Causal connections of this type are impossible to forge with confidence, but we venture a few speculative remarks. First, we suspect that the weakened *Unocal* standard probably accounts—at least in part—for the limited litigation in this area. Despite several recent decisions by Vice Chancellor Strine, litigation in the Delaware courts over issues relating to hostile takeovers has slowed considerably. From 1985 through 1990, the Delaware courts decided an average of 3.5 cases per year in which they employed the *Unocal* analysis. From 1991 through

---

[20] Ronald J. Gilson, *Unocal Fifteen Years Later (and What We Can Do About It)*, 26 DEL. J. CORP. L. 491 (2001).

2000, the Delaware courts decided just over one such case per year.

The decline in *Unocal* litigation might be thought to be related to a decline in hostile-takeover activity. This explanation might explain litigation patterns in the early 1990s. But from 1994 through 1998 there were an average of 40 hostile bids per year. Moreover, there were 68 hostile bids in 1995, "nearly as many as any year in the 1980s." The bottom line is that during the 1990s the number of hostile transactions returned to levels nearly equal to those of the 1980s, and the number of Delaware corporations remains as high as ever, but neither participants in those takeover battles nor target-company shareholders seem to be going to court. In the absence of a change in the legal standards, this result would seem particularly puzzling because success rates for hostile bidders have declined over time, suggesting that the need for litigation is stronger than ever. In the next section, we explore a common-sense explanation to that puzzle.

What explains the death of *Unocal* in the Delaware Supreme Court? [T]he dearth of current litigation over the *Unocal* standard stems from the simple fact that outcomes in hostile takeover litigation have become so predictable that the combatants choose to avoid the effort. Although Delaware fiduciary-duty law is notoriously indeterminate, Unocal has become well-settled in the sense that directors win except in extreme cases.

Collectively, the reformulated standards in *Unitrin* seem to have lost the skepticism of incumbent managers that animated *Unocal*, opting instead to consolidate power over takeover decisions in those incumbent managers despite the "omnipresent specter" of self-interest. In light of our prior observations regarding the *Unocal* standard, however, the extreme position taken by the *Unitrin* court seems almost inevitable. Given the expansive notion of "threats" adopted by the Delaware courts, managers can hardly fail (and rarely do) in the first prong of *Unocal*. Additionally, when the courts come around to the second prong, they are forced into the uncomfortable position of speculating about the relative harm posed by the threat as compared to the benefits promised by the defensive action. In lieu of bald speculation, and in harmony with a tradition of deference to directors, courts are driven to seek markers that signal abuse. Short of completely foreclosing shareholder action, there are no such markers. Thus, it is quite understandable for the court to gravitate toward a "preclusive or coercive" standard.

Of course, *Unitrin* retained the "range of reasonableness" inquiry, in the event that an action that is not quite preclusive or coercive might still be objectionable. This standard has been employed only twice (both times by the Court of Chancery) in striking down a defensive action. In one of those cases, the Delaware Supreme Court subsequently affirmed on alternative grounds, and the other case ended prior to any hearing by the court.[21]

As the authors note, *Unocal* challenges almost never prevail; virtually all defenses pass *Unocal* muster. One possible conclusion about the "death" of *Unocal* is that courts stopped interfering in hostile takeover contests. One of this textbook's authors has theorized that there may be political reasons for this change.

> *Unocal*, again as with *Revlon*, could also be painted as a crafted response to the SEC's antitakeover stance in the 1980s. The Delaware court's decision to regulate, and put a limit on, takeover defenses was an olive branch to prevent greater SEC action in this arena. Then in 1995, after the battles of the 1980s had passed and long after the SEC lost interest in takeover regulation, the Delaware Supreme Court relaxed *Unocal's* strictures on takeover defenses in *Unitrin, Inc. v. American General Corp. Unitrin* held that a Delaware court should first ascertain whether a target board's takeover response was preclusive or coercive. If not, then the court should review the decision under a "range of reasonableness."
>
> . . .
>
> The true impact of *Unitrin*, though, was in its facts. In *Unitrin*, the Unitrin board had initiated a self-tender that had the effect of raising the target directors' holdings to a blocking threshold, preventing any merger transaction with a 15 percent or greater shareholder (i.e., the hostile bidder in the case, American General). Unitrin had also adopted a poison pill with a 15 percent threshold, limiting any subsequent bidder's acquisition of the target's shares. The Delaware Supreme Court reversed a lower court finding that this response was unreasonable in relation to the threat posed. The Supreme Court stated: "The adoption of the poison pill and the limited Repurchase Program was not coercive and the Repurchase Program may not be preclusive."
>
> The court then remanded the case for the lower court to consider whether the program made a bid "mathematically impossible or

---

[21] Robert H. Thompson & D. Gordon Smith, *Toward a New Theory of the Shareholder Role: "Sacred Space" in Corporate Takeovers*, 80 TEX. L. REV. 261, 284–294 (2001).

realistically unattainable" and was reasonable in relation to the threat at hand. However, in other parts of the opinion, the court telegraphed the lower court's determination by strongly implying that the Unitrin board had met this new test. The *Unitrin* gloss on *Unocal* accordingly gave target boards wide latitude in their ability to adopt strong, potentially preclusionary takeover defenses, so long as they did not completely preclude a proxy contest.

Unocal review, as subsequently modified by *Unitrin,* is thus quite limited. By one count, the Delaware courts after *Unitrin* have overturned only four takeover defense responses as disproportionate or preclusive solely under the *Unocal* standard. All except *Omnicare* were decided in the Chancery Court. On the edges of *Unocal,* the courts, acting in their takeover supervisory role, repeatedly punished target boards who completely shut off a bid's potential for success, however remote, or who otherwise unfairly acted mid-contest to alter the rules of the game to the same effect. Thus, in two cases, *Carmody v. Toll Brothers, Inc.* and *Mentor Graphics Corp. v. Quickturn Design Systems, Inc.,* the Delaware courts struck down no-hand and dead-head poison pills. Then in *Chesapeake Corp. v. Shore,* the Chancery Court held that a bylaw provision adopted in the middle of a takeover battle that effectively frustrated an unsolicited bidder after its successful proxy battle was not sustainable under *Unocal* and *Unitrin.* However, these decisions were islands in a sea of permissiveness. The Delaware courts have largely upheld the vast majority of takeover defensive action, largely confining *Unocal* to a test of preclusiveness.

The result is twofold. First, litigation remains an element of any hostile as the potential, if not the actuality, for a violation of *Unocal* is present. Delaware courts thus retain their oversight review of hostile transactions. Second, given the Delaware court's strict reading of *Unocal,* the defensive actions that a board can take today outside *Revlon* are vast.[22]

Another explanation is that the change in law is justified due to changes in the M&A market. In the 1980s, both how hostile bidders proceeded, and how companies defended against their bids, was more aggressive and more varied. Hostile bidders would launch coercive two-tiered front loaded tender offers, and companies would respond to hostile bids with equally aggressive tactics, such as leveraged recapitalizations and white knight sales to preferred bidders described in Chapter XV. The *Revlon* case covered in Chapter XVIII aptly summarizes the (extreme)

---

[22] STEVEN M. DAVIDOFF, GODS AT WAR: SHOTGUN TAKEOVERS, GOVERNMENT BY DEAL, AND THE PRIVATE EQUITY IMPLOSION, 208–9 (2009).

lengths that a board would take to fight off a hostile bidder as well as the "take no prisoner" attitude of a hostile bidder. But in the modern day, takeover contests are conducted differently. Some of the strategies used in the 1980s transactions are no longer being used, and others were validated: the strategies thus became less varied. In particular, defenses like the poison pill, which could channel hostile contests to proxy contests, were upheld, and Delaware courts assiduously police the fairness of these proxy contests. Prior court decisions influenced market practices so as to make Unocal's "death" appropriate.

F.   THE "JUST SAY NO" DEFENSE UNDER *UNOCAL: AIR PRODUCTS & CHEMICALS v. AIRGAS*

As discussed in the previous Chapter, perhaps the most powerful defense against an unwanted takeover bid is the combination of a staggered (or classified) board and a poison pill; this combination is the cornerstone of the "just say no" defense. When faced with an unwanted offer, a target with these defenses in place need merely identify a threat, often "substantive coercion," and then the board need just say no to the unwanted offer. Although the defense does not preclude an unwanted bidder from pursuing a proxy contest, with the typical staggered board having three classes of directors and only one class's term expiring at the end of each year, a bidder can only replace at most one third of the target's board in any one election cycle. A bidder must wait for two election cycles in order to overcome the defense. The wait is costly for many reasons, including the distraction of the bidder's management.

The validity of the just say no defense has been at issue for many years. In *Airgas*, the court was asked to determine whether the just say no defense comports with *Unocal*'s enhanced scrutiny standard: as used by Airgas, was it a reasonable response in relation to the threat posed? The threat identified by the Airgas board was "substantive coercion"—an all-cash all-shares fully financed offer that the board considered to be too low but that shareholders might nevertheless mistakenly accept. Since Airgas had a staggered board, Air Products would have had to have waited two years to replace the Airgas board and force redemption of the poison pill, something Air Products asserted it would not do. In his opinion ruling in favor of Airgas's board, Chancellor Chandler made it clear that although he "agreed theoretically" with a view less inclined to characterize the offer as substantively coercive so as to warrant Airgas's response, he nevertheless felt constrained by Delaware Supreme Court precedent.

AIR PRODUCTS & CHEMICALS, INC. V. AIRGAS, INC.

Delaware Court of Chancery
16 A.3d 48 (2011)

CHANDLER, CHANCELLOR.

This case poses the following fundamental question: Can a board of directors, acting in good faith and with a reasonable factual basis for its decision, when faced with a structurally non-coercive, all-cash, fully financed tender offer directed to the stockholders of the corporation, keep a poison pill in place so as to prevent the stockholders from making their own decision about whether they want to tender their shares—even after the incumbent board has lost one election contest, a full year has gone by since the offer was first made public, and the stockholders are fully informed as to the target board's views on the inadequacy of the offer? If so, does that effectively mean that a board can "just say never" to a hostile tender offer?

The answer to the latter question is "no." A board cannot "*just* say no" to a tender offer. Under Delaware law, it must first pass through two prongs of exacting judicial scrutiny by a judge who will evaluate the actions taken by, and the motives of, the board. Only a board of directors found to be acting in good faith, after reasonable investigation and reliance on the advice of outside advisors, which articulates and convinces the Court that a hostile tender offer poses a legitimate threat to the corporate enterprise, may address that perceived threat by blocking the tender offer and forcing the bidder to elect a board majority that supports its bid.

In essence, this case brings to the fore one of the most basic questions animating all of corporate law, which relates to the allocation of power between directors and stockholders. That is, "when, if ever, will a board's duty to 'the corporation and its shareholders' require [the board] to abandon concerns for 'long term' values (and other constituencies) and enter a current share value maximizing mode?" More to the point, in the context of a hostile tender offer, who gets to decide when and if the corporation is for sale? . . .

. . . I conclude that, as Delaware law currently stands, the answer must be that the power to defeat an inadequate hostile tender offer ultimately lies with the board of directors. As such, I find that the Airgas board has met its burden under *Unocal* to articulate a legally cognizable threat (the allegedly inadequate price of Air Products' offer, coupled with the fact that a majority of Airgas's stockholders would likely tender into that inadequate offer) and has taken defensive measures that fall within a range of reasonable responses proportionate to that threat. I thus rule in favor of defendants. Air Products' and the Shareholder Plaintiffs' requests for relief are denied, and all claims asserted against defendants are dismissed with prejudice.

This is the Court's decision . . . in this long-running takeover battle between Air Products & Chemicals, Inc. ("Air Products") and Airgas, Inc. ("Airgas"). The now very public saga began quietly in mid-October 2009 when John McGlade, President and CEO of Air Products, privately approached Peter McCausland, founder and CEO of Airgas, about a potential acquisition or combination. After McGlade's private advances were rebuffed, Air Products went hostile in February 2010, launching a public tender offer for all outstanding Airgas shares.

Now, over a year since Air Products first announced its all-shares, all-cash tender offer, the terms of that offer (other than price) remain essentially unchanged. After several price bumps and extensions, the offer currently stands at $70 per share and is set to expire today, February 15, 2011—Air Products' stated "best and final" offer. The Airgas board unanimously rejected that offer as being "clearly inadequate." The Airgas board has repeatedly expressed the view that Airgas is worth at least $78 per share in a sale transaction—and at any rate, far more than the $70 per share Air Products is offering. . . .

Airgas continues to maintain its defenses, blocking the bid and effectively denying shareholders the choice whether to tender their shares. Air Products and Shareholder Plaintiffs now ask this Court to order Airgas to redeem its poison pill and other defenses that are stopping Air Products from moving forward with its hostile offer, and to allow Airgas's stockholders to decide for themselves whether they want to tender into Air Products' (inadequate or not) $70 "best and final" offer.

  . . . .

Although I have a hard time believing that inadequate price alone (according to the target's board) in the context of a non-discriminatory, all-cash, all-shares, fully financed offer poses any "threat"—particularly given the wealth of information available to Airgas's stockholders at this point in time—under existing Delaware law, it apparently does. Inadequate price has become a form of "substantive coercion" as that concept has been developed by the Delaware Supreme Court in its takeover jurisprudence. That is, the idea that Airgas's stockholders will disbelieve the board's views on value (or in the case of merger arbitrageurs who may have short-term profit goals in mind, they may simply ignore the board's recommendations), and so they may mistakenly tender into an inadequately priced offer. Substantive coercion has been clearly recognized by our Supreme Court as a valid threat. . . .

Here, even using heightened scrutiny, the Airgas board has demonstrated that it has a reasonable basis for sustaining its long term corporate strategy—the Airgas board is independent, and has relied on the advice of three different outside independent financial advisors in concluding that Air Products' offer is inadequate. Air Products' *own three nominees* who were elected to the Airgas board in September 2010 [*Editor: Air Products engaged in a successful proxy fight and got three of its nominees, who it noted were independent, with no prior relationship to Air Products, elected to the board*] have joined wholeheartedly in the Airgas board's determination, and when the Airgas board met to consider the $70 "best and final" offer in December 2010, it was one of those Air Products Nominees who said, "We have to protect the pill." Indeed, one of Air Products' *own directors* conceded at trial that the Airgas board members had acted within their fiduciary duties in their desire to "hold out for the proper price," and that "if an offer was made for Air Products that [he] considered to be unfair to the stockholders of Air Products . . . [he would likewise] use every legal mechanism available" to hold out for the proper price as well. Under Delaware law, the Airgas directors have complied with their fiduciary duties. Thus, as noted above, and for the reasons more fully described in the remainder of this Opinion, I am constrained to deny Air Products' and the Shareholder Plaintiffs' requests for relief. . . .

[*The court includes this description of Airgas's Anti-Takeover Devices:*

B. Airgas's Anti-Takeover Devices

As a result of Airgas's classified board structure, it would take two annual meetings to obtain control of the board. In addition to its staggered board, Airgas has three main takeover defenses: (1) a shareholder rights plan ("poison pill") with a 15% triggering threshold, (2) Airgas has not opted out of Delaware General Corporation Law ("DGCL") § 203, which prohibits business combinations with any interested stockholder for a period of three years following the time that such stockholder became an interested stockholder, unless certain conditions are met, and (3) Airgas's Certificate of Incorporation includes a supermajority merger approval provision for certain business combinations. Namely, any merger with an "Interested Stockholder" (defined as a stockholder who beneficially owns 20% or more of the voting power of Airgas's outstanding voting stock) requires the approval of 67% or more of the voting power of the then-outstanding stock entitled to vote, unless approved by a majority of the disinterested directors or certain fair price and procedure requirements are met.

Together, these are Airgas's takeover defenses that Air Products and the Shareholder Plaintiffs challenge and seek to have removed or deemed inapplicable to Air Products' hostile tender offer.]

III. ANALYSIS

A. Has the Airgas Board Established That It Reasonably Perceived the Existence of a Legally Cognizable Threat?

1. Process

Under the first prong of *Unocal*, defendants bear the burden of showing that the Airgas board, "after a reasonable investigation . . . determined in good faith, that the [Air Products offer] presented a threat . . . that warranted a defensive response." I focus my analysis on the defendants' actions in response to Air Products' current $70 offer, but I note here that defendants would have cleared the *Unocal* hurdles with greater ease when the relevant inquiry was with respect to the board's response to the $65.50 offer. . . .

2. What is the "Threat?"

Although the Airgas board meets the threshold of showing good faith and reasonable investigation, the first part of *Unocal* review requires more than that; it requires the board to show that its good faith and reasonable investigation ultimately gave the board "grounds for concluding that a threat to the corporate enterprise existed." . . .

The reality is that the Airgas board discussed essentially none of these alleged "threats" in its board meetings, or in its deliberations on whether to accept or reject Air Products' $70 offer, or in its consideration of whether to keep the pill in place. The board did not discuss "coercion" or the idea that Airgas's stockholders would be "coerced" into tendering. . . .

Airgas's board members testified that the concepts of coercion, threat, and the decision whether or not to redeem the pill were nonetheless "implicit" in the board's discussions due to their knowledge that a large percentage of Airgas's stock is held by merger arbitrageurs who have short-term interests and would be willing to tender into an inadequate offer. But the only threat that the board discussed—the threat that has been the central issue since the beginning of this case—is the inadequate price of Air Products' offer. Thus, inadequate price, coupled with the fact that a majority of Airgas's stock is held by merger arbitrageurs who might be willing to tender into such an inadequate offer, is the only real "threat" alleged. In fact, Airgas directors have admitted as much. . . .

a. Structural Coercion

Air Products' offer is not structurally coercive. A structurally coercive offer involves "the risk that disparate treatment of non-tendering shareholders might distort shareholders' tender decisions." *Unocal*, for example, "involved a two-tier, highly coercive tender offer" where stockholders who did not tender into the offer risked getting stuck with junk bonds on the back end. "In such a case, the threat is obvious: shareholders may be compelled to tender *to avoid being treated adversely in the second stage of the transaction*." Air Products' offer poses no such structural threat. It is for all shares of Airgas, with consideration to be paid in all cash. The offer is backed by secured financing. There is regulatory approval . . .

b.   Opportunity Loss

Opportunity loss is the threat that a "hostile offer might deprive target stockholders of the opportunity to select a superior alternative offered by target management or . . . offered by another bidder. . . . Air Products' offer poses no threat of opportunity loss. The Airgas board has had, at this point, over sixteen months to consider Air Products' offer and to explore "strategic alternatives going forward as a company." And after all that time there is no alternative offer currently on the table. . . . The "superior alternative" Airgas is pursing is simply to continue [ ] on its current course and execute [ ] its strategic [five year, long term] plan."

c.   Substantive Coercion

Inadequate price and the concept of substantive coercion are inextricably related. The Delaware Supreme Court has defined substantive coercion, as discussed in Section II.C, as "the risk that [Airgas's] stockholders might accept [Air Products'] inadequate Offer because of 'ignorance or mistaken belief' regarding the Board's assessment of the long-term value of [Airgas's] stock." In other words, if management advises stockholders, in good faith, that it believes Air Products' hostile offer is inadequate because in its view the future earnings potential of the company is greater than the price offered, Airgas's stockholders might nevertheless reject the board's advice and tender.

The next question is, if a majority of stockholders *want* to tender into an inadequately priced offer, is that substantive coercion? Is that a threat that justifies continued maintenance of the poison pill? Put differently, is there evidence in the record that Airgas stockholders are so "focused on the short-term" that they would "take a smaller harvest in the swelter of August over a larger one in Indian Summer"? Air Products argues that there is none whatsoever. . . .

But there is at least some evidence in the record suggesting that this risk may be real. Moreover, both Airgas's expert and well as *Air Products' own expert* testified that a large number—if not all—of the arbitrageurs who bought into Airgas's stock at prices significantly below the $70 offer price would be happy to tender their shares at that price regardless of the potential long-term value of the company. Based on the testimony of both expert witnesses, I find sufficient evidence that a majority of stockholders might be willing to tender their shares regardless of whether the price is adequate or not—thereby ceding control of Airgas to Air Products. This is a clear "risk" under the teachings of *TW Services* and *Paramount* because it would essentially thrust Airgas into *Revlon* mode.

Ultimately, it all seems to come down to the Supreme Court's holdings in *Paramount* and *Unitrin*. In *Unitrin*, the Court held: "[T]he directors of a Delaware corporation have the prerogative to determine that the market undervalues its stock and to protect its stockholders from offers that do not reflect the long-term value of the corporation under its present management plan." When a company is not in *Revlon* mode, a board of directors "is not under any *per se* duty to maximize shareholder value in the short term, even in the context of a takeover." . . . I find that the Airgas board acted in good faith and relied on the advice of its financial and legal advisors in coming to the conclusion that Air Products' offer is inadequate. And as the Supreme Court has held, a board that in good faith believes that a hostile offer is inadequate may "properly employ [ ] a poison pill as a proportionate defensive response to protect its stockholders from a 'low ball' bid."

B.   Is the Continued Maintenance of Airgas's Defensive Measures Proportionate to the "Threat" Posed by Air Products' Offer?

Turning now to the second part of the *Unocal* test, I must determine whether the Airgas board's defensive measures are a proportionate response to the threat posed by Air Products' offer. Where the defensive measures "are inextricably related, the principles of *Unocal* require that [they] be scrutinized collectively as a unitary response to the perceived threat." Defendants bear the burden of showing that their defenses are not preclusive or coercive, and if neither, that they fall within a "range of reasonableness."

1.   Preclusive or Coercive

A defensive measure is coercive if it is "aimed at 'cramming down' on its shareholders a management-sponsored alternative." Airgas's defensive measures are certainly not coercive in this respect, as Airgas is specifically *not* trying to cram down a management sponsored alternative, but rather, simply wants to maintain the status quo and manage the company for the long term.

A response is preclusive if it "makes a bidder's ability to wage a successful proxy contest and gain control [of the target's board] . . . 'realistically unattainable.'" . . . [The Delaware Supreme Court has held that]: *the combination of a classified board and a Rights Plan do not constitute a preclusive defense.*"

The Supreme Court explained its reasoning as follows:

Classified boards are authorized by statute and are adopted for a variety of business purposes. Any classified board also operates as an antitakeover defense by preventing an insurgent from obtaining control of the board in one election. More than a decade ago, in *Carmody* [*v. Toll Brothers, Inc.*], the Court of Chancery noted "because only one third of a classified board would stand for election each year, a classified board would *delay—but not prevent—a hostile acquiror from obtaining control of the board,* since a determined acquiror could wage a proxy contest and obtain control of two thirds of the target board over a two year period, as opposed to seizing control in a single election."

The [*Versata*] Court concluded: "The fact that a combination of defensive measures makes it more difficult for an acquirer to obtain control of a board does not make such measures realistically unattainable, i.e., preclusive."

. . .

I am . . . bound by . . . precedent to proceed on the assumption that Airgas's defensive measures are not preclusive if they delay Air Products from obtaining control of the Airgas board (even if that delay is significant) so long as obtaining control at some point in the future is realistically attainable. I now examine whether the ability to obtain control of Airgas's board in the future is realistically attainable

Air Products has already run one successful slate of insurgents. Their three independent nominees were elected to the Airgas board in September. Airgas's next annual meeting will be held sometime around September 2011. Accordingly, if Airgas's defensive measures remain in place, Air Products has two options if it wants to continue to pursue Airgas at this time: (1) It can call a special meeting and remove the entire board with a supermajority vote of the outstanding shares, or (2) It can wait until Airgas's 2011 annual meeting to nominate a slate of directors. I will address the viability of each of these options in turn.

a. Call a Special Meeting to Remove the Airgas Board by a 67% Supermajority Vote

. . . Airgas's charter allows for 33% of the outstanding shares to call a special meeting of the stockholders, and to remove the entire board without cause by a vote of 67% of the outstanding shares. . . .

[A] poison pill is assuredly preclusive in the everyday common sense meaning of the word; indeed, its *rasion d'etre* is preclusion—to stop a bid (or *this* bid) from progressing. That is what it is intended to do and that is what the Airgas pill has done successfully for over sixteen months.

Whether it is realistic to believe that Air Products can, at some point in the future, achieve a 67% vote necessary to remove the entire Airgas board at a special meeting is (in my opinion) impossible to predict given the host of variables in this setting, but the sheer lack of historical examples where an insurgent has ever achieved such a percentage in a contested control election must mean something. Commentators who have studied actual hostile takeovers for Delaware companies have, at least in part, essentially corroborated this common sense notion that such a victory is not realistically attainable. Nonetheless, while the special meeting may not be a realistically attainable mechanism for circumventing the Airgas defenses, that assessment does not end the analysis under existing precedent.

b. Run Another Proxy Contest

Even if Air Products is unable to achieve the 67% supermajority vote of the outstanding shares necessary to remove the board in a special meeting, it would only need a simple majority of the voting stockholders to obtain control of the board at next year's annual meeting. . . . The reality is that obtaining a simple majority of the voting stock is significantly less burdensome than obtaining a supermajority vote of the outstanding shares, and considering the current composition of Airgas's stockholders (and the fact that, as a result of that shareholder composition, a majority of the voting shares today would likely tender into Air Products' $70 offer), if Air Products and those stockholders choose to stick around, an Air Products victory at the next annual meeting is very realistically attainable.

. . . Air Products is unwilling to wait another eight months to run another slate of nominees . . . [T]hat is a business decision of the Air Products board, but as the Supreme Court has held, waiting until the next annual meeting "delay[s]—but [does] not prevent—[Air Products] from obtaining control of the board." I thus am constrained to conclude that Airgas's defensive measures are not preclusive.

2. *Range of Reasonableness*

"If a defensive measure is neither coercive nor preclusive, the *Unocal* proportionality test requires the focus of enhanced judicial scrutiny to shift to the range of reasonableness." The reasonableness of a board's response is evaluated in the context of the specific threat identified—the "specific nature of the threat [ ] 'sets the parameters for the range of permissible defensive tactics' at any given time."

Here, the record demonstrates that Airgas's board, composed of a majority of outside, independent directors, acting in good faith and with numerous outside advisors concluded that Air Products' offer clearly undervalues Airgas in a sale transaction. The board believes in good faith that the offer price is inadequate by no small margin. Thus, the board is responding to a legitimately articulated threat.

This conclusion is bolstered by the fact that the three Air Products Nominees on the Airgas board have now wholeheartedly joined in the board's determination—what is more, they believe it is their fiduciary duty to keep Airgas's defenses in place. And Air Products' *own directors* have testified that (1) they have no reason to believe that the Airgas directors have breached their fiduciary duties, (2) even though plenty of information has been made available to the stockholders, they "agree that Airgas management is in the best position to understand the intrinsic value of the company," and (3) if the shoe were on the other foot, they would act in the same way as Airgas's directors have. . . .

CONCLUSION

Vice Chancellor Strine recently suggested that:

> The passage of time has dulled many to the incredibly powerful and novel device that a so-called poison pill is. That device has no other purpose than to give the board issuing the rights the leverage to prevent transactions it does not favor by diluting the buying proponent's interests.

There is no question that poison pills act as potent anti-takeover drugs with the potential to be abused. Counsel for plaintiffs (both Air Products and Shareholder Plaintiffs) make compelling policy arguments in favor of redeeming the pill in this case—to do otherwise, they say, would essentially make all companies with staggered boards and poison pills "takeover proof." The argument is an excellent sound bite, but it is ultimately not the holding of this fact-specific case, although it does bring us one step closer to that result.

As this case demonstrates, in order to have any effectiveness, pills do not—and can not—have a set expiration date. To be clear, though, this case does not endorse "just say never." What it does endorse is Delaware's long-understood respect for reasonably exercised managerial discretion, so long as boards are found to be acting in good faith and in accordance with their fiduciary duties (after rigorous judicial fact-finding and enhanced scrutiny of their defensive actions). The Airgas board serves as a quintessential example.

Directors of a corporation still owe fiduciary duties to *all stockholders*—this undoubtedly includes short-term as well as long-term holders. At the same time, a board cannot be forced into *Revlon* mode any time a hostile bidder makes a tender offer that is at a premium to market value. The mechanisms in place to get around the poison pill—even a poison pill in combination with a staggered board, which no doubt makes the process prohibitively more difficult—have been in place since 1985, when the Delaware Supreme Court first decided to uphold the pill as a legal defense to an unwanted bid.

For the foregoing reasons, Air Products' and the Shareholder Plaintiffs' requests for relief are denied, and all claims asserted against defendants are dismissed with prejudice.

———————————

Immediately after the issuance of this decision Air Products dropped its hostile offer, preferring not to appeal the decision to the Delaware Supreme Court.

G. DEFENDING THE DEAL

Until now, we have discussed the application of *Unocal*'s intermediate standard in the context of defenses against an unsolicited tender offer. However, defending the corporation against the threat of a hostile offer is not the only application of *Unocal*. Since the 1980s, target boards have generally changed their view on selling the corporation. More often than not, rather than resist a transaction, boards will now find a preferred buyer with which to enter into a transaction and then seek to protect the transaction. The merger agreements entered into with these preferred buyers will typically include deal protection measures such as termination fees to protect the transaction from interference by other bidders.

Deal protections in merger agreements can be seen as defending a "corporate policy" (to merge with the preferred buyer). Consistent with *Unocal*'s reasonableness limits on director action, directors are not free to use any means available to them to defend their corporate policies, including mergers. When challenged, merger agreements, and the deal protection measures included in them, are subject to *Unocal*'s intermediate scrutiny.

Common deal protection measures fall into one of three general categories: voting protections, exclusivity measures, and compensatory devices.[23]

1. VOTING PROTECTIONS

Voting protections enable a seller to "bank" a high percentage of the shareholders' votes in favor of the agreed upon transaction prior to an actual shareholder vote. A seller can ensure the success of its preferred transaction by securing voting agreements from shareholders holding a majority of the shares or voting power. Where ownership of the seller is

———————————

[23] The following material is adapted from Brian JM Quinn, *Bulletproof: Mandatory Rules for Deal Protection*, 32 J. Corp. L. 865 (2007).

closely held, the transaction costs associated with assembling a majority bloc in support of the transaction can be reasonably low: many of the major shareholders are often directly represented on the seller's board of directors, and the universe of shareholders is small. Where voting agreements are used, the merger agreement is usually signed contingent upon or contemporaneous with their delivery.

In public company transactions, where a controlling bloc of shares cannot be easily assembled in favor of the sale, sellers are not able to offer many voting protections. The most attractive from the buyer's point of view is the commitment that the seller's board will continue to recommend the transaction and, in the event of a better subsequent offer, that the seller's shareholders must be given an opportunity to vote on the initial transaction before being allowed to terminate the merger agreement. The "force-the-vote" provision, which requires boards to call such votes prior to terminating a merger agreement, can be an effective deterrent to a subsequent bid. In particular, it can reduce the incentive of a seller's board to pursue alternative transactions or to re-open negotiations with buyers once an initial transaction is agreed upon.

A number of other voting protections help defend the deal so as to protect buyers. These measures include provisions that require sellers to call shareholder meetings, or set time limits on how long a selling board may delay its obligation to call a meeting. Other provisions include "best efforts" provisions relating to regulatory approvals. Though these provisions provide buyers with some additional deal security, voting agreements and force-the-vote provisions are clearly the most valuable with respect to securing protection of the vote required to approve the transaction.

The "quick consent" strategy represents what may be an extreme example of voting protections. Where controlling or majority shareholders are easily accessible to the seller's board, the seller's board can eschew a shareholder meeting and substitute an action by written consent pursuant to DGCL § 228. Unlike statutory voting requirements, there is no required notice prior to undertaking a shareholder action by written consent. Therefore, it is possible to sign a merger agreement and then, nearly simultaneously, receive shareholder approval via written consent for the merger agreement. The intent of the immediate or near immediate delivery of shareholder consent is to head off any potential second bid before it has a chance to appear. Indeed, with this strategy, shareholders often deliver their consents before the transaction is announced to the public. As a consequence, the quick consent strategy formally complies with the requirements of *Unocal* by making a second bid theoretically possible, without giving up much in the way of transactional certainty.

2. EXCLUSIVITY MEASURES

Exclusivity measures prevent selling boards from considering or negotiating with a potential rival acquirer. We discussed no-shop provisions in Chapter XIV.H.3 No-shop and no-talk provisions are the most common types of exclusivity measures. No-shop, also called no-solicitation, provisions restrict selling boards from actively seeking an alternative buyer. No-shop provisions allow a seller to respond to an unsolicited bid but do not allow a seller to initiate discussions with a potential bidder, or to shop itself. No-talk provisions go further, prohibiting sellers from sharing proprietary and non-public information or engaging in any discussions with another potential bidder. In preventing a seller from sharing any non-public information or speaking with subsequent bidders, no-talk provisions can shut down a potential bid by denying a subsequent bidder the information he would need to generate a competitive bid. Common versions of no-shop and no-talk provisions prohibit sellers from initiating any contact with a potential subsequent bidder, but do allow sellers to terminate the initial transaction in order to respond to unsolicited superior offers from subsequent bidders.

Rights of first refusal, or matching rights, are another type of exclusivity measure. A right of first refusal provides that in the event that a subsequent bid is made, the buyer with a right of first refusal has the right to match the subsequent bid. The presence of rights of first refusal can be a strong deterrent against subsequent bids and is therefore a potentially potent protective measure. A subsequent bidder faces a risk of incurring the expense of evaluating a target and making a bid, only to see the initial bidder exercise its right of first refusal and buy the company. While a subsequent bidder is always free to make a topping bid, it may have only limited access to information regarding the seller. The subsequent bidder knows that it can win only in the event its bid, which is based on limited information regarding the seller, is higher than the bid of the original buyer, a party who has far more extensive information about the seller. "Success" under these circumstances may involve paying too much and suffering the "winner's curse." The Delaware courts have repeatedly held that matching rights are valid exclusivity measures, notwithstanding the strong effect such rights have.[24]

The courts have held that strict exclusivity measures which prevent the board of the seller from learning about or considering subsequent bids are illegal due to their pernicious effect: they "involve[ ] an abdication by the board of its duty to determine what its own fiduciary obligations require at precisely that time in the life of the company when the board's

---

[24] *See In re Toys "R" Us, Inc. Sh'lder Litig.,* 877 A.2d 975 (Del. Ch. 2005) (upholding the use of matching rights as "not unusual" and a reasonable exercise of the board's discretion).

own judgment is most important." *ACE Ltd. v. Capital Re Corporation,* 747 A.2d 95,106 (Del. Ch. 1999). In *Ace*, the challenged merger agreement included a "no talk" provision that allowed the board to engage in discussions with a potential third party bidder if the board concluded "in good faith . . . based upon the written advice of its outside legal counsel, that participating in such negotiations or discussion or furnishing such information is required in order to prevent the Board of Directors of [the target] from breaching its fiduciary duties to its stockholders." Then-Vice Chancellor Strine stated that: "[a] ban on considering such a proposal, even one with an exception where legal counsel opines in writing that such consideration is 'required,' comes close to self-disablement by the board. Our case law takes a rather dim view of restrictions that tend to produce such a result."

Similarly, in *Phelps Dodge Corp. v. Cyprus Amax Minerals Co.*, Nos. CIV.A 17398, CIV.A 17383, CIV.A 17427, 1999 WL 1054255 (Del. Ch. Sept. 27, 1999), the Chancery Court observed that although sellers are "under no duty to negotiate [with subsequent bidders] . . . nevertheless, even the decision not to negotiate . . . must be an informed one." Chancellor Chandler held that strict no-talk provisions are troubling because they "prevent a board from meeting its duty to make an informed judgment with respect to even considering whether to negotiate with a third party." In that respect, strict no-shop and no-talk provisions fail to meet even the relatively low duty of care standard, much less more searching intermediate scrutiny. Boards may not simply close their eyes to potential subsequent transactions or changes in conditions without violating their duties as directors. Entry into a merger agreement that requires them to do so will earn court disfavor.

3. COMPENSATORY DEVICES

The final general category of deal protection devices is compensatory devices. Stock lockups, termination fees, and topping fees are intended not just to protect the deal by deterring third party bids. They are also intended to compensate the bidder with whom the seller enters into the merger agreement. A stock lockup is an option granted to the buyer entering into the merger agreement to purchase shares of the seller's stock upon the occurrence of a triggering event, such as the seller's termination of the merger agreement in order to pursue an alternative transaction. A termination fee is a cash payment to the buyer in the event the merger agreement with the seller is terminated due to a triggering event. A topping fee is a cash payment made to the buyer by the seller in event the seller terminates the transaction with the buyer in order to accept a topping bid from another buyer. The size of the fee is equal to a percentage of the difference between the price offered by the initial buyer and the topping bid. An asset lockup is an option issued to the initial bidder to purchase a division or other asset of the seller; such an asset may be the "crown jewel" of the seller, may involve assets that are of particular interest to the non-preferred bidder, or may simply be at a below-market price (or some combination of these things).[25]

From the point of view of a subsequent bidder, compensatory devices act as a tax on its bid. Depending on the size of the compensatory device, the third party's valuation of the seller and the price at which the third party can acquire the seller, these mechanisms can render a seller unattractive to a third party. A topping fee can have a particularly perverse incentive effect. In its most extreme form, a topping fee pays the initial bidder the value of the difference between the initial bid and the subsequent sale price in the event the initial bidder's bid is "topped." This device not only deters subsequent bidders, but it also removes the seller's incentive to pursue potential (higher) third party bids because the potential gains from a subsequent bid will accrue to the initial bidder and not the seller.

Because it may be difficult to ascertain at first glance whether a board has been properly motivated to protect a deal with termination fees or other deal protection measures or is motivated by self-interest to protect its preferred transaction from other possible deals, the adoption of deal protection measures in merger agreements rightly falls within the purview of *Unocal's* intermediate standard.

4. *BRAZEN V. BELL ATLANTIC CO.*

In the case that follows, *Brazen v. Bell Atlantic Co.*, the court is asked to determine whether the board of the seller violated its fiduciary duties when it included termination fees in a merger agreement. Notice how the court applies the language of liquidated damages in its review of the reasonableness of a termination fee used to protect the merger. Although the court relies on the language of liquidated damages, the analysis closely mirrors *Unocal's* intermediate standard of review. The

---

[25] A post on the Harvard Corporate Governance blog notes: "After a long period of dormancy, lock-ups—"crown jewel" or otherwise—have seen a recent creative rebirth with some structural twists. What remains clear is that, absent extreme circumstances (such as Bear Stearns [which gave an option for JPMorgan, who was "rescuing" it by acquiring it, to buy its Manhattan headquarters for $1.1 billion], an old-fashioned "crown jewel" asset lock-up that serves only to end an auction by virtue of its preclusive impact on other bidders will be subject to significant judicial scrutiny under basic *Revlon* and *Unocal* principles." [Indeed, the lock-up in Revlon itself was enjoined.] "However, a small sampling of recent case law, coupled with developing market practice, suggest that in appropriate circumstances there may be room in the dealmaking toolkit for modern and creative variations on traditional lock-up arrangements (more so where there is demonstrable business benefit to one or both parties beyond the resulting deal protection)." Daniel E. Wolf, *Crown Jewels—Restoring the Luster to Creative Deal Lock-ups?* HARV. L. SCH. FORUM ON CORP. GOVERNANCE & FIN., February 22, 2013, http://corp gov.law.harvard.edu/2013/02/22/crown-jewels-restoring-the-luster-to-creative-deal-lock-ups/. *See also* Christina M. Sautter, *Fleecing the Family Jewels,* forthcoming 90 TUL L. REV. (2016), available at http://ssrn.com/abstract=2625412.

case involves a stock for stock merger such that each party is in a sense acquiring the other. As a result, the parties negotiated reciprocal termination fees in the event of a termination pursuant to a fiduciary out.

BRAZEN V. BELL ATLANTIC CORP.

Supreme Court of Delaware
695 A.2d 43 (1997)

VEASEY, CHIEF JUSTICE:

In this appeal, the issues facing the Court surround the question of whether a two-tiered $550 million termination fee in a merger agreement is a valid liquidated damages provision or whether the termination fee was an invalid penalty and tended improperly to coerce stockholders into voting for the merger.

. . . [W]e do not apply the business judgment rule as such. We hold that the termination fee should be analyzed as a liquidated damages provision because the merger agreement specifically so provided. Under the appropriate test for liquidated damages, the provisions at issue here were reasonable in the context of this case. We further find that the fee was not a penalty and was not coercive. Accordingly, we affirm the judgment of the Court of Chancery, but upon an analysis that differs somewhat from the rationale of that Court.

Facts

In 1995, defendant below-appellee, Bell Atlantic Corporation, and NYNEX Corporation entered into merger negotiations. In January 1996, NYNEX circulated an initial draft merger agreement that included a termination fee provision. Both parties to the agreement determined that the merger should be a stock-for-stock transaction and be treated as a merger of equals. Thus, to the extent possible, the provisions of the merger agreement, including the termination fee, were to be reciprocal.

Representatives of Bell Atlantic and NYNEX agreed that a two-tiered $550 million termination fee was reasonable for compensating either party for damages incurred if the merger did not take place because of certain enumerated events. The termination fee was divided into two parts. First, either party would be required to pay $200 million if there were both a competing acquisition offer for that party and either (a) a failure to obtain stockholder approval, or (b) a termination of the agreement. Second, if a competing transaction were consummated within eighteen months of termination of the merger agreement, the consummating party would be required to pay an additional $350 million to its disappointed merger partner.

In the negotiations where such a fee was discussed, the parties took into account the losses each would have suffered as a result of having focused attention solely on the merger to the exclusion of other significant opportunities for mergers and acquisitions in the telecommunications industry. The parties concluded that, with the recent passage of the national Telecommunications Act of 1996, the entire competitive landscape had been transformed for the regional Bell operating companies, creating a flurry of business combinations. The parties further concluded that the prospect of missing out on alternative transactions due to the pendency of the merger was very real. The "lost opportunity" cost issue loomed large. The negotiators also considered as factors in determining the size of the termination fee (a) the size of termination fees in other merger agreements found reasonable by Delaware courts, and (b) the lengthy period during which the parties would be subject to restrictive covenants under the merger agreement while regulatory approvals were sought.

Bell Atlantic and NYNEX decided that $550 million, which represented about 2% of Bell Atlantic's approximately $28 billion market capitalization, would serve as a "reasonable proxy" for the opportunity cost and other losses associated with the termination of the merger. In addition, senior management advised Bell Atlantic's board of directors that the termination fee was at a level consistent with percentages approved by Delaware courts in earlier transactions, and that the likelihood of a higher offer emerging for either Bell Atlantic or NYNEX was very low.

The termination fee provision states:

If (I) this Agreement (A) is terminated by NYNEX pursuant to Section 9.1(f) hereof or NYNEX or Bell Atlantic pursuant to Section 9.1(g) hereof because of the failure to obtain the required approval from the Bell Atlantic stockholders or by Bell Atlantic pursuant to Section 9.1(h) hereof, or (B) is terminated as a result of Bell Atlantic's material breach of Section 7.2 hereof which is not cured within 30 days after notice thereof to Bell Atlantic and (ii) at the time of such termination or prior to the meeting of Bell Atlantic's stockholders there shall have been an Acquisition Proposal (as defined in Section 6.3 hereof) involving Bell Atlantic or any of its Significant Subsidiaries (whether or not such offer shall have been rejected or shall have been withdrawn prior to the time of such termination or of the meeting), Bell Atlantic shall pay to NYNEX a termination fee of $200 million (the "Initial Bell Atlantic Termination Fee"). In addition, if, within one and one-half years of any such termination described in clause (I) of the immediately preceding sentence that gave rise to the obligation to pay the Initial Bell Atlantic Termination Fee, Bell Atlantic, or the Significant Subsidiary of Bell Atlantic which was the subject of such Acquisition Proposal (the "Bell Atlantic Target Party"), becomes a subsidiary of the person which made (or the affiliate of which made) an Acquisition Proposal described in clause (ii) of the immediately preceding sentence or of any Offering Person or accepts a written offer to consummate or consummates an Acquisition Proposal with such person or any Offering Person, then, upon the signing of a definitive agreement relating to any such Acquisition Proposal, or, if no such agreement is signed then at the closing (and as a condition to the closing) of such Bell Atlantic Target Party becoming such a subsidiary or of any such Acquisition Proposal, Bell Atlantic shall pay to NYNEX an additional termination fee equal to $350 million.

In addition, section 9.2(e) of the merger agreement states,

NYNEX and Bell Atlantic agree that the agreements contained in Sections 9.2(b) and (c) above are an integral part of the transactions contemplated by this Agreement and *constitute liquidated damages and not a penalty*. If one Party fails to promptly pay to the other any fee due under such Sections 9.2(b) and (c), the defaulting Party shall pay the costs and expenses (including legal fees and expenses) in connection with any action, including the filing of any lawsuit or other legal action, taken to collect payment, together with interest on the amount of any unpaid fee at the publicly announced prime rate of Citibank, N.A. from the date such fee was required to be paid.

Finally, section 9.2(a), also pertinent to this appeal, states,

In the event of termination of this Agreement as provided in Section 9.1 hereof, and subject to the provisions of Section 10.1 hereof, this Agreement shall forthwith become void and there shall be no liability on the part of any of the Parties except (I) as set forth in this Section 9.2 . . . and (ii) nothing herein shall relieve any Party from liability for any willful breach hereof.

Plaintiff below-appellant, Lionel L. Brazen, a Bell Atlantic stockholder, filed a class action against Bell Atlantic and its directors for declaratory and injunctive relief. Plaintiff alleged that the termination fee was not a valid liquidated damages clause because it failed to reflect an estimate of actual expenses incurred in preparation for the merger. Plaintiffs alleged that the $550 million payment was "an unconscionably high termination or 'lockup' fee," employed "to restrict and impair the exercise of the fiduciary duty of the Bell Atlantic board and coerce the shareholders to vote to approve the proposed merger. . . ."

The parties filed cross-motions for summary judgment. Bell Atlantic sought a declaration that the decision to include and structure the termination fee was a valid exercise of business judgment. The Court of Chancery denied the relief sought by plaintiff after concluding that the termination fee structure and terms were protected by the business judgment rule and that plaintiff failed to rebut its presumptions.

* * *

Termination Fee as Liquidated Damages

The Court of Chancery determined that the proper method for analyzing the termination fee in this merger agreement was to employ the business judgment rule rather than the test accepted by Delaware courts for analyzing the validity of liquidated damages provisions. In arriving at this determination, the Court of Chancery concluded that a liquidated damages analysis was not appropriate in this case because, notwithstanding section 9.2(e) of the merger agreement, which states that the $550 million fee constitutes liquidated damages, the event which triggers payment of the fees is not a breach but a termination. Liquidated damages, by definition, are damages paid in the event of a breach. . . . In addition, the Merger Agreement clearly provides that nothing in the Agreement (including the payment of termination fees) "shall relieve any Party from liability for any willful breach hereof." Accordingly, the Boards' decision to include these termination fees, which are triggered by a *termination* of the Merger Agreement and payment of which will not hinder either party's ability to recover damages from a breach, is protected by the business judgment rule and the fees will not be struck down unless plaintiff demonstrates that their inclusion was the result of disloyal or grossly negligent acts.

Plaintiff argued below and argues again here that the proper analysis for determining the validity of the termination fee in section 9.2(c) of the merger agreement is to analyze it as a liquidated damages clause employing a test different from the business judgment rule. We agree.

The express language in section 9.2(e) of the agreement unambiguously states that the termination fee provisions "constitute liquidated damages and not a penalty." The Court of Chancery correctly found that liquidated damages, by definition, are damages paid in the event of a breach of a contract. While a breach of the merger agreement is not the only event that would trigger payment of the termination fee, the express language of section 9.2(c) states that a party's breach of section 7.2 (which provides that the parties are required to take all action necessary to convene a stockholders' meeting and use all commercially reasonable efforts to secure proxies to be voted in favor of the merger), coupled with other events, may trigger a party's obligation to pay the termination fee.

Thus, we find no compelling justification for treating the termination fee in this agreement as anything but a liquidated damages provision, in light of the express intent of the parties to have it so treated.

Analyzing the Validity of Liquidated Damages

In *Lee Builders v. Wells*, a case involving a liquidated damages provision equal to 5% of the purchase price in a contract for the sale of land, the Court of Chancery articulated the following two-prong test for analyzing the validity of the amount of liquidated damages: "Where the damages are uncertain and the amount agreed upon is reasonable, such an agreement will not be disturbed."

Plaintiff argues that the termination fee, if properly analyzed as liquidated damages, fails the *Lee Builders* test because both portions of the fee are punitive rather than compensatory, having nothing to do with actual damages but instead being designed to punish Bell Atlantic stockholders and the subsequent third-party acquirer if Bell Atlantic were ultimately to agree to merge with another entity. We find, however, that the termination fee safely passes both prongs of the *Lee Builders* test.

To be a valid liquidated damages provision under the first prong of the test, the damages that would result from a breach of the merger agreement must be uncertain or incapable of accurate calculation. Plaintiff does not attack the fee on this ground. Given the volatility and uncertainty in the telecommunications industry due to enactment of the Telecommunications Act of 1996 and the fast pace of technological change, one is led ineluctably to the conclusion that advance calculation of actual damages in this case approaches near impossibility.

Plaintiff contends, however, that the $550 million fee violates the second prong of the *Lee Builders* test, i.e., that it is not a reasonable forecast of actual damages, but rather a penalty intended to punish the stockholders of Bell Atlantic for not approving the merger. Plaintiff's attack is without force. Two factors are relevant to a determination of whether the amount fixed as liquidated damages is reasonable. The first factor is the anticipated loss by either party should the merger not occur. The second factor is the difficulty of calculating that loss: the greater the difficulty, the easier it is to show that the amount fixed was reasonable. In fact, where the level of uncertainty surrounding a given transaction is high, "[e]xperience has shown that . . . the award of a court or jury is no more likely to be exact compensation than is the advance estimate of the parties themselves." Thus, to fail the second prong of *Lee Builders,* the amount at issue must be unconscionable or not rationally related to any measure of damages a party might conceivably sustain.

Here, in the face of significant uncertainty, Bell Atlantic and NYNEX negotiated a fee amount and a fee structure that take into account the following: (a) the lost opportunity costs associated with a contract to deal exclusively with each other; (b) the expenses incurred during the course of negotiating the transaction; (c) the likelihood of a higher bid emerging for the acquisition of either party; and (d) the size of termination fees in other merger transactions. The parties then settled on the $550 million fee as reasonable given these factors. Moreover, the $550 million fee represents 2% of Bell Atlantic's market capitalization of $28 billion. This percentage falls well within the range of termination fees upheld as reasonable by the courts of this State. We hold that it is within a range of reasonableness and is not a penalty.

This is not strictly a business judgment rule case. If it were, the Court would not be applying a reasonableness test. . . .

Since we are applying the liquidated damages rubric, and not the business judgment rule, it is appropriate to apply a reasonableness test, which in some respects is analogous to some of the heightened scrutiny processes employed by our courts in certain other contexts. Even then, courts will not substitute their business judgment for that of the directors, but will examine the decision to assure that it is, "on balance, within a range of reasonableness." Is the liquidated damages provision here within the range of reasonableness? We believe that it is, given the undisputed record showing the size of the transaction, the analysis of the parties concerning lost opportunity costs, other expenses and the arms-length negotiations.

Plaintiff further argues that the termination fee provision was coercive. Plaintiff contends that (a) the stockholders never had an option to consider the merger agreement without the fee, and (b) regardless of what the stockholders thought of the merits of the transaction, the stockholders knew that if they voted against the transaction, they might well be imposing a $550 million penalty on their company. Plaintiff contends that the termination fee was so enormous that it "influenced" the vote. Finally, plaintiff argues that the fee provision was meant to be coercive because the drafters deliberately crafted the termination fees to make them applicable when Bell Atlantic's stockholders decline to approve the transaction as opposed to a termination resulting from causes other than the non-approval of the Bell Atlantic stockholders. We find plaintiff's arguments unpersuasive.

First, the Court of Chancery properly found that the termination fee was not egregiously large. Second, the mere fact that the stockholders knew that voting to disapprove the merger may result in activation of the termination fee does not by itself constitute stockholder coercion. Third, we find no authority to support plaintiff's proposition that a fee is coercive because it can be triggered upon stockholder disapproval of the merger agreement, but not upon the occurrence of other events resulting in termination of the agreement.

In *Williams v. Geier*, this Court enunciated the test for stockholder coercion. Wrongful coercion that nullifies a stockholder vote may exist "where the board or some other party takes actions which have the effect of causing the stockholders to vote in favor of the proposed transaction for some reason other than the merits of that transaction." But we also stated in *Williams v. Geier* that "[i]n the final analysis ... the determination of whether a particular stockholder vote has been robbed of its effectiveness by impermissible coercion depends on the facts of the case."

In this case, the proxy materials sent to stockholders described very clearly the terms of the termination fee. Since the termination fee was a valid, enforceable part of the merger agreement, disclosure of the fee provision to stockholders was proper and necessary. Plaintiff has not produced any evidence to show that the stockholders were forced into voting for the merger for reasons other than the merits of the transaction. To the contrary, it appears that the reciprocal termination fee provisions, drafted to protect both Bell Atlantic and NYNEX in the event the merger was not consummated, were an integral part of the merits of the transaction. Thus, we agree with the finding of the Court of Chancery that, although the termination fee provision may have influenced the stockholder vote, there were "no structurally or situationally coercive factors" that made an otherwise valid fee provision impermissibly coercive in this setting.

Conclusion

Because we find that actual damages in this case do not lend themselves to reasonably exact calculation, and because we further find that the $550 million termination fee was a reasonable forecast of damages and that the fee was neither coercive nor unconscionable, we hold that the fee is a valid liquidated damages provision in this merger agreement.

In light of the foregoing, we affirm, albeit on somewhat different grounds, the judgment of the Court of Chancery.

In subsequent cases, courts have regularly been called upon to analyze the validity of termination fees. In particular, courts have been asked to determine whether particular termination fee are so large as to run afoul of the intermediate standard. To date, courts have been extremely reluctant to specify an outer limit on the size of termination fees. In *Louisiana Municipal Police Employees' Retirement System v. Crawford,* 918 A.2d 1172 (Del. Ch. 2007), the Chancery Court, refusing to establish a bright line rule for termination fees, noted in dicta that the reasonableness of termination fees as well as any other lock-up would be subject to a highly fact-intensive review under *Unocal's* reasonableness analysis.

The parties make passionate arguments with respect to the appropriateness of the deal protections. Defendants maintain that these are no more than a customary set of devices employed regularly by market participants and their lawyers. Particularly with respect to the termination fee, this argument by custom fails to convince.

It is true, as defendants note, that this Court has upheld termination fees of greater than three percent of total deal value. [*Editor: The cases include examples mostly around 3%, with some at 3.5%, and one example, with expense reimbursement, coming to 4.167%.*]

Defendants attempt to build a bright line rule upon treacherous foundations, relying upon carefully-selected comments to contradict a clear principle of Delaware law. Our courts do not "presume that all business circumstances are identical or that there is any naturally occurring rate of deal protection, the deficit or excess of which will be less than economically optimal." . . . Rather, a court focuses upon "the real world risks and prospects confronting [directors] when they agreed to the deal protections." . . . That analysis will, by necessity, require the Court to consider a number of factors, including without limitation: the overall size of the termination fee, as well as its percentage value; the benefit to shareholders, including a premium (if any) that directors seek to protect; the absolute size of the transaction, as well as the relative size of the partners to the merger; the degree to which a counterparty found such protections to be crucial to the deal, bearing in mind differences in bargaining power; and the preclusive or coercive power of *all* deal protections included in a transaction, taken as a whole. The inquiry, by its very nature fact intensive, cannot be reduced to a mathematical equation. Though a "3% rule" for termination fees might be convenient for transaction planners, it is simply too blunt an instrument, too subject to abuse, for this Court to bless as a blanket rule.

Nor may plaintiffs rely upon some naturally-occurring rate or combination of deal protection measures, the existence of which will invoke the judicial blue pencil. Rather, plaintiffs must specifically demonstrate how a given set of deal protections operate in an unreasonable, preclusive, or coercive manner, under the standards of this Court's *Unocal* jurisprudence, to inequitably harm shareholders.

Nevertheless, because I conclude that plaintiffs are not subject to any irreparable harm so long as shareholders are given the opportunity to exercise a fully-informed vote, I need not address the specific deal protections at this stage in litigation.[26]

The "3% rule" that the court refers to in this opinion is a historical rule of thumb that transactional lawyers use that termination fees should be roughly 3% of the transaction value. However, with the refusal of Delaware courts to adopt this norm there has been some drift upwards from this norm in recent years. According to FactSet MergerMetrics in 2014, the average termination fee was 4.43% of transaction value while the median termination fee was 3.6% of transaction value.

H. *OMNICARE* AND THE FURTHER DEVELOPMENT OF *UNOCAL*

In 2003, the Delaware Supreme Court decided *Omnicare, Inc. v. NCS Healthcare, Inc.*, 818 A.2d 914 (Del. 2003), a decision which sent shock waves through the legal community for its seeming prohibition on lock-ups that might prevent other bidders from making a competing bid and its bright-line requirement that every deal include an effective fiduciary termination right.

NCS Healthcare was in bad financial condition, and had been seeking a suitor for several years. It was negotiating a merger with Genesis. Just before the board was getting ready to sign an agreement with Genesis, Omnicare made what the dissent characterized as a "conditional eleventh hour bid." There had been some previous negotiating history with both Omnicare and Genesis, but the Omnicare proposals were characterized by the dissent as being at "fire sale prices." The board tried to elicit better terms from both Genesis and Omnicare. With Omnicare, there were enough conditions that the board feared that the deal might not close. Genesis improved its terms considerably.

The board decided to do a deal with Genesis. It "resolved that the merger agreement and the transactions contemplated thereby were advisable and fair and in the best interest of all the NCS stakeholders. The NCS board further resolved to recommend the transaction to the stockholders for their approval and adoption." It signed a merger agreement with Genesis which had a "force the vote" provision under § 251(c) requiring NCS to hold a shareholder vote even if NCS's board subsequently recommended against the transaction. At Genesis's insistence, the agreement did not have a "fiduciary out," allowing NCS to terminate the merger agreement to accept a higher, competing offer. Also, two NCS shareholders, holding in the aggregate a majority of NCS's voting power, had agreed unconditionally to vote for the Genesis merger, giving an irrevocable proxy. Genesis required that this voting agreement

---

[26] *Louisiana Municipal Police Employee Retirement System v. Crawford*, 918 A.2d 1172, 1181 at n.10 (Del. Ch. 2007).

be entered into simultaneously with the merger agreement. The net effect of the "force the vote" provision and the voting agreement was that NCS was required to hold a shareholder vote and the vote was assured of being favorable to Genesis. In the parlance of M&A attorneys, this is known as a fully-locked up deal. NCS could not escape even if a higher competing bid emerged.

Sure enough, a higher bid did emerge. Omnicare bid a significantly higher price. Before the shareholder vote could take place, the board withdrew its recommendation in order to support the Omnicare bid, which it decided was a superior transaction. Omnicare sued in Delaware court to invalidate the merger agreement on fiduciary duty grounds, and also challenged the voting agreements.[27] The Chancery Court noted that force-the-vote provisions and shareholder voting agreements were legal. It held that the deal protection measures passed muster under Unocal. The Delaware Supreme Court reversed, stating:

> [w]e have concluded that, in the absence of an effective fiduciary out clause, those defensive measures are both preclusive and coercive. Therefore, we hold that those defensive measures are invalid and unenforceable. . . . Those tripartite defensive measures—the Section 251(c) provision, the voting agreements, and the absence of an effective fiduciary out clause—made it 'mathematically impossible' and 'realistically unattainable' for the Omnicare transaction or any other proposal to succeed, no matter how superior the proposal. . . . The defensive measures that protected the merger transaction are unenforceable not only because they are preclusive and coercive but, alternatively, they are unenforceable because they are invalid as they operate in this case. Given the specifically enforceable irrevocable voting agreements, the provision in the merger agreement requiring the board to submit the transaction for a shareholder vote and the omission of a fiduciary out clause in the merger agreement completely prevented the board from discharging its fiduciary responsibilities to the minority shareholders when Omnicare presented its superior transaction.[28]

At the time it was decided, and continuing afterwards, *Omnicare* was derided by some as one of the worst corporate law opinions since *Smith v. Van Gorkom* (a decision we discuss in the next Chapter). Indeed, the Delaware Supreme Court's decision was, quite unusually for the court, a

---

[27] The action was consolidated with an action brought by NCS shareholders, which sought to "invalidate the merger primarily on the ground that the directors of NCS violated their fiduciary duty of care in failing to establish an effective process designed to achieve the transaction that would produce the highest value for the NCS stockholders." *Omnicare, Inc. v. NCS Healthcare, Inc.*, 818 A.2d 914, 919 (Del. 2003). The Chancery Court opinion is *Omnicare, Inc. v. NCS Healthcare, Inc.*, 809 A.2d 1163 (Del. Ch. 2002).

[28] *Omnicare, Inc. v. NCS Healthcare, Inc.*, 818 A.2d 914, 936 (Del. 2003).

3–2 split decision, with a vigorous dissent written by Chief Justice Myron Steele. The essence of Chief Justice Steele's objection was that bidders are reasonable in wanting some deal certainty, and boards should sometimes be allowed to give it to them—especially when the alternative to granting a buyer deal certainty is losing a desirable deal.

So contentious was the *Omnicare* opinion that Chief Justice Steele remarked at a conference not long after that the opinion would likely have the life span of a "fruit fly."[29] Now all these years later, practitioners have learned to live with—or more precisely, work around—the *Omnicare* decision. Deal protections are perhaps as formidable as they have ever been. Following the opinion, the courts could have taken *Omnicare* as a cue to move the needle on a long-standing debate about the proper limits on board action, but they collectively decided against that course of action. While the Supreme Court has not had an opportunity to directly revisit the issue, the Chancery Court has taken the opportunities that have been regularly presented to it to peel back the ruling's effect and distinguish the facts before it from *Omnicare*'s holding. In recent years, as practitioners have introduced transactional innovations in response to *Omnicare* that limit its effect, the courts have regularly blessed them.

Transactional innovations developed and used since *Omnicare* pay lip service to the ruling by technically complying with a narrow interpretation of *Unocal*'s requirements while still ensuring the maximum amount of certainty for buyers as possible. Among the techniques validated by the Chancery Court have been an agreement between a buyer and controlling shareholder that the agreement would be terminated if there were a higher bid, but that "the shareholder could not sell to another bidder for 18 months" and a merger agreement entered into by the company and, the same day, approved by the shareholders by written consent.[30] Another case validating the quick delivery of written consents in conjunction with the signing of a merger agreement was *In re OPENLANE, Inc. Shareholders Litigation*.[31] Indeed, where controlling or majority shareholders are easily accessible to the seller's board, sellers can eschew a shareholder meeting and substitute an action by written consent pursuant to § 228. Unlike statutory voting requirements, there is

---

[29] "So while I don't suggest that you rip the *Omnicare* pages out of your notebook . . . I do suggest that there's the possibility, one could argue, that the decision has the life expectancy of a fruit fly." *See* David Marcus, *Man of Steele*, D & O ADVISOR, Sept. 2004 at 16 (quoting Justice Steele).

[30] The cases are, respectively, *Orman v. Cullen*, 794 A.2d 5 (Del. Ch. 2002), and *Optima International of Miami v. WCI Steel, Inc.*, C.A. No. 3833–VCL (Del. Ch. June 27, 2008). *See generally* Steven M. Davidoff, *The Long, Slow Death of Omnicare*, N.Y. TIMES, August 28, 2008, available at http://dealbook.nytimes.com/2008/08/28/the-long-slow-death-of-omnicare/?module=ArrowsNav&contentCollection=Business%20Day&action=keypress&region=FixedLeft&pgtype=Blogs.

[31] *In re* OPENLANE, Inc. S'holder Litig., No 6849 VCN, 2011 WL 4599662 (Dcl. Ch. Sept.30, 2011).

no required notice prior to seeking written consent. Therefore, it is possible to sign a merger agreement and then, nearly simultaneously, to receive shareholder approval via written consent for the merger agreement. By this action, the board intends immediate or near immediate delivery of shareholder consent to head off any potential second bid before such a bid has a chance to appear. Indeed, shareholders typically deliver their consents before the transaction is announced to the public. As a consequence, the quick consent strategy formally complies with the requirements of *Omnicare* that the transaction include an effective fiduciary out without giving up much in the way of transactional certainty.

Notwithstanding the Chancery Court's validation of the quick consent strategy, the strategy is preclusive by design. As part of the strategy, buyers negotiate the right to terminate the merger agreement without paying a fee in the event the board does not deliver consents sufficient to approve the agreement within a designated window, typically 24 hours. In such a situation, shareholders are under extreme pressure to consent quickly to the merger agreement or risk losing the transaction altogether. The board will present minority shareholders who are likely not at the negotiating table with a *fait accompli* after the acquirer secures written consents sufficient to approve the merger agreement. A subsequent bid might be made during the interim period between delivery of consents and closing. At that stage, however, unless the seller's board has negotiated a right to terminate the merger following shareholder approval and before closing, the transaction may be practically immune to a topping bid.

In the years since *Omnicare*, there have been a series of subtle doctrinal changes that have tended to reduce *Unocal's* scope. It appears that, having given itself the power to review deal protections in merger transactions, the court has since backed away from an aggressive application of that oversight. Rather than an inquiry into the substance of threats presented to a corporation followed by a substantive review of board actions taken in response, *Unocal* has been largely supplanted by what one might understand as a preliminary inquiry into the competitive posture of a transaction. Where transactions are not subject to multiple bids, courts will be highly deferential to board decisions to grant buyers deal protections. If there are multiple bids, courts will be less deferential, looking more closely at a board's decision to protect a preferred transaction to the exclusion of other bids.

Because of this narrowing of *Unocal's* application, the courts have been largely left to focus only on *Unocal's* coercion prong when examining deal protection measures. Coercive deal protections that implicate statutory obligations of the board and shareholders are, by now, the only deal protection measures likely to run afoul of *Unocal*. This approach to deal protections limits *Unocal*'s scope dramatically and generates a troublesome incentive for dealmakers to innovate and deploy deal protection measures that fall just short of *Omnicare*'s bright-line requirement of an effective fiduciary termination right, but are still powerful enough to deter second bids.

QUESTIONS

Unocal Questions:

1. According to the court, how much was Mesa's second-tier consideration (i.e., the "junk bonds") worth? On what basis did the court make this assessment? How would an investment banker make this assessment? How would a shareholder make this assessment?

2. What were the Unocal shareholders going to get in exchange for their shares if they tendered to Unocal? How was Unocal going to finance its self-tender?

3 How did Unocal's defense work?

4. Why did Unocal's bankers tell them to remove the Mesa Purchase Condition?

5. How would Unocal be affected by the exchange offer? Who would be better off? Who would be worse off?

Moran Questions:

1. Describe how the poison pill in *Moran* worked. What kind of plan was it?

2. What is the statutory source of the board's authority to craft the rights described in the *Moran* poison pill?

3. What role did the proxy contest play in the court's decision approving use of the poison pill in *Moran*?

4. If a board adopts a poison pill "under a blue sky" when no threat is present, will that pill ever be subject to review under *Unocal*?

Unitrin Questions:

1. How does the Delaware Supreme Court's approach to the *Unocal* standard compare to that of the Chancery Court?

2. Describe the defenses Unitrin adopted in response to the American General offer.

3. The Chancellor in *Unitrin* described the threat faced by Unitrin as "mild," how did the Delaware Supreme Court react to that characterization?

4. How does the Delaware Supreme Court define "substantive coercion" and how does that compare to the way that term is used by Professors Gilson and Kraakman?

Airgas **Questions:**

1.   What did the suite of takeover defenses in place for Airgas look like? Describe how each of them worked alone and in combination to deter an unwanted takeover.

2.   What was the nature of the "threat" identified by the Airgas board?

3.   Is a board ever justified in saying "never" to a takeover offer? Why or why not?[32]

Brazen **Questions:**

1.   Describe the termination fee adopted by the parties in *Brazen*. How did it work?

2.   Compare the liquidated damages approach the court took to rationalizing the termination fee to an analysis of the same fee under *Unocal*. Are the two approaches consistent or inconsistent?

3.   Does the court's reasoning in *Brazen* suggest there is a limit to the size of a termination fee? If so, how large?

Omnicare **Questions:**

1.   When the board of NCS agreed to do a deal with Genesis, it agreed to include deal protection measures in the merger agreement. Why are such deal protections subject to *Unocal*'s intermediate scrutiny? Why did Revlon not apply to the NCS's board decision to sell to Genesis?

2.   Describe the defenses the board of NCS adopted to protect its deal with Genesis. How did they work to prevent a bid by Omnicare?

3.   The *Omnicare* opinion has been derided by many. Why might one fairly be critical of the court's opinion?

PROBLEM

Beta Corporation has 95 million shares outstanding, and that the market price is $20/share. Alpha Co., run by Fred Jones, who Beta's management would like to see acquire Beta, makes an offer to buy 100% of Beta for $35/share. Beta's board accepts the offer; Beta and Alpha make a deal pursuant to which Alpha will buy Beta for $35/share. The deal includes an option to buy 5 million shares at the then-market price ($20/share).

The market price of Beta's stock goes up to reflect Alpha's offer. Assume it goes up to $34/share. A second bidder, competing with Alpha, comes along and offers more, assume $40/share. How much will Jones pay for all of Beta's stock if Alpha succeeds in buying Beta? How much would the second bidder have to pay to acquire Beta? What is the result for Alpha if the new bidder buys Beta? Does the Beta's deal with Alpha need the approval of Beta's shareholders? If so, why? If not, why not?

---

[32] For an example of a "just say never" defense used by Mylan Pharmaceuticals to fight off a hostile bid from Teva Pharmaceuticals, albeit under the laws of the Netherlands, *see* Steven Davidoff Solomon. *Mylan's Too Harsh Takeover Defense*, N.Y TIMES, May 18, 2015, available at http://www.nytimes.com/2015/05/09/business/dealbook/mylans-too-harsh-takeover-defense.html.

CHAPTER XVII

THE SALE PROCESS

■ ■ ■

In the previous two Chapters, we examined the board's decision to reject a takeover offer. In this Chapter and the next, we discuss the board's fiduciary duties as to both the decision to sell a corporation and the process by which the sale is to be conducted. When a disinterested and independent board decides to engage in a merger or a sale of all or part of the corporation, courts will generally give that decision business judgment deference: courts will presume that directors made the decision on an informed basis, in good faith, and in the best interests of the corporation. But, as we will see in this Chapter, the manner in which the sale is made is nevertheless subject to considerable scrutiny.

In this Chapter, we discuss the board's duty of care in the sales process. The cases below, along with the *Unocal* case, form part of the background against which the *Revlon* doctrine was developed. *Revlon* governs the board process as to a sale of control or break up of the company. We discuss *Revlon* in the next Chapter.

A. *SMITH v. VAN GORKOM* AND THE BOARD'S DUTY OF CARE

In 1985, during the height of the 1980s takeover boom, the Delaware Supreme Court decided *Smith v. Van Gorkom*. *Van Gorkom* was the first in a set of cases, together with *Unocal, Moran,* and *Revlon,* which make up the core of Delaware's M&A and takeover jurisprudence. In *Van Gorkom,* the court struggled with its existing vocabulary—business judgment deference, on the one hand, and heightened scrutiny for entire fairness, on the other—to adjudicate a situation that did not easily fit into the then-traditional categories.

At the time it was decided, the result in *Van Gorkom* was highly controversial. In a court that typically enjoys a norm of unanimity, *Van Gorkom* was an unusual 3–2 split decision. While *Van Gorkom* is typically studied as an example of a board failing to live up to its obligations under the duty of care, it also provides guidance as to how a board must proceed in selling a company. The ruling as to what the duty of care requires is of limited legal viability: soon after the case, the Delaware legislature responded by eliminating directors' monetary liability for breaches of the duty of care (although equitable relief for such breaches is still available).

But the sale procedures discussed in the opinion remain highly influential. As we have discussed in Chapter X.C.3 in our review of fairness opinions, Van Gorkom continues to influence selling companies to get such opinions. In other respects as well, companies take care to "abide by" *Van Gorkom*'s "dictates" as to what the duty of care requires, even though the directors no longer face monetary liability if they do not abide by that duty.

SMITH V. VAN GORKOM

Supreme Court of Delaware
488 A.2d 858 (1985)

HORSEY, JUSTICE (for the majority):

[*Editor: The case is a class action in which Trans Union shareholders were claiming that the directors violated their fiduciary duties in connection with TransUnion's $55 cash-out merger transaction. The shareholders were seeking rescission or damages.*]

Trans Union was a publicly-traded, diversified holding company, the principal earnings of which were generated by its railcar leasing business. During the period here involved, the Company had a cash flow of hundreds of millions of dollars annually. However, the Company had difficulty in generating sufficient taxable income to offset increasingly large investment tax credits (ITCs). Accelerated depreciation deductions had decreased available taxable income against which to offset accumulating ITCs. The Company took these deductions, despite their effect on usable ITCs, because the rental price in the railcar leasing market had already impounded the purported tax savings. [*Editor: This situation, in which the company could not take full advantage of tax credits, was continuing; one solution discussed and ultimately pursued (via the transaction at issue in this case) was to sell Trans Union to a company with significant taxable income against which the credits could be used.*]

. . .

On the record before us, we must conclude that the Board of Directors did not reach an informed business judgment on September 20, 1980 in voting to "sell" the Company for $55 per share pursuant to the Pritzker cash-out merger proposal. Our reasons, in summary, are as follows:

The directors (1) did not adequately inform themselves as to Van Gorkom's role in forcing the "sale" of the Company and in establishing the per share purchase price [*Editor: Van Gorkom was the Chairman and CEO of Trans Union.*]; (2) were uninformed as to the intrinsic value of the Company; and (3) given these circumstances, at a minimum, were grossly negligent in approving the "sale" of the Company upon two hours' consideration, without prior notice, and without the exigency of a crisis or emergency.

. . . [T]he Board based its September 20 decision to approve the cash-out merger primarily on Van Gorkom's representations. None of the directors, other than Van Gorkom and Chelberg [President and Chief Operating Officer], had any prior knowledge that the purpose of the meeting was to propose a cash-out merger of Trans Union. No members of Senior Management were present, other than Chelberg, Romans [Chief Financial Officer] and Peterson [Controller]; and the latter two had only learned of the proposed sale an hour earlier. Both general counsel Moore and former general counsel Browder attended the meeting, but were equally uninformed as to the purpose of the meeting and the documents to be acted upon.

Without any documents before them concerning the proposed transaction, the members of the Board were required to rely entirely upon Van Gorkom's 20-minute oral presentation of the proposal. No written summary of the terms of the merger was presented; the directors were given no documentation to support the adequacy of $55 price per share for sale of the Company; and the Board had before it nothing more than Van Gorkom's statement of his understanding of the substance of an agreement which he admittedly had never read, nor which any member of the Board had ever seen. [*Editor: The portion of the opinion describing the origins of the deal is omitted. In brief, Van Gorkom decided on his own to meet with Pritzker, "a well-known corporate takeover specialist and social acquaintance," (the Pritzker family owns, among other things, the Hyatt hotel chain) and had Peterson do some preliminary computations "to calculate the feasibility of a leveraged buy-out at an assumed price per share of $55." Van Gorkom worked a bit more with Peterson on numbers, and proposed a deal to Pritzker at $55/share. Among Van Gorkom's motivations may have been that he had 75,000 shares of Trans Union and was nearing retirement age.*]

Under 8 Del.C. § 141(e), "directors are fully protected in relying in good faith on reports made by officers." . . . The term "report" has been liberally construed to include reports of informal personal investigations by corporate officers, . . . However, there is no evidence that any "report," as defined under § 141(e), concerning the Pritzker proposal, was presented to the Board on September 20. Van Gorkom's oral presentation of his understanding of the terms of the proposed Merger Agreement, which he had not seen, and Romans' brief oral statement of his preliminary study regarding the feasibility of a leveraged buy-out of Trans Union do not qualify as § 141(e) "reports" for these reasons: The former lacked substance because Van Gorkom was basically uninformed as to the essential provisions of the very document about which he was talking. Romans' statement was irrelevant to the issues before the Board since it did not purport to be a valuation study. At a minimum for a report to enjoy the status conferred by § 141(e), it must be pertinent to the subject matter upon which a board is called to act, and otherwise be entitled to good faith, not blind, reliance. Considering all of the surrounding circumstances—hastily calling the meeting without prior notice of its subject matter, the proposed sale of the Company without any prior consideration of the issue or necessity therefor, the urgent time constraints imposed by Pritzker, and the total absence of any documentation whatsoever—the directors were duty bound to make reasonable inquiry of Van Gorkom and Romans, and if they had done so, the inadequacy of that upon which they now claim to have relied would have been apparent.

The defendants rely on the following factors to sustain the Trial Court's finding that the Board's decision was an informed one: (1) the magnitude of the premium or spread between the $55 Pritzker offering price and Trans Union's current market price of $38 per share; (2) the amendment of the Agreement as submitted on September 20 to permit the Board to accept any better offer during the "market test" period; (3) the collective experience and expertise of the Board's "inside" and "outside" directors; and (4) their reliance on Brennan's legal advice that the directors might be sued if they rejected the Pritzker proposal. We discuss each of these grounds *seriatim:*

(1)

A substantial premium may provide one reason to recommend a merger, but in the absence of other sound valuation information, the fact of a premium alone does not provide an adequate basis upon which to assess the fairness of an offering price. Here, the judgment reached as to the adequacy of the premium was based on a comparison between the historically depressed Trans Union market price and the amount of the Pritzker offer. Using market price as a basis for concluding that the premium adequately reflected the true value of the Company was a clearly faulty, indeed fallacious, premise, as the defendants' own evidence demonstrates.

The record is clear that before September 20, Van Gorkom and other members of Trans Union's Board knew that the market had consistently undervalued the worth of Trans Union's stock, despite steady increases in the Company's operating income in the seven years preceding the merger. The Board related this occurrence in large part to Trans Union's inability to use its ITCs as previously noted. Van Gorkom testified that he did not believe the market price accurately reflected Trans Union's true worth; and several of the directors testified that, as a general rule, most chief executives think that the market undervalues their companies' stock. Yet, on September 20, Trans Union's Board apparently believed that the market stock price accurately reflected the value of the Company for the purpose of determining the adequacy of the premium for its sale.

In the Proxy Statement, however, the directors reversed their position. There, they stated that, although the earnings prospects for Trans Union were "excellent," they found no basis for believing that this would be reflected in future stock prices. With regard to past trading, the Board stated that the prices at which the Company's common stock had traded in recent years did not reflect the "inherent" value of the Company. But having referred to the "inherent" value of Trans Union, the directors ascribed no number to it. Moreover, nowhere did they disclose that they had no basis on which to fix "inherent" worth beyond an impressionistic reaction to the premium over market and an unsubstantiated belief that the value of the assets was "significantly greater" than book value. By their own admission they could not rely on the stock price as an accurate measure of value. Yet, also by their own admission, the Board members assumed that Trans Union's market price was adequate to serve as a basis upon which to assess the adequacy of the premium for purposes of the September 20 meeting.

The parties do not dispute that a publicly-traded stock price is solely a measure of the value of a minority position and, thus, market price represents only the value of a single share. Nevertheless, on September 20, the Board assessed the adequacy of the premium over market, offered by Pritzker, solely by comparing it with Trans Union's current and historical stock price.

Indeed, as of September 20, the Board had no other information on which to base a determination of the intrinsic value of Trans Union as a going concern. As of September 20, the Board had made no evaluation of the Company designed to value the entire enterprise, nor had the Board ever previously considered selling the Company or consenting to a buy-out merger. Thus, the adequacy of a premium is indeterminate unless it is assessed in terms of other competent and sound valuation information that reflects the value of the particular business.

Despite the foregoing facts and circumstances, there was no call by the Board, either on September 20 or thereafter, for any valuation study or documentation of the $55 price per share as a measure of the fair value of the Company in a cash-out context. It is undisputed that the major asset of Trans Union was its cash flow. Yet, at no time did the Board call for a valuation study taking into account that highly significant element of the Company's assets.

We do not imply that an outside valuation study is essential to support an informed business judgment; nor do we state that fairness opinions by independent investment bankers are required as a matter of law. Often insiders familiar with the business of a going concern are in a better position than are outsiders to gather relevant information; and under appropriate circumstances, such directors may be fully protected in relying in good faith upon the valuation reports of their management. *See* 8 Del.C. § 141(e).

Here, the record establishes that the Board did not request its Chief Financial Officer, Romans, to make any valuation study or review of the proposal to determine the adequacy of $55 per share for sale of the Company. On the record before us: The Board rested on Romans' elicited response that the $55 figure was within a "fair price range" within the context of a leveraged buy-out. No director sought any further information from Romans. No director asked him why he put $55 at the bottom of his range. No director asked Romans for any details as to his study, the reason why it had been undertaken or its depth. No director asked to see the study; and no director asked Romans whether Trans Union's finance department could do a fairness study within the remaining 36-hour period available under the Pritzker offer.

Had the Board, or any member, made an inquiry of Romans, he presumably would have responded as he testified: that his calculations were rough and preliminary; and, that the study was not designed to determine the fair value of the Company, but rather to assess the feasibility of a leveraged buy-out financed by the Company's projected cash flow, making certain assumptions as to the purchaser's borrowing needs. Romans would have presumably also informed the Board of his view, and the widespread view of Senior Management, that the timing of the offer was wrong and the offer inadequate. The record also establishes that the Board accepted without scrutiny Van Gorkom's representation as to the fairness of the $55 price per share for sale of the Company—a subject that the Board had never previously considered. The Board thereby failed to discover that Van Gorkom had suggested the $55 price to Pritzker and, most crucially, that Van Gorkom had arrived at the $55 figure based on calculations designed solely to determine the feasibility of a leveraged buy-out. No questions were raised either as to the tax implications of a cash-out merger or how the price for the one million share option granted Pritzker was calculated. [*Editor: The opinion contains more details as to the haste in which the transaction was conceived and pursued, how Van Gorkom did much of the early negotiation without informing the board, and that Pritzker imposed very short deadlines.*]

We do not say that the Board of Directors was not entitled to give some credence to Van Gorkom's representation that $55 was an adequate or fair price. Under § 141(e), the directors were entitled to rely upon their chairman's opinion of value and adequacy, provided that such opinion was reached on a sound basis. Here, the issue is whether the directors informed themselves as to all information that was reasonably available to them. Had they done so, they would have learned of the source and derivation of the $55 price and could not reasonably have relied thereupon in good faith.

None of the directors, Management or outside, were investment bankers or financial analysts. Yet the Board did not consider recessing the meeting until a later hour that day (or requesting an extension of Pritzker's Sunday evening deadline) to give it time to elicit more information as to the sufficiency of the offer, either from inside Management (in particular Romans) or from Trans Union's own investment banker, Salomon Brothers, whose Chicago specialist in merger and acquisitions was known to the Board and familiar with Trans Union's affairs.

Thus, the record compels the conclusion that on September 20 the Board lacked valuation information adequate to reach an informed business judgment as to the fairness of $55 per share for sale of the Company.

(2)

This brings us to the post-September 20 "market test" upon which the defendants ultimately rely to confirm the reasonableness of their September 20 decision to accept the Pritzker proposal. In this connection, the directors present a two-part argument: (a) that by making a "market test" of Pritzker's $55 per share offer a condition of their September 20 decision to accept his offer, they cannot be found to have acted impulsively or in an uninformed manner on September 20; and (b) that the adequacy of the $17 premium for sale of the Company was conclusively established over the following 90 to 120 days by the most reliable evidence available—the marketplace. Thus, the defendants impliedly contend that the "market test" eliminated the need for the Board to perform any other form of fairness test either on September 20, or thereafter.

Again, the facts of record do not support the defendants' argument. There is no evidence: (a) that the Merger Agreement was effectively amended to give the Board freedom to put Trans Union up for auction sale to the highest bidder; or (b) that a public auction was in fact permitted to occur. The minutes of the Board meeting make no reference to any of this. Indeed, the record compels the conclusion that the directors had no rational basis for expecting that a market test was attainable, given the terms of the Agreement as executed during the evening of September 20. We rely upon the following facts which are essentially uncontradicted:

The Merger Agreement, specifically identified as that originally presented to the Board on September 20, has never been produced by the defendants, notwithstanding the plaintiffs' several demands for production before as well as during trial. No acceptable explanation of this failure to produce documents has been given to either the Trial Court or this Court. Significantly, neither the defendants nor their counsel have made the affirmative representation that this critical document has been produced. Thus, the Court is deprived of the best evidence on which to judge the merits of the defendants' position as to the care and attention which they gave to the terms of the Agreement on September 20.

Van Gorkom states that the Agreement as submitted incorporated the ingredients for a market test by authorizing Trans Union to receive competing offers over the next 90-day period. However, he concedes that the Agreement barred Trans Union from actively soliciting such offers and from furnishing to interested parties any information about the Company other than that already in the public domain. Whether the original Agreement of September 20 went so far as to authorize Trans Union to receive competitive proposals is arguable. The defendants' unexplained failure to produce and identify the original Merger Agreement permits the logical inference that the instrument would not support their assertions in this regard. It is a well-established principle that the production of weak evidence when strong is, or should have been, available can lead only to the conclusion that the strong would have been adverse. Van Gorkom, conceding that he never read the Agreement, stated that he was relying upon his understanding that, under corporate law, directors always have an inherent right, as well as a fiduciary duty, to accept a better offer notwithstanding an existing contractual commitment by the Board.

The defendant directors assert that they "insisted" upon including two amendments to the Agreement, thereby permitting a market test: (1) to give Trans Union the right to accept a better offer; and (2) to reserve to Trans Union the right to distribute proprietary information on the Company to alternative bidders. Yet, the defendants concede that they did not seek to amend the Agreement to permit Trans Union to solicit competing offers.

Several of Trans Union's outside directors resolutely maintained that the Agreement as submitted was approved on the understanding that, "if we got a better deal, we had a right to take it." Director Johnson so testified; but he then added, "And if they didn't put that in the agreement, then the management did not carry out the conclusion of the Board. And I just don't know whether they did or not." The only clause in the Agreement as finally executed to which the defendants can point as "keeping the door open" is the following underlined statement found in subparagraph (a) of section 2.03 of the Merger Agreement as executed:

The Board of Directors shall recommend to the shareholders of Trans Union that they approve and adopt the Merger Agreement ('the shareholders' approval') and to use its best efforts to obtain the requisite votes therefor. *GL acknowledges that Trans Union directors may have a competing fiduciary obligation to the shareholders under certain circumstances.*

Clearly, this language on its face cannot be construed as incorporating either of the two "conditions" described above: either the right to accept a better offer or the right to distribute proprietary information to third parties. The logical witness for the defendants to call to confirm their construction of this clause of the Agreement would have been Trans Union's outside attorney, James Brennan. The defendants' failure, without explanation, to call this witness again permits the logical inference that his testimony would not have been helpful to them. The further fact that the directors adjourned, rather than recessed, the meeting without incorporating in the Agreement these important "conditions" further weakens the defendants' position. As has been noted, nothing in the Board's Minutes supports these claims. No reference to either of the so-called "conditions" or of Trans Union's reserved right to test the market appears in any notes of the Board meeting or in the Board Resolution accepting the Pritzker offer or in the Minutes of the meeting itself. That evening, in the midst of a formal party which he hosted for the opening of the Chicago Lyric Opera, Van Gorkom executed the Merger Agreement without he or any other member of the Board having read the instruments.

The defendants attempt to downplay the significance of the prohibition against Trans Union's actively soliciting competing offers by arguing that the directors "understood that the entire financial community would know that Trans Union was for sale upon the announcement of the Pritzker offer, and anyone desiring to make a better offer was free to do so." Yet, the press release issued on September 22, with the authorization of the Board, stated that Trans Union had entered into "definitive agreements" with the Pritzkers; and the press release did not even disclose Trans Union's limited right to receive and accept higher offers. Accompanying this press release was a further public announcement that Pritzker had been granted an option to purchase at any time one million shares of Trans Union's capital stock at 75 cents above the then-current price per share. [*Editor: Such an agreement is called a "stock lock-up." Pritzker got this stock lock-up after saying that he did not want to be a "stalking horse," simply serving to attract other, higher bids. If someone other than Pritzker was the successful bidder, that bidder would presumably have to pay a higher price to acquire the Trans Union shares than Pritzker had paid to acquire his shares. If Pritzker did not succeed in buying Trans Union, he would be compensated because the other bidder would have to buy the shares Pritzker acquired under the lock-up (as well as Pritzker's other shares) at that bidder's higher price. Moreover, because another bidder would have to pay Pritzker as well as the other Trans Union shareholders, the other bidder's cost to acquire Trans Union would be considerably larger than Pritzker's, making it more likely there would not be other bids.]*

Thus, notwithstanding what several of the outside directors later claimed to have "thought" occurred at the meeting, the record compels the conclusion that Trans Union's Board had no rational basis to conclude on September 20 or in the days immediately following, that the Board's acceptance of Pritzker's offer was conditioned on (1) a "market test" of the offer; and (2) the Board's right to withdraw from the Pritzker Agreement and accept any higher offer received before the shareholder meeting.

(3)

The directors' unfounded reliance on both the premium and the market test as the basis for accepting the Pritzker proposal undermines the defendants' remaining contention that the Board's collective experience and sophistication was a sufficient basis for finding that it reached its September 20 decision with informed, reasonable deliberation. [In another case,] the Court of Chancery preliminary enjoined a board's sale of stock of its wholly-owned subsidiary for an alleged grossly inadequate price. It did so based on a finding that the business judgment rule had been pierced for failure of management to give its board "the opportunity to make a reasonable and reasoned decision."

The Court there reached this result notwithstanding the board's sophistication and experience; the company's need of immediate cash; and the board's need to act promptly due to the impact of an energy crisis on the value of the underlying assets being sold—all of its subsidiary's oil and gas interests. The Court found those factors denoting competence to be outweighed by evidence of gross negligence; that management in effect sprang the deal on the board by negotiating the asset sale without informing the board; that the buyer intended to "force a quick decision" by the board; that the board meeting was called on only one-and-a-half days' notice; that its outside directors were not notified of the meeting's purpose; that during a meeting spanning "a couple of hours" a sale of assets worth $480 million was approved; and that the Board failed to obtain a *current* appraisal of its oil and gas interests. The analogy of [that case] to the case at bar is significant.

(4)

Part of the defense is based on a claim that the directors relied on legal advice rendered at the September 20 meeting by James Brennan, Esquire, who was present at Van Gorkom's request. . . .

Several defendants testified that Brennan advised them that Delaware law did not require a fairness opinion or an outside valuation of the Company before the Board could act on the Pritzker proposal. If given, the advice was correct. However, that did not end the matter. Unless the directors had before them adequate information regarding the intrinsic value of the Company, upon which a proper exercise of business judgment could be made, mere advice of this type is meaningless; and, given this record of the defendants' failures, it constitutes no defense here.

* * *

We conclude that Trans Union's Board was grossly negligent in that it failed to act with informed reasonable deliberation in agreeing to the Pritzker merger proposal on September 20; and we further conclude that the Trial Court erred as a matter of law in failing to address that question before determining whether the directors' later conduct was sufficient to cure its initial error.

A second claim is that counsel advised the Board it would be subject to lawsuits if it rejected the $55 per share offer. It is, of course, a fact of corporate life that today when faced with difficult or sensitive issues, directors often are subject to suit, irrespective of the decisions they make. However, counsel's mere acknowledgement of this circumstance cannot be rationally translated into a justification for a board permitting itself to be stampeded into a patently unadvised act. While suit might result from the rejection of a merger or tender offer, Delaware law makes clear that a board acting within the ambit of the business judgment rule faces no ultimate liability. Thus, we cannot conclude that the mere threat of litigation, acknowledged by counsel, constitutes either legal advice or any valid basis upon which to pursue an uninformed course.

[*The court also ruled that the majority shareholder vote approving the transaction did not ratify it because the proxy statement on the basis of which the shareholders voted on the transaction had material deficiencies.*]

* * *

REVERSED and REMANDED for proceedings consistent herewith.

McNEILLY, JUSTICE, dissenting:

The majority opinion reads like an advocate's closing address to a hostile jury. And I say that not lightly. Throughout the opinion great emphasis is directed only to the negative, with nothing more than lip service granted the positive aspects of this case. In my opinion Chancellor Marvel (retired) should have been affirmed. The Chancellor's opinion was the product of well reasoned conclusions, based upon a sound deductive process, clearly supported by the evidence and entitled to deference in this appeal. Because of my diametrical opposition to all evidentiary conclusions of the majority, I respectfully dissent.

It would serve no useful purpose, particularly at this late date, for me to dissent at great length. I restrain myself from doing so, but feel compelled to at least point out what I consider to be the most glaring deficiencies in the majority opinion. The majority has spoken and has effectively said that Trans Union's Directors have been the victims of a "fast shuffle" by Van Gorkom and Pritzker. That is the beginning of the majority's comedy of errors. The first and most important error made is the majority's assessment of the directors' knowledge of the affairs of Trans Union and their combined ability to act in this situation under the protection of the business judgment rule.

Trans Union's Board of Directors consisted of ten men, five of whom were "inside" directors and five of whom were "outside" directors. The "inside" directors were Van Gorkom, Chelberg, Bonser, William B. Browder, Senior Vice-President—Law, and Thomas P. O'Boyle, Senior Vice-President—Administration. At the time the merger was proposed the inside five directors had collectively been employed by the Company for 116 years and had 68 years of combined experience as directors. The "outside" directors were A.W. Wallis, William B. Johnson, Joseph B. Lanterman, Graham J. Morgan and Robert W. Reneker. With the exception of Wallis, these were all chief executive officers of Chicago based corporations that were at least as large as Trans Union. The five "outside" directors had 78 years of combined experience as chief executive officers, and 53 years cumulative service as Trans Union directors.

The inside directors wear their badge of expertise in the corporate affairs of Trans Union on their sleeves. But what about the outsiders? Dr. Wallis is or was an economist and math statistician, a professor of economics at Yale University, dean of the graduate school of business at the University of Chicago, and Chancellor of the University of Rochester. Dr. Wallis had been on the Board of Trans Union since 1962. He also was on the Board of Bausch & Lomb, Kodak, Metropolitan Life Insurance Company, Standard Oil and others.

William B. Johnson is a University of Pennsylvania law graduate, President of Railway Express until 1966, Chairman and Chief Executive of I.C. Industries Holding Company, and member of Trans Union's Board since 1968.

Joseph Lanterman, a Certified Public Accountant, is or was President and Chief Executive of American Steel, on the Board of International Harvester, Peoples Energy, Illinois Bell Telephone, Harris Bank and Trust Company, Kemper Insurance Company and a director of Trans Union for four years.

Graham Morgan is a chemist, was Chairman and Chief Executive Officer of U.S. Gypsum, and in the 17 and 18 years prior to the Trans Union transaction had been involved in 31 or 32 corporate takeovers.

Robert Reneker attended University of Chicago and Harvard Business Schools. He was President and Chief Executive of Swift and Company, director of Trans Union since 1971, and member of the Boards of seven other corporations including U.S. Gypsum and the Chicago Tribune.

Directors of this caliber are not ordinarily taken in by a "fast shuffle." I submit they were not taken into this multi-million dollar corporate transaction without being fully informed and aware of the state of the art as it pertained to the entire corporate panoroma [sic] of Trans Union. True, even directors such as these, with their business acumen, interest and expertise, can go astray. I do not believe that to be the case here. These men knew Trans Union like the back of their hands and were more than well qualified to make on the spot informed business judgments concerning the affairs of Trans Union including a 100% sale of the corporation. Lest we forget, the corporate world of then and now operates on what is so aptly referred to as "the fast track". These men were at the time an integral part of that world, all professional business men, not intellectual figureheads.

The majority of this Court holds that the Board's decision, reached on September 20, 1980, to approve the merger was not the product of an informed business judgment, that the Board's subsequent efforts to amend the Merger Agreement and take other curative action were legally and factually ineffectual, and that the Board did not deal with complete candor with the shareholders by failing to disclose all material facts, which they knew or should have known, before securing the shareholders' approval of the merger. I disagree.

The Delaware Supreme Court's decision in *Smith v. Van Gorkom* was controversial, especially since it held that the directors of Trans Union would be personally liable "to the extent that the fair value of Trans Union exceed[ed] $55 per share." The case was subsequently settled, with the directors being assessed $23.5 million in damages. However, insurance paid $10 million of the amount and Pritzker agreed to pay the remainder, despite having no legal obligation to do so.

That directors could be found personally liable on these facts sent fear through the corporate community, as boards worried about the huge potential liability exposure from making a decision to sell a company. In the wake of the decision, Professor Daniel Fischel wrote that it was "one of the worst decisions in the history of corporate law." In this excerpt, he explained what he viewed as the perverse and problematic effects of the decision:

THE BUSINESS JUDGMENT RULE AND THE TRANS UNION CASE

Daniel R. Fischel

40 BUS. LAW. 1437, 1439–54 (1985)

The business judgment rule is one of the most fundamental doctrines in corporate law. Although courts and commentators have articulated different formulations of the rule, its effect is clear. The rule limits the scope of judicial review of the merits of managerial decisions in a wide variety of situations. Implicit in the rule is the recognition that liability rules enforced by shareholder litigation play a relatively minor role in aligning the interests of managers with those of shareholders. Precisely why liability rules enforced by shareholder litigation should play such a minor role is less clear. The standard justifications for the business judgment rule are that judges lack competence in making business decisions, and that the fear of personal liability will cause corporate managers to be more cautious and also result in fewer talented people being willing to serve as directors. These standard justifications are helpful but not entirely satisfactory. They do not explain, for example, why the same judges who presumably are able to resolve other commercial disputes are unable to decide whether a business decision was made negligently. Nor do they explain why causing corporate managers to be more cautious is not beneficial much in the same manner that the effect of tort suits causing automobile drivers to be more careful is beneficial.

Thus the rationale of the business judgment rule, and the correspondingly limited role of liability rules in the corporate context, must rest on something more. My argument is that the role of liability rules is more limited in the corporate than other contexts because of several factors, including the cost of contracting which makes it extremely difficult to distinguish adequate or reasonable performance from a breach of fiduciary duty; the specialization of function in public corporations; the role of contractual and market mechanisms in rewarding good business decisions and penalizing inferior ones coupled with the absence of similar mechanisms to discipline judges' decisions; and the weak incentive of small shareholders and their attorneys to maximize the value of the firm. I discuss these concepts below in the context of the main issue in the Trans Union case—whether there should be a judicially enforceable requirement that directors acquire information before making a decision or whether the decision to acquire information itself should be shielded from judicial review by the business judgment rule. I focus on the duty to make an informed decision for illustrative purposes only; the same analysis can be used to explain the business judgment rule in other contexts.

. . .

One obvious problem with the court's holding that the directors acted improperly was the fifty percent premium received by Trans Union's shareholders. Presumably, the directors would have incurred no legal liability if they had turned down Pritzker's offer or even if they had successfully resisted a hostile tender offer made by Pritzker or someone else. Thus, the rule seems to be that if directors increase shareholders' wealth by fifty percent, they face personal liability; if on the other hand, they prevent shareholders from increasing their wealth by the same amount, they are protected. Shareholders should be forgiven for being somewhat confused about how they, the supposed beneficiaries, are protected by this interpretation of fiduciary duties.

The court was not troubled by this glaring anomaly, however, at least in part because it dismissed the premium paid by Pritzker over the market price as irrelevant. While the court's analysis was not entirely clear on this point, the court apparently relied on statements by the directors that Trans Union's stock price was depressed and did not represent its true value and on the distinction between the trading price of a single share and the value of the entire company.

Neither ground for dismissing the significance of the premium is plausible. The statement by the directors that the market price of Trans Union's shares was depressed and did not reflect its true value was simply a recognition of the investment tax credit problem. The stock price was "depressed" relative to what it would have been if the benefits of the unused investment tax credits had been realized. The merger at a premium over the market price was a method of selling the investment tax credit to an entity that could use it. Thus, the premium reflected the existence of a value-increasing exchange. Moreover, even assuming the market price was depressed, it still represented the amount shareholders could realize for their shares. And if "the market" is so stupid today as to set an artificially low price for Trans Union's shares, how can it be said that this same stupidity will not cause the market to set an even lower price tomorrow? Unless the directors could predict future stock price movements with certainty, a very unlikely possibility, they were entirely justified in concluding that the merger, whether or not the market price was depressed, increased shareholders' wealth by fifty percent.

. . .

WINNERS AND LOSERS

The most immediate effect of Trans Union will be that no firm considering a fundamental corporate change will do so without obtaining a fairness letter or other similar documentation from outside consultants. Indeed, these outside consultants are the biggest winners after Trans Union. The decision requires their participation as a type of insurance no matter how worthless their opinion is or how much it will cost.

Shareholders are the biggest losers after Trans Union. Firms will have no difficulty finding an "expert" who is willing to state that a price at a significant premium over the market price in an arm's-length transaction is "fair." (I wish someone would pay me several hundred thousand dollars to state that $55 is greater than $35.) But the cost of obtaining such an opinion is, in effect, a judicially imposed tax on fundamental corporate changes. The inevitable consequence will be that fewer transactions will occur and that when they do occur, returns to investors will be lower.

A less direct effect of Trans Union will be to decrease the amount of risk taking by corporate managers in general. Because the decision increases the probability that managers will be sued and held personally liable for damages, managers will naturally want to minimize their exposure by avoiding activities in which they are likely to be sued. They will be less willing to serve (the best protection against getting sued), and when they do serve, will overinvest in information and be less entrepreneurial. One of the major problems in the principal-agent relationship between managers and shareholders, however, is, as discussed above, that managers already have incentives to avoid risk because of their inability to diversify the value of their human capital. Liability rules that reinforce this incentive will operate to shareholders' detriment.

B. THE LEGISLATIVE RESPONSE TO *VAN GORKOM*

The Delaware legislature apparently agreed with Mr. Fischel. In the wake of *Smith v. Van Gorkom*, the Delaware legislature adopted § 102(b)(7), which provides that a corporation's certificate of incorporation may contain:

> A provision eliminating or limiting the personal liability of a director to the corporation or its shareholders for monetary damages for breach of fiduciary duty as a director, provided that such provision shall not eliminate or limit the liability of a director: (i) For any breach of the director's duty of loyalty to the corporation or its shareholders; (ii) for acts or omissions not in good faith or which involve intentional misconduct or a knowing violation of law; (iii) under § 174 of this title[relating to unlawful

payment of dividends]; or (iv) for any transaction from which the director derived an improper personal benefit.

The legislature also amended § 141(e) to expand the scope of individuals on which a board is entitled to rely. Section 141(e) as amended now states:

> A member of the board of directors, or a member of any committee designated by the board of directors, shall, in the performance of such member's duties, be fully protected in relying in good faith upon the records of the corporation and upon such information, opinions, reports or statements presented to the corporation by any of the corporation's officers or employees, or committees of the board of directors, or by any other person as to matters the member reasonably believes are within such other person's professional or expert competence and who has been selected with reasonable care by or on behalf of the corporation.

Almost every corporation incorporated in Delaware promptly adopted § 102(b)(7) provisions exculpating directors.[1] The result is that directors are not personally liable for monetary damages if they violate their fiduciary duty of care. In *Malpiede v. Townson*, 780 A.2d 1075 (Del. 2001), the Delaware Supreme Court ruled that when plaintiffs' claims solely implicate the duty of care and they are only seeking monetary damages, and where the subject corporation has a § 102(b)(7) provision in its corporate charter, plaintiffs' claims will be dismissed for failure to state a claim for which relief can be granted. A defendant corporation and its directors therefore can eliminate these claims on a motion to dismiss, avoiding costly litigation and discovery. Suits for injunctive and other equitable relief are still permitted, though the judges on the Delaware Chancery Court are often loath to enjoin transactions.

Delaware judges' reluctance to enjoin transactions was illustrated in *In re CheckFree Corporation Shareholders Litigation*, No. CIV.A 3193–CC 2007 WL 3262188 (Del. Ch. Nov. 1, 2007). In *CheckFree* a group of shareholder plaintiffs moved for a preliminary injunction to enjoin a

---

[1]   Other jurisdictions have generally adopted comparable statutory exculpation provisions, which have been commonly used by companies in those jurisdictions. *See* Bryn R. Vaaler, *2.02(B)(4) Or Not 2.02(B)(4): That Is The Question*, 74 LAW & CONTEMP. PROBS. 79 (2011), at 82, 84 and notes 18 and 19. ("Over the next several years [after Section 102(b)(7) was enacted], two things happened. First, section 102(b)(7) exculpation provisions became standard features in Delaware certificates of incorporation, as stockholders of hundreds of existing corporations approved the addition of exculpation clauses in the certificate of incorporation and such provisions became routine in new incorporations. Second, other state legislatures included director-exculpation provisions in their respective corporation statutes." "In the more than two decades since statutory authorization of exculpation swept the country, exculpation provisions have become a crucially important part of the balance that U.S. corporate law has maintained between holding directors' feet to the fire and attracting the best and the brightest into the corporate boardroom.").

transaction between CheckFree Corporation and Fiserv, Inc. on grounds that the proxy materials were defective. In the proposed transaction, CheckFree's stockholders would receive a premium over the market price for their stock; moreover, there were no competing bids. Chancellor Chandler refused to grant the injunction, stating that "the public interest requires an especially strong showing" to enjoin an acquisition transaction where there is "a premium" being paid and in "the absence of a competing bid." As one law firm noted, "[t]he *CheckFree* decision largely reaffirms settled Delaware law on these and other issues, while sending a strong signal to the plaintiffs' bar that shareholder plaintiffs face a very high burden when challenging 'a premium transaction in the absence of a competing bid.'"[2] The end result is that in the case of a breach of duty of care, shareholders have no claim against directors for monetary relief, and a very high hurdle to obtain injunctive relief.[3]

In addition to the legislative response, after *Van Gorkom*, parties entering into merger transactions began to negotiate strong indemnification provisions for directors and officers. Here is the indemnification provision from the Dell merger agreement:

Section 5.10 Indemnification and Insurance.

(b) From and after the Effective Time, the Surviving Corporation shall, and Parent shall cause the Surviving Corporation to, to the fullest extent permitted under applicable Law, indemnify and hold harmless (and advance funds in respect of each of the Indemnified Parties) each current and former director or officer of the Company or any of its Subsidiaries and each Person who served, at the request of the Company or any of its Subsidiaries, as a director, officer, member trustee, or fiduciary of another corporation, partnership, joint venture, trust, pension or other employee benefit plan or enterprise (each, together with such Person's heirs, executors or administrators, an "Indemnified Party") against any costs or expenses (including advancing reasonable attorneys' fees and expenses in advance of the final disposition of any claim, suit, proceeding or investigation to each Indemnified Party to the fullest extent permitted by Law), judgments, fines, losses, claims, damages, liabilities and amounts paid in settlement (collectively, "Losses") in connection

---

[2] *Delaware Chancery Court Declines to Enjoin Merger, Recognizing High Burden to Succeed in Enjoining Premium Transaction in Absence of Competing Bid*, SHEPPARD MULLIN CORPORATE & SECURITIES LAW BLOG, Nov. 15, 2007, available at http://www.corporatesecuritieslawblog.com/2007/11/delaware-chancery-court-declines-to-enjoin-merger-recognizing-high-burden-to-succeed-in-enjoining-premium-transaction-in-absence-of-competing-bid/.

[3] Shareholders instead have tried to couch their claims under the rubric of (non-exculpable) good faith, but as you will have learned in your Corporations or Business Associations class and as we discuss later in this textbook, this strategy has generally not been successful.

with any actual or threatened claim, action, suit, litigation, proceeding or investigation, whether civil, criminal, administrative or investigative (an "Action"), arising out of, relating to or in connection with any action or omission occurring or alleged to have occurred whether before or after the Effective Time in connection with such Indemnified Party's service as a director or officer of the Company or any of its Subsidiaries (including acts or omissions in connection with such Indemnified Party's service as officer, director, member, trustee or other fiduciary in any other entity if such services were at the request or for the benefit of the Company); provided that any Person to whom any funds are advanced pursuant to the foregoing must, if required by Law, provide an undertaking to repay such advances if it is ultimately determined that such Person is not entitled to indemnification. In the event of any such Action, Parent, the Surviving Corporation and the Indemnified Party shall cooperate with each other in the defense of any such Action.

Comparable provisions can be found in almost every merger agreement for the acquisition of a public company.[4] There is also typically a second provision requiring that the acquirer maintain directors' and officers' insurance. Although the issue has not been squarely addressed in the Delaware courts, this indemnification seems to be permissible even if it extends beyond the normal statutory limits on director indemnification under § 145. This is because it is provided contractually by the acquirer, not by the corporation for its own directors and officers.[5]

C. *VAN GORKOM* AND THE DUTY OF CARE IN MODERN TIMES

Given § 102(b)(7)'s exculpation of directors from monetary liability for breach of their duty of care, *Smith v. Van Gorkom*'s holding is not an important legal precedent as to what the duty of care requires. The kinds of claims that would have been brought as duty of care claims before § 102(b)(7) was enacted are now brought as good faith claims since good faith claims are not exculpable, as we further discuss below and in the next Chapter.

Nevertheless, as noted at the beginning of this Chapter, the language in *Van Gorkom* that directors needed to "fully inform" themselves has very much influenced the M&A process. Lawyers and market participants talk about what the duty of care "requires" notwithstanding § 102(b)(7).

---

[4] Note that this is quite different from the indemnification provisions we discussed in Chapter XIV.L, relating to selling shareholders' indemnification of the acquirer.

[5] *See, e.g., Louisiana Mun. Police Employees' Ret. Sys. v. Crawford*, 918 A.2d 1172, 1180 at n.8 (Del. Ch. 2007) (stating that acquirer indemnification provisions in a merger agreement "arguably arise[ ] under contract law and outside the restrictions of statutory corporate law").

Among the practices that *Van Gorkom* made standard are: providing copies of the merger agreement and related documents sufficiently in advance of the meeting at which the transaction will be discussed, typically on a Thursday for a Sunday meeting; providing copies of adviser reports at the meeting, to ensure the availability of the § 141(e) reliance; holding more than one meeting about a transaction; ensuring active involvement of the board in the negotiation of any sale transaction; and formally retaining financial advisors and obtaining a fairness opinion for the transaction. That these practices are now standard notwithstanding the lack of a legal "stick" demonstrates the extent to which corporate actors are highly influenced by the norms of the transactional community sometimes as much as by formal legal rules. This does not mean that these norms are always followed, however, as the following blog post by Professor Stephen Bainbridge about Facebook's acquisition of Instagram demonstrates:

DID FACEBOOK'S ZUCKERBERG JUST HAVE A VAN GORKOM MOMENT?

Stephen Bainbridge
PROFESSOR BAINBRIDGE.COM
Apr. 18, 2012

The WSJ reports that:

On the morning of Sunday, April 8, Facebook Inc.'s youthful chief executive, Mark Zuckerberg, alerted his board of directors that he intended to buy Instagram, the hot photo-sharing service. It was the first the board heard of what, later that day, would become Facebook's largest acquisition ever.... Mr. Zuckerberg and his counterpart at Instagram, Kevin Systrom, had already been talking over the deal for three days, these people said.

Negotiating mostly on his own, [at his home,] Mr. Zuckerberg had fielded Mr. Systrom's opening number, $2 billion, and whittled it down over several meetings.... Later that Sunday, the two 20-somethings would agree on a sale valued at $1 billion.

It was a remarkably speedy three-day path to a deal for Facebook—a young company taking pains to portray itself as blue-chip ahead of its initial public offering of stock in a few weeks that could value it at up to $100 billion. Companies generally prefer to bring in ranks of lawyers and bankers to scrutinize a deal before proceeding, a process that can eat up days or weeks.

Mr. Zuckerberg ditched all that. By the time Facebook's board was brought in, the deal was all but done. The board, [said a person who knew the situation], "Was told, not consulted."

Ah, the hubris of youth.

Many of the facts call to mind the classic corporate law case, *Smith v. Van Gorkom* . . .

Smith v. Van Gorkom, 488 A.2d 858 (Del. 1985), was one of the most important corporate law decisions of the 20th century. The supreme court of a state widely criticized for allegedly leading the race to the bottom held that directors who make an uninformed decision are unprotected by the business judgment rule and, accordingly, face substantial personal liability exposure:

According to the court's opinion, Pritzker had imposed a tight time deadline on the negotiations in order to prevent leaks and the increased stock price that usually follows such leaks. According to Robert Pritzker's subsequent account, however, the timetable was initiated by Van Gorkom.

In any case, the process in fact went quite quickly and many decisions were made under significant time constraints. All of which evidently troubled the court, as it several times noted that there was no crisis or emergency justifying such speed.

Sounds a lot like the Facebook deal, doesn't it?

In the *Trans Union* case, a disgruntled shareholder brought suit, claiming that the board of directors had violated its duty of care in approving the deal. The court agreed, stating that, of all the preconditions that must be satisfied in order for the business judgment rule to insulate a board of director decision from judicial review the most important is the requirement that the decision be an informed one. Put another way, the board of directors must exercise what has been called "process due care." Accordingly, the *Van Gorkom* opinion explained that "[i]n the specific context of a proposed merger of domestic corporations, a director has a duty . . . along with his fellow directors, to act in an informed and deliberate manner in determining whether to approve an agreement of merger before submitting the proposal to the shareholders." The court further explained that "[t]he determination of whether a business judgment is an informed one turns on whether the directors have informed themselves 'prior to making a business decision, of all material information reasonably available to them.'"

On the facts of the case before it, the court concluded that the board had abdicated its responsibilities in these areas and, instead, had allowed itself to be railroaded by management to so great an extent that deference became inappropriate.

Sounds a lot like the Facebook deal, doesn't it?

By so focusing its opinion, the *Van Gorkom* court established a set of legal rules that disfavors agenda control by senior management and penalizes boards that simply go through the motions. The decision encourages inquiry, deliberation, care, and process. The decision strongly encourages boards to seek outside counsel and financial advice. None of which was done by the Trans Union board.[6]

In *McPadden v. Sihdu*, which follows, plaintiffs challenged a board's decision to sell the corporation to a group led by the CEO. In the court's opinion, you can see how § 102(b)(7) affected the board's liability. As you read the case, consider whether you think the board would have been liable had § 102(b)(7) not been in effect.

McPadden v. Sidhu

Delaware Court of Chancery
964 A.2d 1262 (2008)

Chandler, Chancellor.

. . .

In June 2005, the board of directors of i2 Technologies, Inc. ("i2" or the "Company") approved the sale of i2's wholly owned subsidiary, Trade Services Corporation ("TSC"), to a management team led by then-TSC vice president, defendant Anthony Dubreville ("Dubreville") for $3 million. Two years later, after first rejecting an offer of $18.5 million as too low just six months after the sale, Dubreville sold TSC to another company for over $25 million. These transactions engendered this lawsuit and the motions to dismiss presently before me. Plaintiff alleges that the Company's directors caused the Company to sell TSC to Dubreville's team for a price that the directors knew to be a mere fraction of TSC's fair market value. . . . [P]laintiff . . . asserts a breach of fiduciary duty claim against the directors who approved the sale of TSC and against Dubreville. [*Editor: Another allegation was made: of unjust enrichment against Dubreville. We have mostly omitted the discussion of that allegation.*] [A]ll defendants, including nominal defendant i2, together move to dismiss plaintiff's complaint pursuant to Chancery Rule 12(b)(6) for failure to state a claim and Chancery Rule 23.1 for failure to plead

---

[6] Available at http://www.professorbainbridge.com/professorbainbridgecom/2012/04/did-facebooks-zuckerburg-just-have-a-van-gorkom-moment.html. The Wall Street Journal article from which Bainbridge is quoting is Shayndi Raice, Spencer E. Ante & Emily Glazer, *In Facebook Deal, Board Was All But Out of Picture*, WALL ST. J., April 18, 2012, available at http://www.wsj.com/articles/SB10001424052702304818404577350191931921290.

particularized facts excusing plaintiff's failure to make a demand upon the board.

The Parties

Nominal defendant i2, a Delaware corporation headquartered in Dallas, Texas, sells supply chain management software and related consulting services. i2's charter includes an exculpatory provision, which protects i2's directors from liability to the fullest extent under Delaware law. The Company operated a division known as the Content and Data Services Division ("CDSD"), which included both TSC and another subdivision known as CDS. TSC occupied a niche market unrelated to i2's main line of business.

Defendants Sanjiv S. Sidhu ("Sidhu"), Stephen Bradley ("Bradley"), Harvey B. Cash ("Cash"), Richard L. Clemmer ("Clemmer"), Michael E. McGrath ("McGrath"), Lloyd G. Waterhouse ("Waterhouse"), Jackson L. Wilson, Jr. ("Wilson"), and Robert L. Crandall ("Crandall" and, together, the "Director Defendants") were or still are members of the i2 board of directors. All Director Defendants approved the 2005 sale of TSC. Of these directors, defendants Cash, Crandall, Clemmer, Bradley, Waterhouse, and Wilson were members of the board's special committee that was charged with reviewing the Sonenshine fairness opinion. Defendant Dubreville was not a director of i2; he was vice president of CDCS, which, as described above, was a division of i2 that included TSC.

. . .

The Facts

In June 2002, Dubreville caused TSC to sue VisionInfoSoft and its sister company, Material Express.com, (together, "VIS/ME"), competitors of TSC, for copyright infringement. In 2002 and 2003, while the copyright litigation was pending, VIS/ME inquired about purchasing TSC, apparently for the purpose of resolving the lawsuit. On July 12, 2002, VIS/ME's chairman, Earl Beutler ("Beutler"), sent certified letters to i2 directors, including Sidhu, Cash, and Crandall, informing them that VIS/ME had made several inquiries regarding its interest in acquiring TSC, communicating VIS/ME's strong interest so the board would be aware of it before approving a sale to another party, and suggesting that VIS/ME was prepared to outbid other offerors. . . .

In January 2003, Beutler sent a letter to Sidhu and i2's CFO stating that VIS/ME would be willing to pay up to $25 million for TSC. The letter repeated that there was significant organizational overlap between TSC and VIS/ME, and that Beutler believed the combined operations would produce significant additional cash flow within a short period of time. The i2 board discussed TSC—its business and its effect on i2—at a meeting held a few days later. Director defendants Sidhu, Cash, and Crandall attended the meeting. Later, in June 2004, TSC and VIS/ME settled their copyright infringement dispute with VIS/ME agreeing to pay quarterly licensing fees to TSC. . . .

Plaintiff alleges a litany of actions purportedly taken by Dubreville (and allegedly permitted by the Director Defendants) to drive down the earnings of TSC, including incurring unnecessary expenses (such as leasing twice the necessary office space); artificially depressing TSC's EBITDA through use of a printing company that Dubreville partially owned (and thereby reaping windfall profits); and causing TSC to incur significant legal expenses in its copyright dispute with VIS/ME though the new owners of TSC (once it was sold in June 2005) were permitted to retain the benefits of the settlement.

In November 2004, i2 conducted a review of CDSD. Dubreville headed CDSD, which included TSC and the other subdivision, CDS. Under Dubreville's direction, CDSD prepared a presentation that included projections of TSC's FY 2005 revenue at $16 million, which was an increase of 2% over FY 2004, and FY 2006 revenue of $16.8 million. . . .

Plaintiff alleges that these inaccurate allocations enabled Dubreville to make TSC's earnings appear lower than they actually were and that, though not disruptive to day to day operations, such improper cost allocations negatively impacted TSC's value when it was sold.

In December 2004, the i2 board decided to sell TSC. An offering memorandum was prepared in January 2005 to convey information about TSC to prospective purchasers. At a board meeting on February 1, 2005, i2's investment banker, Sonenshine Partners ("Sonenshine"), gave a presentation that included various options for the sale of TSC. One of these options was to sell TSC for $4.2 million to TSC employees. At this meeting, the board was also apprised of the plan to let Dubreville conduct the sale process of TSC. By this time, Dubreville was aware that VIS/ME earlier had expressed interest in buying TSC for up to $25 million and Dubreville had already discussed with i2 the possibility of leading a management buyout of TSC. Sidhu, Clemmer, Cash, Crandall, and McGrath discussed the idea of a management buyout at the February 1, 2005 board meeting. Nevertheless, no business broker or investment banker was hired; the board charged Dubreville with finding a buyer for TSC.

In mid-February, the February 2005 version of the offering memorandum was created. This version altered the projections used in the January 2005 offering memorandum; these revised projections were significantly reduced. The February 2005 offering memorandum was ultimately used by Dubreville to solicit bids for TSC.

Plaintiff recounts Dubreville's limited efforts to market TSC. Dubreville did not solicit interest from any of TSC's direct competitors, which were its most likely buyers. In particular, Dubreville did not solicit interest from VIS/ME though he and at least three directors (Sidhu, Cash, and Crandall) knew VIS/ME had indicated a strong interest in buying TSC and had offered as much as $25 million for TSC in 2003. Though Dubreville did contact Reed Elsevier Inc. (owner of LexisNexis information services), he did not contact that company's largest competitor, Thomson Corporation (owner of Westlaw), because plaintiff alleges that Dubreville knew that contacting Thomson would alert VIS/ME that TSC was for sale.

While the search for a buyer for TSC was ongoing, on March 9, 2005, the board again discussed Dubreville's proposal to lead a management buyout of TSC. By this point, Dubreville had solicited only two bids for TSC. The process Dubreville employed ultimately produced three offers for TSC. First, an electronic parts distributor, HIS, offered $12 million for the entire CDSD division, of which $4.3 million was allocated to TSC. Because i2 did not want to bundle these two businesses for sale, it rejected IHS's offer. Ultimately, in 2006 IHS purchased CDS (the other CDSD subdivision) for approximately $29 million. A second offer was from an entity named Sunrise Ventures, the principal of which was Dubreville's former boss at TSC and his partner in a printing company. Sunrise Ventures offered $1.8 million for TSC, which plaintiff alleges was a "lowball" offer designed to make the Dubreville-led group's offer of $3 million appear generous. The third offer was from the Dubreville-led group, Trade Service Holdings, LLC ("TSH"), of which Dubreville was a principal owner. On March 18, 2005, TSH offered to buy TSC for $2 million in cash and $1 million in software licensing agreements, with TSH keeping all outstanding receivables and repayments. The offer also contemplated that TSC would sublease half its existing office space, that i2 would pay for TSC's relocation within its building, and that i2 would bear the costs of the office space that TSC would not use.

About four days before the board's April 18, 2005 meeting to discuss the offers for TSC, Sonenshine distributed a document (the "Sonenshine Document") that included two sets of TSC projections: the projections from the original January 2005 offering memorandum; and the revised February 2005 projections, which were significantly less profitable. Plaintiff alleges that the board knew that these projections were "inherently unreliable" because they were "buyer" projections; both sets of projections were created by TSC management under Dubreville's direction when the possibility of a management acquisition of TSC had already been contemplated. In addition, the Sonenshine Document, reporting the results of the "internally-led sale process," notes that, of the thirteen potential buyers that were contacted, most were large corporations that would be uninterested in acquiring TSC's niche business. Notably, no TSC competitors were contacted during the sale process.

On April 18, 2005, the board met to discuss the proposed management buyout of TSC and the other two offers for TSC that had been received. As detailed in the Sonenshine Document, Sonenshine confirmed to the board that its preliminary valuation of TSC was around $3 to $7 million using the February management projections; and $6 to $10.8 million using the January projections. The board then authorized management to move forward with discussions to sell TSC to TSH (the company partially owned by Dubreville), even though the board knew that Dubreville had been responsible for conducting the sale of TSC and that TSC had not been offered to competitors. In addition, plaintiff contends that neither the board nor the special committee negotiated with Dubreville before the letter of intent was signed on April 22, 2005.

Plaintiff states that the TSH offer was at the lowest end of Sonenshine's range using even the February projections and was half as much as the minimum estimated value of TSC using the January projections. In addition, plaintiff alleges gross irregularities in the approval of the sale, including that the special committee of the board (which was charged with reviewing the fairness of the transaction) never met with Sonenshine until June 21, 2005, which was a week before the sale was finally approved. At this point, under the terms of the agreement, if the special committee or i2 had decided not to go forward with the transaction, the breakup fee would have been $716,000.

Sonenshine made a preliminary presentation to the special committee on June 21, 2005, and then an advisory presentation to the special committee and the board on June 23, 2005. On June 28, 2005, the special committee and the board met and approved the transaction. Plaintiff alleges that the fairness opinion that the board relied upon was "on its face grossly and blatantly unreliable" for a litany of reasons. Specifically, the two sets of financial projections used in the discounted cash flow valuation analysis were both lower than the January projections: the "seller" projections, which had never been presented to the board and which were more pessimistic than the buyer projections, and the "re-forecasted buyer" projections, which were similar to the February projections. The source of this set of projections was, as with the earlier projections, TSC's management who were, here, the buyers. In addition, plaintiff contends that the fairness opinion was flawed because it made use of unreliable, inconsistent, and unaudited financial statements, which resulted in valuations extremely favorable to the buyer and which failed to account for the improper allocation of costs between TSC and CDS. The fairness opinion also failed to include TSC's competitors on the list of "potential suitors" and omitted the fees paid to TSC by VIS/ME as part of the litigation settlement.

In sum, the effect of these numerous alleged deficiencies is that the fairness opinion, because it was based on financial information, including projections and financial statements, provided or prepared by the buyers, favored the interests of Dubreville and TSH and produced a valuation that supported a sale at a price exceedingly favorable to the buyers. Because of the unreliability of the fairness opinion, plaintiff contends, the special committee and the board could not have relied in good faith on that opinion in its approval of the sale of TSC to Dubreville at an offer that represented 0.2X sales. . . .

H. TSC's Sale for Its Allegedly True Value

In the fall of 2005, TSH offered to sell TSC to VIS/ME. In December 2005, VIS/ME offered $18.5 million. TSH, through Dubreville, rejected this offer as too low and later, in 2007, sold TSC for more than $25 million. Plaintiff contends that no significant changes to TSC's business occurred during that period of time to justify the price difference and instead attributes it to the use of accurate financial statements, which supported a higher valuation of TSC. . . .

IV. ANALYSIS

. . .

A. Demand Futility Under the Second Prong of Aronson

In his complaint, plaintiff alleges neither interest nor lack of independence and the parties agree that the question of demand futility is properly considered under the second prong of *Aronson*. [*Editor: Recall from your Corporations or Business Associations class that for a plaintiff to bring a derivative action—a suit to force the corporation to sue its directors and perhaps officers—it must either make demand or argue that demand is excused as futile. Where what is at issue is a board decision, the relevant doctrine is Aronson, the first prong of which is about independence and interest and the second prong of which is about business judgment, as further explained in the text.*] Plaintiff avers that demand is excused as futile because the board's approval of the sale was not fully informed, not duly considered, and not made in good faith for the best interests of the Company. For the reasons described below, I conclude that, because plaintiff has pleaded a duty of care violation with particularity sufficient to create a reasonable doubt that the transaction at issue was the product of a valid exercise of business judgment, demand is excused as futile.

In evaluating the decisions of boards, the courts of this State have consistently noted the limited nature of such judicial determinations of due care: "Due care in the decisionmaking context is *process* due care only." Where, as here, the board has retained an expert to assist the board in its decision making process, the Delaware Supreme Court has specified that a complaint will survive a motion to dismiss in a due care case if it alleges particularized facts that, if proven, would show that "the subject matter ... that was material and reasonably available was so obvious that the board's failure to consider it was grossly negligent regardless of the expert's advice or lack of advice." Contrary to defendants' cursory treatment of this argument, I conclude that the complaint does plead particularized facts demonstrating that material and reasonably available information was not considered by the board and that such lack of consideration constituted gross negligence, irrespective of any reliance on the Sonenshine fairness opinion.

The challenged transaction at issue—the sale of TSC to Dubreville's group—is analytically a series of discrete board actions. Plaintiff has sufficiently alleged facts to create a reasonable doubt that they, together, cannot be the product of a valid exercise of the board's business judgment. The board's first step in the series of actions culminating in the sale of TSC to Dubreville was also its most egregious: tasking Dubreville with the sale process of TSC when the board knew that Dubreville was interested in purchasing TSC. Certainly Dubreville's interest as a potential purchaser was material to the board's decision in determining to whom to assign the task of soliciting bids and offers for TSC. It would be in Dubreville's own self-interest to obtain low offers for TSC; the more diligent he was about seeking the best offers for TSC, the higher Dubreville himself would have to bid. Had the board not known of Dubreville's interest in the sale, its decision to charge him with finding a buyer for TSC might be less perplexing. Yet, this material information was not merely reasonably available to the board, it was actually known. Dubreville had already discussed with i2 the possibility of leading a management buyout of TSC, an idea that Sidhu, Clemmer, Cash, Crandall, and McGrath discussed at the February 1, 2005 board meeting (and a topic that was later revisited during the March 9, 2005 meeting). Nevertheless, the board decided that Dubreville, whom the board knew was conflicted, would conduct the sale process. From this point forward, the board's actions only exacerbated a misstep that was presumably otherwise correctable or perhaps even unactionable.

Despite having tasked a potential purchaser of TSC with its sale, the board appears to have engaged in little to no oversight of that sale process, providing no check on Dubreville's half-hearted (or, worse, intentionally misdirected) efforts in soliciting bids for TSC. Dubreville's limited attempts to find a buyer for TSC did not include contacting the most obvious potential buyers: TSC's direct competitors, particularly a competitor that had previously offered as much as $25 million for TSC in 2003. Perhaps unsurprisingly, Dubreville's group emerged as the highest bidder for TSC from the sale process.

The board, during its consideration of the offers for TSC at the April 18, 2005 meeting, discussed the Sonenshine Document, which clearly described Dubreville's efforts in selectively contacting potential buyers. Thus, the Director Defendants knew that Dubreville did not contact any TSC competitors. Yet the Director Defendants did nothing to remedy the situation they created by tasking an interested purchaser with the sale of an asset of the Company. Instead, they authorized further discussions with TSH and, on April 22, 2005, signed a letter of intent for i2 to sell TSC to Dubreville and his group and, in doing so, missed another opportunity to rectify the situation they had created.

In addition, the two sets of projections described in the Sonenshine Document should have alerted the board to carefully consider whether Dubreville's offer was high enough. The Directors Defendants knew that Sonenshine's preliminary valuation of TSC was based on projections provided by management, which were prepared at the direction of Dubreville. The Director Defendants therefore also knew that the valuation was calculated using these "buyer" projections. The January projections valued TSC at $6 to $10.8 million. Even the February projections, which plaintiff alleges were adjusted to make TSC appear significantly less profitable than it was, valued TSC at $3 to $7 million. Despite this, the board agreed to proceed with an offer of $3 million, which would only ultimately result in a net gain of $2.2 million because of terms in the agreement favorable to Dubreville. The entire offer of $3 million, not even considering its ultimate net value, was at the lowest end of the valuation range of TSC using even the February projections.

The board's actions, to this point, are quite puzzling. In making its decisions, the board had no shortage of information that was both material—because it affected the process and ultimate result of the sale—and reasonably available (or, even, actually known as evidenced by the discussions at the board meetings): Dubreville's interest in leading a management buyout of TSC; Dubreville's limited efforts in soliciting offers for TSC, including his failure to contact TSC competitors, including one he knew had previously expressed concrete interest in purchasing TSC; the circumstances under which the January and February projections were produced; the use of those projections in Sonenshine's preliminary valuations of TSC; and that TSH was a group led by Dubreville. That the board would want to consider this information seems, to me, so obvious that it is equally obvious that the Directors Defendants' failure to do so was grossly negligent.

Finally, on June 28, 2008, the board and the special committee approved the sale of TSC to Dubreville. As detailed above, plaintiff argues strenuously that the Sonenshine fairness opinion was flawed and that the Director Defendants cannot reasonably have relied on it. Because, however, I conclude that the Director Defendants' actions, culminating with the approval of the sale of TSC, were grossly negligent, I need not further consider the board's reliance on the Sonenshine fairness opinion or the reliability of the opinion in finding that demand is excused as futile.

B.   Failure to State a Claim

Though plaintiff has demonstrated that it would have been futile to make a demand upon the board, plaintiff fails to state a claim against the Director Defendants, who have the benefit of a section 102(b)(7) exculpatory provision in the i2 certificate, because plaintiff has not adequately alleged that the Director Defendants acted in bad faith. In contrast, however, plaintiff has stated a claim for both breach of fiduciary duty and unjust enrichment as to Dubreville. Dubreville, though he, as an officer, owes the same duties to the Company as the Director Defendants, does not benefit from the same protections as the Director Defendants because the section 102(b)(7) provision operates to exculpate only directors, not officers.

1.   The 102(b)(7) Provision Exculpates the Director Defendants

As authorized by Section 102(b)(7), i2's certificate of incorporation contains an exculpatory provision, limiting the personal liability of directors for certain conduct. Certain conduct, however, cannot be exculpated, including bad faith actions. Gross negligence, in contrast, is exculpated because such conduct breaches the duty of care. Traditionally, "[i]n the duty of care context gross negligence has been defined as 'reckless indifference to or a deliberate disregard of the whole body of shareholders or actions which are without the bounds of reason.'" Recently, however, the Supreme Court has modified Delaware's understanding of the definition of gross negligence in the context of fiduciary duty. In analyzing "three different categories of fiduciary behavior [that] are candidates for the 'bad faith' pejorative label," the Court made quite clear that gross negligence cannot be such an example of bad faith conduct: "[t]here is no basis in policy, precedent or common sense that would justify dismantling the distinction between gross negligence and bad faith." Instead, the Court concluded that conduct motivated by subjective bad intent and that resulting from gross negligence are at opposite ends of the spectrum. The Court then considered a third category of conduct: the intentional dereliction of duty or the conscious disregard for one's responsibilities. The Court determined that such misconduct must be treated as a non-exculpable, non-indemnifiable violation of the fiduciary duty to act in good faith, a duty that the Court later confirmed was squarely within the duty of loyalty. Thus, from the sphere of actions that was once classified as grossly negligent conduct that gives rise to a violation of the duty of care, the Court has carved out one specific type of conduct—the intentional dereliction of duty or the conscious disregard for one's responsibilities—and redefined it as bad faith conduct, which results in a breach of the duty of loyalty. Therefore, Delaware's current understanding of gross negligence is conduct that constitutes reckless indifference or actions that are without the bounds of reason.

The conduct of the Director Defendants here fits precisely within this revised understanding of gross negligence. In finding that demand is excused as futile, I have already concluded that plaintiff has pleaded with particularity so as to raise a reasonable doubt that the actions of the board were a product of the valid exercise of their business judgment. Thus, for the reasons explained above, the Director Defendants' actions, beginning with placing Dubreville in charge of the sale process of TSC and continuing through their failure to act in any way so as to ensure that the sale process employed was thorough and complete, are properly characterized as either recklessly indifferent or unreasonable. Plaintiff has not, however, sufficiently alleged that the Director Defendants acted in bad faith through a conscious disregard for their duties. Instead, plaintiff has ably pleaded that the Director Defendants quite clearly were not careful enough in the discharge of their duties—that is, they acted with gross negligence or else reckless indifference. Because such conduct breaches the Director Defendants' duty of care, this violation is exculpated by the Section 102(b)(7) provision in the Company's charter and therefore the Director Defendants' motion to dismiss for failure to state a claim must be granted. . . .

V. CONCLUSION

Though this board acted "badly"—with gross negligence—and in doing so provided the basis for my denial of defendants' motion to dismiss pursuant to Rule 23.1, this board did not act in bad faith. Therefore, with the benefit of the protections of the Company's exculpatory provision, the motion to dismiss Count I (breach of fiduciary duty) pursuant to Rule 12(b)(6) is granted as to the Director Defendants. . . .

QUESTIONS

1.   What does the *Van Gorkom* court think the "leveraged buyout (LBO) value" measured? How did the court think the LBO value was different from the "intrinsic value?" How do you think it is different from the intrinsic value?

2.   Why did the *Van Gorkom* court focus as little as it did on the size of the premium? Do you think the court was correct in its reasoning about the premium?

3.   How would the result in *Van Gorkom* have been different if the directors had more carefully read the merger agreement? Would that have sufficed for the court to not find them liable?

4.   Why did Pritzker pay amounts he wasn't liable to pay?

5.   Today, how would you advise a board as to what is must do to approve a takeover transaction? In particular, what information must the board receive?

6.   How has DGCL § 102(b)(7) changed the way that boards consider a potential sale of the company? If you were a shareholder how would you feel about this statute? Does § 102(b)(7) provide any benefits to you, as a shareholder?

7.   Why do you think the Delaware General Assembly amended DGCL § 141(e) in the wake of *Van Gorkom*?

8.   How did the board's conduct in *McPadden* follow the dictates of *Van Gorkom*? How did it not?

9.   Do you agree or disagree with Daniel Fischel's opinion of *Van Gorkom*? Do you agree with the rationale behind the *Van Gorkom* decision?

10.   Why wasn't interest or lack or independence at issue in *McPadden*? Should it have been? Why did the board allow Dubreville to run the sales process?

11.   Given § 102(b)(7), was there a way to find the directors in *McPadden* liable? Should there have been?

PROBLEM

The board of Epsilon Inc., a publicly traded Delaware corporation, is considering a sale transaction. Please draft a memo to the board of Epsilon, describing how the board should go about structuring the sales process.

CHAPTER XVIII

SELLING THE CORPORATION

■ ■ ■

As we have seen, the sale of a company (or some or all of its business or assets) is a highly coordinated process governed by law, but also informed by norms of the deal community. The sales process is led by the board of directors of the company. The directors make the decision as to whether to engage in a sale and, if a sale is to take place, the process to be utilized. In making these decisions, the board typically takes advice from the company's investment bankers, who advise on the process from a financial point of view, and the company's attorneys, who advise the board on how they must proceed under the law. In prior Chapters, we explored the board's fiduciary duties in the context of resisting an unwanted takeover offer. We also considered how the board's fiduciary duties inform its decision to sell the company and the process it adopts. This Chapter more fully explores the obligations of the board after having decided to sell the company.

The duties of directors as regards a sale of the company or substantially all the assets of its business have been shaped by a series of cases decided by the Delaware courts dating back to the 1980s. These cases provide guidance as to how directors should proceed; they address both the process and substance of the sale transaction.

A. MAXIMIZING SHAREHOLDER VALUE: *REVLON DUTIES*

A year after it decided *Unocal*, the Delaware Supreme Court decided *Revlon, Inc. v. MacAndrews & Forbes Holdings, Inc.*, 506 A.2d 173 (Del. 1986). *Revlon* has shaped much of the takeover jurisprudence with its admonition to boards that they must "seek the highest price reasonably available" when engaging in a sale of a company. In order to understand the *Revlon* case, it is important to understand something about the personalities involved; to some extent, the personalities dictated how Revlon and its board responded.

1. SETTING THE STAGE: PERLMAN AND BERGERAC MEET

In the early evening of June 14, 1985, Ronald Perelman appeared at the lavish penthouse apartment of Michel Bergerac. Perelman had just acquired control of Pantry Pride, Inc., a supermarket chain [with assets of less than $410 million and a net worth of less than $150 million]. Bergerac was . . . chairman and CEO . . . of Revlon Inc., the cosmetics and health-care giant, which as of December 1984 had over $2.3 billion in assets and net worth in excess of $1 billion. . . . [T]he small-time, unimpressive Perelman, transfigured by a wave of Milken's wand, had come courting.

[*Editor's note: Milken is Michael Milken, discussed in Chapter I. In the 1980s, Milken, then working at the now-defunct investment bank Drexel Burnham Lambert, transformed the capital markets, making it possible for people who hadn't been able to borrow from traditional funding sources to borrow using lower quality debt known as high-yield bonds, referred to more colloquially as "junk bonds."*]

The chemistry, however, was all wrong. According to Bergerac, Perelman told him about MacAndrews and Forbes Holdings, the mini-conglomerate he had amassed in the preceding eight years . . . [Bergerac said:] "I'd never heard of it," . . . "He told me that the dream of his life was to buy Revlon." "I said that that was wonderful, but it was not for sale . . . He said that he would do wonderful things for me. I said that I didn't have much taste for being bribed, and goodbye."

Associates of both men agree that their personal styles must have blended like oil and water. Bergerac is a courtly, somewhat imperious, urbane, witty Frenchman. Perelman is crude, brusque, humorless, speaks in a staccato manner and perpetually puffs an enormous cigar. "They didn't hit it off," declared Perelman's lawyer and constant cohort, [lawyer at Skadden, Arps, Slate, Meagher & Flom, a leading corporate law firm] Donald Drapkin. "Bergerac with his Château Lafite, and Ronnie with his diet Coke."[1]

2. THE REVLON CASE

The personality clashes foreshadowed by the initial meeting between Bergerac and Perelman were much in evidence in the subsequent battle

---

[1] CONNIE BRUCK, THE PREDATORS' BALL: THE INSIDER STORY OF DREXEL BURNHAM AND THE RISE OF THE JUNK BOND RAIDERS 193–4 (1988).

for control over Revlon. The Delaware Supreme Court opinion below recounts much of the back and forth, including the reasons the Revlon board articulated for not selling the corporation to Perelman. Notice how the court deals with the Revlon board's preference for Forstmann's lower bid over Perelman's higher bid.

REVLON, INC. V. MACANDREWS & FORBES HOLDINGS, INC.

Supreme Court of Delaware
506 A.2d 173 (1986)

MOORE, JUSTICE:

. . . The prelude to this controversy began in June 1985, when Ronald O. Perelman, chairman of the board and chief executive officer of Pantry Pride, met with his counterpart at Revlon, Michel C. Bergerac, to discuss a friendly acquisition of Revlon by Pantry Pride. Perelman suggested a price in the range of $40–50 per share, but the meeting ended with Bergerac dismissing those figures as considerably below Revlon's intrinsic value. All subsequent Pantry Pride overtures were rebuffed, perhaps in part based on Mr. Bergerac's strong personal antipathy to Mr. Perelman.

Thus, on August 14, Pantry Pride's board authorized Perelman to acquire Revlon, either through negotiation in the $42–$43 per share range, or by making a hostile tender offer at $45. Perelman then met with Bergerac and outlined Pantry Pride's alternate approaches. Bergerac remained adamantly opposed to such schemes and conditioned any further discussions of the matter on Pantry Pride executing a standstill agreement prohibiting it from acquiring Revlon without the latter's prior approval.

On August 19, the Revlon board met specially to consider the impending threat of a hostile bid by Pantry Pride. At the meeting, Lazard Freres, Revlon's investment banker, advised the directors that $45 per share was a grossly inadequate price for the company. Felix Rohatyn and William Loomis of Lazard Freres explained to the board that Pantry Pride's financial strategy for acquiring Revlon would be through "junk bond" financing followed by a break-up of Revlon and the disposition of its assets. With proper timing, according to the experts, such transactions could produce a return to Pantry Pride of $60 to $70 per share, while a sale of the company as a whole would be in the "mid 50" dollar range. Martin Lipton, special counsel for Revlon, recommended two defensive measures: first, that the company repurchase up to 5 million of its nearly 30 million outstanding shares; and second, that it adopt a Note Purchase Rights Plan. Under this plan, each Revlon shareholder would receive as a dividend one Note Purchase Right (the Rights) for each share of common stock, with the Rights entitling the holder to exchange one common share for a $65 principal Revlon note at 12% interest with a one-year maturity.

The Rights would become effective whenever anyone acquired beneficial ownership of 20% or more of Revlon's shares, unless the purchaser acquired all the company's stock for cash at $65 or more per share. In addition, the Rights would not be available to the acquiror, and prior to the 20% triggering event the Revlon board could redeem the rights for 10 cents each. Both proposals were unanimously adopted.

Pantry Pride made its first hostile move on August 23 with a cash tender offer for any and all shares of Revlon at $47.50 per common share and $26.67 per preferred share, subject to (1) Pantry Pride's obtaining financing for the purchase, and (2) the Rights being redeemed, rescinded or voided.

The Revlon board met again on August 26. The directors advised the stockholders to reject the offer. Further defensive measures also were planned. On August 29, Revlon commenced its own offer for up to 10 million shares, exchanging for each share of common stock tendered one Senior Subordinated Note (the Notes) of $47.50 principal at 11.75% interest, due 1995, and one-tenth of a share of $9.00 Cumulative Convertible Exchangeable Preferred Stock valued at $100 per share. Lazard Freres opined that the notes would trade at their face value on a fully distributed basis. Revlon stockholders tendered 87 percent of the outstanding shares (approximately 33 million), and the company accepted the full 10 million shares on a pro rata basis. The new Notes contained covenants which limited Revlon's ability to incur additional debt, sell assets, or pay dividends unless otherwise approved by the "independent" (non-management) members of the board.

At this point, both the Rights and the Note covenants stymied Pantry Pride's attempted takeover. The next move came on September 16, when Pantry Pride announced a new tender offer at $42 per share, conditioned upon receiving at least 90% of the outstanding stock. Pantry Pride also indicated that it would consider buying less than 90%, and at an increased price, if Revlon removed the impeding Rights. While this offer was lower on its face than the earlier $47.50 proposal, Revlon's investment banker, Lazard Freres, described the two bids as essentially equal in view of the completed exchange offer.

The Revlon board held a regularly scheduled meeting on September 24. The directors rejected the latest Pantry Pride offer and authorized management to negotiate with other parties interested in acquiring Revlon. Pantry Pride remained determined in its efforts and continued to make cash bids for the company, offering $50 per share on September 27, and raising its bid to $53 on October 1, and then to $56.25 on October 7.

In the meantime, Revlon's negotiations with Forstmann and the investment group Adler & Shaykin had produced results. The Revlon directors met on October 3 to consider Pantry Pride's $53 bid and to examine possible alternatives to the offer. Both Forstmann and Adler & Shaykin made certain proposals to the board. As a result, the directors unanimously agreed to a leveraged buyout by Forstmann. The terms of this accord were as follows: each stockholder would get $56 cash per share; management would purchase stock in the new company by the exercise of their Revlon "golden parachutes"; Forstmann would assume Revlon's $475 million debt incurred by the issuance of the Notes; and Revlon would redeem the Rights and waive the Notes covenants for Forstmann or in connection with any other offer superior to Forstmann's. The board did not actually remove the covenants at the October 3 meeting, because Forstmann then lacked a firm commitment on its financing, but accepted the Forstmann capital structure, and indicated that the outside directors would waive the covenants in due course. Part of Forstmann's plan was to sell Revlon's Norcliff Thayer and Reheis divisions to American Home Products for $335 million. Before the merger, Revlon was to sell its cosmetics and fragrance division to Adler & Shaykin for $905 million. These transactions would facilitate the purchase by Forstmann or any other acquiror of Revlon.

When the merger, and thus the waiver of the Notes covenants, was announced, the market value of these securities began to fall. The Notes, which originally traded near par, around 100, dropped to 87.50 by October 8. One director later reported (at the October 12 meeting) a "deluge" of telephone calls from irate noteholders, and on October 10 the Wall Street Journal reported threats of litigation by these creditors.

Pantry Pride countered with a new proposal on October 7, raising its $53 offer to $56.25, subject to nullification of the Rights, a waiver of the Notes covenants, and the election of three Pantry Pride directors to the Revlon board. On October 9, representatives of Pantry Pride, Forstmann and Revlon conferred in an attempt to negotiate the fate of Revlon, but could not reach agreement. At this meeting Pantry Pride announced that it would . . . top any Forstmann offer by a slightly higher one. It is also significant that Forstmann, to Pantry Pride's exclusion, had been made privy to certain Revlon financial data. . . .

[P]rivately armed with Revlon data, Forstmann met on October 11 with Revlon's special counsel and investment banker. On October 12, Forstmann made a new $57.25 per share offer, based on several conditions. The principal demand was a lock-up option to purchase Revlon's Vision Care and National Health Laboratories divisions for $525 million, some $100–$175 million below the value ascribed to them by Lazard Freres, if another acquiror got 40% of Revlon's shares. Revlon also was required to accept a no-shop provision. The Rights and Notes covenants had to be removed as in the October 3 agreement. There would be a $25 million cancellation fee to be placed in escrow, and released to Forstmann if the new agreement terminated or if another acquiror got more than 19.9% of Revlon's stock. Finally, there would be no participation by Revlon management in the merger. In return, Forstmann agreed to support the par value of the Notes, which had faltered in the market, by an exchange of new notes. Forstmann also demanded immediate acceptance of its offer, or it would be withdrawn. The board unanimously approved Forstmann's proposal because: (1) it was for a higher price than the Pantry Pride bid, (2) it protected the noteholders, and (3) Forstmann's financing was firmly in place. The board further agreed to redeem the rights and waive the covenants on the preferred stock in response to any offer above $57 cash per share. The covenants were waived, contingent upon receipt of an investment banking opinion that the Notes would trade near par value once the offer was consummated.

Pantry Pride . . . [challenged] the lock-up, the cancellation fee, and the exercise of the Rights and the Notes covenants. Pantry Pride also sought a temporary restraining order to prevent Revlon from placing any assets in escrow or transferring them to Forstmann. Moreover, on October 22, Pantry Pride again raised its bid, with a cash offer of $58 per share conditioned upon nullification of the Rights, waiver of the covenants, and an injunction of the Forstmann lock-up.

On October 15, the Court of Chancery prohibited the further transfer of assets, and eight days later enjoined the lock-up, no-shop, and cancellation fee provisions of the agreement. The trial court concluded that the Revlon directors had breached their duty of loyalty by making concessions to Forstmann, out of concern for their liability to the noteholders, rather than maximizing the sale price of the company for the stockholders' benefit. . . .

[W]hen a board implements anti-takeover measures there arises "the omnipresent specter that a board may be acting primarily in its own interests, rather than those of the corporation and its shareholders . . ." [citing *Unocal*] This potential for conflict places upon the directors the burden of proving that they had reasonable grounds for believing there was a danger to corporate policy and effectiveness, a burden satisfied by a showing of good faith and reasonable investigation. In addition, the directors must analyze the nature of the takeover and its effect on the corporation in order to ensure balance—that the responsive action taken is reasonable in relation to the threat posed.

B.

The first relevant defensive measure adopted by the Revlon board was the Rights Plan, which would be considered a "poison pill" in the current language of corporate takeovers—a plan by which shareholders receive the right to be bought out by the corporation at a substantial premium on the occurrence of a stated triggering event. . . .

The Revlon board approved the Rights Plan in the face of an impending hostile takeover bid by Pantry Pride at $45 per share, a price which Revlon reasonably concluded was grossly inadequate. Lazard Freres had so advised the directors, and had also informed them that Pantry Pride was a small, highly leveraged company bent on a "bust-up" takeover by using "junk bond" financing to buy Revlon cheaply, sell the acquired assets to pay the debts incurred, and retain the profit for itself. In adopting the Plan, the board protected the shareholders from a hostile takeover at a price below the company's intrinsic value, while retaining sufficient flexibility to address any proposal deemed to be in the stockholders' best interests.

To that extent the board acted in good faith and upon reasonable investigation. Under the circumstances it cannot be said that the Rights Plan as employed was unreasonable, considering the threat posed. Indeed, the Plan was a factor in causing Pantry Pride to raise its bids from a low of $42 to an eventual high of $58. . . . [T]he measure spurred the bidding to new heights, a proper result of its implementation.

[The Plan's] continued usefulness was rendered moot by the directors' actions on October 3 and October 12. At the October 3 meeting the board redeemed the Rights conditioned upon consummation of a merger with Forstmann, but further acknowledged that they would also be redeemed to facilitate any more favorable offer. On October 12, the board unanimously passed a resolution redeeming the Rights in connection with any cash proposal of $57.25 or more per share. Because all the pertinent offers eventually equaled or surpassed that amount, the Rights clearly were no longer any impediment in the contest for Revlon. . . .

C.

The second defensive measure adopted by Revlon to thwart a Pantry Pride takeover was the company's own exchange offer for 10 million of its shares. . . . [W]hen exercising [their power to deal with the stock of their company] in an effort to forestall a hostile takeover, the board's actions are strictly held to the fiduciary standards outlined in *Unocal*. . . .

The Revlon directors concluded that Pantry Pride's $47.50 offer was grossly inadequate. In that regard the board acted in good faith, and on an informed basis, with reasonable grounds to believe that there existed a harmful threat to the corporate enterprise. . . .

D.

However, when Pantry Pride increased its offer to $50 per share, and then to $53, it became apparent to all that the break-up of the company was inevitable. The Revlon board's authorization permitting management to negotiate a merger or buyout with a third party was a recognition that the company was for sale. The duty of the board had thus changed from the preservation of Revlon as a corporate entity to the maximization of the company's value at a sale for the stockholders' benefit. This significantly altered the board's responsibilities under the *Unocal* standards. It no longer faced threats to corporate policy and effectiveness, or to the stockholders' interests, from a grossly inadequate bid. The whole question of defensive measures became moot. The directors' role changed from defenders of the corporate bastion to auctioneers charged with getting the best price for the stockholders at a sale of the company.

III.

This brings us to the lock-up with Forstmann and its emphasis on shoring up the sagging market value of the Notes in the face of threatened litigation by their holders. Such a focus was inconsistent with the changed concept of the directors' responsibilities at this stage of the developments. The impending waiver of the Notes covenants had caused the value of the Notes to fall, and the board was aware of the noteholders' ire as well as their subsequent threats of suit. The directors thus made support of the Notes an integral part of the company's dealings with Forstmann, even though their primary responsibility at this stage was to the equity owners.... [T]he Revlon board could not make the requisite showing of good faith by preferring the noteholders and ignoring its duty of loyalty to the shareholders. The rights of the former already were fixed by contract. The noteholders required no further protection, and when the Revlon board entered into an auction-ending lock-up agreement with Forstmann on the basis of impermissible considerations at the expense of the shareholders, the directors breached their primary duty of loyalty.

The Revlon board argued that it acted in good faith in protecting the noteholders because *Unocal* permits consideration of other corporate constituencies.... A board may have regard for various constituencies in discharging its responsibilities, provided there are rationally related benefits accruing to the stockholders. However, such concern for non-stockholder interests is inappropriate when an auction among active bidders is in progress, and the object no longer is to protect or maintain the corporate enterprise but to sell it to the highest bidder ... [W]e must conclude that the merger agreement with Forstmann was unreasonable in relation to the threat posed.

A lock-up is not *per se* illegal under Delaware law.... Such options can entice other bidders to enter a contest for control of the corporation, creating an auction for the company and maximizing shareholder profit. Current economic conditions in the takeover market are such that a "white knight" like Forstmann might only enter the bidding for the target company if it receives some form of compensation to cover the risks and costs involved. However, while those lock-ups which draw bidders into the battle benefit shareholders, similar measures which end an active auction and foreclose further bidding operate to the shareholders' detriment. . . .

The Forstmann option had a . . . destructive effect on the auction process. Forstmann had already been drawn into the contest on a preferred basis, so the result of the lock-up was not to foster bidding, but to destroy it. The board's stated reasons for approving the transactions were: (1) better financing, (2) noteholder protection, and (3) higher price. As the Court of Chancery found, and we agree, any distinctions between the rival bidders' methods of financing the proposal were nominal at best, and such a consideration has little or no significance in a cash offer for any and all shares. The principal object, contrary to the board's duty of care, appears to have been protection of the noteholders over the shareholders' interests.

While Forstmann's $57.25 offer was objectively higher than Pantry Pride's $56.25 bid, the margin of superiority is less when the Forstmann price is adjusted for the time value of money. In reality, the Revlon board ended the auction in return for very little actual improvement in the final bid. The principal benefit went to the directors, who avoided personal liability to a class of creditors to whom the board owed no further duty under the circumstances. Thus, when a board ends an intense bidding contest on an insubstantial basis, and where a significant by-product of that action is to protect the directors against a perceived threat of personal liability for consequences stemming from the adoption of previous defensive measures, the action cannot withstand the enhanced scrutiny which *Unocal* requires of director conduct.

In addition to the lock-up option, the Court of Chancery enjoined the no-shop provision as part of the attempt to foreclose further bidding by Pantry Pride. The no-shop provision, like the lock-up option, while not *per se* illegal, is impermissible under the *Unocal* standards when a board's primary duty becomes that of an auctioneer responsible for selling the company to the highest bidder. The agreement to negotiate only with Forstmann ended rather than intensified the board's involvement in the bidding contest.

It is ironic that the parties even considered a no-shop agreement when Revlon had dealt preferentially, and almost exclusively, with Forstmann throughout the contest. After the directors authorized management to negotiate with other parties, Forstmann was given every negotiating advantage that Pantry Pride had been denied: cooperation from management, access to financial data, and the exclusive opportunity to present merger proposals directly to the board of directors. Favoritism for a white knight to the total exclusion of a hostile bidder might be justifiable when the latter's offer adversely affects shareholder interests, but when bidders make relatively similar offers, or dissolution of the company becomes inevitable, the directors cannot fulfill their enhanced *Unocal* duties by playing favorites with the contending factions. Market forces must be allowed to operate freely to bring the target's shareholders the best price available for their equity. Thus, as the trial court ruled, the shareholders' interests necessitated that the board remain free to negotiate in the fulfillment of that duty.

The court below similarly enjoined the payment of the cancellation fee, pending a resolution of the merits, because the fee was part of the overall plan to thwart Pantry Pride's efforts. We find no abuse of discretion in that ruling. . . .

The decision of the Court of Chancery, therefore, is AFFIRMED.

———

In the wake of the *Revlon* case, Revlon accepted Perlman's offer and MacAndrews & Forbes Holding acquired the company for $1.8 billion. Bergerac, who had run Revlon for a decade, departed as CEO with a severance payment of $35 million.

B. WHAT TRIGGERS *REVLON*?

In *Revlon*, in response to an unwanted takeover offer, the board decided to sell the corporation to a white knight, Forstmann Little. The *Revlon* court ruled that once a sale or break-up of the corporation in response to an unwanted offer became inevitable, the board became an "auctioneer," obligated to seek the highest price reasonably available for shareholders.

The *Revlon* case left a number of open questions, including what sorts of fact settings it applies to, when it is triggered, and what procedures it requires. In the two cases that follow, *Paramount v. Time* and *QVC v. Paramount,* the Delaware Supreme Court provided more guidance as to when *Revlon* duties apply. *QVC* also discusses what the duties require.

In the first of these cases, *Paramount v. Time*, the court considered whether *Revlon* duties applied to a strategic combination which the parties did not characterize as a sale.

1. *PARAMOUNT v. TIME*

PARAMOUNT COMMUNICATIONS, INC. V. TIME INCORPORATED

Supreme Court of Delaware
571 A.2d 1140 (1989)

HORSEY, JUSTICE:

Paramount Communications, Inc. ("Paramount") and two other groups of plaintiffs ("Shareholder Plaintiffs"), shareholders of Time Incorporated ("Time"), a Delaware corporation, separately filed suits in the Delaware Court of Chancery seeking a preliminary injunction to halt Time's tender offer for 51% of Warner Communication, Inc.'s ("Warner") outstanding shares at $70 cash per share. The court below . . . denied plaintiffs' motion. [This court affirms.]

I

Time is a Delaware corporation with its principal offices in New York City. Time's traditional business is publication of magazines and books; however, Time also provides pay television programming through its Home Box Office, Inc. and Cinemax subsidiaries. In addition, Time owns and operates cable television franchises through its subsidiary, American Television and Communication Corporation. During the relevant time period, Time's board consisted of sixteen directors. Twelve of the directors were "outside," nonemployee directors. Four of the directors were also officers of the company. . . .

As early as 1983 and 1984, Time's executive board began considering expanding Time's operations into the entertainment industry. In 1987, Time established a special committee of executives to consider and propose corporate strategies for the 1990s. The consensus of the committee was that Time should move ahead in the area of ownership and creation of video programming. . . . Some of Time's outside directors, especially Luce and Temple, had opposed this move as a threat to the editorial integrity and journalistic focus of Time. Despite this concern, the board recognized that a vertically integrated video enterprise to complement Time's existing HBO and cable networks would better enable it to compete on a global basis.

In late spring of 1987, a meeting took place between Steve Ross, CEO of Warner Brothers, and Nicholas of Time. Ross and Nicholas discussed the possibility of a joint venture between the two companies through the creation of a jointly-owned cable company. Time would contribute its cable system and HBO. Warner would contribute its cable system and provide access to Warner Brothers Studio. The resulting venture would be a larger, more efficient cable network, able to produce and distribute its own movies on a worldwide basis. Ultimately the parties abandoned this plan, determining that it was impractical for several reasons, chief among them being tax considerations.

On August 11, 1987, Gerald M. Levin, Time's vice chairman and chief strategist, wrote J. Richard Munro a confidential memorandum in which he strongly recommended a strategic consolidation with Warner. In June 1988, Nicholas and Munro sent to each outside director a copy of the "comprehensive long-term planning document" prepared by the committee of Time executives that had been examining strategies for the 1990s. The memo included reference to and a description of Warner as a potential acquisition candidate.

Thereafter, Munro and Nicholas held meetings with Time's outside directors to discuss, generally, long-term strategies for Time and, specifically, a combination with Warner. Nearly a year later, Time's board reached the point of serious discussion of the "nuts and bolts" of a consolidation with an entertainment company. On July 21, 1988, Time's board met, with all outside directors present. The meeting's purpose was to consider Time's expansion into the entertainment industry on a global scale. Management presented the board with a profile of various entertainment companies in addition to Warner, including Disney, 20th Century Fox, Universal, and Paramount.

Without any definitive decision on choice of a company, the board approved in principle a strategic plan for Time's expansion. The board gave management the "go-ahead" to continue discussions with Warner concerning the possibility of a merger. With the exception of Temple and Luce, most of the outside directors agreed that a merger involving expansion into the entertainment field promised great growth opportunity for Time. Temple and Luce remained unenthusiastic about Time's entry into the entertainment field.

The board's consensus was that a merger of Time and Warner was feasible, but only if Time controlled the board of the resulting corporation and thereby preserved a management committed to Time's journalistic integrity. To accomplish this goal, the board stressed the importance of carefully defining in advance the corporate governance provisions that would control the resulting entity. Some board members expressed concern over whether such a business combination would place Time "in play." The board discussed the wisdom of adopting further defensive measures to lessen such a possibility.

Of a wide range of companies considered by Time's board as possible merger candidates, Warner Brothers, Paramount, Columbia, M.C.A., Fox, MGM, Disney, and Orion, the board, in July 1988, concluded that Warner was the superior candidate for a consolidation. Warner stood out on a number of counts [for reasons described at length in the opinion].

In August 1988, Levin, Nicholas, and Munro, acting on instructions from Time's board, continued to explore a business combination with Warner. By letter dated August 4, 1988, management informed the outside directors of proposed corporate governance provisions to be discussed with Warner. The provisions incorporated the recommendations of several of Time's outside directors.

From the outset, Time's board favored an all-cash or cash and securities acquisition of Warner as the basis for consolidation. Bruce Wasserstein, Time's financial advisor, also favored an outright purchase of Warner. However, Steve Ross, Warner's CEO, was adamant that a business combination was only practicable on a stock-for-stock basis. Warner insisted on a stock swap in order to preserve its shareholders' equity in the resulting corporation. Time's officers, on the other hand, made it abundantly clear that Time would be the acquiring corporation and that Time would control the resulting board. Time refused to permit itself to be cast as the "acquired" company.

Eventually Time acquiesced in Warner's insistence on a stock-for-stock deal, but talks broke down over corporate governance issues. Time wanted Ross' position as a co-CEO to be temporary and wanted Ross to retire in five years. Ross, however, refused to set a time for his retirement and viewed Time's proposal as indicating a lack of confidence in his leadership. Warner considered it vital that their executives and creative staff not perceive Warner as selling out to Time. Time's request of a guarantee that Time would dominate the CEO succession was objected to as inconsistent with the concept of a Time-Warner merger "of equals." Negotiations ended when the parties reached an impasse. Time's board refused to com-promise on its position on corporate governance. Time, and particularly its outside directors, viewed the corporate governance provisions as critical for preserving the "Time Culture" through a pro-Time management at the top. . . .

Warner and Time resumed negotiations in January 1989. [*One development that permitted the negotiations to resume was Ross's agreement to retire in five years and let Nicholas succeed him.*] . . . Many of the details of the original stock-for-stock exchange agreement remained intact. In addition, Time's senior management agreed to long-term contracts.

Time insider directors Levin and Nicholas met with Warner's financial advisors to decide upon a stock exchange ratio. Time's board had recognized the potential need to pay a premium in the stock ratio in exchange for dictating the governing arrangement of the new Time-Warner. Levin and outside director Finkelstein were the primary proponents of paying a premium to protect the "Time Culture." The board discussed premium rates of 10%, 15% and 20%. Wasserstein also suggested paying a premium for Warner due to Warner's rapid growth rate. The market exchange ratio of Time stock for Warner stock was .38 in favor of Warner. Warner's financial advisors in-formed its board that any exchange rate over .400 was a fair deal and any exchange rate over .450 was "one hell of a deal." The parties ultimately agreed upon an exchange rate favoring Warner of .465. On that basis, Warner stockholders would have owned approximately 62% of the common stock of Time-Warner.

On March 3, 1989, Time's board, with all but one director in attendance, met and unanimously approved the stock-for-stock merger with Warner. Warner's board likewise approved the merger. The agreement called for Warner to be merged into a wholly-owned Time subsidiary with Warner becoming the surviving corporation. The common stock of Warner would then be converted into common stock of Time at the agreed upon ratio. Thereafter, the name of Time would be changed to Time-Warner, Inc.

The rules of the New York Stock Exchange required that Time's issuance of shares to effectuate the merger be approved by a vote of Time's stockholders. The Delaware General Corporation Law required approval of the merger by a majority of the Warner stockholders. Delaware law did not require any vote by Time stockholders.

The resulting company would have a 24-member board, with 12 members representing each corporation. The company would have co-CEO's, at first Ross and Munro, then Ross and Nicholas, and finally, after Ross' retirement, by Nicholas alone. The board would create an editorial committee with a majority of members representing Time. A similar entertainment committee would be controlled by Warner board members. . . . [The court discussed a few other governance arrangements.]

At its March 3, 1989 meeting, Time's board adopted several defensive tactics. Time entered an automatic share exchange agreement with Warner. Time would receive 17,292,747 shares of Warner's outstanding common stock (9.4%) and Warner would receive 7,080,016 shares of Time's outstanding common stock (11.1%). Either party could trigger the exchange. Time sought out and paid for "confidence" letters from various banks with which it did business. In these letters, the banks promised not to finance any third-party attempt to acquire Time. . . .

Time representatives lauded the lack of debt to the United States Senate and to the President of the United States. Public reaction to the announcement of the merger was positive. Time-Warner would be a media colossus with international scope. . . . On May 24, 1989, Time sent out extensive proxy statements to the stockholders regarding the approval vote on the merger. . . . Time's board was unanimously in favor of the proposed merger with Warner; and, by the end of May, the Time-Warner merger appeared to be an accomplished fact.

On June 7, 1989, these wishful assumptions were shattered by Paramount's surprising announcement of its all-cash offer to purchase all outstanding shares of Time for $175 per share. The following day, June 8, the trading price of Time's stock rose from $126 to $170 per share. Paramount's offer was said to be "fully negotiable."

Time found Paramount's "fully negotiable" offer to be in fact subject to at least three conditions. First, Time had to terminate its merger agreement and stock exchange agreement with Warner, and remove certain other of its defensive devices, including the redemption of Time's shareholder rights. Second, Paramount had to obtain the required cable franchise transfers from Time in a fashion acceptable to Paramount in its sole discretion. Finally, the offer depended upon a judicial determination that section 203 of the General Corporate Law of Delaware (The Delaware Anti-Takeover Statute) was inapplicable to any Time-Paramount merger. . . .

On June 8, 1989, Time formally responded to Paramount's offer. Time's chairman and CEO, J. Richard Munro, sent an aggressively worded letter to Paramount's CEO, Martin Davis. Munro's letter attacked Davis' personal integrity and called Para-mount's offer "smoke and mirrors." . . . [A]ll [board] members endorsed management's response as well as the letter's content.

[The Time board met several times in June] to discuss Paramount's $175 offer. The board viewed Paramount's offer as inadequate and concluded that its proposed merger with Warner was the better course of action. [They are advised by financial advisors that "on an auction basis, Time's per share value was materially higher than Warner's $175 per share offer.] Therefore, the board declined to open any negotiations with Paramount and held steady its course toward a merger with Warner.

At these June meetings, certain Time directors expressed their concern that Time stockholders would not comprehend the long-term benefits of the Warner merger. Large quantities of Time shares were held by institutional investors. The board feared that even though there appeared to be wide support for the Warner transaction, Paramount's cash premium would be a tempting prospect to these investors. In mid-June, Time sought permission from the New York Stock Exchange to alter its rules and allow the Time-Warner merger to proceed without stockholder approval. Time did so at Warner's insistence. The New York Stock Exchange rejected Time's request on June 15; and on that day, the value of Time stock reached $182 per share.

The following day, June 16, Time's board met to take up Paramount's offer. The board's prevailing belief was that Paramount's bid posed a threat to Time's control of its own destiny and retention of the "Time Culture.". . . Time's advisors suggested various options, including defensive measures. . . . Time's board formally rejected Paramount's offer.

At the same meeting, Time's board decided to recast its consolidation with Warner into an outright cash and securities acquisition of Warner by Time; and Time so informed Warner. Time accordingly restructured its proposal to acquire Warner as follows: Time would make an immediate all-cash offer for 51% of Warner's outstanding stock at $70 per share. The remaining 49% would be purchased at some later date for a mixture of cash and securities worth $70 per share. To provide the funds required for its outright acquisition of Warner, Time would assume 7–10 billion dollars worth of debt, thus eliminating one of the principal transaction-related benefits of the original merger agreement. Nine billion dollars of the total purchase price would be allocated to the purchase of Warner's goodwill.

Warner agreed but insisted on certain terms. Warner sought a control premium and guarantees that the governance provisions found in the original merger agreement would remain intact. . . .

On June 23, 1989, Paramount raised its all-cash offer to buy Time's outstanding stock to $200 per share. Paramount still professed that all aspects of the offer were negotiable. Time's board met on June 26, 1989 and formally rejected Paramount's $200 per share second offer. The board reiterated its belief that, despite the $25 increase, the offer was still inadequate. The Time board maintained that the Warner transaction offered a greater long-term value for the stockholders and, unlike Paramount's offer, did not pose a threat to Time's survival and its "culture." Paramount then filed this action in the Court of Chancery.

II

The Shareholder Plaintiffs first assert a *Revlon* claim. They contend that the March 4 Time-Warner agreement effectively put Time up for sale, triggering *Revlon* duties, requiring Time's board to enhance short-term shareholder value and to treat all other interested acquirors on an equal basis. The Shareholder Plaintiffs base this argument on two facts: (i) the ultimate Time-Warner exchange ratio of .465 favoring Warner, resulting in Warner shareholders' receipt of 62% of the combined company; and (ii) the subjective intent of Time's directors as evidenced in their statements that the market might perceive the Time-Warner merger as putting Time up "for sale" and their adoption of various defensive measures.

The Shareholder Plaintiffs further contend that Time's directors, in structuring the original merger transaction to be "takeover-proof," triggered *Revlon* duties by foreclosing their shareholders from any prospect of obtaining a control premium. In short, plaintiffs argue that

Time's board's decision to merge with Warner imposed a fiduciary duty to maximize immediate share value and not erect unreasonable barriers to further bids. Therefore, they argue, the Chancellor erred in finding: that Paramount's bid for Time did not place Time "for sale;" that Time's transaction with Warner did not result in any transfer of control; and that the combined Time-Warner was not so large as to preclude the possibility of the stockholders of Time-Warner receiving a future control premium.

[Discussion of Paramount's *Unocal* claim omitted.]

The Court of Chancery posed the pivotal question presented by this case to be: Under what circumstances must a board of directors abandon an in-place plan of corporate development in order to provide its shareholders with the option to elect and realize an immediate control premium? As applied to this case, the question becomes: Did Time's board, having developed a strategic plan of global expansion to be launched through a business combination with Warner, come under a fiduciary duty to jettison its plan and put the corporation's future in the hands of its shareholders?

While we affirm the result reached by the Chancellor, we think it unwise to place undue emphasis upon long-term versus short-term corporate strategy. . . . [T]he question of "long-term" versus "short-term" values is largely irrelevant because directors, generally, are obliged to chart a course for a corporation which is in its best interests without regard to a fixed investment horizon. [Moreover], absent a limited set of circumstances as defined under *Revlon*, a board of directors, while always required to act in an informed manner, is not under any per se duty to maximize shareholder value in the short term, even in the context of a takeover. In our view, the pivotal question presented by this case is: "Did Time, by entering into the proposed merger with Warner, put itself up for sale?"

A.

We first take up plaintiffs' principal *Revlon* argument, summarized above. In rejecting this argument, the Chancellor found the original Time-Warner merger agreement not to constitute a "change of control" and concluded that the transaction did not trigger *Revlon* duties. The Chancellor's conclusion is premised on a finding that "[b]efore the merger agreement was signed, control of the corporation existed in a fluid aggregation of unaffiliated shareholders representing a voting majority— in other words, in the market." The Chancellor's findings of fact are supported by the record and his conclusion is correct as a matter of law. However, we premise our rejection of plaintiffs' *Revlon* claim on different grounds, namely, the absence of any substantial evidence to conclude that

Time's board, in negotiating with Warner, made the dissolution or break-up of the corporate entity inevitable, as was the case in *Revlon*.

Under Delaware law there are, generally speaking and without excluding other possibilities, two circumstances which may implicate *Revlon* duties. The first, and clearer one, is when a corporation initiates an active bidding process seeking to sell itself or to effect a business reorganization involving a clear break-up of the company. However, *Revlon* duties may also be triggered where, in response to a bidder's offer, a target abandons its long-term strategy and seeks an alternative transaction involving the breakup of the company.[13] Thus, in *Revlon*, when the board responded to Pantry Pride's offer by contemplating a "bust-up" sale of assets in a leveraged acquisition, we imposed upon the board a duty to maximize immediate shareholder value and an obligation to auction the company fairly. If, however, the board's reaction to a hostile tender offer is found to constitute only a defensive response and not an abandonment of the corporation's continued existence, *Revlon* duties are not triggered, though *Unocal* duties attach.[14]

The plaintiffs insist that even though the original Time-Warner agreement may not have worked "an objective change of control," the transaction made a "sale" of Time inevitable. Plaintiffs rely on the subjective intent of Time's board of directors and principally upon certain board members' expressions of concern that the Warner transaction might be viewed as effectively putting Time up for sale. Plaintiffs argue that the use of a lock-up agreement, a no-shop clause, and so-called "dry-up" agreements prevented shareholders from obtaining a control premium in the immediate future and thus violated *Revlon*.

We agree with the Chancellor that such evidence is entirely insufficient to invoke *Revlon* duties; and we decline to extend *Revlon*'s application to corporate transactions simply because they might be construed as putting a corporation either "in play" or "up for sale." The adoption of structural safety devices alone does not trigger *Revlon*. . . .

Finally, we do not find in Time's recasting of its merger agreement with Warner from a share exchange to a share purchase a basis to conclude that Time had either abandoned its strategic plan or made a sale of Time inevitable. The Chancellor found that although the merged

---

[13] As we stated in *Revlon*, in both such cases, "[t]he duty of the board [has] changed from the preservation of . . . [the] corporate entity to the maximization of the company's value at a sale for the stockholder's benefit. . . . [The board] no longer face[s] threats to corporate policy and effectiveness, or to the stockholders' interests, from a grossly inadequate bid."

[14] Within the auction process, any action taken by the board must be reasonably related to the threat posed or reasonable in relation to the advantage sought. Thus, a *Unocal* analysis may be appropriate when a corporation is in a *Revlon* situation and *Revlon* duties may be triggered by a defensive action taken in response to a hostile offer. Since *Revlon*, we have stated that differing treatment of various bidders is not actionable when such action reasonably relates to achieving the best price available for the stockholders.

Time-Warner company would be large (with a value approaching approximately $30 billion), recent takeover cases have proven that acquisition of the combined company might nonetheless be possible. . . . [*Unocal* therefore applies; *Unocal* analysis omitted.]

C.

Conclusion

Applying the test for grant or denial of preliminary injunctive relief, we find plaintiffs failed to establish a reasonable likelihood of ultimate success on the merits. Therefore, we affirm.

———————————

Time's decision to ignore its own shareholders, spurn Paramount's offer and combine with Warner turned out to be a terrible one. It took until 1997 for Time Warner's stock to reach the same price as Paramount had offered.[2] Time Warner then proceeded to engage in one of the worst deals in history, the combination of AOL and Time Warner discussed in Chapter I. Today Time, with its the well-known magazine brands such as People, Sports Illustrated, Time, Entertainment weekly, and Horse & Hound, among others, has been spun off from Time Warner and trades as a separate company, Time, Inc. AOL, Inc. was spun off by Time Warner in 2009 and was later acquired by Verizon. Time would thus seem to be back where it was prior to the Warner combination. And, due to the decline of print media, as this book goes to press, Time's fortunes scarcely seem assured. An article written in mid-2014 noted:

> Sometime late next year Time Inc., the company that all but created the modern magazine business, will leave its home of more than five decades, the Time & Life Building in Rockefeller Center, and head to new quarters in downtown Manhattan. It is a pragmatic move aimed at reducing costs, but one filled with symbolism for a company that is starting over in fundamental ways.
>
> On Monday, the nation's largest magazine publisher will begin trading as an independent company—stock symbol: TIME—with an uncertain future. What was once a jewel in terms of profit and stature is now a drag on the share price of Time Warner, its parent company, and is being spun off with little ceremony and a load of debt. . . . The new entity will start off with $1.3 billion in debt, including $600 million that will go toward a one-time cash dividend to Time Warner shareholders. . . . Time Inc.'s debt is

———————————

[2] *Time Warner Stock Price Reaches $50*, N.Y TIMES, June 12, 1997, available at http://www.nytimes.com/1997/06/12/business/time-warner-stock-price-reaches–50.html ("Now, after eight years, the value of Time Warner's stock is equal to that fateful Paramount bid—at least, after accounting for a 4-for-1 stock split.").

high-risk, and Moody's has rated it at less than investment grade. As recently as 2006, Time Inc. produced about $1 billion in earnings, a figure that is now down to $370 million."[3]

The *Time* opinion set up a dichotomous world. It appeared to hold that when a company was acquired by another company, Revlon would apply. However, when the company would continue to exist as part of a strategic combination, *Revlon* did not apply since there had been no change of control or break-up of the company. To what transactions *Revlon* would apply was left uncertain; the question was resolved in *QVC v. Paramount*.

2.   *QVC v. PARAMOUNT*

In the mid-1980s, the media industry began consolidating around content and the "pipes" to deliver that content into people's homes. Part of the motivating factor for the Time-Warner merger was what seemed to be a distant prospect of being able to offer consumers a "triple play," combined phone, cable television and interactive content, through a single service. In the late 1970s Warner had already tested its interactive "Qube" technology with some of its cable subscribers in the Northeast. At the same time, Time was also testing its own version of interactive cable technology, "Time Teletext." A race began among cable companies to consolidate horizontally and vertically to prepare for the interactive future. (By now, of course, that distant vision of an interactive future has become commonplace.) The quest to consolidate content with the technology to deliver the content into consumer homes was Paramount's primary motivation for attempting to acquire Time. With the failure of the Time acquisition, Paramount came to the attention of Viacom.

Paramount and Viacom had had discussions about a business combination in 1990. At the time, Paramount was a widely held public company while Viacom was controlled by its CEO, Sumner Redstone. The discussions between Paramount and Viacom do not seem to have proceeded continuously, but in April of 1993, the two came to a tentative agreement. Negotiations then broke down. Before they resumed, Morton Davis, the CEO of Paramount, learned that QVC, headed by Barry Diller, might be interested in Paramount, and Mr. Davis told QVC's Diller that Paramount was not for sale. In August 1993, Paramount and Viacom resumed discussions. In September 1993, Paramount approved a merger agreement with Viacom. Under the terms of the transaction, Viacom would issue stock to acquire Paramount. Mr. Redstone would maintain control of the combined corporation. Shortly thereafter, QVC jumped in, attempting to acquire Paramount.

---

[3]   David Carr & Ravi Somaiya, *Time Inc. to Set a Lonely Course After a Spinoff*, N.Y. TIMES, Jun. 8, 2014, available at http://www.nytimes.com/2014/06/09/business/media/time-inc-to-set-a-lonely-course-after-a-spinoff.html.

PARAMOUNT COMMUNICATIONS, INC. V. QVC NETWORK, INC.

Supreme Court of Delaware
637 A.2d 34 (1994)

VEASEY, CHIEF JUSTICE.

. . .

I. FACTS

. . .

Paramount is a Delaware corporation with its principal offices in New York City. . . . The majority of Paramount's stock is publicly held by numerous unaffiliated investors. Paramount owns and operates a diverse group of entertainment businesses, including motion picture and television studios, book publishers, professional sports teams, and amusement parks. . . .

Viacom is a Delaware corporation with its headquarters in Massachusetts. Viacom is controlled by Sumner M. Redstone ("Redstone"), its Chairman and Chief Executive Officer, who owns indirectly approximately 85.2 percent of Viacom's voting Class A stock and approximately 69.2 percent of Viacom's nonvoting Class B stock through National Amusements, Inc. ("NAI"), an entity 91.7 percent owned by Redstone. Viacom has a wide range of entertainment operations, including a number of well-known cable television channels such as MTV, Nickelodeon, Showtime, and The Movie Channel. Viacom's equity co-investors in the Paramount-Viacom transaction include NYNEX Corporation and Blockbuster Entertainment Corporation.

QVC is a Delaware corporation with its headquarters in West Chester, Pennsylvania. QVC has several large stockholders, including Liberty Media Corporation, Comcast Corporation, Advance Publications, Inc., and Cox Enterprises Inc. Barry Diller ("Diller"), the Chairman and Chief Executive Officer of QVC, is also a substantial stockholder. QVC sells a variety of merchandise through a televised shopping channel. QVC has several equity co-investors in its proposed combination with Paramount including BellSouth Corporation and Comcast Corporation.

Beginning in the late 1980s, Paramount investigated the possibility of acquiring or merging with other companies in the entertainment, media, or communications industry. Paramount considered such transactions to be desirable, and perhaps necessary, in order to keep pace with competitors in the rapidly evolving field of entertainment and communications. Consistent with its goal of strategic expansion, Paramount made a tender offer for Time Inc. in 1989, but was ultimately unsuccessful.

Although Paramount had considered a possible combination of Paramount and Viacom as early as 1990, recent efforts to explore such a transaction began at a dinner meeting between Redstone and [Paramount CEO Martin] Davis [("Davis")] on April 20, 1993. Robert Greenhill ("Greenhill"), Chairman of Smith Barney Shearson Inc. ("Smith Barney"), attended and helped facilitate this meeting. After several more meetings between Redstone and Davis, serious negotiations began taking place in early July.

It was tentatively agreed that Davis would be the chief executive officer and Redstone would be the controlling stockholder of the combined company, but the parties could not reach agreement on the merger price and the terms of a stock option to be granted to Viacom. With respect to price, Viacom offered a package of cash and stock (primarily Viacom Class B nonvoting stock) with a market value of approximately $61 per share, but Paramount wanted at least $70 per share.

Shortly after negotiations broke down in July 1993, two notable events occurred. First, Davis apparently learned of QVC's potential interest in Paramount, and told Diller over lunch on July 21, 1993, that Paramount was not for sale. Second, the market value of Viacom's Class B nonvoting stock increased from $46.875 on July 6 to $57.25 on August 20. QVC claims (and Viacom disputes) that this price increase was caused by open market purchases of such stock by Redstone or entities controlled by him.

On August 20, 1993, discussions between Paramount and Viacom resumed when Greenhill arranged another meeting between Davis and Redstone. After a short hiatus, the parties negotiated in earnest in early September, and performed due diligence with the assistance of their financial advisors, Lazard Freres & Co. ("Lazard") for Paramount and Smith Barney for Viacom. On September 9, 1993, the Paramount Board was informed about the status of the negotiations and was provided information by Lazard, including an analysis of the proposed transaction.

On September 12, 1993, the Paramount Board met again and unanimously approved the Original Merger Agreement whereby Paramount would merge with and into Viacom. The terms of the merger provided that each share of Paramount common stock would be converted into 0.10 shares of Viacom Class A voting stock, 0.90 shares of Viacom Class B nonvoting stock, and $9.10 in cash. In addition, the Paramount Board agreed to amend its "poison pill" Rights Agreement to exempt the proposed merger with Viacom. The Original Merger Agreement also contained several provisions designed to make it more difficult for a potential competing bid to succeed. We focus, as did the Court of Chancery, on three of these defensive provisions: a "no-shop" provision (the "No-Shop Provision"), the Termination Fee, and the Stock Option Agreement.

First, under the No-Shop Provision, the Paramount Board agreed that Paramount would not solicit, encourage, discuss, negotiate, or endorse any competing transaction unless: (a) a third party "makes an unsolicited written, bona fide proposal, which is not subject to any material contingencies relating to financing"; and (b) the Paramount Board determines that discussions or negotiations with the third party are necessary for the Paramount Board to comply with its fiduciary duties.

Second, under the Termination Fee provision, Viacom would receive a $100 million termination fee if: (a) Paramount terminated the Original Merger Agreement because of a competing transaction; (b) Paramount's stockholders did not approve the merger; or (c) the Paramount Board recommended a competing transaction.

The third and most significant deterrent device was the Stock Option Agreement, which granted to Viacom an option to purchase approximately 19.9 percent (23,699,000 shares) of Paramount's outstanding common stock at $69.14 per share if any of the triggering events for the Termination Fee occurred. In addition to the customary terms that are normally associated with a stock option, the Stock Option Agreement contained two provisions that were both unusual and highly beneficial to Viacom: (a) Viacom was permitted to pay for the shares with a senior subordinated note of questionable marketability instead of cash, thereby avoiding the need to raise the $1.6 billion purchase price (the "Note Feature"); and (b) Viacom could elect to require Paramount to pay Viacom in cash a sum equal to the difference between the purchase price and the market price of Paramount's stock (the "Put Feature"). Because the Stock Option Agreement was not "capped" to limit its maximum dollar value, it had the potential to reach (and in this case did reach) unreasonable levels.

After the execution of the Original Merger Agreement and the Stock Option Agreement on September 12, 1993, Paramount and Viacom announced their proposed merger. In a number of public statements, the parties indicated that the pending transaction was a virtual certainty. Redstone described it as a "marriage" that would "never be torn asunder" and stated that only a "nuclear attack" could break the deal. Redstone also called Diller and John Malone of Tele-Communications Inc., a major stockholder of QVC, to dissuade them from making a competing bid.

Despite these attempts to discourage a competing bid, Diller sent a letter to Davis on September 20, 1993, proposing a merger in which QVC would acquire Paramount for approximately $80 per share, consisting of 0.893 shares of QVC common stock and $30 in cash. QVC also expressed its eagerness to meet with Paramount to negotiate the details of a transaction. When the Paramount Board met on September 27, it was advised by Davis that the Original Merger Agreement prohibited Paramount from having discussions with QVC (or anyone else) unless certain conditions were satisfied. In particular, QVC had to supply evidence that its proposal was not subject to financing contingencies. The Paramount Board was also provided information from Lazard describing QVC and its proposal.

On October 5, 1993, QVC provided Paramount with evidence of QVC's financing. The Paramount Board then held another meeting on October 11, and decided to authorize management to meet with QVC . . . In response to Paramount's request for information, QVC provided two binders of documents to Paramount on October 20.

On October 21, 1993, QVC filed this action and publicly announced an $80 cash tender offer for 51 percent of Paramount's outstanding shares (the "QVC tender offer"). Each remaining share of Paramount common stock would be converted into 1.42857 shares of QVC common stock in a second-step merger. The tender offer was conditioned on, among other things, the invalidation of the Stock Option Agreement, which was worth over $200 million by that point. . . .

Confronted by QVC's hostile bid, which on its face offered over $10 per share more than the consideration provided by the Original Merger Agreement, Viacom realized that it would need to raise its bid in order to remain competitive. Within hours after QVC's tender offer was announced, Viacom entered into discussions with Paramount concerning a revised transaction. These discussions led to serious negotiations concerning a comprehensive amendment to the original Paramount-Viacom transaction. In effect, the opportunity for a "new deal" with Viacom was at hand for the Paramount Board. With the QVC hostile bid offering greater value to the Paramount stockholders, the Paramount Board had considerable leverage with Viacom.

At a special meeting on October 24, 1993, the Paramount Board approved the Amended Merger Agreement and an amendment to the Stock Option Agreement. The Amended Merger Agreement was, however, essentially the same as the Original Merger Agreement, except that it included a few new provisions. One provision related to an $80 per share cash tender offer by Viacom for 51 percent of Paramount's stock, and another changed the merger consideration so that each share of Paramount would be converted into 0.20408 shares of Viacom Class A voting stock, 1.08317 shares of Viacom Class B nonvoting stock, and 0.20408 shares of a new series of Viacom convertible preferred stock. The Amended Merger Agreement also added a provision giving Paramount the right not to amend its Rights Agreement to exempt Viacom if the

Paramount Board determined that such an amendment would be inconsistent with its fiduciary duties because another offer constituted a "better alternative." Finally, the Paramount Board was given the power to terminate the Amended Merger Agreement if it withdrew its recommendation of the Viacom transaction or recommended a competing transaction.

Although the Amended Merger Agreement offered more consideration to the Paramount stockholders and somewhat more flexibility to the Paramount Board than did the Original Merger Agreement, the defensive measures designed to make a competing bid more difficult were not removed or modified. In particular, there is no evidence in the record that Paramount sought to use its newly-acquired leverage to eliminate or modify the No-Shop Provision, the Termination Fee, or the Stock Option Agreement when the subject of amending the Original Merger Agreement was on the table.

. . .

On November 6, 1993, Viacom unilaterally raised its tender offer price to $85 per share in cash and offered a comparable increase in the value of the securities being proposed in the second-step merger. At a telephonic meeting held later that day, the Paramount Board agreed to recommend Viacom's higher bid to Paramount's stockholders.

QVC responded to Viacom's higher bid on November 12 by increasing its tender offer to $90 per share and by increasing the securities for its second-step merger by a similar amount. In response to QVC's latest offer, the Paramount Board scheduled a meeting for November 15, 1993. Prior to the meeting, [Paramount board member and Executive VP, Chief Administrative Officer and General Counsel] Oresman sent the members of the Paramount Board a document summarizing the "conditions and uncertainties" of QVC's offer. One director testified that this document gave him a very negative impression of the QVC bid.

At its meeting on November 15, 1993, the Paramount Board determined that the new QVC offer was not in the best interests of the stockholders. The purported basis for this conclusion was that QVC's bid was excessively conditional. The Paramount Board did not communicate with QVC regarding the status of the conditions because it believed that the No-Shop Provision prevented such communication in the absence of firm financing. Several Paramount directors also testified that they believed the Viacom transaction would be more advantageous to Paramount's future business prospects than a QVC transaction. Although a number of materials were distributed to the Paramount Board describing the Viacom and QVC transactions, the only quantitative analysis of the consideration to be received by the stockholders under each proposal was based on then-current market prices of the securities involved, not on the anticipated value of such securities at the time when the stockholders would receive them.

The preliminary injunction hearing in this case took place on November 16, 1993. On November 19, Diller wrote to the Paramount Board to inform it that QVC had obtained financing commitments for its tender offer and that there was no antitrust obstacle to the offer. On November 24, 1993, the Court of Chancery issued its decision granting a preliminary injunction in favor of QVC and the plaintiff stockholders. This appeal followed.

II.   APPLICABLE PRINCIPLES OF ESTABLISHED DELAWARE LAW

. . . Under normal circumstances, neither the courts nor the stockholders should interfere with the managerial decisions of the directors. The business judgment rule embodies the deference to which such decisions are entitled.

Nevertheless, there are rare situations which mandate that a court take a more direct and active role in overseeing the decisions made and actions taken by directors. In these situations, a court subjects the directors' conduct to enhanced scrutiny to ensure that it is reasonable. The decisions of this Court have clearly established the circumstances where such enhanced scrutiny will be applied. *E.g., Unocal*; and *Revlon*. The case at bar implicates two such circumstances: (1) the approval of a transaction resulting in a sale of control, and (2) the adoption of defensive measures in response to a threat to corporate control.

A.   The Significance of a Sale or Change of Control

When a majority of a corporation's voting shares are acquired by a single person or entity, or by a cohesive group acting together, there is a significant diminution in the voting power of those who thereby become minority stockholders. Under the statutory framework of the General Corporation Law, many of the most fundamental corporate changes can be implemented only if they are approved by a majority vote of the stockholders. Such actions include elections of directors, amendments to the certificate of incorporation, mergers, consolidations, sales of all or substantially all of the assets of the corporation, and dissolution. 8 Del.C. §§ 211, 242, 251–258, 263, 271, 275. Because of the overriding importance of voting rights, this Court and the Court of Chancery have consistently acted to protect stockholders from unwarranted interference with such rights.

In the absence of devices protecting the minority stockholders, stockholder votes are likely to become mere formalities where there is a majority stockholder. For example, minority stockholders can be deprived of a continuing equity interest in their corporation by means of a cash-out merger. Absent effective protective provisions, minority stockholders must rely for protection solely on the fiduciary duties owed to them by the directors and the majority stockholder, since the minority stockholders have lost the power to influence corporate direction through the ballot. The acquisition of majority status and the consequent privilege of exerting the powers of majority ownership come at a price. That price is usually a control premium which recognizes not only the value of a control block of shares, but also compensates the minority stockholders for their resulting loss of voting power.

In the case before us, the public stockholders (in the aggregate) currently own a majority of Paramount's voting stock. Control of the corporation is not vested in a single person, entity, or group, but vested in the fluid aggregation of unaffiliated stockholders. In the event the Paramount-Viacom transaction is consummated, the public stockholders will receive cash and a minority equity voting position in the surviving corporation. Following such consummation, there will be a controlling stockholder who will have the voting power to: (a) elect directors; (b) cause a break-up of the corporation; (c) merge it with another company; (d) cash-out the public stockholders; (e) amend the certificate of incorporation; (f) sell all or substantially all of the corporate assets; or (g) otherwise alter materially the nature of the corporation and the public stockholders' interests. Irrespective of the present Paramount Board's vision of a long-term strategic alliance with Viacom, the proposed sale of control would provide the new controlling stockholder with the power to alter that vision.

Because of the intended sale of control, the Paramount-Viacom transaction has economic consequences of considerable significance to the Paramount stockholders. Once control has shifted, the current Paramount stockholders will have no leverage in the future to demand another control premium. As a result, the Paramount stockholders are entitled to receive, and should receive, a control premium and/or protective devices of significant value. There being no such protective provisions in the Viacom-Paramount transaction, the Paramount directors had an obligation to take the maximum advantage of the current opportunity to realize for the stockholders the best value reasonably available.

B.   The Obligations of Directors in a Sale or Change of Control Transaction

The consequences of a sale of control impose special obligations on the directors of a corporation. . . . [T]he directors must focus on one primary objective—to secure the transaction offering the best value reasonably available for the stockholders—and they must exercise their fiduciary duties to further that end. The decisions of this Court have consistently emphasized this goal. . . .

In pursuing this objective, the directors must be especially diligent. In particular, this Court has stressed the importance of the board being adequately informed in negotiating a sale of control: "The need for adequate information is central to the enlightened evaluation of a transaction that a board must make." This requirement is consistent with the general principle that "directors have a duty to inform themselves, prior to making a business decision, of all material information reasonably available to them." . . . Moreover, the role of outside, independent directors becomes particularly important because of the magnitude of a sale of control transaction and the possibility, in certain cases, that management may not necessarily be impartial.

Barkan [*Barkan v. Amsted Indus., Inc.,* 567 A.2d 1279 (Del. 1989)] teaches some of the methods by which a board can fulfill its obligation to seek the best value reasonably available to the stockholders. . . . These methods are designed to determine the existence and viability of possible alternatives. They include conducting an auction, canvassing the market, etc. Delaware law recognizes that there is "no single blueprint" that directors must follow. . . .

In determining which alternative provides the best value for the stockholders, a board of directors is not limited to considering only the amount of cash involved, and is not required to ignore totally its view of the future value of a strategic alliance. . . . Instead, the directors should analyze the entire situation and evaluate in a disciplined manner the consideration being offered. Where stock or other non-cash consideration is involved, the board should try to quantify its value, if feasible, to achieve an objective comparison of the alternatives. In addition, the board may assess a variety of practical considerations relating to each alternative, including:

> [an offer's] fairness and feasibility; the proposed or actual financing for the offer, and the consequences of that financing; questions of illegality; . . . the risk of [nonconsummation]; . . . the bidder's identity, prior background and other business venture experiences; and the bidder's business plans for the corporation and their effects on stockholder interests.

These considerations are important because the selection of one alternative may permanently foreclose other opportunities. While the assessment of these factors may be complex, the board's goal is straightforward: Having informed themselves of all material information reasonably available, the directors must decide which alternative is most likely to offer the best value reasonably available to the stockholders.

C.   Enhanced Judicial Scrutiny of a Sale or
Change of Control Transaction

Board action in the circumstances presented here is subject to enhanced scrutiny. Such scrutiny is mandated by: (a) the threatened diminution of the current stockholders' voting power; (b) the fact that an asset belonging to public stockholders (a control premium) is being sold and may never be available again; and (c) the traditional concern of Delaware courts for actions which impair or impede stockholder voting rights. In *Macmillan* [*Mills Acquisition Co. v. Macmillan, Inc.*, 559 A.2d 1261 (Del. 1989)], this Court held:

> When *Revlon* duties devolve upon directors, this Court will continue to exact an enhanced judicial scrutiny at the threshold, as in *Unocal,* before the normal presumptions of the business judgment rule will apply.

The *Macmillan* decision articulates a specific two-part test for analyzing board action where competing bidders are not treated equally:

> In the face of disparate treatment, the trial court must first examine whether the directors properly perceived that shareholder interests were enhanced. In any event the board's action must be reasonable in relation to the advantage sought to be achieved, or conversely, to the threat which a particular bid allegedly poses to stockholder interests.

The key features of an enhanced scrutiny test are: (a) a judicial determination regarding the adequacy of the decisionmaking process employed by the directors, including the information on which the directors based their decision; and (b) a judicial examination of the reasonableness of the directors' action in light of the circumstances then existing. The directors have the burden of proving that they were adequately informed and acted reasonably.

Although an enhanced scrutiny test involves a review of the reasonableness of the substantive merits of a board's actions, a court should not ignore the complexity of the directors' task in a sale of control. There are many business and financial considerations implicated in investigating and selecting the best value reasonably available. The board of directors is the corporate decisionmaking body best equipped to make these judgments. Accordingly, a court applying enhanced judicial scrutiny should be deciding whether the directors made a reasonable decision, not a perfect decision. If a board selected one of several reasonable alternatives, a court should not second-guess that choice even though it might have decided otherwise or subsequent events may have cast doubt on the board's determination. Thus, courts will not substitute their business judgment for that of the directors, but will determine if the directors' decision was, on balance, within a range of reasonableness.

D. *Revlon* and *Time-Warner* Distinguished

The Paramount defendants and Viacom assert that the fiduciary obligations and the enhanced judicial scrutiny discussed above are not implicated in this case in the absence of a "break-up" of the corporation, and that the order granting the preliminary injunction should be reversed. This argument is based on their erroneous interpretation of our decisions in *Revlon* and *Time-Warner*.

In *Revlon,* we reviewed the actions of the board of directors of Revlon, Inc. ("Revlon"), which had rebuffed the overtures of Pantry Pride, Inc. and had instead entered into an agreement with Forstmann Little & Co. ("Forstmann") providing for the acquisition of 100 percent of Revlon's outstanding stock by Forstmann and the subsequent break-up of Revlon. Based on the facts and circumstances present in *Revlon,* we held that "[t]he directors' role changed from defenders of the corporate bastion to auctioneers charged with getting the best price for the stockholders at a sale of the company." We further held that "when a board ends an intense bidding contest on an insubstantial basis, . . . [that] action cannot withstand the enhanced scrutiny which *Unocal* requires of director conduct."

It is true that one of the circumstances bearing on these holdings was the fact that "the break-up of the company . . . had become a reality which even the directors embraced." *Revlon.* It does not follow, however, that a "break-up" must be present and "inevitable" before directors are subject to enhanced judicial scrutiny and are required to pursue a transaction that is calculated to produce the best value reasonably available to the stockholders. In fact, we stated in *Revlon* that "when bidders make relatively similar offers, or dissolution of the company becomes inevitable, the directors cannot fulfill their enhanced *Unocal* duties by playing favorites with the contending factions." *Revlon* thus does not hold that an inevitable dissolution or "break-up" is necessary.

The decisions of this Court following *Revlon* reinforced the applicability of enhanced scrutiny and the directors' obligation to seek the best value reasonably available for the stockholders where there is a pending sale of control, regardless of whether or not there is to be a break-up of the corporation.

In *Barkan,* we observed further:

> We believe that the general principles announced in *Revlon,* in *Unocal*, and in *Moran v. Household International* govern this case and every case in which a fundamental change of corporate control occurs or is contemplated.

Although *Macmillan* and *Barkan* are clear in holding that a change of control imposes on directors the obligation to obtain the best value reasonably available to the stockholders, the Paramount defendants have interpreted our decision in *Time-Warner* as requiring a corporate break-up in order for that obligation to apply. The facts in *Time-Warner,* however, were quite different from the facts of this case, and refute Paramount's position here. In *Time-Warner,* the Chancellor held that there was no change of control in the original stock-for-stock merger between Time and Warner because Time would be owned by a fluid aggregation of unaffiliated stockholders both before and after the merger . . .

The existence of a control block of stock in the hands of a single shareholder or a group with loyalty to each other does have real consequences to the financial value of "minority" stock. The law offers some protection to such shares through the imposition of a fiduciary duty upon controlling shareholders. But here, effectuation of the merger would not have subjected Time shareholders to the risks and consequences of holders of minority shares. This is a reflection of the fact that no control passed to anyone in the transaction contemplated. The shareholders of Time would have "suffered" dilution, of course, but they would suffer the same type of dilution upon the public distribution of new stock. Moreover, the transaction actually consummated in *Time-Warner* was not a merger, as originally planned, but a sale of Warner's stock to Time.

In our affirmance of the Court of Chancery's well-reasoned decision, this Court held that "The Chancellor's findings of fact are supported by the record and his conclusion is correct as a matter of law." *Time-Warner.* Nevertheless, the Paramount defendants here have argued that a break-up is a requirement and have focused on the following language in our *Time-Warner* decision:

> However, we premise our rejection of plaintiffs' *Revlon* claim on different grounds, namely, the absence of any substantial evidence to conclude that Time's board, in negotiating with Warner, made the dissolution or break-up of the corporate entity inevitable, as was the case in *Revlon.*

> Under Delaware law there are, generally speaking and without excluding other possibilities, two circumstances which may implicate *Revlon* duties. The first, and clearer one, is when a corporation initiates an active bidding process seeking to sell itself or to effect a business reorganization involving a clear break-up of the company. However, *Revlon* duties may also be triggered where, in response to a bidder's offer, a target abandons its long-term strategy and seeks an alternative transaction involving the breakup of the company.

The Paramount defendants have misread the holding of *Time-Warner.* Contrary to their argument, our decision in *Time-Warner* expressly states that the two general scenarios discussed in the above-quoted paragraph are not the only instances where "*Revlon* duties" may be implicated. The Paramount defendants' argument totally ignores the phrase "without excluding other possibilities." Moreover, the instant case is clearly within the first general scenario set forth in *Time-Warner*. The Paramount Board, albeit unintentionally, had "initiate[d] an active bidding process seeking to sell itself" by agreeing to sell control of the corporation to Viacom in circumstances where another potential acquiror (QVC) was equally interested in being a bidder.

The Paramount defendants' position that both a change of control and a break-up are required must be rejected. Such a holding would unduly restrict the application of *Revlon,* is inconsistent with this Court's decisions in *Barkan* and *Macmillan,* and has no basis in policy. There are few events that have a more significant impact on the stockholders than a sale of control or a corporate breakup. Each event represents a fundamental (and perhaps irrevocable) change in the nature of the corporate enterprise from a practical standpoint. It is the significance of each of these events that justifies: (a) focusing on the directors' obligation to seek the best value reasonably available to the stockholders; and (b) requiring a close scrutiny of board action which could be contrary to the stockholders' interests.

Accordingly, when a corporation undertakes a transaction which will cause: (a) a change in corporate control; or (b) a breakup of the corporate entity, the directors' obligation is to seek the best value reasonably available to the stockholders. This obligation arises because the effect of the Viacom-Paramount transaction, if consummated, is to shift control of Paramount from the public stockholders to a controlling stockholder, Viacom. Neither *Time-Warner* nor any other decision of this Court holds that a "break-up" of the company is essential to give rise to this obligation where there is a sale of control.

III. BREACH OF FIDUCIARY DUTIES
BY PARAMOUNT BOARD

We now turn to duties of the Paramount Board under the facts of this case and our conclusions as to the breaches of those duties which warrant injunctive relief.

A. The Specific Obligations of the Paramount Board

Under the facts of this case, the Paramount directors had the obligation: (a) to be diligent and vigilant in examining critically the Paramount-Viacom transaction and the QVC tender offers; (b) to act in good faith; (c) to obtain, and act with due care on, all material information reasonably available, including information necessary to compare the two offers to determine which of these transactions, or an alternative course of action, would provide the best value reasonably available to the stockholders; and (d) to negotiate actively and in good faith with both Viacom and QVC to that end.

Having decided to sell control of the corporation, the Paramount directors were required to evaluate critically whether or not all material aspects of the Paramount-Viacom transaction (separately and in the aggregate) were reasonable and in the best interests of the Paramount stockholders in light of current circumstances, including: the change of control premium, the Stock Option Agreement, the Termination Fee, the coercive nature of both the Viacom and QVC tender offers, the No-Shop Provision, and the proposed disparate use of the Rights Agreement as to the Viacom and QVC tender offers, respectively.

These obligations necessarily implicated various issues, including the questions of whether or not those provisions and other aspects of the Paramount-Viacom transaction (separately and in the aggregate): (a) adversely affected the value provided to the Paramount stockholders; (b) inhibited or encouraged alternative bids; (c) were enforceable contractual obligations in light of the directors' fiduciary duties; and (d) in the end would advance or retard the Paramount directors' obligation to secure for the Paramount stockholders the best value reasonably available under the circumstances.

The Paramount defendants contend that they were precluded by certain contractual provisions, including the No-Shop Provision, from negotiating with QVC or seeking alternatives. Such provisions, whether or not they are presumptively valid in the abstract, may not validly define or limit the directors' fiduciary duties under Delaware law or prevent the Paramount directors from carrying out their fiduciary duties under Delaware law. To the extent such provisions are inconsistent with those duties, they are invalid and unenforceable.

Since the Paramount directors had already decided to sell control, they had an obligation to continue their search for the best value reasonably available to the stockholders. This continuing obligation included the responsibility, at the October 24 board meeting and thereafter, to evaluate critically both the QVC tender offers and the Paramount-Viacom transaction to determine if: (a) the QVC tender offer was, or would continue to be, conditional; (b) the QVC tender offer could be improved; (c) the Viacom tender offer or other aspects of the Paramount-Viacom transaction could be improved; (d) each of the respective offers would be reasonably likely to come to closure, and under what circumstances; (e) other material information was reasonably available for consideration by the Paramount directors; (f) there were viable and realistic alternative courses of action; and (g) the timing constraints could be managed so the directors could consider these matters carefully and deliberately.

B.   The Breaches of Fiduciary Duty by the Paramount Board

The Paramount directors made the decision on September 12, 1993, that, in their judgment, a strategic merger with Viacom on the economic terms of the Original Merger Agreement was in the best interests of Paramount and its stockholders. Those terms provided a modest change of control premium to the stockholders. The directors also decided at that time that it was appropriate to agree to certain defensive measures (the Stock Option Agreement, the Termination Fee, and the No-Shop Provision) insisted upon by Viacom as part of that economic transaction. Those defensive measures, coupled with the sale of control and subsequent disparate treatment of competing bidders, implicated the judicial scrutiny of *Unocal, Revlon, Macmillan,* and their progeny. We conclude that the Paramount directors' process was not reasonable, and the result achieved for the stockholders was not reasonable under the circumstances.

When entering into the Original Merger Agreement, and thereafter, the Paramount Board clearly gave insufficient attention to the potential consequences of the defensive measures demanded by Viacom. The Stock Option Agreement had a number of unusual and potentially "draconian" provisions, including the Note Feature and the Put Feature. Furthermore, the Termination Fee, whether or not unreasonable by itself, clearly made Paramount less attractive to other bidders, when coupled with the Stock Option Agreement. Finally, the No-Shop Provision inhibited the Paramount Board's ability to negotiate with other potential bidders, particularly QVC which had already expressed an interest in Paramount.

Throughout the applicable time period, and especially from the first QVC merger proposal on September 20 through the Paramount Board meeting on November 15, QVC's interest in Paramount provided the opportunity for the Paramount Board to seek significantly higher value for the Paramount stockholders than that being offered by Viacom. QVC persistently demonstrated its intention to meet and exceed the Viacom offers, and frequently expressed its willingness to negotiate possible further increases.

The Paramount directors had the opportunity in the October 23–24 time frame, when the Original Merger Agreement was renegotiated, to take appropriate action to modify the improper defensive measures as well as to improve the economic terms of the Paramount-Viacom transaction. Under the circumstances existing at that time, it should have been clear to the Paramount Board that the Stock Option Agreement, coupled with the Termination Fee and the No-Shop Clause, were impeding the realization of the best value reasonably available to the Paramount stockholders. Nevertheless, the Paramount Board made no effort to eliminate or modify these counterproductive devices, and instead continued to cling to its vision of a strategic alliance with Viacom. Moreover, based on advice from the Paramount management, the Paramount directors considered the QVC offer to be "conditional" and asserted that they were precluded by the No-Shop Provision from seeking more information from, or negotiating with, QVC.

By November 12, 1993, the value of the revised QVC offer on its face exceeded that of the Viacom offer by over $1 billion at then current values. This significant disparity of value cannot be justified on the basis of the directors' vision of future strategy, primarily because the change of control would supplant the authority of the current Paramount Board to continue to hold and implement their strategic vision in any meaningful way. Moreover, their uninformed process had deprived their strategic vision of much of its credibility.

When the Paramount directors met on November 15 to consider QVC's increased tender offer, they remained prisoners of their own misconceptions and missed opportunities to eliminate the restrictions they had imposed on themselves. Yet, it was not "too late" to reconsider negotiating with QVC. The circumstances existing on November 15 made it clear that the defensive measures, taken as a whole, were problematic: (a) the No-Shop Provision could not define or limit their fiduciary duties; (b) the Stock Option Agreement had become "draconian;" and (c) the Termination Fee, in context with all the circumstances, was similarly deterring the realization of possibly higher bids. Nevertheless, the Paramount directors remained paralyzed by their uninformed belief that the QVC offer was "illusory." This final opportunity to negotiate on the stockholders' behalf and to fulfill their obligation to seek the best value reasonably available was thereby squandered.

[The court considers, and rejects, an argument by Viacom that it had "certain 'vested' contract rights with respect to the No-Shop Provision and the Stock Option Agreement," holding that because both were invalid, Viacom "never had any vested contract rights" in the provision or the Agreement.]

V.   CONCLUSION

The realization of the best value reasonably available to the stockholders became the Paramount directors' primary obligation under these facts in light of the change of control. That obligation was not satisfied, and the Paramount Board's process was deficient. The directors' initial hope and expectation for a strategic alliance with Viacom was allowed to dominate their decisionmaking process to the point where the arsenal of defensive measures established at the outset was perpetuated (not modified or eliminated) when the situation was dramatically altered. QVC's unsolicited bid presented the opportunity for significantly greater value for the stockholders and enhanced negotiating leverage for the directors. Rather than seizing those opportunities, the Paramount directors chose to wall themselves off from material information which was reasonably available and to hide behind the defensive measures as a rationalization for refusing to negotiate with QVC or seeking other alternatives. Their view of the strategic alliance likewise became an empty rationalization as the opportunities for higher value for the stockholders continued to develop. . . .

For the reasons set forth herein, the November 24, 1993, Order of the Court of Chancery has been AFFIRMED, . . .

The following quote gives some color to the bidding war between QVC and Viacom and describes how the battle ended.

> In the end, the biggest takeover war of the 1990s boiled down to five words penned personally by QVC Chairman Barry Diller: "They won. We lost. Next."
>
> By 1993, Paramount was a ripe takeover candidate . . . Investors were impatient. Paramount's film slate was sparse, and the company's earnings were regularly full of unpleasant surprises. Its stock was trading at about half the value that Viacom eventually agreed to pay.
>
> Diller . . . [had] surprised people by signing on to head QVC, a home shopping channel. Although he often touts home shopping as a place that allows viewers to "shop for underwear in their underwear," his real goal was to use QVC as leverage to build an entertainment/technology company at the forefront of the "information superhighway" explosion. . . .
>
> [Paramount Chairman and CEO Davis ran into Diller more than once,] each time trying to squeeze information out of him to determine if Diller had anything planned. Acting carefully to avoid legal problems, Diller didn't bite.
>
> "The turning point was very clearly the Delaware court system," Davis said Tuesday. "The Delaware court is creating new law . . . to fit the climate. The Delaware decision is one that I respectfully and at the same time vehemently disagree with."[4]

---

[4]   James Bates, *Paramount Deal: As Show Closes, a Look at the Script,* L.A. TIMES, Feb. 16, 1994, available at http://articles.latimes.com/1994-02-16/news/mn-23560_1_paramount-communications.

C. *REVLON* TODAY

1. IN GENERAL

What types of transactions would *Revlon* apply to? The *QVC* case largely answered the question. In transactions where the consideration is all cash and where the company experiences a change of control, *Revlon* will apply. In transactions where the consideration is all stock and where "[c]ontrol of the corporation is not vested in a single person, entity, or group, but vested in the fluid aggregation of unaffiliated stockholders," *Revlon* will not apply. Under the *QVC* holding, *Revlon* applied to the Paramount/Viacom transaction even though the consideration for Paramount was stock, because after the transaction, control would have been "vested in" Sumner Redstone, the controlling shareholder of Viacom.

There were still open questions concerning *Revlon*. The first concerned when *Revlon* duties were triggered. Were they triggered when the board began to consider a change of control transaction, when one was proposed, or only when the board definitively decided to sell itself? The second question concerned the sale process itself. If *Revlon* duties applied, how did the board go about satisfying them? Was an auction required in all circumstances? And if not, when was a single bidder negotiation permissible?

Lyondell Chemical Company v. Ryan is an important case addressing when *Revlon* is triggered and what *Revlon* requires. *Lyondell* was one of a number of cases in which plaintiffs alleged that the directors' conduct fell so far short of what *Revlon* requires that it amounted to a violation of the duty of good faith, thus giving rise to a non-exculpable claim for damages. In *Lyondell*, plaintiffs, Lyondell shareholders, filed a lawsuit following the announcement of a merger in which the board agreed to sell Lyondell in a cash merger. The plaintiffs argued that the deal announced by the board clearly triggered scrutiny under *Revlon*, and that *Revlon* required the board to take specific actions with respect to the sale process. By failing to such actions, the board "failed to act in the face of a known duty" and thus violated its duty of good faith. Among the questions raised in the case were: exactly when was *Revlon* triggered? And what did *Revlon* require of the board?

The Chancery Court denied the defendants' motion to dismiss, concluding that "the process chosen by the Board is troubling under *Revlon*. It is difficult for the Court to conclude on this record, after giving Ryan the benefit of all reasonable inferences, that the process employed by the Board was a 'reasonable' effort to create value for the Lyondell shareholders under these circumstances." *Ryan v. Lyondell Chem. Co.*, C.A. No. 3176–VCN, 2008 WL 2923427 (Del. Ch. July 29, 2008). On appeal, the Delaware Supreme Court reversed the Chancery Court's ruling, taking the opportunity to set forth when *Revlon* is triggered, and what *Revlon* requires.

a. *Lyondell Chemical v. Ryan*

LYONDELL CHEMICAL COMPANY V. WALTER E. RYAN, JR.
Supreme Court of Delaware
970 A.2d 235 (2009)

BERGER, JUSTICE.

. . .

Before the merger at issue, Lyondell Chemical Company ("Lyondell") was the third largest independent, publicly traded chemical company in North America. Dan Smith ("Smith") was Lyondell's Chairman and CEO. Lyondell's other ten directors were independent and many were, or had been, CEOs of other large, publicly traded companies. Basell AF ("Basell") is a privately held Luxembourg company owned by Leonard Blavatnik ("Blavatnik") through his ownership of Access Industries. Basell is in the business of polyolefin technology, production and marketing.

In April 2006, Blavatnik told Smith that Basell was interested in acquiring Lyondell. A few months later, Basell sent a letter to Lyondell's board offering $26.50–$28.50 per share. Lyondell determined that the price was inadequate and that it was not interested in selling. During the next year, Lyondell prospered and no potential acquirors expressed interest in the company. In May 2007, an Access affiliate filed a Schedule 13D with the Securities and Exchange Commission disclosing its right to acquire an 8.3% block of Lyondell stock owned by Occidental Petroleum Corporation. The Schedule 13D also disclosed Blavatnik's interest in possible transactions with Lyondell.

In response to the Schedule 13D, the Lyondell board immediately convened a special meeting. The board recognized that the 13D signaled to the market that the company was "in play," but the directors decided to take a "wait and see" approach. A few days later, Apollo Management, L.P. contacted Smith to suggest a management-led LBO, but Smith rejected that proposal. In late June 2007, Basell announced that it had entered into a $9.6 billion merger agreement with Huntsman Corporation ("Huntsman"), a specialty chemical company. Basell apparently reconsidered, however, after Hexion Specialty Chemicals, Inc. made a topping bid for Huntsman. Faced with competition for Huntsman, Blavatnik returned his attention to Lyondell.

On July 9, 2007, Blavatnik met with Smith to discuss an all-cash deal at $40 per share. Smith responded that $40 was too low, and Blavatnik raised his offer to $44–$45 per share. Smith told Blavatnik that he would present the proposal to the board, but that he thought the board would reject it. Smith advised Blavatnik to give Lyondell his best offer, since Lyondell really was not on the market. The meeting ended at that point, but Blavatnik asked Smith to call him later in the day. When Smith called, Blavatnik offered to pay $48 per share. Under Blavatnik's proposal, Basell would require no financing contingency, but Lyondell would have to agree to a $400 million break-up fee and sign a merger agreement by July 16, 2007.

Smith called a special meeting of the Lyondell board on July 10, 2007 to review and consider Basell's offer. The meeting lasted slightly less than one hour, during which time the board reviewed valuation material that had been prepared by Lyondell management for presentation at the regular board meeting, which was scheduled for the following day. The board also discussed the Basell offer, the status of the Huntsman merger, and the likelihood that another party might be interested in Lyondell. The board instructed Smith to obtain a written offer from Basell and more details about Basell's financing.

Blavatnik agreed to the board's request, but also made an additional demand. Basell had until July 11 to make a higher bid for Huntsman, so Blavatnik asked Smith to find out whether the Lyondell board would provide a firm indication of interest in his proposal by the end of that day. The Lyondell board met on July 11, again for less than one hour, to consider the Basell proposal and how it compared to the benefits of remaining independent. The board decided that it was interested, authorized the retention of Deutsche Bank Securities, Inc. ("Deutsche Bank") as its financial advisor, and instructed Smith to negotiate with Blavatnik.

Basell then announced that it would not raise its offer for Huntsman, and Huntsman terminated the Basell merger agreement. From July 12–July 15 the parties negotiated the terms of a Lyondell merger agreement; Basell conducted due diligence; Deutsche Bank prepared a "fairness" opinion; and Lyondell conducted its regularly scheduled board meeting. The Lyondell board discussed the Basell proposal again on July 12, and later instructed Smith to try to negotiate better terms. Specifically, the board wanted a higher price, a go-shop provision, and a reduced break-up fee. As the trial court noted, Blavatnik was "incredulous." He had offered his best price, which was a substantial premium, and the deal had to be concluded on his schedule. As a sign of good faith, however, Blavatnik agreed to reduce the break-up fee from $400 million to $385 million.

On July 16, 2007, the board met to consider the Basell merger agreement. Lyondell's management, as well as its financial and legal advisers, presented reports analyzing the merits of the deal. The advisors explained that, notwithstanding the no-shop provision in the merger agreement, Lyondell would be able to consider any superior proposals that might be made because of the "fiduciary out" provision. In addition, Deutsche Bank reviewed valuation models derived from "bullish" and more conservative financial projections. Several of those valuations yielded a range that did not even reach $48 per share, and Deutsche Bank opined that the proposed merger price was fair. Indeed, the bank's managing director described the merger price as "an absolute home run." Deutsche Bank also identified other possible acquirors and explained why it believed no other entity would top Basell's offer. After considering the presentations, the Lyondell board voted to approve the merger and recommend it to the stockholders. At a special stockholders' meeting held on November 20, 2007, the merger was approved by more than 99% of the voted shares.

[Ryan, the plaintiff, brought suit.] . . . The Court of Chancery issued its opinion on July 29, 2008, denying summary judgment as to the *"Revlon"* and the "deal protection" claims. This Court accepted the Lyondell directors' application for certification of an interlocutory appeal on September 15, 2008.

DISCUSSION

The class action complaint challenging this $13 billion cash merger [made a variety of claims.] . . . The trial court rejected all claims except those directed at the process by which the directors sold the company and the deal protection provisions in the merger agreement.

The remaining claims are but two aspects of a single claim, under *Revlon,* that the directors failed to obtain the best available price in selling the company. As the trial court correctly noted, *Revlon* did not create any new fiduciary duties. It simply held that the "board must perform its fiduciary duties in the service of a specific objective: maximizing the sale price of the enterprise." The trial court reviewed the record, and found that Ryan might be able to prevail at trial on a claim that the Lyondell directors breached their duty of care. But Lyondell's charter includes an exculpatory provision, pursuant to 8 Del. C. § 102(b)(7), protecting the directors from personal liability for breaches of the duty of care. Thus, this case turns on whether any arguable shortcomings on the part of the Lyondell directors also implicate their duty of loyalty, a breach of which is not exculpated. Because the trial court determined that the board was independent and was not motivated by self-interest or ill will, the sole issue is whether the directors are entitled to summary judgment on the claim that they breached their duty of loyalty by failing to act in good faith.

This Court examined "good faith" in two recent decisions. In *In re Walt Disney Co. Deriv Litig.,* the Court discussed the range of conduct that might be characterized as bad faith, and concluded that bad faith encompasses not only an intent to harm but also intentional dereliction of duty:

> [A]t least three different categories of fiduciary behavior are candidates for the "bad faith" pejorative label. The first category involves so-called "subjective bad faith," that is, fiduciary conduct motivated by an actual intent to do harm. . . . [S]uch conduct constitutes classic, quintessential bad faith. . . .

> The second category of conduct, which is at the opposite end of the spectrum, involves lack of due care—that is, fiduciary action taken solely by reason of gross negligence and without any malevolent intent. . . . [W]e address the issue of whether gross negligence (including failure to inform one's self of available material facts), without more, can also constitute bad faith. The answer is clearly no.

> * * *

> That leaves the third category of fiduciary conduct, which falls in between the first two categories. . . . This third category is what the Chancellor's definition of bad faith—intentional dereliction of duty, a conscious disregard for one's responsibilities—is intended to capture.

> The question is whether such misconduct is properly treated as a non-exculpable, nonindemnifiable violation of the fiduciary duty to act in good faith. In our view, it must be. . . .

The *Disney* decision expressly disavowed any attempt to provide a comprehensive or exclusive definition of "bad faith."

A few months later, in *Stone v. Ritter,* this Court addressed the concept of bad faith in the context of an "oversight" claim. We adopted the standard articulated ten years earlier, in *In re Caremark Int'l Deriv. Litig.*:

> [W]here a claim of directorial liability for corporate loss is predicated upon ignorance of liability creating activities within the corporation . . . only a sustained or systematic failure of the board to exercise oversight—such as an utter failure to attempt to assure a reasonable information and reporting system exists— will establish the lack of good faith that is a necessary condition to liability.

The *Stone* Court explained that the *Caremark* standard is fully consistent with the *Disney* definition of bad faith. *Stone* also clarified any possible ambiguity about the directors' mental state, holding that "imposition of liability requires a showing that the directors knew that they were not discharging their fiduciary obligations."

The Court of Chancery recognized these legal principles, but it denied summary judgment in order to obtain a more complete record before deciding whether the directors had acted in bad faith. Under other circumstances, deferring a decision to expand the record would be appropriate. Here, however, the trial court reviewed the existing record under a mistaken view of the applicable law. Three factors contributed to that mistake. First, the trial court imposed *Revlon* duties on the Lyondell directors before they either had decided to sell, or before the sale had become inevitable. Second, the court read *Revlon* and its progeny as creating a set of requirements that must be satisfied during the sale process. Third, the trial court equated an arguably imperfect attempt to carry out *Revlon* duties with a knowing disregard of one's duties that constitutes bad faith.

Summary judgment may be granted if there are no material issues of fact in dispute and the moving party is entitled to judgment as a matter of law. The facts, and all reasonable inferences, must be considered in the light most favorable to the nonmoving party. The Court of Chancery identified several undisputed facts that would support the entry of judgment in favor of the Lyondell directors: the directors were "active, sophisticated, and generally aware of the value of the Company and the conditions of the markets in which the Company operated." They had reason to believe that no other bidders would emerge, given the price Basell had offered and the limited universe of companies that might be interested in acquiring Lyondell's unique assets. Smith negotiated the price up from $40 to $48 per share—a price that Deutsche Bank opined was fair. Finally, no other acquiror expressed interest during the four months between the merger announcement and the stockholder vote.

Other facts, however, led the trial court to "question the adequacy of the Board's knowledge and efforts. . . ." After the Schedule 13D was filed in May, the directors apparently took no action to prepare for a possible acquisition proposal. The merger was negotiated and finalized in less than one week, during which time the directors met for a total of only seven hours to consider the matter. The directors did not seriously press Blavatnik for a better price, nor did they conduct even a limited market check. Moreover, although the deal protections were not unusual or preclusive, the trial court was troubled by "the Board's decision to grant considerable protection to a deal that may not have been adequately vetted under *Revlon*."

The trial court found the directors' failure to act during the two months after the filing of the Basell Schedule 13D critical to its analysis of their good faith. The court pointedly referred to the directors' "two months of slothful indifference despite *knowing* that the Company was in play," and the fact that they "languidly awaited overtures from potential suitors. . . ." In the end, the trial court found that it was this "failing" that warranted denial of their motion for summary judgment:

> [T]he Opinion clearly questions whether the Defendants "engaged" in the sale process. . . . This is where the 13D filing in May 2007 and the subsequent two months of (apparent) Board inactivity become critical. . . . [T]he Directors made *no apparent effort to* arm themselves with *specific knowledge* about the present value of the Company in the May through July 2007 time period, despite *admittedly knowing* that the 13D filing . . . effectively put the Company "in play," and, therefore, presumably, also knowing that an offer for the sale of the Company could occur at any time. It is these facts that raise the specter of "bad faith" in the present summary judgment record. . . .

The problem with the trial court's analysis is that *Revlon* duties do not arise simply because a company is "in play." The duty to seek the best available price applies only when a company embarks on a transaction— on its own initiative or in response to an unsolicited offer—that will result in a change of control. Basell's Schedule 13D did put the Lyondell directors, and the market in general, on notice that Basell was interested in acquiring Lyondell. The directors responded by promptly holding a special meeting to consider whether Lyondell should take any action. The directors decided that they would neither put the company up for sale nor institute defensive measures to fend off a possible hostile offer. Instead, they decided to take a "wait and see" approach. That decision was an entirely appropriate exercise of the directors' business judgment. The time for action under *Revlon* did not begin until July 10, 2007, when the directors began negotiating the sale of Lyondell.

The Court of Chancery focused on the directors' two months of inaction, when it should have focused on the one week during which they considered Basell's offer. During that one week, the directors met several times; their CEO tried to negotiate better terms; they evaluated Lyondell's value, the price offered and the likelihood of obtaining a better price; and then the directors approved the merger. The trial court acknowledged that the directors' conduct during those seven days might not demonstrate anything more than lack of due care. But the court remained skeptical about the directors' good faith—at least on the present record. That lingering concern was based on the trial court's synthesis of the *Revlon* line of cases, which led it to the erroneous conclusion that directors must follow one of several courses of action to satisfy their *Revlon* duties.

There is only one *Revlon* duty—to "[get] the best price for the stockholders at a sale of the company." No court can tell directors exactly how to accomplish that goal, because they will be facing a unique combination of circumstances, many of which will be outside their control. As we noted in *Barkan,* "there is no single blueprint that a board must follow to fulfill its duties." That said, our courts have highlighted both the positive and negative aspects of various boards' conduct under *Revlon.* The trial court drew several principles from those cases: directors must "engage actively in the sale process," and they must confirm that they have obtained the best available price either by conducting an auction, by conducting a market check, or by demonstrating "an impeccable knowledge of the market."

The Lyondell directors did not conduct an auction or a market check, and they did not satisfy the trial court that they had the "impeccable" market knowledge that the court believed was necessary to excuse their failure to pursue one of the first two alternatives. As a result, the Court of Chancery was unable to conclude that the directors had met their burden under *Revlon.* In evaluating the totality of the circumstances, even on this limited record, we would be inclined to hold otherwise. But we would not question the trial court's decision to seek additional evidence if the issue were whether the directors had exercised due care. Where, as here, the issue is whether the directors failed to act in good faith, the analysis is very different, and the existing record mandates the entry of judgment in favor of the directors.

As discussed above, bad faith will be found if a "fiduciary intentionally fails to act in the face of a known duty to act, demonstrating a conscious disregard for his duties." The trial court decided that the *Revlon* sale process must follow one of three courses, and that the Lyondell directors did not discharge that "known set of *[Revlon]* 'duties'." But, as noted, there are no legally prescribed steps that directors must follow to satisfy their *Revlon* duties. Thus, the directors' failure to take any specific steps during the sale process could not have demonstrated a conscious disregard of their duties. More importantly, there is a vast difference between an inadequate or flawed effort to carry out fiduciary duties and a conscious disregard for those duties.

Directors' decisions must be reasonable, not perfect. "In the transactional context, [an] extreme set of facts [is] required to sustain a disloyalty claim premised on the notion that disinterested directors were intentionally disregarding their duties." The trial court denied summary judgment because the Lyondell directors' "unexplained inaction" prevented the court from determining that they had acted in good faith. But, if the directors failed to do all that they should have under the circumstances, they breached their duty of care. Only if they knowingly and completely failed to undertake their responsibilities would they breach their duty of loyalty. The trial court approached the record from the wrong perspective. Instead of questioning whether disinterested, independent directors did everything that they (arguably) should have done to obtain the best sale price, the inquiry should have been whether those directors utterly failed to attempt to obtain the best sale price.

Viewing the record in this manner leads to only one possible conclusion. The Lyondell directors met several times to consider Basell's premium offer. They were generally aware of the value of their company and they knew the chemical company market. The directors solicited and followed the advice of their financial and legal advisors. They attempted to negotiate a higher offer even though all the evidence indicates that Basell had offered a "blowout" price. Finally, they approved the merger agreement, because "it was simply too good not to pass along [to the stockholders] for their consideration." We assume, as we must on summary judgment, that the Lyondell directors did absolutely nothing to prepare for Basell's offer, and that they did not even consider conducting a market check before agreeing to the merger. Even so, this record clearly establishes that the Lyondell directors did not breach their duty of loyalty by failing to act in good faith. In concluding otherwise, the Court of Chancery reversibly erred. . . . [The court granted summary judgment to the defendants.]

———————

Lyondell held that *Revlon* duties were only triggered once the board decided to sell the company. Boards therefore control when *Revlon* is triggered, and can decide when (if ever) they are subject to *Revlon* duties. Additionally, *Lyondell* provided wide latitude to a board as to how it satisfied its *Revlon* duties. Compare the actions of the Lyondell board to the actions of the board in *Smith v. Van Gorkom*. Is the difference solely that *Van Gorkom* is a duty of care case while *Lyondell* considers whether a breach of the duty of good faith occurred? We will discuss this point in the next subsection.

Ironically, the *Lyondell* case arose from the ashes of the Huntsman transaction discussed below. After Basell lost in the bidding for Huntsman, it turned its attentions to acquiring Lyondell. Basell succeeded acquiring Lyondell in a deal valued at $12.7 billion. Initially, the acquisition was a disaster. Two years later, in the wake of the financial crisis LyondellBasell (the name of the merged company) filed for bankruptcy. Lawsuits were brought against various parties, including Blavatnik as well as the Lyondell shareholders, in effect alleging that the price paid was too high—because Lyondell ultimately had to pay the amounts from its corporate coffers, it had enormous amounts of debt, which, coupled with management fees to Blavatnik's firm, were significant contributors to its bankruptcy. At this writing, a suit against large shareholders is proceeding. But LyondellBasell itself has since recovered spectacularly. An article in mid-2014 recounted:

In the history of Wall Street there haven't been too many moneymaking machines quite like LyondellBasell, which has seen its shares return 500% since it emerged from bankruptcy four years ago. And that's been especially lucrative for Blavatnik, 57, who cobbled the company together, saw it fail and plunge into bankruptcy court, and then doubled down on the same assets, personally investing another $2.37 billion in LyondellBasell the second time around. . . .

Basell bought Lyondell in a $20 billion leveraged buyout in December 2007 to create LyondellBasell, the world's third-biggest independent chemicals company. The timing couldn't have been worse. Within months the financial crisis hit and the deal looked like a debacle. Weighed down by more than $20 billion in debt, LyondellBasell hit the wall as the economy crumbled. . . . In early 2009 Blavatnik pushed LyondellBasell into bankruptcy. It was a humiliating moment for Blavatnik. . . . In bankruptcy court LyondellBasell shed the weight that brought it down . . . It reduced its debt load to $2.5 billion, slashing annual interest expenses by $1.7 billion . . .

[Blavatnik's] investment is now worth more than $10 billion . . . LyondellBasell has been a cash machine. In the past three years the company returned $8.4 billion to shareholders via share repurchases and dividends.[5]

Since LyondellBasell emerged from bankruptcy in 2010, its stock price has increased considerably, from $22.30, rising at times to almost $115; at this writing, even with the recent drop in the markets, it is still around $75. But its success was apparently built on "fracking," a controversial technology to extract oil. Given the controversy, and with oil prices considerably lower than their historic highs as this book goes to press, the future of LyondellBasell may not be as rosy.

b. Has *Revlon* Become a Good Faith Test?

At several points in the opinion, *Revlon* characterizes the directors' conduct as breaching the duty of care. But DGCL Section 102(b)(7), enacted in the wake of *Smith v. Van Gorkom* (and discussed in Chapter XVII) allows corporations to include in their certificates of incorporation provisions exculpating directors for monetary liability for breaches of the duty of care, something most corporations have done. *Lyondell* is a *Revlon* case, but it is not a duty of care case. Rather, it examined whether the board violated its duty of good faith in the manner in which they

---

[5] Nathan Vardi, *How One Billionaire's Bet On LyondellBasell Turned Into The Greatest Deal In Wall St. History*, FORBES, Aug. 18, 2014, available at http://www.forbes.com/sites/nathanvardi/2014/07/30/the-greatest-deal-of-all-time/.

proceeded in the sale of the company. Indeed, in order to provide a basis for liability now that breaches of the duty of care are generally exculpated, *Revlon* claims are now often brought as breaches of the duty of good faith.

The courts have contributed to this transformation, and in recent years, have tended to refer to *Revlon* duties in the context of the duty of good faith. An example is the case of *Koehler v. NetSpend,* C.A. No. 8373–VCG (Del. Ch. May 21, 2013). In *NetSpend,* the target's board had chosen to negotiate with only one party, attempting to get that party to increase its bid, rather than soliciting competing bids. NetSpend's CEO had justified this approach in his deposition stating "if you know that running an auction process isn't going to produce any serious bona fide bidders, then you don't go out and run an auction. You stick with what we've been saying [to the bidder who they hoped would increase its bid] . . . I ain't selling. So if you want it, you got to pay for it."

Emphasizing the lack of a single blueprint for the sale of a company, Vice Chancellor Glasscock focused instead on the directors' good faith intent to follow the dictates of *Revlon.* The Vice Chancellor found that given "the lack of a market check at any stage in this process; the Board's reliance on a weak fairness opinion; the deal protections which were incorporated into the Merger Agreement; and the lack of an anticipated leisurely post-agreement process which would give other suitors the opportunity to appear," he believed that the Defendants would "fail to meet their burden at trial of proving that they acted reasonably to maximize share price."[6] While the Vice Chancellor in *Netspend* found that the single bidder strategy was unjustified because of these other indicia that the board had failed to negotiate properly, holdings finding violations of *Revlon* are rare. The Delaware courts have generally found that procedures used by boards are appropriate and satisfy *Revlon*—that the boards acted in good faith.

Take for example then-Vice-Chancellor Strine (now Chief Justice Strine)'s opinion in *In re Dollar Thrifty,* Consol. C.A. No. 5458–VCS (Del. Ch. Sept. 8, 2010). In that case, the board of Dollar Thrifty had decided to negotiate with Hertz but not Avis, entering into an agreement to be acquired by Hertz. Dollar Thrifty's shareholders sued, contending that "by failing to take affirmative steps to draw Avis into a bidding contest with Hertz *before* signing up a definitive merger agreement with Hertz, the Dollar Thrifty directors breached their duty to take a reasonable approach to immediate value maximization, as required by *Revlon.*"

---

[6] That being said, the court did not grant an injunction against the deal, holding that "because the injunction requested presents a possibility that the stockholders will lose their chance to receive a substantial premium over market for their shares . . . and because no other potential bidders have appeared, I find that the Plaintiff has failed to demonstrate that the equities of the matter favor injunctive relief." *Id.* at 3.

Strine rejected this argument. He stated that "although the level of judicial scrutiny under *Revlon* is more exacting than the deferential rationality standard applicable to run-of-the-mill decisions governed by the business judgment rule, at bottom *Revlon* is a test of reasonableness; directors are generally free to select the path to value maximization, so long as they choose a reasonable route to get there." *Revlon* thus represents a middle ground under which a court has "leeway to examine the reasonableness of the board's actions under a standard that is more stringent than business judgment review and yet less severe than the entire fairness standard." *Revlon* requires a court to take a "nuanced and realistic look at the possibility that personal interests short of pure self-dealing have influenced the board to block a bid or to steer a deal with one bidder rather than another." Strine concluded that "[w]hen directors who are well motivated, have displayed no entrenchment motivation over several years, and who diligently involve themselves in the deal process choose a course of action, this court should be reluctant to second-guess their actions as unreasonable."

2. *REVLON*'S SUBSTANTIVE REQUIREMENTS

When a board is no longer defending the corporate bastion but has instead decided to sell the company *Revlon* requires the board to act as "auctioneers charged with getting the best price for the shareholders". But what does this mean? Again, one thing it does *not* mean is that the board actually has to auction the company. Following *Lyondell*, the courts have provided further guidance on the contours of *Revlon*'s requirements. One post-*Lyondell Revlon* case is *C&J Energy Services*, 107 A.3d 1049 (Del. 2014), in which the Delaware Supreme Court explained what *Revlon* does—and does not—require.

> *Revlon* involved a decision by a board of directors to chill the emergence of a higher offer from a bidder because the board's CEO disliked the new bidder, after the target board had agreed to sell the company for cash. *Revlon* made clear that when a board engages in a change of control transaction, it must not take actions inconsistent with achieving the highest immediate value reasonably attainable.

> But *Revlon* does not require a board to set aside its own view of what is best for the corporation's stockholders and run an auction whenever the board approves a change of control transaction. As this Court has made clear, "there is no single blueprint that a board must follow to fulfill its duties," and a court applying *Revlon*'s enhanced scrutiny must decide "whether the directors made a *reasonable* decision, not a *perfect* decision."

In a series of decisions in the wake of *Revlon,* Chancellor Allen correctly read its holding as permitting a board to pursue the transaction it reasonably views as most valuable to stockholders, so long as the transaction is subject to an effective market check under circumstances in which any bidder interested in paying more has a reasonable opportunity to do so. Such a market check does not have to involve an active solicitation, so long as interested bidders have a fair opportunity to present a higher-value alternative, and the board has the flexibility to eschew the original transaction and accept the higher-value deal. The ability of the stockholders themselves to freely accept or reject the board's preferred course of action is also of great importance in this context.[7]

Notwithstanding *Revlon's* charge to seek the highest price, target boards nevertheless retain considerable discretion in choosing among potential bidders. If several bids were made that were identical except as to price, the board would be constrained to choose the highest bid. However, in real life bidding contests, the choices presented to boards are rarely so simple.

Take the case where Bidder 1 is offering $15 per share in cash and Bidder 2 is offering $16 per share of its securities. $16 seems higher than $15. But Bidder 2's bid effectively requires the shareholders of the target to make an investment in Bidder 2. The target board must accordingly assess the prospects for Bidder 2's securities to determine the value of the bid. Upon further scrutiny, the target's board may conclude that they value the securities of Bidder 2 less than the $15 in cash offered by Bidder 1. Boards must inform themselves as to the value of each of the offers, but they are ultimately given great latitude to make their best judgment as to which bid offers shareholders the most value.

Another complexity in comparing bids involves completion risk. If Bidder A offers what is clearly a higher price than Bidder B, but a deal with Bidder A may not close because it may not get required regulatory approval, such as antitrust approval, the board may reasonably decide that Bidder B's bid offers shareholders a higher value. Alternatively, there might be uncertainty as to whether Bidder A will be able to finance its acquisition. If Bidder B has or is more certain of getting the necessary funds to close the transaction, the board may reasonably decide that Bidder B's bid is better for shareholders.

A good example of the difficulties boards face in making these assessments can be seen in the bidding in 2007 for Huntsman Chemical Corp. Huntsman had negotiated with Basell Holdings, a Netherlands-based chemical company (and the company that later bought Lyondell

---

[7] *Id* at 1067–68.

Chemical in the case discussed above), to be acquired by Basell for $25.25 per share in cash; the transaction was signed and announced on June 26, 2007. On July 12, 2007, the board of Huntsman terminated that deal to accept a higher offer of $28 per share in cash from Hexion Specialty Chemical, a company owned by the private equity firm Apollo. While Hexion's bid was clearly higher, Hexion needed to borrow substantial amounts of money in order to fund the transaction. When the financial crisis hit in the fall of 2007, Hexion was no longer able to borrow the necessary funds to acquire Huntsman. The parties sued each other, and in a litigation settlement, the transaction was terminated. (This case is discussed in Chapter XIV.G of this book.) Huntsman received approximately $1 billion in connection with the settlement of the litigation. But at the time of the settlement, Basell was no longer interested in acquiring Huntsman, and Huntsman's share price slipped to $3.00 per share. The loss to shareholders was far in excess of the $1 billion payment Huntsman received.

The story of Huntsman demonstrates the importance of assessing completion risk. A target board's decision to accept a "lower" bid may be difficult to justify to its shareholders, but so long as the decision is fully-informed and well-considered, Delaware courts are not likely to find directors to have breached their *Revlon* duties. In *In re Cogent*, C.A. No. 57810–VCP (Del. Ch. Oct. 5, 2010), Cogent's board had accepted an offer of $10.50 per share from 3M at the same time that another company, "Company D," was offering a higher amount. The Delaware Chancery Court found the Cogent board's decision acceptable under *Revlon*, stating that "[t]he Board could, and did, consider the long length of time Cogent was perceived as being for sale without having received a firm purchase offer besides 3M's, the perception that Company D was dragging its feet, Company D's history of start-stop negotiations, the risk that Company D, like an earlier suitor, would withdraw its offer upon completing due diligence, and the risk of losing 3M's bid. . . . [A]fter being fully informed as to the benefits and risks associated with each of its two potential suitors, Cogent's Board reasonably could conclude that the greater certainty associated with 3M's bid outweighed the risk of waiting for a potentially higher offer from Company D that might never materialize."

3. THE MARKET CHECK

In the years immediately following the *Revlon* decision, some practitioners and academics argued that *Revlon's* dictate to obtain the highest price reasonably available had given rise to a board duty to auction the company.[8] As we have discussed, subsequent pronouncements by the Delaware courts have made clear that this is not so. But

---

[8]   See Evelyn Sroufe, *A Bird in the Hand or Pie in the Sky: The Market Checks in the '90's,* 5 No. 10 INSIGHTS 12, 12 (Oct. 1991).

practitioners, aware of the ubiquitous litigation risk accompanying merger transactions, counsel clients that while an auction is not required, some form of market check—sufficient to demonstrate "impeccable knowledge" of the target's value—may be required, and is certainly strongly advisable in situations where the board has dealt only with one bidder.

A market check may take place either before or after the announcement of the transaction. Pre-announcement and post-announcement market checks differ significantly. In a pre-announcement market check, the target has yet to make any commitment to any bidder, and is therefore free to accept a competing bid or generate an auction. Post-announcement, the target has already agreed to be acquired. It typically also has agreed to pay the original bidder a termination fee if a competing bidder emerges and the target then terminates the deal. Termination fees are deal protection measures. As we have discussed, deal protection measures are intended to deter subsequent bids; courts therefore look upon them especially warily when *Revlon* is implicated. But courts have approved the use of post-announcement market checks in many circumstances. The following excerpt from a client memo from Delaware law firm Potter Anderson elaborates on the issues involved:

> In the context of a sale of control transaction, a board of directors of a target corporation generally may satisfy its fiduciary duties to obtain the best transaction reasonably available under the circumstances for the corporation and its stockholders by engaging in one of several general types of transactions: (i) a transaction with the highest bidder after a full public auction of the target corporation, i.e. a pre-agreement market check, (ii) a transaction with the highest bidder after a more limited pre-agreement market check in which multiple potential bidders are contacted and participate in the bidding, (iii) a transaction with a single bidder where the target board has reliable evidence demonstrating that the board has obtained the best transaction reasonably available, or (iv) a transaction with a single bidder where the target board, due to the absence of reliable evidence that the board has obtained the best transaction reasonably available, bargains for a post-agreement market check. A transaction that follows a full auction or involves multiple bidders may warrant more restrictive deal protections, such as a higher termination fee, a matching right and a more limited no shop provision, because the market has been canvassed for potential bidders. By contrast, when a target board lacks sufficiently reliable evidence to permit it to conclude that a transaction with a single bidder is the best transaction reasonably available, the use of a post-agreement market check

(coupled with modest deal protection provisions) will permit interested competing bidders to emerge, thus ensuring that the target corporation obtains the best transaction reasonably available under the circumstances.

A post-agreement market check is effective because it establishes a "floor" for the transaction and, by providing for a limited period of time after the announcement of the transaction for a competing bidder to emerge, allows the reasonableness of the transaction to be tested. A post-agreement market check typically includes the following components: (i) a period of time, longer than the time period legally required, following the announcement of the deal for competing bidders to emerge, (ii) a "window shop" prohibiting a target company from actively soliciting bids, but allowing a target company to negotiate with bidders who make superior proposals, (iii) a "fiduciary termination right" that allows the target company to terminate the deal in favor of a superior proposal, (iv) the use of limited deal protection devices (such as termination fees that fall significantly below the normal threshold for acceptable termination fees), and (v) a press release announcing the deal and inviting competing bids.[9]

In a series of cases, the Delaware courts validated post-announcement market-checks. In *In re Fort Howard Corp. S'holders Litig.*, C.A. No. 9991 1988 WL 83147 (Del. Ch. Aug. 8, 1988), the board of Fort Howard had agreed that the company would be sold in a single-bidder negotiation. The merger agreement was with a management affiliated buyout group. It contained a "window shop" provision allowing Fort Howard to consider, but not solicit, other proposals, as well as a termination fee equal to 1.9% of the transaction value. The board of Fort Howard had also issued a press releasing saying it would entertain and cooperate with competing bids. The court validated this approach, stating that it made logical sense for "negotiations with the management affiliated buyout group to be completed before turning to the market in any respect [and that] [t]o start a bidding contest before it was known that an all cash bid for all shares could and would be made, would increase the risk of a possible takeover attempt at less than a 'fair' price or for less than all shares." The court also determined that the "alternative 'market check' that was achieved was not so hobbled by lock-ups, termination fees or topping fees; so constrained in time or so administered as to permit the inference that this alternative was a sham designed from the outset to be ineffective or minimally effective."

[9] Michael K. Reilly, *The Post-Agreement Market-Check Revisited*, POTTER ANDERSON CORROON, LLP, Mar. 1, 2004, available at http://www.potteranderson.com/publication/the-post-agreement-market-check-revisited.

Since that time, Delaware courts have repeatedly stated that there is "no single blueprint" to sell a company.[10] A market check is only necessary where "the directors [do not] possess a body of reliable evidence with which to evaluate the fairness of a transaction."[11] Consequently, in Delaware it is acceptable to negotiate with a single bidder and to conduct the market check after the transaction is announced. Delaware courts have validated this single bidder negotiation strategy even when the termination fee is more than three percent, and other lock-ups are in place, where the target justified the lock-ups for strategic and competitive reasons.[12]

In re Plains Exploration & Production Company Shareholder Litigation, C.A. No. 8090–VCN (Del. Ch. May 9, 2013) provides a good example of the present Delaware approach. In that case, Vice Chancellor Noble held that a board's decision to "(i) not form a special committee, (ii) allow the target's CEO to run the negotiations, (iii) not conduct a pre-signing market check and (iv) agree to various deal protections devices in the merger agreement, were in each case reasonable under the circumstances and satisfied the Board's *Revlon* duties."[13] The court continued: "as long as the Board retained 'significant flexibility to deal with any later-emerging bidder and ensured that the market would have a healthy period of time to digest the proposed transaction,' [if] no other bidder emerged, the Board could be assured that it had obtained the best transaction reasonably attainable." Despite the market having known about the sale for five months, no competing offers had emerged for Plains. Under those circumstances, Vice Chancellor Noble held that the plaintiffs had not established that the board's failure to undertake a

---

[10] The "blueprint" terminology originated in *Barkan v. Amsted Industries, Inc.* 567 A.2d 1279, 1286 (Del. 1989).

[11] The language from *Barkan* warrants being quoted at length: "When the board is considering a single offer and has no reliable grounds upon which to judge its adequacy, this concern for fairness demands a canvas of the market to determine if higher bids may be elicited [citing *Fort Howard Corp.*] When, however, the directors possess a body of reliable evidence with which to evaluate the fairness of a transaction, they may approve that transaction without conducting an active survey of the market. As the Chancellor recognized, the circumstances in which this passive approach is acceptable are limited. "A decent respect for reality forces one to admit that . . . advice [of an investment banker] is frequently a pale substitute for the dependable information that a canvas of the relevant market can provide." [citing *In re Amsted Indus. Litig.*, letter op. at 19–20.] The need for adequate information is central to the enlightened evaluation of a transaction that a board must make. Nevertheless, there is no single method that a board must employ to acquire such information. *Id.* at 1287.

[12] *See also In re MONY Group Inc. Shareholder Litigation*, 852 A.2d 9 (Del. Ch. 2004) (3.3% termination fee as measured by equity value upheld with single bidder negotiation and post-announcement market check); *In re Pennaco Energy, Inc.,* 787 A.2d 691 (Del. Ch. 2001) (3% termination fee as measured by equity value upheld with single bidder negotiation and post-announcement market check). For more on termination fees see Chapter XVI.G.

[13] Milbank Client Alert: Corporate Governance Group: *Delaware Chancery Court Denies Summary Judgment on Revlon Claims*, available at http://www.milbank.com/images/content/1/3/13207/NY–GC–Del–Chancery–Court–Denies–Summary–Judgment-on-Revlon–Claim.pdf.

market check raised a reasonable likelihood that their claim would be successful on the merits.

Revlon requires selling boards to justify any favoritism or exclusion from the sale process. This question implicates whether and under what circumstances a market check is required. In *In re Netsmart Technologies, Inc. Shareholders Litigation,* 924 A.2d 171 (Del. Ch. 2007), the target entered into a merger agreement, on which shareholders were to vote. The board had charged the Chief Executive Officer with running the bidding. On plaintiff's motion to preliminarily enjoin the shareholder vote on the merger, the court found that the CEO had deliberately steered the bidding towards certain private equity firms in preference to strategic buyers. Ultimately, the board, as advised by the CEO, decided to exclude all strategic buyers. The plaintiff shareholders alleged that the CEO preferred this course of action in part because he was more likely to maintain his job in the acquired company if a private equity firm was the acquirer.

The Delaware Chancery Court severely criticized this conduct, finding that the board "failed to take any reasonable steps to explore whether strategic buyers might be interested in Netsmart." The court stated that "[h]aving embarked on the pursuit of a cash sale, it was incumbent upon the board to make a reasonable effort to maximize the return to Netsmart's investors." "'When...directors possess a body of reliable evidence with which to evaluate the fairness of a transaction, they may approve that transaction without conducting an active survey of the market.' (quoting *Barkan*.) The corollary is clear: when they do not possess reliable evidence of the market value of the entity as a whole, the lack of an active sales effort is strongly suggestive of a *Revlon* breach.'" The court ultimately concluded that the plaintiffs had "demonstrated a reasonable probability that they [would] later prove that the board's failure to engage in any logical efforts to examine the universe of possible strategic buyers and to identify a select group for targeted sales overtures was unreasonable and a breach of their *Revlon* duties." The court did not enjoin the merger, but it did enjoin the vote until the shareholders were provided with more complete disclosure.

These cases suggest that a board aiming to obtain the highest price reasonably available for shareholders can satisfy its duties under *Revlon* in many ways, so long as it acts reasonably and in good faith. Even when boards fall short of that requirement, as evidenced by *Netsmart*, courts are hesitant to permanently enjoin premium single bidder transactions if shareholders still have the ability to consider all the information with respect to the board's failure to comport with its fiduciary obligations and then reject the merger agreement.

D. GO-SHOPS

Under the "no single blueprint" mantra, Delaware courts have repeatedly stated that boards are free to structure their own reasonable sale processes. Go-shop provisions (also discussed in Chapter XIV.H), or active post-announcement market checks, are not required. If a go-shop provision is fairly administered, however, it can go a long way to helping boards meet their obligation to demonstrate knowledge of the firm's value as they seek to obtain the highest price reasonably available for shareholders. The following excerpt from a law firm memorandum discusses two cases, *In Re Lear Shareholder Litigation,* 926 A.2d 94 (Del. Ch. 2007), and *In Re Topps Shareholder Litigation,* 926 A.2d 58 (Del. Ch. 2007), in which the fair administration of go-shop provisions was at issue:

Lear: Adequate Post-Signing Market Check

In contrast to *Netsmart*, *Lear* holds that a widely traded public company may rely primarily on a post-signing market check to comply with *Revlon* duties. Lear was a widely traded Fortune 200 company with an extensive analyst following. Lear was considered to be "in play" because it had rescinded its poison pill and the noted financier Carl Icahn had taken a substantial equity stake, which caused the trading price to rise substantially (from $17 to about $30). Icahn offered to buy the company at $36 per share, provided that the company did not conduct an auction. Nevertheless, the Lear board quickly contacted eight potential investors over a few days, in a process that the court did not regard as a genuine pre-signing market check, but no alternative bidder emerged. Accordingly, the Lear board relied on a post-signing market check consisting of a 45 day go shop provision, with a reduced termination fee for any deal signed in that period and a higher fee for any deal signed thereafter. Lear conducted an extensive, active canvassing of 41 potential buyers in the go shop period. The court held that because Lear was so visible and well known, this post-signing market check did comply with *Revlon* in that it was reasonable and provided adequate assurance that no bidder willing to materially top Icahn existed. The Lear board viewed this approach as locking in Icahn's bid, while securing a chance to prospect for more. In that context, Icahn's agreement to vote his shares in favor of a topping bid was strong evidence that the post-signing market check was designed to result in the best value.

Topps: Baseball Card Company Uses
A Non-Level Playing Field!

In *Topps*, the family-controlled public company had a management friendly bid from a buyer group consisting of former Walt Disney Company CEO Michael Eisner and a private equity firm, Madison Dearborn Partners, and the prospect of a competing higher bid from its primary competitor in the baseball card business, Upper Deck. In essence, the Topps board acted as if it was doing management's bidding by favoring the lower Eisner group bid over Upper Deck's higher bid, particularly after a merger agreement with the Eisner group had been signed. Questionable actions by the Topps board included not exempting the Upper Deck offer from the no shop provision in the signed Eisner group merger agreement (which the Topps board had the right to do), not seeking to negotiate a resolution of the aspects of the Upper Deck bid that troubled the Topps board relating to deal certainty associated with antitrust and financing issues, not allowing Upper Deck relief from a standstill agreement to enable it to bring its higher bid directly to the Topps stockholders, and including misleading statements in the proxy that cast doubt on Upper Deck's intentions. The court indicated that accepting the lower Eisner group bid alone was not a *Revlon* breach given the noted concerns about the certainty of the Upper Deck deal and the risk that Upper Deck was just seeking competitive information or to kill the Eisner group bid, which are legitimate non-price considerations under *Revlon*. However, the court held that the Topps board was required to negotiate in good faith to seek to resolve its concerns about Upper Deck's bid, rather than simply refusing to engage with Upper Deck, and that its failure to do so (along with the misleading statements in the proxy statement) could be attributed to the board seeking to help management remain in control, rather than a good faith desire to maximize price. The court found that these motivations combined to cause the directors to favor the Eisner group over Upper Deck without regard for the price ultimately received by Topps' stockholders, thus breaching their fiduciary duties. As *Topps* demonstrates, when directors have made the decision to sell the company, any favoritism they display towards a particular bidder must be justified solely by reference to permissible objectives such as maximizing deal value and improving deal certainty.[14]

While go-shops are increasingly common, they are also commonly criticized, by some practitioners and academics, as ineffective, or worse. Subsequent bidders seldom emerge, and go-shops may be serving to make the board seem far more open to other bids than it actually is. The

---

[14] David W. Healy, *Corporate and Securities Update: M&A Development—Deal Process and Protections (Netsmart, Lear and Topps): Lessons on What Not to Do When Selling Your Company*, Fenwick & West LLP (2007), available at https://www.fenwick.com/FenwickDocuments/M-A_Developments_Deal_Process.pdf.

target's preference for a particular bidder can thus be cosmetically covered up by use of a go-shop. Recall that the Dell transaction contained a go-shop provision (included in Chapter XIV.H). Given that Dell had signed an agreement with Michael Dell, it needed to demonstrate that the company and its management, including Michael Dell, truly was open to other offers. Indeed, Dell's press release stated that: "[t]he Special Committee . . . noted that Michael Dell has confirmed to the Committee his willingness to explore in good faith the possibility of working with third parties regarding alternative acquisition proposals."[15] But, as critics would have predicted, the go-shop did not yield a successful alternative transaction, and Michael Dell succeeded in taking Dell private.

Professor Guhan Subramanian has published a study on the effectiveness of go-shops. His data—every "going-private" deal between January 2006 and August 2007 with a private equity sponsor:

> reveals two different kinds of go-shops: a "pure" go-shop, in which the seller negotiates exclusively with a single buyer and then shops after the deal is announced; and . . . an "add-on" go-shop, in which the go-shop provision is included after the target has already conducted a pre-signing canvass of the marketplace. . . . [I]n my sample, I find that the pure go-shops (but not add-on go-shops) yield approximately 5% higher returns to target shareholders. [But practitioners] . . . generally [view] the go-shop process as simply "window dressing" and "illusory."

> [G]o-shop provisions, appropriately structured, can satisfy a target board's *Revlon* duties . . . [and can be a] "win-win" for both buyer and seller. [T]he go-shop process induces a full price from the first bidder, which is meaningfully shopped post-signing.

> [For management buyouts, by contrast, t]he data . . . indicate[s] some reason to be wary. Non-MBOs with a pure go-shop clause are jumped 23% of the time, while MBO go-shops are never jumped. While the sample is small, this finding is consistent with practitioner impressions that potential bidders are generally unwilling to bid when management has publicly signed on with a preferred buyout partner.[16]

E. *REVLON* AND DEAL PROTECTIONS

Deal protection measures, like termination fees, matching rights and other lock-ups, raise some interesting issues when *Revlon* is the standard

---

[15] *Dell Special Committee Receives Two Alternative Acquisition Proposals in "Go-Shop" Process,* Dell, Mar. 25, 2013, available at http://www.dell.com/learn/us/en/uscorp1/secure/2013–03–25–dell-go-shop-proposals.

[16] Guhan Subramanian, *Go-Shops vs. No-Shops in Private Equity Deals: Evidence and Implications,* 63 BUS. LAW. 729 (2008).

of review. Deal protections function to deter subsequent bids that would compete with the incumbent bid from emerging, and may therefore run afoul of the board's obligation to seek the highest price for shareholders. When challenged in the context of a change of control transaction, such measures are subject to *Revlon*'s enhanced scrutiny.

In *In re Toys R Us Shareholder Litigation*, 877 A.2d 975 (Del. Ch. 2005), the board of Toys R Us had agreed to sell the corporation to KKR in a change of control transaction. Shareholders challenged the decision of the board to include in the merger agreement a series of deal protection measures, including a 3.75% termination fee as well as matching rights, arguing that use of such measures ran afoul of the board's obligation to seek the highest price reasonably available to shareholders.

[The plaintiffs argue] that the board acted unreasonably by signing a merger agreement with the KKR Group that, in their view, includes deal protection measures that preclude other bidders from making a topping offer. In support of this argument, the plaintiffs offer up expert testimony from two professors, R. Preston McAfee, an economist at the California Institute of Technology, and Guhan Subramanian, a professor at Harvard Law School.

Together, the professors advance the position that the deal protection measures in the merger agreement might have deterred some superior offers for the Company. For his part, McAfee believes matching rights are a stiff barrier to rival bidders. Subramanian concentrates more on termination fees, and argues that those fees, when combined with matching rights, are a potent obstacle to emerging bidders. In a series of rapidly evolving affidavits, Subramanian claims to have developed data that suggests that the termination fee in the merger agreement—which is 3.75% of equity value and 3.25% of total transaction value—exceeds that which is typical of deals this size. Consistent with work he has done with Professor Coates, Subramanian claims that any termination fee of 3% or more "has a reasonable likelihood of foreclosing higher value bidders."

Furthermore, in his scholarly work Subramanian argues that combination of a termination fee and matching rights raises the fears second bidders have of suffering a "winner's curse." This is the anxiety that a first bidder will match the initial topping bid, only to refuse to match the next topping gambit, leaving the second bidder having paid more than was economically rational. This fear, Subramanian points out, is further exacerbated by the common circumstance that first bidders often have superior

future takeover premium. Only if there has been a change of control is that option foreclosed.

In any event . . . the relevant policy concern is not whether there is a tomorrow. To be sure, *QVC* spoke of "an asset belonging to public shareholders"; i.e., "a control premium." As we saw above, although he did not cite *QVC*, Vice Chancellor Laster implicated this concern by holding that *Revlon* was triggered because the transaction at issue was the "only chance [the target shareholders would have to have their fiduciaries bargain for a premium for their shares."

If *QVC* is properly understood, however, the Supreme Court was not showing concern for whether there will be a tomorrow for the shareholders. Instead, as discussed above, the court was concerned in *QVC* with the division of gains between target and acquirer shareholders because the post-transaction company would have a dominating controlling shareholder.

. . . [T]he relevant concern thus is the potential that conflicted interests will affect the target's board of directors' decisions. Indeed, as we have seen, even Vice Chancellor Lamb's opinion in *Lukens* recognized that the motivating concern underlying *Revlon* is "the omnipresent specter that a board may be acting primarily in its own interest, rather than those of the corporation and its shareholders." Curiously, however, Vice Chancellor Lamb brought that policy concern into play only with respect to whether the directors had satisfied their *Revlon* duties, while ignoring it when deciding whether those duties have triggered. But nothing in *Revlon* or *QVC* suggests that that policy is limited to the former issue rather than both inquiries.

Because the conflict of interest policy concern is the underlying driver of both aspects of *Revlon*, the Chancery Court in *Lukens* and its progeny should have considered whether the all- or partial-cash transactions necessarily implicate conflicts of interest akin to those at issue in *Revlon* and *QVC*. If the various Vice Chancellors had done so, they would have recognized that, so long as acquisitions of publicly held corporations are conducted by other publicly held corporations, diversified shareholders will be indifferent as to the allocations of gains between the parties. In turn, those shareholders also will be indifferent as to the form of consideration.

In contrast, if the transaction results in a privately held entity, a diversified shareholder cannot be on both sides of the transaction. If the post-transaction entity remains publicly held, but will be dominated by a controlling shareholder, there is a substantial risk that the control shareholder will be able to extract non-pro rata benefits in the future and get a sweetheart deal from target directors in the initial acquisition. In either situation, the division of gain matters a lot. As such, investors would prefer to see gains in such transactions allocated to the target. It is in these situations that *Revlon* therefore should come into play.

G. *REVLON* IN OTHER STATES, AND OTHER CONSTITUENCY PROVISIONS

The *Revlon* doctrine is the law in Delaware. But it has had a mixed reception in other states. Professor Michal Barzuza finds that four states adopted *Revlon* (California, Illinois, Michigan and Texas) while nine states have explicitly rejected it (Indiana, Ohio, Pennsylvania, North Carolina, Maryland, Virginia, New York, Wisconsin and Missouri).[20] States that reject the *Revlon* doctrine largely adopt the business judgment rule to assess board decisions to sell their companies. But while the legal standard of review is the business judgment rule, in application it often appears that some type of *Revlon* scrutiny is applied.

Moreover, some 33 states (including New York, but not Delaware) have "other constituency" statutes that, typically, allow, and sometimes require, boards to take into consideration interests others than shareholders.'[21] These statutes can give boards the statutory authority to say no to unwanted bids or to prefer one bid over another for reasons other than securing the highest price for shareholders in the short run.

For example, the Wisconsin constituency statute, which is representative of these kinds of statutes, states that:

> In discharging his or her duties to the corporation and in determining what he or she believes to be in the best interests of the corporation, a director or officer may, in addition to considering the effects of any action on shareholders, consider the following: (1) The effects of the action on employees, suppliers and customers of the corporation; (2) The effects of the action on communities in which the corporation operates; (3) Any other factors that the director or officer considers pertinent.[22]

---

[20] Michal Barzuza, *The State of Antitakeover Law*, 95 VA. L. REV. 1973 (2009).

[21] See Matthew D. Cain, Stephen B. McKeon, & Steven Davidoff Solomon, *Do Takeover Laws Matter? Evidence from Five Decades of Hostile Takeovers* (2015), available at http://ssrn.com/abstract=2517513.

[22] Wis. Stat. § 180.0827.

Wisconsin courts have stated *Revlon* is not the law in Wisconsin. Rejecting "the plaintiff's contention that heightened scrutiny applied," a Wisconsin court held that "in Wisconsin it's the business judgment rule plain and simple. I think that's a high burden that plaintiffs have to get over. So is there heightened scrutiny? Yeah, on [the plaintiff's] behalf."[23] In *Dixon v. Ladish Co.*, in Federal court (the Eastern District of Wisconsin), the court reasoned that the Wisconsin constituency statute "is in direct conflict with a rule that would require directors to focus solely on maximizing value for the benefit of shareholders." The court further stated that it was "not implying that the value secured in a merger transaction is irrelevant, it is one of a number of considerations a board may take into account and is properly reviewed through the lens of the business judgment rule."[24] That being said, while constituency statutes generally provide boards the protection of the business judgment rule in their decisions to decline to accept a premium bid, they may come up against real world norms that look a lot like *Revlon* when challenged.

QUESTIONS

The *Revlon* Case

1. Why do you think Bergerac did not want to do a deal with Perelman?

2. Can you defend the proposition that Mr. Bergerac's reaction to Perelman's offer was in the Revlon shareholders' best interests? What does your answer suggest about how courts should scrutinize the conduct of a target company and its directors and officers?

3. What do you think really motivated the directors to favor Forstmann Little? Why did the court think that motivation was problematic? Whose interests most needed protecting here?

4. Whose interests does the court think the board should be protecting? Whose interests does the court think the board should *not* be protecting?

5. What liability could the directors have had to the noteholders? How were the noteholders harmed?

6. Why did the deal change so that management were no longer participating?

---

[23] *Ponds Edge Capital LLC v. Outlook Group Corp.,* No. 06–cv–489 (Winnebago County Cir. Ct. Nov. 29, 2006), summary judgment granted, March 9, 2007.

[24] *Dixon v. Ladish Co.,* 785 F.Supp.2d 746 (E.D.Wis.2011), *aff'd, Dixon v. ATI Ladish LLC,* 667 F.3d 891, (7th Cir. 2012). *See generally* Richard B. Kapnick, Courtney A. Rosen & Veena Gursahani, *Wisconsin Courts Reject Heightened Scrutiny in Mergers and Acquisitions Litigation,* SIDLEY AUSTIN LLP (2011), available at http://www.sidley.com/~/media/Files/Publications/2011/08/Wisconsin%20Courts%20Reject%20Heightened%20Scrutiny%20in%20M__/Files/View%20Article/FileAttachment/Wisconsin%20Courts%20Reject%20Heightened%20Scrutiny.

7.   How does the court's reasoning in *Revlon* relate to Manne's theory of a "market for corporate control" described in Chapter I?

The *Time* Case

1.   What did restructuring the deal accomplish?

2.   What does the court think of the capacities and motivations of the board? The shareholders?

3.   Do you think there is something problematic about the "confidence" letters obtained by Time?

4.   Time repeatedly referenced (in its dealings with Warner and Paramount) the importance of preserving its "culture." How much deference should courts accord such a determination? How much deference did the court afford to the determination in the case?

5.   Why does the court say that Paramount could have bought the combined Time-Warner? What legal importance does that "fact" have?

6.   Who owned Time before this deal? Who owned Warner before this deal? Who would own Time Warner as the deal was originally structured? What about as the deal was restructured?

The *QVC* Case

1.   How does the court's emphasis on whether there is a change in control comport with the *Revlon* decision?

2.   How does the court's description of a board's obligations in *QVC* differ from how those same obligations were described in *Revlon*?

3.   Why do you think Sumner Redstone made the statement that the merger of Viacom and QVC would survive anything but a "nuclear attack"? Do you think it was a wise statement to make?

4.   Paramount became a target of QVC and Viacom after losing a bidding war for Time. What does this say about the market for takeovers and why companies and executives sometimes engage in acquisitions? What reasons do you think QVC and Viacom had for engaging in a bidding war for Paramount?

The *Lyondell* Case

1.   Post-*Lyondell*, how do you think the *Revlon* standard as applied by the Delaware courts is different than the *Unocal* standard?

2.   Interestingly, as you can see, the Supreme Court reversed the Chancery Court's ruling. Where the Supreme Court saw 'good' facts for the directors, the Chancery Court saw 'bad' facts. What was the Chancery Court's *Revlon* analysis? When did it think *Revlon* was triggered, and why? What did it think *Revlon* required? Which analysis do you agree with more, the Chancery Court's or the Supreme Court's, and why?

PROBLEMS

1. In a sale of control, the board of Apex Tech is faced with the following two competing offers:

    a. Beta Corp, a strategic competitor, is offering $15/share in stock as consideration.

    b. Gamma Group, a private equity buyer, is offering $12/share in cash as consideration.

Is the board required to select one of these? If so, which should the board select? What considerations should the board take into account in coming to its conclusion?

2. In a sale of control, the board of Apex Tech is faced with the following two competing offers:

    a. Beta Corp, a strategic competitor, is offering $15/share in cash as consideration. Beta has made commitments to maintain current employment in Apex Tech's factories and facilities.

    b. Epsilon Energy Corp., a competitor, is offering $17/share in cash as consideration. Epsilon has publicly committed to closing existing factories and facilities and moving production overseas.

Is the board required to select one of these? If not, which should the board select? What are the considerations that the board should take into account in coming to that conclusion?

3. In a sale of control, the board of Apex Tech is faced with the following two competing offers:

    a. Delta Fund, a private equity buyer, is offering $12.50/ share in cash as consideration.

    b. Gamma Group, a private equity buyer, is offering $12/share in cash as consideration.

Is the board required to select one of these? If not, which should the board select? What are the considerations that the board should take into account in coming to that conclusion?

4. In a sale of control, the board of Apex Tech is faced with the following two competing offers:

    a. Delta Fund, a private equity buyer, is offering $12/share in cash as consideration. Delta has publicly committed to keeping the current CEO in place in order to maintain stability and increase the likelihood of success in implementing Apex's long term strategy.

    b. Gamma Group, a private equity buyer, is offering $16/share in cash as consideration. Gamma has made no statements with respect to the future of the corporation.

Is the board required to select one of these? If not, which should the board select? What are the considerations that the board should take into account in coming to that conclusion?

5.   A client comes to you and tells you that they are interested in selling their company, a publicly traded ice cream manufacturer that is incorporated in Delaware and publicly traded. The board of the company asks you to advise them on the appropriate sale process. In particular, what does the board need to do in speaking with bidders? The board thinks that the most likely buyer is a private equity firm. Please draft a memo advising them on what procedures they should use to satisfy their obligations under *Revlon*.

CHAPTER XIX

CONFLICTS OF INTEREST: ENTIRE FAIRNESS

■ ■ ■

As was discussed in the previous Chapters, when companies are being taken over or sold, courts are concerned that shareholder interests be sufficiently taken into account, especially given the possible conflicts of interest of management and the board. In this Chapter, we explore the regulation of conflicts in three specific areas: transactions with controlling shareholders, sometimes known as freeze-outs or squeeze-outs; transactions with management, also known as management buy-outs; and private equity buy-outs.

Courts in both Delaware and other jurisdictions recognize the conflict inherent in takeovers: that directors and officers may lose their positions as a result of a takeover.. Consequently, directors' and officers' interests may not necessarily align with those of shareholders. Courts developed the *Unocal* and *Revlon* standards in order to help resolve those potential conflicts.

Other conflicts may apply only to a subset of directors or officers. When a company has a controlling shareholder, some or all of the directors may have been effectively appointed by that shareholder, and are perhaps subject to the shareholder's control. When the controlling shareholder seeks to do a freeze-out—that is, purchase the remaining shares of the company—*Revlon* duties may not apply because there is no change of control or other Revlon trigger, but a conflict still exists due to the presence of directors with dual loyalties and the controlling shareholder's ability to cause the transaction to occur. If a chief executive officer proposes a management buy-out, she is obviously conflicted. What about the (other) directors? How should the additional conflict presented by a management buy-out be regulated? Courts have sought to deal with these conflicts and give guidance to dealmakers.

As we will see in this Chapter, the courts have given a prominent role to independent and disinterested directors in MBO and freeze-out transactions, hoping that such directors will be free of conflicts that commonly arise in these types of transactions. But as we will also see, reality may be different than what was hoped for.

A. THE ORIGINS OF CONFLICT OF INTEREST REGULATION

As you may remember from your Corporations or Business Associations class, transactions such as a management buy-out or a squeeze-out are essentially interested director or officer (or shareholder) transactions. Under the common law, corporate transactions with a director or officer were void or voidable merely due to the involvement of the director or officer. State law conflict of interest statutes provide a mechanism for saving such transactions from being void or voidable.

Here is Delaware's conflict of interest statute, DGCL § 144:

> (a) No contract or transaction between a corporation and 1 or more of its directors or officers, or between a corporation and any other corporation, . . . in which 1 or more of its directors or officers, are directors or officers, or have a financial interest, shall be void or voidable solely for this reason . . . if:
>
>> (1) The material facts as to the director's or officer's relationship or interest and as to the contract or transaction are disclosed or are known to the board of directors or the committee, and the board or committee in good faith authorizes the contract or transaction by the affirmative votes of a majority of the disinterested directors, even though the disinterested directors be less than a quorum; or
>>
>> (2) The material facts as to the director's or officer's relationship or interest and as to the contract or transaction are disclosed or are known to the shareholders entitled to vote thereon, and the contract or transaction is specifically approved in good faith by vote of the shareholders; or
>>
>> (3) The contract or transaction is fair as to the corporation as of the time it is authorized, approved or ratified, by the board of directors, a committee or the shareholders.

The statute sets forth three different ways for a conflict not to render a transaction void or voidable. The first is the approval of a majority of the disinterested directors, either acting through a committee or the full board. The second is approval of a majority of shareholders. The statute does not expressly provide that this approval must be by the disinterested shareholders, but Delaware courts have generally read into the statute a requirement that disinterested shareholders approve conflict transactions as consistent with the common law. Other states specifically set forth a disinterestedness requirement in their statute. The third and final way for a conflict not to render a conflict transaction void or voidable is for the transaction to be deemed "fair." As we will see below, fairness is determined in a judicial proceeding, and encompasses both fair price and fair dealing.

The § 144(a)(2) safe harbor resembles, but is not exactly the same as, the common law doctrine of ratification. Section 144 requires approval by a majority of shareholders (not a majority of the disinterested shareholders). Because it is possible that shareholder approval for purposes of § 144 can be accomplished by a controlling shareholder alone, a transaction relying on the § 144 safe harbor may still be subject to entire fairness review since it is not approved by the disinterested shareholders.

Common law ratification doctrine requires approval of a conflicted director transaction by a majority of the disinterested shareholders. The effect of fully informed approval by a majority of the disinterested shareholders is that "the entire atmosphere is freshened and a new set of rules invoked."[1] In an atmosphere freshened by approval of a majority of disinterested shareholders, a conflicted director transaction receives the protection of the business judgment presumption.

In combination, the interested director statute and the common law ratification doctrine permit conflicted director transactions, and where robust procedural protections mimicking an arm's length approval process—approval of a majority of either fully-informed disinterested directors or fully-informed disinterested shareholders—are in place, give these conflict transactions the protection of business judgment deference.

Because obtaining disinterested director approval is much more manageable, practitioners have focused on obtaining such approval as the way to cleanse conflicted director transactions. By contrast, approval by the shareholders requires a shareholder vote, a cumbersome and expensive process. This does not mean that approval by the disinterested shareholders is not also sought in conflicted director transactions, but it may be being done as a matter of good practice rather than because it is legally required to "cleanse" the otherwise interested transaction. Director approval is also preferred to a judicial determination of fairness. An ex post judicial determination of "fairness" involves litigation, which is time-consuming, costly, and uncertain.

Given that approval of a conflicted director transaction by disinterested directors is often the preferred route, the definition of disinterested director takes on particular importance. It is explored in the following excerpt:

> In Delaware, the core notion is that directors must be able to exercise their own independent judgment in approving a transaction. If they have a relationship with someone else that

---

[1]   *Gottlieb v. Heyden Chemical Corp.*, 91 A.2d 57, 59 (Del. 1952).

would cause their independence to be impaired, they are not independent. The inquiry is highly fact-dependent. However, in most contexts Delaware courts have been unwilling to infer a lack of independence unless the interested party is able to inflict a material financial punishment upon the director. Social ties, even close ones, have generally (though not quite always) not been enough.

Independence is defined quite differently in stock exchange listing rules and federal securities law. Independence is defined ex ante for a director generally, not ex post for particular transactions as in Delaware. The MBCA does not use the term "independent directors." But, it does require that where an interested transaction is sought to be cleansed by director approval, that approval must be by "qualified directors." A qualified director must not have "a familial, financial, professional, employment or other relationship that would reasonably be expected to impair the objectivity of the director's judgment when participating in the action to be taken." (a definition quite close to Delaware's definition of independence). The ALI's Principles of Corporate Governance speak of approval by "disinterested directors." However, disinterest is defined broadly, and excludes directors who have:

> a business, financial, or familial relationship with a party to the transaction or conduct, and that relationship would reasonably be expected to affect the director's or officer's judgment with respect to the transaction or conduct in a manner adverse to the corporation; [or who are] . . . subject to a controlling influence by a party to the transaction or conduct or a person who has a material pecuniary interest in the transaction or conduct, and that controlling influence could reasonably be expected to affect the director's or officer's judgment with respect to the transaction or conduct in a manner adverse to the corporation.

Thus, the ALI's definition of "disinterested director" resembles Delaware's definition of "independent director" and the MBCA's definition of "qualified director."[2]

The concepts of independence and (dis)interest are related, but distinct. As the excerpt discusses and as the phraseology of DGCL § 144 indicates, "interest" relates more to a particular matter, while "independence" is a more general status. Articulations of seminal doctrines, such as when a court will excuse demand in a derivative case or

---

[2]   Claire A. Hill & Brett H. McDonnell, *Sanitizing Interested Transactions*, 36 DEL. J. CORP. L. 903, 911–915 (2011).

accept a special litigation committee (SLC)'s judgment to discontinue litigation against the directors when demand has been or would be excused, use both terms. For our purposes, there is considerable overlap.[3]

The article excerpted above describes the varying approaches to defining what makes a director interested or disinterested, and independent or not independent. Objective ties such as employment or monetary compensation can be readily assessed. Softer ties such as friendship, collegiality or even shared affinity to an educational or other organization, such as the college the parties attended, may also implicate independence, but are harder, if not impossible, to effectively take into account. The article notes that except as to independence in the specialized context of special litigation committees deciding whether the company should pursue litigation against its directors, the trend in Delaware and elsewhere is to assess independence in terms of monetary and other objective indicia, rather than social ties.[4]

In reading the materials in the next Sections, think about whether a more "objective" definition based on money, employment, and familial ties suffices, or whether a more fine-grained assessment that takes into account the complexities of human behavior is warranted or even feasible.[5]

---

[3] One example of overlap is where references to independence are made in opinions or other legal analyses with respect to a particular transaction or other matter.

[4] In significant part, this is a function of who bears the burden of showing independence and disinterest. In cases involving special litigation committees deciding on litigation against directors, demand has been or would be excused, so it is not surprising that the committee has the burden to demonstrate its independence and disinterest. In most other contexts, including those involving conflicted director transactions, the plaintiff has the burden of showing independence and disinterest are lacking. One other point should be made. Definitions of independence for purposes of the NYSE and other like organizations increasingly include more subjective determinations. *See* the following commentary from NYSE 303A.02: "It is not possible to anticipate, or explicitly to provide for, all circumstances that might signal potential conflicts of interest, or that might bear on the materiality of a director's relationship to a listed company (references to "listed company" would include any parent or subsidiary in a consolidated group with the listed company). Accordingly, it is best that boards making "independence" determinations broadly consider all relevant facts and circumstances. In particular, when assessing the materiality of a director's relationship with the listed company, the board should consider the issue not merely from the standpoint of the director, but also from that of persons or organizations with which the director has an affiliation. Material relationships can include commercial, industrial, banking, consulting, legal, accounting, charitable and familial relationships, among others."

[5] See generally *In re Oracle Corp. Derivative Litigation*, 824 A.2d 917 (Del. Ch. 2003) for then-Vice-Chancellor Strine's elaboration on why a more nuanced perspective on human nature is more realistic, and using such a perspective in a case in which he rejected a special litigation committee's determination to terminate a lawsuit against the corporation's directors.

B. FREEZE-OUTS

1. HISTORY OF FREEZE-OUTS

In a freeze-out, a controlling shareholder purchases the shares held by the minority shareholders. Courts are concerned that minority shareholders be treated fairly. The controlling shareholder has often appointed a majority of the directors, and has substantial ties with those directors. The controlling shareholder can make her offer the only viable one by refusing to sell her shares to a third party. Her control means, as well, that just by voting her shares she can approve a transaction or block an unwanted third party offer. Minority shareholders may thus be frozen out at a price below fair value.

Because of the potential for abuse, freeze-outs are subject to heightened procedural requirements and judicial scrutiny in Delaware and other states. The law in this area is still in flux and hotly debated. To understand the current debate, we first review the development of the law on "going-private" transactions, in which a controller acquires the rest of a company's shares:

> The third wave of merger activity subsided in the early 1970s with the popping of the conglomerate stock bubble and repeated U.S. economic recession. These two events combined to birth the next major issue of takeover regulation: the abusive going-private. These were largely "take 'em public high-buy 'em out low" affairs; controlling affiliates of corporations who had only recently engaged in initial public offerings when stock market prices were substantially higher offered to buy out their own publicly held stock at markedly lower prices. Because there was an inherently coercive element in these transactions and the opportune timing was at the affiliates' discretion, these purchases engendered cries of fraud and unjust enrichment. The states' response was, at least initially, relatively sluggish, and the SEC again took the wheel maintaining its role as the nation's primary takeover regulator.
>
> In 1975, the SEC launched a fact-finding investigation and simultaneously proposed rules to govern going-private transactions. One form of the proposed rule would have required that a price paid in such a transaction be no lower than "the consideration recommended jointly by two qualified independent persons." Adoption of this rule was delayed, largely due to allegations that the SEC lacked rulemaking authority under the Williams Act. Then in 1977, the Supreme Court in *Santa Fe Industries v. Green* overruled the Second Circuit's holding that Rule 10b–5 constituted a basis to challenge a going-private

decision on substantive grounds. This decision, and continued dissatisfaction with state regulation of going-privates-primarily the Delaware Supreme Court's decision in *Singer v. Magnavox Co.* led the SEC to repropose rules. These rules were finally adopted by the SEC in 1979, and, although not as far-reaching as originally proposed, established a new disclosure-based regime for going-privates. Most notably, the rules now obligated corporations in going-private transactions to express an opinion as to the "fairness" of the transaction to unaffiliated shareholders. The SEC conduct was particularly noteworthy given the view of many that it did not have the legal authority to adopt even this scaled-back regulation.

Regulation of going-privates thus was initially driven by the SEC. In a polemical speech made at Notre Dame law school, SEC Commissioner A.A. Sommer, Jr., initiated the SEC charge against going-private transactions. He labeled them as "serious, unfair, and sometimes disgraceful, a perversion of the whole process of public financing."

Academics also joined in and this was the topic du jour of the 1970s. The SEC adopted the so-called going-private rules. The requirement that the controlling shareholder express an opinion as to the fairness of the transaction was designed to ensure that there was quality control. But the rules also required enhanced disclosure including disclosure of all presentations to the board. The remedy thus offered a disclosure based solution to going-privates.

But dissatisfaction with going-privates remained. In *Singer*, the Delaware Supreme Court held that a going-private transaction must have a valid business purpose. A transaction "made for the sole purpose of freezing out minority shareholders" lacked such purpose and therefore was "an abuse of the corporate process." The court further held that even if a valid business purpose was existent, a Delaware court should still "scrutinize the circumstances for compliance with the ... rule of 'entire fairness'...." The business purpose test was popular among other states at the time, and was adopted by many. Though it did not succeed, *Singer* was arguably Delaware's attempt to forestall SEC rulemaking and was in reaction to the SEC's heated criticism of going-privates.[6]

---

[6]   Steven M. Davidoff, *The SEC and The Failure of Federal Takeover Litigation,* 34 FLA. ST. U. L. REV. 211, 219–22 (2007).

2. *WEINBERGER v. UOP*

The debate over going-private transactions did not subside with the SEC's actions. In 1983, in *Weinberger v. UOP, Inc.*, the Delaware Supreme Court issued what has become an extremely important opinion on the subject. The case defined "fairness" as including fair price and fair dealing; it also expressly reversed the holding in *Singer v. Magnavox,* 380 A.2d 969 (Del. 1977) that a controller needed to demonstrate a valid business purpose to effect a freeze-out.

WEINBERGER V. UOP, INC.

Supreme Court of Delaware
457 A.2d 701 (1983)

MOORE, JUSTICE:

This post-trial appeal was reheard en banc from a decision of the Court of Chancery. It was brought by the class action plaintiff below, a former shareholder of UOP, Inc., who challenged the elimination of UOP's minority shareholders by a cash-out merger between UOP and its majority owner, The Signal Companies, Inc. . . . The present Chancellor held that the terms of the merger were fair to the plaintiff and the other minority shareholders of UOP. Accordingly, he entered judgment in favor of the defendants. . . .

The Chancellor . . . held that even though the ultimate burden of proof is on the majority shareholder to show by a preponderance of the evidence that the transaction is fair, it is first the burden of the plaintiff attacking the merger to demonstrate some basis for invoking the fairness obligation. We agree with that principle. However, where corporate action has been approved by an informed vote of a majority of the minority shareholders, we conclude that the burden entirely shifts to the plaintiff to show that the transaction was unfair to the minority. But in all this, the burden clearly remains on those relying on the vote to show that they completely disclosed all material facts relevant to the transaction.

I.

. . .

Signal is a diversified, technically based company operating through various subsidiaries. Its stock is publicly traded on the New York, Philadelphia and Pacific Stock Exchanges. UOP, formerly known as Universal Oil Products Company, was a diversified industrial company engaged in various lines of business, including petroleum and petro-chemical services and related products, construction, fabricated metal products, transportation equipment products, chemicals and plastics, and other products and services including land development, lumber products and waste disposal. Its stock was publicly held and listed on the New York Stock Exchange.

In 1974 Signal sold one of its wholly-owned subsidiaries for $420,000,000 in cash. While looking to invest this cash surplus, Signal became interested in UOP as a possible acquisition. Friendly negotiations ensued, and Signal proposed to acquire a controlling interest in UOP at a price of $19 per share. UOP's representatives sought $25 per share. In the arm's length bargaining that followed, an understanding was reached whereby Signal agreed to purchase from UOP 1,500,000 shares of UOP's authorized but unissued stock at $21 per share.

This purchase was contingent upon Signal making a successful cash tender offer for 4,300,000 publicly held shares of UOP, also at a price of $21 per share. This combined method of acquisition permitted Signal to acquire 5,800,000 shares of stock, representing 50.5% of UOP's outstanding shares. The UOP board of directors advised the company's shareholders that it had no objection to Signal's tender offer at that price. Immediately before the announcement of the tender offer, UOP's common stock had been trading on the New York Stock Exchange at a fraction under $14 per share.

The negotiations between Signal and UOP occurred during April 1975, and the resulting tender offer was greatly oversubscribed. However, Signal limited its total purchase of the tendered shares so that, when coupled with the stock bought from UOP, it had achieved its goal of becoming a 50.5% shareholder of UOP.

Although UOP's board consisted of thirteen directors, Signal nominated and elected only six. Of these, five were either directors or employees of Signal. The sixth, a partner in the banking firm of Lazard Freres & Co., had been one of Signal's representatives in the negotiations and bargaining with UOP concerning the tender offer and purchase price of the UOP shares.

However, the president and chief executive officer of UOP retired during 1975, and Signal caused him to be replaced by James V. Crawford, a long-time employee and senior executive vice president of one of Signal's wholly-owned subsidiaries. Crawford succeeded his predecessor on UOP's board of directors and also was made a director of Signal.

By the end of 1977 Signal basically was unsuccessful in finding other suitable investment candidates for its excess cash, and by February 1978 considered that it had no other realistic acquisitions available to it on a friendly basis. Once again its attention turned to UOP.

The trial court found that at the instigation of certain Signal management personnel, including William W. Walkup, its board chairman, and Forrest N. Shumway, its president, a feasibility study was made concerning the possible acquisition of the balance of UOP's outstanding shares. This study was performed by two Signal officers, Charles S. Arledge, vice president (director of planning), and Andrew J. Chitiea, senior vice president (chief financial officer). Messrs. Walkup, Shumway, Arledge and Chitiea were all directors of UOP in addition to their membership on the Signal board.

Arledge and Chitiea concluded that it would be a good investment for Signal to acquire the remaining 49.5% of UOP shares at any price up to $24 each. Their report was discussed between Walkup and Shumway who, along with Arledge, Chitiea and Brewster L. Arms, internal counsel for Signal, constituted Signal's senior management. . . . It was ultimately agreed that a meeting of Signal's executive committee would be called to propose that Signal acquire the remaining outstanding stock of UOP through a cash-out merger in the range of $20 to $21 per share.

The executive committee meeting was set for February 28, 1978. As a courtesy, UOP's president, Crawford, was invited to attend, although he was not a member of Signal's executive committee. On his arrival, and prior to the meeting, Crawford was asked to meet privately with Walkup and Shumway. He was then told of Signal's plan to acquire full ownership of UOP and was asked for his reaction to the proposed price range of $20 to $21 per share. Crawford said he thought such a price would be "generous", and that it was certainly one which should be submitted to UOP's minority shareholders for their ultimate consideration. [Crawford does ask that employees be assured of continuing employment and accommodation for any stock options they had] . . .

Thus, it was the consensus that a price of $20 to $21 per share would be fair to both Signal and the minority shareholders of UOP. Signal's executive committee authorized its management "to negotiate" with UOP "for a cash acquisition of the minority ownership in UOP, Inc., with the intention of presenting a proposal to [Signal's] board of directors . . . on March 6, 1978". Immediately after this February 28, 1978 meeting, Signal issued a press release stating:

The Signal Companies, Inc. and UOP, Inc. are conducting negotiations for the acquisition for cash by Signal of the 49.5 per cent of UOP which it does not presently own, announced Forrest N. Shumway, president and chief executive officer of Signal, and James V. Crawford, UOP president.

Price and other terms of the proposed transaction have not yet been finalized and would be subject to approval of the boards of directors of Signal and UOP, scheduled to meet early next week, the stockholders of UOP and certain federal agencies.

The announcement also referred to the fact that the closing price of UOP's common stock on that day was $14.50 per share.

Two days later, on March 2, 1978, Signal issued a second press release stating that its management would recommend a price in the range of $20 to $21 per share for UOP's 49.5% minority interest. This announcement referred to Signal's earlier statement that "negotiations" were being conducted for the acquisition of the minority shares.

Between Tuesday, February 28, 1978 and Monday, March 6, 1978, a total of four business days, Crawford spoke by telephone with all of UOP's non-Signal, i.e., outside, directors. Also during that period, Crawford retained Lehman Brothers to render a fairness opinion as to the price offered the minority for its stock. . . .

During this period Crawford also had several telephone contacts with Signal officials. In only one of them, however, was the price of the shares discussed. In a conversation with Walkup, Crawford advised that as a result of his communications with UOP's non-Signal directors, it was his feeling that the price would have to be the top of the proposed range, or $21 per share, if the approval of UOP's outside directors was to be obtained. But again, he did not seek any price higher than $21. . . .

On Monday morning, March 6, 1978, Glanville and the senior member of the Lehman Brothers team flew to Des Plaines to attend the scheduled UOP directors meeting. Glanville looked over the assembled information during the flight. The two had with them the draft of a "fairness opinion letter" in which the price had been left blank. Either during or immediately prior to the directors' meeting, the two-page "fairness opinion letter" was typed in final form and the price of $21 per share was inserted.

On March 6, 1978, both the Signal and UOP boards were convened to consider the proposed merger. Telephone communications were maintained between the two meetings. Walkup, Signal's board chairman, and also a UOP director, attended UOP's meeting with Crawford in order to present Signal's position and answer any questions that UOP's non-Signal directors might have. Arledge and Chitiea, along with Signal's other designees on UOP's board, participated by conference telephone. All of UOP's outside directors attended the meeting either in person or by conference telephone.

First, Signal's board unanimously adopted a resolution authorizing Signal to propose to UOP a cash merger of $21 per share as outlined in a certain merger agreement and other supporting documents. This proposal required that the merger be approved by a majority of UOP's outstanding minority shares voting at the stockholders meeting at which the merger would be considered, and that the minority shares voting in favor of the merger, when coupled with Signal's 50.5% interest would have to comprise at least two-thirds of all UOP shares. Otherwise the proposed merger would be deemed disapproved.

UOP's board then considered the proposal. [The board had copies of the agreement and other financial and other information, and the Lehman letter.] . . . [T]he Lehman Brothers partner, and UOP director, commented on the information that had gone into preparation of the letter.

Signal also suggests that the Arledge-Chitiea feasibility study, indicating that a price of up to $24 per share would be a "good investment" for Signal, was discussed at the UOP directors' meeting. The Chancellor made no such finding, and our independent review of the record, detailed infra, satisfies us by a preponderance of the evidence that there was no discussion of this document at UOP's board meeting. Furthermore, it is clear beyond peradventure that nothing in that report was ever disclosed to UOP's minority shareholders prior to their approval of the merger.

After consideration of Signal's proposal, Walkup and Crawford left the meeting to permit a free and uninhibited exchange between UOP's non-Signal directors. Upon their return a resolution to accept Signal's offer was then proposed and adopted. While Signal's men on UOP's board participated in various aspects of the meeting, they abstained from voting. However, the minutes show that each of them "if voting would have voted yes."

On March 7, 1978, UOP sent a letter to its shareholders advising them of the action taken by UOP's board with respect to Signal's offer. This document pointed out, among other things, that on February 28, 1978 "both companies had announced negotiations were being conducted."

Despite the swift board action of the two companies, the merger was not submitted to UOP's shareholders until their annual meeting on May 26, 1978. In the notice of that meeting and proxy statement sent to shareholders in May, UOP's management and board urged that the merger be approved. The proxy statement also advised:

> The price was determined after *discussions* between James V. Crawford, a director of Signal and Chief Executive Officer of UOP, and officers of Signal which took place during meetings on February 28, 1978, and in the course of several subsequent telephone conversations. (Emphasis added.)

In the original draft of the proxy statement the word "negotiations" had been used rather than "discussions". However, when the Securities and Exchange Commission sought details of the "negotiations" as part of its review of these materials, the term was deleted and the word "discussions" was substituted. The proxy statement indicated that the vote of UOP's board in approving the merger had been unanimous. It also advised the shareholders that Lehman Brothers had given its opinion that the merger price of $21 per share was fair to UOP's minority.

However, it did not disclose the hurried method by which this conclusion was reached.

As of the record date of UOP's annual meeting, there were 11,488,302 shares of UOP common stock outstanding, 5,688,302 of which were owned by the minority. At the meeting only 56%, or 3,208,652, of the minority shares were voted. Of these, 2,953,812, or 51.9% of the total minority, voted for the merger, and 254,840 voted against it. When Signal's stock was added to the minority shares voting in favor, a total of 76.2% of UOP's outstanding shares approved the merger while only 2.2% opposed it.

By its terms the merger became effective on May 26, 1978, and each share of UOP's stock held by the minority was automatically converted into a right to receive $21 cash.

II.

A.

A primary issue mandating reversal is the preparation by two UOP directors, Arledge and Chitiea, of their feasibility study for the exclusive use and benefit of Signal. This document was of obvious significance to both Signal and UOP. Using UOP data, it described the advantages to Signal of ousting the minority at a price range of $21–$24 per share. . . . [I]t is clear from the record that neither Arledge nor Chitiea shared this report with their fellow directors of UOP. We are satisfied that no one else did either. This conduct hardly meets the fiduciary standards applicable to such a transaction . . .

. . .

Given the absence of any attempt to structure this transaction on an arm's length basis, Signal cannot escape the effects of the conflicts it faced, particularly when its designees on UOP's board did not totally abstain from participation in the matter. There is no "safe harbor" for such divided loyalties in Delaware. When directors of a Delaware corporation are on both sides of a transaction, they are required to demonstrate their utmost good faith and the most scrupulous inherent fairness of the bargain. The requirement of fairness is unflinching in its demand that where one stands on both sides of a transaction, he has the burden of establishing its entire fairness, sufficient to pass the test of careful scrutiny by the courts.

There is no dilution of this obligation where one holds dual or multiple directorships, as in a parent-subsidiary context. Thus, individuals who act in a dual capacity as directors of two corporations, one of whom is parent and the other subsidiary, owe the same duty of good management to both corporations, and in the absence of an independent negotiating structure, or the directors' total abstention from any participation in the matter, this duty is to be exercised in light of what is best for both companies. The record demonstrates that Signal has not met this obligation.

C.

The concept of fairness has two basic aspects: fair dealing and fair price. The former embraces questions of when the transaction was timed, how it was initiated, structured, negotiated, disclosed to the directors, and how the approvals of the directors and the stockholders were obtained. The latter aspect of fairness relates to the economic and financial considerations of the proposed merger, including all relevant factors: assets, market value, earnings, future prospects, and any other elements that affect the intrinsic or inherent value of a company's stock. However, the test for fairness is not a bifurcated one as between fair dealing and price. All aspects of the issue must be examined as a whole since the question is one of entire fairness. However, in a non-fraudulent transaction we recognize that price may be the preponderant consideration outweighing other features of the merger. Here, we address the two basic aspects of fairness separately because we find reversible error as to both.

Part of fair dealing is the obvious duty of candor. Moreover, one possessing superior knowledge may not mislead any stockholder by use of corporate information to which the latter is not privy. Delaware has long imposed this duty even upon persons who are not corporate officers or directors, but who nonetheless are privy to matters of interest or significance to their company. . . .

How did this merger evolve? It is clear that it was entirely initiated by Signal. The serious time constraints under which the principals acted were all set by Signal. It had not found a suitable outlet for its excess cash and considered UOP a desirable investment, particularly since it was now in a position to acquire the whole company for itself. For whatever reasons, and they were only Signal's, the entire transaction was presented to and approved by UOP's board within four business days. Standing alone, this is not necessarily indicative of any lack of fairness by a majority shareholder. It was what occurred, or more properly, what did not occur, during this brief period that makes the time constraints imposed by Signal relevant to the issue of fairness.

The structure of the transaction, again, was Signal's doing. So far as negotiations were concerned, it is clear that they were modest at best. Crawford, Signal's man at UOP, never really talked price with Signal, except to accede to its management's statements on the subject, and to convey to Signal the UOP outside directors' view that as between the $20–$21 range under consideration, it would have to be $21. The latter is not a surprising outcome, but hardly arm's length negotiations.

As we have noted, the matter of disclosure to the UOP directors was wholly flawed by the conflicts of interest raised by the report of Arledge and Chitiea. All of those conflicts were resolved by Signal in its own favor without divulging any aspect of them to UOP. . . .

Finally, the minority stockholders were denied the critical information that Signal considered a price of $24 to be a good investment. Since this would have meant over $17,000,000 more to the minority, we cannot conclude that the shareholder vote was an informed one. Under the circumstances, an approval by a majority of the minority was meaningless.

Given these particulars and the Delaware law on the subject, the record does not establish that this transaction satisfies any reasonable concept of fair dealing, and the Chancellor's findings in that regard must be reversed.

E.

Turning to the matter of price, plaintiff also challenges its fairness. His evidence was that on the date the merger was approved the stock was worth at least $26 per share. In support, he offered the testimony of a chartered investment analyst who used two basic approaches to valuation: a comparative analysis of the premium paid over market in ten other tender offer-merger combinations, and a discounted cash flow analysis.

In this breach of fiduciary duty case, the Chancellor perceived that the approach to valuation was the same as that in an appraisal proceeding. Consistent with precedent, he rejected plaintiff's method of proof and accepted defendants' evidence of value as being in accord with practice under prior case law. This means that the so-called "Delaware block" or weighted average method was employed wherein the elements of value, i.e., assets, market price, earnings, etc., were assigned a particular weight and the resulting amounts added to determine the value per share. This procedure has been in use for decades. However, to the extent it excludes other generally accepted techniques used in the financial community and the courts, it is now clearly outmoded. It is time we recognize this in appraisal and other stock valuation proceedings and bring our law current on the subject.

While the Chancellor rejected plaintiff's discounted cash flow method of valuing UOP's stock, as not corresponding with "either logic or the existing law", it is significant that this was essentially the focus, i.e., earnings potential of UOP, of Messrs. Arledge and Chitiea in their evaluation of the merger. Accordingly, the standard "Delaware block" or weighted average method of valuation, formerly employed in appraisal and other stock valuation cases, shall no longer exclusively control such proceedings. We believe that a more liberal approach must include proof of value by any techniques or methods which are generally considered acceptable in the financial community and otherwise admissible in court . . . .

The plaintiff has not sought an appraisal, but rescissory damages of the type contemplated by *Lynch v. Vickers Energy Corp.* (*Lynch II*). In view of the approach to valuation that we announce today, we see no basis in our law for *Lynch II*'s exclusive monetary formula for relief. On remand the plaintiff will be permitted to test the fairness of the $21 price by the standards we herein establish, in conformity with the principle applicable to an appraisal—that fair value be determined by taking "into account all relevant factors". In our view this includes the elements of rescissory damages if the Chancellor considers them susceptible of proof and a remedy appropriate to all the issues of fairness before him. To the extent that Lynch II purports to limit the Chancellor's discretion to a single remedial formula for monetary damages in a cash-out merger, it is overruled.

While a plaintiff's monetary remedy ordinarily should be confined to the more liberalized appraisal proceeding herein established, we do not intend any limitation on the historic powers of the Chancellor to grant such other relief as the facts of a particular case may dictate. The appraisal remedy we approve may not be adequate in certain cases, particularly where fraud, misrepresentation, self-dealing, deliberate waste of corporate assets, or gross and palpable overreaching are involved. Under such circumstances, the Chancellor's powers are complete to fashion any form of equitable and monetary relief as may be appropriate, including rescissory damages. Since it is apparent that this long completed transaction is too involved to undo, and in view of the Chancellor's discretion, the award, if any, should be in the form of monetary damages based upon entire fairness standards, i.e., fair dealing and fair price. . . .

III.

Finally, we address the matter of business purpose. The defendants contend that the purpose of this merger was not a proper subject of inquiry by the trial court. The plaintiff says that no valid purpose existed—the entire transaction was a mere subterfuge designed to eliminate the minority. . . .

In view of the fairness test which has long been applicable to parent-subsidiary mergers, the expanded appraisal remedy now available to shareholders, and the broad discretion of the Chancellor to fashion such relief as the facts of a given case may dictate, we do not believe that any additional meaningful protection is afforded minority shareholders by the business purpose requirement of the trilogy of *Singer, Tanzer, Najjar,* and their progeny. Accordingly, such requirement shall no longer be of any force or effect.

The judgment of the Court of Chancery, finding both the circumstances of the merger and the price paid the minority shareholders to be fair, is reversed. The matter is remanded for further proceedings consistent herewith. Upon remand the plaintiff's post-trial motion to enlarge the class should be granted.

---

3. *WEINBERGER* AND THE ENTIRE FAIRNESS AND BUSINESS PURPOSE TESTS

Weinberger established an "entire fairness" test for freeze-outs. Controlling shareholders would henceforth have the burden of showing that the transaction was "fair." Fair for these purposes meant fair price and fair dealing. *Weinberger* was notable in that it went beyond Delaware's conflict of interest statute, holding that the "entire fairness" test applied even if the transaction was approved by the independent and disinterested directors or shareholders.

Weinberger was also notable for rejecting the "business purpose" test. This test required controlling shareholders to provide a proper business reason for squeezing out minority shareholders. The rationale was that this would prevent the controller from squeezing out minority shareholders simply because the price of the company was at a cyclical low.

The business purpose test is still utilized in other states such as Massachusetts and New York. In *Coggins v. New England Patriots Football Club, Inc.*, 397 Mass. 525, 492 N.E.2d 1112 (1986), a holder of 10 non-voting shares of the New England Patriots sued when the controlling shareholder squeezed out his shares for cash. Coggins brought a suit challenging the transaction. The Massachusetts Supreme Court, in a ruling shortly after the *Weinberger* opinion, stated that "the 'fairness' test to which the Delaware court now has adhered [in *Weinberger*] is . . . closely related to the views expressed in our decisions. Unlike the Delaware court [in *Weinberger*], however, we believe that the 'business-purpose' test is an additional useful means under our statutes and case law for examining a transaction in which a controlling shareholder eliminates the minority interest in a corporation."[7]

The court ultimately found that the "the sole reason for the merger was to effectuate a restructuring of the Patriots that would enable the repayment of the [personal] indebtedness incurred by" the controlling shareholder. This type of personal interest did not suffice to establish a

---

[7]   *Id.* at 531, 492 N.E.2d at 1117.

sufficient business purpose. While the Massachusetts Supreme Court held for the plaintiff, it also held that rescission was an inappropriate remedy after 10 years, the amount of time it took for the case to be decided by the Massachusetts Supreme Court, and instead awarded money damages.

What is a proper business purpose? In *Alpert v. 28 Williams Street Corporation*, 63 N.Y.2d 557, 573 (1984) the New York Court of Appeals stated that:

> In the context of a freeze-out merger, variant treatment of the minority shareholders—i.e., causing their removal—will be justified when related to the advancement of a general corporate interest. The benefit need not be great, but it must be for the corporation. For example, if the sole purpose of the merger is reduction of the number of profit sharers—in contrast to increasing the corporation's capital or profits, or improving its management structure—there will exist no "independent corporate interest." All of these purposes ultimately seek to increase the individual wealth of the remaining shareholders. What distinguishes a proper corporate purpose from an improper one is that, with the former, removal of the minority shareholders furthers the objective of conferring some general gain upon the corporation. Only then will the fiduciary duty of good and prudent management of the corporation serve to override the concurrent duty to treat all shareholders fairly

4. APPRAISAL AS AN EXCLUSIVE REMEDY

Notably, the *Weinberger* case considered whether appraisal was the exclusive remedy available in a freeze-out merger. In some states such as Ohio, courts appear to have rejected the *Weinberger* doctrine and instead, where price is the only issue, only allow appraisal rights. In *Weinberger*, the Delaware courts instead permitted both an action for breach of fiduciary duties and for appraisal rights.

As a practical matter, the *Weinberger* court's refusal to limit remedies to appraisal opened the door for more relief to shareholders. As discussed in Chapter III, until recently, because of the costs and hurdles involved in exercising the appraisal remedy, including retaining and paying for a lawyer, appraisal proceedings were rarely brought. In contrast, a *Weinberger* quasi-appraisal action can be brought as a class action by a plaintiffs' law firm, without any up-front costs incurred by shareholders.[8] The *Weinberger* decision therefore facilitates a more active

---

[8] In a "quasi-appraisal" action, like *Weinberger*, the plaintiff's theory is that the board's failure to make certain disclosures directly affected the shareholder's decision not to seek appraisal rights. Had the board been truthful, a larger class of shareholders would have sought

market in challenging freeze-outs in court, a fact with which courts have grappled extensively.

5. *WEINBERGER*'S BURDEN OF PROOF

In *Kahn v. Lynch Communication Systems*, 638 A.2d 1110 (Del. 1994), the Delaware Supreme Court further refined its *Weinberger* holding. In *Kahn*, controlling shareholder Alcatel wished to freeze out minority shareholders of Lynch through a merger. The court held that entire fairness review was the appropriate standard of review for the merger even though it had been approved by Lynch's independent (special) committee. The committee approval merely shifted the burden of proof from the acquirer to the shareholders challenging the transaction. The decision was interpreted as requiring "entire fairness" review of every freeze-out transaction, including one approved by a committee of disinterested directors, or by disinterested shareholders. As so interpreted, the decision was criticized by some commentators on grounds that it failed to incentivize a controlling shareholder to use procedures that might better protect the other shareholders. Instead, no matter what the controlling shareholder did to mimic an arm's length transaction, the exacting "entire fairness" standard would apply. The fact that plaintiffs were left to bear the burden of proving unfairness turned out not to be a "bug" but a "feature" from the point of view of enterprising plaintiffs' counsel. Bearing the burden of proving unfairness simply meant that even a flimsy case had to be permitted to advance as far as trial in order to allow plaintiffs to attempt to bear their burden in court, even if they were ultimately unsuccessful. For plaintiffs, this meant that any transaction involving a controlling shareholder, no matter how cleanly implemented, was a lawsuit with a settlement value.

6. *WEINBERGER* IN THE MODERN AGE

As academics, practitioners and regulators all began to embrace the independent director as a panacea for many corporate ills, the Delaware Chancery Court began reigning in the expansive use of entire fairness review established by the holding of *Weinberger* and its extension in *Kahn*. In a series of opinions, various different judges on Delaware's Chancery Court began to revisit *Weinberger*'s requirements. In the first of these opinions, *In re Siliconix Inc. Shareholders Litigation,* 2001 WL 716787 (Del. Ch. June 19, 2001), Vice Chancellor Noble held that as to a tender offer, "unless coercion or disclosure violations can be shown, no defendant has the duty to demonstrate the entire fairness of [the] proposed tender transaction." The Vice Chancellor justified this finding on the grounds that tender offers, unlike mergers, did not require board

---

to perfect their appraisal rights under the statute. The plaintiff in the quasi-appraisal seeks a remedy equivalent to an appraisal for the entire class.

approval to proceed and therefore did not implicate a board's fiduciary duties. The *Siliconix* opinion was followed by an opinion by Vice Chancellor Strine the next year. The opinion further described the parameters under which a squeeze-out via tender offer could avoid "entire fairness" review.

IN RE PURE RESOURCES, INC. SHAREHOLDERS LITIGATION

Delaware Court of Chancery
808 A.2d 421 (2002)

STRINE, VICE CHANCELLOR.

This is the court's decision on a motion for preliminary injunction. The lead plaintiff in the case holds a large block of stock in Pure Resources, Inc., 65% of the shares of which are owned by Unocal Corporation. The lead plaintiff and its fellow plaintiffs seek to enjoin a now-pending exchange offer (the "Offer") by which Unocal hopes to acquire the rest of the shares of Pure in exchange for shares of its own stock. . . .

A.

Unocal Corporation is a large independent natural gas and crude oil exploration and production company with far-flung operations. In the United States, its most important operations are currently in the Gulf of Mexico. Before May 2000, Unocal also had operations in the Permian Basin of western Texas and southeastern New Mexico. During that month, Unocal spun off its Permian Basin unit and combined it with Titan Exploration, Inc. Titan was an oil and gas company operating in the Permian Basin, south central Texas, and the central Gulf Coast region of Texas. It also owned mineral interests in the southern Gulf Coast.

The entity that resulted from that combination was Pure Resources, Inc. Following the creation of Pure, Unocal owned 65.4% of Pure's issued and outstanding common stock. . . .

II.

A.

I now turn to the course of events leading up to Unocal's offer.

From its formation, Pure's future as an independent entity was a subject of discussion within its board. Although Pure's operations were successful, its status as a controlled subsidiary of another player in the oil and gas business suggested that the day would come when Pure either had to become wholly-owned by Unocal or independent of it. . . .

B.

On August 20, 2002, Unocal sent the Pure board a letter that stated in pertinent part that:

> It has become clear to us that the best interests of our respective stockholders will be served by Unocal's acquisition of the shares of Pure Resources that we do not already own. . . .
>
> Unocal recognizes that a strong and stable on-shore, North America production base will facilitate the execution of its North American gas strategy. The skills and technology required to maximize the benefits to be realized from that strategy are now divided between Union Oil and Pure. Sound business strategy calls for bringing those assets together, under one management, so that they may be deployed to their highest and best use. For those reasons, we are not interested in selling our shares in Pure. Moreover, if the two companies are combined, important cost savings should be realized and potential conflicts of interest will be avoided.
>
> Consequently, our Board of Directors has authorized us to make an exchange offer pursuant to which the stockholders of Pure (other than Union Oil) will be offered 0.6527 shares of common stock of Unocal for each outstanding share of Pure common stock they own in a transaction designed to be tax-free. Based on the $34.09 closing price of Unocal's shares on August 20, 2002, our offer provides a value of approximately $22.25 per share of Pure common stock and a 27% premium to the closing price of Pure common stock on that date.
>
> Unocal's offer is being made directly to Pure's stockholders. . . .
>
> Our offer will be conditioned on the tender of a sufficient number of shares of Pure common stock such that, after the offer is completed, we will own at least 90% of the outstanding shares of Pure common stock and other customary conditions. . . . Assuming that the conditions to the offer are satisfied and that the offer is completed, we will then effect a "short form" merger of Pure with a subsidiary of Unocal as soon as practicable thereafter. In this merger, the remaining Pure public stockholders will receive the same consideration as in the exchange offer, except for those stockholders who choose to exercise their appraisal rights.
>
> We intend to file our offering materials with the Securities and Exchange Commission and commence our exchange offer on or about September 5, 2002. Unocal is not seeking, and as the offer is being made directly to Pure's stockholders, Delaware law does

not require approval of the offer from Pure's Board of Directors. We, however, encourage you to consult with your outside counsel as to the obligations of Pure's Board of Directors under the U.S. tender offer rules to advise the stockholders of your recommendation with respect to our offer. . . .

. . . [The next day] . . . the Pure board voted to establish a Special Committee [of, effectively, independent directors] . . . The precise authority of the Special Committee to act on behalf of Pure was left hazy at first, but seemed to consist solely of the power to retain independent advisors, to take a position on the offer's advisability on behalf of Pure, and to negotiate with Unocal to see if it would increase its bid. Aside from this last point, this constrained degree of authority comported with the limited power that Unocal had desired.

During the early days of its operation, the Special Committee was aided by company counsel, Thompson & Knight, and management in retaining its own advisors and getting started. Soon, though, the Special Committee had retained two financial advisors and legal advisors to help it.

For financial advisors, the Special Committee hired Credit Suisse First Boston ("First Boston"), the investment bank assisting Pure with its consideration of the Royalty Trust, and Petrie Parkman & Co., Inc., a smaller firm very experienced in the energy field. . . .

For legal advisors, the Committee retained Baker Botts and Potter Anderson & Corroon . . .

After the formation of the Special Committee, Unocal formally commenced its Offer, which had these key features:

- An exchange ratio of 0.6527 of a Unocal share for each Pure share.

- A non-waivable majority of the minority tender provision, which required a majority of shares not owned by Unocal to tender. . . .

- A waivable condition that a sufficient number of tenders be received to enable Unocal to own 90% of Pure and to effect a short-form merger 8 Del.C. § 253.

- A statement by Unocal that it intends, if it obtains 90%, to consummate a short-form merger as soon as practicable at the same exchange ratio.

Thereafter, the Special Committee sought to, in its words, "clarify" its authority. The clarity it sought was clear: the Special Committee wanted to be delegated the full authority of the board under Delaware law to respond to the Offer. With such authority, the Special Committee could have searched for alternative transactions, speeded up consummation of the Royalty Trust [*Editor: "The Royalty Trust would monetize the value of certain mineral rights owned by Pure by selling portions of those interests to third parties."* Unocal apparently had "genuine concerns" about the *Trust.*], evaluated the feasibility of a self-tender, and put in place a shareholder rights plan (*a.k.a.,* poison pill) to block the Offer. . . .

After discussions between Counsel for Unocal and the Special Committee, the bold resolution drafted by Special Committee counsel was whittled down to take out any ability on the part of the Special Committee to do anything other than study the Offer, negotiate it, and make a recommendation on behalf of Pure in the required 14D–9.

The record does not illuminate exactly why the Special Committee did not make this their Alamo. . . . At best, the record supports the inference that the Special Committee believed some of the broader options technically open to them under their preferred resolution (*e.g.,* finding another buyer) were not practicable. As to their failure to insist on the power to deploy a poison pill—the by-now *de rigeur* tool of a board responding to a third-party tender offer—the record is obscure. The Special Committee's brief suggests that the Committee believed that the pill could not be deployed consistently [with an agreement in place with Unocal that gave it preemptive rights][although the court seems to think the Committee was wrong on this point.]. The Special Committee also argues that the pill was unnecessary because the Committee's ability to make a negative recommendation—coupled with Hightower's and Staley's by-then apparent opposition to the Offer [*Editor: Hightower is Pure's CEO and Chairman and owns 6.1% of Pure; Staley is Pure's Chief Operating Officer and also a large stockholder; both were members of the "minority" for purposes of the majority of the minority provision*],—were leverage and protection enough. . . .

The most reasonable inference that can be drawn from the record is that the Special Committee was unwilling to confront Unocal as aggressively as it would have confronted a third-party bidder. . . .

III. *The Plaintiffs' Demand For A Preliminary Injunction*

. . . Distilled to the bare minimum, the plaintiffs argue that the Offer should be enjoined because: (i) the Offer is subject to the entire fairness standard and the record supports the inference that the transaction cannot survive a fairness review; (ii) in any event, the Offer is actionably coercive and should be enjoined on that ground; [Discussion of deficient disclosures omitted.] . . .

B. *The Plaintiffs' Substantive Attack on the Offer*

. . . In the plaintiffs' mind, the Offer poses the same threat of (what I will call) "inherent coercion" that motivated the Supreme Court in *Kahn v. Lynch Communication Systems, Inc.* to impose the entire fairness standard of review on any interested merger involving a controlling stockholder, even when the merger was approved by an independent board majority, negotiated by an independent special committee, and subject to a majority of the minority vote condition. . . .

2.

This case . . . involves an aspect of Delaware law fraught with doctrinal tension: what equitable standard of fiduciary conduct applies when a controlling shareholder seeks to acquire the rest of the company's shares? In considering this issue, it is useful to pause over the word "equitable" and to capture its full import . . .

At present, the Delaware case law has two strands of authority that answer these questions differently. In one strand, which deals with situations in which controlling stockholders negotiate a merger agreement with the target board to buy out the minority, our decisional law emphasizes the protection of minority stockholders against unfairness. In the other strand, which deals with situations when a controlling stockholder seeks to acquire the rest of the company's shares through a tender offer followed by a short-form merger under 8 Del.C. § 253, Delaware case precedent facilitates the free flow of capital between willing buyers and willing sellers of shares, so long as the consent of the sellers is not procured by inadequate or misleading information or by wrongful compulsion.

These strands appear to treat economically similar transactions as categorically different simply because the method by which the controlling stockholder proceeds varies. This disparity in treatment persists even though the two basic methods (negotiated merger versus tender offer/short-form merger) pose similar threats to minority stockholders. Indeed, it can be argued that the distinction in approach subjects the transaction that is more protective of minority stockholders when implemented with appropriate protective devices—a merger negotiated by an independent committee with the power to say no and conditioned on a majority of the minority vote—to more stringent review than the more dangerous form of a going-private deal—an unnegotiated tender offer made by a majority stockholder. The latter transaction is arguably less protective than a merger of the kind described, because the majority stockholder-offeror has access to inside information, and the offer requires disaggregated stockholders to decide whether to tender quickly, pressured by the risk of being squeezed out in a short-form merger at a different price later or being left as part of a much smaller public minority. This disparity creates a possible incoherence in our law.

3.

To illustrate this possible incoherence in our law, it is useful to sketch out these two strands. I begin with negotiated mergers. In *Kahn v. Lynch Communication Systems, Inc.,* the Delaware Supreme Court addressed the standard of review that applies when a controlling stockholder attempts to acquire the rest of the corporation's shares in a negotiated merger pursuant to 8 Del.C. § 251. The Court held that the stringent entire fairness form of review governed regardless of whether: i) the target board was comprised of a majority of independent directors; ii) a special committee of the target's independent directors was empowered to negotiate and veto the merger; and iii) the merger was made subject to approval by a majority of the disinterested target stockholders.

The Supreme Court concluded that even a gauntlet of protective barriers like those would be insufficient protection because of (what I will term) the "inherent coercion" that exists when a controlling stockholder announces its desire to buy the minority's shares. In colloquial terms, the Supreme Court saw the controlling stockholder as the 800-pound gorilla whose urgent hunger for the rest of the bananas is likely to frighten less powerful primates like putatively independent directors who might well have been hand-picked by the gorilla (and who at the very least owed their seats on the board to his support).

All in all, the Court was convinced that the powers and influence possessed by controlling stockholders were so formidable and daunting to independent directors and minority stockholders that protective devices like special committees and majority of the minority conditions (even when used in combination with the statutory appraisal remedy) were not trustworthy enough to obviate the need for an entire fairness review. The Court did, however, recognize that these safety measures had utility and should be encouraged. Therefore, it held that their deployment could shift the burden of persuasion on the issue of fairness from the controlling stockholders and the target board as proponents of the transaction to shareholder-plaintiffs seeking to invalidate it.

The policy balance struck in *Lynch* continues to govern negotiated mergers between controlling stockholders and subsidiaries. If anything, later cases have extended the rule in *Lynch* to a broader array of transactions involving controlling shareholders.

4.

The second strand of cases involves tender offers made by controlling stockholders—*i.e.,* the kind of transaction Unocal has proposed. The prototypical transaction addressed by this strand involves a tender offer by the controlling stockholder addressed to the minority stockholders. In that offer, the controlling stockholder promises to buy as many shares as the minority will sell but may subject its offer to certain conditions. For example, the controlling stockholder might condition the offer on receiving enough tenders for it to obtain 90% of the subsidiary's shares, thereby enabling the controlling stockholder to consummate a short-form merger under 8 Del.C. § 253 at either the same or a different price.

As a matter of statutory law, this way of proceeding is different from the negotiated merger approach in an important way: neither the tender offer nor the short-form merger requires any action by the subsidiary's board of directors. The tender offer takes place between the controlling shareholder and the minority shareholders so long as the offering conditions are met. And, by the explicit terms of § 253, the short-form merger can be effected by the controlling stockholder itself, an option that was of uncertain utility for many years because it was unclear whether § 253 mergers were subject to an equitable requirement of fair process at the subsidiary board level. That uncertainty was recently resolved in *Glassman v. Unocal Exploration Corp.*, an important recent decision, which held that a short-form merger was not reviewable in an action claiming unfair dealing, and that, absent fraud or misleading or inadequate disclosures, could be contested only in an appraisal proceeding that focused solely on the adequacy of the price paid.

Before *Glassman*, transactional planners had wondered whether the back-end of the tender offer/short-form merger transaction would subject the controlling stockholder to entire fairness review. *Glassman* seemed to answer that question favorably from the standpoint of controlling stockholders, and to therefore encourage the tender offer/short-form merger form of acquisition as presenting a materially less troublesome method of proceeding than a negotiated merger.

Why? Because the legal rules that governed the front end of the tender offer/short-form merger method of acquisition had already provided a more flexible, less litigious path to acquisition for controlling stockholders than the negotiated merger route. Tender offers are not addressed by the Delaware General Corporation Law ("DGCL"), a factor that has been of great importance in shaping the line of decisional law addressing tender offers by controlling stockholders—but not, as I will discuss, tender offers made by third parties.

Because no consent or involvement of the target board is statutorily mandated for tender offers, our courts have recognized that "[i]n the case of totally voluntary tender offers . . . courts do not impose any right of the shareholders to receive a particular price. Delaware law recognizes that, as to allegedly voluntary tender offers (in contrast to cash-out mergers), the determinative factors as to voluntariness are whether coercion is present, or whether there are materially false or misleading disclosures made to stockholders in connection with the offer." In two recent cases, this court has followed *Solomon* [*Solomon v. Pathe Communications*

Corp., 672 A.2d 35 (Del.1996)]*'s* articulation of the standards applicable to a tender offer, and held that the "Delaware law does not impose a duty of entire fairness on controlling stockholders making a non-coercive tender or exchange offer to acquire shares directly from the minority holders."

The differences between this approach, which I will identify with the *Solomon* line of cases, and that of *Lynch* are stark. To begin with, the controlling stockholder is said to have no duty to pay a fair price, irrespective of its power over the subsidiary. Even more striking is the different manner in which the coercion concept is deployed. In the tender offer context addressed by *Solomon* and its progeny, coercion is defined in the more traditional sense as a wrongful threat that has the effect of forcing stockholders to tender at the wrong price to avoid an even worse fate later on, a type of coercion I will call structural coercion. The inherent coercion that *Lynch* found to exist when controlling stockholders seek to acquire the minority's stake is not even a cognizable concern for the common law of corporations if the tender offer method is employed. . . .

The debate about that issue was complex and exciting (at least for those interested in corporate law). . . .

7.

The absence of convincing reasons for [the] disparity in treatment [between the *Lynch* and *Solomon* line of cases] inspires the plaintiffs to urge me to apply the entire fairness standard of review to Unocal's offer. Otherwise, they say, the important protections set forth in the *Lynch* line of cases will be rendered useless, as all controlling stockholders will simply choose to proceed to make subsidiary acquisitions by way of a tender offer and later short-form merger.

I admit being troubled by the imbalance in Delaware law exposed by the *Solomon/Lynch* lines of cases . . .

. . . [T]he preferable policy choice is to continue to adhere to the more flexible and less constraining *Solomon* approach, while giving some greater recognition to the inherent coercion and structural bias concerns that motivate the *Lynch* line of cases. Adherence to the *Solomon* rubric as a general matter, moreover, is advisable in view of the increased activism of institutional investors and the greater information flows available to them. Investors have demonstrated themselves capable of resisting tender offers made by controlling stockholders on occasion, and even the lead plaintiff here expresses no fear of retribution. This does not mean that controlling stockholder tender offers do not pose risks to minority stockholders; it is only to acknowledge that the corporate law should not be designed on the assumption that diversified investors are infirm but instead should give great deference to transactions approved by them voluntarily and knowledgeably . . .

8.

. . . The potential for coercion and unfairness posed by controlling stockholders who seek to acquire the balance of the company's shares by acquisition requires some equitable reinforcement, in order to give proper effect to the concerns undergirding *Lynch*. In order to address the prisoner's dilemma problem, our law should consider an acquisition tender offer by a controlling stockholder non-coercive only when: 1) it is subject to a non-waivable majority of the minority tender condition; 2) the controlling stockholder promises to consummate a prompt § 253 merger at the same price if it obtains more than 90% of the shares; and 3) the controlling stockholder has made no retributive threats. Those protections—also stressed in this court's recent *Aquila* decision—minimize the distorting influence of the tendering process on voluntary choice. . . .

9.

Turning specifically to Unocal's Offer, I conclude that the application of these principles yields the following result. The Offer, in its present form, is coercive because it includes within the definition of the "minority" those stockholders who are affiliated with Unocal as directors and officers. It also includes the management of Pure, whose incentives are skewed by their employment, their severance agreements, and their Put Agreements. [*Editor: "The Put Agreements give the managers—including Hightower and Staley—the right to put their Pure stock to Unocal upon the occurrence of certain triggering events—among which would be consummation of Unocal's Offer."*] This is, of course, a problem that can be cured if Unocal amends the Offer to condition it on approval of a majority of Pure's unaffiliated stockholders. Requiring the minority to be defined exclusive of stockholders whose independence from the controlling stockholder is compromised is the better legal rule (and result). Too often, it will be the case that officers and directors of controlled subsidiaries have voting incentives that are not perfectly aligned with their economic interest in their stock and who are more than acceptably susceptible to influence from controlling stockholders. Aside, however, from this glitch in the majority of the minority condition, I conclude that Unocal's Offer satisfies the other requirements of "non-coerciveness." Its promise to consummate a prompt § 253 merger is sufficiently specific, and Unocal has made no retributive threats.

Although Unocal's Offer does not altogether comport with the above-described definition of non-coercive, it does not follow that I believe that the plaintiffs have established a probability of success on the merits as to their claim that the Pure board should have blocked that Offer with a pill or other measures. Putting aside the shroud of silence that cloaked the board's (mostly, it seems, behind the scenes) deliberations, there appears to have been at least a rational basis to believe that a pill was not necessary to protect the Pure minority against coercion, largely, because Pure's management had expressed adamant opposition to the Offer. Moreover, the board allowed the Special Committee a free hand: to recommend against the Offer—as it did; to negotiate for a higher price—as it attempted to do; and to prepare the company's 14D–9—as it did.

[The court found that the plaintiffs did "not have a probability of success on the merits of their attack on the Offer" although they did have a probability of success on the merits as to part of their disclosure claim. But, because the majority of the minority condition was flawed, rendering the Offer coercive, and because "an injunction can be issued that can be lifted in short order if Unocal and the Pure board respond[ed] to the concerns addressed in th[e] opinion," the court granted plaintiffs' motion for a preliminary injunction, and enjoined the consummation of the Offer.]

---

7. POST-*PURE RESOURCES*/*SILICONIX* PRACTICES

In the wake of the *Pure Resources* and *Siliconix* decisions, there now existed a fractured path for a freeze-out transaction.

The first route was via a merger, as in *Kahn*, in which the controlling shareholder would announce its offer and seek to negotiate with the board. The board would form a special committee which would hire its own advisers, both legal and financial. The controller would then negotiate a transaction price with the special committee. These protections were designed to respond to the mandate in *Weinberger* that a freeze-out meet the requisites of "entire fairness," meaning fair price and fair dealing. In *Kahn* the court had also held that approval by an independent committee of directors would be a signal that the deal was approved pursuant to a "fair" process, as was conditioning the merger on the approval of the majority of the outstanding minority shares. However, while the *Kahn* Court embraced these procedural devices, it did not go so far as to sketch a route to avoid an "entire fairness" review; rather the use of these devices simply shifted the burden to the plaintiff to show that the transaction was not fair.

The Delaware courts adopted a different standard for freeze-outs pursuant to a tender offer. The standard erected procedural devices to stem the coercion problem. Under the *Pure Resources* standard, a controlling shareholder could obtain business judgment review of such a transaction. A 2011 article written by practitioners stated that to meet the *Pure Resources* standard, "a controlling shareholder pursuing a unilateral tender offer would have to: (1) condition the offer on a non-waivable majority of the minority condition; (2) ensure that the transaction was accompanied by a special committee process in which independent directors of the target board had "adequate time" and "free rein" to react to the tender offer; (3) not make retributive threats; (4) agree to a short-form merger at the tender price promptly after the tender accomplished a 90% ownership threshold; and (5) adequately and accurately disclose information related to the offer. Only if these conditions were satisfied would a defendant-controlling shareholder be able to utilize the business judgment rule presumption and obtain dismissal on the pleadings."[9]

8. THE LITIGATION DYNAMICS OF FREEZE-OUTS

The differing standards for tender offers and mergers were not just about differing burdens being placed on freeze-outs based on how they were structured. The requirements of *Kahn* created a dynamic in many going-private transactions that worked to the detriment of the controlling shareholder without providing any real benefits to other parties. Vice Chancellor Strine described this dynamic in *In re Cox Communications Shareholder Litigation,* 879 A.2d 604, 619–20 (Del. Ch. 2005):

> Unlike any other transaction one can imagine—even a *Revlon* deal—it was impossible after *Lynch* to structure a merger with a controlling stockholder in a way that permitted the defendants to obtain a dismissal of the case on the pleadings. Imagine, for example, a controlled company on the board of which sat Bill Gates and Warren Buffett. Each owned 5% of the company and had no other business dealings with the controller. The controller announced that it was offering a 25% premium to market to buy the rest of the shares. The controlled company's board meets and appoints Gates and Buffett as a special committee. The board also resolves that it will not agree to a merger unless the special committee recommends it and unless the merger is conditioned on approval by two-thirds of the disinterested stockholders. The special committee hires a top five investment bank and top five law firm and negotiates the price up to a 38% premium. The special committee then votes to approve the deal and the full board accepts their recommendation. The disinterested stockholders vote to approve the deal by a huge margin that satisfies the two-thirds Minority Approval Condition.
>
> After that occurs, a lawsuit is filed alleging that the price paid is unfair. The filing party can satisfy Rule 11 as to that allegation because financial fairness is a debatable issue and the plaintiff has at least a colorable position. The controller and the special

---

[9]   Suneela Jain, et al., *Examining Data Points in Minority Buy-outs: A Practitioners Report,* 36 DEL. J. CORP. LAW 939, 958–963 (2011).

committee go to their respective legal advisors and ask them to get this frivolous lawsuit dismissed. What they will be told is this, "We cannot get the case dismissed. We can attempt to show the plaintiffs that we are willing to beat them on this and persuade them to drop it voluntarily because they will, after great expense, lose. But if they want to fight a motion to dismiss, they will win, see Lynch. At the very least, therefore, if the plaintiffs are willing to fight, it would be rational for you to pay an amount to settle the case that reflects not only the actual out-of-pocket costs of defense to get the case to the summary judgment stage, but the (real but harder to quantify) costs of managerial and directorial time in responding to discovery over a past transaction."

For both the proponents of mergers with controlling stockholders (i.e., controllers and the directors involved in the transactions, all of whom become defendants in lawsuits attacking those transactions) and the plaintiffs' lawyers who file suits, this incentive effect of Lynch manifested itself in a unique approach to "litigation." Instead of suing once a controller actually signs up a merger agreement with a special committee of independent directors, plaintiffs sue as soon as there is a public announcement of the controller's intention to propose a merger.

---

9. TOWARDS HARMONY IN FREEZE-OUTS

The Chancery Court's dissatisfaction with the dual standard led to an attempt at harmonization. The Chancery Court's focus was on cutting back *Kahn's* "entire fairness" mandate, but with the Delaware Supreme Court refusing to reconsider its standards, the Chancery Court had to content itself with tinkering around the edges of *Weinberger* while still attempting to abide by its holding. The Chancery Court's efforts are described in the following excerpt:

The Court of Chancery progressed more slowly with respect to scaling back plaintiff-stockholder advantages in the negotiated merger context. In a footnote to the *Pure Resources* decision, then-Vice Chancellor Strine suggested the possibility of a "slight easing" of the *Lynch* standard to create a business judgment rule safe harbor for deals structured as negotiated mergers. Three years later, in *Cox Communications*, then-Vice Chancellor Strine explicitly proposed that the courts develop a "unified ... standard" for the treatment of negotiated mergers and tender offers that would provide both transactions with the same safe harbor from "entire fairness." Five years later, in the 2010 context of a stockholder challenge to the tender offer by CONSOL for the publicly held shares of CONSOL's subsidiary, CNX Gas, Vice Chancellor Laster responded to former Vice Chancellor Strine's call and adopted a unified standard for a safe harbor from "entire fairness" for both tender offers and negotiated mergers. In *CNX Gas*, the Court of Chancery held that business judgment review would be available in all controlling stockholder buyout transactions, regardless of form, that were both (1) negotiated and recommended by a special committee with the full authority of the Board (including authority to negotiate, consider alternatives, and adopt a stockholder rights plan), and (2) approved by a majority of the minority stockholders in satisfaction of an unwaivable condition to this effect."[10]

Vice Chancellor Laster's attempt to adopt a unified standard in *CNX* was echoed by then-Chancellor Strine in *MFW Worldwide Shareholders Litigation*, 67 A.3d 496 (Del. Ch. 2013). (Note that MFW was affirmed by the Delaware Supreme Court; the case is discussed in subsection 12 below.) In *MFW*, the Chancellor stated that "[a]lthough rational minds may differ on the subject, the court concludes that when a controlling stockholder merger has, from the time of the controller's first overture, been subject to (i) negotiation and approval by a special committee of independent directors fully empowered to say no, and (ii) approval by an uncoerced, fully informed vote of a majority of the minority investors, the business judgment rule standard of review applies." Strine distinguished *Weinberger* and *Kahn*, stating that "[i]n no prior case was our Supreme Court given the chance to determine whether a controlling stockholder merger conditioned on both independent committee approval and a majority-of-the-minority vote should receive the protection of the business judgment rule."[11]

The standards adopted by then-Chancellor Strine and Vice Chancellor Laster were similar but not identical. The Vice Chancellor would require that the independent committee be permitted to take defensive actions while Chancellor Strine did not make such a requirement. Still the aim of both of the jurists was to adopt a unified standard for both tender offers and mergers.

10. FREEZE-OUTS IN PRACTICE

Before *CNX*, controllers might have been expected to prefer the *Pure Resources* route for freeze-outs over the more arduous and litigation-

---

[10] *Id.* at 947–48.

[11] In re *MFW Shareholders Litigation*, 67 A. 3d 496, 502 (Del. Ch. 2013). The case was affirmed by the Delaware Supreme Court, *Kahn v. M&F Worldwide Corp.*, 88 A.3d 635 (Del. 2014).

eliciting *Weinberger/Kahn* route. However, as the following, from an article by three attorneys at the law firm Cleary Gottlieb Steen & Hamilton, shows, this turned out not to be true.

EXAMINING DATA POINTS IN MINORITY BUY-OUTS: A PRACTITIONERS' REPORT

Suneela Jain, et al.
36 DEL. J. CORP. LAW 939, 949–53 (2011)

Recently, we reviewed controlling stockholder buyout transactions announced between January 1, 2006 and December 31, 2010, in which the controlling stockholder held more than 40% of the target company at the commencement of the transaction, the value paid for the minority stake was in excess of $50 million, and the transaction was successfully completed. Of the approximately forty-five transactions that met these parameters, we narrowed the deals examined to twenty-seven, excluding situational outliers, foreign or non-corporate targets, and a few transactions in which full information was not publicly available. Among the variables we examined were how the deal was structured, whether it included a majority of the minority condition and/or a special committee, whether stockholder litigation was filed, and, as applicable, the amount of plaintiffs' counsel fees and expenses related to settlement. . . . While the limited sample size and inherently complex nature of the transaction processes preclude any claims as to scientific significance, the review did reveal some interesting and instructive findings.

III. THE FAILURE OF PURE RESOURCES AND THE DIM PROSPECTS OF *CNX*

Few controlling stockholders bother to take advantage of the protection of the *Pure Resources* safe harbor from entire fairness review. Of the twenty-seven deals we reviewed, only eight were structured as unilateral tender offers. The remaining nineteen involved signed merger agreements, providing for either a one-step or two-step (tender offer followed by short-form merger) structure, and therefore triggered automatic application of "entire fairness" and loss of the ability to prevail on the pleadings. At its most basic level, this means that 70% of the controlling stockholders in our review felt that the benefits of the *Pure Resources* safe harbor from "entire fairness" review were not worth the costs of pursuing it.

The decision not to pursue the *Pure Resources* safe harbor involves multiple considerations, but the most meaningful is the distastefulness of the majority of the minority closing condition, a mandatory and unwaivable element of the *Pure Resources* safe harbor, but optional in the "entire fairness"/negotiated merger agreement context when combined with a special committee. Even for corporations with fairly large market caps, there exist real risks that hedge funds and arbitrageurs will engage in open market purchases of equity sufficient to prevent the satisfaction of a majority of the minority condition. The execution risks that arise from subjecting a transaction's success to the whims of "minority" stockholders are often equally unattractive to both controlling stockholders and the special committee; the former concerned about the risk that they may have to pay ransom in the form of increased offer prices to satisfy the demands of minority stockholders, and the latter wary about the stigma of stockholder rejection of an offer recommended by them after good faith negotiations with the controlling stockholder or, less egotistically, genuinely concerned that the public stockholders will reject an offer that really is in their best interests.

These baseline concerns about the risks inherent with an unwaivable majority of the minority condition were supplemented by the Court of Chancery's decision in the *CNX* decision, which injected doctrinal uncertainty into calculations regarding how and when the condition would be deemed satisfied. Specifically, in *CNX*, the court questioned the inclusion of T. Rowe Price, the largest minority stockholder of CNX Gas (the target company) and the holder of roughly equivalent equity shares of both CONSOL (the controlling stockholder) and CNX Gas, as part of the "minority" stockholders required to approve the transaction. Observing T. Rowe Price's holdings and the fact that it had pre-negotiated merger terms with CONSOL in exchange for its promise to tender, the Court of Chancery determined that T. Rowe Price had "materially different incentives" from the other "minority" holders of CNX stock, and, therefore, their tender should not be counted for the purposes of determining whether the majority of the minority condition was satisfied. The Court of Chancery rejected the defendants' protest that delving into a particular stockholder's incentives, in a world where "[s]ophisticated institutional investors . . . often have diverse holdings that could include shares of both parent and subsidiary[,] . . . have complex hedging arrangements, [and] possess holdings in competitor corporations," was "unworkable as well as unwarranted." Unwarranted or not, by increasing the uncertainty regarding satisfaction of the majority of the minority condition, the *CNX* court created an additional burden for those who might otherwise have attempted to require it.

CNX also complicated the landscape for merger parties considering whether to seek protection of a *Pure Resources* safe harbor by heightening the standards required to satisfy the second prong of the safe harbor: the special committee process. In *CNX*, the Court of Chancery determined that a special committee must be accorded the right not only to recommend against and refuse to adopt any proposed transaction, but also the extraordinary right to adopt a stockholder rights plan that would, if implemented, block completely any buyout transaction that the special committee did not adopt or recommend. The right to adopt a stockholder rights plan creates a particularly significant risk for the controlling stockholder: If the controlling stockholder runs into a dead-end in its negotiations with the special committee, and the special committee adopts a rights plan, the controlling stockholder will be prevented from presenting its case directly to the other stockholders by way of a unilateral tender offer. If implemented, the rights plan would preclude even a unilateral tender offer that would have had a reasonable chance of satisfying entire fairness. Indeed, such a tender offer under the (pre-*CNX*) *Pure Resources* paradigm would have qualified for deferential, business judgment rule treatment.

In sum, to the extent that our research of past transactions reflects an already-existing skepticism of the net benefit of the *Pure Resources* safe harbor, the heightened standards of the *CNX* safe harbor may well further encourage a controlling stockholder to take its chances with "entire fairness." Accordingly, we predict that the Court of Chancery will not see any meaningful movement among merger parties toward embracing the business judgment rule safe harbor outlined in *CNX*.

---

11. CAN A SPECIAL COMMITTEE SAY NO? THE CASE OF iBASIS AND KPN

A company with a controlling shareholder who would like to freeze out the other shareholders has very few options. The company can stay public and say no to the controlling shareholder, or sell to the controlling shareholder. A sale to a third party is not possible, since Delaware law permits a controlling shareholder to refuse to sell its shares. A controller wishing to engage in a freeze-out will thus almost always assert that it is unwilling to sell its shares to a third party. A special committee will therefore be unable to confirm through a canvass of the market that the controller is willing to pay the highest price reasonably available.

The premise of *Weinberger* is that independent directors on the board will act as gatekeepers. They will refuse to approve a transaction unless it meets the requirements of fairness. But *Weinberger* also reflects skepticism that when there is bargaining by the board and the price is accepted by the minority shareholders that the result will always be a "fair price." The push-back in the Delaware Chancery Court's opinions in *CNX* and *MFW* reflect a different view—that independent committees in such a circumstance can effectively negotiate a fair price, if not the highest price reasonably available, and that courts should defer to properly motivated independent committees who have negotiated on behalf of minority shareholders.

If a controlling shareholder does not own at least 90% of the target company, it needs board approval for a merger. But it does not need board approval to make a tender offer: under the *Pure Resources/Siliconix* line of cases, a controlling shareholder can effectively bypass the board and make a tender offer directly to shareholders. What can the independent directors of a board do to prevent a tender offer by a controlling shareholder? Can they adopt a shareholder rights plan, also known as a poison pill, or take other measures to stop a non-coercive tender offer by a controlling shareholder? How much independence from a controller should a board have?

In 2009, the issue was brought to the forefront in a bid by Royal KPN of the Netherlands to purchase for $2.25 per share the portion of iBasis it did not own. Royal KPN launched a tender offer that complied with the dictates of Pure Resources. However, the iBasis special committee responded by adopting a poison pill, attempting to forestall Royal KPN's tender offer. iBasis brought a lawsuit in Delaware Chancery Court in which it claimed that "KPN had failed to fully disclose the internal projections and estimates that the company and its banker, Morgan Stanley, used to price this offer and declare it fair to the minority shareholders. KPN countersued in Delaware to have the poison pill judicially nullified or redeemed."[12]

In a hearing in the case, then-Vice Chancellor Leo E. Strine Jr. seemed to think that iBasis board's response to KPN's "noncoercive" tender offer was not a reasonable one under the *Unocal* standard. iBasis had contended that its response, a poison pill, was justified by, among other things, KPN's failures to make full disclosure, and KPN's actions to drive iBasis's stock down. Before Strine could rule, the parties settled their litigation, KPN raised its offer to $3 a share, and the iBasis board recommended the offer. Strine became the Chancellor of the Delaware Chancery Court in 2011, and the Chief Justice of the Delaware Supreme Court in 2014.

Vice Chancellor Laster appears to take a different view than Strine does. In *CNX*, Laster specifically conditioned the application of the business judgment rule on the special committee of independent directors being allowed to consider defensive measures such as a poison pill.

Many open questions remain as to what a board can and cannot do in the face of a tender offer by a controller. Especially as to a non-coercive such offer, what defensive measures can it take? What if it wishes to accept the offer? The courts continue to grapple with these issues.

---

[12] Steven M. Davidoff, *A Missed Chance for a Ruling on Poison Pills,* N.Y. TIMES, Nov. 23, 2009, available at http://dealbook.nytimes.com/2009/11/23/handicapping-a-ruling-the-ibasis-kpn-case/.

12. TOWARDS RESOLUTION OF THE WEINBERGER SPLIT: *KAHN v. M&F WORLDWIDE*

By 2014, the Delaware courts had moved towards resolving the split in the standards of review over freeze-outs. In *Kahn v. M&F Worldwide*, the Delaware Supreme Court adopted procedural protections on par with those adopted in *Pure Resources*, trying for some measure of convergence on this issue.

KAHN V. M&F WORLDWIDE CORP.

Supreme Court of Delaware
88 A.3d 635 (2014)

HOLLAND, JUSTICE:

. . .

ANALYSIS

What Should Be The Review Standard?

Where a transaction involving self-dealing by a controlling stockholder is challenged, the applicable standard of judicial review is "entire fairness," with the defendants having the burden of persuasion. In other words, the defendants bear the ultimate burden of proving that the transaction with the controlling stockholder was entirely fair to the minority stockholders. In *Kahn v. Lynch Communication Systems, Inc.*, however, this Court held that in "entire fairness" cases, the defendants may shift the burden of persuasion to the plaintiff if either (1) they show that the transaction was approved by a well-functioning committee of independent directors; or (2) they show that the transaction was approved by an informed vote of a majority of the minority stockholders.

This appeal presents a question of first impression: what should be the standard of review for a merger between a controlling stockholder and its subsidiary, where the merger is conditioned ab initio upon the approval of both an independent, adequately-empowered Special Committee that fulfills its duty of care, and the uncoerced, informed vote of a majority of the minority stockholders. The question has never been put directly to this Court.

Almost two decades ago, in *Kahn v. Lynch*, we held that the approval by either a Special Committee or the majority of the noncontrolling stockholders of a merger with a buying controlling stockholder would shift the burden of proof under the entire fairness standard from the defendant to the plaintiff. Lynch did not involve a merger conditioned by the controlling stockholder on both procedural protections. The Appellants submit, nonetheless, that statements in *Lynch* and its progeny could be (and were) read to suggest that even if both procedural protections were used, the standard of review would remain entire fairness. However, in *Lynch* and the other cases the controller did not give up its voting power by agreeing to a non-waivable majority-of-the-minority condition. That is the vital distinction between those cases and this one. The question is what the legal consequence of that distinction should be in these circumstances.

The Court of Chancery held that the consequence should be that the business judgment standard of review will govern going-private mergers with a controlling stockholder that are conditioned *ab initio* upon (1) the approval of an independent and fully-empowered Special Committee that fulfills its duty of care and (2) the uncoerced, informed vote of the majority of the minority stockholders.

The Court of Chancery rested its holding upon the premise that the common law equitable rule that best protects minority investors is one that encourages controlling stockholders to accord the minority both procedural protections. A transactional structure subject to both conditions differs fundamentally from a merger having only one of those protections, in that:

> By giving controlling stockholders the opportunity to have a going-private transaction reviewed under the business judgment rule, a strong incentive is created to give minority stockholders much broader access to the transactional structure that is most likely to effectively protect their interests. . . . That structure, it is important to note, is critically different than a structure that uses only one of the procedural protections. The "or" structure does not replicate the protections of a third-party merger under the DGCL approval process, because it only requires that one, and not both, of the statutory requirements of director and stockholder approval be accomplished by impartial decisionmakers. The "both" structure, by contrast, replicates the arm's-length merger steps of the DGCL by "requir[ing] two independent approvals, which it is fair to say serve independent integrity-enforcing functions."

Before the Court of Chancery, the Appellants acknowledged that "this transactional structure is the optimal one for minority shareholders." Before us, however, they argue that neither procedural protection is adequate to protect minority stockholders, because "possible ineptitude and timidity of directors" may undermine the special committee protection, and because majority-of-the-minority votes may be unduly influenced by arbitrageurs that have an institutional bias to approve virtually any transaction that offers a market premium, however insubstantial it may be. Therefore, the Appellants claim, these protections, even when combined, are not sufficient to justify "abandon[ing]" the entire fairness standard of review.

With regard to the Special Committee procedural protection, the Appellants' assertions regarding the MFW directors' inability to discharge their duties are not supported either by the record or by well-established principles of Delaware law. As the Court of Chancery correctly observed:

> Although it is possible that there are independent directors who have little regard for their duties or for being perceived by their company's stockholders (and the larger network of institutional investors) as being effective at protecting public stockholders, the court thinks they are likely to be exceptional, and certainly our Supreme Court's jurisprudence does not embrace such a skeptical view.

Regarding the majority-of-the-minority vote procedural protection, as the Court of Chancery noted, "plaintiffs themselves do not argue that minority stockholders will vote against a going-private transaction because of fear of retribution." Instead, as the Court of Chancery summarized, the Appellants' argued as follows:

> [Plaintiffs] just believe that most investors like a premium and will tend to vote for a deal that delivers one and that many long-term investors will sell out when they can obtain most of the premium without waiting for the ultimate vote. But that argument is not one that suggests that the voting decision is not voluntary, it is simply an editorial about the motives of investors and does not contradict the premise that a majority-of-the-minority condition gives minority investors a free and voluntary opportunity to decide what is fair for themselves.

Business Judgment Review Standard Adopted

We hold that business judgment is the standard of review that should govern mergers between a controlling stockholder and its corporate subsidiary, where the merger is conditioned ab initio upon both the approval of an independent, adequately-empowered Special Committee that fulfills its duty of care; and the uncoerced, informed vote of a majority of the minority stockholders. We so conclude for several reasons. . . .

[T]he dual procedural protection merger structure optimally protects the minority stockholders in controller buyouts. As the Court of Chancery explained:

> [W]hen these two protections are established up-front, a potent tool to extract good value for the minority is established. From inception, the controlling stockholder knows that it cannot bypass the special committee's ability to say no. And, the

controlling stockholder knows it cannot dangle a majority-of-the-minority vote before the special committee late in the process as a deal-closer rather than having to make a price move.

. . . [A]pplying the business judgment standard to the dual protection merger structure

. . . is consistent with the central tradition of Delaware law, which defers to the informed decisions of impartial directors, especially when those decisions have been approved by the disinterested stockholders on full information and without coercion. Not only that, the adoption of this rule will be of benefit to minority stockholders because it will provide a strong incentive for controlling stockholders to accord minority investors the transactional structure that respected scholars believe will provide them the best protection, a structure where stockholders get the benefits of independent, empowered negotiating agents to bargain for the best price and say no if the agents believe the deal is not advisable for any proper reason, plus the critical ability to determine for themselves whether to accept any deal that their negotiating agents recommend to them. A transactional structure with both these protections is fundamentally different from one with only one protection.

. . . [T]he underlying purposes of the dual protection merger structure utilized here and the entire fairness standard of review both converge and are fulfilled at the same critical point: price. Following *Weinberger v. UOP, Inc.*, this Court has consistently held that, although entire fairness review comprises the dual components of fair dealing and fair price, in a non-fraudulent transaction "price may be the preponderant consideration outweighing other features of the merger." The dual protection merger structure requires two price-related pretrial determinations: first, that a fair price was achieved by an empowered, independent committee that acted with care; and, second, that a fully-informed, uncoerced majority of the minority stockholders voted in favor of the price that was recommended by the independent committee.

The New Standard Summarized

To summarize our holding, in controller buyouts, the business judgment standard of review will be applied if and only if: (i) the controller conditions the procession of the transaction on the approval of both a Special Committee and a majority of the minority stockholders; (ii) the Special Committee is independent; (iii) the Special Committee is empowered to freely select its own advisors and to say no definitively; (iv) the Special Committee meets its duty of care in negotiating a fair price; (v) the vote of the minority is informed; and (vi) there is no coercion of the minority.[14]

13. THE FUTURE OF GOING-PRIVATE TRANSACTIONS

The effect of *MFW* is to move towards greater uniformity in the standards of review that the courts will apply to controller going-private transactions. This more uniform approach will provide boards adopting robust procedural protections that attempt to mimic an arm's length deal with the protection of business judgment. At the same time, transactions that eschew these procedural protections will still be subject to the more exacting entire fairness standard. This more unified approach to review of these transactions creates an incentive for boards to rely more on independent special committees and approvals of unaffiliated shareholders. And these protections, in turn, should yield better deals for unaffiliated shareholders.

The more uniform standard may also lessen the incentive for plaintiffs to bring lawsuits when controller freeze-out transactions are announced. Rather than permit plaintiffs the opportunity at trial to prove that a transaction was unfair, the deferential *MFW* standard permits boards complying with the robust procedural protections required for the business judgment presumption to escape litigation at a much earlier stage, making this kind of litigation less valuable for plaintiffs to pursue. How will *MFW* change the volume and type of controller freeze-out cases that are brought? To some extent, the answer to this question turns on the effect of footnote 14 of the MFW opinion. The footnote seems to suggest that the number of suits will be less affected than the nature of the suits, an issue discussed in the blog post reproduced below:

> In footnote 14, the Supreme Court notes that MFW could not
> have [been] decided on the pleadings and would have survived a
> motion to dismiss even under the new standard. The pleadings,

---

[14] The Verified Consolidated Class Action Complaint would have survived a motion to dismiss under this new standard. First, the complaint alleged that Perelman's offer [*Editor: Perelman is the owner of the controlling shareholder. This is the same Perelman as was involved in the Revlon case.*] "value[d] the company at just four times" MFW's profits per share and "five times 2010 pre-tax cash flow," and that these ratios were "well below" those calculated for recent similar transactions. Second, the complaint alleged that the final Merger price was two dollars per share lower than the trading price only about two months earlier. Third, the complaint alleged particularized facts indicating that MWF's share price was depressed at the times of Perelman's offer and the Merger announcement due to short-term factors such as MFW's acquisition of other entities and Standard & Poor's downgrading of the United States' creditworthiness. Fourth, the complaint alleged that commentators viewed both Perelman's initial $24 per share offer and the final $25 per share Merger price as being surprisingly low. These allegations about the sufficiency of the price call into question the adequacy of the Special Committee's negotiations, thereby necessitating discovery on all of the new prerequisites to the application of the business judgment rule.

the court noted, were sufficient to require discovery in the application of the standard . . .

Ultimately we'll see to what degree footnote 14 matters. But, it does seem a little disconcerting that Strine's project to provide a pathway to early dismissal of these kinds of cases might just move the locus of the argument to the functioning of the special committee.

Sure, that's obviously better, but it's not yet clear that MFW and footnote 14 will dramatically reduce incentives to bring these cases. Perhaps we will just be battling the same fight on new ground. Of course, the Chancery Court is likely to want to find ways to rule on the pleadings and my guess is that now that Chief Justice Strine is in a place to influence how the MFW standard is going to roll out that he won't be looking to increase incentives for plaintiffs to bring these cases.[13]

14. EMPIRICAL EVIDENCE ON GOING-PRIVATE TRANSACTIONS

Is there empirical evidence that any of these standards result in greater value for shareholders? There have been several studies addressing this issue. In a 2005 article, Guhan Subramanian analyzed practices under the *Pure Resources* and *Weinberger* standards. He found that aggregate takeover premiums were lower for tender offers conducted under the *Pure Resources/Siliconix* standard than for mergers subject to *Weinberger*.[14] A recent paper by Fernan Restrepo also found that freeze-outs via tender offers result in lower wealth effects for shareholders.[15]

These findings are disputed by Bates et al., who found in a sample of freeze-outs from 1988 through 2003 that there was no evidence that freeze-outs pursuant to tender offers were detrimental to shareholders. The authors concluded that "[o]verall, our results suggest that legal standards and economic incentives are sufficient to deter self-dealing by controllers during freeze-out bids."[16] A 2015 paper by both Professor Restrepo and Professor Subramanian examines the wealth effects of freeze-outs pre- and post-*Cox Communications*. In *Cox* then-Vice Chancellor Strine first suggested applying the business judgment rule to

---

[13] Brian JM Quinn, *MFW—Just Half a Loaf*, M&A LAW PROF BLOG, March 18, 2014, available at http://lawprofessors.typepad.com/mergers/2014/03/mfw-just-half-a-loaf.html.

[14] Guhan Subramanian, *Post-Siliconix Freezeouts: Theory and Evidence*, 36 J. LEG. STUD. 1 (2007).

[15] Fernan Restrepo, *Do Different Standards of Judicial Review Affect the Gains of Minority Shareholders in Freezeout Transactions? A Re-examination of Siliconix*, 3 HARV. BUS. LAW REV. 321 (2013).

[16] Thomas W. Bates, Michael Lemmon & James S. Linck, *Shareholder Wealth Effects and Bid Negotiation in Freeze-Out Deals: Are Minority Shareholders Left Out in the Cold?* 81 J. FIN. ECON. 681 (2006), at Abstract.

freeze-outs conducted by merger according to similar standards as were used in *Pure Resources*. Restrepo and Subramanian found that the deleterious wealth effects of tender offer squeeze-outs disappeared post-*Cox*. However, the authors find that about half of merger freeze-outs still do not have a majority of the minority condition. The authors therefore recommend adoption of the unified standard.[17]

C. MANAGEMENT BUY-OUTS

In contrast to a freeze-out, which involves a controlling shareholder, in a management buy-out, a member of management is in the buy-out group. This member of management may (or may not) have a controlling interest in the acquiring company. Whether or not she does, the conflict here is quite clear. One or more of the managers are seeking to acquire the company they had been hired to run as fiduciaries for shareholders. Managers involved in an MBO typically justify taking the company private by arguing that the presence of public shareholders makes the company rigid, less able to be innovative, and otherwise difficult to manage. Michael Dell gave precisely this explanation for why he wanted to take Dell private: "[U]nder a new private company structure we will have the flexibility to accelerate our strategy and purse organic and inorganic investment without the scrutiny, quarterly targets and other limitations of operating as a public company."[18] Management buy-outs have received less attention under Delaware law than freeze-outs and transactions implicating director conflicts because the courts presume that disinterested directors are able to police the managers they hire.

1. BACKGROUND ON MBOS

The following excerpt provides a historical overview of management buy-outs. It sets forth arguments for and against permitting these types of transactions. As is the case with much in M&A, events in the 1980s very much shaped both the current regulatory regime and the prevailing views of management buy-outs:

---

[17] See Fernan Restrepo & Guhan Subramanian, *The Effect of Delaware Doctrine on Freezeout Structure and Outcomes: Evidence on the Unified Approach* 5 HARV. BUS. L. REV. 205 (2015).("Taken together, these findings suggest that: (1) transactional planners seem to respond to even dicta in Delaware case law regarding standards of judicial review; and (2) the social welfare loss identified by Subramanian seems no longer to be present in the post-Cox era. This result in turn suggests that the Delaware Supreme Court seems to have adopted the correct policy by endorsing the unified approach for merger freezeouts in Kahn v. M&F Worldwide Corp., and moreover, that the court should also explicitly endorse that approach in the context of tender offer freezeouts when presented with such facts." *Id.* at 207–8).

[18] Nathan Vardi, *Michael Dell: We Are Going Back To Our Roots Taking Dell Private,* FORBES, Sept. 12, 2013, *available at* http://www.dell.com/learn/us/en/uscorp1/about-dell-investor. See also http://www.sec.gov/Archives/edgar/data/826083/000119312513266621/d558010ddfan14a. htm.

FORM OVER SUBSTANCE? THE VALUE OF CORPORATE PROCESS AND MANAGEMENT BUY-OUTS

Matthew D. Cain & Steven M. Davidoff
36 DEL. J. CORP. L. 849, 855–67 (2011)

MBOs became a prominent fixture on the takeover landscape during the 1980s due primarily to the increased viability of the leveraged buy-out ("LBO"). In its most basic form the LBO involves a private equity firm, or other acquirer, borrowing approximately 60 to 90% of the transaction value to acquire a company's outstanding equity. During the 1980s, LBOs constituted approximately 24.5% of all takeovers. . . .

The appearance of MBOs was similarly attributed to the increased availability of debt and a more active takeover market. Management, either alone or with another acquisition group, would acquire a company under their control by arranging debt financing in leverage ranges equivalent to an LBO. Due to this leverage and need for debt financing, MBOs were often structured similar to LBOs.

The impact of the MBO on the public and popular imagination was greater than its frequency. Proposed MBOs for RJR/Nabisco and MacMillan & Co. were subject to harsh media and judicial scrutiny. In both cases, management was portrayed in the press as greedy agents seeking to obtain private benefits at the expense of shareholders. The view that management was obtaining undue amounts of wealth was affirmed in public opinion as particularly lucrative MBOs emerged. One such example was the Gibson Greetings MBO. In 1982, the management of Gibson Greetings Inc., a subsidiary of the conglomerate RCA Corp., arranged an MBO of their own company for $80 million. The overwhelming portion of this was financed by $79 million in debt. Only eighteen months later the company went public, selling itself at a price that valued the company at more than $290 million. Conversely, the 1988 bankruptcy of Revco D.S., Inc., only nineteen months after its MBO, anecdotally affirmed in the public mind the risky nature of these transactions, and led to outcries that LBOs generally destroyed wealth. . . .

The controversy over management involvement during this time led to calls for heightened regulation of MBOs. Louis Lowenstein called for an open bidding regime prior to a management takeover. Victor Brudney called for banning these transactions altogether. Other commentators called for varying levels of increased judicial scrutiny of MBOs. These calls were countered by those who argued that MBOs were simply part of an efficient capital market, and that heightened regulation would diminish MBO rates and prevent wealth-increasing transactions. Despite the fomentation, no significant regulation particular to MBOs was adopted during this time. The only major proposal was one by the

American Law Institute ("ALI") to mandate an open bidding regime similar to the one advocated by Professor Lowenstein. It was never adopted by the ALI, or by any state. . . .

The form and structure of MBOs changed in the new millennium. Management became less likely to be the primary equity capital provider or organizing force in these transactions. Instead, a private equity firm would initiate discussions to acquire the company in partnership with management. As part of the acquisition, management would cash out a portion of their equity interests, but also receive an ownership interest and employment agreements with the newly private company. Technically, these were management buy-ins ("MBIs"), not MBOs, and they allowed management to profit while simultaneously diversifying their portfolio and reducing their investment risk profile. . . .

III. The Underpinnings of MBOs

The return of the MBO and the early public scrutiny of these transactions belied a more fundamental debate about the efficacy of management participation in buy-outs. These objections largely center around differing and over-lapping arguments based on fairness and economic grounds. The validity of these theories was challenged by many, and studies, mostly from the 1980s, came to differing conclusions as to the effect of these transactions on shareholder wealth and their driving forces. The result is that even today there is uncertainty over the reasons for, and economic utility and effects of these transactions.

A.   Theoretical Objections to MBOs

A principal objection to an MBO transaction is that it breaches a species of the public trust doctrine. This doctrine is today most often cited as a land use principle; but it traces its conception to democratic notions of public trust in government and the faith the public consequently puts in its representative officials. In the MBO context, the doctrine can be applied as follows: Managers as agents are entrusted by public shareholders with the task of operating and monitoring the corporate enterprise. When management profits at the expense of shareholders through an MBO it violates a public trust. More particularly, such actions dilute public faith and reliance in the capital markets. Economically this can result in less demand for public securities, lower aggregate pricing of securities, and an increased cost of capital for companies as the public seeks ex ante compensation for a perceived prospective, inappropriate wealth transfer through a potential MBO.

Distinct from this economic rationale, though, is an "integrity of the markets" argument undergirding the public trust doctrine. If management could operate the company for a profit themselves, why should this profit not go to the shareholders? After all, management has been hired and placed in this position as agents for shareholders. Any profit they derive is therefore owed to the shareholders. The integrity of the markets requires that manager agents place their fiduciary duty above their own economic interest.

There is a more concrete argument against MBOs on fairness grounds. It is the prospect that management is utilizing inside information when it arranges an MBO. Management by its inherent position has in its possession non-public knowledge of the corporation, and management can use this informational asymmetry between itself and public shareholders to time the buy-out process. MBOs can thus be arranged at advantageous times in the business cycle or history of the corporation. Management can further manipulate this process through its control of the proxy machinery and ability to under-disclose information or otherwise manipulate company projections or even company earnings and revenues leading up to the transaction. This view has been buttressed by studies that find MBO firms are different than other public targets and possibly more prone to such manipulation. . . .

The position of management as agent for the shareholders provides them with additional ability to manipulate the corporate process to arrange an MBO and another objection to MBOs. Directors, who are often appointed with management influence, can be swayed to otherwise approve conflicted interest transactions. Managers often sua sponte propose these transactions to directors. The board is then faced with the decision of catering to management or rejecting the proposal and possibly having to replace the entire management team. Faced with this difficult decision, directors decide to take the easier course and sell the company. Meanwhile, open bidding does not occur due to management's ability to negotiate protective lock-ups in acquisition contracts. During the private equity boom of 2004 to 2007, there came new charges that management, aware its ability to obtain both protective lock-up provisions and director approval, would often steer the acquisition process away from strategic buyers and towards a private equity firm that would provide an MBI opportunity to management. This accusation was supported by antitrust claims and studies which found that private equity firm consortiums were loath to trump bids of other private equity firms, resulting in a diminished market for corporate control.

Objections to MBOs not only focus on shareholders but also other corporate constituents, particularly employees and bondholders. The objections concerning the ability of managers to extract wealth benefits from employees and bondholders are similar to those raised concerning traditional LBOs. In the case of employees, management can be claimed to be expropriating wealth by arranging for employee cut-backs and other expenditure reductions management was otherwise unwilling to make when the company was public. This can further extend to an under-investment in capital resources in order to service the additional debt acquired in an MBO. . . .

In the 1980s, some in the Chicago law and economics school argued that the debate over these transactions was immaterial. The existence of any takeover premium was a net gain to shareholders, and any loss to shareholders was simply lost surplus. Accordingly, wealth effects were created in any takeover, and the law and economic jurisprudence had nothing more to add. While an important argument in the 1980s, this argument has faded away against claims that there is value and a property right in the firm's cash flows generally, and a takeover premium more specifically, which should be allocated to shareholders. This counter-argument is buttressed in the MBO context by the fact that the inside information management uses in the transaction is legally the property of the corporation and all of its shareholders, not management, and the value of this right is thus allocable to shareholders.

Related to these two arguments is the contention that MBOs can be viewed as a form of a venture capital transaction. Management's larger ownership and capacity to control the corporate enterprise incentivize them to act in an entrepreneurial manner. Even when they are not the primary capital provider, the release from agency costs and the better incentivizing compensation create opportunities for innovation. The gains and social wealth created by management are attributable to this conduct.

Separately, there is the argument that management may be owed some of this premium in light of the risk they are accruing by leveraging the company. The increased debt and management ownership concentrates the wealth of the managers and creates excessive risk for them. Management is compensated for this risk through an outsize share of the takeover premium. The gains accrued are not the property of the shareholders, but rather surplus or created wealth.

The argument that shareholder wealth is appropriated by managers is not mutually exclusive with the above arguments. This point is often addressed by the argument that the MBO process is subject to the general market for corporate control. If managers are indeed underbidding, this would be corrected in an efficient market by other interloping bids. These bidders would not be deterred by break fees, lock-ups, or the head start provided by management.

---

2. REGULATING MBOS

The most prominent legal case bearing on the appropriate legal standard for an MBO is *In re Wheelabrator Technologies, Inc.*

Shareholders Litigation, 663 A.2d 1194 (Del. Ch. 1995). Waste Management, Inc. owned 22% of Wheelabrator, and was attempting to acquire the remaining shares. Wheelabrator had an 11 member board with 3 Wheelabrator officers, 4 Waste designees, and 4 independent directors. After discussion and then a vote by all directors other than the Waste designees approving the merger, the full board, including those designees, also approved the merger.

Vice Chancellor Jacobs considered what standard should apply— *Weinberger*'s entire fairness standard or the business judgment rule. The court concluded that "[i]n this case, there is no contention or evidence that Waste, a 22% stockholder of WTI, exercised de jure or de facto control over WTI. Therefore, neither the holdings of or policy concerns underlying *Kahn* [*Kahn v. Lynch*] and *Stroud* [where "certain charter amendments [were] proposed by the board whose members were also the corporation's controlling stockholders"] are implicated here." In those transactions, the applicable law was that upon approval by fully-informed disinterested shareholders, the burden shifted to plaintiffs to prove the transaction was unfair, but the entire fairness standard still applied. Here, where there was no controlling shareholder, the effect of approval by the majority of disinterested shareholders, was that the applicable standard of review was "business judgment, with the plaintiffs having the burden of proof." In the footnote to this text, the court stated that:

> That result is reached not only by process of elimination but also by application of 8 Del.C. § 144(a)(1). That statute provides that when a majority of fully informed, disinterested directors (even if less than a quorum) approve a transaction in which other directors are interested, the transaction will not be void or voidable by reason of the conflict of interest. Under § 144(a)(1), a ratifying disinterested director vote has the same procedural effect as a ratifying disinterested shareholder vote under § 144(a)(2). Here, it is undisputed that the merger was approved by the fully informed vote of WTI's disinterested directors. Those directors were fully aware of both the obvious conflict of the Waste designees and of the conflict of three other directors, created by the prospect of accelerated stock options and of future employment.

In *Wheelabrator,* critically, there was no controlling shareholder. *Wheelabrator* held that in such a case, the applicable rule would be the business judgment rule. While no court has expressly addressed the level of scrutiny applicable to an MBO, there is no reason to suppose that a court would decide that more scrutiny was warranted. For example, in a case challenging the management buyout of Dell organized by Michael Dell, then-Chancellor Strine observed that with his 14% share of Dell's equity, Michael Dell was "not anywhere close" to being a controlling shareholder. Consequently, even though it involved a significant shareholder who was also the company's CEO and founder, the Dell transaction was accorded the protection of the business judgment rule because the transaction had been approved by Dell board, which had a majority of disinterested directors.

3. ADDITIONAL PROCESS IN MBOS

Beyond the process the court described in *Wheelabrator*, additional protections to minimize the potential conflict in MBOs have developed as "best practices." These best practices in many ways mimic the robust procedural protections that have found favor with the courts in controller freeze-out transactions. The following excerpt discusses these practices:

> The statutory conflict standards for MBOs in light of the *Wheelabrator* opinion have been supplemented by a set of normative protections. These norms are a response to this regulation and the channeling process it creates. These protections go beyond what Delaware and other states require, and are often implemented in response to best practices put forth by academics and proxy ratings agencies. They create a contractual structure that is bargained over by boards and MBO-sponsors, and is designed to protect and empower shareholders in the MBO process. They consist of both substantive and procedural devices:
>
> ***Special Committee of Independent Directors.*** Committees of independent directors are formed to consider these transactions. In order to buttress their independence, these committees typically retain their own set of legal and financial advisors to assist them in considering and negotiating the transaction.
>
> ***Majority of the Minority Condition.*** This requirement placed in the acquisition agreement specifies that approval of the transaction shall be by a majority of the disinterested or unaffiliated shareholders. Like the independent director requirement it is formulated in regard to conflict of interest statutes. This is generally a higher requirement than the fifty-percent shareholder approval requirement to approve a merger since it excludes shares held by management and other interested parties. This condition can be formulated in two ways: (1) as a majority of those voting, or (2) of the entire outstanding minority shareholder base. The latter formulation is a more powerful shareholder check on the MBO transaction since it has a higher threshold of shareholder approval. In MBO transactions, these conditions are less likely to be negotiated since in many instances the interested management stake is well

below a majority control level, and therefore the need for this condition is diminished.

Reduced Lock-ups. Lock-ups are normative contractual devices which are designed to compensate an initial bidder in an ordinary change of control context. In an MBO, these devices are sometimes reduced or eliminated. This theoretically should permit more active third-party bidding for the MBO target as it eliminates or reduces potentially preclusive lock-ups. The main type of lock-up typically at issue in an MBO is the breakup or termination fee. The amount of a termination fee is typically limited by Delaware law and normative practices to approximately three-percent of the transaction value, though in some circumstances Delaware has allowed lock-ups that exceed this amount. In an MBO transaction, this breakup fee is sometimes reduced below this amount or eliminated in order to create more open bidding.

Auctions. This is a pre-announcement procedure whereby a company, usually through its retained financial advisors, auctions itself. The goal is to maximize pricing and bidding for the company. In the MBO context, an auction is also a part of the open bidding process.

Go-shop. . . . A go-shop purportedly substitutes for a pre-announcement auction process by allowing a post-auction solicitation of offers for the company after announcement of the initial takeover transaction.

All of these mechanisms have their flaws, drawbacks, and complexities. For example, in the case of an independent committee, the question is how independent must the committee be? A director who meets the legal standards is still subject to heuristic biases and other conflicts which could force him or her to unintentionally favor a management bidding group. There is a lack of consensus on just how independent these directors need to be, both in general and for purposes of assessing the MBO transaction.

Go-shops have been viewed as cosmetic and enabling management to paper over the head start they gain in announcing a transaction with an agreement and without an auction. Meanwhile, the auction processes can be subtly manipulated through the information provided, potential bidder awareness of management preferences, and the initial bidders contacted.

To our knowledge, the role of ex ante court review of these devices when used in MBOs has yet to be examined. Ultimately, the question is whether these processes add value and if that value is warranted in an MBO.[19]

One of the biggest concerns presented by an MBO is that the managers can buy "their" company too cheaply. In the Dell management buy-out, Dell and the buying group, which included Michael Dell and a private equity firm, Silver Lake, included all of the procedural protections described above, precisely to prevent that result. Among the protections were a 45 day go-shop period, and the ability to sell to a bidder emerging during that period with a superior proposal, even after the period ended, by paying a termination fee of $180 million, less than 1 percent of the transaction value. (Dell could accept another bid, but would have to pay a termination fee of $450 million). Moreover, Dell could reimburse other bidders' expenses. Dell had two banks involved; JPMorgan Chase, which could not provide financing for the transaction (but could finance a deal approved by Dell's board with a higher bidder), and Evercore, whose fee was significantly dependent on its ability to find a higher bidder during the no-shop period. By contrast with the terms applicable for many original bidders who enter into merger agreements, Michael Dell and Silver Lake had the right to match competing offers only once. Often, original bidders' agreements allow them to match such offers as often as they would like to, dissuading competing bidders, who know that the original bidders can repeatedly make slightly better offers than the competitors do. The transaction with Michael Dell and Silver Lake had to be approved by a majority of the shares other than shares held by Michael Dell. Moreover, Michael Dell agreed to vote his shares for another accepted bid in the same proportions as other shareholders voted. He was not involved in the deal price negotiations, leaving Silver Lake to handle them.

If Michael Dell and Silver Lake did not put in enough money to consummate the deal, they would have had to pay Dell a reverse termination fee of $750 million, an amount within, albeit on the low end of, the range then (and now) common in transactions, and amounting to 3 percent of the transaction value.[20]

An article written at the time of the deal by one of this book's co-authors noted: "[T]he lawyers for Dell's special committee of independent directors . . . appear to have put in every contractual mechanism ever invented to address th[e] problem [that company management was

---

[19] Matthew D. Cain & Steven M. Davidoff, *Form Over Substance? The Value of Corporate Process and Management Buy-outs*, 36 DEL. J. CORP. L. 849, 876–78 (2011).

[20] This description of the facts is based on Steven M. Davidoff, *How Dell Tried to Avoid Potential Buyout Pitfalls*, N.Y. TIMES, Feb. 8, 2013, available at http://dealbook.nytimes.com/2013/02/08/how-dell-tried-to-avoid-potential-buyout-pitfalls/.

conflicted]. But does it really matter when there is only one real possible buyer, namely Michael S. Dell and Silver Lake?"

In that regard, the article also noted that giving these protections probably was not very costly for Michael Dell since it was quite unlikely that there would be another bidder. First, there usually aren't other bidders for deals of this sort, done by management and a private equity firm. Second, in this particular deal, others who might have been potential bidders did not seem likely to bid. Other private equity firms either didn't do technology deals or had decided against this deal; bidders also might have been deterred by the transaction's size. And there didn't seem to be a willing and interested strategic bidder. The author correctly predicted that shareholders were likely to approve the deal. He concluded that "the decision to sell . . . may be the one that is most controversial despite these procedural protections."[21]

4. EMPIRICAL EVIDENCE ON MBOS

The most recent articles to examine the wealth effects of MBOs in the last two decades have conflicting findings. The first study found that "the stock ownership of buyout managers is negatively associated with the buyout premiums." The authors cite this as "very strong evidence that buyout managers expropriate shareholder wealth when they purchase a firm."[22] In contrast, the second study found that in a sample of completed MBO acquisitions from 1995 to 2007, management involvement in a takeover reduces pre-bidding competition. However, despite this reduction, the authors did not find any evidence indicating that target management involvement negatively affects shareholder returns throughout the announcement period.[23]

Earlier articles also had conflicting findings. Yakov Amihud surveyed the evidence prior to 1990 and conducted his own analysis. Amihud found that the "evidence on the premiums offered in MBOs does not support the hypothesis that management exploits the shareholders."[24] Amihud's findings were later corroborated by a subsequent study. However, a 1985 study by Louis Lowenstein had conflicting findings. Lowenstein studied twenty-eight MBOs from 1979 to 1984, and found reduced premiums in

---

[21] *Id.*

[22] Kai Chen, Yong-Cheol Kim, & Richard D. Marcus, *Hands in the Cookie Jar? The Case of Management Buyouts,* 3 INT'L. REV ACCTG., BANKING & FIN. 43, 46 (2011).

[23] Sridhar Gogineni & John Puthenpurackal, *Target Management Involved Buyouts: Impact on Takeover Competition, Litigation Risk and Shareholder Returns,* 37 J. FIN. RESEARCH 323 (2014). ("Using a sample of 295 completed buyouts by financial buyers from 1995 to 2007, we find that management involvement does not appear to reduce target buyout announcement returns.") *Id.* at 323.

[24] *See* Yakov Amihud, *Leveraged Management Buyouts and Shareholders' Wealth* 3, 13–18, in LEVERAGED MANAGEMENT BUYOUTS: CAUSES AND CONSEQUENCES (Yakov Amihud, ed. 2002).

MBOs without competitive bidding. Lowenstein cited these findings to argue for an open bidding regime in MBOs.[25]

The results of a study by Easterwood et al., which examined 184 MBOs from 1978 through 1988, lends support to Lowenstein's argument for open bidding. The authors found that "explicit competition for control" in the form of a competing bid resulted in higher bid revisions and cumulative abnormal returns for shareholders. This competition resulted in more shareholder aggregate wealth production than did litigation or the effect of board negotiations. Easterwood et al. also found that negotiations with independent directors improve bid revisions.[26]

The evidence is similarly mixed on whether management times the buy-out process to its advantage, unduly manipulates the corporate process, or utilizes inside information to arrange an MBO. DeAngelo found no evidence of manipulation of management earnings in a study of sixty-four firms from 1973 to 1982.[27] In contrast, a 2008 study found that management with greater external MBO financing tend to report significantly fewer abnormal accruals. This provides support for the argument that the board of directors and shareholders serve as weak gatekeepers of the MBO process.[28]

Finally, Cain and Davidoff examine a sample of MBO transactions announced between 2003 and 2009. They find that procedural devices such as special committees and majority of the minority provisions are positively associated with higher MBO premiums. Among transactions with low initial offer premiums, bid failures are more likely when target shareholders benefit from competitive contracts. The authors also find that bid premiums are lower when management initiates the deal publicly, reinforcing the notion that management can clear the field in an MBO. Ultimately, they find evidence to support management buy-outs as potentially beneficial to shareholders, but also reasons for shareholders to be wary and support procedural protections in merger agreements.[29]

D. PRIVATE EQUITY AND LBOS

Private equity transactions also potentially involve conflicts. A common conflict is that the private equity firm will also include

---

[25] Louis Lowenstein, *Management Buyouts*, 85 COLUM. L. REV. 730, 731 (1985).

[26] John C. Easterwood et al., *Controlling the Conflict of Interest in Management Buyouts*, 76 REV. ECON. STAT. 512, 513 (1994).

[27] *See* Linda Elizabeth DeAngelo, *Accounting Numbers as Market Valuation Substitutes: A Study of Management Buyouts of Public Shareholders*, 61 ACCT. REV. 400, 401, 417–18 (1986). In his 1989 study, Steven Kaplan found that managers consistently project outsized gains in their post-MBO forecasts. *See* Steven N. Kaplan, *The Effects of Management Buyouts on Operating Performance and Value*, 24 J. FIN. ECON. 217, 217 (1989).

[28] Paul E. Fischer & Louis Henock, *Financial Reporting and Conflicting Managerial Incentives: The Case of Management Buyouts*, 54 MGMT. SCI. 1700, 1713 (2008).

[29] Cain & Davidoff, *supra* note 19.

management as part of the buying group. Such transactions thus raise many of the concerns that are present in a management buyout deal. The presence of incumbent management cooperating with a private equity bidder can adversely affect the sale process in many ways, as is demonstrated by the 2011 J. Crew transaction. In that transaction, CEO (and significant shareholder) Millard Drexler did not inform the J. Crew board for seven weeks that he was discussing a buyout with TPG Capital and Leonard Green & Partners, two private equity firms, in which he would participate. Moreover, the investment bank that had previously worked for J. Crew began to work for the buyout group. The securities filings made clear that Mr. Drexler would be receiving a great deal of cash in the transaction and a significant interest in the new company. There was a go-shop provision, but with Mr. Drexler apparently unwilling to consider other deals, the provision was not of great benefit to J. Crew. Mr. Drexler refused to "sterilize" his shares—that is, he refused to agree that his shares would not count towards the vote needed to approve the transaction. Indeed, TPG and Leonard Green had even proposed that he agree to vote his shares for the transaction, something that was only changed in later negotiations as the bidders were lowering their bid. The article below describes other flaws in the sale process:

> Cravath, Swaine & Moore [one of the top New York law firms] represented the special committee, and was retained. . . , five days after the committee was formed and seven weeks after TPG had first raised the possibility of a buyout with Mr. Drexler. . . . Cravath [apparently] realized that the buyout process was out of control as they immediately sent an e-mail out to TPG saying that all talks would be halted until the committee "got up to speed." Cravath also arranged for [a prominent Delaware law firm] to get involved on fiduciary duty issues . . . another sign that Cravath did not like the process and was in damage-control mode.

> [Five days later] TPG was...talking again with Cravath about providing confidential information to [buyout participant] Leonard Green. . . . No confidentiality agreement was signed with either firm until [approximately three weeks later]. . . . Other than arrange for the formalities of a committee, what did the special committee do during this time? . . . Shouldn't it have first considered whether a sale was even appropriate and if so laid out the process and taken control?

The author concluded:

> [T]he special committee was [apparently] attempting to stabilize a situation that was out of control and that Mr. Drexler and his private equity buyers were attempting to do an end-run around. The special committee may have even made the best decision for

shareholders despite the flawed process. And it appears that committee members and their counsel were struggling in good faith to do so.[30]

But struggling may not be sufficient. The many intimations that the special committee was hamstrung, combined with incomplete information in the public filings, suggest that Mr. Drexler and his buy-out partners were taking advantage of their positions to purchase the company at too low a price.

The J. Crew buy-out raises the main issue private equity deals raise. Because management is often employed by the private equity buyer after the buy-out occurs, they may have incentives to favor a private equity firm in a change of control transaction precisely at the time when the board is obliged to seek the highest price reasonably available for shareholders. Where managers appear to have committed themselves to a private equity buyer early in the process, courts have taken a skeptical view of the ability of managers to fairly manage a sale process. Shareholder litigation over the J. Crew buy-out was settled for $16 million.

We discuss these issues and the law of Delaware on this matter further in Chapter XVIII.

QUESTIONS

Freeze-Outs

1.   Is there a functional difference between "entire fairness" review and the "business purpose" test? What problem is each test attempting to address?

2.   Who decides whether the business purpose test is met? Who decides whether the entire fairness test is met?

3.   Can you trace the origins of the "entire fairness" test from DGCL § 144? How would you compare the entire fairness test with DGCL Section 144?

4.   What is the "conflict" that the court in *Weinberger* is trying to regulate?

5.   What do you think is the effect of burden-shifting under *Kahn*?

6.   Do you agree with the distinction that then-Vice Chancellor Strine made in *Pure Resources* between mergers and tender offers? Do you agree with the effective conclusion of the Vice Chancellor that the protections he specifies for a tender offer freeze-out transaction are sufficient to protect minority shareholders?

---

[30] Steven M. Davidoff, *J. Crew Buyout Raises Questions*, N.Y. TIMES, Dec. 10, 2010, available at http://dealbook.nytimes.com/2011/01/21/j-crew-buyout-settlement-still-leaves-some-questions/. The description of the J. Crew deal is also taken from this article.

7.   Why might controllers still prefer mergers over tender offers for a freeze-out?

8.   What further changes would you recommend to doctrine to encourage the use of tender offers? Would this affect how minority shareholders are treated?

9.   How is *Kahn v. M&F* as decided by the Delaware Supreme Court different than the standard enunciated by then-Chancellor Strine in the lower court opinion? How are both different than the standard in *CNX*? Why are there so many different standards?

10.   Do you agree with the Delaware courts that there is no need for "entire fairness" review if certain procedural protections are put in place? Is this a question of who polices these transactions—courts, or boards comprised of independent directors?

11.   Why do you think that the Delaware Supreme Court added footnote 14 in *Kahn v. M&F*?

Management Buy-Outs

1.   What different concerns are implicated in freeze-outs than in management buy-outs? Should different standards apply for the two types of transactions?

2.   How should management buy-outs be regulated? Is the present level of regulation sufficient?

3.   What would you advise a CEO who was thinking of making an offer to purchase her company to do before contacting a private equity firm to be a partner in the bid?

4.   Given that Dell adopted many of the recommended procedural protections, why do you think the boards of other companies in an MBO do not adopt these protections?

PROBLEM

National Insurance Industries is an Ohio corporation publicly traded on the New York Stock Exchange. It is 53% controlled by American Financial Group. Six of the ten directors on the National Insurance Industries board are affiliated with American Financial. Ohio has not adopted the Weinberger test and instead, the exclusive remedy in a freeze-out is for a shareholder to seek appraisal rights. How would you advise American Financial to structure their freeze-out? Please advise whether a merger or tender offer is preferable. How would your answer change if National Insurance were a Delaware corporation? If you think that only the legalities matter in this decision you may want to read Steven M. Davidoff, *A Buyout Offer That Raises Questions of Board Fairness and Duty*, N.Y. TIMES, Feb. 25, 2014, available at http://dealbook.nytimes.com/2014/02/25/a-buyout-offer-that-raises-questions-of-board-fairness-and-duty/.

PART V

OTHER M&A ISSUES
■ ■ ■

CHAPTER XX

SHAREHOLDER ACTIVISM

■ ■ ■

A. INTRODUCTION

Why would shareholder activism be covered in an M&A casebook? After all, it is not a merger or an acquisition transaction. But the most prominent form of shareholder activism at this writing, "economic" activism, involves trying to change how particular companies are run, and what they do, which is the aim of many, and probably most, M&A transactions. Moreover, companies sometimes react to economic activists with the same sorts of defenses they use for hostile bids. Thus, economic activism presents many of the same issues as do M&A transactions.

Economic activists are principally hedge funds and other institutional funds. Both the funds and the companies they target are creative in their tactics and strategy. The law has to deal with what activists do as well as how companies respond.

Sometimes, activism and M&A overlap. As we have mentioned previously, and as we will discuss in this Chapter, a prominent hedge fund, Pershing Square, teamed up with a pharmaceutical corporation, Valeant, to support Valeant's offer to purchase another pharmaceutical corporation, Allergan. In this Chapter, we provide an overview of shareholder activism and discuss the relevant law.

B. WHAT IS SHAREHOLDER ACTIVISM?

As noted above, this Chapter is about the most prominent type of shareholder activism today, "economic activism." Economic activism is aimed at changing the direction of corporate strategy. Activists extensively research particular companies, identify ways in which those companies should, in the activists' view, be conducting their businesses, and press the companies to proceed in accordance with strategies that the activists have identified.[1]

---

[1] That being said, some critics of economic activism argue that there is really only one 'activist playbook.' "Activist investors are like UPS drivers. They turn in only one direction. By now, the activists' rise is remarkable for its sheer scale and ferocity, with some $119 billion placed in their hands. Last year, they pursued 343 companies, up 27% from the year before, according to FactSet. Their rise is also remarkable for another thing: their intellectual sameness. Plot a map of the 10 largest activist firms and you will find that seven of them are based within 17 blocks of each other in midtown Manhattan. The vast majority are making similar demands of

Another type of shareholder activism, "governance activism," is focused on getting companies to adopt certain practices and policies that give more power to shareholders, including governance practices that make companies easier to take over, as well as social proposals that may be favored by some groups. While economic activists, who are principally hedge funds and other institutional funds, tend to be quite well funded, governance activists are often less well funded. The economic activists have strong views about things a particular company should be doing to improve its performance; by contrast, the governance activists are typically trying to get particular companies to do things they think companies generally should do, such as adopting governance practices that make companies easier to take over, or pursuing certain social aims. Like economic activism, governance activism has been, and remains, controversial.

One focus of governance activism has been to influence companies to de-stagger their boards, thus making them easier to take over. The governance activists argue that ease in unseating entrenched management should help maximize shareholder value. Another focus of governance activism concerns the debate we mentioned earlier, and return to in this Chapter, regarding § 13(d) of the Williams Act, notably how quickly disclosure of a 5% stake has to be made, and what additional acquisitions can be made prior to the required disclosure. The present situation, in which the disclosure need not be made for ten days and unlimited additional shares can be acquired during that period, has been praised by some governance activists as strengthening the power of shareholders vis a vis entrenched managers.

Economic activists try to influence companies to pursue strategies they think will maximize shareholder value. They commonly recommend some of the following business strategies:

Selling the Company. One strategy activists recommend is that the target's board sell the company. The rationale is that the company's value can be maximized if it is sold instead of continuing as an independent operating entity. For example, Carl Icahn often engages in this type of activism, advocating it successfully at over 20 companies in the past decades according to FactSet SharkRepellent.

Spin-Off. Another strategy activists recommend is that a company should be broken up into divisions or that some of its businesses should be spun off. They argue that the market will value the separate businesses more highly than it does the whole. Examples of this type of activism include Pershing Square's activism at Fortune Brands, which

their targets, delivered with what now feels like a dull percussion: Raise the dividend, buy back shares, cut these costs, spin off that division, sell the company." Dennis K. Berman, *A Radical Idea for Activist Investors*, WALL ST. J., January 27, 2015, available at http://www.wsj.com/articles/a-radical-idea-for-activist-investors–1422370260.

resulted in the company breaking up into four different companies, including Jim Beam Brands (which was later sold, combining two activist strategies) and Carl Icahn's activism at eBay, which successfully advocated spinning off eBay's PayPal division.

Strategic and Governance Changes. Activists sometimes also advocate long-term changes in either the strategy or governance of a company in order to enhance the company's financial performance. These can include economic changes, as well as the addition of new board members selected by the activists, or the replacement of the CEO. An example is Dan Loeb's activism at Sotheby's, discussed below. Governance changes can also include distributing cash to shareholders, often in the form of a special dividend or share repurchase. The cash can come from amounts the company already has on hand—an example is of Carl Icahn's at least somewhat successful campaign to get Apple to make cash payouts to its shareholders—or amounts borrowed for that purpose.

M&A Related Activism. Historically, this type of activism has involved taking a position in a company that is a party to an agreement to be acquired, and advocating that the buyer pay a higher price. An example of this is Carl Icahn's activism at Dell: Icahn succeeded in getting the merger consideration increased from $13.25 per share to $13.88 per share. Another example is when Pershing Square and Valeant teamed up to help Valeant acquire Allergan. This new type of M&A activism, in which activists and bidders team up to force a sale to a pre-selected bidder, may become more frequent.

Economic activism by hedge funds has achieved particular prominence in recent years. Hedge funds like Bill Ackman's Pershing Square, Dan Loeb's Third Point and David Einhorn's Greenlight Capital, as well as Carl Icahn's fund, have brought activist campaigns at a multitude of companies, including Apple, eBay, Microsoft, Sotheby's, and JCPenney. These activists have wrought tremendous change at these companies. Companies not targeted have also been affected, especially insofar as they make pre-emptive changes in hopes of avoiding being targeted.

In a 1976 letter to prospective investors that has been called the Icahn Manifesto, Carl Icahn laid out the basic investment strategy for shareholder activists, a strategy that is still used today:

> It is our opinion that the elements in today's economic environment have combined in a unique way to create large profit making opportunities with relatively little risk . . . It is our contention that sizable profits can be earned by taking large positions in "undervalued" stocks and then attempting to control the destinies of these companies by:

a. Trying to convince management to liquidate or sell the company to a "white knight;"

b. Waging a proxy contest;

c. Making a tender offer; and/or

d. Selling back our position to the company.[2]

According to Forbes, at this writing (in late 2015), Carl Icahn is worth over $20 billion.[3] In this Chapter, we will discuss the law governing the strategies Carl Icahn outlined almost four decades ago, strategies which still form the core of the shareholder activist's campaign.

Economic activism has become increasingly prominent over the past decade. In part, this activism has been spurred by the increasingly concentrated ownership of U.S. public companies. It is now not uncommon for the top ten shareholders of a company to be institutional investors, principally mutual funds; together, these shareholders might own a majority of the company. Activists thus only have to convince a small number of shareholders to side with them to achieve a successful outcome.

As shareholder activists seek to change the strategic direction of a company, they not infrequently seek to change its management. The company will not infrequently resist the activist's "suggestions," leading the activist to attempt to replace some of the company's directors by means of a proxy contest.

The following chart sets forth the number of proxy contests from 2001 to 2015 (through November 20, 2015). Almost all of these were initiated by hedge fund activists. As the chart shows, proxy contests peaked in 2009, at 133, and declined in 2012 to 77, rising in 2014 to 93 and in 2015 to 105. Proxy contests are the most prominent form of shareholder activism, and the most M&A-like activity. Recall our discussion of proxy fights as a means by which hostile bidders would try to replace a board of a company with a poison pill; the bidder-selected directors would presumably be willing to remove the pill.

The chart shows a decline in the number of proxy fights from the 2009 peak. This decline does not reflect a decline in activism. Indeed, FactSet SharkRepellent reports that the number of hedge fund activist "events" (that is, attempts to influence a particular company) rose from 140 in 2009 to 241 in 2014. The decline in the number of proxy fights may reflect that companies are increasingly settling with the activists rather than fighting an expensive contest that they are likely to lose.

---

[2] The letter is quoted in Tobias E. Carlisle, *The Insight That Enabled Carl Icahn to Become a Corporate Raider*, CRAIN'S WEALTH, December 8, 2014, available at http://www.crains wealth.com/article/20141208/WEALTH/312089997.

[3] *The World's Most Powerful People*, FORBES, http://www.forbes.com/profile/carl-icahn/.

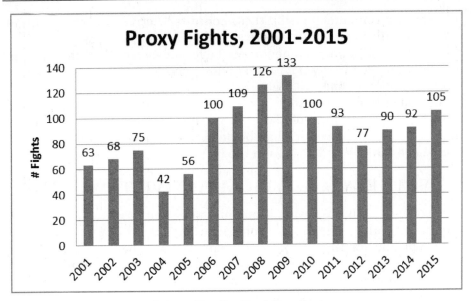

Source: FactSet SharkRepellent

The chart below shows that in 2014, activists won 73% of proxy contests, including those that ended in settlements and that as of November 20, 2015, they had won 64%. A "win" for the activist is defined as placing a dissident director on the board; a "win" for the activist is a "loss" for the board. This high "loss" rate is pushing many companies to avoid a costly and hostile proxy contest by simply settling with the activists.

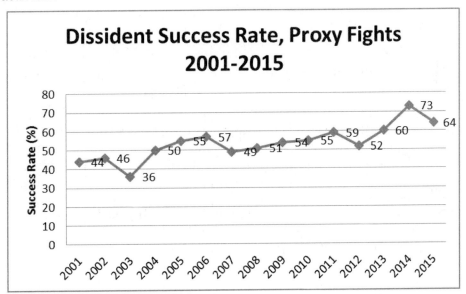

Source: FactSet SharkRepellent

Why are companies losing these contests? Activists normally target underperforming companies where shareholders might be more accepting of change. And some commentators have suggested that institutional investors, and the proxy advisory services who advise these investors as to how to vote, might have a general view that activists' ideas are better than those of companies (that is, incumbent management), and might be inclined to vote in favor of those ideas and directors who would follow them. The rise in economic shareholder activism has spurred a vigorous debate, one that we will discuss in the last Subsection of this Chapter.

C. SOTHEBY'S: A TYPICAL ACTIVIST CAMPAIGN

Economic activists target companies they think are not maximizing shareholder value. They try to convince companies to pursue strategies and adopt policies they think will maximize shareholder value. Among their tactics are pressuring company management, privately and publicly, to pursue different business strategies and sometimes, to appoint particular people to the board, and running proxy contests to elect their desired board members.

This Section discusses a recent prominent activist campaign by one of the best-known shareholder activists, Dan Loeb and the hedge fund he founded and runs, the $17.5 billion Third Point hedge fund, involving the venerable auction house Sotheby's. Sotheby's has a long and storied history. It was founded in 1744, and is the oldest of all the publicly traded companies presently listed on the NYSE.

1. THE INITIAL ACTIVIST STEPS

Typically, an activist's first step is to take a (stock) position in the company. This action implicates the Williams Act and more particularly, § 13(d) of the Securities Exchange Act of 1934. Upon acquiring a greater than 5% position in the target, the activist will be required to file a Schedule 13D within 10 days.

The filing of the Schedule 13D is typically the activists' announcement to the world that it has taken a position and may advocate for change at the targeted company. Investors and the public will scrutinize the Schedule 13D's Item 4 disclosure and statement of purpose to see what the activist is intending. After acquiring its position, the activist then typically sends a letter to management, known as a poison pen letter, outlining objections to the company's current state of affairs and demanding a new course of action.

Whether through the Schedule 13D or a poison pen letter, the activist will publicly announce its presence and set forth its agenda. Implicit (or explicit) in the activist's statements is a threat that if the company does not respond adequately, the activist will launch a proxy campaign to unseat the directors. These initial activist steps shape the trajectory of future dealings between the activist and the company.

Third Point began acquiring shares of Sotheby's in mid-2013. It approached Sotheby's in early August, and the two companies had discussions concerning Third Point's ideas for changes at Sotheby's. At that time, the Sotheby's board was also holding internal discussions, and discussions with other activist shareholders. On August 15, 2013, Third Point's acquisitions of Sotheby's shares had passed the 5% threshold, triggering the 13D filing requirement. On August 26, 2013, Third Point filed its 13D.

Here is the Item 4 Disclosure from Third Point's Schedule 13D with respect to Sotheby's:

Item 4. Purpose of Transaction

The Reporting Persons originally acquired their shares of Common Stock subject to this Schedule 13D for investment purposes.

The Reporting Persons intend to engage in a dialogue with members of the Board or management of the Issuer or other representatives of the Issuer. The Reporting Persons may also engage in a dialogue and other communications regarding the Issuer with other stockholders of the Issuer, knowledgeable industry or market observers (including art market participants), or other persons. Any dialogue or communications with any of the foregoing persons may relate to potential changes of strategy and leadership at the Issuer and proposals that, if effected, may result in one or more of the events described in Item 4 of Schedule 13D. Except as set forth herein, the Reporting Persons have no present plans or proposals that relate to or would result in any of the matters set forth in subparagraphs (a)–(j) of Item 4 of Schedule 13D.

The Reporting Persons intend to review their investment in the Issuer's shares of Common Stock on a continuing basis. Depending on various factors including, without limitation, the Issuer's financial position and investment strategy, the price levels of the shares, conditions in the securities markets and general economic and industry conditions, the Reporting Persons may in the future take such actions with respect to their investment in the Issuer as they deem appropriate including, without limitation, purchasing additional shares of Common Stock, selling some or all of their shares of Common Stock, or changing their intention with respect to any and all matters set forth in subparagraphs (a)–(j) of Item 4 of Schedule 13D.

This disclosure is written to give Third Point maximum flexibility for future action. The filing itself was probably enough to signal to the market that Third Point was about to launch an activist campaign. As noted above, in other cases, the activist will accompany the Schedule 13D filing with a letter to management, known as a poison pen letter, outlining objections to the company's current state of affairs and demanding a new course of action.

In the Sotheby's case, Mr. Loeb waited almost another two months before issuing his poison pen letter. On October 2, 2013, Third Point filed an amended Schedule 13D reporting that its holdings of Sotheby's had risen to 9.3%. Attached to the schedule as an exhibit was a letter written by Loeb (on behalf of Third Point) to Sotheby's CEO, William Ruprecht. Following is an excerpt from the letter:

Dear Mr. Ruprecht:

Funds managed by Third Point LLC ("Third Point") recently received Hart-Scott-Rodino approval to increase our stake in Sotheby's (the "Company") and now hold 9.3% of the outstanding shares, making us the Company's largest shareholder. Notwithstanding Sotheby's recent efforts—a belated announcement partially addressing poor capital allocation practices and the hiring of a new Chief Financial Officer—we remain concerned about its leadership, shareholder misalignment, strategic direction, and Board governance.

In particular, we are troubled by the Company's chronically weak operating margins and deteriorating competitive position relative to Christie's, as evidenced by each of the Contemporary and Modern art evening sales over the last several years . . .

Pressing Issues at Sotheby's

We acknowledge that you, Mr. Ruprecht, were an able steward for the Company following both the price fixing scandal in 2000 and the financial crisis in 2008. Unfortunately, you have not led the business forward in today's art market. It is apparent to us from our meeting that you do not fully grasp the central importance of Contemporary and Modern art to the Company's growth strategy, which is highly problematic since these are the categories expanding most rapidly among new collectors. This is not to say that Sotheby's entire portfolio of art, antique, and collectible departments is not critically important—it is. However, Sotheby's success will be defined in large part by its ability to generate sales and profits in Contemporary and

Modern art, as this is where the greatest growth potential lies
. . .

<u>Management's Lack of Alignment with Shareholders</u>

Emblematic of the Company's misalignment with shareholder interests are both your own generous pay package and scant stock holdings by virtually all Board members. Third Point's current stake represents nearly 10 times the number of fully-vested shares held by Sotheby's directors and executive officers. Your personal holding of 152,683 shares, representing a mere 0.22% interest, is particularly noteworthy because you have been an employee of the Company since 1980 and its CEO since 2000.

In sharp contrast to your limited stock holdings is a generous package of cash pay, perquisites, and other compensation. We see little evidence justifying your 2012 total compensation of $6,300,399 in both salary and PSU awards valued at over $4 million, seemingly based on a mysterious target not disclosed in any of the Company's public filings. Your compensation award compares quite favorably to companies offered as peers in your own proxy statement: $3.9 million for the CEO of Nordstrom Inc. and $6.1 million for the CEO of Tiffany & Co.—both companies more than three times the size of Sotheby's—and yet Sotheby's has clearly underperformed these "comparables."

A review of the Company's proxy statement reveals a perquisite package that invokes the long-gone era of imperial CEOs: a car allowance, coverage of tax planning costs, and reimbursement for membership fees and dues to elite country clubs. What example does this set for Sotheby's hard-working employees, who see leaders at the top collecting guaranteed perks rather than rewards delivered for growing earnings? In our experience, skewed compensation programs approved by a Board with little oversight inevitably result in exactly the type of lackadaisical corporate culture evident at Sotheby's today.

. . .

A Prescription for Repairing Sotheby's

Sotheby's is like an old master painting in desperate need of restoration. Auctions, private and internet sales all need to be reinvigorated or revamped. Sotheby's global footprint must expand, and opportunities to exploit the Sotheby's brand through adjacent businesses should be considered. Sotheby's can also use its unique position and potential excess capital to judiciously take principal positions in works of art when doing so would not conflict with its clients' interests.

As with any important restoration, Sotheby's must first bring in the right technicians. Third Point is not only Sotheby's largest shareholder but also has significant experience and a successful track record of serving on public company boards. I am willing to join the board immediately and help recruit several new directors who have experience increasing shareholder value, share a passion for art, understand technology and luxury brands, or have operated top-performing sales organizations. Importantly, our candidates would also better represent Sotheby's expanding geographic footprint. We support the Company placing a designee from another large shareholder on the Board as well. Once installed, these new directors would determine what other steps are necessary to ensure that the Company benefits from the rigor and direction that comes with having an "owners' perspective" in the boardroom.

It is also time, Mr. Ruprecht, for you to step down from your positions as Chairman, President and Chief Executive Officer and for the role of Chairman to be separated for your successor.

. . .

Sincerely,
/s/ Daniel S. Loeb
Daniel S. Loeb

Chief Executive Officer

The poison pen letter has become a bit of an art form, just as is the case with the bear hug letter discussed in Chapter XV.B.1. The activist will highlight its concerns with, and perhaps, plans for, the company; he may also criticize the company's management, as Mr. Loeb did. In fact, Loeb is known for his venomous letters, including one that referred to a CEO as a "CVD," or chief value destroyer, and another that referred to two great-grandsons of one company's founder as part of the "Lucky Sperm Club." In a letter to Irik Sevin, CEO of fuel distributor Star Gas Partners LP, Mr. Loeb wrote: "Do what you do best: Retreat to your waterfront mansion in the Hamptons where you can play tennis and hobnob with your fellow socialites."[4] The idea behind the poison pen letter is not only to highlight a new agenda, but to embarrass the company and warn them that the activist is not about to go away.

----

[4] Among the articles discussing and quoting Loeb's letters are Ben McGrath, *The Angry Investor*, THE NEW YORKER, April 18, 2005, available at http://www.newyorker.com/magazine/2005/04/18/the-angry-investor and Jaime LaLinde, *Dan Loeb's Top Ten Most Scathing Letters*, VANITY FAIR, October 31, 2013, available at http://www.vanityfair.com/news/2013/10/dan-loeb-mean-letters.

Mr. Loeb's letter outlined a new management vision for Sotheby's. Third Point's goal was to make Sotheby's more competitive in the marketplace by pursuing a new direction with new management He advocated that the CEO resign and be replaced with a new CEO. Mr. Loeb asked for directors from his firm to be placed on the Sotheby's board. Both of these requests are common in activist campaigns, and are one reason why companies fear being targeted by such campaigns. After all, the activist is sometimes asking that the company's management and board resign, and is almost always asking that they acknowledge failures.

In litigation arising from the Sotheby's case, Vice Chancellor Parsons discussed Mr. Loeb's letters:

> Loeb apparently made several of the accusations in his letter without actual knowledge of their veracity. In addition, the record supports an inference that Loeb included the letter with the Schedule 13D as part of an "all out assault" meant to destabilize the Company. In contemporaneous emails, Loeb described his letter as both part of a "holy jihad" intended to "make sure all the Sotheby's infidels are made aware that there is only one true God" and part of a "Special Operation on Sotheby's," which was intended to "shock and awe" the Company and "undermine the credibility" of Ruprecht.[5]

2. THE COMPANY RESPONSE

Following receipt of the activist's opening, the target company faces the choice of whether or not to respond. In some cases, and more often as of late, the company will settle with the activist, adopting the activist's preferred strategy and appointing the activist's preferred directors. In a not-insignificant number of cases, the companies simply settle, without further action by the activist. In other cases, the company will attempt to ignore the activist. A third option, which is more common than simply ignoring the activist, is for the company to announce its own strategic plan to increase the company's value—a plan which may or may not incorporate all or part of the activists' plan. In both the second and third options, the company may also adopt defensive measures typical of those adopted by a target responding to a hostile takeover offer.

In the case of Sotheby's, the company initially refused to engage with Mr. Loeb and Third Point. Instead, the Sotheby's board reacted, not only to Third Point, but to their perceived vulnerability to shareholder activists generally, including another fund that had filed a Schedule 13D on July 30, 2013, Marcato Capital Management, by announcing a poison pill. The pill contained two different triggering events. One was the

---

[5] *Third Point LLC v. William F. Ruprecht and Sotheby's*, C.A. No. 9469–VCP, memo. op., p.20 (Del. Ch. May 2, 2014).

acquisition of a 10% stake by a shareholder whose ownership was to be reported on Schedule 13D; the other was the acquisition of a 20% stake by a shareholder whose ownership was to be reported on Schedule 13G, the schedule that is applicable for an acquirer who did not acquire the securities "with any purpose, or with the effect of, changing or influencing the control of the issuer, or in connection with or as a participant in any transaction having that purpose or effect."

In January of 2014, Sotheby's announced its alternative plan, a $300 million special dividend to shareholders, and a $150 million share buyback. The court decision in the parties' subsequent litigation discusses what happened next:

> In February of 2014, Third Point and Sotheby's began negotiating in earnest in an attempt to avoid a proxy contest. The "core" of Third Point's settlement proposal was that: (1) the Company redeem or modify the Rights Plan to allow 15% ownership; (2) the roles of CEO and Chairman be separated; and (3) Loeb and "1 other Loeb designee" join the Board. Loeb also emphasized that, as a director, he would focus on instituting annual "360 degree director reviews," and a mandatory Board retirement age. On the issues of separating the CEO and Chairman roles, 360 degree reviews, and a mandatory retirement age, Dodge [Sotheby's director, and lead director until December 1, 2013] "strongly favored" Third Point's position and noted "[w]e can fault Loeb for his ego, his rough edges, for his 'ready, fire, aim' approach, but on the substance he is far from all wrong, and he is with us already on the core issue of returning capital in measured amounts." On the more controversial issue of representation on the Board, Sotheby's responded that it was prepared to offer Third Point one nominee, who could not be Loeb. Third Point rejected this offer. The Company later offered to allow just Loeb on to the Board if he agreed to abide by certain terms, including a standstill agreement that would cap Third Point's holdings at around the 10% mark. This offer was also rejected.[6]

3. THE PROXY CONTEST

The negotiations between Sotheby's and Third Point broke down, and in February of 2014, Third Point announced that it would nominate three directors to the Sotheby's board. This constituted a material change to the information in Third Point's Schedule 13D, necessitating an amendment: Third Point's revised Item 4 disclosure, filed on February 27, 2014, included the following:

---

[6]   *Id.* at 26.

The Reporting Persons initially filed a Schedule 13D in August after concluding that Sotheby's—one of the world's foremost luxury brands—was languishing and lacked the resolve to change despite the obvious need to do so. We commend the Company for taking some action following our filing and believe these expeditious improvements demonstrate the benefits of engaging with shareholders. Today, much remains to be done to enhance the Company's competitive position, improve its strategy and boost shareholder value. As Sotheby's largest shareholder, the Reporting Persons remain firm in their conviction that the current Board will benefit greatly from new perspectives and different expertise to move the Company forward. Therefore we are nominating three new Directors to the Board. . . .

[T]he Reporting Persons today provided formal notice to the Issuer that they will nominate Daniel S. Loeb, Harry J. Wilson, and Olivier Reza (the "Third Point Nominees") for election to the Board at the 2014 Annual Meeting.

The Item 4 disclosure not only amends Third Point's Schedule 13D to include the director nomination; it also serves as Third Point's talking points to shareholders and the public to explain why it is taking this action. In essence, Third Point triggered the "nuclear option" by nominating directors to the board. Third Point did not seek to replace the entire board; this is rarely done by activists. Nor did they seek to acquire majority control. Institutional shareholders are loath to support such a step and generally, the proxy advisory services will not support such a step either.

Once an activist nominates dissident directors, it is in a proxy "fight" with the company. The activist and the company make their case to win the fight, in the court of public opinion as well as with shareholders. Often, as in the Sotheby's case, there is accompanying litigation. As an article by one of this book's authors on the litigation between Third Point and Sotheby's noted: "Sotheby's knew that it had the upper hand and Delaware law was on its side. But for Mr. Loeb, winning the litigation wasn't as important as deposing the Sotheby's directors in the hope that he could find some ammunition for his fight. In other words, Sotheby's overreached with the poison pill and gave Mr. Loeb an opening to inflict damage."[7]

Ultimately, Sotheby's won in court, but its victory was pyrrhic. Emails emerged in the discovery process in which Mr. Ruprecht referred to Mr. Loeb as "scum." Steven B. Dodge, the lead independent director,

---

[7]   Steven M. Davidoff, *A Truce at Sotheby's After a Costly and Avoidable Battle*, N.Y. TIMES, May 5, 2014, http://dealbook.nytimes.com/2014/05/05/a-truce-at-sothebys-after-a-costly-and-avoidable-battle/.

said to another director that the board was "too comfortable, too chummy and not doing its job." In another email Dodge stated that at least in part, Mr. Loeb was "right on the merits." (This should serve as yet another reminder to be careful what you write in emails and remind your clients of the same—they should assume anything they write may come out in litigation).

On May 5, 2013, a few days after the decision was issued, Sotheby's gave Loeb much of what he asked for. Sotheby's had been advised that Third Point's nominees had a good chance of prevailing in the proxy fight. Faced with Institutional Shareholder Services' recommendation of Loeb and one other Third Point nominee, Sotheby's agreed to appoint Loeb and Third Point's other two nominees to its board. Moreover, Sotheby's agreed to pay Third Point $10 million to reimburse it for its expenses during the proxy battle. Sotheby's conducted an expensive battle. What did it get for its money? Arguably, nothing. The article quoted above concluded:

> In these situations, the rule is to compromise and give the hedge funds the seats.
>
> [In 2013], 80 percent of activists were granted a seat before a proxy campaign was even completed. And 60 percent of proxy contests that went the distance were won by activists. According to SharkRepellent, even Carl C. Icahn has stated that he is "surprised" that he is being offered board seats so often to forestall a campaign.
>
> This not only means that compromise is the preferred route, but it is becoming the case before a proxy contest gains traction.[8]

Six months after the settlement and the placement of Mr. Loeb's nominees on the Sotheby's board, Mr. Ruprecht resigned as CEO.

In the next Subsections we explore some of the defenses companies commonly employ against activists—defenses that often resemble those a company adopts to prevent or fight off a hostile takeover.

D.   DEFENSES AGAINST SHAREHOLDER ACTIVISM

A company's primary defense against activism is to argue that the activist's plan is not a good one, or that it has a better plan. After all, if the company can get its own shareholders' support, the activist cannot force through its agenda. Companies often will also take defensive actions to protect themselves. Two significant defensive actions are:

Adopting a poison pill. As in the Sotheby's case, a company can adopt a poison pill, if it does not already have one in place. The poison pill

---

[8]   *Id.*

does not stop the activist from acquiring shares below the threshold, but it puts a cap on accumulations above the threshold. In addition, the provisions in the pill defining a "group" (discussed in Chapter IV.B.3) will be drafted so as to limit as much as possible hedge fund communications with other shareholders, particularly other activists.

Companies are becoming more aggressive in their adoption of language defining a group that goes beyond the § 13(d) definition. For example, Barnes & Noble adopted a poison pill to fend off Ronald W. Burkle's Yucaipa Group; for purposes of the pill, "group" was defined to include shareholders with "any agreement, arrangement or understanding (written or oral) to cooperate in obtaining, changing or influencing the control of the company."[9] The provision effectively chilled almost all shareholder communication, and its validity was challenged in court by Mr. Burkle. Barnes & Noble eliminated it before the court could rule on whether the provision violated the board's fiduciary duties. Other companies have been even more aggressive. According to a memo by the law firm Latham & Watkins, companies have adopted broad definitions of "group," using phrases such as "acting with conscious parallelism," "acting in concert" or "cooperating" in order to prevent activist hedge funds and indeed any shareholders from working together.[10] The Delaware courts have yet to rule on the validity of this type of language, and it is likely to be heavily scrutinized if and when it is challenged.

Advance Notice Bylaw Restrictions. In recent years, companies have adopted intricate advance bylaw notice provisions which place burdens on activists seeking to nominate directors. The following, excerpted from a memo by a law firm which specializes in representing hedge funds in activist situations, discusses the bylaws now being written:

SECOND GENERATION ADVANCE NOTIFICATION BYLAWS
Marc Weingarten & Erin Magnor
Schulte Roth & Zabel
March 2009

IN THE SPRING 2005 ISSUE of Activist Investing Developments, we wrote about the special bylaw provisions regulating the ability of shareholders to nominate directors or place items on the agenda for consideration at a company's annual or special meeting or by consent, typically referred to as advance notification bylaws ("ANBs"). At the time,

---

[9] *Yucaipa American Alliance Fund II, L.P. v. Riggio,* 1 A.3d 310 (Del. Ch. 2010), aff'd by *Yucaipa American Alliance Fund II, L.P. v. Riggio,* 15 A.3d 218 (Del. 2011).

[10] Charles Nathan, *Adoption of Poison Pill to Deter Activist Investor Opposition to Negotiated Mergers,* M&A COMMENTARY, LATHAM & WATKINS, February 2011, available at http://corpgov.law.harvard.edu/2011/03/04/adoption-of-poison-pill-to-deter-activist-investor-opposition-to-negotiated-mergers/.

most ANBs were straightforward. They typically advanced the date by which a shareholder was obligated to notify the company to 60 or 90 days prior to the expected meeting date. These ANBs, or First Generation ANBs, also typically required the proponent shareholder to include in the notification the same basic information about the shareholder, and if applicable the nominees, as required by the proxy rules.

More recently, however, many companies, at the urging of counsel "defending" against activist investors, have adopted new forms of ANBs, or Second Generation ANBs, that demand far more extensive disclosure from, and in some cases purport to establish eligibility qualifications for, proponent shareholders. These ANBs have been expanded to include not only longer advance notice requirements, but also requirements for the completion of company-drafted director nominee questionnaires, submission of broad undertakings by nominees to comply with company "policies," minimum size and/or duration of holding requirements, continuous disclosure of derivative positions, disclosure of otherwise confidential compensation information, and even information regarding shareholders with whom the proponent has merely had conversations regarding the company.

Advance Notice Periods

In our prior article, we noted that courts had determined that 90-day advance-notice requirements had become commonplace Since then, some companies have adopted ANBs requiring notice of 150, or even 180, days prior to the annual meeting (in some cases keyed off the mailing date of the prior year's proxy statement).

Company-Drafted Questionnaires and Undertakings

Many companies have adopted Second Generation ANBs that require shareholder nominees to complete and submit company-prepared director questionnaires along with the nomination notification. The nominating shareholder is required to request a copy of the questionnaire from the corporate secretary, in effect pushing the advance notification deadline even further back by giving the company even earlier notice of a potential contest.

The questionnaire requirement is generally a pointless waste of time. ANBs already uniformly require a nominating shareholder to include in its notice all information with regard to itself and its nominees that would be required to be disclosed in a proxy statement, which includes information about the nominees' shareholdings, backgrounds and any relationships they may have with the company. The questionnaire generally will yield no additional relevant information. But so long as the company uses the same form for shareholder-proposed nominees as for its own candidates, without adding burdensome or troublesome questions targeted to frustrate shareholder nominations, the questionnaire requirement is merely an annoyance but not legally objectionable.

Many companies also now require, as a condition of eligibility, that shareholder-proposed director nominees agree to various undertakings. They may have to sign an agreement that they will not join in voting agreements, that they will not enter into undisclosed indemnification or compensation agreements, and that they will comply with all company policies and guidelines applicable to directors, which may include subjects such as corporate governance, conflicts of interest, confidentiality and stock ownership.

Minimum Holding Periods and Levels of Ownership

Currently, under Rule 14a–8 of the Securities Exchange Act of 1934, in order to be eligible to submit a proposal to be included on a company proxy card, a shareholder must have continuously held, for at least one year prior to the date the proposal is submitted, a minimum of $2,000 in market value, or 1%, of the company's securities entitled to be voted on the proposal. Such a requirement is justified on the basis that the company is being put to expense and burden (albeit minimal), in including these proposals in its proxy materials, and should not have to do so for frivolous or harassing shareholders with de minimus or short-term holdings. Regardless of the merits of such rationale, it has no applicability where the shareholder utilizes its own proxy materials at its own expense. Any attempt to establish minimum holding periods or level-of-ownership requirements in ANBs as applicable outside the 14a–8 context should be an invalid and unenforceable limitation on shareholder rights. The adoption of such requirements as part of a federally mandated proxy-access regime similarly should have no bearing on shareholders seeking to take action utilizing their own proxy materials.

Disclosure of Derivative Positions

Another common trend in Second Generation ANBs is the adoption of requirements that the nominating shareholders disclose not only their beneficial ownership position but also any derivative positions, such as cash-settled swaps, that they may hold. Such holdings were not historically believed to confer beneficial ownership of any underlying counterparty-held shares, and so did not trigger the filing of a Schedule 13D when the shareholder held less than 5% in physical shares. As a result of the 2008 decision in *CSX Corporation v. The Children's Investment Fund (UK) LLP,* corporate counsel have decried this supposed "loophole" in the 13D rules, and have urged companies to require swap disclosure in their ANBs. These ANBs now include laundry lists of security interests that the shareholder must disclose, including options, swaps, warrants and convertible securities, as well as broad catch-all phrases that seek to capture any economic interest that the company has not specifically named.

Such increased disclosure requirements should not be problematic for shareholder proponents, or objectionable. While such disclosures may provide a company with more information than it would have based on SEC filings alone, the overall consequence of companies learning more about the holdings of proponent shareholders should not significantly affect the ability of proponents to nominate directors or propose business for shareholder meetings.

However, one prominent defense-side law firm has suggested to its corporate clients that they adopt an ANB disclosure requirement for derivatives that we believe has been designed as a trap to disenfranchise shareholders and should therefore be invalidated. Specifically, the bylaw provision requires that, once a shareholder has obtained a certain percentage of economic interest in the company (the drafters suggest 7.5% or 10% as possible threshold amounts), combining long ownership with any derivative or synthetic interest, the shareholder must continuously inform the company of its "interest" level, even if the shareholder at that time has no intention whatsoever of taking governance action. If the shareholder does not comply with the provision, the company will disqualify the shareholder from later seeking to take action at a shareholder meeting.

This provision would require shareholders to review, in advance, the bylaws of every company in which they intend to purchase shares to determine whether they contain any custom-designed ownership-reporting requirement, since failure to do so may result in forfeiture of their rights to nominate directors or propose other corporate action should they later wish to exercise them. If this type of bylaw were valid, shareholders would be subject to a crazy quilt of reporting requirements with differing thresholds at different companies, and forced to comply at a time when they aren't even seeking to take governance action, to avoid forfeiting fundamental shareholder rights. Rather than relying on uniform SEC-mandated disclosure requirements, every company would be making up its own rules and reporting regimes to trap unwary investors. Such provisions should not be upheld.

Acting in Concert

In September 2008, another defense-side firm published sample ANBs for its clients that define the term "Proposing Person" to include any person with whom the proposing shareholder or beneficial owner is "Acting in Concert," and require proponent shareholders to disclose any such persons. These proposed bylaws provide that a person should be deemed to be Acting in Concert with another person if "such person knowingly acts (whether or not pursuant to an express agreement, arrangement or understanding) in concert with, or towards a common goal relating to the management, governance or control of the Corporation in parallel with, such other person where (a) each person is conscious of the other person's conduct or intent and this awareness is an element of their decision-making processes and (b) at least one additional factor suggests that such persons intend to act in concert or in parallel, which such additional factors may include, without limitation, exchanging information (whether publicly or privately), attending meetings, conducting discussions, or making or soliciting invitations to act in concert or in parallel. . . . A person Acting in Concert with another person shall be deemed to be Acting in Concert with any third party who is also Acting in Concert with such other person."

The above "Acting in Concert" definition takes the federal securities law definition, which requires an agreement between the parties, and stretches it to cover mere consciousness of each other plus discussion. The plain intention of this provision is to force activist shareholders to disclose the identity of every other shareholder they've spoken to as a "concert party," or risk forfeiture of their shareholder rights. The provision is intended to chill protected and legitimate shareholder communication, encouraged by the SEC and enables companies to disenfranchise shareholders by arguing that adequate disclosure has not been made. The bylaw does nothing to create a more orderly process for shareholder nominations, or serve any other legitimate purpose of the company. Discouraging shareholders from sharing their viewpoints on the management or governance of a company is not a legitimate purpose, and shareholders should have the right to discuss the actions of a company in which they are invested without having to disclose the participants in all such conversations to the company simply in order to be eligible to exercise shareholder rights.

Compensation Information

Several companies have adopted Second Generation ANBs requiring disclosure of compensation arrangements and "any other material relationships" between the nominating shareholder and its affiliates and concert-parties, on the one hand, and its nominees and their affiliates and concert-parties, on the other hand.[11]

In addition to adopting advance notice bylaws, companies are also acting pre-emptively, before an activist appears on the scene, adopting other governance restrictions designed to deter both shareholder activism and hostile takeovers. These actions include limitations on shareholder

---

[11] Available at http://www.srz.com/files/News/9f6f664b-2067-4417-8285-09052737b28a/Presentation/NewsAttachment/49aee1dc-912e-4dd9-b030-0019bb7412e0/AIDev_Winter09_Bylaws.pdf (internal citations omitted).

action by written consent and removal of directors, special meeting restrictions, restrictions on replacement of directors, and voting requirements. Ultimately, though, a company can only make it more difficult for activists to prevail; it cannot prevent activist campaigns against it, nor can it prevent those campaigns from succeeding. In the absence of a dual-class share structure or other mechanism which concentrates the majority voting in the hands of a friendly force, companies will have to face the threat that an activist may bring a proxy contest—a contest that the activist may very well win.

The next two Subsections explore federal and state law issues with respect to shareholder activism.

E. FEDERAL ISSUES

The principal securities laws that affect activism should already be familiar: the Williams Act, mostly § 13(d) and its rules and regulations, and proxy regulations. The short swing profits rule under § 16 of the '34 Act also affects and potentially constrains shareholder activism.

1. SECTION 13(d)

Activists must take care to abide by § 13(d). The four principal respects in which they must be particularly mindful are:

Accumulations before Filing. If an activist is to be successful, it must accumulate a sufficiently large stake. Recall that filing is required within 10 days of acquiring a more than 5% stake, but that additional acquisitions can be made during the 10 day period. A hedge fund will often accumulate a 5% stake and accumulate stock during the ten-day window. In some circumstances, as discussed in Chapter IV.B.2 and 3, a hedge fund may enter into cash-settled derivatives in order to avoid triggering Section 13(d)'s filing requirements.

Group Issues. The activist will need to be careful in its interactions with other parties in order to avoid triggering the group requirements under Section 13(d) (as well as the group requirements under the provisions of any poison pill the company has in place). This will require careful monitoring and limiting of communications with other shareholders, particularly hedge funds.

Initial Filing. The activist will have to ensure that its initial filing, particularly the Item 4 disclosure, accurately reflects the activist's intent with respect to the company. This is often done as a coordinated effort to push the company towards quick action: the Schedule 13D will be filed on the same day a poison pen letter is sent to the issuer.

Updates. The Schedule 13D must be kept up to date. This can be a tricky task, as it requires that the filer amend the filing to record material events, such as negotiations with the company or a change in strategy or goals. The filing of the Schedule 13D thus marks a milestone in the campaign, as it will force any negotiations or communications with the company into the public sphere, and make them subject to these updating requirements.

These and other requirements under Section 13(d) are more fully discussed in Chapter IV.

2.   PROXY ISSUES

An activist faces two main issues under the proxy rules. First, the activist must avoid triggering the proxy rules through an inadvertent solicitation of shareholder votes. Attorneys for the activist will closely monitor communications to ensure that they do not appear to be a solicitation. In this regard, § 14(a)2–b(2) of the Exchange Act states that if "the total number of persons solicited is not more than ten," then the solicitation will not trigger the proxy filing requirements. This rule permits activists to freely speak to up to ten shareholders without concern that the proxy filing rules will be unintentionally triggered. The rule is particularly important in light of the typically concentrated nature of a public company's shareholder ownership, often allowing an activist to speak to shareholders holding a majority of a company's shares without fear of inadvertently triggering these requirements.

The second issue is compliance with the proxy rules, since these rules will also govern any actual proxy contest. These rules require the hedge fund to prepare, file and clear a proxy statement with the SEC. In addition, the proxy statement communication rules will apply, requiring certain communications to be filed with the SEC. As the proxy contest progresses, the hedge fund will also be required to update its proxy statement if there are any material changes. We discussed the legal requirements applicable to a proxy contest in Chapter VI.

3.   SECTION 16

Activists generally limit their stake to 10% of a target company in order to avoid application of § 16 of the '34 Act, the short swing profit rule. The rule applies to any officer, director or more than 10% shareholder of a company, and provides that any profit realized by such person from any purchase or sale of a security within any period of less than six months is recoverable by the company. These persons are also subject to a filing regime requiring them report their sales and purchases of a security.

An example helps explain the rule.

A 10.1% shareholder buys $1 million worth of shares on day 1. Three months later, the shareholder sells the shares for a

$500,000 profit. The $500,000 profit is forfeited to the company because the profit was realized within a six month period of time.

Hedge fund activists, in particular, value liquidity—the ability to sell their positions, rather than having to hold them. They prefer not to lock themselves into a position that they cannot sell for a six month period. Additionally, once the activist goes over the 10% level triggering application of § 16, it may be deemed to be an affiliate of the company and subject to the Securities Act affiliate resale restrictions. These restrictions combine to impose an effective, though not absolute, 10% limit on most activist stakes.

F. STATE ISSUES

Activists face two main state law issues. The first involves the internal organization of the company and the nomination procedures for a proxy contest. The second set of state law issues involves the fiduciary duties of a board in responding to an activist shareholder. *Unocal* is applicable to the company's response to an unsolicited takeover offer. In addition, because a shareholder vote is often involved, the "*Blasius* doctrine," which requires a "compelling justification" for board actions intending to interfere with the shareholder franchise, may apply.

1. INTERNAL ORGANIZATION ISSUES WITH SHAREHOLDER ACTIVISM

The solicitation of votes to remove and replace directors is governed by the federal securities laws. But the corporation's internal organizational documents and state statutory law govern the procedures for nomination and replacement of directors. These set the "rules of the road" for any director nomination and the proxy contest itself. As discussed above, companies are increasingly responding to shareholder activism by adopting sophisticated advance notice bylaws and other mechanisms to inhibit, and if possible, prevent, shareholder activism. The following case highlights the issues involved when there is a dispute over how those mechanisms work.

JANA MASTER FUND, LTD. V. CNET NETWORKS, INC.
Delaware Court of Chancery
954 A.2d 335 (2008)

CHANDLER, CHANCELLOR.

The storm of words in this case, which ranged in rhetorical heft from allusions to Lewis Carroll's Through the Looking Glass to incantations of "the bloody shirt of *Blasius*," has proven to be a tempest in a teapot. For reasons I explain below, I have determined that the unambiguous language of the bylaw at the heart of this case renders the bylaw inapplicable to nominations and proposals plaintiff JANA Master Fund seeks to put forth at the annual meeting of defendant CNET Networks. Consequently, I need not and do not address the hypothetical validity of the bylaw were it to operate as CNET contended it would.

I.   FACTUAL AND PROCEDURAL BACKGROUND

Plaintiff JANA Master Fund, Ltd. ("JANA"), an investment fund, owns with its affiliates approximately eleven percent of the outstanding common stock of defendant CNET Networks, Inc. ("CNET"). CNET, a Delaware corporation, is an interactive media company whose ventures include news.com, MP3.com, GameSpot, ZDNet, and Urban Baby. CNET has a staggered, eight-member board, and two of the current directors are up for reelection this year. Motivated by what it perceives to be poor financial performance on the part of CNET stock, JANA seeks to replace the two current directors, expand the size of the board from eight to thirteen, and nominate five individuals to fill the newly created positions. Such actions, if successful, will result in a new majority in control of the board of CNET.

On December 26, 2007, JANA wrote to CNET to advise the current board of its intention to solicit proxies from the other CNET shareholders in favor of its nominees and proposals and to request inspection of stocklist materials pursuant to section 220 of the Delaware General Corporation Law for the purpose of communicating with shareholders and for soliciting proxies. On January 3, 2008, CNET responded by letter and refused to provide the requested stocklist materials. CNET took the position that JANA failed to state a proper purpose because JANA's proposed proxy solicitation violated provisions of the company's bylaws. Specifically, CNET's letter cited JANA's "fail[ure] to comply with the provisions of the Company's bylaws which require a shareholder seeking to nominate candidates for director election or seeking to transact other corporate business at an annual meeting to beneficially own $1,000 of the Company's common stock for at least one year."

JANA reasonably assumed that this sentence referred to two sections of the CNET bylaws: Article III, Section 6, entitled "Nominations for Directors," and Article II, Section 3, entitled "Notice of Annual Meeting." Because JANA made its initial investment in CNET in October 2007, JANA will have held shares of the company for only eight months at the time of the meeting if CNET holds its annual meeting in June 2008 as expected. If the bylaw provisions apply to JANA's proposals and nominations, JANA will be unable to bring them to the attention of shareholders at the 2008 meeting.

On January 7, 2008, JANA filed a complaint with this Court that seeks a declaration either that the bylaws are inapplicable to JANA or that CNET's interpretation of the bylaws is invalid . . .

II. BYLAWS

Although JANA initially thought that CNET contended two separate provisions of the company bylaws operated to prevent JANA's proposals, CNET ultimately conceded that the "Nominations for Directors" bylaw of Article III, Section 6 did not apply. Instead, CNET argues that the so-called "Notice Bylaw" of Article II, Section 3 governs both shareholder nominations for directors and other shareholder proposals. This provision provides, in part:

> Any stockholder of the Corporation that has been the beneficial owner of at least $1,000 of securities entitled to vote at an annual meeting for at least one year may seek to transact other corporate business at the annual meeting, provided that such business is set forth in a written notice and mailed by certified mail to the Secretary of the Corporation and received no later than 120 calendar days in advance of the date of the Corporation's proxy statement released to security-holders in connection with the previous year's annual meeting of security holders (or, if no annual meeting was held in the previous year or the date of the annual meeting has been changed by more than 30 calendar days from the date contemplated at the time of the previous year's proxy statement, a reasonable time before the solicitation is made). Notwithstanding the foregoing, such notice must also comply with any applicable federal securities laws establishing the circumstances under which the Corporation is required to include the proposal in its proxy statement or form of proxy.

Thus, the language indicates that a shareholder must have owned stock in CNET for a full year before it "may seek to transact other corporate business" under this provision.

JANA contends that this provision does not or cannot apply to its nominations and proposals. First, JANA argues, this bylaw only applies to nominations and proposals made under Rule 14a–8 of the federal securities laws; i.e., this bylaw only governs nominations and proposals a shareholder wishes to have included on management's form of proxy. Because JANA intends to independently finance its own proxy materials, it claims this bylaw is inapplicable. Second, JANA suggests that if this bylaw can be read to apply, it is invalid under Delaware law because it is an unreasonable restriction on shareholder franchise.

CNET takes the opposite position, arguing that the bylaw is both applicable and valid. First, CNET cites the plain language of the provision, which it says contains nothing that limits the scope of the bylaw's requirements to proposals and nominations under Rule 14a–8. Second, CNET argues that this bylaw is valid because it was adopted by the shareholders of the corporation and reasonably serves a valid corporate purpose. . . .

IV. ANALYSIS

The language of the Notice Bylaw leads to only one reasonable conclusion: the bylaw applies solely to proposals and nominations that are intended to be included in the company's proxy materials pursuant to Rule 14a–8. One may parse the bylaw as follows: (1) notice of CNET's annual meeting will be provided to stockholders sometime between ten and sixty days before the meeting is held; (2) any stockholder who has owned $1,000 of stock for at least a year before the meeting may seek to transact other corporate business at the meeting; (3) to do so, that stockholder must send the CNET secretary notice of what business he/she plans to conduct a certain number of days before CNET needs to send out its proxy materials; and, finally, (4) in addition, such notice must also comply with the federal securities laws governing shareholder proposals a corporation must include in its own proxy materials. There are three related reasons I conclude this bylaw can be read only to apply to proposals under Rule 14a–8. First, the notion that a stockholder "may seek to transact other corporate business" does not make sense outside the context of Rule 14a–8. Second, it is reasonable to conclude this bylaw applies only to proposals shareholders want included on management's proxy materials because the bylaw sets the deadline for notice specifically in advance of the release of management's proxy form. Third, and most importantly, the explicit language of the final sentence makes clear that the scope of the bylaw is limited to proposals and nominations a shareholder wishes to have included on management's form of proxy.

A.   Shareholders "may seek" to bring proposals under Rule 14a–8; outside that rule, shareholders simply "may bring" such proposals.

. . .

[T]he real action in corporate elections is in the proxy solicitation process, and that process is heavily regulated by both state and federal law. More importantly, the solicitation process is extraordinarily expensive. The traditional proxy contest "involve[s] a fight between management and insurgent shareholders over the control of the corporation in the annual election of directors." Generally, although management is reimbursed for its proxy expenses from the corporate coffers, insurgent shareholders finance their own bid and can hope for reimbursement only if that bid is successful. Such a rule undoubtedly proves intimidating and likely discourages many shareholders from attempting to wage a proxy contest.

To attempt to give shareholders a greater ability to bring proposals without the cost associated with a fully waged proxy contest, the Securities Exchange Commission in 1942 adopted Rule 14a–8. The current version of Rule 14a–8 describes the circumstances under which management must include a shareholder proposal in its own proxy materials. Permitting a shareholder access to the company's proxy greatly reduces the cost that would otherwise be associated with a proxy fight, but the SEC gave and the SEC hath taken away. Rule 14a–8 may allow a shareholder access to management's proxy, but such access comes at a price. First, to be eligible to even submit a proposal for inclusion, a shareholder must own a certain amount of equity and have been a holder for a year. Second, a shareholder can submit only one proposal per year and the text of the proposal cannot exceed 500 words. Third, and most importantly, management may exclude a shareholder proposal for any of thirteen reasons enumerated in the Rule. Thus, although Rule 14a–8 does open the doors to management's proxy materials, management retains significant power as a gatekeeper. . . .

It is in this sense, then, that one understands the use of the phrase "any stockholder of the corporation . . . *may seek to transact* other corporate business at the annual meeting." To the extent a shareholder wishes to submit a proposal that will be reported in management's proxy, the shareholder *may seek* inclusion. To the extent a shareholder wishes to put a proposal before his or her fellow shareholders in the form of an independently financed proxy solicitation, however, the federal securities laws do not require the shareholder to seek management's approval.

The language itself is key here, particularly the predicate of the sentence: *may seek to transact . . . business.* The business of an annual meeting is the election and voting process. Thus, the bylaw says that a qualified shareholder may seek to transact an election—in other words, *may seek* to put an issue or nominations up for an election. The phrase "may seek" suggests that the shareholder must ask for permission or approval to make such a proposal. A shareholder essentially requests the inclusion of a proposal in management's proxy materials under Rule 14a–8; outside that rule, however, a shareholder simply makes a proposal. Thus, the "may seek to transact" language of the bylaw envisions use of Rule 14a–8. Because JANA intends to finance its own proxy solicitation, such language indicates that the bylaw does not apply to JANA's proposals.

B.   The bylaw establishes a deadline that would permit the corporation to include approved proposals in its form of proxy.

The second indication that the Notice Bylaw does not apply to JANA's independently funded proxy solicitation is that the bylaw establishes its deadline for notice by reference to the date on which the

CNET will mail its own proxy materials. Specifically, a shareholder seeking to make a proposal under the bylaw is required to inform the CNET corporate secretary via written notice "received no later than 120 calendar days in advance of the state of the Corporation's proxy statement" or, if there was no annual meeting the previous year or if this year's meeting date has changed significantly from the previous year, "a reasonable time before the solicitation is made."

In other words, this bylaw requires a shareholder bringing a proposal to give advance notice, but ties the deadline for that notice explicitly to the release of CNET's proxy materials. The most reasonable explanation for so requiring is that the bylaw is designed to allow management time to include the shareholder proposal in its own proxy materials. A similar requirement is established by Rule 14a–8 itself.

CNET's contention that this bylaw merely acts as an advance notice bylaw is undercut by this Court's previous encounters with advance notice bylaws. An advance notice bylaw is one that requires stockholders wishing to make nominations or proposals at a corporation's annual meeting to give notice of their intention in advance of so doing. This Court has upheld such bylaws in the past, but has warned that "when advance notice bylaws unduly restrict the stockholder franchise or are applied inequitably, they will be struck down." This Court cannot find a single example of a permissible advance notice bylaw that has set the notice required by reference to the release of the company's proxy statement. Although not dispositive, this suggests that the CNET Notice Bylaw is designed to govern shareholder proposals under Rule 14a–8 rather than to operate as an advance notice bylaw. CNET is correct that it has no other advance notice provision and that if the Notice Bylaw is interpreted to apply only to 14a–8 proposals, then "any of CNET's thousands of stockholders are free to raise for the first time and present any proposals they desire at the Annual Meeting." Although this may sound daunting, it is the default rule in Delaware. . . .

V. CONCLUSION

CNET's Notice Bylaw unambiguously applies only to proposals and nominations a shareholder wishes to have included in the corporate proxy materials. The language of the provision-construed as required by law-mandates this conclusion. First, the bylaw notes that a shareholder "may seek" to have an issue brought to a vote. The precatory nature of the bylaw recalls the inherently precatory nature of Rule 14a–8. Second, a shareholder who seeks to make a proposal under the bylaw must submit notice to the company in time to have the company include the proposal on its own form of proxy. This timing requirement only makes sense in the context of Rule 14a–8 and does not mirror any of the generally applicable advance notice bylaws that this Court has previously found valid. Finally, the last sentence of the bylaw purportedly grafts onto the bylaw all of the requirements of Rule 14a–8. Those requirements far exceed the default rules under Delaware law and were designed by the SEC only to apply in the context of Rule 14a–8. Under this Court's rules of construction favoring the free exercise of shareholders' electoral rights, I must read that final sentence to set the scope of the bylaw narrowly and, therefore, conclude that the bylaw does not apply outside the context of Rule 14a–8.

Because JANA does not request CNET to include its proposals or nominations in the corporate proxy materials, JANA need not comply with the Notice Bylaw's requirements. Because I have concluded that the bylaw does not apply to JANA in this circumstance, I will not consider its hypothetical validity were it to apply as CNET contended.

The *JANA* case concerned a bylaw requiring that a shareholder hold shares of a certain minimum value (at least $1000) for a specified period of time (at least one year) before being able to "transact other corporate business"—that is, bring forth a proposal for other shareholders to vote upon at the annual meeting. Holding period bylaws are popular with companies because they require hedge funds to operate on a far longer timeframe than the funds would like.

JANA sought to nominate directors and make several other proposals. It was going to prepare and distribute a proxy statement at its own expense. CNET argued that its bylaw required that JANA hold its shares for a full year before being able to nominate directors or make other proposals; it noted that JANA had owned its shares for far less than a year. But the court held that CNET's bylaw only applied to shareholder proposals made pursuant to Rule 14a–8, a rule which allows shareholders to include a proposal in the company's proxy statement if the rule's requirements are met.

Including a proposal in the company's proxy is far cheaper than the alternative, preparing and circulating another proxy statement. For that reason, corporate governance activists use the Rule 14a–8 route. But JANA was not using the Rule 14a–8 route—it was preparing and distributing its own proxy statement, at its own expense. [12]

The *JANA* opinion was based on the court's interpretation of CNET's bylaw. In the wake of *JANA*, though, a company could simply adopt a

---

[12] Rules adopted pursuant to authority granted in Dodd-Frank potentially allow shareholders to use management's proxy to nominate some directors. But Rule 14a–8 as amended pursuant to Dodd-Frank is not a substitute for proxy contests. Director nominations that are part of activist campaigns may not fall within the types of nominations allowed, and the expense and other disadvantages proxy fights entail are far less important factors for activists than for many other types of shareholders potentially seeking to nominate directors.

holding period bylaw that expressly applied to all shareholder proposals, regardless of whether they were proposals to be included in management's proxy under Rule 14a–8. Delaware has yet to rule on the appropriate parameters of such a bylaw, particularly the maximum holding period before nominations can be made, a matter we discuss further below.

2. FIDUCIARY DUTIES AND SHAREHOLDER ACTIVISM

To date, Delaware has yet to adopt a special fiduciary duty standard to govern board action in response to or anticipation of shareholder activism. Instead, the same standards that are applicable in an M&A transaction have been applied to shareholder activism: the *Unocal* standard governing board responses to potential threats to the corporation, and the *Blasius* standard, mentioned in the beginning of the *JANA* opinion above, governing board actions intended to interfere with the shareholder vote. *Blasius* provides for additional court scrutiny for such actions: there must be a "compelling justification" to interfere with the shareholder franchise. It had been thought for a time that no justification was sufficiently compelling. But sufficiently compelling justifications have been found in recent cases, as explained in a blog post by one of this book's authors.[13]

STRINE STRIKES AGAIN: MERCIER, ET AL. V. INTER-TEL
Steven M. Davidoff
August 21, 2007

On August 14 in *Mercier, et al. v. Inter-Tel,* [929 A.2d 786 (Del. Ch. 2007] Vice Chancellor Strine upheld the decision of a special committee to postpone a shareholder meeting to vote on an acquisition proposal which was made on the day of that meeting. In his opinion, Strine held that postponement was appropriate under the "compelling justification" test of *Blasius Industries, Inc. v. Atlas Corp.*, 564 A.2d 651 (Del. Ch. 1988), since "compelling circumstances are presented when independent directors believe that: (1) stockholders are about to reject a third-party merger proposal that the independent directors believe is in their best interests; (2) information useful to the stockholders' decision-making process has not been considered adequately or not yet been publicly disclosed; and (3) if the stockholders vote no . . . the opportunity to receive the bid will be irretrievably lost."

[Strine] uses the opportunity presented to attempt a rewrite of the *Blasius* standard. [T]he opinion [also] provides important guidance for a board wishing to postpone a shareholder meeting on an acquisition

---

[13] Available at http://lawprofessors.typepad.com/mergers/2007/08/strine-strikes-.html.

proposal. Ultimately, the decision increases a target board's ability to control an acquisition process and influence its outcome.

The summary facts are these: Inter-Tel had agreed to be acquired by Mitel Networks Corporation for $25.60 a share in a cash merger. A competing proposal was put forth for a recapitalization of Inter-Tel by the founder of the company who was also a director. Institutional Shareholder Services and several shareholders also subsequently came out in opposition to the Mitel merger. Faced with certain defeat, the special committee of the board of Inter-Tel voted on the actual day of the meeting to postpone it in order to attempt to persuade sufficient shareholders to change their vote. In the postponed meeting, the shareholders voted to approve the merger based in part on the changed recommendation of ISS and subsequent deteriorated financial condition of Inter-Tel.

First, the technical points in the opinion concerning the shareholder meeting postponement:

1. The board here "postponed" the meeting rather than adjourning it once it had been convened. The Delaware General Corporation Law does not address this practice, but practitioners have generally believed that this is permissible. Strine's acceptance of this postponement without comment in his opinion implicitly confirms this. This, together with Strine's ultimate holding, opens up a wide technical loop-hole for future boards to "postpone" shareholder meetings when faced with an uncertain vote rather than adjourning them. Given today's market volatility and the uncertainty behind a number of deals, expect this option to be exercised in the near-future (e.g., a likely candidate is Topps).

2. Inter-Tel ultimately set the new shareholder meeting date twenty days after the old one. The Delaware long form merger statute (DGCL 251(c)) requires twenty days' notice prior to the date of the meeting. The opinion thus leaves the question open whether a postponed meeting is a new one for these purposes such that the full twenty days' notice period starts anew.

3. Inter-Tel's proxy had included a provision granting the board the power to "adjourn or postpone the special meeting" to solicit more proxies. This provision was included due to informal SEC proxy requirements that shareholders must approve any adjournment. In the case of Inter-Tel there were insufficient votes voting to adjourn the meeting. In footnote 38 of the opinion, Strine stated that "[i]f the

special meeting had actually been convened, Inter-Tel's bylaws would seem to have required stockholder consent to adjourn." Section 2.8 of Inter-Tel's bylaws states that "The stockholders entitled to vote at the meeting, present in person or represented by proxy, shall have the power to adjourn the meeting form time to time." Thus, Inter-Tel side-stepped this dilemma through a postponement. Note that a separate bylaw would have been required to give the Chair of the meeting power to adjourn the board in the absence of the necessary shareholder vote.

Now for the more interesting part, the doctrinal issues:

... Strine ... then concluded by stating that the *Blasius* approach should be "reserved largely for director election contests or election contests having consequences for corporate control." Here, Strine judicially constricted the reach of *Blasius* from that decision itself and the Delaware Supreme Court's decision in *MM Companies, Inc. v. Liquid Audio, Inc.*, 813 A.2d 1118 (Del. 2003) which speak of applying the standard to board actions which have "the primary purpose of interfering with or impeding the effective exercise of a shareholder vote." Accordingly, his holding here may not be one the Delaware Supreme Court ultimately agrees with.

Strine then attempted to recast *Blasius* as interpreted by *Liquid Audio* itself:

Although it does not use those precise words, *Liquid Audio* can be viewed as requiring the directors to show that their actions were reasonably necessary to advance a compelling corporate interest. ... Consistent with the directional impulse of *Liquid Audio*, I believe that the standard of review that ought to be employed in this case is a reasonableness standard consistent with the *Unocal* standard.

Strine ... concludes by applying this "compelling justification" standard to the facts at hand to find that the following factors were sufficient to justify a same-day meeting postponement: (i) ISS's suggestion that it might change its negative recommendation if it had more time to study recent market events (including the debt market's volatility and the bidder's refusal to increase the consideration), (ii) the founder's competing proxy proposal for a recapitalization that was still being reviewed by the SEC, and (iii) the desire to announce the company's negative second-quarter results. Strine found that the directors acted with "honesty of purpose" and noted that they did not have any entrenchment motive because they would not serve with the surviving entity. Thus, the *Blasius* standard was satisfied and the plaintiff's request for a preliminary injunction of the merger denied.

. . . [P]erhaps the most interesting point in the opinion was Strine's observations on arbitrageurs and their effect on acquisition proposals. Here, the board had specifically based its postponement in part to permit arbitrageurs more time to increase their positions so as to vote in favor of the merger, though, ultimately it appears that they did not effect the vote. Strine addressed this issue by specifically refusing to:

> premise an injunction on the notion that some stockholders are 'good' and others are 'bad short-termers'. . . .

And while Strine left open the door for future challenges if arbitrageurs do indeed [a]ffect the outcome in such circumstances, the difficulty of proving who are the shareholders voting may open a small gate here for undue influence. Hopefully, this is a gate that the Delaware courts will police thoroughly so as to prevent boards from unduly shifting a shareholder vote.

---

a.   *Third Point v. Ruprecht*

The following case discusses how *Unocal* and *Blasius* have been applied in the shareholder activism context. The issue in the case is the poison pill Sotheby's adopted to fend off Dan Loeb's Third Point and another hedge fund, Marcato Capital Management. Marcato also took a position in Sotheby's but did not launch a proxy contest, perhaps preferring to "free-ride" off the work of Third Point and Mr. Loeb.

THIRD POINT LLC v. WILLIAM F. RUPRECHT, ET AL.

Delaware Chancery Court
C.A. No. 9469–VCP 2014 WL 1922029 (May 2, 2014)

PARSONS, VICE CHANCELLOR.

This action arises from a corporation's alleged misuse of a stockholder rights plan. In response to an apparent threat posed by increasing hedge fund activity in its stock, the corporation adopted a rights plan that would be triggered at a lower percentage of ownership for those stockholders who file a Schedule 13D with the U.S. Securities and Exchange Commission ("SEC") than those stockholders who file a Schedule 13G. The rights plan has remained in full force since its adoption despite at least one entity, the primary plaintiff in this litigation, having sought a waiver from certain of its requirements.

The primary plaintiff is an activist hedge fund and stockholder of the corporation. According to the hedge fund, the corporation's board violated their fiduciary duties by adopting the rights plan and refusing to provide it with a waiver from the rights plan's terms, so that the Board could obtain an impermissible advantage in an ongoing proxy contest with the hedge fund.

In response, the defendant directors, who comprise the corporation's board, assert that, at all relevant times, the hedge fund posed a number of different legally cognizable threats to the corporation, and that the board responded proportionately to those threats in both adopting the rights plan and refusing to grant the hedge fund a waiver from certain of its provisions. The defendants also argue that the rights plan's two-tiered structure is reasonable based on the source of the threats to the corporation.

This matter is before me on the plaintiffs' motion for a preliminary injunction. The plaintiffs seek to enjoin the corporation's annual meeting, which is scheduled to take place on May 6, 2014, until an expedited trial can be conducted to determine the merits of the challenged board actions.

. . .

11. The terms of the Rights Plan

By its own terms, the Rights Plan expires in one year unless it is approved by a stockholder vote. Nothing in the Rights Plan, however, appears to prohibit the Board from re-adopting it in whole or in part after it expires. In addition, the Rights Plan contains a "qualifying offer" exception, in which the Rights Plan will not apply to an "any-and-all" shares offer for the Company that cashes out all Sotheby's stockholders and gives them at least 100 days to consider the offer.

Of greater relevance to the current litigation, however, is the Rights Plan's two-tiered structure. Under the Rights Plan's definition of "Acquiring Person," those who report their ownership in the Company pursuant to Schedule 13G may acquire up to a 20% interest in Sotheby's. A person is eligible to file a Schedule 13G only if, among other things, they have "not acquired the securities with any purpose, or with the effect of, changing or influencing the control of the issuer, or in connection with or as a participant in any transaction having that purpose or effect" and they own less than 20% of the issuer's securities. All other stockholders, including those who report their ownership pursuant to Schedule 13D, such as Third Point are limited to a 10% stake in the Company before triggering the Rights Plan or "poison pill."

. . .

15. Third Point requests a waiver of the 10% trigger

On March 13, 2014, the Company announced that Dodge [a director of Sotheby's] would not stand for reelection at the upcoming annual meeting. The same day, Third Point again amended its Schedule 13D, revealing that it owned, directly or beneficially, 9.62% of Sotheby's stock.

In addition, Third Point sent a letter to Sotheby's requesting that the Company grant it a waiver from the Rights Plan's 10% trigger, and allow it to purchase up to a 20% stake in the Company.

Also that same day, Ruprecht [Sotheby's CEO] and McClymont [Sotheby's CFO] met with Tom Hill of Blackrock. Hill recommended that Sotheby's settle for two seats with Loeb because he was "going to win." Hill also told Ruprecht and McClymont that "I really like Marcato, he is very smart, and while Dan's current position is polar opposite to Mick's, that won't last and he will change his mind." Ruprecht did not "have a conclusion" based on his meeting with Hill.

The Board met six days later on March 19 to, among other things, receive an update from its advisors about "possible voting outcomes" in the ongoing proxy contest with Third Point and to consider Third Point's waiver request. As to the proxy contest, Morrow [Sotheby's proxy solicitor] expressed the view that in the likely event that ISS, an influential proxy firm, supported Third Point, the proxy contest would be "a dead heat." Goldman agreed with Morrow's assessment and described the proxy contest as "a very close race." The Company's third proxy-related advisor, CamberView, also agreed and noted that "investors could perceive there to be compelling arguments on both sides."

According to the meeting minutes, which not unexpectedly appear to have been prepared by Sotheby's lawyers and which were finalized after this litigation began:

> Mr. McClymont updated the Board on a conversation that he had had with Mr. Loeb regarding [the waiver] letter. The directors discussed among themselves and with their advisors the Board's rationale for putting the Rights Plan in place in October 2013: the Board's determination that the rapid accumulation of shares by Marcato and Third Point constituted a threat to the Company's corporate policy and effectiveness and might be evidence of an attempt to achieve a change in effective control of the Company without having to pay any premium to shareholders. The directors then considered whether the same rationale still applied in determining how to respond to Third Point's request. With its advisors, the Board considered the basis for the Rights Plan in the context of Third Point's letter and discussed at length whether Third Point and other activist investors continued to pose a threat to corporate policy and effectiveness and a risk of creeping control. The Board reviewed the interactions over the past eight months between Sotheby's, on the one hand, and Third Point and Mr. Loeb, on the other, including the risk that Third Point could obtain "negative control" or effectively a controlling influence without paying a

premium with respect to certain matters if it achieved a 20% stake. . . . The Board considered Mr. Brownstein's advice and ultimately concluded that nothing had changed that would warrant a change in the Rights Plan, including the exemption requested by Third Point.

[The opinion then discusses deposition testimony of Sotheby's director Taylor, which told "somewhat of a different story:" that the proxy advisors had advised Sotheby's that if Third Point did not have a 20% stake, it was "totally up in the air" who would win a proxy contest, but that with a 20% stake, Third Point likely would win the contest, so that denying the waiver request was, while not "per se" about the board seats, it was "about the control and the seats are part of that."]

. . .

Two days later, on March 21, 2014, Sotheby's notified Third Point that the Board had denied its request to waive the 10% trigger.

. . .

The fundamental dispute between the parties in this litigation is whether Sotheby's Board breached its fiduciary duties either: (1) in adopting the Rights Plan in October 2013; or (2) by refusing to grant Third Point a waiver from the Rights Plan's 10% trigger in March 2014. As a threshold issue, however, I must determine the proper legal standard under which to analyze the conduct of Sotheby's Board.

A. Reasonable Probability of Success on the Merits

1. The legal standard

a. *Unocal* provides the proper legal framework for this dispute

Nearly thirty years ago, in the seminal case *Moran v. Household International, Inc.*, the Supreme Court validated the concept of a rights plan. In reaching that conclusion, the Supreme Court's analysis was guided by, and in accordance with, the teachings of its then-recent decision in *Unocal Corp. v. Mesa Petroleum Co.* Since *Moran,* both this Court and the Supreme Court have used Unocal exclusively as the lens through which the validity of a contested rights plan is analyzed. This includes cases in which a rights plan has been used outside of the hostile takeover context. Thus, it is settled law that the Board's compliance with their fiduciary duties in adopting and refusing to amend or redeem the Rights Plan in this case must be assessed under *Unocal.*

b. It is possible, but unlikely, that *Blasius* nevertheless may be implicated within the *Unocal* framework in this case

"Famously, and under very unusual facts, [the case of] *Blasius Industries, Inc. v. Atlas Corp.* held that the board of directors must provide a 'compelling justification' for its actions where the board acted 'for the primary purpose of interfering with the effectiveness of a stockholder vote.' " In *MM Cos. v. Liquid Audio, Inc.*, the Supreme Court reemphasized that "the *Blasius* and *Unocal* standards of enhanced judicial review ('tests') are not mutually exclusive." The Court held that the "compelling justification" standard set out in *Blasius* could be applied within the *Unocal* framework, but only where " 'the primary purpose of the board's action is to interfere with or impede exercise of the shareholder franchise and the shareholders are not given a full and fair opportunity to vote' effectively." The Court noted specifically, however, that because of its strict criteria, the "compelling justification" standard announced in *Blasius* "is rarely applied either independently or within the *Unocal* standard of review."

In that regard, Plaintiffs have not cited to any case in which this Court or the Supreme Court has invoked *Blasius* to examine a rights plan. There are any number of possible explanations for this dearth of authority, including, but not limited to, that: (1) no Delaware court has ever found that a board of directors adopted a rights plan for the "primary purpose" of interfering with or impeding the exercise of the stockholder franchise; (2) while rights plans can interfere with the franchise, they do not do so in the manner that *Blasius* was concerned with so long as a proxy contest remains a viable option; or (3) to the extent a stockholder rights plan does adversely affect the franchise, that circumstance is adequately dealt with under the *Unocal* standard such that application of *Blasius* has proven unnecessary. Therefore, although *Blasius* might have some theoretical application to the facts of this case, it appears that, based on the relevant precedent, or more precisely, the lack thereof, *Unocal* provides the appropriate framework.

c. The *Unocal* standard

The well-known *Unocal* standard consists of two prongs. The first is "a reasonableness test, which is satisfied by a demonstration that the board of directors had reasonable grounds for believing that a danger to corporate policy and effectiveness existed." In other words, a board must articulate a legally cognizable threat. This first prong "is essentially a process-based review." "Directors satisfy the first part of the *Unocal* test by demonstrating good faith and reasonable investigation." A good process standing alone, however, is not sufficient if it does not lead to the finding of an objectively reasonable threat. "[N]o matter how exemplary the board's process, or how independent the board, or how reasonable its investigation, to meet their burden under the first prong of *Unocal* defendants must actually articulate some legitimate threat to corporate policy and effectiveness."

The second prong of *Unocal* is a "proportionality test, which is satisfied by a demonstration that the board of directors' defensive response was reasonable in relation to the threat posed." Proportionality review itself consists of two parts. First, the Court must consider whether a board's defensive actions were "draconian, by being either preclusive or coercive." Next, if the board's response to the threat was not draconian, the Court then must decide whether its actions fell "within a range of reasonable responses to the threat" posed. The defendant board bears the burden of proving the reasonableness of its actions under *Unocal*.

2. The October 2013 adoption of the Rights Plan and the March 2014 refusal to grant Third Point a waiver

As *Moran* makes clear, the Board's decision to adopt the Rights Plan in October 2013 and its subsequent election to refuse to provide Third Point with a waiver from the plan's conditions each independently must pass muster under *Unocal*.

a. The October 2013 adoption of the Rights Plan

1. Plaintiffs do not have a reasonable probability of success as to the first prong of *Unocal*

Plaintiffs here make no serious argument that the Sotheby's Board will be unlikely to meet its burden of demonstrating that it conducted a good faith and reasonable investigation into the threat posed by Third Point. The Board undeniably is comprised of a majority of independent directors. In addition, it is undisputed that the Board retained competent outside financial and legal advisors, which it appears to have utilized and relied on frequently. "The presence of a majority of outside directors, coupled with a showing of reliance on advice by legal and financial advisors, 'constitute[s] a prima facie showing of good faith and reasonable investigation.'"

Having determined that the Board probably can demonstrate on a full record that it conducted the requisite investigation, the next relevant inquiry is whether the Board determined that Third Point presented an objectively reasonable and legally cognizable threat to Sotheby's. While the Board has asserted that, at all relevant times, Third Point has presented a multitude of threats to the Company, for purposes of the October 2013 adoption, I need focus only on one: "creeping control." At the time the Board elected to adopt the Rights Plan in October 2013, it had several hedge funds accumulating its stock simultaneously, and at least as to Third Point, the accumulation was occurring on a relatively rapid basis. The Board also was informed by its advisors that it was not uncommon for activist hedge funds to form a group or "wolfpack," for the purpose of jointly acquiring large blocks of a target company's stock. Based on these facts, and the profiles of Third Point and Marcato presented to the Board in materials prepared by its financial and legal advisors, I cannot conclude that there is a reasonable probability that the Board did not make an objectively reasonable determination that Third Point posed a threat of forming a control block for Sotheby's with other hedge funds without paying a control premium. That is, on the record before me, there is sufficient support for the Board's assertion that its good faith investigation led it to determine that Third Point posed a legally cognizable threat, and I consider that threat objectively reasonable. Thus, Plaintiffs have not demonstrated a reasonable probability of success with respect to the first prong of the *Unocal* analysis for the October 2013 adoption of the Rights Plan.

2. The "primary purpose" of the October 2013 adoption of the Rights Plan was not to interfere with the stockholder franchise

For the reasons stated previously, the role of *Blasius* in the stockholder rights plan context is not entirely clear. Nevertheless, I address Plaintiffs' argument regarding the Board's intent in adopting the Rights Plan because, at a minimum, the use of the *Unocal* standard is intended to "smoke out" impermissible pre-textual justifications for defensive actions.

On this truncated record, there is sufficient evidence to support a reasonable inference that the Company has been concerned with the prospect of a proxy fight with an activist stockholder since the Summer of 2013. But the facts here do not support the conclusion that Plaintiffs have a reasonable probability of demonstrating that the Board adopted the Rights Plan in October 2013 for the primary purpose of interfering with the franchise of any stockholder, including Third Point, several months later. As stated previously, the Company was facing a rapid increase in hedge fund ownership in its stock that at least one Sotheby's insider believed was "collusive." Based on the advice of its outside legal and financial advisors, it appears, at least at this stage of the proceedings, that the Company believed certain hedge funds were attempting to gain effective control of the Company without paying a premium, and that it was objectively reasonable for the Company to perceive that threat. Because it is reasonably likely that the Board will be able to show that they were motivated to adopt the Rights Plan in response to this control threat and that "any effect of electoral rights was an incident to that end," Plaintiffs have not shown that it is reasonably probable that Plaintiffs will be able to establish that interference with the franchise was a major, let alone primary, purpose behind the Board's decision.

. . .

Because Plaintiffs do not have a reasonable probability of demonstrating the Board acted with animus or an entrenchment motive in adopting the Rights Plan, it begs the question, what end would be served by a course of action taken for the primary purpose of disenfranchising Third Point and Sotheby's other stockholders? The fact that this question remains unanswered at this point militates against the conclusion that the Board acted with the requisite improper "primary purpose" that would be necessary for the Board's actions to have to pass muster under the compelling justification standard set forth in *Blasius*.

Finally, the apparent effect of the Rights Plan itself also weighs against a conclusion that there is a reasonable probability that Plaintiffs can show it was adopted for the primary purpose of interfering with the stockholder franchise. As stated by Chief Justice Strine, then writing as Vice Chancellor in *Mercier v. Inter-Tel*:

> In prior decisions, this court has decided that because board action influencing the election process did not have the effect of precluding or coercing stockholder choice, that action was not taken for the primary purpose of disenfranchising stockholders. Because non-preclusive, non-coercive action did not have the primary purpose of disenfranchisement, the *Blasius* standard did not apply and thus no compelling justification for the board's action had to be shown. That is, the lack of disenfranchising effect provided that the trigger for the test was not pulled.

In this case, Plaintiffs have not shown a reasonable likelihood that they will be able to demonstrate that the Rights Plan is either coercive or preclusive. This Rights Plan does not contain any features that would outright force a stockholder to vote in favor of the Board or allow the Board to induce votes in its favor through more subtle means. Said differently, the Rights Plan does not impose any consequences on stockholders for voting their shares as they wish. Thus, the Rights Plan is not "coercive." Nor is the Rights Plan here preclusive. It is undisputed that Third Point's proxy contest with the Board is eminently winnable by either side. Therefore, even with a 10% cap on the number of shares it can acquire, there is no credible argument that Third Point's success in the pending proxy contest is "realistically unattainable." Because the Rights Plan at issue here is not coercive or preclusive, the effect of the Rights Plan is another consideration that weighs against finding that Plaintiffs have a reasonable probability of showing that the Rights Plan was adopted for the primary purpose of interfering with the stockholder franchise.

In sum, on the record before me I cannot conclude that Plaintiffs have a reasonable probability of being able to establish that the Board acted with the necessary "primary purpose" to invoke *Blasius*'s compelling justification standard. Accordingly, I turn to the issue of whether the adoption of the Rights Plan in October 2013 satisfies the second prong of the *Unocal* standard.

3. Plaintiffs have not shown they have a reasonable probability of success as to the second prong of *Unocal*

For the reasons stated supra, the Rights Plan at issue here is neither preclusive nor coercive. Because it is not draconian, proportionality review turns on whether the Rights Plan adopted by the Board falls within the "range of reasonableness." "The reasonableness of a board's response is evaluated in the context of the specific threat identified—the 'specific nature of the threat [ ] 'sets the parameters for the range of permissible defensive tactics' at any given time.'" When evaluating whether a defensive measure falls within the range of reasonableness, the role of the Court is to decide "whether the directors made a reasonable decision, not a perfect decision." Courts applying enhanced scrutiny under Unocal should "not substitute their business judgment for that of the directors" and if, on balance, "a board selected one of several reasonable alternatives, a court should not second-guess that choice."

In this case there is a reasonable probability that the Board will be able to show that in October 2013 it was faced with the legally cognizable and objectively reasonable threat that Third Point, alone or with others, could acquire a controlling interest in the Company without paying Sotheby's other stockholders a premium. Thus, the relevant inquiry is whether the adoption of the Rights Plan was a reasonable and proportionate response to that threat of creeping control.

I consider it reasonably probable that the Board will be able to meet its burden to demonstrate that the adoption of the Rights Plan in October 2013 was a proportionate response to the control threat posed by Third Point. Plaintiffs here have not litigated the issue of or whether a 10% rights plan comports with Delaware law. Because the entire Board, collectively, owns less than 1% of Sotheby's stock, a 10% threshold allows activist investors to achieve a substantial ownership position in the Company.

Based on the record before me, Plaintiffs have not shown that there is a reasonable probability that the Board will be unable to establish that the adoption of the Rights Plan in response to a legitimate control threat was a reasonable and proportionate response. As such, Plaintiffs have not demonstrated a likelihood of success on the merits of their claim that the Board breached its fiduciary duties in adopting the Rights Plan in October 2013. I turn next to the Plaintiffs' fiduciary duty claim pertaining to the Board's refusal to grant Third Point a waiver from the 10% trigger in March 2014.

b. The refusal to waive the 10% trigger in March 2014

1. Plaintiffs have not shown they have a reasonable probability of success as to the first prong of *Unocal*

As with the Board's October 2013 decision to adopt the Rights Plan, I find that the Board likely will be able to meet its burden of demonstrating that it undertook a good faith and reasonable investigation in response to Third Point's request to waive the 10% trigger in the Rights Plan. The majority of the Board still were independent and disinterested directors and had utilized their outside legal and financial advisors continuously since the adoption of the Rights Plan in October 2013. Thus, the key inquiry in terms of the first prong of Unocal is whether the Board determined there was an objectively reasonable and legally cognizable threat to the Company in March 2014 when Third Point made its waiver request.

This presents a much closer question than the Board's original decision to adopt the Rights Plan in October 2013. Had Third Point asked the Board to waive the Rights Plan in its entirety, rather than just the 10% trigger, based on the record before me, it would have been relatively easy to determine that Third Point posed at least the same threat to the Company that it did when the plan was adopted in the first place. That, however, is not what happened.

Third Point asked only for a waiver of the 10% trigger for Schedule 13D filers so that it could buy up to a 20% interest in the Company. Third Point did not ask, for example, that the Rights Plan be redeemed or that the Company waive the Rights Plan's proscription of concerted action. It is not clear, therefore, that the Board did or should have had the exact same concerns in March 2014 that it did in October 2013 when it adopted the Rights Plan. As a result, I am skeptical that there is a reasonable probability that the Board could establish that when it rejected the request for a waiver, it had an objectively reasonable belief that Third Point continued to pose a "creeping control" risk to the Company, either individually or as part of a "wolf pack."

Nevertheless, despite the change in circumstances, I am persuaded that Sotheby's has made a sufficient showing as to at least one objectively reasonable and legally cognizable threat: negative control. Plaintiffs are correct that the Delaware case law relating to the concept of negative control addresses situations in which a person or entity obtains an explicit veto right through contract or through a level of share ownership or board representation at a level that does not amount to majority control, but nevertheless is sufficient to block certain actions that may require, for example, a supermajority vote. The evidence currently available indicates that Sotheby's may have had legitimate real-world concerns that enabling individuals or entities, such as Loeb and Third

Point, to obtain 20% as opposed to 10% ownership interests in the Company could effectively allow those persons to exercise disproportionate control and influence over major corporate decisions, even if they do not have an explicit veto power. . . .

2. Plaintiffs have not shown they have a reasonable probability of success as to the second prong of *Unocal*

For the reasons already discussed supra, the Rights Plan does not implicate issues of preclusion or coercion. Consequently, the relevant inquiry is whether the Board's refusal to grant Third Point a waiver from the 10% trigger falls within the range of reasonableness. The Board's refusal to grant Third Point a waiver was a response to the threat that it posed to the Company of obtaining, at least, negative control and threatening corporate policy and effectiveness. The refusal to waive the Rights Plan's 10% trigger level is consistent with the Board's stated purposes, and the operation of the Rights Plan at the 10% level would help the Board achieve that end. While it is of course conceivable that there is some level of ownership between 10% and 20% that the Board could have allowed Third Point to increase its stake in the Company to without allowing it to obtain negative control, the 10% cap must be reasonable, not perfect. Based on the record before me, I find that Plaintiffs have not shown that there is a reasonable probability that the Board will be unable to demonstrate that its refusal to waive the 10% trigger in the Rights Plan was within the "range of reasonable" responses to the negative control threat posed by Third Point. Therefore, Plaintiffs have not established a likelihood of success on the merits of their claim that the Board breached its fiduciary duties by refusing to allow Third Point in March 2014 to acquire up to 20% of the Company's stock.

. . .

For the foregoing reasons, Plaintiffs' motions for a preliminary injunction are denied.

———

The Third Point decision applies the *Unocal* and *Blasius* standards to a poison pill in a shareholder activist situation. How would these standards apply to second-generation advance notice bylaws? As of this writing, the Delaware courts have not analyzed their validity under either *Unocal* or *Blasius*. Valeant and Pershing Square's Allergan campaign almost led to a decision on this point. A number of years before Valeant and Pershing Square announced their position in Allergan, Allergan's board adopted an advance notice bylaw which required a person nominating directors to provide two years of trading history and disclose all their associates—any person, property or entity in which they hold a stake of more than 10 percent. Allergan's bylaw treated each of these associates as also making the proposal, and their own holdings in Allergan and other information about them, including their officers and directors, had to be disclosed. As one of the authors of this book wrote, "[t]his is unbelievably broad, and as the proxy advisory firm Institutional Shareholder Services put it, 'a term which apparently extends to the L.L.C. through which the C.E.O. of one shareholder owns a vacation home.' "[14] It also would force institutional investors making a proposal to examine their investments and obtain this information, an almost impossible task for a big mutual fund like Fidelity which could have thousands of investment positions. Allergan ultimately dropped the bylaw after litigating the issue with Valeant and Pershing Square. The company did so after the judge in the case, Chancellor Bouchard, called it "a horse-choker of a bylaw" at a preliminary hearing.[15]

The Delaware courts will probably allow advance notice bylaw provisions which require information that is reasonably related to assessing a director nomination, even if such information is burdensome to collect, so long as the burden is not excessive. Bylaws which create impossible or near-impossible hurdles will be suspect. In addition to excessive information requirements, bylaws which require a long holding period may also be invalid. In a 2013 arbitration involving Commonwealth REIT, a Maryland real estate investment trust, two activists had challenged a bylaw that provided for a holding period of three years. One of the arbitrators was Bill Chandler, who in 2008 decided *JANA;* he retired from the bench in 2011. In dicta, Chancellor Chandler stated that he thought the bylaw was unreasonable and that under *Unocal,* grounds existed for striking it down.[16] How Delaware courts will treat advance notice bylaws remains uncertain, though it seems likely that they will closely scrutinize, if not invalidate, significantly long holding periods such as the one in Commonwealth REIT.

b. The Case of the Poison Put: *Pontiac* and *SandRidge*

In *Pontiac General Employees Retirement System v. John W. Ballantine,*[17] plaintiffs challenged as a breach of fiduciary duty a

---

[14] Steven M. Davidoff, *In Botox Maker Fight, Focus on Clever Strategy Overshadows the Goal,* N.Y TIMES, August 12, 2014, available at http://dealbook.nytimes.com/2014/08/12/in-allergan-fight-a-focus-on-clever-strategy-overshadows-the-goal/.

[15] Steven M. Davidoff, *Allergan-Valeant Fight Holds Lessons for All Corporate Shareholders,* N.Y. TIMES, September 18, 2014, available at http://dealbook.nytimes.com/2014/09/18/allergan-valeant-fight-holds-lessons-for-all-corporate-shareholders/.

[16] *In the Matter of an Arbitration Between Commonwealth REIT et al. v. Corvex Management L.P. et al,* AAA No 11–512–Y–276–13, November 18, 2013, available at http://www.bergermontague.com/media/421630/arbitration-order-re-CommonWealth-reit.pdf.

[17] *Pontiac General Employees Retirement System v. John W. Ballantine,* No. 9789–VCL. (Del. Ch. Oct 14, 2014), 2014 WL 6633634 (Del. Ch.) (Trial Transcript). *See also* http://blogs.law.harvard.edu/corpgov/2014/11/17/pontiac-general-employees-retirement-system-v-healthways-inc/ and http://www.sullcrom.com/pontiac-general-employees-retirement-system-v-healthways-inc.

company's inclusion in its loan agreement of a particular default provision. Under the provision, the company would be in default if there was a "change in control," where the definition of "change in control" included that a majority of the directors were not "Continuing Directors." The defined term "Continuing Directors" excludes those elected in a proxy contest. The name for this type of provision is a "dead hand proxy put." If the proxy contest yields a board the majority of which consists of directors who were elected as a result of the contest, the company is not only put into default, but must buy back its debt at face value if creditors so demand. The company may not have the money to make this repurchase, and it may have to pay creditors a significant amount of money to waive the default. The court refused to dismiss the case on the pleadings, allowing it to proceed, while noting that a plaintiff victory at trial was not assured.

A dead hand proxy put has, as the court noted, an "entrenching effect"—default on a loan is clearly an undesirable outcome, and a successful proxy contest for a large enough number of directors would yield such an outcome, thus making such contests less likely. Vice Chancellor Laster noted:

> Given the facts here, as alleged, including that there was a historic credit agreement that had a proxy put but not a dead hand proxy put, and then that under pressure from shareholders, including the threat of a potential proxy contest, the debt agreements were modified so that the change-in-control provision now included a dead hand proxy put, and considering that all of this happened well after Sandridge and Amylin [*Editor: both cases are discussed below; they concern board conduct regarding the election of dissident directors whose election might trigger a poison put*] let everyone know that these provisions were something you ought to really think twice about, I believe that, as pled, this complaint satisfies the requirement to survive a motion to dismiss.

> It may well be that there's ultimately no claim and that SunTrust [a defendant] wins. It may well be that they didn't aid and abet anything. But for pleading-stage purposes, what they are is they're a party to an agreement containing an entrenching provision that creates a conflict of interest on the part of the fiduciaries on the other side of the negotiation. And that provision arose in the context of a series of pled events and after decisions of this Court that should have put people on notice that

there was a potential problem here such that the inclusion of the provision was, for pleading-stage purposes, knowing.[18]

In *Kallick v. SandRidge Energy, Inc.,* which was mentioned by Vice Chancellor Laster in *Pontiac,* quoted above, the board approved a series of defensive measures, including a "poison put." These defenses were challenged by shareholders. In his review of the appropriateness of such measures , then-Chancellor Strine applied the *Unocal* standard..

KALLICK V. SANDRIDGE ENERGY, INC.

Delaware Court of Chancery
68 A.3d 242 (2013)

STRINE, CHANCELLOR.

The incumbent management and board of SandRidge Energy, an oil and natural gas business focusing on domestic exploration and production, face a serious proxy fight. A hedge fund, TPG-Axon ("TPG"), which holds a 7% stake in SandRidge, has launched a consent solicitation to destagger SandRidge's seven-member board by amending the company's bylaws, remove all the directors, and install its own slate. TPG claims that SandRidge's performance has been abysmal during the past six years, resulting in a performance that is extremely poor in comparison to other U.S. oil and gas companies. TPG also alleges that, during the same period, SandRidge's incumbent board has lavished compensation on the corporation's CEO, Tom Ward, paying him $150 million despite the company's subpar performance.

By its consent solicitation, TPG wishes to seat a new SandRidge board majority that has committed to change the management of the company and explore strategic alternatives for the company, including an asset sale. The incumbent board, whose members, along with SandRidge, are the defendants in this action, has resisted the consent solicitation and has energetically campaigned to convince SandRidge's stockholders not to give consents to TPG. Even further, it has tried to obtain revocations from stockholders who have given TPG consents. The incumbent board contends that TPG's slate is less qualified to run SandRidge than it is because TPG's nominees lack expertise in "upstream" oil and gas exploration and have no specific experience with the company's principal asset, a 2.2 million acre oil and gas play in Kansas and Oklahoma (the "Mississippian Play").

For present purposes, what is most relevant is that in originally opposing the consent solicitation, the incumbent board warned the

---

[18] *Pontiac General Employees Retirement System v. Healthways, Inc.,* C.A. No. 9789–VCL (Del. Ch. Oct. 14, 2014) (transcript ruling). *See generally* Daniel E. Wolf & Micheal P. Brueck, *Finding the Antidote—Addressing Poison Put Provisions in Debt Instruments,* KIRKLAND M&A UPDATE, available at http://www.kirkland.com/siteFiles/Publications/MAUpdate_060815.pdf.

stockholders that the election of TPG's proposed slate would constitute a "Change of Control" for the purposes of SandRidge's credit agreements simply because it involved the election of a new board majority not approved by the incumbent board, and that such a Change of Control would trigger the requirement in SandRidge's note indentures that SandRidge offer to repurchase its existing debt (the "Proxy Put"). That is, the incumbent board clearly told stockholders that if they chose to elect a new board majority, the Proxy Put would cause a material economic harm because SandRidge's lenders would have the right to put $4.3 billion worth of notes back to the company.

After taking that position, the incumbent board faced this litigation from the plaintiff, Gerald Kallick, a SandRidge stockholder who supports the TPG consent solicitation. Kallick argues that the incumbent board is breaching its fiduciary duties by failing to approve the TPG slate, which, under the indentures governing SandRidge's notes, would mean that the SandRidge stockholders could replace the incumbent board without triggering the Proxy Put. Because the incumbent board has been unable to identify any rational question about the integrity of the TPG slate, about their qualifications to serve as public company directors, or about the propriety of their motives, Kallick says there is no proper basis for the incumbent board to fail to approve them. At best, the incumbent board believes it is more qualified than the TPG slate, and believes that TPG's plans for SandRidge are not wise. Such mere differences in policy, says Kallick, are not a proper basis for failing to approve the TPG slate for purposes of the Proxy Put. Kallick therefore argues that the incumbent board should be enjoined from soliciting consent revocations until it approves the TPG slate, because otherwise it is able to inequitably exploit its incumbency to pressure voters to keep the directors in office simply to avoid the negative consequences of triggering the Proxy Put.

Since TPG first indicated that it would carry out a consent solicitation at the end of November last year, the incumbent board has wiggled and squirmed in order to avoid dealing with this litigation, or the discretion given it to approve the TPG slate for purposes of the Proxy Put. Facing Kallick's suit, the incumbent board assented to a schedule culminating in a preliminary injunction hearing. An order scheduling that argument was entered on February 7, 2013. But, having warned its stockholders twice in its SEC filings that triggering the Proxy Put would be "extreme" and "risky," the incumbent board then reversed direction, and stated in an 8–K the very next day that there was *no* danger posed by the Proxy Put. That was because SandRidge's debt was trading at prices above the repurchase price set in the indentures, and thus debtholders were not likely to tender at a below-market price. The record shows, however, that SandRidge's debt was trading well above par even when the incumbent board declared that triggering the Proxy Put would be "extreme" and "risky."

The incumbent board then sought to cancel the preliminary injunction hearing to which they just had assented, claiming that there was no material likelihood of harm to the company in not approving the TPG slate. But it failed to decide, one way or the other, whether it approved the TPG slate for purposes of the Proxy Put. That remains true as of today. As a default matter, therefore, the incumbent board has left the TPG slate unapproved. Likewise, although the defendants admit that credit markets can move quickly and although the defendants' estimates of the costs of refinancing the debt keep shifting, the defendants claim that the doubt their own disclosures have created over the consequences of voting for the TPG slate is too insubstantial for the court to worry that the electoral playing field has been unfairly tilted.

In keeping with this state's public policy of stringent policing of the fairness of corporate elections, this court's decision in *San Antonio Fire & Police Pension Fund v. Amylin Pharmaceuticals* made clear that a board deciding whether to approve directors for the purposes of a Proxy Put could not act consistently with its fiduciary duties by simply failing to approve any director candidates who ran against the incumbent slate. Rather, the incumbent board must respect its primary duty of loyalty to the corporation and its stockholders and may refuse to grant approval only if it determines that the director candidates running against them posed such a material threat of harm to the corporation that it would constitute a "breach of the directors' duty of loyalty to the corporation and its stockholders" to "pass[ ] control" to them. In other words, unless the incumbent board determined, by way of example, that the rival candidates lacked ethical integrity, fell within the category of known looters, or made a specific determination that the rival candidates proposed a program that would have demonstrably material adverse effects for the corporation's ability to meet its legal obligations to its creditors, the incumbent board should approve the rival slate and allow the stockholders to choose the corporation's directors without fear of adverse financial consequences, and also eliminate the threat to the corporation of a forced refinancing. Notably, absent any determination by the incumbents that the rival slate has suspect integrity or specific plans that would endanger the corporation's ability to repay its creditors, there is no harm threatened to the creditors by the election of the slate. Rather, the only "harm" threatened is that the stockholders will choose to seat a new board of directors. The incumbents' expected view that they are better suited to run the company effectively is, without substantially more, not a sufficient fiduciary basis to deny approval to their opponents.

Given that the incumbent board has admitted it has no basis to doubt the integrity of the TPG slate or the basic qualifications of that slate to serve with competence as the directors of a public company, the incumbent board is merely basing its refusal to make a decision on its contention that the incumbents are the better choice at the ballot box. Not only has the incumbent board failed to identify any threat the TPG slate poses to the company's creditors or ability to meet its legal obligations, its financial advisor, Morgan Stanley, has generously offered to pay off the existing debt holders and become the company's lender itself, if the TPG slate is elected. That is, Morgan Stanley told the board that its own financial institution would risk $4.3 billion lent to SandRidge even if TPG's slate controlled the board. The incumbent board's further contention that the SandRidge stockholders will be too stupid not to be confused if the board approves the TPG slate for the sole purpose of alleviating the risk of the Proxy Put is one premised on a view of stockholder cognition inconsistent with giving them a right to vote at all on important matters like elections and mergers. That self-serving, paternalist explanation cannot justify the doubt that the Proxy Put creates in an electoral contest in which each voting decision may turn out to matter immensely.

Having failed to exercise its discretion in a reasonable manner, the incumbent board should be enjoined from soliciting consent revocations, voting any proxies it received from the consent revocations, and impeding TPG's consent solicitation in any way until the incumbent board has approved the TPG slate. The equities here weigh heavily in favor of the stockholders' right to make a free, uncoerced choice. . . .

II. *Kallick's Motion For Injunctive Relief*

The incumbent board has refused to decide whether to approve TPG's slate for purposes of the Proxy Put, claiming that it would be confusing to the company's stockholders and detrimental to its position in the credit markets. As a result of the incumbent board's non-decision, the electorate must consider the potential risks in electing a new slate of directors, an event that depending on which version of the incumbent board's own shifting view of reality one embraces, would either be of no consequence or be one that has an "extreme" deal of financial risk and cost. . . . Kallick seeks (i) to enjoin the defendants from soliciting any consent revocations; (ii) to have any consent revocations obtained to date declared invalid; and (iii) to enjoin the defendants from taking any steps to hinder TPG's consent solicitation until they have complied with their fiduciary duties and have approved the TPG slate, or have explained in full why they will not approve it.

. . .

A. *The Incumbent Board's Unconvincing Justification For Its Refusal To Approve TPG's Slate*

In defense of its non-decision as to whether to approve the TPG slate, the incumbent board makes a variety of cursory arguments. I now analyze them and make findings of fact as to them consistent with the appropriate procedural standard, which requires me to determine, from the record before me, what would likely be the state of reality found to exist after trial. For reasons that may reflect the expedited nature of the case, but may also reflect the fact that the SandRidge board has engaged in inadequate deliberations concerning the Proxy Put, the record is decidedly spare. There are only two depositions in the record: one is of Daniel Jordan, a SandRidge director who is independent under New York Stock Exchange rules, and one is of Michael Johnson, a managing director at Morgan Stanley who is a financial advisor to SandRidge.

First, the defendants claim that the TPG slate does not consist of directors with sufficient energy industry experience.... [The portion of the case detailing specifics of the experience of the slate is omitted.]

Although the defendants admit that "five" of the directors in fact have "some" energy experience, they fault three of the five members for not having "upstream" oil and gas experience and the directors with upstream experience for not having experience with the Mississippian Play. Despite these very particular arguments, the incumbent board has no reason to doubt the integrity of the TPG slate, as Jordan admitted in his deposition:

Q: Did the board find out anything that would lead you to believe TPG-Axon's nominees are people of ill repute?

A: No. I mean, that's—that's—no.

Q: Did the board's internal investigation reveal that TPG-Axon's nominees were anything other than respected and well-accomplished business people?

A: I'm sure they are in their own fields. . . .

Taken as a whole, therefore, the record supports nothing more than the conclusion that the incumbent board, as expected, believes that it is managing the company in an optimal manner, that it has better qualifications than the TPG slate, that the TPG slate's plans for the company are not wise, and that the incumbents should therefore continue to run the company. In other words, the incumbent board has simply made the same determination that all incumbents who seek to continue in office make: we are better than the new guys and gals, so keep us in office. Such self-belief does not come close to a reasoned conclusion that the electoral rivals lack the integrity, character, and basic competence to serve in office. Nothing in this record indicates that any incumbent board member or incumbent board advisor has any reasonable basis to dispute the basic qualifications of the TPG slate.

Second, the defendants used a leading question at a deposition to elicit the concern from Jordan that the company would be sued by noteholders if they approved of the nominees in bad faith:

> Q: Now, if the board were to approve the TPG-Axon slate even though it believed that the election of that slate would be harmful to SandRidge, would it be possible that bondholders could sue the company for making that approval decision in bad faith?
>
> A: Yeah. That's possible. Absolutely.

But Jordan, while he was being examined by the opposing counsel, and before an hour-long break in the deposition, had already testified to a *diametrically opposite* conclusion:

> Q: Would approving TPG-Axon's director nominees for the limited purpose of the change of control provision violate any duties the company owes to its bondholders?
>
> A: *Violate any duties that we owe to our bondholders? Approving their slate? I don't think it does.*

Relatedly, the incumbent board suggests that if it approves TPG's slate, this approval would compromise the company's ability to obtain financing because, presumably, such lenders would charge a higher price for credit, perceiving SandRidge as a company that "circumvents" change of control provisions The sum and substance of the record support for this proposition is this testimony by Johnson, the incumbent board's financial advisor:

> Q: Would it be more difficult or expensive for a company like SandRidge to obtain financing without such a change of control provision?
>
> A: Yes.
>
> Q: If SandRidge were perceived as having approved the TPG-Axon slate simply in order to neutralize the change of control provisions in its debt instruments, could that have an effect on its ability to obtain financing in the future?
>
> [Objection.]
>
> A: It would—it would be highly likely in my opinion that it would have an impact on the price at which they could obtain financing. I'm not prepared to speculate on whether it would impact whether they could obtain financing or not.

But, before he gave that answer, Johnson had testified as follows:

Q: Would a change in control at SandRidge affect market conditions for their bonds?

A: No.

Q: And why is that?

A: The market conditions for the bonds are driven by factors that are separate from whether SandRidge has a change in control or not.

At the same time as the incumbent board is arguing that creditors will exact a penalty for SandRidge's approval of a dissident slate, it also now argues to the court that, if the Proxy Put is triggered, there will be no harm even if the company does have to refinance, because the froth has returned to the debt markets, credit is easy to obtain, providers are competing to lend, and there will be insubstantial costs to refinance. These arguments bring to mind one definition of genius, I suppose. But viewed more realistically, these are fundamentally inconsistent propositions put forward to justify the incumbents' refusal to make an approval decision, one way or the other. In that regard, the lengths to which the incumbents' loyal financial advisor would go to aid their litigation aims were great but constrained: he refused to directly answer if it would be "harmful" to SandRidge to elect TPG's nominees.

Notably, the incumbent board and its financial advisors have failed to provide any reliable market evidence that lenders place a tangible value on a Proxy Put trigger—not a change in board composition accompanying a merger or acquisition or another type of event having consequences for the company's capital structure, but a mere change in the board majority. In fact, the evidence in the record indicates that credit providers would be happy to keep lending to the company if the board changed majority. Johnson's own employer, Morgan Stanley has offered to refinance SandRidge's debt for a 1% fee if the board majority turned over. Thus, Johnson's suggestion that the incumbent board's approval of the TPG slate might have an effect on the price at which SandRidge could obtain financing is *inconsistent with his own presentation to the SandRidge board that Morgan Stanley would be happy to provide financing to SandRidge even if the TPG slate was in control.*

. . .

Taken as a whole, the record, such as it is, reveals the following. The incumbent board has no reasonable basis to conclude that the TPG slate is unqualified to serve with basic competence and integrity as the directors of a public energy company. The incumbent board has identified no specific threat that the TPG slate's plans have on the ability of

SandRidge to repay its creditors. To the contrary, its own current argument that the triggering of the Proxy Put is no longer an "extreme" financial risk, but a yawn, because lenders will be glad to cheaply refinance SandRidge's debt if the TPG slate wins, refutes any rational basis for the refusal to approve the TPG slate for purposes of relieving SandRidge of any harm from triggering the Proxy Put. Nonetheless, the board refuses to make a decision whether to approve the TPG slate for purposes of the Proxy Put, a protection that is supposedly for the benefit of the lenders, and thus leaves the corporation exposed to the potential for a mandatory refinancing of its $4.3 billion in long-term debt if the TPG slate is elected.

Regrettably, I am left with the impression that this condition of piquant ambiguity is one that the incumbent board, for tactical electoral reasons, finds of utility in its attempt to remain in power. That impression is reinforced by the shifts in position by the incumbents as this litigation has progressed, positions that seem more convenient than principled. In this context where the importance of the stockholders' right to choose is paramount, games-playing is not something our law takes lightly.

With those basic facts in mind, I turn to resolving the application before me, which is neatly framed by the parties' starkly different views of what standard applies to determining whether the incumbent directors have likely breached their fiduciary duties by failing to approve the TPG slate for purposes of the Proxy Put.

B.   *The Standard Of Review*

For their part, the incumbent board argues that the standard of review is the plain vanilla business judgment rule, which requires that their decision be approved if it can be attributed to any rational business purpose. Thus, the incumbent board argues for something as close to non-review as our law contemplates.

Not unexpectedly, Kallick comes playing the Sousa-inspired sounds of *Blasius,* arguing that the incumbents may only fail to approve the TPG slate if they can prove that there is a "compelling justification" for their decision. Kallick argues that, because the effect of the Proxy Put is to place a toll on the voting decision of the electorate, the primary purpose of such a provision is disenfranchising within the meaning of the *Blasius* standard. As readers familiar with *Blasius* are well-aware, that standard of review is a potent one and its express trigger was stated in correspondingly stark terms. For the *Blasius* standard to be invoked, the challenged action had to be "taken for the sole or primary purpose of thwarting a shareholder vote."] If that predicate was laid, then the defendants could only justify their actions by showing a compelling justification, a very high standard drawing on the closest scrutiny used in cases involving racial discrimination and restrictions on political speech.

For reasons I have explained elsewhere, and will not repeat in detail, *Blasius'* importance rests more in its emphatic and enduring critical role in underscoring the serious scrutiny that Delaware law gives to director action that threatens to undermine the integrity of the electoral process, than in its articulation of a useful standard of review to decide actual cases. Precisely because our law embraces a republican model giving directors substantial authority to use their own judgment while in office, it is vital that the stockholders have a genuinely fair opportunity to elect new directors.

But the standard of review *Blasius* offers does little to address situations like this, where a contractual provision cannot be said to have the "sole or primary purpose" of impeding the stockholders' vote, because it might have a legitimate purpose of protecting creditors who in fact insisted on its inclusion for their own good-faith reasons, but does have the obvious potential to tilt the electoral playing field toward the incumbent board.

For reasons I have previously explained, our Supreme Court's invocation of a flexible, intermediate standard of review—*Unocal*—to address situations where boards of directors make decisions that have clear implications for their continued control was explicitly designed to give this court the ability to use its equitable tools to protect stockholders against unreasonable director action that has a defensive or entrenching effect. By enabling the Court of Chancery to examine whether the directors taking actions have acted in a circumstantially reasonable way, the Supreme Court provided a responsible form of review that smokes out self-interest and pretext, by requiring boards that face the omnipresent specter of *Unocal* to justify their actions as reasonable in relationship to a threat faced by the corporation. This Court has followed the Delaware Supreme Court and applied *Unocal* in these situations with a special sensitivity towards the stockholder franchise.

By definition, a contract that imposes a penalty on the corporation, and therefore on potential acquirers, or in this case, simply stockholders seeking to elect a new board, has clear defensive value. Such contracts are dangerous because, as will be seen here, doubt can arise whether the change of control provision was in fact sought by the third party creditors or willingly inserted by the incumbent management as a latent takeover and proxy contest defense. *Unocal* is the proper standard of review to examine a board's decision to agree to a contract with such provisions and to review a board's exercise of discretion as to the change of control provisions under such a contract.

Of course, the mere fact that the court uses a heightened reasonableness standard does not mean that the directors will fail to satisfy it. A reasonableness standard is just that. But it does mean that the directors must comply with their *Unocal* duties by identifying a circumstantially proper and non-pretextual basis for their actions, particularly when their actions have the effect of tilting the electoral playing field against an opposition slate. Relatedly, *Unocal* implements, and does not displace, *Schnell*'s generalized insistence that any director action be in fact taken for a proper purpose. By smoking out the directors' reasons, *Unocal* surfaces the issues at stake, including the possibility of bad faith. With these thoughts in mind, I now explain why the defendants' actions cannot pass the *Unocal* test.

C. *The Incumbent Board's Actions Are Likely A Violation Of Its Fiduciary Duty*

Here, the directors have failed to demonstrate a reasonable justification for their refusal to consider whether to approve the TPG slate for purposes of the good faith standard of *Unocal.* In *Amylin,* this court made plain that the board's duty in exercising its discretion under such a contract was focused on the best interests of the corporation and its stockholders, and that its only duty to the creditors was to honor the implied covenant of good faith and fair dealing. The crucial issue for the board's determination is the board's obligation to act in good faith: as Vice Chancellor Lamb held, the board could approve the new slate if "passing control would not constitute a breach of the directors' duty of loyalty to the corporation and its stockholders." Because, as Vice Chancellor Lamb also noted, the failure to approve a new slate might "impinge on the free exercise of the stockholder franchise," and because a board that acts in good faith must seek to protect the stockholders' ability to make an uncoerced choice of directors, it follows that a board may only *fail* to approve a dissident slate if the board determines that passing control to the slate would constitute a breach of the duty of loyalty, in particular, because the proposed slate poses a danger that the company would not honor its legal duty to repay its creditors.

Thus, this court in *Amylin* focused on the nature of the Proxy Put as a provision giving the creditors protection against a new board that would threaten their legitimate interests in getting paid. Such situations could arise, for example, because the proposed new board consists of "known looters" or persons of suspect integrity. Or, the insurgent slate could have plans for the company posing a genuine and specific threat to the corporation and its ability to honor its obligations to its creditors that prevent the incumbent board from approving them in good conscience for purposes of the Proxy Put. By contrast, where an incumbent board cannot identify that there is a specific and substantial risk to the corporation or its creditors posed by the rival slate, and approval of that slate would therefore not be a breach of the contractual duty of good faith owed to noteholders with the rights to the Proxy Put, the incumbent board must approve the new directors as a matter of its obligations to the company and its stockholders, even if it believes itself to be better qualified and have better plans for the corporation than the rival slate. The stockholders, after all, have a fundamental interest in freely choosing for themselves who should constitute the board.

In other words, the duty of loyalty requires the incumbent board to exercise their contractual discretion with the best interests of SandRidge and its stockholders firmly in mind, to the extent that it can do so without breaching the very limited obligations it owes to its noteholders. The parties do not dispute that, under *Amylin,* the incumbent board has the power to approve of TPG's nominees without endorsing the dissident's slate and maintaining its ability to run its own campaign. Thus, it is undisputed that the incumbent board can neutralize any adverse consequences from the Proxy Put if TPG prevails in its proxy contest without signaling its support for the election of TPG's nominees. In this case, the corporation's best interest seems rather obvious, which is in letting its stockholders choose without fear of a compelled refinancing. From a purely financial standpoint, it is clear that SandRidge is not advantaged from being compelled to make an offer to redeem its long-term debt. There is only possible pain, and no possible gain, to SandRidge from triggering the Proxy Put.

Regrettably, as I have discussed, the thin and shifting arguments of the incumbent board do not persuade me that any legitimate interest of SandRidge was served by the board's failure to make an approval decision. Rather, the incumbent board's behavior is redolent more of the pursuit of an incremental advantage in a close contest, where a small margin may determine the outcome, than of any good faith concern for the company, its creditors, or its stockholders. That self-interested, tactical reason for withholding approval implicates *Amylin*'s basic premise because an "eviscerating" threat to the shareholder franchise exists when the board retains the power to approve the dissident slate, but refuses to exercise that power to protect itself or give itself an advantage in a proxy context. I therefore conclude that the board has likely acted with an absence of good faith and reasonableness inconsistent with their fiduciary duties. . . .

G. ASSESSING SHAREHOLDER ACTIVISM

Shareholder activism is highly influential—and highly controversial. There is a fierce debate about whether shareholder activism is economically beneficial for companies, capital markets, and our economy as a whole. To date, academic studies of the matter have mostly found that shareholder activism provides economic benefits to the companies targeted. One 2008 paper discussing hedge funds' activist campaigns from 2001–2006[19] "found that activism that targeted the sale of the company or changes in business strategy returned 8.54 percent and 5.95 percent, respectively," and "that hedge funds that regularly engaged in this type of activity or other hostile activity also experienced higher returns."

> Hedge fund activism was found to have other beneficial effects, such as overall improved performance, including increased return on assets and operating margins. It also resulted in reduced executive pay, the bête noire of the agency theorists. The 2007 paper found that the year before the hedge fund activity occurred, the target companies' average CEO pay was $914,000 higher than the average CEO compensation at the targets' peer companies. In the year after the hedge fund's dissident activity, CEO compensation was reduced to a level in line with the target's peer companies.[20]

This led stock prices of companies that were targeted by activists to increase; hedge funds engaging in these types of activities increased as well, both in number and in volume of assets under management.

Among the concerns expressed about shareholder activism are that hedge funds are focusing on the short term, and will seek to benefit themselves notwithstanding the effects on other shareholders. One suggested response has been that hedge funds should have "special fiduciary duties" to the target. But early statistics did not suggest that this was necessary.

> [T]he benefits for companies appear to be widespread. The . . . typical hedge fund position, a minority one on the board of directors, also provides a mechanism for oversight of hedge fund activities. The remaining majority directors can not only look out for the interests of the company but also prevent any private gains from accruing to the hedge funds' activities.[21]

A 2015 paper also found that shareholder activism provides economic benefits to shareholders. In *The Long-Term Effects of Shareholder Activism*,[22] Professor Lucian Bebchuk, a noted shareholder advocate, and Professors Alon Brav and Wei Jiang, the latter two also having been co-authors of the 2008 paper mentioned above, examine activist activity and

---

[19] Alon Brav, Wei Jiang, Frank Partnoy & Randall Thomas, *Hedge Fund Activism, Corporate Governance, and Firm Performance*, 63. J. FIN. 1729 (2008).

[20] STEVEN M. DAVIDOFF, GODS AT WAR: SHOTGUN TAKEOVERS, GOVERNMENT BY DEAL AND THE PRIVATE EQUITY IMPLOSION 169 (2009).

[21] *Id.* at 169–171.

[22] Lucian Bebchuk, Alon Brav & Wei Jiang, *The Long-Term Effects of Shareholder Activism*, 115 COLUM. L. REV. 1085 (2015).

the performance of targets over a five year period after the announcement of the activist position. Examining Tobin's Qs (a measure of performance) for the targets, the authors find that targets have improved operating performance over this five-year period, higher than peer companies.

A recent paper by Professors Coffee and Palia argues that the evidence does not yet support the view that shareholder activism is a net benefit:

THE IMPACT OF HEDGE FUND ACTIVISM: EVIDENCE AND IMPLICATIONS

John C. Coffee, Jr. & Darius Palia
European Corporate Governance Institute (ECGI)—Law Working Paper No. 266/2014
Columbia Law and Economics Working Paper No. 489
5–9, (2014)

Even if one concludes that hedge fund activism is associated on average with stock price gains for shareholders, any conclusion that hedge fund activism is therefore efficiency-enhancing is still premature because of four limitations on these studies:

(1) These studies tend to ignore or downplay the distribution of short-term returns and the fact that a significant proportion of firms experience losses as a result of hedge fund activism;

(2) The positive abnormal stock returns on which the proponents of hedge fund activism rely do not truly establish causality or demonstrate that hedge fund activism has reduced agency costs; instead, improved results at target firms may be attributable to other factors (including market speculation about an expected takeover or simply a regression to the mean);

(3) These studies overlook (or give only inadequate attention to) the possibility that whatever shareholder wealth is created by hedge fund activism may reflect only a wealth transfer from bondholders, employees, or other claimants; and

(4) The impact of hedge fund activism on American corporations (and long-term investment) cannot be adequately measured by looking only to the post-intervention performance at those companies that experience a hedge fund intervention; this ignores the general deterrent impact of such activism on the many more companies that experience no such intervention, but that increase leverage and dividends or reduce long-term investment in fear of the growing risk of such an intervention.

These limitations are important. If the distribution of short-term returns shows that a significant number of firms experience losses (and sizeable ones), then hedge fund activism looks very different depending on whether one examines it from the perspective of the hedge fund manager or the corporate director. To the diversified fund manager, a tactic is justified if it produces a portfolio-wide positive return. In contrast, a corporate director is responsible for, and must consider the welfare of, only one company. Thus, the possibility of a negative return (particularly when the upside return may be only modest) may reasonably cause a board of directors to reject a strategy favored by a group of hedge funds that, like them, also wants to maximize shareholder value.

Similarly, others have suggested that the post-intervention gains in stock price experienced by the subjects of hedge fund activism may reflect simply a regression to the mean. We do not purport to know if that is true, but this possibility can only be investigated adequately if a more carefully selected control group is used that has the same characteristics as those firms that were the targets of activism (and this has not yet been done).

In order to establish causality on the part of hedge fund activists, these studies would need to use a method such as propensity score matching. In such methodologies, one can examine what is often referred to as the "but for" explanation. In our context, targets and non-targets would be matched in all observable firm characteristics in the pre-Schedule 13D filing period (that is, they would have the closest propensity score). Thus, rather than simply controlling for size and industry group (as many studies do), other variables, such as life cycle liquidity effects, would also be considered. This approach should permit the investigator to determine whether, "but for" the intervention of the activist hedge fund, shareholder value would have been created in the post Schedule 13D filing period. This refinement has not, however, been used in any existing study of which we are aware.

Finally, although shareholders are basically entitled to seek gains from any source (including bondholders), public policy has little reason to encourage wealth transfers. Public policy is ultimately our focus. Although we do not doubt that some hedge fund interventions promote efficiency, there are likely diminishing returns to increased activism, and, at some point, more interventions may only produce decreasing gains for shareholders at the expense of growing costs to other constituencies. Thus, from a policy perspective, we will argue that new rules promote greater transparency with regard to hedge funds' activities would come at an acceptable cost, even if they were to chill certain kinds of "creeping control" acquisitions.

Above all, our concern is with the possibility that hedge fund activism may exacerbate an important externality: namely, it may encourage corporate boards and managements to forego long-term investments (particularly in research and development) in favor of a short-term policy of maximizing dividend payouts and stock buybacks. Such a shift away from long-term investment could ultimately prove costly to the American economy, but those costs would not necessarily be observable within the time periods examined by the existing studies. As more activists chase a constant or declining number of inefficient targets, the prospect for overdeterrence grows. Nor would the costs from over-deterrence be borne only by the actual subjects of hedge fund activism that these studies cover, as other corporations would predictably take similar defensive measures. Worse yet, if such a short-term investment horizon were to be imposed (or at least encouraged) by hedge fund activism and if the gains to shareholders were primarily wealth transfers from bondholders and others, then on the macro level the American economy would suffer an injury with little compensating benefit.[23]

Contrasting with both Bebchuk and others' positive views of shareholder activism and Coffee and Palia's more skeptical view are the views of opponents of shareholder activism. Some opponents argue that the pro-shareholder activism "evidence" is either wrong or ignores other evidence. Martin Lipton, one of the founders of the law firm Wachtell, Lipton Rosen & Katz, a law firm which regularly represents companies in their defenses against activist hedge funds (and against hostile acquirers), has been a vocal opponent of activism on these grounds, arguing that instead of offering economic benefits to shareholders, shareholder activism results in short term focused decisions by companies which are ultimately harmful, a concern which Professors Coffee and Palia also raise.

In the following memorandum, Mr. Lipton comments on the recent shareholder activism at Apple by Carl Icahn and Dan Loeb's Third Point fund. The two activists commenced a successful campaign to get Apple to distribute to its shareholders over $100 billion in excess cash:

> The activist-hedge-fund attack on Apple—in which one of the most successful, long-term-visionary companies of all time is being told by a money manager that Apple is doing things all wrong and should focus on short-term return of cash—is a clarion call for effective action to deal with the misuse of shareholder power. Institutional investors on average own more than 70% of the shares of the major public companies. Their voting power is being harnessed by a gaggle of activist hedge funds who troll through SEC filings looking for opportunities to demand a change in a company's strategy or portfolio that will create a short-term profit without regard to the impact on the

---

[23] Available at http://papers.ssrn.com/sol3/papers.cfm?abstract_id=2496518. See also http://papers.ssrn.com/sol3/papers.cfm?abstract_id=2656325.

company's long-term prospects. These self-seeking activists are aided and abetted by Harvard Law School Professor Lucian Bebchuk who leads a cohort of academics who have embraced the concept of "shareholder democracy" and close their eyes to the real-world effect of shareholder power, harnessed to activists seeking a quick profit, on a targeted company and the company's employees and other stakeholders.

They ignore the fact that it is the stakeholders and investors with a long-term perspective who are the true beneficiaries of most of the funds managed by institutional investors. Although essentially ignored by Professor Bebchuk, there is growing recognition of the fiduciary duties of institutional investors not to seek short-term profits at the expense of the pensioners and employees who are the beneficiaries of the pension and welfare plans and the owners of shares in the managed funds. In a series of brilliant speeches and articles, the problem of short-termism has been laid bare by Chancellor Leo E. Strine, Jr. of the Delaware Court of Chancery, e.g., One Fundamental Corporate Governance Question We Face: Can Corporations Be Managed for the Long Term Unless Their Powerful Electorates Also Act and Think Long Term?, and is the subject of a continuing Aspen Institute program, Overcoming Short-Termism.

In his drive to enhance the shift of power over the management of companies from directors to shareholders, Professor Bebchuk has announced that he is pursuing empirical studies to prove his thesis that shareholder demand for short-term performance enforced by activist hedge funds is good for the economy. We have been debating director-centric corporate governance versus shareholder-centric corporate governance for more than 25 years. Because they are inconvenient to his theories, Professor Bebchuk rejects the decades of my and my firm's experience in advising corporations and the other evidence of the detrimental effects of pressure for short-term performance. I believe that academics' self-selected stock market statistics are meaningless in evaluating the effects of short-termism. Our debates, which extend over all aspects of corporate governance, have of late focused on my effort to obtain early disclosure of block accumulations by activist hedge funds and my endorsement of an effort to require institutional shareholders to report their holdings two days, rather than 45 days, after each quarter. It is in the context of these efforts, opposed by the activists who benefit from lack of transparency, that Professor Bebchuk has announced his research project.

If Professor Bebchuk is truly interested in meaningful research to determine the impact of an activist attack (and the fear of an activist attack) on a company, he must first put forth a persuasive (or even just coherent) theory as to why the judgments as to corporate strategy and operations of short-term-focused professional money managers should take precedence over the judgments of directors and executives charged with maximizing the long-term success of business enterprises. There is nothing persuasive about his view, whether as theory or experience. Furthermore, he must take into account the following:

1.   As to all companies that were members of the Fortune 500 during the period January 1, 2000 to December 31, 2012, what was the impact on the price of the shares of a company that missed the "street estimate" or "whisper number" for its earnings for a quarter and what adjustment did each of those companies make to its capital expenditures, investment in research and development and number of employees for the balance of the year of the miss and the following year.

2.   For companies that are the subject of hedge fund activism and remain independent, what is the impact on their operational performance and stock price performance relative to the benchmark, not just in the short period after announcement of the activist interest, but after a 24-month period.

3.   Interviews with the CEOs of the Fortune 500 as to whether they agree or disagree with the following statements:

a) From the Aspen paper, "We believe that short-term objectives have eroded faith in corporations continuing to be the foundation of the American free enterprise system, which has been, in turn, the foundation of our economy. Restoring that faith critically requires restoring a long-term focus for boards, managers, and most particularly, shareholders—if not voluntarily, then by appropriate regulation."

b) From a 2002 interview with Daniel Vasella, CEO of Novartis in Fortune Magazine,

"The practice by which CEOs offer guidance about their expected quarterly earnings performance, analysts set 'targets' based on that guidance, and then companies try to meet those targets within the penny is an old one. But in recent years the practice has been so enshrined in the culture of Wall Street that the men and women running public companies often think of little else. They become preoccupied with short-term 'success,' a mindset that can hamper or even destroy long-term performance for shareholders. I call this the tyranny of quarterly earnings."[24]

The debate over economic shareholder activism thus is about whether activists provide long-term value. When they seek to change a company's management or direction, does this benefit the company, or only boost shareholder returns in the short run? Do they have better ideas as to how to run companies, or are they using what is now a well-worn formula to 'take the money and run'? Notwithstanding attempts to resolve this matter empirically, the debate is certain to continue.

QUESTIONS

1.   Describe how company responses to shareholder activism may also act to inhibit a hostile takeover.

2.   Can a board "just say no" in response to a shareholder activist? What are the pluses and the minuses of such a strategy?

3.   Describe how the Sotheby's and CNET cases might apply to actions of a company defending itself against a hostile takeover.

4.   What are the arguments for shareholder activism? What are the arguments against it? Who do you think is correct, and why?

5.   If Dan Loeb had shown you the poison pen letter he wrote in Sotheby's and asked whether he should send it, what would you have told him? If you would have advised him not to send the letter, what reasons would you have given, and how strongly would you have told him you felt about the advice?

6.   Are the *Unocal* and *Blasius* standards appropriate tools for monitoring companies' responses to activism? Can you think of another approach?

7.   How are the arguments over reform of § 13(d) to change the 10-day reporting window and reporting of cash-settled derivatives outlined in Chapter IV applicable to the case of shareholder activism? Does the prevalence of shareholder activism argue in favor of reform, or against it?

8.   Do you think that companies should adopt defensive measures to protect themselves against shareholder activism? Why or why not? If you were a shareholder, would you want your company to adopt such mechanisms?

---

[24]   Martin Lipton, *Bite the Apple; Poison the Apple; Paralyze the Company; Wreck the Economy,* http://blogs.law.harvard.edu/corpgov/2013/02/26/bite-the-apple-poison-the-apple-paralyze-the-company-wreck-the-economy/.

CHAPTER XXI

INTERNATIONAL ISSUES

■ ■ ■

A. INTRODUCTION

In today's global capital markets, M&A transactions not infrequently have an international component even if both the buyer and target are U.S. companies. Most often, this involves obtaining antitrust or other regulatory clearances in other jurisdictions, as discussed in Chapter VIII. Other statutory schemes, notably the Foreign Corrupt Practices Act of 1977 (FCPA), often loom large. For example, a buyer of a foreign company, or a U.S. company with non-U.S. operations, now commonly conducts significant due diligence with respect to FCPA compliance as well as obtaining representations and warranties in the merger agreement concerning this issue.

In this Chapter, we focus on U.S. companies' acquisitions of non-U.S. companies. U.S. law may be implicated on multiple levels. First, non-U.S. companies may have U.S. operations, often requiring U.S. regulatory clearances to be obtained. But U.S. legal issues more frequently arise when a foreign company has shareholders located in the United States. In such a case, the Williams Act and other laws applicable to public company acquisitions may apply. This can raise complicated issues, particularly as applicable U.S. laws may sometimes conflict with the laws of the home country jurisdiction. For example, the Williams Act rules require that an offeror "promptly" pay for shares accepted in a tender offer, while many jurisdictions such as Germany have a payment mechanism that only allows for payment weeks after the offer has been completed. Moreover, if a U.S. company issues shares to acquire a non-U.S. company, the registration requirements of the Securities Act of 1933 may apply.

In this Chapter we explore how companies deal with the U.S. legal issues involved in the acquisition of non-U.S. companies. We conclude by discussing the differences between the U.K. and U.S. takeover regimes; doing so illustrates how different takeover systems can regulate takeovers in very different ways.

B. THE SCOPE OF U.S. JURISDICTION

The SEC has typically asserted a broad view of the application of U.S. securities laws abroad. The SEC has taken the position that U.S.

jurisdiction is appropriate when foreign conduct has a substantial effect on the United States or on U.S. persons. Historically, this broad view of jurisdiction has been upheld in the courts. The main case addressing the issue in the takeover context is *Consolidated Gold Fields, PLC v. Minorco, S.A.*[1] Minorco, a Luxembourg company, launched a tender offer to acquire all of the outstanding shares of Consolidated Gold Fields, a British company. Two and a half percent of Consolidated Gold Fields' shares were held by U.S. residents, but Consolidated Gold Fields had no U.S. stock exchange listing. Some of the shares were held directly, through "depository receipts" (ADRs) but more were held indirectly, through nominees. Consolidated Gold Fields sued Minorco, accusing it of violating the antifraud provisions of the U.S. federal securities laws by misstating Minorco's ties to South African companies, and requesting corrective disclosure. Consolidated Gold also claimed that the transaction would violate antitrust law; it requested that the transaction be preliminarily enjoined.

Minorco raised a jurisdictional defense. It argued that U.S. securities laws did not apply since Minorco had taken steps to exclude U.S. residents from the offer, including by sending the tender offer documents to British nominees of U.S. persons and not directly to U.S. persons who held ADRs. The District Court ruled that there was no jurisdiction over the securities law claims, but the Second Circuit Court of Appeals disagreed, holding that there were "substantial effects" in the U.S. The Second Circuit held that "the District Court should have asserted jurisdiction once it noted that Minorco knew that the British nominees were required by law to forward the tender offer documents to Gold Fields' shareholders and ADR depository banks in the United States."[2] The applicable test is known as the "conduct and effects" test.

The *Minorco* case represents an expansive view of federal jurisdiction abroad. So long as conduct had substantial effects in the U.S.—broadly interpreted—U.S. jurisdiction was appropriate. Consider that neither the bidder nor the target in *Minorco* had a U.S. listing, and that only 2.5% of Consolidated Gold's shares were held by U.S. residents. Despite many companies' protests that expanding federal jurisdiction to this extent was unwarranted and inadvisable, especially since almost any foreign company of any significant size had at least some U.S. shareholders, the Second Circuit test remained the law until 2010. In that year, in *Morrison v. National Australia Bank, Ltd.*,[3] the Supreme Court rejected the long-standing Second Circuit test, holding that for purposes of the extraterritorial reach of § 10(b) of the Exchange Act, the test was instead whether the purchase or sale of the security occurred in the United States

---

[1]   871 F.2d 252 (2d Cir. 1989).

[2]   *Id.* at 262.

[3]   561 U.S. 247 (2010).

or on a U.S. stock exchange; if neither of these were the case, there would be no U.S. securities law jurisdiction, at least for a private cause of action under § 10(b) of the Exchange Act. *Morrison* has marked a revolution in the prosecution of foreign securities fraud class actions in the United States. Scores of pending cases were dismissed and the scope to bring new cases based on foreign conduct is now severely circumscribed. To opponents of frivolous securities fraud litigation, this has been a significantly positive development. Congress, though, was not ready to abandon the conduct and effects test. *Morrison* applies to private rights of action under § 10(b), and the Dodd-Frank Act explicitly rejected *Morrison* in suits under § 10(b) brought by the SEC or the DOJ.[4] Indeed, the Dodd-Frank Act expressly affirmed the conduct and effects tests as the proper scope of jurisdiction for such suits. Dodd-Frank also directed further study by the SEC into the proper scope of jurisdiction for private suits, apparently leaving open the possibility of reinstating some type of conduct and effects test.

The result of the *Morrison* decision and the Dodd-Frank provision is that when a transaction involves U.S. shareholders or may involve the issuance of securities into the United States, U.S. laws will presumably apply. However, compliance with U.S. law can sometimes be quite difficult for foreign issuers, as the case of Gaz de France and Suez, both French companies, highlights. Neither company had a listing on a U.S. stock exchange. But Gaz de France was going to acquire Suez by issuing shares—indeed, shares worth $13 billion—to Suez shareholders in the U.S., and to holders of Suez's American Depository Receipts. Those shares therefore had to be registered with the SEC. Gaz de France filed its 571 page Form F–4 registration statement (the equivalent of an S–4, to register securities issued by a foreign private issuer in a business combination).

> Why [were offering documents] even filed in the United States, you might ask?
>
> Gaz de France is not listed in the United States, nor are its shares registered with the SEC. Suez historically had shares listed and registered in the United States, but in September 2007 it elected to delist from the New York Stock Exchange and deregister its shares.
>
> After the offering, the combined company's shares will not be listed on a U.S. exchange and Gaz de France will likely deregister them as soon as possible.
>
> That is a lot of paper—not to mention the lawyer and printer bills—for such a transitory benefit. (It could have been much

---

[4] The Dodd-Frank Wall Street Reform and Consumer Protection Act § 929P(b) (Pub.L. 111–203, H.R. 4173).

worse: Gaz de France saved months of time and accountants' bills by not having to prepare U.S. GAAP-reconciled financial statements.)

Gaz de France . . . was required to make this filing under U.S. securities law since approximately 15 percent of Suez's shareholders are located in the United States. Gaz de France thus did not qualify to use the SEC's cross-border exemptions [discussed in the next Subsection].[5]

Because of these sorts of difficulties, U.S. takeover lawyers have adopted a number of strategies to exclude U.S. shareholders and prevent U.S. jurisdiction over a foreign takeover.

C. THE EXCLUSIONARY OFFER

The principal means to avoid application of the U.S. takeover rules is to exclude shareholders located in the U.S. from the foreign takeover offer. If shareholders located in the United States are excluded and no securities are issued into the U.S., then under either the Second Circuit "conduct" and "effects" test or *Morrison,* the U.S. federal securities laws presumably do not apply, lacking jurisdictional reach. The following, from a memorandum by the law firm Davis Polk & Wardwell, describes how a tender offer for a Japanese company with U.S. shareholders can be structured so that the U.S. rules do not apply:

> The [United States] Tender Offer Rules will generally not apply to a tender offer that excludes U.S. holders and avoids the use of U.S. jurisdictional means (an "Exclusionary Offer"). In evaluating this approach, the bidder and target should also consider, as a business matter, whether the success of the offer may be impaired and whether they are comfortable with potential ill will that may be generated among U.S. holders excluded from the tender offer.

> If the bidder wishes to conduct an Exclusionary Offer, it should review the following general considerations and procedures. Even if the bidder takes the precautionary steps outlined below to avoid U.S. jurisdictional means, there will be some risk that the SEC or a U.S. court may nonetheless deem the Exclusionary Offer to be subject to U.S. jurisdiction. The SEC has recently indicated that it will more closely monitor Exclusionary Offers to determine whether SEC action is necessary to protect U.S. holders of the target's securities.

---

[5] Steven M. Davidoff, *French Deal, American Red Tape*, N.Y. TIMES, June 17, 2008, available at http://dealbook.nytimes.com/2008/06/17/french-deal-american-red-tape/.

. . .

A.   General Considerations and Procedures

In order to avoid the application of the Tender Offer Rules, an Exclusionary Offer must be conducted without implicating U.S. jurisdictional means. However, the term "U.S. jurisdictional means" is interpreted very broadly. It may include, for example:

- mailing tender offer materials to the agents in Japan acting as standing proxies (*jonin dairi nin*) if the agents are required or expected to forward the materials to beneficial holders resident in the United States;

- making tender offer materials available, electronically or physically, in the United States, including by means of posting the documentation on a company's website;

- directing communications with respect to a tender offer into the United States;

- permitting the participation of U.S. securities analysts or reporters in telephone conferences, meetings or other similar events relating to the tender offer;

- permitting tenders to be mailed from the United States; or

- sending the payment for the shares into the United States.

The SEC has stated that it will skeptically view exclusionary offers for securities of foreign private issuers that trade on a U.S. exchange, where the participation of U.S. holders is necessary to meet the minimum acceptance condition in the tender offer. Where purportedly exclusionary offers are made under those circumstances, the SEC has said that it will look closely to determine whether bidders are taking reasonable measures to keep the offer out of the United States. It is possible that the SEC will challenge the exclusion of U.S. holders in transactions where the participation of U.S. investors is necessary to make the transaction successful.

In addition, the bidder may implicate U.S. jurisdictional means if it fails to take adequate measures to prevent tenders by U.S. holders of the target's securities, while purporting to exclude such U.S. holders. If the bidder seeks to avoid the application of the Tender Offer Rules, it should take special precautions to assure that an Exclusionary Offer is not made in the United States, for example by:

- including legends on the tender offer materials themselves and on any Internet website on which they are posted;

- putting in place measures to ensure that tenders are not accepted from U.S. holders, including, when responding to inquiries and processing letters of transmittal, obtaining adequate information to identify U.S. holders;

- obtaining representations from tendering investors, or nominees or other persons tendering on investors' behalf, that the investors tendering are not U.S. holders;

- avoiding the mailing into the United States of cash or other consideration to tendering holders; and

- checking for indications that the tendering holder is a U.S. holder, including receipt of payment drawn on a U.S. bank, or provision of a U.S. taxpayer identification number or other statements by the tendering holder suggesting that, notwithstanding a foreign address, the holder is a U.S. holder.

. . .

C.   Use of the Internet and U.S. Jurisdictional Means

Materials relating to Exclusionary Offers are often posted on the websites of the parties involved and thus widely accessible on the Internet. If the bidder uses a website to publicize an Exclusionary Offer, it must take special care that the website is not used as a means to induce indirect participation in the tender offer by U.S. holders. As a general matter, however, we believe that website materials in the Japanese language are of less concern than those in the English language.

In addition to the general precautions described above, certain other measures should be adopted if tender offer documents are posted to a website, such as utilizing technology to obtain adequate information (such as the location of internet access, a mailing address or a telephone number) to determine whether persons attempting to access the documents are U.S. holders before providing access, responding to inquiries or processing letters of transmittal.[6]

The exclusionary offer by its terms excludes U.S. shareholders. In reality this exclusion may not be significant for most offers, since a foreign issuer may have few U.S. holders. In addition, these holders will likely sell their shares to non-U.S. holders who can tender. Alternatively,

---

[6] *U.S. Securities Laws Considerations and Options for Japanese Cash Tender Offers*, DAVIS, POLK & WARDWELL, Oct. 2009, available at http://www.davispolk.com/publications/us-securities-laws-considerations-and-options-japanese-cash-tender-offers/.

a U.S. holder may designate an off-shore proxy to receive and tender their shares.

D. REGULATION S

As the above discussion with respect to the Gaz de France/Suez combination notes, the registration process for securities can be time-consuming and arduous. If possible, in a non-U.S. transaction, the party issuing securities will seek to avoid this process. The principal means to do so is by making an exclusionary offer whereby the securities to be issued outside the United States are issued under Regulation S, as the following, excerpted from a memorandum by the law firm Dorsey & Whitney, discusses:

SUMMARY OF SEC REGULATION S
Dorsey & Whitney LLP

Regulation S under the Securities Act of 1933, as amended (the "Securities Act") is a safe harbour rule that defines when an offering of securities would be deemed to come to rest abroad so as not to be subject to the registration obligations imposed under § 5 of the Securities Act. The General Statement to Regulation S applies a territorial approach to Securities Act registration by providing that offers and sales subject to § 5 include offers and sales that occur within the United States and do not include offers and sales that occur outside the United States. Regulation S also includes several safe harbour exemptions addressing specified transactions.

Each safe harbour is subject to two general conditions:

1. The offer or sale must occur in an "offshore transaction." This means that (i) the seller reasonably believes that the buyer is offshore at the time of the offer or sale or (ii) the transaction occurs on certain "designated offshore securities markets," which includes each of the Canadian stock exchanges participating in the Committee, and the transaction is not pre-arranged with a buyer in the United States.

2. That no "directed selling efforts" may be made in the United States by the issuer, a distributor, any of their respective affiliates, or any person acting on behalf of any of the foregoing. These activities consist of efforts reasonably expected to condition the U.S. market for the securities.

Rule 903 provides specific rules for offerings by issuers, distributors and their respective affiliates:

Category 1: (a) securities of a "foreign issuer" for which there is no "substantial U.S. market interest" (as defined below), (b) securities offered by a "foreign issuer" in "overseas directed offerings" (as defined below, (c) non-convertible debt securities of a domestic issuer offered in overseas directed offerings that are denominated in a currency other than U.S. dollars, and (d) securities backed by the full faith and credit of a foreign government. . . .

In these cases, only the general conditions referred to above must be observed.

Category 2: (a) equity offerings by reporting foreign issuers, and (b) offerings of debt securities and non-convertible, non-participating preferred stock by reporting issuers or non-reporting foreign issuers. To be treated as a qualified reporting issuer, the issuer must have filed all required reports for at least twelve months prior to the offer or sale, or such shorter period during which the issuer was subject to the reporting obligation.

Offering Restrictions must be observed, which include prohibitions on resales to U.S. Persons during the distribution compliance period, in addition to the application of the general conditions. Generally, a 40 day distribution compliance period (i.e., the period during which the restrictions required by the particular category remain in effect) will apply, which will have to be codified in a written agreement with each distributor and reflected in the offering documentation and on all confirmations issued to distributors and others receiving transaction-based compensation and to purchasers during the distribution compliance period.

Category 3: offerings of all other securities, including (a) equity offerings by domestic reporting issuers, (b) offerings of equity securities by non-reporting foreign issuers for which there is a substantial U.S. market interest and (c) offerings by U.S. issuers that are not reporting issuers. These offerings are subject to the most stringent conditions.

For debt securities the offering restrictions are the same as for Category 2, plus the need to use a temporary global certificate to support the 40-day distribution compliance period.

For equity securities, the distribution compliance period is increased to one year, and the purchaser must also provide a certification as to its non-U.S. status and must agree not to resell to a U.S. Person except in accordance with U.S. requirements, in addition to compliance with the restrictions applicable to Category 2.

The securities of a domestic issuer must bear a restrictive legend, supported by stop transfer instructions. The documentation required in the case of such issuers must refer to the prohibition on certain hedging transactions during the distribution compliance period that would have the effect of pre-selling, the securities into the United States and distributors must agree in writing to observe this prohibition.

Rule 904 provides a safe harbour for certain resale transactions by persons other than the issuer, a distributor, any of their respective affiliates (except any officer or director who is an affiliate solely by virtue of such office), or any person acting on their behalf. They are subject to the following conditions:

1. All permitted sellers are subject to the general conditions.

2. In the case of a seller who is a dealer or a person receiving any remuneration, a resale cannot be knowingly made to a U.S. Person prior to the end of the relevant distribution compliance period. A confirmation stating the applicable securities law restrictions must be sent to any other dealer or person receiving selling compensation person.

3. No special compensation can be paid if the seller is an officer or director of the issuer.

4. The safe harbour is not available to "affiliates" of the issuer, except where affiliation arises solely from the status of the seller as an officer or director. An "affiliate" is any person controlling, controlled by or under common control with the issuer. "Control" for this purpose means de facto control. A strong inference of control based upon voting influence often arises at the 10% threshold, although other factors may demonstrate or point away from control.

5. Transactions must be effected through a "designated offshore securities market" in a transaction not pre-arranged with a U.S. Person or in a transaction involving a buyer outside of the United States at the time the buy order is originated.

6. Care must be taken to ensure that the transaction does not involve a scheme to evade the Securities Act registration requirements, including for the purpose of washing off transfer restrictions.

Rule 905 provides that equity securities of domestic issuers acquired from the issuer, distributor, or any of their respective affiliates in a transaction subject to the safe harbour rules discussed above are deemed to be restricted securities, and resales by any offshore purchaser must be made pursuant to Regulation S or another exemption from Securities Act registration.[7]

Regulation S can provide a foreign offering an exemption from the U.S registration requirements, so long as the issuer is not a domestic issuer and an exclusionary offer is possible. Domestic issuers face a distribution compliance period of one year. Monitoring the one-year compliance period is quite difficult, as is ensuring that there are no resales back into the U.S. Consequently, when used in takeovers, Regulation S is for the most part used only by foreign issuers which do not have a U.S. listing or shares registered in the United States. For these foreign companies, there is no distribution compliance period, primarily because there is no active U.S. trading market for the company's securities. However, if the foreign issuer is registered in the United States, there is still a distribution compliance period, albeit one that is only 40 days, shorter than the one-year period for domestic issuers. This 40-day period is typically also hard to enforce; these foreign private issuers also rarely use Regulation S.

Regulation S also requires that no activities can be directed into the United States. As a practical matter, compliance with this requirement is not onerous if the foreign issuer is acquiring another foreign issuer. It involves proper legending of the materials, and limitations on access to the materials from the United States. In the case of the Gaz de France/Suez transaction, though, the parties could not use Regulation S because the number of shares held by U.S. shareholders was high enough that their participation in the transaction was needed for the transaction to succeed.

E. A NOTE ABOUT SCHEMES OF ARRANGEMENT

England and some other common law jurisdictions have a transaction structure called a "scheme of arrangement" that can be used in lieu of a tender offer. A scheme of arrangement is a reorganization of a company's capital structure or its debts which is binding on creditors and shareholders. It is not available or utilized in the United States, but it is common in England and in countries with law modeled upon the English company law system (Australia, New Zealand, South Africa, etc.). The relevant English statute is § 425 of the English Companies Act 1985. The structure can be best analogized to a U.S. merger, although there are distinct differences between the two.

---

[7]   Available at http://www.dorsey.com/files/tbl_s21Publications%5CPDFUpload141%5C1052%5CSummary_of_SEC_Regulation_S.pdf.

There are two types of scheme of arrangement: a creditors' scheme and a members' or shareholders' scheme. A creditors' scheme is generally used by companies in financial difficulty; the creditors can agree to defer payments and effect a restructuring of the indebtedness of the corporation. A members' scheme is used to effect corporate reorganizations, particularly a combination with another company. In general, a scheme of arrangement is carried out in three steps:

1. The court is approached to order a meeting of creditors or shareholders directly affected;

2. The scheme in general must be approved by a vote of more than 50 per cent of the creditors or members present and voting who represent 75 per cent of the total debts or nominal value of the shares of those present and voting at the meeting (the law may vary depending upon the country but this is the law in England); and

3. The scheme is referred back to the court for confirmation.

The most important element of a scheme of arrangement for U.S. transactional purposes is that the securities issued pursuant to the scheme are exempt under § 3(a)(10) of the Securities Act. Section 3(a)(10) of the Securities Act states:

> Except with respect to a security exchanged in a case under title 11 of the United States Code, any security which is issued in exchange for one or more bona fide outstanding securities, claims or property interests, or partly in such exchange and partly for cash, where the terms and conditions of such issuance and exchange are approved, after a hearing upon the fairness of such terms and conditions at which all persons to whom it is proposed to issue securities in such exchange shall have the right to appear, by any court, or by any official or agency of the United States, or by any State or Territorial banking or insurance commission or other governmental authority expressly authorized by law to grant such approval. . . .

The exemption was initially promulgated for state fairness hearings, discussed in Chapter VII.B.2; such hearings were prevalent prior to the adoption of the Securities Act. U.S. lawyers practicing outside of the U.S. realized that the exemption could also apply with respect to schemes of arrangement, and began petitioning the SEC for no-action relief for schemes under the laws of different countries. In the early 1990s, the SEC would generally issue no-action relief, doing so on a case-by-case basis for each scheme as to which such relief had been requested. In October 1999, the SEC issued a legal bulletin specifying the circumstances in which a foreign scheme of arrangement could qualify for the 3(a)(10) exemption.[8] Today, almost all schemes qualify such that the practice is no longer to seek no-action relief from the SEC, but instead to rely upon the requirements set forth in the October 1999 bulletin.

The scheme of arrangement is a particularly advantageous way to extend an offer into the United States because there are no filing requirements with the SEC and no substantive requirements other than that the judge be informed of the exemption and rule specifically on the fairness of the terms and conditions of the transaction. These are lesser information and filing requirements than are contained in even the SEC's Cross-Border exemptions (discussed in the next Subsection). U.S. lawyers therefore often advise their non-U.S. clients that in order to avoid being subject to most U.S. securities law requirements, they should pursue a scheme of arrangement, even when U.S. holders number less than 10% such that the cross-border exemptions can be met.[9] The antifraud provisions under the U.S. securities laws still apply, however, and the lawyers will want to ensure that transaction documentation is drafted so as to avoid liability under these laws.

F. TIER I AND TIER II OFFERS

In some cases an exclusionary offer is not possible. In order for the offer to succeed, the target may have a significant number of U.S. shareholders who need to be included. Alternatively, the buyer may be a U.S. company or a foreign company with shares registered in the United States. Additionally, not all jurisdictions have a scheme of arrangement structure which can be used to avoid the U.S. registration requirements. To address these issues, in 2000 the SEC adopted cross-border exemptions designed to facilitate the extension of offers into the United States. The SEC's goal was to encourage issuers to include U.S. holders in foreign takeover offers. The following article excerpt explains the historical origins of the cross-border exemptions and how they function. Pay attention to the myriad mechanical difficulties an acquirer faces when trying to conduct an offer in several different jurisdictions at the same time, and how the SEC addressed the issues involved:

---

[8]   Division of Corporate Finance: Revised Staff Legal Bulletin No. 3 (CF), Oct. 20, 1999.

[9]   This Subsection is based on Steven M. Davidoff, *Better Know a Deal Structure*, M&A LAW PROF. BLOG, Oct. 22, 2007, available at http://lawprofessors.typepad.com/mergers/2007/10/better-know-a-1.html.

GETTING U.S. SECURITY HOLDERS TO THE PARTY: THE SEC'S CROSS-BORDER RELEASE FIVE YEARS ON

Brett Carron & Steven M. Davidoff
12 U. PA J. INT'L ECON L. 455 (2005)

Prior to 1989, the U.S. regulatory and practical experience with integrated cross-border takeovers had been haphazard at best. The conflicts between the U.S. takeover rules and similar non-U.S rules, the perception that compliance with U.S. rules would be unduly onerous, and a concern about the active plaintiff's bar in the United States discouraged the development of an integrated cross-border regime in which U.S. and non-U.S. holders could participate equally. In transactions where U.S. share ownership was minimal, the benefit of excluding U.S. security holders was often perceived as outweighing the benefit of greater shareholder participation. As a result, participants in cross-border takeovers often decided to exclude U.S. holders from participation therein, what we refer to in this Article as an "exclusionary offer."

The harbinger of an integrated cross-border regime would be a nonpareil transaction in which the number of securities held by an acquiree's U.S. security holders was substantial enough that U.S. security holders could not, on either a commercial or legal basis, be ignored. This most certainly occurred in 1989 with the announced takeover of Jaguar plc by the Ford Motor Company. On November 2, 1989, Ford announced an agreed $2.38 billion cash tender offer for all of Jaguar's outstanding ordinary securities. Jaguar's primary market was the London Stock Exchange. However, unlike in other prior cross-border takeovers, Jaguar had a large U.S. shareholder presence: Jaguar's American Depositary Securities ("ADSs") were quoted on the Nasdaq National Market System, its ordinary securities were registered under Section 12 of the Securities Exchange Act of 1934 ("Exchange Act"), at least 25% of Jaguar's security holders were located in the United States, and Ford itself, a U.S. domiciled company, held approximately 13.4% of Jaguar's securities. Faced with this substantial U.S. presence, Ford decided to extend its offer into the United States to U.S. security holders.

The Ford offer was required to comply with the governing takeover codes in two jurisdictions: the Williams Act in the United States and the U.K. City Code on Takeovers and Mergers and the Rules Governing Substantial Acquisition of Securities ("City Code") issued by the U.K. Panel on Takeovers and Mergers in the United Kingdom ("Takeover Panel"). Under the Williams Act, the acquiror, in this case Ford, was required to prepare and file with the SEC a tender offer statement on Schedule TO (at that time known as a Schedule 14D–1). The acquiree, in this case, Jaguar, was also required to file a response statement on Schedule 14D–9. In addition, the Williams Act imposes, and imposed on Ford, numerous procedural requirements, including that the offer commence within five U.S. business days of its announcement, be kept open for a minimum of twenty U.S. business days, and be open to all holders. The Williams Act also requires that the acquiror and its affiliates make no purchases outside the offer. Among other things, these U.S. requirements were designed to provide U.S. security holders with procedural and substantive protections from potentially abusive and manipulative practices through clear rules of conduct. In the Ford offer (and in subsequent cross-border takeovers) the U.S. requirements existed alongside sometime conflicting and differing U.K. disclosure and procedural requirements.

The applicable U.S. rules conflicted in several aspects with the City Code. Under the City Code, for example, tendered securities cannot be withdrawn in the period after the offer conditions have been satisfied or waived and the offer has been declared "unconditional, as to acceptances." This City Code restriction on withdrawal rights conflicts, and conflicted at the time of the Ford offer, with the U.S. requirement under the Williams Act that withdrawal rights be available at all times during the pendency of an offer. In addition, in order to comply with the differing disclosure and procedural requirements in the United Kingdom and the United States, Ford used a common technique in non-exclusionary cross-border takeovers and structured its offer as two distinct offers cross-conditional on each other: a U.K. offer for U.K. and non-U.S. persons made in compliance with the City Code using a U.K. compliant disclosure document, and a U.S. offer for U.S. persons made in compliance with the Williams Act using a disclosure document compliant with Schedule TO (at that time known as a Schedule 14D–1). However, this dual offer structure technically violated the all-holders rule set forth in Rule 14d–10 of the Exchange Act which provides that an offer must be made to all acquiree security holders wherever located and the prohibition on purchases outside the offer set forth in Rule 14e–5 of the Exchange Act (then Rule 10b–13), since U.K. holders could not tender into the U.S. offer and the purchases made in the U.K. offer constituted purchases outside the U.S. offer and vice-versa.

These and other issues that to this day vex practitioners in cross-border takeovers had to be confronted and solved as matters of first impression: differing and conflicting U.K. and U.S. rules sorted and harmonized, offering documentation prepared to comport with the requirements of multiple jurisdictions, and timing differentials between the U.K. and U.S. rules reconciled. All of the foregoing needed to occur among parties and legal advisors of variant nationalities from differing cultures, operating using different terminology, and pursuant to different and sometimes conflicting legal regimes. U.K. and U.S. regulators were also forced to interact on unprecedented levels and to consider and grant new types of relief from the strict application of national takeover rules.

Both the SEC and the Takeover Panel would eventually provide exemptive and no-action relief on both a formal and informal basis to permit the Ford offer to legally proceed in its respective jurisdictions.

In the end, the Ford offer was successful, and a full-fledged, U.S. inclusionary, cross-border takeover, at least in the English-speaking Western world, was now a possibility. But success had been difficult.

The staff of the SEC recognized this, and in the summer of 1991 made its first attempt in the International Tender and Exchange Offers Release ("International Release"), albeit a failed one, to establish rules governing cross-border takeovers. Although [the early proposals were] unsuccessful, the [1990s attempts at rule-making] . . . established the outlines of the SEC staff's thinking on and approach to these transactions, and provided commentators, practitioners, and regulators a basis to comparatively assess the need for additional rules and their scope. The unintended delay from the time of the International Release to the Cross-Border Release may have been sound for this reason alone, but also because it permitted further experience in other jurisdictions, such as France, Germany and the United Kingdom, to accumulate, be measured and applied. It also permitted the SEC to develop and refine its approach to other related areas of cross-border securities law. The rules that were ultimately adopted in the Cross-Border Release bear a remarkable similarity to the International Release, but also reflect a more nuanced approach borne out by experience and other continued ancillary rulemaking.

The eight-year wait also permitted pattern and practice to take hold. In cross-border takeovers where the acquiree company had a small number of U.S. security holders, or compliance with U.S. laws was simply too difficult or burdensome, U.S. persons typically were excluded by acquirors and the U.S. rules rendered inapplicable through the avoidance of U.S. jurisdictional means. However, when U.S. ownership was significant or material, U.S. persons were generally included. As previously noted, the inclusion of U.S. persons led to a developing body of precedent transactions—patterns of necessary SEC relief that harmonized conflicting rules and raised familiarity among lawyers and regulators of different countries. These were all taken into account when the Cross-Border Rules were ultimately adopted in 1999.

Additionally, the exclusionary offer was not necessarily deleterious to U.S. security holders. U.S. security holders could still sell into the market upon announcement, albeit without the benefit of the offer documentation, which was prohibited from being distributed to them. Arguably, the U.S. security holders' loss (or, more aptly, lost opportunity) was primarily the vanished benefit of the risk arbitrage spread between the offer consideration and the trading price of the security in the market, the opportunity of a higher second takeover bid, and any brokerage fees. This loss, however, may be inconsequential when marked against the actual premium received by the shareholder and the traded risk of a broken deal and no premium whatsoever. In fact, investment professionals have historically recommended that small holders sell upon announcement of a takeover transaction, a "take the money and run" approach—it is for the arbitrageurs and more sophisticated financial investors to better assume the risk of completion. In any event, the number of individual investors who invested directly in non-U.S. issuers during the 1990s was relatively small compared to U.S. domestic investment. Consequently, the aggregate number of U.S. security holders who were adversely affected in an exclusionary offer was arguably immaterial in most cases.

Nor were the larger U.S. domiciled institutional holders, the Qualified Institutional Buyers ("QIBs"), or other classes of sophisticated institutional investors (those that typically hold the bulk of securities in non-U.S. companies) usually affected. These investors could often tender into exclusionary offers by transferring their investment discretion to an offshore affiliate who could then make the investment decision to tender. Such investors were sufficiently sophisticated to know of this procedure and how to use it.

Nonetheless, the SEC has historically disfavored the exclusionary offer approach, especially for unsophisticated investors. The SEC's traditional focus has been on protecting the average, rather than the financially sophisticated, investor. . . .

In addition, the number of U.S. investors in non-U.S. companies increased exponentially during this period, and cross-border takeovers increased with the general rise of mergers and acquisitions activity in the 1990s—the culmination undoubtedly being the approximately $127 billion unsolicited cross-border, U.S. inclusionary takeover of Mannesmann AG, a German company with significant U.S. holdings and listed on the New York Stock Exchange ("NYSE"), by Vodafone plc, an English public limited company also listed on the NYSE.

Addressing these transactions on an ad hoc basis increased the drain on the SEC staff's resources, and, from the vantage point of the late 1990s, such a drain was expected to increase further as the number of non-U.S. companies listed on the NYSE and quoted on the Nasdaq increased. It was against this backdrop that the SEC proposed and adopted the new Cross-Border Rules.

3.   THE CROSS-BORDER RULES

3.1. *The Exemptions*

The exemptions created by the Cross-Border Rules can be set forth in three strokes. Tender offers for the securities of non-U.S. companies (defined as "foreign private issuers") became exempt from most of the provisions of the Williams Act, so long as U.S. holders held 10% or less of the class of securities sought in the offer. This exemption is typically referred to as the "Tier I exemption." Similarly, in exchange offers and business combinations, where new securities were being offered as consideration to security holders of the non-U.S. acquiree company, acquirors became exempt from the registration requirements under Section 5 of the Securities Act that applied to new securities offerings, and from the qualification requirements of the U.S. Trust Indenture Act of 1939, so long as U.S. holders held 10% or less of the class of securities sought in the offer. This exemption is typically referred to as the "Rule 802 exemption." Finally, tender offers for the securities of a non-U.S. acquiree company received limited exemptive relief of a procedural nature to eliminate frequent areas of conflict between U.S. and non-U.S. regulatory requirements in situations where U.S. holders held 40% or less of the class of securities sought in the offer. This exemption is typically referred to as the "Tier II exemption."

3.1.1. *Tier I Exemption*

Under the Tier I exemption, qualifying tender and exchange offers are exempt from almost all of the requirements of the Williams Act, including the provisions therein concerning disclosure, filing, dissemination, minimum offering period, equal treatment, material amendments, withdrawal rights, and proration requirements. In order to qualify for the Tier I exemption, an offer must meet the following requirements: (i) the acquiree must be a foreign private issuer as defined in Rule 3b–4 of the Exchange Act; (ii) U.S. holders of the acquiree must hold 10% or less of the securities subject to the offer; (iii) the acquiror must submit an English language translation of the offering materials to the SEC under cover of Form CB and, in the case of an acquiror who is a foreign private issuer, submit to service of process on Form F–X; (iv) U.S. holders must be treated on terms at least as favorable as those offered to any other security holders of the acquiree; and (v) U.S. holders of the acquiree must be provided the offering circular or other offering materials, in English, on a comparable basis as non-U.S. acquiree security holders.

The creation and availability of the Tier I exemption significantly reduces the burden of complying with U.S. federal securities laws and provides incentives for acquirors to include U.S. holders in cross-border takeover offers. In addition, subject to certain conditions, the prohibition in Rule 14e–5 under the Exchange Act relating to purchases outside of the offer does not apply to offers qualifying for the Tier I exemption. This provides an acquiror and its advisors flexibility in an offer qualifying for the Tier I exemption to make such purchases in accordance with local rules. Consequently, under the Tier I exemption, it was and is the SEC's design that an acquiror could include U.S. holders in its cross-border takeover offer without significant additional cost or other burden above what is normally required by the home jurisdiction of the acquiree.

3.1.2. Rule 802 Exemption

In a similar fashion, the SEC also adopted Rule 802 under the Securities Act. Rule 802 exempts from the registration requirements of Section 5 of the Securities Act any exchange offer for a class of securities of a foreign private issuer or any securities issued in exchange for those of a foreign private issuer in any business combination.

The exemption from Section 5 is applicable only if: (i) the subject company is a foreign private issuer; (ii) U.S. holders hold no more than 10% of the subject securities, or in the case of a business combination in which the securities are to be issued by a successor registrant, U.S. holders hold no more than 10% of the class of securities of the successor registrant, as measured immediately after the business combination; (iii) U.S. holders are permitted to participate on terms at least as favorable as those offered any other holder of the subject securities; (iv) the acquiror is a foreign private issuer, it must file a Form F–X with the SEC appointing an agent for service of process in the United States; and (v) the acquiror complies with the SEC filing and informational dissemination requirements . . .

Rule 802 is not an exclusive exemption. An issuer may also rely on any other applicable exemption from the registration requirements of the Securities Act. In adopting Rule 802, the SEC enunciated a strict approach towards its use and the use of the accompanying Tier I exemption. The SEC stated that these exemptions would not be available for any transaction or series of transactions that technically complies with the exemption but is part of a plan or a scheme to evade the registration requirements of the Securities Act.

3.1.3. Tier II Exemption

Under the Tier II exemption, qualifying tender and exchange offers receive only limited exemptions from the Williams Act and Rule 14e–5 of the Exchange Act to harmonize SEC-perceived common areas of conflict with non-U.S. regulatory takeover schemes. The reason for differing treatment under the Tier I exemption and the Tier II exemption stems, in part, from the view that the greater the extent of U.S. ownership, the greater the extent to which U.S. investors need the protection of the U.S. securities rules. The Tier II exemption is available for both issuer and third party tender and exchange offers when the acquiree is a foreign private issuer and U.S. holders of the acquiree hold more than 10% and less than or equal to 40% of the securities subject to the cross-border takeover offer.

The Tier II exemptions are, in the words of the SEC, simply "codifications of exemptive and interpretive positions" that currently apply in cross-border acquisitions. These exemptions include harmonizing relief under the prompt payment rule and notice rule, an exemption under the all-holders/best price rule for the common cross-border dual-offer structure, and the adoption of a rule with respect to waiver or reduction of minimum conditions in cross-border takeovers. Takeover offers qualifying for the Tier II exemption are still subject to the substantive rules set forth in the Williams Act, including the disclosure and filing requirements thereof. It should be noted that these are only the codified exemptions. Since the adoption of the Cross-Border Rules, the SEC has been amenable to providing other harmonizing relief as necessary and stated as such in the Cross-Border Release.

In 2008, the SEC adopted further amendments to the rules, "to expand and enhance the utility of these exemptions"—to provide further encouragement for the extension of cross-border M&A transactions into the United States. Most of the new rule changes are intended to make more transactions qualify for the exemptions. One change relates to the manner of computation of beneficial ownership; more flexibility is now allowed, such that more transactions now qualify. Tier I exemptions are now available for more forms of types of affiliated transactions than previously had been the case: they are now available for, among other sorts of transactions, cash mergers and schemes of arrangement. There were additional Tier II changes, but they were largely technical and designed to further harmonize foreign legal rules with United States requirements. The changes include, for instance, the ability to not pay for securities tendered in a subsequent offering period on a rolling basis when the securities are tendered as required under US law, but instead, to make payment in accordance with foreign law or, if earlier, 20 days from the date the securities are tendered.[10] Indeed, for the most part the changes were not substantive, but rather further codified prior SEC positions taken in exemptive orders and no-action letters.[11]

---

[10] *See generally* Scott Ashton, SEC Adopts Revisions to its Cross-Border Transaction Exemptions and Beneficial Ownership Reporting Rules, MORRISON & FOERSTER, October 22, 2008, available at http://www.mofo.com/resources/publications/2008/10/sec-adopts-revisions-to-its-cross_border-transac.

[11] Final Rules, SEC Guidance And Revisions To The Cross-Border Tender Offer, Exchange Offer, Rights Offerings, And Business Combination Rules And Beneficial Ownership Reporting

In the years since the passage, of the cross-border exemptions, they have facilitated some offers, particularly in cases where U.S. holders hold less than 10% of the shares. However, the need to file documents in English has deterred some foreign issuers due to the costs of translation. In addition, compliance with these rules requires that a U.S. lawyer be hired; the costs are not insignificant. Therefore, if possible, foreign transactions are still generally structured to exclude U.S. holders. They typically only include these holders and comply with the cross-border exemptions if the number of shareholders in the U.S. is so large that the transaction effectively requires the offer to be extended into the U.S.

G. U.K. TAKEOVER CODE

The prior Subsection discusses Ford's historic offer for Jaguar, which at the time was subject to the U.S. rules as well as the U.K. rules, in the form of the U.K. Takeover Code. The following excerpt discusses in more depth how the U.K. Takeover Code works. In reading this excerpt, note how different the U.K. takeover regulation scheme is from the scheme in the United States. Consider, too, that the differences will be far more meaningful in some circumstances than in others.

THE TAKEOVER CODE
THE TAKEOVER PANEL

The City Code on Takeovers and Mergers (the "Code") has been developed since 1968 to reflect the collective opinion of those professionally involved in the field of takeovers as to appropriate business standards and as to how fairness to shareholders and an orderly framework for takeovers can be achieved. Following the implementation of the Takeovers Directive (2004/25/EC) (the "Directive") by means of Part 28 of the Companies Act 2006 (the "Act"), the rules set out in the Code have a statutory basis in relation to the United Kingdom and comply with the relevant requirements of the Directive.

The rules set out in the Code also have a statutory basis in relation to the Isle of Man, Jersey and Guernsey.

GENERAL PRINCIPLES AND RULES

The Code is based upon six General Principles, which are essentially statements of standards of commercial behaviour. These General Principles are the same as the general principles set out in Article 3 of the Directive. They apply to takeovers and other matters to which the Code applies. They are expressed in broad general terms and the Code does not define the precise extent of, or the limitations on, their application. They

Rules For Certain Foreign Institutions, available at http://www.sec.gov/rules/final/2008/33–8957.pdf.

are applied in accordance with their spirit in order to achieve their underlying purpose.

In addition to the General Principles, the Code contains a series of rules. Although most of the rules are expressed in less general terms than the General Principles, they are not framed in technical language, and like the General Principles, are to be interpreted to achieve their underlying purpose. Therefore, their spirit must be observed as well as their letter.

The following is a brief summary of some of the most important Rules:

- When a person or group acquires interests in shares carrying 30% or more of the voting rights of a company, they must make a cash offer to all other shareholders at the highest price paid in the 12 months before the offer was announced (30% of the voting rights of a company is treated by the Code as the level at which effective control is obtained).

- When interests in shares carrying 10% or more of the voting rights of a class have been acquired by an offeror (i.e. a bidder) in the offer period and the previous 12 months, the offer must include a cash alternative for all shareholders of that class at the highest price paid by the offeror in that period. Further, if an offeror acquires for cash any interest in shares during the offer period, a cash alternative must be made available at that price at least.

- If the offeror acquires an interest in shares in an offeree company (i.e. a target) at a price higher than the value of the offer, the offer must be increased accordingly.

- The offeree company must appoint a competent independent adviser whose advice on the financial terms of the offer must be made known to all the shareholders, together with the opinion of the board.

- Favourable deals for selected shareholders are banned.

- All shareholders must be given the same information.

- Those issuing takeover circulars must include statements taking responsibility for the contents.

- Profit forecasts, quantified financial benefits statements and asset valuations must be made to specified standards and must be reported on by professional advisers.

- Misleading, inaccurate or unsubstantiated statements made in documents or to the media must be publicly corrected immediately.

- Actions during the course of an offer by the offeree company which might frustrate the offer are generally prohibited unless shareholders approve these plans.

- Stringent requirements are laid down for the disclosure of dealings in relevant securities during an offer.

- Employees of both the offeror and the offeree company and the trustees of the offeree company's pension scheme must be informed about an offer. In addition, the offeree company's employee representatives and pension scheme trustees have the right to have a separate opinion on the effects of the offer on employment appended to the offeree board's circular or published on a website.[12]

The Takeover Code is administered by a Takeover Panel which is primarily comprised of industry experts. The Takeover Panel is quite active in supervising any takeover, and willing to act quickly to enforce rules and liaise with practitioners. One way the Takeover Panel derives significant power over takeovers is through the principle-based nature of the Takeover Code, which gives the Takeover Panel wide latitude to act to stem conduct it sees as violative of these principles. In this regard the Code is different than the Williams Act, which is specifically rule based. The Takeover Code's six guiding principles are:

1. All holders of the securities of an offeree company of the same class must be afforded equivalent treatment; moreover, if a person acquires control of a company, the other holders of securities must be protected.

2. The holders of the securities of an offeree company must have sufficient time and information to enable them to reach a properly informed decision on the bid; where it advises the holders of securities, the board of the offeree company must give its views on the effects of implementation of the bid on employment, conditions of employment and the locations of the company's places of business.

3. The board of an offeree company must act in the interests of the company as a whole and must not deny the holders of securities the opportunity to decide on the merits of the bid.

---

[12] Available at http://www.thetakeoverpanel.org.uk/the-code/download-code.

4.   False markets must not be created in the securities of the offeree company, of the offeror company or of any other company concerned by the bid in such a way that the rise or fall of the prices of the securities becomes artificial and the normal functioning of the markets is distorted.

5.   An offeror must announce a bid only after ensuring that he/she can fulfil in full any cash consideration, if such is offered, and after taking all reasonable measures to secure the implementation of any other type of consideration.

6.   An offeree company must not be hindered in the conduct of its affairs for longer than is reasonable by a bid for its securities.[13]

H. A CONCLUDING REMARK

Given the increasing globalization of markets, we can expect increasing efforts to accommodate deals that involve multiple jurisdictions. These accommodations can be technically difficult, as well as controversial. Simply figuring out the mechanics is challenging; adding in different views (one might even say, philosophies) about the extent to which form or substance should dictate regulatory treatment, the relative role of various stakeholders (including government), and many other things complicates the task exponentially. Efforts towards standardization in various M&A-relevant realms continue, with some successes, but obstacles will not be easily surmounted.

QUESTIONS

1.   Under what circumstances might a transaction involving a foreign buyer and a foreign target be subject to U.S. securities laws?

2.   What is an exclusionary offer and how does it avoid the jurisdiction of U.S. securities laws?

3.   What is the Reg. S safe harbor and why does a transaction involving a Reg. S safe harbor avoid U.S. registration requirements?

4.   Is there any rationale justifying why a bidder is able to sidestep many of the applicable federal securities laws by using a scheme of arrangement when it would have to comply with the Williams Act if the same acquisition were made via a tender offer?

5.   What problem were the cross-border exemptions trying to solve? If you were advising an acquirer, would you recommend they comply with these rules or do an exclusionary offer?

---

[13]   The U.K. Takeover Code at B1 (2015).

6.   How does the U.K. Takeover Code differ than the Williams Act? What do you think are the main differences? What reasons can you think of for the differences?

7.   What is the role of "principles" in the U.K. Takeover Code? What are the benefits of principles (as versus rules)? What are the costs?

8.   What do you think motivated the U.K. requirement that someone who acquires 30% of a company must make an offer to acquire the rest? Is the rule a good one? Who is helped, and who is hurt? What would you expect to be the economic effects?

9.   If you were a regulator in a country with relatively stricter laws (requiring, for instance, more disclosure), how would you balance the desirability of more cross-border activity with the policies that underlie your regulatory regime?

PROBLEMS

1.   Your client, Delta Inc., a publicly-traded U.S. corporation, would like to expand into Europe. It has identified a possible target, Romeo Co., a U.K. firm traded on the London Stock Exchange. What options might be available to your client for structuring an acquisition of Rome? Which regulating authorities will likely be in play? Please draft a memo for the board of Delta.

2.   Your client, Tango, a German company, would like to acquire Beta Corp., a publicly-traded U.S. corporation. What options might be available to your client for structuring an acquisition of Beta? Which regulating authorities will likely be in play? Please draft a memo for the board of Tango.

3.   British Plc., a public limited corporation organized under the laws of England and Wales, wishes to acquire French SA, a société anonyme (literally, anonymous society; a civil law organizational form resembling a public company) organized under the laws of France. French SA is listed on the New York and Euronext Paris Stock Exchanges. British Plc is listed on the London Stock Exchange. British Plc will use stock consideration in the acquisition; the acquisition will be pursuant to a tender offer conducted under French law. Approximately 15% of French SA's shares are held in the United States. Your client is British Plc. How would you advise them with respect to including or excluding U.S. shareholders? Based on your advice, what filings must British Plc make in the United States and what U.S. rules must it follow? How would your advice change if only 5% of French SA's shares were held in the United States? How would your answers to the prior questions change if French SA was instead organized under the laws of England and Wales and a scheme of arrangement structure was utilized?

ONLINE APPENDIX

■ ■ ■

Available at:
http://www.HillMergersandAcquisitions.com

1. Dell Certificate of Incorporation, prior to Merger

2. Amended and Restated Certificate of Incorporation of Dell Inc., following Merger

3. Sample Bulk Sales Opinion

4. Merger Agreement, dated as of August 11, 2013, among DFC Holdings, LLC, DFC Merger Corp., David H. Murdock and Dole Food Company, Inc.

5. Press Release of the Dell Special Committee of the Board of Directors of Dell Inc. issued on July 11, 2013

6. Dell Notice of Special Meeting of Stockholders with their Rights, May 30, 2013

7. The Williams Act Sections 13(d) [15 U.S.C. 78m(d)]

8. Men's Wearhouse's Tender Offer for Joseph A. Bank

9. Dell, Inc., Form 10–K (2013)

10. Fairness Opinions of JP Morgan and Evercore, a more lengthy reference to their analysis in a preliminary proxy statement filed on March 29, 2013, Board book

11. Form of Confidentiality Agreement, Martin Marietta Materials, Inc. v. Vulcan Materials Company

12. Sample Letter of Intent

13. Sample Change of Control Provisions in the three contracts

14. Annotated Form of an Investment Bank Engagement Letter

15. Dell: Agreement and Plan of Merger, dated as of February 5, 2013; Agreement and Plan of Merger, dated as of May 31, 2015, by and among Intel and Altera

16. Representations and Warranties of the Company (Altera to Intel)

17. Representations and Warranties of Parent and Acquisition Sub (Intel to Altera)

18. Indemnification provision from eBay's Acquisition of Skype

19. Shareholder Rights Plan/Poison Pill of Allergan, Form 8–K (the Certificate of Designation and the Indenture Agreement)

20. Form of Certificate of Merger

INDEX

References are to Pages

NATIONAL SECURITY REVIEW (EXON-FLORIO AMENDMENT)

NO-SHOP

NON-DISCLOSURE AND CONFIDENTIALITY AGREEMENTS

NOT-FOR-PROFIT CORPORATIONS

NOTICE